The Arms Race and Nuclear War

William M. Evan
University of Pennsylvania

Stephen Hilgartner
Cornell University

Editors

Prentice-Hall, Inc., Englewood Cliffs, New Jersey 07632

Library of Congress Cataloging-in-Publication Data

Evan, William M.
   The arms race and nuclear war.

  Bibliography:
   1. Nuclear disarmament. 2. Nuclear arms control.
I. Hilgartner, Stephen.   II. Title.
JX1974.7.E9 1987   327.1'74   86-25157
ISBN 0-13-046301-9

Editorial/production supervision and interior design:
  Ann L. Mohan, WordCrafters Editorial Services, Inc.
Cover design: George Cornell
Manufacturing buyer: John B. Hall

© 1987 by Prentice-Hall, Inc.
A Division of Simon & Schuster
Englewood Cliffs, New Jersey 07632

Printed in the United States of America.
10 9 8 7 6 5 4 3 2 1

ISBN   0-13-046301-9   01

Prentice-Hall International (UK) Limited, *London*
Prentice-Hall of Australia Pty. Limited, *Sydney*
Prentice-Hall Canada, Inc., *Toronto*
Prentice-Hall Hispanoamericana, S.A., *Mexico*
Prentice-Hall of India Private Limited, *New Delhi*
Prentice-Hall of Japan, Inc., *Tokyo*
Prentice-Hall of Southeast Asia Pte. Ltd., *Singapore*
Editora Prentice-Hall do Brasil, Ltda., *Rio de Janeiro*

Contents

iii

Preface

This book presents an interdisciplinary perspective on the subject of nuclear war, exploring a wide range of issues and approaches to policies in the nuclear age. Through a carefully selected set of readings, the book examines the risks of a nuclear world, the dynamics of the nuclear arms race, and a number of alternative strategies for preventing nuclear war. Our goal is to expose the reader to a concise but intellectually stimulating overview of the contemporary debate over nuclear policy, surveying a broad range of topics and points of view. To accomplish this, the book includes selections from classic works as well as more recent writings. Special emphasis is placed on issues of great importance in the late 1980s, such as current developments in space weaponry, strategic doctrine, and peace movements. In addition, the book devotes much attention to specific proposals for reducing the risks of nuclear war. It is our hope that this text will provide the attentive reader with an introduction to nuclear issues that will enable and encourage ongoing participation in the critical debate over public policies in a nuclear-armed world.

This text is organized into four parts. Part One addresses the risks of a nuclear world, examining some ways nuclear war could start and the potential effects of such a calamity. Part Two examines the weapons of the nuclear age. Subjects covered include the development of the A- and H-bombs, the scope and types of existing nuclear weapons systems, and the new generation of space weapons currently under development. Part Three explores the dynamics of the nuclear arms race from a number of perspectives, addressing such topics as nuclear strategy, United States–Soviet relations, and the bureaucratic, economic and psychological aspects of the arms race. Finally, Part Four presents a number of strategies that have been proposed for preventing or reducing the risks of nuclear war, with chapters on contemporary peace movements, arms control and disarmament negotiations, unilateral initiatives for peace, economic conversion, and international law.

Books, especially edited collections, are the work of many people. Our first, and greatest, debt is to the authors of works that we have excerpted and reprinted here. We also owe special thanks to the students at the University of Pennsylvania who enrolled in the survey course on nuclear war taught there by William M. Evan in 1984, 1985, and 1986. Their reactions to the assigned readings helped us in making selections for this text. In addition, we want to thank the following colleagues and friends who made valuable suggestions and comments: Richard C. Bell, Jonathan Luskin, R. Craig Nation, Kathleen O'Neil, Judith Reppy, and Jonathan Root. The book benefited from their assistance; any shortcomings are, of course, our own responsibility. We also wish to express our indebtedness to Dean Ivar Berg of the University of Pennsylvania for his intellectual and material encouragement in the preparation of a new course on nuclear war. Finally, we owe special thanks to Bill Webber, our editor at Prentice-Hall, who saw the need for a book of this type and initiated the project.

The nuclear arms race is the subject of heated debate. But whatever the views of our readers, we hope that this book will stimulate them to scrutinize the premises of, and evidence for, their beliefs.

W.M.E.
S.H.

The Threat of Nuclear War

How likely is nuclear war? How might a nuclear war start? What would happen if one did? These questions—like most of those surrounding the nuclear arms race—are the subject of much debate.

Some analysts argue that nuclear war is becoming more likely. They point to the growth of nuclear arsenals, to the development of increasingly accurate and deadly weapons, and to the expansion of the arms race into space. They suggest that the sheer size and complexity of today's nuclear forces raises the risk of accidental nuclear war. They argue that the current generation of sophisticated missiles—which can strike targets quickly and accurately—increase the risk that military leaders will resort to nuclear weapons in a crisis. They believe that if conventional war ever broke out in Europe, NATO would use nuclear weapons to counter the Warsaw Pact's superiority in conventional forces. They worry that the proliferation of nuclear technology will make it possible for a growing number of countries to develop nuclear weapons, charging that the "nuclear club" is in danger of becoming a "nuclear-armed crowd." They are concerned about the current state of United States–Soviet relations, arguing that today's hostile relationship stands in the way of mutually-beneficial negotiations that could reduce the risk of war. They also worry that this "new cold war" makes international crises between the U.S. and the Soviet Union more likely, while at the same time raising the likelihood that nuclear weapons would be employed during a crisis.

Other analysts believe that the foregoing diagnosis is alarmist. They point out that forty years have elapsed since nuclear bombs have been used in warfare, and they argue that it is unlikely that nuclear weapons will be used anytime soon, claiming that most "scenarios" for the outbreak of nuclear war are far-fetched or implausible. They are confident that the large nuclear arsenals built up by the superpowers will deter military leaders from being the first to resort to nuclear weapons. They believe that nuclear war is unlikely to begin by accident, arguing that precautions taken by both sides make accidental or unauthorized use of nuclear weapons unlikely. Similarly, they claim that it is improbable that unintentional war will occur as a result of miscalculation or irrational decision-making during an international crisis. They doubt that a regional war—even one between two fledgling nuclear powers—would be likely to escalate into a nuclear war between the U.S. and the USSR. They suggest that no matter how tense the relationship between Washington and Moscow becomes, it is unlikely that either country will elect to use nuclear weapons to settle their differences.

Predicting the future is a dangerous venture, and most analysts—whatever their views—readily admit that assessments of the likelihood of nuclear war are fraught with uncertainty. Similarly, it is difficult to estimate the effects that a nuclear war would have. This much, however, is certain: a full-scale nuclear war between the superpowers would be an unprecedented disaster, killing many millions of people, destroying cities, and causing economic ruin. There is also the distinct possibility that a large number of nuclear explosions would produce devastating environmental effects, such as "nuclear winter," that could destroy the crops, livestock and ecosystem upon which human life depends. In the aftermath of a nuclear war, the continued existence of the human species cannot be taken for granted.

Part One examines the threat of nuclear war. Chapter I, "The Risks of a Nuclear World," examines some ways nuclear wars could begin. Chapter II looks at the potential effects of nuclear war—on individual human beings, on cities, on the economic infrastructure, and on the environment.

The Risks of a Nuclear World

The existence of nuclear weapons poses unique risks for humanity. This chapter explores those risks, and examines some of the ways nuclear war might start.

We begin with a reading that looks at the level of military preparedness that marks today's nuclear world. In this reading, William M. Arkin and Richard W. Fieldhouse point out that "every minute of every day, at thousands of locations around the world . . . nuclear missiles sit ready to be launched." Describing the vast nuclear infrastructure that penetrates into every corner of the globe and even into outer space, they argue we live in a "state of war," in a world that is "only nominally at peace."

Next comes an excerpt on the "Causes of War in the Atomic Age" from Quincy Wright's *A Study of War*. This classic work examines the long and unfortunate history of warfare, reaching some general conclusions about the causes of war. In this discussion of atomic warfare, Wright argues that although the problem of war has grown more acute, the causes of war—and the obstacles to peace—remain similar. He concludes that conditions of peace can never be taken for granted, since even in the atomic age political leaders may deem war or threats of war to be useful instruments of policy.

In "Victory is Possible," Colin S. Gray and Keith Payne argue that nuclear weapons can—and should—be used to further U.S. foreign policy objectives. They argue that nuclear war, like any war, can be won or lost, and they propose that "the West needs to devise ways in which it can employ strategic nuclear forces coercively." Rejecting the idea that World War III would be a "nonsurvivable event," they maintain that the U.S. should prepare to fight a nuclear war—both by developing detailed war-fighting plans and by providing for the protection of American territory.

Robert S. McNamara and Hans Bethe take issue with the notion of nuclear war-fighting. They argue that U.S. and Soviet efforts to improve their nuclear war-fighting capabilities have shaken confidence in the ability of deterrence to prevent war. They believe that proponents of controlled, rational nuclear war-fighting are deluding themselves, since no one can predict what would happen during the chaos of nuclear war.

Daniel Frei discusses the risk of unintentional nuclear war. He argues that an acute international crisis could lead to nuclear war even when no government wanted one. He notes that such factors as organizational and individual failures, erratic behavior under stress, misperceptions, mishandling of information, and confusion could lead to bad decision-making and hence to nuclear war. Moreover, he points out that the frequency of international crises has not declined in the nuclear age, so the threat of unintentional nuclear war must be taken very seriously.

Finally, Leonard S. Spector examines the danger of the proliferation of nuclear weapons. A growing number of nations are acquiring the technology and raw materials necessary to make nuclear bombs, and this poses a serious threat to world peace. If proliferation continues—and many analysts believe it will—then the use of nuclear weapons in regional wars or by terrorist groups will grow increasingly likely.

1 State of War

William M. Arkin and Richard W. Fieldhouse

Every minute of every day, at thousands of locations around the world—from the plains of North Dakota and Montana, from the Ukraine and Siberia, from southern France and central China, to beneath the Arctic icepack, to the Sea of Okhotsk, to the Yellow Sea—nuclear missiles sit ready to be launched. In Western Europe nuclear aircraft sit cocked on alert. On and under the high seas, nuclear-armed ships and submarines patrol, waiting for their day to go into battle. The weapons could reach their targets thousands of miles away quicker than it takes most people to get to work in the morning.

At scores of military command centers around the world, nuclear war plans are continuously tested, revised, and updated. Planners record the latest personnel and equipment strengths and enemy dispositions, consult weather forecasts, and sift through and assimilate mountains of constantly arriving data giving the details of the next war.

In the air, endless streams of dispatches fly back and forth between bureaucracies, naval vessels, and military forces dispersed around the globe. Spy satellites, ships, and airplanes keep a close watch, covertly intercepting, recording, and photographing. The five nuclear powers and many military alliances work in rhythm, feeding off each other's actions. It is "a world that's only nominally at peace," says Admiral James Watkins, U.S. Chief of Naval Operations.[1] "Peace, crisis, conflict: often in today's world there are

no clear demarcations," he told Congress in early 1984.[2]

To support the huge nuclear arsenals and war plans, a global infrastructure has been created. It comprises much more than the 50,000 warheads the five nuclear nations have stockpiled. The infrastructure includes hundreds of laboratories, testing sites, and electronic support facilities. It encompasses the factories, military bases, transportation networks, command centers, computers, and satellites that feed the system. It is the lifeblood of the war plans. The infrastructure knows no boundaries and observes no borders; the battlefields are virtually everywhere. Scores of nations are linked, wittingly and unwittingly; all of them are on the front lines. Just as the distinction between peace and war is blurred, so is the distinction between military and civilian. The nuclear infrastructure has a priority claim on all resources. To recognize the full scope of this infrastructure is to fathom the true extent of the arms race. Simply tallying up the number of nuclear weapons in a nation's arsenal does not indicate how ready or able it is to use nuclear weapons in a war.

Most of us go about our daily lives unaware of how close to war we constantly are. Every day, all over the globe, endless military activity insures that war planners never let down their guard. On a normal day, U.S. military radars and command centers must catalog and distinguish between 1,700 flights that enter and leave U.S. airspace. They must determine whether each flight is a valid civilian aircraft or a covert military one. A difference of five minutes or twenty-five miles between flight plans and radar contacts will cause interceptor jets to "scramble" and investigate. In a typical year, there are also over 500 "major" rocket launches around the

5

world, at least one every day. Last year, about 400 were Soviet launches, and for each one, the U.S. early-warning system clicked into operation. Within five minutes, officers in command posts had to determine whether a satellite was being propelled into orbit, whether a routine missile test was taking place, or whether World War III had just begun.

The level of peacetime military preparedness has reached wartime dimensions. This is most clearly seen with naval forces, the focus of superpower signaling and posturing. U.S. and Soviet naval operations routinely include provocative maneuvers such as shadowing and mock attacks. The superpowers continually use geographic advantages such as "choke points" for peacetime positioning. Recently, for instance, the United States resumed aircraft-carrier operations in the Sea of Japan after a thirteen-year absence, and U.S. attack submarines have conducted patrols in such protected Soviet waters as the Sea of Okhotsk. The Soviets have responded by using naval bombers for simulated strikes against U.S. ships and by increasing the tempo and range of their own naval operations.

The two sides carry out these cat-and-mouse antics in a cavalier fashion. In September 1982 the U.S. Navy conducted an unprecedented exercise in the north Pacific with two aircraft-carrier battle groups. Admiral Watkins, Chief of Naval Operations, stated that the exercise was "to show the Soviet Union we were back in the vicinity of our western reaches of the Aleutian Islands within 500 miles of Petropavlovsk."[3] The exercise was enough, according to Admiral S.R. Foley, Jr., Commander of the Pacific Fleet, for the Soviets to have "Backfires conduct flights against our carrier battle force in the North Pacific . . . the first such use of Backfires anywhere." The United States then followed with another exercise in April 1983, this time with three carrier battle groups off the Aleutian Islands, to deliberately simulate the conditions of the Falklands conflict, Admiral Foley stated. "I believe the Soviets were surprised to see us conduct such a large-scale exercise, nearly back to back with the annual 'Team Spirit' exercise in Korea." In his words, the exercise "gave the Soviets a few more things to ponder."[4]

Even in the absence of these provocative maneuvers, conflicts rage on among more than forty-five nations in forty wars around the globe. That the nuclear powers are among those involved in these conflicts is often ignored. In the past few years, all of the five nuclear powers have been (or continue to be) at war: the Soviet Union in Afghanistan, China against Vietnam, France against Libya and in Lebanon, Britain against Argentina, the United States in Grenada, Central America, and Lebanon.

The links between the nuclear powers in these conflicts are significant. The United States and China provide covert assistance to Afghani guerilla fighters. The Soviet Union provides military support to Cuba, Nicaragua, Vietnam, Syria, and Libya. The United States, committed by treaty to both Britain's and Argentina's defense, provided intelligence and communications assistance to Britain during the Falklands War. The United States also provided satellite reconnaissance information to France for its operations in Chad. Meanwhile, French aircraft and missiles were the most potent weapons used by the Argentines against the British.

The five nuclear powers have spread the arms race beyond their own soil by placing nuclear-related facilities in sixty-five countries and territories. Some 11,800 nuclear weapons are stored or deployed outside the homelands of these five powers. About 70 percent of U.S. tactical nuclear weapons are stored in foreign countries or on ships at sea. The Soviet Union has 15 percent of its Navy at sea (presumed to be nuclear-armed) and stores nuclear weapons in four Eastern European countries. Britain has nuclear weapons in West Germany. The infrastructure extends underground and into the oceans, across the land, and into the atmosphere and space. No continent is immune; no border, river, mountain range, or political frontier divides one battlefield from another. A new geography has been created.

NOTES

1. U.S., Congress, House Armed Services Committee, Fiscal Year 1985 Department of Defense, pt. 1, p. 563.

2. Ibid., p. 567.

3. U.S., Congress, House Appropriations Committee, Fiscal Year 1984 Department of Defense, pt. 2, p. 454.

4. Admiral S.R. Foley, Jr., Commander-in-Chief, U.S. Pacific Fleet, *Current Strategy Forum*, (Newport, R.I.: Naval War College, June 23, 1983).

2   Causes of War in the Atomic Age

Quincy Wright

The problem of war has become more acute. . . . Quantitative changes have been of such magnitude that the relations of nations have become qualitatively different. A new world has emerged. Nevertheless, my conclusions in regard to the causes of war still seem valid.

Among the specific causes of war frequently noted by historians, I referred (a) to reaction to perceived threats; (b) to enthusiasm for ideals; (c) to frustration over unsatisfactory conditions attributed to a foreign scapegoat; (d) to belief in the utility of threats of war or war itself as an instrument of independence, policy, prestige, or power; and (e) to conviction that military self-help is necessary to vindicate justice, law, and rights if peaceful negotiation proves ineffective.[1]

a) *Reaction to perceived threats.*—The urge to preserve the self and the territory, the group, the means of livelihood, and the way of life with which the self is identified threatened war after World War II, as it always had among animals,[2] primitive peoples,[3] and historic civilizations.[4] Many people on both sides of the iron curtain were obsessed by the fear that the government on the other side was determined to attack or subvert them and that war might be necessary to assure their survival. Many Americans and Europeans perceived a threat from the superior land army of the Soviet bloc backed by formidable missiles with nuclear warheads, and many Soviet citizens perceived a threat from the superior nuclear missiles controlled by the United States on submarines and land bases surrounding Soviet territory. Although the American government said these weapons were only for defense in a counterforce strategy, the Soviet Union interpreted this policy as designed to destroy Soviet retaliatory capability by a first strike after all launching sites had been pinpointed by espionage from the air or outer space.[5] The arms race resulting from these perceived threats tended to augment fear on each side and the demand for a position of strength, for superior power, or for dominance.[6]

b) *Enthusiasm for ideals.*—To some people, obsessed by ideological convictions, which have often been emphatic in proportion as the revolution that gave political support to their ideology was recent, war seemed laudable to contain or to eliminate a society, whether communist or capitalist, which they considered wicked or to convert the world to values which they considered good for everyone.[7]

c) *Frustration over unsatisfactory conditions.*— Frustrated by continued disorder and poverty after independence (Indonesia) or by the failure of economic planning inspired by revolution (China), some governments developed aggressive policies against their neighbors, their ideological opponents, or those "imperialist" states generally considered responsible for their difficulties.[8]

d) *Belief in the utility of threats of war.*—To people demanding self-determination, such as the Vietnamese, Algerians, and Angolans, war seemed necessary if the demand was resisted, and to some mature states war or threats of war seemed useful for promoting the policy of the government, whether that of the Soviet

From Quincy Wright, *A Study of War*, Second Edition, with a Commentary on War since 1942 (pp. 1512–1518). Copyright © 1965 by University of Chicago. Reprinted with permission.

7

Union in Korea or Hungary or that of the United States in Vietnam or Cuba.[9]

e) *Belief in the necessity of military self-help.*— Some governments thought military resistance or attack reasonable or necessary to maintain justice or a right, such as that claimed by France in Indochina and Algeria, by the United States and the Soviet Union in Berlin, by Israel and the Arab states in Palestine, and by Britain and France in Suez.[10]

It is still true that no single cause of war can be identified. Recent hostilities, although attributable primarily to specific causes, have arisen because of the changing relation of numerous factors—psychological, economic, ideological, social, political, and legal. It is still true that peace results from an equilibrium among many forces.[11] Among these forces, appreciation of the cost of nuclear war and the intervention of international organizations assumed great importance after World War II.

Apart from specific causes of war, certain general conditions have made for war. Among these have been the lag of procedures for peaceful adjustment behind technological and ideological change.[12] Such a lag was especially notable after World War II because of the extraordinary rapidity of such change. Neither diplomacy nor the United Nations was wholly adequate to deal with the problems posed by atomic energy and guided missiles, ideological differences, the breakup of empires, and territorial disputes. Military self-help at Suez in 1956 was said to be justifiable, in spite of the UN Charter prohibitions against the use or threat of force in international relations, because neither diplomacy nor the United Nations had been able to protect Israel against fedayeen raids or to settle the Suez dispute to the satisfaction of the British and French.[13] In justification of the Cuban quarantine in 1962, some jurists suggested, in spite of the Charter limitation of the right of defense to armed attack, that modern military technology justified anticipatory defensive action.[14]

Another general condition inducing war has been the inherent aggressiveness of particular rulers or states, like Hitler and Nazi Germany, and the attribution of such aggressiveness by their opponents to the communist and imperialist states during the "cold war."[15]

A traditional feud between two states has frequently induced war in the past.[16] Such a feud developed between Russia and the West at the time of the Soviet Revolution and was aug-

mented by mutual provocations in spite of their alliance during World War II. Feuds have also developed between Israel and the Arab states, between Greece and Turkey, and between India and Pakistan.

Another general condition unfavorable to peace has been the bipolarization of power through rival alliances. Bipolarization has in the past made the power situation extremely unstable because each side believes eventual war is inevitable and calculates the influence of time on its relative power position. The side that becomes convinced that time is against it is likely to initiate a preventive war.[17] The conviction of each side in the "cold war" that time is favoring it together with the extreme risks of nuclear war has made deliberate initiation of preventive war improbable in the nuclear age. But bipolarization has created great concern with relative power positions, has made each side unwilling to make the concessions necessary to settle disputes for fear they may compromise that position, and has developed a disposition in times of crises, as in Berlin and Vietnam, to retaliate, countering threats with threats and intervention with counterintervention. Furthermore bipolarization developed the concept of security through mutual deterrence by nuclear threats. But as counterforce strategy develops with the increased destructive power of weapons and the greater speed in delivering them, a premium is placed on the first strike which may destroy the enemy's retaliatory capacity; and pre-emptive war (i.e., preventive war, when it is believed the enemy is about to strike) becomes a real danger. Some hope to counter it by protective second-strike capability of both sides in hardened bases or submarines so that devastating retaliation against a first strike is certain.[18]

The most persistent condition of war, however, has been the inherent difficulty, which I have emphasized in this book, of organizing peace.[19] In spite of earnest efforts, this difficulty has not been overcome in the postwar period. Peace has not been made the most important symbol or goal in the policy of governments and the opinions of peoples. Particular symbols, such as justice and self-determination, and particular drives, such as security and power, continue to urge action which produces hostilities. It is still impossible for all persons or groups to satisfy, and difficult for them to sublimate, the human urge to dominate over others, particularly the urge of great powers to dominate over small neighbors.[20] Sovereign states are still reluctant to recognize that objective justice implies submission to impartial third-party adjudication.

It has proved no less difficult in recent years than in the past to maintain either a stable equilibrium of power or a system of collective security among the rapidly changing political and military forces within the state system. Each great power confronted by a rival deemed it necessary to increase its power in order to survive. Each could not negotiate from a position of superior strength, but each tried to do so, with the result of an arms race in which each became less secure.[21] Power must balance power in a stable system but the balance must be complicated, utilizing elements other than military and centers of power other than states.[22]

Today, as in the past, states, especially new states, have found it difficult to organize political authority sufficient to maintain internal order unless they are in hostile relations to outside states. War or fear of war has often been used to integrate states. On occasion, multinational states, like the Soviet Union, India, Pakistan, Israel, and Indonesia, have sought to maintain their solidarity by convincing all their people of the need for united defense from external enemies, actual or created. Regional organizations —NATO, the Warsaw Pact, and the Arab League—have manifested internal solidarity only when all members feared attack from outside. The world-society has no external enemy, so the United Nations, like the League of Nations, has found it difficult to maintain order and stability within that society.[23] The advantages of cooperation must play a larger role than fear of aggression if states and international organizations are to enjoy both stability within and peace without.

It has always been difficult to develop the sources and sanctions of international law so as to keep that law an effective analysis of the changing interests of states, of the changing conceptions of justice, and of the changing values of humanity.[24] This difficulty has continued, in spite of the efforts of the International Court of Justice, the International Law Commission, and the United Nations. Each sovereign state still claims to be the legislator, judge, and executor of its own rights. If it acknowledges the existence of international law, it reserves the right to interpret it in its own interest, as did Britain in the Suez crisis of 1956, the United States in the Cuban crisis of 1962, and the Soviet Union in the Hungarian crisis of 1956, or to decide what matters are within its domestic jurisdiction, as

did the United States Senate by the Connally amendment to its acceptance of the optional clause of the World Court Statute. There has been progress both in developing international law and international adjudication, but the balance of law and politics is still overweighted on the side of the latter.[25]

These difficulties in the realms of psychology and opinion, of politics and power, of government and authority, and of law and sovereignty have in the past frustrated efforts to create conditions of secure peace. Until they are surmounted, states may continue, however irrationally in the atomic age, to regard war or threats of war as instruments of policy and necessary supports to diplomacy and justice. They may deem war necessary when political obstruction will not yield to persuasion or threats.[26] These difficulties will never be wholly surmounted. Conditions of peace can never be taken for granted. They will have to be continually reconstructed and maintained by human efforts. Peace is artificial: war is natural.[27]

NOTES

1. Quincy Wright, *A Study of War, Second Edition, with a Commentary on War since 1942.* (Chicago: University of Chicago Press, 1965) pp. 138, 720 –27, 1236. (Unless otherwise indicated, all page numbers in citations below refer to Wright, *A Study of War.*)

2. Pp. 43, 487 ff.

3. Pp. 76 ff.

4. Pp. 131 ff., 138 ff.

5. Speech at Ann Arbor, Michigan, by Secretary of Defense Robert McNamara, June 16, 1963; John Strachey, *On the Prevention of War* (London: Macmillan, 1962) pp. 30 ff., 63 ff.; Albert Wohlstetter, "The Delicate Balance of Terror," *Foreign Affairs,* vol. 37 (January, 1959), 241 ff.

6. See Appendix G, pp. 1562–1563.

7. Pp. 761; Strachey, *op. cit.,* pp. 234 ff., 240, 244 ff.

8. Pp. 132, 357, 1460; John Dollard, *Frustration and Aggression* (New Haven, Conn.: Yale University Press, 1939).

9. Quincy Wright, "The Cuban Quarantine," *American Journal of International Law,* vol. 57 (July, 1963), 564. See also pp. 1221, 1236, 1291.

10. Julius Stone, "Law, Force and Survival," *Foreign Affairs,* vol. 39 (July, 1961), 553; Stone, *Aggression and World Order* (Berkeley: University of California Press, 1958), pp. 110 ff. See also Quincy Wright, *The Role of International Law in the Elimination of War* (Manchester, England: Manchester University Press, 1961), pp. 6, 48. See also p. 1294.

11. Pp. 1284 ff. and n. 22 below.

12. *Ibid.*

13. See n. 10 above and Quincy Wright, "Interventions, 1956," *American Journal of International Law*, vol. 51 (April, 1957) 257 ff.

14. Myres MacDougal, "Remarks," *Proceedings of the American Society of International Law*, 1963, pp. 15, 164; MacDougal, "The Soviet-Cuban Quarantine and Self-Defense," *American Journal of International Law*, vol. 57 (July, 1963), 597 ff.

15. Pp. 1311 ff.

16. Pp. 1316 ff.

17. Pp. 382, 399, 690, 763, 774 ff., 1318 ff.

18. Strachey, *op. cit.*, p. 32 ff., 60 ff.

19. Pp. 733, 1236.

20. Pp. 139 ff., 815, 1079 ff., 1233, 1288, and n. 9 above.

21. Pp. 690, 743 ff., 1228, 1291, 1482; Lewis F. Richardson, *Arms and Insecurity* (Pittsburgh: Boxwood Press, 1960), p. 10 ff.; Strachey, *op. cit.*, pp. 117 ff.; Coral Bell, *Negotiation from Strength* (New York: Alfred A. Knopf, 1963).

22. P. 747; Quincy Wright, *The Strengthening of International Law* (Recueil, Academy of International Law [The Hague, 1959]), pp. 99 ff.

23. Pp. 955 ff., 1231, 1287.

24. Pp. 863 ff., 1229, 1294.

25. Quincy Wright, *Problems of Stability and Progress in International Relations* (Berkeley: University of California Press, 1954), pp. 251 ff.; Wright, "Law and Politics in the World Community," in *Law and Politics in the World Community*, ed. George Lipsky (Berkeley: University of California Press, 1953), pp. 3 ff.

26. Pp. 1236 ff.

27. Pp. 163, 285, 379, 1090 ff., 1332; Quincy Wright, *The Study of International Relations* (New York: Appleton-Century-Crofts, 1955) p. 150.

3 Victory Is Possible

Colin S. Gray and Keith Payne

Nuclear war is possible. But unlike Armageddon, the apocalyptic war prophesied to end history, nuclear war can have a wide range of possible outcomes. Many commentators and senior U.S. government officials consider it a nonsurvivable event. The popularity of this view in Washington has such a pervasive and malign effect upon American defense planning that it is rapidly becoming a self-fulfilling prophecy for the United States.

Recognition that war at any level can be won or lost, and that the distinction between winning and losing would not be trivial, is essential for intelligent defense planning. Moreover, nuclear war can occur regardless of the quality of U.S. military posture and the content of American strategic theory. If it does, deterrence, crisis management, and escalation control might play a negligible role. Through an inability to communicate or through Soviet disinterest in receiving and acting upon American messages, the United States might not even have the option to surrender and thus might have to fight the war as best it can. Furthermore, the West needs to devise ways in which it can employ strategic nuclear forces coercively, while minimizing the potentially paralyzing impact of self-deterrence.

If American nuclear power is to support U.S. foreign policy objectives, the United States must possess the ability to wage nuclear war rationally. This requirement is inherent in the geography of East-West relations, in the persisting deficiencies in Western conventional and theater nuclear forces, and in the distinction between

the objectives of a revolutionary and status quo power.

U.S. strategic planning should exploit Soviet fears insofar as is feasible from the Soviet perspective; take full account of likely Soviet responses and the willingness of Americans to accept those responses; and provide for the protection of American territory. Such planning would enhance the prospect for effective deterrence and survival during a war. Only recently has U.S. nuclear targeting policy been based on careful study of the Soviet Union as a distinct political culture, but the U.S. defense community continues to resist many of the policy implications of Soviet responses to U.S. weapons programs. In addition, the U.S. government simply does not recognize the validity of attempting to relate its freedom of offensive nuclear action and the credibility of its offensive nuclear threat to the protection of American territory.

Critics of such strategic planning are vulnerable in two crucial respects: They do not, and cannot, offer policy prescriptions that will insure that the United States is never confronted with the stark choice between fighting a nuclear war or surrendering, and they do not offer a concept of deterrence that meets the extended responsibilities of U.S. strategic nuclear forces. No matter how elegant the deterrence theory, a question that cannot be avoided is what happens if deterrence mechanisms fail? Theorists whose concept of deterrence is limited to massive retaliation after Soviet attack would have nothing of interest to say to a president facing conventional defeat in the Persian Gulf or in Western Europe. Their strategic environment exists only in peacetime. They can recommend very limited, symbolic options but have no theory of how a large-scale Soviet response is to be deterred.

Reprinted with permission from *Foreign Policy* 39 (Summer 1980), pp. 14–27. Copyright © 1980 by Carnegie Endowment for International Peace.

Because many believe that homeland defense will lead to a steeper arms race and destabilize the strategic balance, the U.S. defense community has endorsed a posture that maximizes the prospect for self-deterrence. Yet the credibility of the extended U.S. deterrent depends on the Soviet belief that a U.S. president would risk nuclear escalation on behalf of foreign commitments.

In the late 1960s the United States endorsed the concept of strategic parity without thinking through what that would mean for the credibility of America's nuclear umbrella. A condition of parity or essential equivalence is incompatible with extended deterrent duties because of the self-deterrence inherent in such a strategic context. However, the practical implications of parity may be less dire in some areas of U.S. vital interest. Western Europe, for example, is so important an American interest that Soviet leaders could be more impressed by the character and duration of the U.S. commitment than by the details of the strategic balance.

A THREAT TO COMMIT SUICIDE

Ironically, it is commonplace to assert that war-survival theories affront the crucial test of political and moral acceptability. Surely no one can be comfortable with the claim that a strategy that would kill millions of Soviet citizens and would invite a strategic response that could kill tens of millions of U.S. citizens would be politically and morally acceptable. However, it is worth recalling the six guidelines for the use of force provided by the "just war" doctrine of the Catholic Church: Force can be used in a just cause; with a right intent; with a reasonable chance of success; in order that, if successful, its use offers a better future than would have been the case had it not been employed; to a degree proportional to the goals sought, or to the evil combated; and with the determination to spare noncombatants, when there is a reasonable chance of doing so.

These guidelines carry a message for U.S. policy. Specifically, as long as nuclear threat is a part of the U.S. diplomatic arsenal and provided that threat reflects real operational intentions—it is not a total bluff—U.S. defense planners are obliged to think through the probable course of a nuclear war. They must also have at least some idea of the intended relationship between force applied and the likelihood that political goals will be achieved—that is, a strategy.

Current American strategic policy is not compatible with at least three of the six just-war guidelines. The policy contains no definition of success aside from denying victory to the enemy, no promise that the successful use of nuclear power would insure a better future than surrender, and no sense of proportion because central war strategy in operational terms is not guided by political goals. In short, U.S. nuclear strategy is immoral.

Those who believe that a central nuclear war cannot be waged for political purposes because the destruction inflicted and suffered would dwarf the importance of any political goals can construct a coherent and logical policy position. They argue that nuclear war will be the end of history for the states involved, and that a threat to initiate nuclear war is a threat to commit suicide and thus lacks credibility. However, they acknowledge that nuclear weapons cannot be abolished. They maintain that even incredible threats may deter, provided the affront in question is sufficiently serious, because miscalculation by an adversary could have terminal consequences; because genuinely irrational behavior is always possible; and because the conflict could become uncontrollable.

In the 1970s the U.S. defense community rejected this theory of deterrence. Successive strategic targeting reviews appeared to move U.S. policy further and further from the declaratory doctrine of mutual assured destruction adopted by former Secretary of Defense Robert S. McNamara. Yet U.S. defense planners have not thoroughly studied the problems of nuclear war nor thought through the meaning of strategy in relation to nuclear war. The U.S. defense community has always tended to regard strategic nuclear war not as war but as a holocaust. Former Secretary of Defense James R. Schlesinger apparently adopted limited nuclear options (LNOs)—strikes employing anywhere from a handful to several dozen warheads—as a compromise between the optimists of the minimum deterrence school and the pessimists of the so-called war-fighting persuasion. By definition, LNOs apply only to the initial stages of a war. But what happens once LNOs have been exhausted? If the Soviets retaliated after U.S. LNOs, the United States would face the dilemma of escalating further or conciliating.

Deterrence may fail to be restored during war for several reasons: The enemy may not grant, in operational practice, the concept of intrawar deterrence and simply wage the war as it is able; and command, control, and communications may be degraded so rapidly that strategic decisions are precluded and both sides execute their war plans. Somewhat belatedly, the U.S. defense community has come to understand that flexibility in targeting and LNOs do not constitute a strategy and cannot compensate for inadequate strategic nuclear forces.

LNOs are the tactics of the strong, not of a country entering a period of strategic inferiority, as the United States is now. LNOs would be operationally viable only if the United States had a plausible theory of how it could control and dominate later escalation.

The fundamental inadequacy of flexible targeting, as presented in the 1970s, is that it neglected to take proper account of the fact that the United States would be initiating a process of competitive escalation that it had no basis for assuming could be concluded on satisfactory terms. Flexible targeting was an adjunct to plans that had no persuasive vision of how the application of force would promote the attainment of political objectives.

WAR AIMS

U.S. strategic targeting doctrine must have a unity of political purpose from the first to the last strikes. Strategic flexibility, unless wedded to a plausible theory of how to win a war or at least insure an acceptable end to a war, does not offer the United States an adequate bargaining position before or during a conflict and is an invitation to defeat. Small, preplanned strikes can only be of use if the United States enjoys strategic superiority—the ability to wage a nuclear war at any level of violence with a reasonable prospect of defeating the Soviet Union and of recovering sufficiently to insure a satisfactory postwar world order.

However, the U.S. government does not yet appear ready to plan seriously for the actual conduct of nuclear war should deterrence fail, in spite of the fact that such a policy should strengthen deterrence. Assured-destruction reasoning is proclaimed officially to be insufficient in itself as a strategic doctrine. However, a Soviet assured-destruction capability continues to exist as a result of the enduring official U.S. disinterest in strategic defense, with potentially paralyzing implications for the United States.

No matter how well designed and articulated, targeting plans that allow an enemy to inflict in retaliation whatever damage it wishes on American society are likely to prove unusable.

Four interdependent areas of strategic policy—strategy, weapons development and procurement, arms control, and defense doctrine—are currently treated separately. Theoretically, strategy should determine the evolution of the other three areas. In practice, it never has. Most of what has been portrayed as war-fighting strategy is nothing of the kind. Instead, it is an extension of the American theory of deterrence into war itself. To advocate LNOs and targeting flexibility and selectivity is not the same as to advocate a war-fighting, war-survival strategy.

Strategists do not find the idea of nuclear war fighting attractive. Instead, they believe that an ability to wage and survive war is vital for the effectiveness of deterrence; there can be no such thing as an adequate deterrent posture unrelated to probable wartime effectiveness; victory or defeat in nuclear war is possible, and such a war may have to be waged to that point; and, the clearer the vision of successful war termination, the more likely war can be waged intelligently at earlier stages.

There should be no misunderstanding the fact that the primary interest of U.S. strategy is deterrence. However, American strategic forces do not exist solely for the purpose of deterring a Soviet nuclear threat or attack against the United States itself. Instead, they are intended to support U.S. foreign policy, as reflected, for example, in the commitment to preserve Western Europe against aggression. Such a function requires American strategic forces that would enable a president to initiate strategic nuclear use for coercive, though politically defensive, purposes.

U.S. strategy, typically, has proceeded from the bottom up. Such targeting does not involve any conception of the war as a whole, nor of how the war might be concluded on favorable terms. The U.S. defense community cannot plan intelligently for lower levels of combat, unless it has an acceptable idea of where they might lead.

Most analyses of flexible targeting options assume virtually perfect stability at the highest levels of conflict. Advocates of flexible targeting assert that a U.S. LNO would signal the beginning of an escalation process that the Soviets would wish to avoid in light of the American threat to Soviet urban-industrial areas. Yet it seems inconsistent to argue that the U.S. threat of assured destruction would deter the Soviets from engaging in escalation following an LNO but that U.S. leaders could initiate the process despite the Soviet threat. What could be the basis of such relative U.S. resolve and Soviet vacillation in the face of strategic parity or Soviet superiority?

Moreover, the desired deterrent effect would probably depend upon the Soviet analysis of the entire nuclear campaign. In other words, Soviet leaders would be less impressed by American willingness to launch an LNO than they would be by a plausible American victory strategy. Such a theory would have to envisage the demise of the Soviet state. The United States should plan to defeat the Soviet Union and to do so at a cost that would not prohibit U.S. recovery. Washington should identify war aims that in the last resort would contemplate the destruction of Soviet political authority and the emergence of a postwar world order compatible with Western values.

The most frightening threat to the Soviet Union would be the destruction or serious impairment of its political system. Thus, the United States should be able to destroy key leadership cadres, their means of communication, and some of the instruments of domestic control. The USSR, with its gross overcentralization of authority, epitomized by its vast bureaucracy in Moscow, should be highly vulnerable to such an attack. The Soviet Union might cease to function if its security agency, the KGB, were severely crippled. If the Moscow bureaucracy could be eliminated, damaged, or isolated, the USSR might disintegrate into anarchy, hence the extensive civil defense preparations intended to insure the survival of the Soviet leadership. Judicious U.S. targeting and weapon procurement policies might be able to deny the USSR the assurance of political survival.

Once the defeat of the Soviet state is established as a war aim, defense professionals should attempt to identify an optimum targeting plan for the accomplishment of that goal. For example, Soviet political control of its territory in Central Asia and in the Far East could be weakened by discriminate nuclear targeting. The same applies to Transcaucasia and Eastern Europe.

THE ULTIMATE PENALTY

Despite a succession of U.S. targeting reviews, Soviet leaders, looking to the mid-1980s, may well anticipate the ability to wage World War III successfully. The continuing trend in the East-West military balance allows Soviet military planners to design a theory of military victory that is not implausible and that may stir hopes among Soviet political leaders that they might reap many of the rewards of military success even without having to fight. The Soviets may anticipate that U.S. self-deterrence could discourage Washington from punishing Soviet society. Even if the United States were to launch a large-scale second strike against Soviet military and economic targets, the resulting damage should be bearable to the Soviet Union given the stakes of the conflict and the fact that the Soviets would control regions abroad that could contribute to its recovery.

In the late 1960s the United States identified the destruction of 20–25 per cent of the population and 50–75 per cent of industrial capacity as the ultimate penalty it had to be able to inflict on the USSR. In the 1970s the United States shifted its attention to the Soviet recovery economy. The Soviet theory of victory depends on the requirement that the Soviet Union survive and recover rapidly from a nuclear conflict. However, the U.S. government does not completely understand the details of the Soviet recovery economy, and the concept has lost popularity as a result. Highly complex modeling of the Soviet economy cannot disguise the fact that the available evidence is too rudimentary to permit any confidence in the analysis. With an inadequate data base it should require little imagination to foresee how difficult it is to determine targeting priorities in relation to the importance of different economic targets for recovery.

Schlesinger's advocacy of essential equivalence called for a U.S. ability to match military damage for military damage. But American strategic development since the early 1970s has not been sufficient to maintain the American end of that balance. Because the U.S. defense community has refused to recognize the importance of the possibility that a nuclear war could be won or lost, it has neglected to think beyond a punitive sequence of targeting options.

American nuclear strategy is not intended to defeat the Soviet Union or insure the survival of the United States in any carefully calculated manner. Instead, it is intended to insure that the Soviet Union is punished increasingly severely. American targeting philosophy today is only a superficial improvement over that prevalent in the late 1960s, primarily because U.S. defense planners do not consider anticipated damage to the United States to be relevant to the integrity of their offensive war plans. The strategic case for ballistic missile defense and civil defense has not been considered on its merits for a decade.

In the late 1970s the United States targeted a range of Soviet economic entities that were important either to war-supporting industry or to economic recovery. The rationale for this targeting scheme was, and remains, fragile. War-supporting industry is important only for a war of considerable duration or for a period of postwar defense mobilization. Moreover, although recovery from war is an integral part of a Soviet theory of victory, it is less important than the achievement of military success. If the USSR is able to win the war, it should have sufficient military force in reserve to compel the surviving world economy to contribute to Soviet recovery. Thus, the current trend is to move away from targeting the recovery economy.

To date, the U.S. government has declined to transcend what amounts to a deterrence-through-punishment approach to strategic war planning. Moreover, the strategic targeting reviews of the 1970s did not address the question of self-deterrence adequately. The United States has no ballistic missile defense and effectively no civil defense, while U.S. air defense is capable of guarding American air space only in peace-time. The Pentagon has sought to compensate for a lack of relative military muscle through more imaginative strategic targeting. Review after review has attempted to identify more effective ways in which the USSR could be hurt. Schlesinger above all sought essential equivalence through a more flexible set of targeting options without calling for extensive new U.S. strategic capabilities. Indeed, he went to some pains to separate the question of targeting design from procurement issues.

The United States should identify nuclear targeting options that could help restore deterrence, yet would destroy the Soviet state and enhance the likelihood of U.S. survival if fully implemented. The first priority of such a targeting scheme would be Soviet military power of all kinds, and the second would be the political, military, and economic control structure of the USSR. Successful strikes against military and political control targets would reduce the Soviet ability to project military power abroad and to sustain political authority at home. However, it would not be in the interest of the United States actually to implement an offensive nuclear strategy no matter how frightening in Soviet perspective, if the U.S. homeland were totally naked to Soviet retaliation.

Striking the USSR should entail targeting the relocation bunkers of the top political and bureaucratic leadership, including those of the KGB; key communication centers of the Communist party, the military, and the government; and many of the economic, political, and military records. Even limited destruction of some of these targets and substantial isolation of many of the key personnel who survive could have revolutionary consequences for the country.

THE ARMAGEDDON SYNDROME

The strategic questions that remain incompletely answered are in some ways more difficult than the practical problems of targeting the political control structure. Is it sensible to destroy the government of the enemy, thus eliminating the option of negotiating an end to the war? In the unlikely event that the United States identifies all of the key relocation bunkers for the central political leadership, who would then conduct the Soviet war effort and to what ends? Since after a large-scale counter-control strike the surviving Soviet leadership would have little else to fear, could this targeting option be anything other than a threat?

The U.S. defense community today believes that the political control structure of the USSR is among the most important targets for U.S. strategic forces. However, just how important such targeting might be for deterrence or damage limitation has not been determined. Current American understanding of exactly how the control structure functions is less than perfect. But that is a technical matter that can in principle be solved through more research. The issue of whether the Soviet control structure should actually be struck is more problematic.

Strategists cannot offer painless conflicts or guarantee that their preferred posture and doctrine promise a greatly superior deterrence posture to current American schemes. But, they can claim that an intelligent U.S. offensive strategy, wedded to homeland defenses, should reduce U.S. casualties to approximately 20 million, which should render U.S. strategic threats more credible. If the United States developed the targeting plans and procured the weapons necessary to hold the Soviet political, bureaucratic, and military leadership at risk, that should serve as the functional equivalent in Soviet perspective of the assured-destruction effect of the late 1960s. However, the U.S. targeting community has not determined how it would organize this targeting option.

A combination of counterforce offensive targeting, civil defense, and ballistic missile and air defense should hold U.S. casualties down to a level compatible with national survival and recovery. The actual number would depend on several factors, some of which the United States could control (the level of U.S. homeland defenses); some of which it could influence (the weight and character of the Soviet attack); and some of which might evade anybody's ability to control or influence (for example, the weather). What can be assured is a choice between a defense program that insures the survival of the vast majority of Americans with relative confidence and one that deliberately permits the Soviet Union to wreak whatever level of damage it chooses.

No matter how grave the Soviet offense, a U.S. president cannot credibly threaten and should not launch a strategic nuclear strike if expected U.S. casualties are likely to involve 100 million or more American citizens. There is a difference between a doctrine that can offer little rational guidance should deterrence fail and a doctrine that a president might employ responsibly for identified political purposes. Existing evidence on the probable consequences of nuclear exchanges suggests that there should be a role for strategy in nuclear war. To ignore the possibility that strategy can be applied to nuclear war is to insure by choice a nuclear apocalypse if deterrence fails. The current U.S. deterrence posture is fundamentally flawed because it does not provide for the protection of American territory.

Nuclear war is unlikely to be an essentially meaningless, terminal event. Instead it is likely to be waged to coerce the Soviet Union to give up some recent gain. Thus, a president must have the ability not merely to end a war, but to end it favorably. The United States would need to be able to persuade desperate and determined Soviet leaders that it has the capability, and the determination, to wage nuclear war at ever higher levels of violence until an acceptable outcome is achieved. For deterrence to function during a war each side would have to calculate whether an improved outcome is possible through further escalation.

An adequate U.S. deterrent posture is one that denies the Soviet Union any plausible hope of success at any level of strategic conflict; offers a likely prospect of Soviet defeat; and offers a reasonable chance of limiting damage to the United States. Such a deterrence posture is often criticized as contributing to the arms race and causing strategic instability, because it would stimulate new Soviet deployments. However, during the 1970s the Soviet Union showed that its weapon development and deployment decisions are not dictated by American actions. Western understanding of what determines Soviet defense procurement is less than perfect, but it is now obvious that Soviet weapon decisions cannot be explained with reference to any simple action-reaction model of arms-race dynamics. In addition, highly survivable U.S. strategic forces should insure strategic stability by denying the Soviets an attractive first-strike target set.

An Armageddon syndrome lurks behind most concepts of nuclear strategy. It amounts either to the belief that because the United States could lose as many as 20 million people, it should not save the 80 million or more who otherwise would be at risk, or to a disbelief in the serious possibility that 200 million Americans could survive a nuclear war.

There is little satisfaction in advocating an operational nuclear doctrine that could result in the deaths of 20 million or more people in an unconstrained nuclear war. However, as long as the United States relies on nuclear threats to deter an increasingly powerful Soviet Union, it is inconceivable that the U.S. defense community can continue to divorce its thinking on deterrence from its planning for the efficient conduct of war and defense of the country. Prudence in the latter should enhance the former.

4   The Situation Today: Nuclear Forces that Reflect War-Fighting Doctrine

Robert S. McNamara and Hans A. Bethe

The superpowers' arsenals hold some 50,000 nuclear warheads. Each, on average, is far more destructive than the bomb that obliterated Hiroshima. Just one of our thirty-six strategic submarines has more firepower than man has shot against man throughout history. Thousands of nuclear weapons are ready for immediate use against targets close to hand or half a globe away, but just a few hundred warheads could utterly demolish the largest nation.

To deter war, each side seeks to persuade the other, and itself, that it is prepared to wage a nuclear war that would have the military objectives of a bygone age. What is known of Soviet nuclear-war plans is open to interpretation, but these plans appear to rely on tactics derived from Russia's pre-nuclear military experience. Current U.S. defense policy calls for nuclear forces that are sufficient to support a "controlled and protracted" nuclear war that could eliminate the Soviet leadership and that would even permit the United States to "prevail."

Nuclear-war-fighting notions lead to enormous target lists and huge forces. Our 11,000 strategic warheads are directed against some 5,000 targets. And NATO's war plans are based on early first use of some 6,000 tactical nuclear weapons in response to a Soviet conventional attack. Both NATO and the Warsaw Pact countries routinely train their forces for nuclear operations. War-fighting doctrines create a desire for increasingly sophisticated nuclear weapons which technology always promises to satisfy but never does. Today both sides are committed to programs that will threaten a growing portion of the adversary's most vital military assets with increasingly swift destruction.

These armories and war plans are more than macabre symbols for bolstering self-confidence. Both Moscow and Washington presume that nuclear weapons are likely to be used should hostilities break out. But neither knows how to control the escalation that would almost certainly follow. No one can tell in advance what response any nuclear attack might bring. No one knows who will still be able to communicate with whom, or what will be left to say, or whether any message could possibly be believed.

When our secretary of defense, Caspar Weinberger, was asked whether it really would be possible to control forces and make calculated decisions amid the destruction and confusion of nuclear battle, he replied, "I just don't have any idea. I don't know that anybody has any idea." Surely it is reckless to stake a nation's survival on detailed plans for something about which no one has any idea.

It would be vastly more reckless to attempt a disarming first strike. Nevertheless, the arms race is driven by deep-seated fears held by each side that the other has, or is seeking, the ability to execute just such a strike.

The large force of powerful and increasingly accurate Soviet ICBMs has created the fear of a first strike in the minds of many U.S. leaders. According to this scenario, the Soviet missiles could, at one stroke, eliminate most of our Minuteman ICBMs; our surviving submarines and bombers would enable us only to retaliate against Soviet cities; but we would not do so because of our fear of a Soviet counterattack on our urban population; and thus we would have no choice but to yield to all Soviet demands.

A more subtle variant of this nightmare would have the Soviets exacting political blackmail by merely threatening such an attack.

Those who accept the first-strike scenario view the Soviet ICBMs and the men who command them as objects in a universe decoupled from the real world. They assume that Soviet leaders are confident that their highly complex systems, which have been tested only individually and in a controlled environment, would perform their myriad tasks in perfect harmony during the most cataclysmic battle in history; that our electronic eavesdropping satellites would detect no hint of the intricate preparations that such a strike would require; that we would not launch our missiles when the attack was detected; and that the thousands of submarine-based and airborne warheads that would surely survive would not be used against a wide array of vulnerable Soviet military targets. Finally, they assume Soviet confidence that we would not use those vast surviving forces to retaliate against the Soviet population, even though tens of millions of Americans had been killed by the Soviet attack on our silos. Only madmen would contemplate such a gamble. Whatever else they may be, the leaders of the Soviet Union are not madmen.

That a first strike is not a rational Soviet option has also been stated by President Reagan's own Scowcroft Commission, which found that no combination of attacks from Soviet submarines and land-based ICBMs could catch our bombers on the ground as well as our Minutemen in their silos. In addition, our submarines at sea, which carry a substantial percentage of our strategic warheads, are invulnerable: in the race between techniques to hide submarines and those to find them, the fugitives have always been ahead and are widening their lead. As the chief of naval operations has said, the oceans are getting "more opaque" as we "learn more about them."

Despite all such facts, the war-fighting mania and the fear of a first strike are eroding confidence in deterrence. Though both sides are aware that a nuclear war that engaged even a small fraction of their arsenals would be an unparalleled disaster, each is vigorously developing and deploying new weapons systems that it will view as highly threatening when the opponent also acquires them. Thus our newest submarines will soon carry missiles accurate enough to destroy Soviet silos. When the Soviets follow suit, as they always do, their offshore submarines will for the first time pose a simultaneous threat to our command centers, bomber bases, and Minuteman ICBMs.

The absurd struggle to improve the ability to wage "the war that cannot be fought" has shaken confidence in the ability to avert that war. The conviction that we must change course is shared by groups and individuals as diverse as the freeze movement, the President, the Catholic bishops, the bulk of the nation's scientists, the President's chief arms-control negotiator, and ourselves. All are saying, directly or by implication, that nuclear warheads serve no military purpose whatsoever. They are not weapons. They are totally useless except to deter one's opponent from using his warheads. Beyond this point the consensus dissolves, because the changes of direction being advocated follow from very different diagnoses of the predicament.

5 Risks of Unintentional Nuclear War

Daniel Frei

The possibility of a nuclear holocaust being triggered unintentionally is a matter of growing concern. Large sectors of the public are increasingly alarmed by the traumatic prospect of a system of strategic deterrence getting out of control and suddenly confronting mankind with a doomsday nightmare.

Ever since the film *Dr. Strangelove* portrayed such a prospect, it has become quite popular to worry about insane colonels ordering an unauthorized missile launch, hapless officers pushing the wrong button, the self-activation of an electronic guidance system, blips on a radar screen showing a flock of geese, which is mistaken for attacking missiles, and so on. Yet popular belief in these and other nuclear-war-by-accident scenarios does not necessarily mean that such scenarios are relevant.

Although the dangers of possible nuclear accidents and incidents must certainly not be underestimated, the conclusion cannot be avoided that the focus on the risk of nuclear war by accident may misrepresent the problem and draw attention away from more serious risks. While redundant and efficient safeguard systems practically rule out any serious possibility of human and technical failure, international crises pose a far greater danger. As the following analysis will show, it is quite conceivable that an acute international crisis may act as a catalyst to trigger a nuclear war not in fact intended by the Governments concerned.

What is being envisaged here is not accidental nuclear war, but rather nuclear war based on false assumptions, i.e. on misjudgement or

Excerpted with permission from Daniel Frei, *Risks of Unintentional Nuclear War* (pp. xi–xiii). United Nations Institute for Disarmament Research (Geneva: 1982).

miscalculation by the persons legitimately authorized to decide on the use of nuclear weapons. Substandard performance by decision-makers in crisis situations is particularly common: more than two decades of crisis research have provided ample evidence of all kinds of individual and organizational failures, such as misperceptions, erratic behaviour under stress, the improper handling of information, the escalation of hostilities by mirror-image mechanisms, the hazards of "group-think", the failure to implement decisions due to their overwhelming complexity, confusion due to organizational bottlenecks and the inflexibility of standard operating procedures. This creates many opportunities for the adoption of fatally wrong decisions. Some authors have recently referred to the 1914 analogy, which in fact continues to constitute a frightening example of the cumulative effect of such mistakes in an acute crisis confrontation. Today, similar situations might involve States armed with nuclear weapons and hence would very likely mean nothing less than the beginning of a nuclear holocaust.

WHY UNINTENTIONAL NUCLEAR WAR? THE ANATOMY OF THE DANGER

When referring to international crises as the possible catalysts of an unintentional nuclear war, it would be quite simplistic to claim that any crisis creates a trigger-happy situation involving the risk of nuclear war. The risks do not originate in the crisis situation alone; they are generated by the crisis if and only if the strategic system has a certain propensity to become destabilized. Strategic instability and a crisis as a catalytic cause are necessary and sufficient conditions for triggering an unintentional nuclear war. It is their combination which creates a synergistic effect that may lead to a nuclear war.

Strategic instability can be said to exist if the Governments facing an international crisis feel that it is extremely urgent to decide on the use of nuclear weapons. The urgency in turn depends on the vulnerability of their strategic weapons and C^3 (command, control and communications) systems. If the strategic forces and/or the command channels which carry the threat of retaliation are vulnerable to sudden destruction, this threat can be removed by a preemptive attack aimed at those forces. On the other hand, strategic stability exists if the overall relation of forces leads potential opponents to conclude that any attempt to settle their conflict by using nuclear weapons entails a clearly unacceptable risk. Related to this is the concept of Mutual Assured Destruction (MAD), which implies that neither country's strategic nuclear deterrent force should be vulnerable to a first strike by the other; therefore, neither country has any incentive whatever to strike first. Some authors very pertinently prefer to replace the term "strategic stability" by the term "crisis stability", meaning a configuration of strategic forces which, in a situation of international crisis, allows each side to wait without any great disadvantage in case the other side attacks. By contrast, crisis *in*stability leads to pre-emption by creating an urge for timely action and the first use of nuclear weapons.

Strategic or crisis stability is a central concept of strategic thinking in both East and West. Although Soviet sources do not use this term as explicitly as is the case in official American sources, the issue of strategic stability can rightly be said to be a matter of common concern. The two major powers formally acknowledged its importance in the Joint Statement of Principles and Basic Guidelines for Subsequent Negotiations on the Limitation of Strategic Arms, signed on 18 June 1979 in the context of the SALT II negotiations. In this Statement, the two signatories reaffirmed that "the strengthening of strategic stability meets the interests of the Parties and the interests of international security". They agreed to "continue for the purpose of reducing and averting the risk of outbreak of nuclear war to seek measures to strengthen strategic stability".

The nature of crisis stability can be further described and illustrated by two familiar paradigms offered by games theory. Under conditions of strategic stability, both opponents recognize that the use of nuclear weapons would inevitably entail destruction and death on both sides and, possibly, mutual annihilation. Therefore, both sides have an interest in choosing a co-operative strategy, i.e. avoiding the use of nuclear weapons. Thus the situation tends to stabilize itself; this is the typical outcome of so-called "chicken" game situations.

If, on the other hand, there is a premium on pre-emptive attack, i.e. if, by a preventive first strike, the opponent's capability to retaliate can be successfully knocked out and if both sides perceive the situation this way, they feel a strong urge to launch a disarming first strike. Under these circumstances peculiar to the so-called "prisoner's dilemma" game, the strategic system is highly unstable. In such a situation, a crisis confrontation is liable to trigger a nuclear war even if the Governments concerned do not intend to do so. It is the simple fear that the opponent might strike first which creates a powerful incentive for each side to keep at least one step ahead on the escalation ladder.

In order to assess the risk of unintentional nuclear war, two main questions have to be asked:

(1)   What factors tend to affect crisis stability in the contemporary international system?

(2)   What are the prospects of the use of force as a "continuation of politics by other means" generating acute international crises?

Account might also be taken of the institutions set up and the multilateral and bilateral agreements signed with a view to mitigating the risks of crisis instability and crisis avoidance and/or crisis management:

(3)   How do existing agreements help to counter the risk of unintentional nuclear war?

FACTORS AFFECTING CRISIS STABILITY

When trying to assess the probability of averting crisis instability, three aspects of the current evolution of the strategic system have to be envisaged: (1) the arms race; (2) the development of strategic doctrines; and (3) nuclear proliferation. These three issues involve serious challenges to future crisis stability.

Arms Race Instability versus Crisis Stability

The current arms race implies the danger that the vulnerability of the strategic systems deployed by the two major Powers will be constantly jeopardized by technological improvements. Qualitative changes thus play a more important role than the quantitative arms race: the retaliatory forces of the other side are being threatened and a pre-emptive first strike becomes potentially feasible as a result of developments such as the introduction of multiple independently targetable re-entry vehicles (MIRVs), higher-yield warheads, the higher accuracy of delivery systems and the improved certainty with which the location of targets can be determined. At the same time, the invulnerability of potential targets is challenged by the development of anti-satellites capable of interfering with early-warning and C³ systems and even more so by potential breakthroughs in anti-submarine warfare jeopardizing the relative invulnerability of sea-based deterrent forces. Furthermore, the feasibility of launching a disarming surprise attack is supported by the ability to fire missiles whose flight time is just a few minutes, owing either to increased speed or to the close stationing of the launchers. A grave threat is thus also posed to the invulnerability of C³ systems, thereby giving rise to fears of a "decapitation" surprise attack against command centers and communications facilities. These prospects may in turn make it tempting to adopt launch-on-warning policies or predelegation measures giving subordinate commanders the competence to decide on the release of nuclear weapons. Finally, new technologies contribute to the strengthening of the defensive protection of strategic forces, especially land-based intercontinental ballistic missiles (ICBMs), as well as civilian targets. If it were possible to establish an operational anti-missile defence system, the first Power having such a system might be tempted to launch a disarming strike against its opponent, which would in such a case be deprived of the capability to punish the attacker by a retaliatory second strike.

Recent official United States and Soviet publications offer ample proof that both sides are afraid that their opponent is acquiring or intends to acquire first-strike capability. They tend to have precisely the same fears, suspicions and nervous attitudes. Their expectations and allegations fuel the arms race, regardless of whether they are correct or false. They prevent the arms race from becoming stabilized; arms-race stability can be said to exist if there appears to be no way for one side to achieve an overwhelming advantage over the other by quickly acquiring any feasible quantity of some weapon and, thus, there is no really strong incentive to do so.

Much has been written about the causal factors that determine the dynamics of the arms race. The armaments process seems to be largely governed by an intrinsic inertia having its own momentum independently of conscious decisions taken by policy-makers. There is also a tendency towards mirror-imaging; scientists and engineers often do not wait for a potential enemy to react, but, operating on "worst case" assumptions, react against their own brain-children by designing counter-weapons designed to neutralize weapons developed previously. The arms race is progressing on an incremental step-by-step basis without proper national, let alone international, control. Whatever the causes of the arms race, it cannot be denied that the arms race instability prevailing in the contemporary international system undermines crisis stability.

This does not mean that the arms race has already succeeded in destroying crisis stability. It must not be overlooked that there are also some mitigating factors. The nuclear Powers are extremely sensitive about and attentive to the potential vulnerability of their retaliatory capacity and C³ systems; consequently, they make enormous efforts to forestall potential "windows of vulnerability". New weapons technologies also require testing because no sane decision-maker would be inclined to launch a pre-emptive attack with a new weapon without having determined its reliability; however, testing mitigates the danger of being surprised by a technological breakthrough achieved by the opponent. The MAD relationship continues to prevail and will do so for the foreseeable future. The risks of arms-race instability are not at present liable to upset crisis stability. Yet they are utterly alarming in the long run.

Destabilizing Effects of Doctrinal Developments

The international strategic system is determined by what Soviet authors call "objective factors"—arms—and "subjective factors"—doctrines. Strategic doctrines are sets of operational beliefs, values and assertions that guide official behaviour with respect to strategic research and development, weapons choices, acquisitions policy, force deployment, operational plans, force employment, arms control, etc. Notwithstanding their high degree of sophistication, they ultimately rest on complex and indissoluble political judgements and are thus subject to all kinds of fallacies, distortions and misjudgements. This has particularly dangerous consequences for United States–Soviet strategic relations because United States strategic doctrine is characterized by a bewildering array of partly contradictory conceptions, while Soviet strategic doctrine is surrounded by a high degree of secrecy. There is every reason to assume that strategic doctrines in East and West are mismatched.

This mismatch has its origin in deep-rooted differences in philosophical and national traditions. Assumptions such as permanent conflict or the "ultimate triumph of socialism" and misrepresentations of the Soviet concept of surprise in the battlefield can hardly be said to promote mutual understanding and harmony in matters of strategic doctrines. Linguistic difficulties only make this problem worse. For instance, the English word "stability" cannot be adequately translated into Russian by the word *stabilnost*; while "stability" in the Western sense corresponds to crisis stability as defined above, the Russian term *stabilnost* seems to be synonymous with "balance" or "parity" in general. In the context of the United States, the debate about "parity", "superiority" and "sufficiency" is a particularly confusing aspect of strategic thinking; the practical usefulness of these terms is rather doubtful.

Mismatch and confusion in the field of strategic doctrine challenge crisis stability in two ways: they lead either to underestimation or overestimation of the opponent's intentions in a situation of acute international crisis.

Underestimating the opponent's intentions means that the deterrent ceases to be credible. A may assume that B is bluffing and thus underestimate B's resolve to honour its commitment; or A may assume that it would be irrational for B to carry out the threat to retaliate. Hence deterrence fails and a crisis may easily escalate into a nuclear war in which the attacker may realize too late that his action was based on miscalculation. On the other hand, overestimating the opponent's intentions is a result of "worst case" assumptions resulting from a strategic relationship dominated by ambiguity and a lack of proper mutual understanding of each other's strategic doctrines. "Worst case" thinking may lead A to infer from everything it sees and hears that B is engaged in preparations for launching a disarming first strike; hence it feels a strong urge to prevent impending disaster by quickly attacking B by surprise according to the logic of "use it or lose it". Again, this kind of reasoning would have disastrous consequences if it prevailed in decision-making during an acute international crisis.

The dilemma generated by the asymmetric and fuzzy nature of strategic doctrines of East and West has particularly grave consequences for the strategic situation in Europe. The Governments of the NATO countries realize that the strategic situation in Europe is characterized by a marked conventional imbalance favouring the Warsaw Treaty Organization (WTO). Since the NATO countries do not, for various reasons, feel in a position to redress this imbalance by an appropriate build-up of conventional armaments, NATO strategy basically refuses to rule out the use of nuclear weapons (mainly tactical nuclear weapons) to counter a WTO attack carried out by conventional or nuclear means against the territory of a NATO ally should NATO's conventional defence be overrun. This doctrine makes it highly uncertain that it would be profitable to attempt to exploit conventional superiority by launching a tank "blitzkrieg" for example.

NATO's strategy creates a two-fold credibility problem: first, the Soviet Union firmly rejects the idea that a nuclear war, once started by NATO's first use of nuclear weapons, could be kept limited or controlled; secondly, Soviet sources threaten to launch a "full-scale devastating and annihilating" retaliation strike against the homeland of the United States, thus casting doubts on the credibility of extended deterrence implying nothing less than the incineration of Chicago and New York for the sake of Hamburg and Hanover. On the other hand, NATO tries to enhance the credibility of its concept of extended deterrence and nuclear deterrence against any kind of attack by introducing a land-based intermediate range nuclear force (INF) in Western Europe; however, this policy is promptly denounced by WTO as an attempt to achieve first-strike capability and even the capability of surprise attack against Soviet strategic forces and C^3 installations by launching highly accurate INF missiles with an extremely short flight time (6 to 8 minutes). By placing emphasis on such prospects and uncertainties, the West's deterrence is in turn being deterred, thus eroding the credibility of the United States "nuclear umbrella" over Europe and, at the same time, accusing the West of preparing a disarming first strike. Both aspects are clear indications of doubt about the crisis stability of nuclear armament and strategic doctrines in and for Europe. It would be naïve to assume that the problem could be solved and stability redressed by suggesting common understanding of strategic doctrines. On the contrary, it seems that the mutual rejection of strategic concepts is part of a deliberate and conscious effort to manipulate each other's deterrence posture and, in particular, its doctrinal underpinnings.

When assessing the risks involved in the problem of strategic doctrines, the mitigating factors should not be overlooked. Nor should tendencies and potential dangers be confused with the actual state of affairs. Doubts about credibility do not automatically lead to a complete breakdown of credible deterrence. For the time being, the threat of retaliation and, thus, the expectation of incalculable damage is still effective and credible. No nuclear Power can expect to escape retaliation if it launches a preemptive strike against its opponents unless its Government engages in insane risk-taking behaviour. Although they are far from satisfactory, strategic doctrines do not destroy crisis stability. Yet this situation of relative stability will not be safe indefinitely. It should also be borne in mind that doubt and the erosion of the credibility of deterrence by the evolution of strategic doctrines tend to generate low-key crises and limited probes which in turn involve a risk of escalation.

Precarious Stability in a World of Many Nuclear Powers

In the very near future, a considerable number of countries might acquire nuclear weapons. The efforts made to halt nuclear proliferation may eventually prove to be insufficient, particularly if the nuclear-weapon States themselves do not start a genuine process of nuclear disarmament. In the context of this contribution, it must be asked whether more nuclear Powers will mean more nuclear wars or a greater risk of international crises triggering nuclear conflagration. When trying to answer this question the problem has to be seen in terms of the likelihood of the outbreak of nuclear war between countries emerging as nuclear Powers, on the one hand, and in terms of the likelihood of a new nuclear Power triggering an all-out nuclear war among other nuclear Powers and, in particular, the United States of America and the Soviet Union, on the other hand.

As far as the first problem is concerned, the arguments put forward in the rapidly growing literature on nuclear proliferation are very con-

troversial. Some specialists argue that an increase in the number of nuclear Powers would reduce the probability of war by providing an additional restraining force and increasing uncertainty about the others' reaction. Other authors, however, refer to the delicate situation of regional crisis instability that exists when a nation is about to become a nuclear Power. As a State develops a nuclear capability, there will be a temptation for its potential enemies to attack it before its nuclear delivery system is operational. That was the rationale underlying the "surgical strike" executed by Israel against Iraq's Osirak research reactor. A similar incentive to pre-empt may also be generated after two regional rival countries have acquired nuclear weapons, which, in the initial stage, will be characterized by a high degree of vulnerability that creates a temptation to launch a pre-emptive strike. Hence there is some probability that local crises will escalate into local nuclear wars.

The second problem relates to the possibility that such a local nuclear war might ignite a general nuclear war. One might assume that the two major Powers would behave with utmost care and circumspection in any such conflict. They might even be tempted to exert pressure on their respective clients not to use nuclear weapons. Nevertheless, any generalized conclusion would be misleading. The outcome of a conflagration of this kind would probably be determined by the nature of the involvement and commitment of the two major Powers. Hence the evolution of a crisis would be different in different regions.

THE FUTURE OF INTERNATIONAL CRISES

Since unintentional nuclear war may result from the cumulative effect of inherent crisis instability and acute crisis confrontation, the prospects for future crises must be examined. In particular, two aspects have to be analysed: (1) the impact of nuclear armaments and nuclear strategy on the nature of crises; and (2) the propensity of the international system to generate crises.

The Nature of Crises in the Nuclear Age

According to a familiar definition, crises are the result of a threat to basic values, the high probability of involvement in military hostility and awareness of a time limit for response to the external threat. There is hardly any need for further explanation in order to conclude that the existence of nuclear weapons and the evolution of nuclear strategic doctrines inevitably intensify the gravity and urgency of crisis situations. The nature of nuclear threat establishes a completely new order of magnitude of a danger never heard of before, virtually leading to terror. (It should be noted, in this context, that the term "terror" has the same etymological root as the term "deterrence".) At worst, terror tends to upset firmly established role structures and traditional patterns of perception and behaviour, thus making it extremely difficult to think clearly and decide properly. In other words, the element of terror inherent in any nuclear threat may cause unsuitable behaviour both in individuals and in organizations faced with an international crisis.

Furthermore, any tendency of nuclear-weapon systems to create urgency due to vulnerability in turn helps to aggravate a crisis. The more serious a crisis, however, the more the decision-makers' capability of making an appropriate, rational analysis of the situation is reduced. This is highly unfortunate at a time when strategic doctrines are becoming increasingly complex and are based on a variety of weapons with different performance characteristics. It must therefore be asked whether the political leaders of the countries concerned, in the hectic situation of a crisis emergency, will still be capable of deciding and acting fully in accordance with the requirements of the complex and infinitely subtle logic of nuclear crisis strategy. Decision-makers may become victims of urgency and commit all kinds of mistakes, miscalculations and misperceptions.

In other words, the propensity of the strategic system to become unstable has additional consequences that aggravate the risk of unintentional war by increasing the probability of inappropriate decisions. Thus, crises in the nuclear age are far more dangerous than in the pre-nuclear age. Of course, contemporary political leaders still remember Hiroshima and therefore adopt a very cautious attitude towards the use of nuclear weapons. Yet the general trend may, in the long run, offset these restraints.

The Use of Force: Tendencies and Prospects

Despite the threat of nuclear disaster, the frequency of international crises has not declined in the nuclear age. "Coercive bargaining" is and continues to be a dominant factor in international politics. The symbolic use of force is general practice in the international system. The use of force for the purpose of conveying signals to the opponent in a situation of coercive bargaining may easily produce incidents of all kinds which have a propensity to escalate. This risk is even more serious if nuclear weapons serve as demonstrations of resolve; there are reports of measures such as putting missiles on various levels of alert status, deploying strategic bombers, placing more bombers in the air on airborne alert, deploying tactical nuclear weapons near the crisis area, sending more nuclear submarines on patrol, etc.

The danger inherent in this type of manipulation of the risks of nuclear war naturally leads statesmen to behave with much more caution whenever nuclear weapons are involved. Both the United States and the Soviet Union are known to be placing more emphasis on the central control of their systems. Also, as soon as a crisis escalates, the political leaders of the countries concerned tend to pay much more attention to minute tactical details than in periods of "normalcy". Nevertheless, the fact that it is very difficult to convey messages credibly through this kind of manipulation of force in a situation dominated by distrust must not be disregarded. There is a possibility of misunderstanding and hence of miscalculation in every step made in this delicate field.

There are many reasons to expect cases of coercive bargaining to continue and even increase. Whenever a situation of rivalry between two nuclear Powers is characterized by a high degree of ambiguity, it invites provocation, i.e., all kinds of "limited probes" and "controlled pressure". Ambiguity is presently growing in third world regions where the two major Powers are increasingly inclined to engage in all kinds of poorly defined commitments. Unlike "classical" alliance commitments, this new type of commitment implies a great deal of uncertainty and unpredictability. This gives the two major Powers more opportunities to "test" each other by means of crisis confrontation and coercive bargaining. Hence the risks involved in unintended consequences of such behaviour become proportionately greater.

6 Nuclear Proliferation Today

Leonard S. Spector

The spread of nuclear weapons poses one of the greatest threats of our time and is among the most likely triggers of a future nuclear holocaust. It is sobering, for example, to reflect on how the superpowers might have responded if Israel had used nuclear weapons against Soviet-backed Egyptian forces in the 1973 Middle East War, a course Israel reportedly considered.

Even if nuclear cataclysm were avoided, the use of nuclear arms in a regional war could cause untold devastation. A handful of nuclear weapons could destroy any country in the Middle East as a national entity, cause hundreds of thousands of casualties in the densely populated cities of India or Pakistan, or, if used against the Persian Gulf oil fields, undermine the economies of the West.

The spread of nuclear arms also raises the risk that new nuclear weapon states may attempt to intimidate their non-nuclearized neighbors. Libya might well use nuclear arms to support its adventurism in Northern Africa, while South Africa's nuclear weapons capability may already be buttressing its efforts to impose a regional settlement on neighboring states. Even the major powers are vulnerable to such pressures: Argentina's possession of nuclear arms, for example, would certainly have entered into British calculations in responding to the invasion of the Falklands.

The spread of nuclear arms also increases the risk of their falling into the hands of dissident military elements or revolutionaries. Indeed, if the Shah's nuclear program had been perhaps

From Spector's *Nuclear Proliferation Today* (pp. 3–14), copyright 1984 by Carnegie Endowment for International Peace. Reprinted with permission from Ballinger Publishing Company.

five years more advanced, Iran's revolutionary government might today have the essentials for nuclear arms. The threat of nuclear terrorism is also growing. Boston, Orlando, Los Angeles, and Spokane have already been the target of apparently credible nuclear threats that later proved to be hoaxes. In the case of a genuine threat, national leaders would face agonizing choices. At the same time, the spread of nuclear weapons heightens the likelihood of conventional war, as governments become tempted to strike preemptively against the nuclear installations of potential adversaries. Israel took such a step in 1981, and some observers believe India may now be contemplating similar action.

Finally, the more nations that possess nuclear weapons, the greater the risk that such arms will be used accidentally or inadvertently. No nuclear command and control system can be fool-proof. The greater the number of such systems, the higher the probability of a failure.

For all these reasons, halting the spread of nuclear arms has been a long-standing priority for the United States and the international community. . . .

THE HISTORICAL SETTING

As of July 1984, five nations—the United States, the Soviet Union, Great Britain, France, and China—are known to possess nuclear weapons (i.e. atomic bombs) and even more powerful thermonuclear arms (i.e. hydrogen bombs).

These nations acquired such weapons by the late 1960s and have openly tested them and incorporated them into their military forces. But disturbing as these arsenals may be, relatively stable nuclear relationships have emerged among the five. In the late 1960s, however, a second wave of proliferation began, as less developed nations in tension-filled regions began to develop nuclear weapons capabilities.

Although it has never acknowledged possessing them, Israel is thought to have obtained such weapons secretly by 1968 and may now possess an arsenal of some twenty untested nuclear weapons (or their easily assembled components). India detonated a single nuclear device in 1974 but has not conducted further tests nor, it is believed, manufactured nuclear weapons. South Africa is thought to have accumulated nuclear material for about fifteen nuclear devices beginning in the mid-1970s and may have built an undeclared nuclear arsenal. In view of developments between mid-1983 and mid-1984, it appears that Pakistan is now on the verge of acquiring a nuclear capability similar to these. Although it is not reported to have accumulated enough nuclear weapons material for a nuclear device, Pakistan may possibly have succeeded in producing a quantity of this material and is thought to have completed much of the remaining work needed to manufacture nuclear explosives.

Argentina, Brazil, Iraq, and Libya, although they lack the ability to manufacture atomic explosives, have all taken important steps at one time or another to develop such a capability.

Nuclear proliferation involving these nations —many of which have fought repeated wars with bordering states and have highly unstable governments—presents a host of new and unpredictable dangers to world peace. One need only recall Iraq's invasion of Iran and subsequent use of chemical weapons, and a recent Libyan threat to destroy U.S. nuclear depots in Europe to appreciate the uncertainties of military decision-making in the emerging nuclear states and the risks this might engender if nuclear weapons were present.

THE INTERNATIONAL NON-PROLIFERATION REGIME

Manufacturing nuclear weapons is a daunting technological challenge. The most difficult obstacle is obtaining nuclear explosive material, either highly enriched uranium or plutonium. To obtain the former, natural uranium must be improved in an enrichment plant to weapons grade. Enrichment plants are particularly complex technologically, and the enriched uranium

route to the bomb is generally considered the most difficult. Plutonium is produced in uranium fuel when it is used in a nuclear reactor. The used fuel must then be transferred to a reprocessing plant where it is dissolved in nitric acid and the plutonium extracted from other fuel constituents with which it is amalgamated. Building the necessary reactor and reprocessing installation also requires considerable technical skill. . . . Generally speaking, the nations arousing proliferation concern today have had to rely on assistance from the industrialized nations to build the facilities necessary to produce nuclear weapons material, although over the years a number of the nuclear threshold countries have developed considerable nuclear engineering and manufacturing capabilities of their own.

Not all nations with the ability to manufacture nuclear weapons have done so, for example, Canada, Sweden, Switzerland, Belgium, West Germany, and Japan. Over the years the United States has sponsored a number of important international initiatives aimed at reducing the motivations for nuclear weapons and limiting the spread of nuclear weapons capabilities.

Immediately after World War II, the U.S. proposed the Baruch plan to establish international control of all nuclear materials and facilities. When negotiations on this proposal foundered because certain aspects were unacceptable to the Soviet Union, the United States turned to a policy of secrecy in the hope that this would prevent other nations from developing nuclear arms. The Soviet Union's first test of an atomic bomb in 1949, and Great Britain's in 1952, made clear that secrecy alone would not halt proliferation.

Accordingly, in 1953 the United States inaugurated the Atoms for Peace program, offering to share peaceful nuclear technology with other nations if they would pledge to use U.S. equipment and material exclusively for peaceful purposes and to accept inspections for verifying their compliance. The United States subsequently signed agreements for nuclear cooperation with some thirty nations under this program.

In 1957 the United States was instrumental in establishing the International Atomic Energy Agency (IAEA), a U.N.-affiliated organization which now has more than one hundred members. The Agency's dual role is to promote the peaceful uses of nuclear energy and to implement a system of audits, physical inventories and inspections, known collectively as safeguards, to nuclear installations around the world to verify they are being used exclusively for peaceful purposes. The United States is also a chief sponsor of the 1968 Treaty on the Non-Proliferation of Nuclear Weapons, which some 121 non-nuclear-weapon states have now ratified, pledging not to manufacture nuclear weapons and to place all of their nuclear installations under the IAEA safeguards system. Argentina, Brazil, India, Israel, Pakistan, and South Africa have not ratified the treaty, however, and have important unsafeguarded nuclear installations that can be used to support nuclear weapons programs without violating any international undertaking.

Finally, in 1974 the United States brought together all of the principal nuclear-supplier nations to try to work out a common set of export control standards. The guidelines adopted by the group specified that IAEA safeguards would be applied to any exported nuclear material and equipment and that the suppliers would "exercise restraint" in making sales of enrichment and reprocessing facilities that, while ostensibly part of a recipient country's civilian nuclear program, could provide direct access to nuclear weapons material. Several individual supplier nations have adopted export policies that go beyond those adopted by the suppliers as a group. The 1978 U.S. Nuclear Non-Proliferation Act, for example, prohibits sales of nuclear reactors and fuel to nations that have not placed *all* of their nuclear installations under IAEA safeguards. . . . Valuable as this regime has been in slowing the spread of nuclear arms, it has not succeeded in halting the process, and the trend toward further proliferation is continuing.

NUCLEAR PROLIFERATION TODAY

From mid-1983 to mid-1984, the period reviewed [here] . . . , no new nation is known to have tested a nuclear device. It is possible, however, that one additional nation—Pakistan—may have acquired the capability for manufacturing nuclear weapons, a grave setback for efforts to curb the spread of these arms. This would mean that the line-up that has prevailed for nearly a decade —five full-fledged nuclear states and three ambiguous ones—may soon have to be recast to include a fourth in the ambiguous category. Moreover, the risk of further proliferation increased significantly over the twelve months ending July 1984, as several other nations near to, or just beyond, the nuclear weapons threshold took important steps to acquire or expand their capabilities to manufacture nuclear weapons and as pressures intensified on at least two such countries to pursue active nuclear weapons programs.

South Asia. Pakistan has been seeking to develop nuclear weapons since 1972 but has lacked the capability to manufacture the necessary nuclear material. In February 1984, however, Pakistan announced that it had mastered the uranium enrichment process, and in July, a senior Reagan administration official was quoted in the press as declaring that Pakistan had produced weapons grade uranium at its unsafeguarded Kahuta enrichment plant. Although other administration sources have questioned this report, U.S. officials have confirmed that Pakistan has continued clandestine efforts to design nuclear weapons and to obtain the equipment and materials needed to manufacture them. Indeed, in April 1984, the Reagan administration advised the Senate Foreign Relations Committee that the $3.2 billion U.S. military and economic aid program for Pakistan, initiated in 1981, would have to be terminated if (as proposed in pending legislation) it were made conditional on a Presidential finding that Pakistan was not engaging in such activities. Press accounts in June 1984 also disclosed that China has provided detailed information on the design of nuclear arms to Pakistan and was continuing to provide technical assistance for the Kahuta uranium enrichment facility. And in July, three Pakistani nationals were indicted in Houston, Texas, for attempting to smuggle electronic parts for nuclear weapons, themselves, out of the United States.

These developments indicate that one objective of the U.S. aid program, persuading Pakistan to forego continued development of nuclear arms by providing it with an alternative means for improving its security, has not been achieved. On the other hand, Pakistan has refrained from conducting a nuclear test and is not known to have violated the IAEA safeguards that cover a portion of its nuclear program, no doubt partly because of the threat that such action would trigger a U.S. aid cutoff.

How India may react to Pakistan's emerging nuclear capability is uncertain. New Delhi is reported to be maintaining a nuclear test site in a high state of readiness and will now be under increasing pressure to resume a nuclear explosives program in earnest after ten years of restraint. In addition, in mid-1983, India acquired a major new source of plutonium usable for nuclear weapons with the inauguration of its Madras I nuclear power plant, the first in India not subject to IAEA safeguards. By taking plutonium-bearing spent fuel from this reactor and extracting the plutonium at its Tarapur reprocessing plant, India could greatly increase its stock of nuclear weapons material that could be used in nuclear explosives without violating any international agreement.

Although it is still possible that an active nuclear arms race in South Asia may be averted, the risk of such a race appears to be dramatically increasing.

Latin America. Argentina announced in November 1983 that for five years it had been secretly building a plant capable of producing weapons-grade uranium in 1985—possibly enough for six weapons per year. The secrecy surrounding the plant, the fact that it is far larger than needed for Argentina's civilian nuclear energy program, and Argentina's refusal to place the facility under IAEA inspection strongly suggest that the installation was built to match Brazil's enrichment activities and to provide the basis for a future Argentine nuclear weapons capability.

It was hoped that with the inauguration of Raul Alfonsín in December 1983, Argentina's first democratically elected leader in over a decade, Argentina might slow development of some of the more provocative parts of its nuclear program or accept IAEA supervision of its currently unsafeguarded nuclear installations. By April 1984, however, the Alfonsín government had rejected both measures, and it appears that, for domestic political reasons, a major change of course in Argentina's nuclear program is not likely for some time.

Brazil, responding to Argentina's enrichment breakthrough, has sharply stepped up its own nuclear research and development activities at its atomic research centers in São Paulo and São Jose dos Campos aimed at producing nuclear weapons material not subject to IAEA safeguards. Indeed, in a series of statements during late 1983 and early 1984, Brazilian military leaders made clear that the purpose of this effort was to give Brazil the capability to produce nuclear weapons by 1990, when a decision on whether to proceed with their manufacture would be made.

Argentina may yet shift to a less provocative nuclear policy, a step that would greatly reduce pressures in Brazil for the acquisition of such a capability; through mid-1984, however, the nuclear competition between the two Latin American powers appeared to be intensifying.

Middle East. The gravest new development in this region from the standpoint of nuclear proliferation may have been Iraq's use of another unconventional weapon—lethal chemical agents—in its war against Iran. The use of chemical agents directly violated the 1925 Geneva Protocol, which Iraq signed in 1931, casting doubt on its commitment to another arms control agreement it has ratified, the Nuclear Non-Proliferation Treaty, which prohibits the manufacture of nuclear weapons. Iraq's action also suggests that Iraq might have little compunction about using nuclear arms in its war against Iran if they were available.

Iraq's actual capability to manufacture nuclear arms was greatly set back by Israel's destruction of the Osirak research reactor in 1981. Nevertheless, in 1984 it was revealed that for several years Iraq had been seeking to purchase 34 kilograms of plutonium—enough for perhaps six nuclear weapons—through a 30-member Italian black market arms smuggling ring. Iraq also continues to hold 12.5 kilograms of highly enriched uranium fuel that France supplied for the now-destroyed reactor. This could be enough for a single nuclear weapon if carefully designed. Although the material is subject to continuing inspections by the IAEA, it could pose a near-term proliferation danger given Iraq's apparent readiness to violate its arms control pledges.

Also during 1984, Libya concluded an agreement for cooperation with Belgium to permit Libya's purchase of a specialized uranium processing plant—a plant for which Libya has no apparent need but which could possibly assist it in a future nuclear weapons development effort. In May 1984, it was revealed that Libya had provided Argentina with one hundred million dollars' worth of arms during the 1982 Falklands War. Some nine months after this transfer, a forty-five-member Argentinian delegation visited Tripoli to discuss increased Argentine nuclear and arms exports to Libya, suggesting the possibility of a nuclear quid pro quo for Tripoli's help during the Falklands crisis.

Israel has maintained its ambiguous nuclear posture while presumably continuing to build up its reported small nuclear arsenal, using plutonium produced in its reactor at Dimona. In addition, Israel began studies to select the site for a nuclear power plant. If, as it has done with its Dimona reactor, it refuses to place this facility under IAEA inspection, the plant could greatly increase Israel's capacity for producing plutonium for nuclear arms.

While no Middle East state thus passed a significant milestone in the pursuit of nuclear arms through mid-1984, pressures for further proliferation in the region remained strong.

Africa. South Africa may be substantially augmenting its store of weapons-usable highly enriched uranium. If reports are accurate that sometime between 1980 and 1982 Pretoria obtained significant quantities of low-enriched uranium not subject to international inspection from China, South Africa may be using this material as feedstock for its Valindaba pilot-scale enrichment plant; in principle, this step could allow Pretoria to triple the amount of highly enriched uranium usable for nuclear weapons produced in that installation.

QUESTIONS FOR DISCUSSION

1. Describe some of the ways a nuclear war could start. What kinds of policies might one advocate to reduce each of these risks?

2. Discuss the risks and benefits of relying on nuclear threats to achieve foreign policy objectives.

3. The approach to nuclear war-fighting proposed by Gray and Payne differs greatly from the views of McNamara and Bethe on this issue. Compare and contrast their perspectives.

SUGGESTED READINGS

ALDRIDGE, ROBERT C. *First Strike! The Pentagon's Strategy for Nuclear War.* Boston: South End Press, 1983.

BLECHMAN, BARRY M. "Containing the Threat of Nuclear Terrorism." In *Preventing Nuclear War*, edited by Barry M. Blechman. Bloomington, Ind.: Indiana University Press, 1985, 52–64.

BLECHMAN, BARRY M. and DOUGLAS M. HART, "The Political Utility of Nuclear Weapons: The 1973 Middle East Crisis." In Steve E. Miller, ed., *Strategy and Nuclear Deterrence.* Princeton: Princeton University Press, 1984.

DRELL, SIDNEY. *Facing the Threat of Nuclear Weapons.* Seattle: University of Washington Press, 1983.

FELDMAN, SHAI. *Israeli Nuclear Deterrence: A Strategy for the 1980s.* New York: Columbia University Press, 1982.

GEORGE, ALEXANDER L. *Managing U.S.–Soviet Rivalry: Problems of Crisis Prevention.* Boulder, Colo.: Westview Press, 1983.

LEBOW, RICHARD NED. *Between Peace and War: The Nature of International Crisis.* Baltimore: Johns Hopkins University Press, 1981.

MANDELBAUM, MICHAEL. *The Nuclear Future.* Ithaca, N.Y.: Cornell University Press, 1983.

MEYER, STEPHEN M. *The Dynamics of Nuclear Proliferation.* Chicago: University of Chicago Press, 1984.

NASHIF, TAYSIR N. *Nuclear Warfare in the Middle East: Dimensions and Responsibilities.* Princeton, NJ: Kingston Press, 1984.

RODERICK, HILLIARD with MAGNUSSON, ULLA, eds. *Avoiding Inadvertent War: Crisis Management.* Lyndon B. Johnson School of Public Affairs, University of Texas at Austin, 1983.

Chapter II

The Effects of Nuclear War

It is difficult for the mind to grasp the power of even a single nuclear explosion. The effects of nuclear war—on cities, on civilian populations, on the economic infrastructure, and on the natural environment—are still harder to comprehend. But understanding the effects of nuclear weapons and of nuclear war is essential to informed debate. This chapter considers the effects of nuclear war, examining recent scientific findings about the consequences of nuclear war.

The Office of Technology Assessment (OTA), a research agency of the U.S. Congress, has conducted a detailed assessment of the effects of nuclear war. We include an excerpt here which discusses the types of energy released by nuclear explosions, such as blast, thermal radiation, electromagnetic pulse, and nuclear fallout. The OTA then describes short-term and long-term effects of nuclear war—on people, buildings, cities, and electronic equipment.

Next, Carl Sagan discusses some new evidence about the effects of a large number of nuclear explosions on the global environment. While there are uncertainties about the magnitude of effects, recent scientific studies suggest that the clouds of smoke from fires caused by nuclear war could block sunlight, causing reductions in global temperatures. This effect, known as "nuclear winter," might be sufficiently large to cause sub-freezing temperatures over much of the globe. The effects of such dramatic climatic changes on crops, plants, and the ecosystem upon which we depend could be devastating. Because of such potentially devastating effects, Sagan and his research collaborators conclude that nuclear war threatens the very survival of the human species.

Finally, Caspar W. Weinberger, Secretary of Defense under the Reagan administration, presents his views on the potential climatic effects of nuclear war. Weinberger argues that there is considerable uncertainty about the nuclear winter hypothesis, contending that there is no need to alter the basic thrust of U.S. nuclear policy.

7 The Effects of Nuclear War

Office of Technology Assessment

The energy of a nuclear explosion is released in a number of different ways:

- an explosive blast, which is qualitatively similar to the blast from ordinary chemical explosions, but which has somewhat different effects because it is typically so much larger;
- direct nuclear radiation;
- direct thermal radiation, most of which takes the form of visible light;
- pulses of electrical and magnetic energy, called electromagnetic pulse (EMP); and
- the creation of a variety of radioactive particles, which are thrown up into the air by the force of the blast, and are called radioactive fallout when they return to Earth.

The distribution of the bomb's energy among these effects depends on its size and on the details of its design, but a general description is possible.

BLAST

Most damage to cities from large weapons comes from the explosive blast. The blast drives air away from the site of the explosion, producing sudden changes in air pressure (called static overpressure) that can crush objects, and high winds (called dynamic pressure) that can move them suddenly or knock them down. In general, large buildings are destroyed by the overpressure, while people and objects such as trees and utility poles are destroyed by the wind.

Reprinted from U.S. Congress, Office of Technology Assessment, *The Effects of Nuclear War*, 1979, pp. 15–23, 26.

For example, consider the effects of a 1-megaton (Mt) air burst on things 4 miles [6 km] away. The overpressure will be in excess of 5 pounds per square inch (psi), which will exert a force of more than 180 tons on the wall of a typical two-story house. At the same place, there would be a wind of 160 mph [255 km]; while 5 psi is not enough to crush a man, a wind of 180 mph would create fatal collisions between people and nearby objects.

The magnitude of the blast effect (generally measured in pounds per square inch) diminishes with distance from the center of the explosion. It is related in a more complicated way to the height of the burst above ground level. For any given distance from the center of the explosion, there is an optimum burst height that will produce the greatest overpressure, and the greater the distance the greater the optimum burst height. As a result, a burst on the surface produces the greatest overpressure at very close ranges (which is why surface bursts are used to attack very hard, very small targets such as missile silos), but less overpressure than an air burst at somewhat longer ranges. Raising the height of the burst reduces the overpressure directly under the bomb, but widens the area at which a given smaller overpressure is produced. Thus, an attack on factories with a 1-Mt weapon might use an air burst at an altitude of 8,000 feet [2,400 m], which would maximize the area (about 28 mi^2 [7,200 hectares]) that would receive 10 psi or more of overpressure.

Table 7-1 shows the ranges of overpressures and effects from such a blast.

When a nuclear weapon is detonated on or near the surface of the Earth, the blast digs out a large crater. Some of the material that used to be in the crater is deposited on the rim of the

TABLE 7–1 Blast Effects on a 1-Mt Explosion 8,000 ft Above the Earth's Surface

DISTANCE FROM GROUND ZERO		*Peak overpressure*	*Peak wind velocity (mph)*	*Typical blast effects*
(stat. miles)	*(kilometers)*			
.8	1.3	20 psi	470	Reinforced concrete structures are leveled.
3.0	4.8	10 psi	290	Most factories and commercial buildings are collapsed. Small wood-frame and brick residences destroyed and distributed as debris.
4.4	7.0	5 psi	160	Lightly constructed commercial buildings and typical residences are destroyed; heavier construction is severely damaged.
5.9	9.5	3 psi	95	Walls of typical steel-frame buildings are blown away; severe damage to residences. Winds sufficient to kill people in the open.
11.6	18.6	1 psi	35	Damage to structures; people endangered by flying glass and debris.

crater; the rest is carried up into the air and returns to Earth as fallout. An explosion that is farther above the Earth's surface than the radius of the fireball does not dig a crater and produces negligible immediate fallout.

For the most part, blast kills people by indirect means rather than by direct pressure. While a human body can withstand up to 30 psi of simple overpressure, the winds associated with as little as 2 to 3 psi could be expected to blow people out of typical modern office buildings. Most blast deaths result from the collapse of occupied buildings, from people being blown into objects, or from buildings or smaller objects being blown onto or into people. Clearly, then, it is impossible to calculate with any precision how many people would be killed by a given blast—the effects would vary from building to building. . . .

DIRECT NUCLEAR RADIATION

Nuclear weapons inflict ionizing radiation on people, animals, and plants in two different ways. Direct radiation occurs at the time of the explosion; it can be very intense, but its range is limited. Fallout radiation is received from particles that are made radioactive by the effects of the explosion, and subsequently distributed at varying distances from the site of the blast. Fallout is discussed in a subsequent section.

For large nuclear weapons, the range of intense direct radiation is less than the range of lethal blast and thermal radiation effects. However, in the case of smaller weapons, direct radiation may be the lethal effect with the greatest range. Direct radiation did substantial damage to the residents of Hiroshima and Nagasaki.

Human response to ionizing radiation is subject to great scientific uncertainty and intense controversy. It seems likely that even small doses of radiation do some harm. To understand the effects of nuclear weapons, one must distinguish between short- and long-term effects:

- **Short-Term Effects.**—A dose of 600 rem within a short period of time (6 to 7 days) has a 90-percent chance of creating a fatal illness, with death occurring within a few weeks. (A rem or "roentgen-equivalent-man" is a measure of biological damage: a "rad" is a measure of radiation energy absorbed; a roentgen is a measure of radiation energy; for our purposes it may be assumed that 100 roentgens produce 100 rads and 100 rem.) The precise shape of the curve showing the death rate as a function of radiation dose is not known in the region between 300 and 600 rem, but a dose of 450 rem within a short time is estimated to create a fatal illness in half the people exposed to it; the other half would get very sick, but would recover. A dose of 300 rem might kill about 10 percent of those exposed. A dose of 200 to 450 rem will cause a severe illness from which most people would recover; however, this illness would render people highly susceptible to other disease or infections. A dose of 50 to 200 rem will cause nausea and lower resistance to other diseases, but medical treatment is not required. A dose below 50 rem will not cause any short-term effects that the victim will notice, but will nevertheless do long-term damage.

- **Long-Term Effects.**—The effects of smaller doses of radiation are long term, and measured in a statistical way. A dose of 50 rem generally produces no short-term effects; however, if a large population were exposed to 50 rems, somewhere between 0.4 and 2.5 percent of them would be expected to contract fatal cancer (after some years) as a result. There would also be serious genetic effects for some fraction of those exposed. Lower doses produce lower effects. There is a scientific controversy about whether any dose of radiation, however small, is really safe. . . . It should be clearly understood, however, that a large nuclear war would expose the survivors, however well sheltered, to levels of radiation far greater than the U.S. Government considers safe in peacetime.

of explosion. A 1-Mt explosion can cause first-degree burns (equivalent to a bad sunburn) at distances of about 7 miles [11 km], second-degree burns (producing blisters that lead to infection if untreated, and permanent scars) at distances of about 6 miles [10 km], and third-degree burns (which destroy skin tissue) at distances of up to 5 miles [8 km]. Third-degree burns over 24 percent of the body, or second-degree burns over 30 percent of the body, will result in serious shock, and will probably prove fatal unless prompt, specialized medical care is available. The entire United States has facilities to treat 1,000 or 2,000 severe burn cases; a single nuclear weapon could produce more than 10,000.

The distance at which burns are dangerous depends heavily on weather conditions. Extensive moisture or a high concentration of particles in the air (smog) absorbs thermal radiation. Thermal radiation behaves like sunlight, so objects create shadows behind which the thermal radiation is indirect (reflected) and less intense. Some conditions, such as ice on the ground or low white clouds over clean air, can increase the range of dangerous thermal radiation.

THERMAL RADIATION

Approximately 35 percent of the energy from a nuclear explosion is an intense burst of thermal radiation, i.e., heat. The effects are roughly analogous to the effect of a 2-second flash from an enormous sunlamp. Since the thermal radiation travels at the speed of light (actually a bit slower, since it is deflected by particles in the atmosphere), the flash of light and heat precedes the blast wave by several seconds, just as lightning is seen before the thunder is heard.

The visible light will produce "flashblindness" in people who are looking in the direction of the explosion. Flashblindness can last for several minutes, after which recovery is total. A 1-Mt explosion could cause flashblindness at distances as great as 13 miles [21 km] on a clear day, or 53 miles [85 km] on a clear night. If the flash is focused through the lens of the eye, a permanent retinal burn will result. At Hiroshima and Nagasaki, there were many cases of flashblindness, but only one case of retinal burn, among the survivors. On the other hand, anyone flashblinded while driving a car could easily cause permanent injury to himself and to others.

Skin burns result from higher intensities of light, and therefore take place closer to the point

FIRES

The thermal radiation from a nuclear explosion can directly ignite kindling materials. In general, ignitible materials outside the house, such as leaves or newspapers, are not surrounded by enough combustible material to generate a self-sustaining fire. Fires more likely to spread are those caused by thermal radiation passing through windows to ignite beds and overstuffed furniture inside houses. A rather substantial amount of combustible material must burn vigorously for 10 to 20 minutes before the room, or whole house, becomes inflamed. The blast wave, which arrives after most thermal energy has been expended, will have some extinguishing effect on the fires. However, studies and tests of this effect have been very contradictory, so the extent to which blast can be counted on to extinguish fire starts remains quite uncertain.

Another possible source of fires, which might be more damaging in urban areas, is indirect. Blast damage to stores, water heaters, furnaces, electrical circuits, or gas lines would ignite fires where fuel is plentiful.

The best estimates are that at the 5-psi level about 10 percent of all buildings would sustain a serious fire, while at 2 psi about 2 percent would have serious fires, usually arising from secondary sources such as blast-damaged utilities rather than direct thermal radiation.

It is possible that individual fires, whether caused by thermal radiation or by blast damage to utilities, furnaces, etc., would coalesce into a mass fire that would consume all structures over a large area. This possibility has been intensely studied, but there remains no basis for estimating its probability. Mass fires could be of two kinds: a "firestorm," in which violent inrushing winds create extremely high temperatures but prevent the fire from spreading radially outwards, and a "conflagration," in which a fire spreads along a front. Hamburg, Tokyo, and Hiroshima experienced firestorms in World War II; the Great Chicago Fire and the San Francisco Earthquake Fire were conflagrations. A firestorm is likely to kill a high proportion of the people in the area of the fire, through heat and through asphyxiation of those in shelters. A conflagration spreads slowly enough so that people in its path can escape, though a conflagration caused by a nuclear attack might take a heavy toll of those too injured to walk. Some believe that firestorms in U.S. or Soviet cities are unlikely because the density of flammable materials ("fuel loading") is too low—the ignition of a firestorm is thought to require a fuel loading of at least 8 lbs/ft^2 (Hamburg had 32), compared to fuel loading of 2 lbs/ft^2 in a typical U.S. suburb and 5 lbs/ft^2 in a neighborhood of two-story brick rowhouses. The likelihood of a conflagration depends on the geography of the area, the speed and direction of the wind, and details of building construction. Another variable is whether people and equipment are available to fight fires before they can coalesce and spread.

ELECTROMAGNETIC PULSE

Electromagnetic pulse (EMP) is an electromagnetic wave similar to radio waves, which results from secondary reactions occurring when the nuclear gamma radiation is absorbed in the air or ground. It differs from the usual radio waves in two important ways. First, it creates much higher electric field strengths. Whereas a radio signal might produce a thousandth of a volt or less in a receiving antenna, an EMP pulse might produce thousands of volts. Secondly, it is a single pulse of energy that disappears completely in a small fraction of a second. In this sense, it is rather similar to the electrical signal from

lightning, but the rise in voltage is typically a hundred times faster. This means that most equipment designed to protect electrical facilities from lightning works too slowly to be effective against EMP.

The strength of an EMP pulse is measured in volts per meter (v/m), and is an indication of the voltage that would be produced in an exposed antenna. A nuclear weapon burst on the surface will typically produce an EMP of tens of thousands of v/m at short distances (the 10-psi range) and thousands of v/m at longer distances (1-psi range). Air bursts produce less EMP, but high-altitude bursts (above 19 miles [21 km]) produce very strong EMP, with ranges of hundreds or thousands of miles. An attacker might detonate a few weapons at such altitudes in an effort to destroy or damage the communications and electric power systems of the victim.

There is no evidence that EMP is a physical threat to humans. However, electrical or electronic systems, particularly those connected to long wires such as powerlines or antennas, can undergo either of two kinds of damage. First, there can be actual physical damage to an electrical component such as shorting of a capacitor or burnout of a transistor, which would require replacement or repair before the equipment can again be used. Second, at a lesser level, there can be a temporary operational upset, frequently requiring some effort to restore operation. For example, instabilities induced in power grids can cause the entire system to shut itself down, upsetting computers that must be started again. Base radio stations are vulnerable not only from the loss of commercial power but from direct damage to electronic components connected to the antenna. In general, portable radio transmitter/receivers with relatively short antennas are not susceptible to EMP. The vulnerability of the telephone system to EMP could not be determined.

FALLOUT

While any nuclear explosion in the atmosphere produces some fallout, the fallout is far greater if the burst is on the surface, or at least low enough for the fireball to touch the ground. . . . The fallout from air bursts alone poses long-term health hazards, but they are trivial compared to the other consequences of a nuclear attack. The significant hazards come from particles scooped up from the ground and irradiated by the nuclear explosion.

The radioactive particles that rise only a short distance (those in the "stem" of the familiar mushroom cloud) will fall back to earth within a matter of minutes, landing close to the center of the explosion. Such particles are unlikely to cause many deaths, because they will fall in areas where most people have already been killed. However, the radioactivity will complicate efforts at rescue or eventual reconstruction.

The radioactive particles that rise higher will be carried some distance by the wind before returning to Earth, and hence the area and intensity of the fallout is strongly influenced by local weather conditions. Much of the material is simply blown downwind in a long plume. . . . Wind direction can make an enormous difference. Rainfall can also have a significant influence on the ways in which radiation from smaller weapons is deposited, since rain will carry contaminated particles to the ground. The areas receiving such contaminated rainfall would become "hot spots," with greater radiation intensity than their surroundings. When the radiation intensity from fallout is great enough to pose an immediate threat to health, fallout will generally be visible as a thin layer of dust.

The amount of radiation produced by fallout materials will decrease with time as the radioactive materials "decay." Each material decays at a different rate. Materials that decay rapidly give off intense radiation for a short period of time while long-lived materials radiate less intensely but for longer periods. Immediately after the fallout is deposited in regions surrounding the blast site, radiation intensities will be very high as the short-lived materials decay. These intense radiations will decrease relatively quickly. The intensity will have fallen by a factor of 10 after 7 hours, a factor of 100 after 49 hours and a factor of 1,000 after 2 weeks. . . .

Some radioactive particles will be thrust into the stratosphere, and may not return to Earth for some years. In this case only the particularly long-lived particles pose a threat, and they are dispersed around the world over a range of latitudes. Some fallout from U.S. and Soviet weapons tests in the 1950's and early 1960's can still be detected. There are also some particles in the immediate fallout (notably Strontium 90 and Cesium 137) that remain radioactive for years. . . .

The biological effects of fallout radiation are substantially the same as those from direct radiation, discussed above. People exposed to enough fallout radiation will die, and those exposed to lesser amounts may become ill.

COMBINED INJURIES (SYNERGISM)

So far the discussion of each major effect (blast, nuclear radiation, and thermal radiation) has explained how this effect in isolation causes deaths and injuries to humans. It is customary to calculate the casualties accompanying hypothetical nuclear explosion as follows: for any given range, the effect most likely to kill people is selected and its consequences calculated, while the other effects are ignored. It is obvious that combined injuries are possible, but there are no generally accepted ways of calculating their probability. What data do exist seem to suggest that calculations of single effects are not too inaccurate for immediate deaths, but that deaths occurring some time after the explosion may well be due to combined causes, and hence are omitted from most calculations. Some of the obvious possibilities are:

- **Nuclear Radiation Combined With Thermal Radiation.**—Severe burns place considerable stress on the blood system, and often cause anemia. It is clear from experiments with laboratory animals that exposure of a burn victim to more than 100 rems of radiation will impair the blood's ability to support recovery from the thermal burns. Hence a sublethal radiation dose could make it impossible to recover from a burn that, without the radiation, would not cause death.

- **Nuclear Radiation Combined With Mechanical Injuries.**—Mechanical injuries, the indirect results of blast, take many forms. Flying glass and wood will cause puncture wounds. Winds may blow people into obstructions, causing broken bones, concussions, and internal injuries. Persons caught in a collapsing building can suffer many similar mechanical injuries. There is evidence that all of these types of injuries are more serious if the person has been exposed to 300 rems, particularly if treatment is delayed. Blood damage will clearly make a victim more susceptible to blood loss and infection. This has been confirmed in laboratory animals in which a borderline lethal radiation dose was followed a week later by a blast overpressure that alone would have produced a low level of prompt lethality. The number of prompt and delayed (from radiation) deaths both increased over what would be expected from the single effect alone.

- **Thermal Radiation and Mechanical Injuries.**—There is no information available about the effects of this combination, beyond the common sense observation that since each can place a great stress on a healthy body, the combination of injuries that are individually tolerable may subject the body to a total stress that it cannot tolerate. Mechanical injuries should be prevalent at about the distance from a nuclear explosion that produces sublethal burns, so this synergism could be an important one.

In general, synergistic effects are most likely to produce death when each of the injuries alone is quite severe. Because the uncertainties of nuclear effects are compounded when one tries to estimate the likelihood of two or more serious but (individually) nonfatal injuries, there really is no way to estimate the number of victims.

A further dimension of the problem is the possible synergy between injuries and environmental damage. To take one obvious example, poor sanitation (due to the loss of electrical power and water pressure) can clearly compound the effects of any kind of serious injury. Another possibility is that an injury would so immobilize the victim that he would be unable to escape from a fire.

8 Nuclear War and Climatic Catastrophe: Some Policy Implications

Carl Sagan

... This article seeks, first, to present a short summary, in lay terms, of the climatic and biological consequences of nuclear war that emerge from extensive scientific studies conducted over the past two years, the essential conclusions of which have now been endorsed by a large number of scientists. These findings were presented in detail at a special conference in Cambridge, Mass., involving almost 100 scientists on April 22–26, 1983, and were publicly announced at a conference in Washington, D.C., on October 31 and November 1, 1983. They have been reported in summary form in the press, and a detailed statement of the findings and their bases will be published in *Science*.[1][2] The present summary is designed particularly for the lay reader.

Following this summary, I explore the possible strategic and policy implications of the new findings. They point to one apparently inescapable conclusion: the necessity of moving as rapidly as possible to reduce the global nuclear arsenals below levels that could conceivably cause the kind of climatic catastrophe and cascading biological devastation predicted by the new studies. Such a reduction would have to be to a small percentage of the present global strategic arsenals.

II

The central point of the new findings is that the long-term consequences of a nuclear war could constitute a global climatic catastrophe. ...

The total number of nuclear weapons (strategic plus theater and tactical) in the arsenals of the two nations is close to 50,000, with an aggregate yield near 15,000 megatons. For convenience, we here collapse the distinction between strategic and theater-weapons, and adopt under the rubric "strategic," an aggregate yield of 13,000 megatons. The nuclear weapons of the rest of the world—mainly Britain, France and China—amount to many hundred warheads and a few hundred megatons of additional aggregate yield.

No one knows, of course, how many warheads with what aggregate yield would be detonated in a nuclear war. Because of attacks on strategic aircraft and missiles, and because of technological failures, it is clear that less than the entire world arsenal would be detonated. On the other hand, it is generally accepted, even among most military planners, that a "small" nuclear war would be almost impossible to contain before it escalated to include much of the world arsenals.[3][4] (Precipitating factors include command and control malfunctions, communications failures, the necessity for instantaneous decisions on the fates of millions, fear, panic and other aspects of real nuclear war fought by real people.) For this reason alone, any serious attempt to examine the possible consequences of nuclear war must place major emphasis on large-scale exchanges in the five-to-seven-thousand-megaton range, and many studies have done so.[5][6][7][8] Many of the effects described below, however, can be triggered by much smaller wars.

The adversary's strategic airfields, missile silos, naval bases, submarines at sea, weapons manufacturing and storage locales, civilian and military command and control centers, attack assessment and early warning facilities, and the like are probable targets ("counter-force attack"). While it is often stated that cities are not targeted "per se," many of the above targets are very near or colocated with cities, especially in Europe. In addition, there is an industrial targeting category ("countervalue attack"). Modern nuclear doctrines require that "war-supporting" facilities be attacked. Many of these facilities are necessarily industrial in nature and engage a work force of considerable size. They are almost always situated near major transportation centers, so that raw materials and finished products can be efficiently transported to other industrial sectors, or to forces in the field. Thus, such facilities are, almost by definition, cities, or near or within cities. Other "war-supporting" targets may include the transportation systems themselves (roads, canals, rivers, railways, civilian airfields, etc.), petroleum refineries, storage sites and pipelines, hydroelectric plants, radio and television transmitters and the like. A major countervalue attack therefore might involve almost all large cities in the United States and the Soviet Union, and possibly most of the large cities in the Northern Hemisphere.[9] There are fewer than 2,500 cities in the world with populations over 100,000 inhabitants, so the devastation of all such cities is well within the means of the world nuclear arsenals.

Recent estimates of the immediate death from blast, prompt radiation, and fires in a major exchange in which cities were targeted range from several hundred million to 1.1 billion people—the latter estimate is in a World Health Organization study in which targets were assumed not to be restricted entirely to NATO and Warsaw Pact countries.[10] Serious injuries requiring immediate medical attention (which would be largely unavailable) would be suffered by a comparably large number of people, perhaps an additional 1.1 billion.[11] Thus it is possible that something approaching half the human population on the planet would be killed or seriously injured by the direct effects of the nuclear war. Social disruption; the unavailability of electricity, fuel, transportation, food deliveries, communications and other civil services; the absence of medical care; the decline in sanitation measures; rampant disease and severe psychiatric disorders would doubtless collectively claim a significant number of further victims. But a range of additional effects—some unexpected, some inadequately treated in earlier studies, some uncovered only recently—now make the picture much more somber still.

Because of current limitations on missile accuracy, the destruction of missile silos, command and control facilities, and other hardened sites requires nuclear weapons of fairly high yield exploded as groundbursts or as low airbursts. High-yield groundbursts will vaporize, melt and pulverize the surface at the target area and propel large quantities of condensates and fine dust into the upper troposphere and stratosphere. The particles are chiefly entrained in the rising fireball; some ride up the stem of the mushroom cloud. Most military targets, however, are not very hard. The destruction of cities can be accomplished, as demonstrated at Hiroshima and Nagasaki, by lower-yield explosions less than a kilometer above the surface. Low-yield airbursts over cities or near forests will tend to produce massive fires, some of them over areas of 100,000 square kilometers or more. City fires generate enormous quantities of black oily smoke which rise at least into the upper part of the lower atmosphere, or troposphere. If firestorms occur, the smoke column rises vigorously, like the draft in a fireplace, and may carry some of the soot into the lower part of the upper atmosphere, or stratosphere. The smoke from forest and grassland fires would initially be restricted to the lower troposphere.

The fission of the (generally plutonium) trigger in every thermonuclear weapon and the reactions in the (generally uranium-238) casing added as a fission yield "booster" produce a witch's brew of radioactive products, which are also entrained in the cloud. Each such product, or radioisotope, has a characteristic "half-life" (defined as the time to decay to half its original level of radioactivity). Most of the radioisotopes have very short half-lives and decay in hours to days. Particles injected into the stratosphere, mainly by high-yield explosions, fall out very slowly—characteristically in about a year, by which time most of the fission products, even when concentrated, will have decayed to much safer levels. Particles injected into the troposphere by low-yield explosions and fires fall out more rapidly—by gravitational settling, rainout, convection, and other processes—before the radioactivity has decayed to moderately safe levels. Thus rapid fallout of tropospheric radioactive debris tends to produce larger doses of ionizing radiation than does the slower fallout of radioactive particles from the stratosphere.

Nuclear explosions of more than one-megaton yield generate a radiant fireball that rises through the troposphere into the stratosphere. The fireballs from weapons with yields between 100 kilotons and one megaton will partially extend into the stratosphere. The high temperatures in the fireball chemically ignite some of the nitrogen in the air, producing oxides of nitrogen, which in turn chemically attack and destroy the gas ozone in the middle stratosphere. But ozone absorbs the biologically dangerous ultraviolet radiation from the Sun. Thus the partial depletion of the stratospheric ozone layer, or "ozonosphere," by high-yield nuclear explosions will increase the flux of solar ultraviolet radiation at the surface of the Earth (after the soot and dust have settled out). After a nuclear war in which thousands of high-yield weapons are detonated, the increase in biologically dangerous ultraviolet light might be several hundred percent. In the more dangerous shorter wavelengths, larger increases would occur. Nucleic acids and proteins, the fundamental molecules for life on Earth, are especially sensitive to ultraviolet radiation. Thus, an increase of the solar ultraviolet flux at the surface of the Earth is potentially dangerous for life.

These four effects—obscuring smoke in the troposphere, obscuring dust in the stratosphere, the fallout of radioactive debris, and the partial destruction of the ozone layer—constitute the four known principal adverse environmental consequences that occur after a nuclear war is "over." There may be others about which we are still ignorant. The dust and, especially, the dark soot absorb ordinary visible light from the Sun, heating the atmosphere and cooling the Earth's surface.

All four of these effects have been treated in our recent scientific investigation.[12] The study, known from the initials of its authors as TTAPS, for the first time demonstrates that severe and prolonged low temperatures would follow a nuclear war. (The study also explains the fact that no such climatic effects were detected after the detonation of hundreds of megatons during the period of U.S.–Soviet atmospheric testing of nuclear weapons, ended by treaty in 1963: the explosions were sequential over many years, not virtually simultaneous; and, occurring over scrub desert, coral atolls, tundra and wasteland, they set no fires.) The new results have been subjected to detailed scrutiny, and half a dozen confirmatory calculations have now been made. A special panel appointed by the National Academy of Sciences to examine this problem has come to similar conclusions.[13]

Unlike many previous studies, the effects do not seem to be restricted to northern mid-latitudes, where the nuclear exchange would mainly take place. There is now substantial evidence that the heating by sunlight of atmospheric dust and soot over northern mid-latitude targets would profoundly change the global circulation. Fine particles would be transported across the equator in weeks, bringing the cold and the dark to the Southern Hemisphere. (In addition, some studies suggest that over 100 megatons would be dedicated to equatorial and Southern Hemisphere targets, thus generating fine particles locally.)[14] While it would be less cold and less dark at the ground in the Southern Hemisphere than in the Northern, massive climatic and environmental disruptions may be triggered there as well. . . .

[The TTAPS] calculations . . . are not, and cannot be, assured prognostications of the full consequences of a nuclear war. Many refinements in them are possible and are being pursued. But there is general agreement on the overall conclusions: in the wake of a nuclear war there is likely to be a period, lasting at least for months, of extreme cold in a radioactive gloom, followed —after the soot and dust fall out—by an extended period of increased ultraviolet light reaching the surface.

We now explore the biological impact of such an assault on the global environment.

III

The immediate human consequences of nuclear explosions range from vaporization of populations near the hypocenter, to blast-generated trauma (from flying glass, falling beams, collapsing skyscrapers and the like), to burns, radiation sickness, shock and severe psychiatric disorders. But our concern here is with longer-term effects.

It is now a commonplace that in the burning of modern tall buildings, more people succumb to toxic gases than to fire. Ignition of many varieties of building materials, insulation and fabrics generates large amounts of such pyrotoxins, including carbon monoxide, cyanides, vinyl chlorides, oxides of nitrogen, ozone, dioxins, and furans. Because of differing practices in the use of such synthetics, the burning of cities in North America and Western Europe will probably generate more pyrotoxins than cities in the Soviet Union, and cities with substantial recent construction more than older, unreconstructed cities. In nuclear war scenarios in which a great many cities are burning, a significant pyrotoxin smog might persist for months. The magnitude of this danger is unknown.

The pyrotoxins, low light levels, radioactive fallout, subsequent ultraviolet light, and especially the cold are together likely to destroy almost all of Northern Hemisphere agriculture.... A 12° to 15° C temperature reduction by itself would eliminate wheat and corn production in the United States, even if all civil systems and agricultural technology were intact.[15] With unavoidable societal disruption, and with the other environmental stresses just mentioned, even a 3,000-megaton "pure" counterforce attack ... might suffice. Realistically, many fires would be set even in such an attack (see below), and a 3,000-megaton war is likely to wipe out U.S. grain production. This would represent by itself an unprecedented global catastrophe: North American grain is the principal reliable source of export food on the planet, as well as an essential component of U.S. prosperity. Wars just before harvesting of grain and other staples would be incrementally worse than wars after harvesting. For many scenarios, the effects will extend ... into two or more growing seasons. Widespread fires and subsequent runoff of topsoil are among the many additional deleterious consequences extending for years after the war.

Something like three-quarters of the U.S. population lives in or near cities. In the cities themselves there is, on average, only about one week's supply of food. After a nuclear war it is conceivable that enough of present grain storage might survive to maintain, on some level, the present population for more than a year. But with the breakdown of civil order and transportation systems in the cold, the dark and the fallout, these stores would become largely inaccessible. Vast numbers of survivors would soon starve to death.

In addition, the sub-freezing temperatures imply, in many cases, the unavailability of fresh water. The ground will tend to be frozen to a depth of about a meter—incidentally making it unlikely that the hundreds of millions of dead bodies would be buried, even if the civil organization to do so existed. Fuel stores to melt snow and ice would be in short supply, and ice surfaces and freshly fallen snow would tend to be contaminated by radioactivity and pyrotoxins.

In the presence of excellent medical care, the average value of the acute lethal dose of ionizing radiation for healthy adults is about 450 rads.

(As with many other effects, children, the infirm and the elderly tend to be more vulnerable.) Combined with the other assaults on survivors in the postwar environment, and in the probable absence of any significant medical care, the mean lethal acute dose is likely to decline to 350 rads or even lower. For many outdoor scenarios, doses within the fallout plumes that drift hundreds of kilometers downwind of targets are greater than the mean lethal dose. (For a 10,000-megaton war, this is true for more than 30 percent of northern mid-latitude land areas.) Far from targets, intermediate-timescale chronic doses from delayed radioactive fallout may be in excess of 100 rads for the baseline case. These calculations assume no detonations on nuclear reactors or fuel-reprocessing plants, which would increase the dose.

Thus, the combination of acute doses from prompt radioactive fallout, chronic doses from the delayed intermediate-timescale fallout, and internal doses from food and drink are together likely to kill many more by radiation sickness. Because of acute damage to bone marrow, survivors would have significantly increased vulnerability to infectious diseases. Most infants exposed to 100 rads as fetuses in the first two trimesters of pregnancy would suffer mental retardation and/or other serious birth defects. Radiation and some pyrotoxins would later produce neoplastic diseases and genetic damage. Livestock and domesticated animals, with fewer resources, vanishing food supplies and in many cases with greater sensitivity to the stresses of nuclear war than human beings, would also perish in large numbers.

These devastating consequences for humans and for agriculture would not be restricted to the locales in which the war would principally be "fought," but would extend throughout northern mid-latitudes and, with reduced but still significant severity, probably to the tropics and the Southern Hemisphere. The bulk of the world's grain exports originate in northern mid-latitudes. Many nations in the developing as well as the developed world depend on the import of food. Japan, for example, imports 75 percent of its food (and 99 percent of its fuel). Thus, even if there were no climatic and radiation stresses on tropical and Southern Hemisphere societies— many of them already at subsistence levels of nutrition—large numbers of people there would die of starvation.

As agriculture breaks down worldwide (possible initial exceptions might include Argentina,

Australia and South Africa if the climatic impact on the Southern Hemisphere proved to be minimal), there will be increasing reliance on natural ecosystems—fruits, tubers, roots, nuts, etc. But wild foodstuffs will also have suffered from the effects of the war. At just the moment that surviving humans turn to the natural environment for the basis of life, that environment would be experiencing a devastation unprecedented in recent geological history.

Two-thirds of all species of plants, animals, and microorganisms on the Earth live within 25° of the equator. Because temperatures tend to vary with the seasons only minimally at tropical latitudes, species there are especially vulnerable to rapid temperature declines. In past major extinction events in the paleontological record, there has been a marked tendency for tropical organisms to show greater vulnerability than organisms living at more temperate latitudes.

The darkness alone may cause a collapse in the aquatic food chain in which sunlight is harvested by phytoplankton, phytoplankton by zooplankton, zooplankton by small fish, small fish by large fish, and, occasionally, large fish by humans. In many nuclear war scenarios, this food chain is likely to collapse at its base for at least a year and is significantly more imperiled in tropical waters. The increase in ultraviolet light available at the surface of the earth approximately a year after the war provides an additional major environmental stress that by itself has been described as having "profound consequences" for aquatic, terrestrial and other ecosystems.[16]

The global ecosystem can be considered an intricately woven fabric composed of threads contributed by the millions of separate species that inhabit the planet and interact with the air, the water and the soil. The system has developed considerable resiliency, so that pulling a single thread is unlikely to unravel the entire fabric. Thus, most ordinary assaults on the biosphere are unlikely to have catastrophic consequences. For example, because of natural small changes in stratospheric ozone abundance, organisms have probably experienced, in the fairly recent geologic past, ten percent fluctuations in the solar near-ultraviolet flux (but not fluctuations by factors of two or more). Similarly, major continental temperature changes of the magnitude and extent addressed here may not have been experienced for tens of thousands and possibly not for millions of years. We have no experimental information, even for aquaria or terraria,

on the simultaneous effects of cold, dark, pyrotoxins, ionizing radiation, and ultraviolet light as predicted in the TTAPS study.

Each of these factors, taken separately, may carry serious consequences for the global ecosystem: their interactions may be much more dire still. Extremely worrisome is the possibility of poorly understood or as yet entirely uncontemplated synergisms (where the net consequences of two or more assaults on the environment are much more than the sum of the component parts). For example more than 100 rads (and possibly more than 200 rads) of external and ingested ionizing radiation is likely to be delivered in a very large nuclear war to all plants, animals and unprotected humans in densely populated regions of northern mid-latitudes. After the soot and dust clear, there can, for such wars, be a 200 to 400 percent increment in the solar ultraviolet flux that reaches the ground, with an increase of many orders of magnitude in the more dangerous shorter-wavelength radiation. Together, these radiation assaults are likely to suppress the immune systems of humans and other species, making them more vulnerable to disease. At the same time, the high ambient-radiation fluxes are likely to produce, through mutation, new varieties of microorganisms, some of which might become pathogenic. The preferential radiation sensitivity of birds and other insect predators would enhance the proliferation of herbivorous and pathogen-carrying insects. Carried by vectors with high radiation tolerance, it seems possible that epidemics and global pandemics would propagate with no hope of effective mitigation by medical care, even with reduced population sizes and greatly restricted human mobility. Plants, weakened by low temperatures and low light levels, and other animals would likewise be vulnerable to preexisting and newly arisen pathogens.

There are many other conceivable synergisms, all of them still poorly understood because of the complexity of the global ecosystem. Every synergism represents an additional assault, of unknown magnitude, on the global ecosystem and its support functions for humans. What the world would look like after a nuclear war depends in part upon the unknown synergistic interaction of these various adverse effects.

We do not and cannot know that the worst would happen after a nuclear war. Perhaps there is some as yet undiscovered compensating effect or saving grace—although in the past, the overlooked effects in studies of nuclear war have almost always tended toward the worst. But in an uncertain matter of such gravity, it is wise to contemplate the worst, especially when its probability is not extremely small. The summary of the findings of the group of 40 distinguished biologists who met in April 1983 to assess the TTAPS conclusions is worthy of careful consideration:[17]

> Species extinction could be expected for most tropical plants and animals, and for most terrestrial vertebrates of north temperate regions, a large number of plants, and numerous freshwater and some marine organisms. . . . Whether any people would be able to persist for long in the face of highly modified biological communities; novel climates; high levels of radiation; shattered agricultural, social, and economic systems; extraordinary psychological stresses; and a host of other difficulties is open to question. It is clear that the ecosystem effects *alone* resulting from a large-scale thermonuclear war could be enough to destroy the current civilization in at least the Northern Hemisphere. Coupled with the direct casualties of perhaps two billion people, the combined intermediate and long-term effects of nuclear war suggest that eventually there might be no human survivors in the Northern Hemisphere.
>
> Furthermore, the scenario described here is by no means the most severe that could be imagined with present world nuclear arsenals and those contemplated for the near future. In almost any realistic case involving nuclear exchanges between the superpowers, global environmental changes sufficient to cause an extinction event equal to or more severe than that at the close of the Cretaceous when the dinosaurs and many other species died out are likely. In that event, the possibility of the extinction of *Homo sapiens* cannot be excluded.

VI

We have, by slow and imperceptible steps, been constructing a Doomsday Machine: Until recently—and then, only by accident—no one even noticed. And we have distributed its triggers all over the Northern Hemisphere. Every American and Soviet leader since 1945 has made critical decisions regarding nuclear war in total ignorance of the climatic catastrophe. Perhaps this knowledge would have moderated the sub-

sequent course of world events and, especially, the nuclear arms race. Today, at least, we have no excuse for failing to factor the catastrophe into long-term decisions on strategic policy.

Since it is the soot produced by urban fires that is the most sensitive trigger of the climatic catastrophe, and since such fires can be ignited even by low-yield strategic weapons, it appears that the most critical ready index of the world nuclear arsenals, in terms of climatic change, may be the total *number* of strategic warheads. (There is some dependence on yield, to be sure, and future very low-yield, high-accuracy burrowing warheads could destroy strategic targets without triggering the nuclear winter, as discussed above.) For other purposes there are other indices—numbers of submarine-launched warheads, throw-weight (net payload deliverable to target), total megatonnage, etc. From different choices of such indices, different conclusions about strategic parity can be drawn. In the total number of strategic warheads, however, the United States is "ahead" of the Soviet Union and always has been.

Very roughly, the level of the world strategic arsenals necessary to induce the climatic catastrophe seems to be somewhere around 500 to 2,000 warheads—an estimate that may be somewhat high for airbursts over cities, and somewhat low for high-yield groundbursts. The intrinsic uncertainty in this number is itself of strategic importance, and prudent policy would assume a value below the low end of the plausible range.

National or global inventories above this rough threshold move the world arsenals into a region that might be called the "Doomsday Zone." If the world arsenals were well below this rough threshold, no concatenation of computer malfunction, carelessness, unauthorized acts, communications failure, miscalculation and madness in high office could unleash the nuclear winter. When global arsenals are above the threshold, such a catastrophe is at least possible. The further above threshold we are, the more likely it is that a major exchange would trigger the climatic catastrophe.

Traditional belief and childhood experience teach that more weapons buy more security. But since the advent of nuclear weapons and the acquisition of a capacity for "overkill," the possibility has arisen that, past a certain point, more nuclear weapons do not increase national security. I wish here to suggest that, beyond the climatic threshold, an increase in the number of strategic weapons leads to a pronounced *decline* in national (and global) security. National security is not a zero-sum game. Strategic insecurity of one adversary almost always means strategic insecurity for the other. Conventional pre-1945 wisdom, no matter how deeply felt, is not an adequate guide in an age of apocalyptic weapons.

If we are content with world inventories above the threshold, we are saying that it is safe to trust the fate of our global civilization and perhaps our species to all leaders, civilian and military, of all present and future major nuclear powers; and to the command and control efficiency and technical reliability in those nations now and in the indefinite future. For myself, I would far rather have a world in which the climatic catastrophe cannot happen, independent of the vicissitudes of leaders, institutions and machines. This seems to me elementary planetary hygiene, as well as elementary patriotism.

Something like a thousand warheads (or a few hundred megatons) is of the same order as the arsenals that were publicly announced in the 1950s and 1960s as an unmistakable strategic deterrent, and as sufficient to destroy either the United States or the Soviet Union "irrecoverably." Considerably smaller arsenals would, with present improvements in accuracy and reliability, probably suffice. Thus it is possible to contemplate a world in which the global strategic arsenals are below threshold, where mutual deterrence is in effect to discourage the use of those surviving warheads, and where, in the unhappy event that some warheads are detonated, there is little likelihood of the climatic catastrophe. . . .

VII

In summary, cold, dark, radioactivity, pyrotoxins and ultraviolet light following a nuclear war—including some scenarios involving only a small fraction of the world strategic arsenals—would imperil every survivor on the planet. There is a real danger of the extinction of humanity. A threshold exists at which the climatic catastrophe could be triggered, very roughly around 500–2,000 strategic warheads. A major first strike may be an act of national suicide, even if no retaliation occurs. Given the magnitude of the potential loss, no policy declarations and no mechanical safeguards can adequately guarantee the safety of the human species. No national rivalry or ideological confrontation justifies putting the species at risk. Accordingly, there is a critical need for safe and verifiable reductions of the world strategic inventories to below threshold. At such levels, still adequate for deterrence, at least the worst could not happen should a nuclear war break out.

National security policies that seem prudent or even successful during a term of office or a tour of duty may work to endanger national—and global—security over longer periods of time. In many respects it is just short-term thinking that is responsible for the present world crisis. The looming prospect of the climatic catastrophe makes short-term thinking even more dangerous. The past has been the enemy of the present, and the present the enemy of the future. . . .

NOTES

1. R.P. Turco, O.B. Toon, T.P. Ackerman, J.B. Pollack, and Carl Sagan, "Global Atmospheric Consequences of Nuclear War," *Science* 222, no. 4630 (23 December 1983).

2. P.R. Ehrlich, M.A. Harwell, Peter H. Raven, Carl Sagan, and G.M. Woodwell, "The Long-term Biological Consequences of Nuclear War," *Science* 222, no. 4630 (23 December 1983).

3. D. Ball, Adelphi Paper 169 (London: International Institute for Strategic Studies, 1981).

4. P. Bracken and M. Shubik, *Technology in Society* (1982) 4:155.

5. National Academy of Sciences/National Research Council, "Long-term Worldwide Effects of Multiple Nuclear Weapons Detonations" (Washington: National Academy of Sciences, 1975).

6. Office of Technology Assessment, "The Effects of Nuclear War" (Washington: Author, 1979).

7. J. Peterson, ed., "Nuclear War: The Aftermath," *Ambio* 11; nos. 2–3 (Royal Swedish Academy of Sciences, 1982).

8. S. Bergstrom, et al. "Effects of nuclear war on health and health services," publication no. A36.12 (Rome: World Health Organization, 1983).

9. See, for example, Peterson, *op. cit.*

10. Bergstrom, et al., *op. cit.*

11. Ibid.

12. Turco, et al., *op. cit.*

13. National Academy of Sciences, *op. cit.*

14. Peterson, *op. cit.*

15. David Pimentel and Mark Sorrells, private communication, 1983.

16. C.H. Kruger, R.B. Setlow, et al., "Causes and Effects of Stratospheric Ozone Reduction: An Update" (Washington: National Academy of Sciences, 1982).

17. Erlich, et al., *op. cit.*

9   The Potential Effects of Nuclear War on the Climate

Caspar W. Weinberger

THE CLIMATIC RESPONSE PHENOMENA

The basic phenomena that could lead to climatic response may be described very simply. In a nuclear attack, fires would be started in and around many of the target areas either as a direct result of the thermal radiation from the fireball or indirectly from blast and shock damage. Examples of the latter would be fires started by sparks from electrical short circuits, broken gas lines and ruptured fuel storage tanks. Such fires could be numerous and could spread throughout the area of destruction and in some cases beyond, depending on the amount and type of fuel available and local meteorological conditions. These fires might generate large quantities of smoke which would be carried into the atmosphere to varying heights, depending on the meteorological conditions and the intensity of the fire.

In addition to smoke, nuclear explosions on or very near the earth's surface can produce dust that would be carried up with the rising fireball. As in the case of volcanic eruptions such as Mt. Saint Helens, a part of the dust would probably be in the form of very small particles that do not readily settle out under gravity and thus can remain suspended in the atmosphere for long periods of time. If the yield of the nuclear explosion were large enough to carry some of the dust into the stratosphere where moisture and precipitation are not present to wash it out, it could remain for months.

Thus, smoke and dust could reach the upper atmosphere as a result of a nuclear attack. In-

Excerpted from Caspar W. Weinberger, "The Potential Effects of Nuclear War on the Climate: A Report to the United States Congress," (U.S., Department of Defense, March 1985, pp. 1–2, 9, 11–12).

itially, they could be injected into the atmosphere from many separate points and to varying heights. At this point, several processes would begin to occur simultaneously. Over time, circulation within the atmosphere would begin to spread the smoke and dust over wider and wider areas. The circulation of the atmosphere would itself be perturbed by absorption of solar energy by the dust and smoke clouds, so it could be rather different from normal atmospheric circulation. There may also be processes that could transport the smoke and dust from the troposphere into the stratosphere. At the same time, the normal processes that cleanse pollution from the lower and middle levels of the atmosphere would be at work. The most obvious of these is precipitation or washout, but there are several other mechanisms also at work. While this would be going on, the physical and chemical characteristics of the smoke and dust could change so that, even though they are still suspended in the atmosphere, their ability to absorb or scatter sunlight would be altered.

Depending upon how the atmospheric smoke and dust generated by nuclear war are ultimately characterized, the suspended particulate matter could act much like a cloud, absorbing and scattering sunlight at high altitude and reducing the amount of solar energy reaching the surface of the earth. How much and how fast the surface of the earth might cool as a result would depend on many of the yet undetermined details of the process, but if there is sufficient absorption of sunlight over a large enough area, the temperature change could be significant. If the smoke and dust clouds remained concentrated over a relatively small part of the earth's surface, they might produce sharp drops in the local temperature under them; but the effect on the hemispheric (or global) temperature would be slight since most areas would be substantially unaffected. However, the natural tendency of the atmosphere, disturbed or not, would be to disperse the smoke and dust over wider and wider areas with time. One to several weeks would probably be required for widespread dispersal over a region thousands of kilometers wide. Naturally, a thinning process would occur as the particulate matter spread. At the end of this dispersal period, some amount of smoke and dust would remain, whose ability to attenuate and/or absorb sunlight would depend on its physical and chemical state at the time. By this time, hemispheric wide effects might occur. Temperatures generally would drop and the normal atmospheric circulation patterns (and normal weather patterns) could change. How long temperatures would continue to drop, how low they would fall, and how rapidly they would recover, all depend on many variables and the competition between a host of exacerbating and mitigating processes.

Uncertainties also pervade the question of the possible spread of such effects to the southern hemisphere. Normally the atmospheres of the northern and southern hemispheres do not exchange very much air across the equator. Thus, the two hemispheres are normally thought of as being relatively isolated from one another. However, for high enough loading of the atmosphere of the northern hemisphere with smoke and dust, the normal atmospheric circulation patterns might be altered and mechanisms have been suggested that would cause smoke and dust from the northern hemisphere to be transported into the southern hemisphere.

There is fairly general agreement, at the present time, that for major nuclear attacks the phenomena could proceed about as we have described, although there is also realization that important processes might occur that we have not yet recognized, and these could work to make climatic alteration either more or less serious. However, the most important thing that must be realized is that even though we may have a roughly correct qualitative picture, what we do not have, as will be discussed later, is the ability to predict the corresponding climatic effect quantitatively; significant uncertainties exist about the magnitude, and persistence of these effects. At this time, for a postulated nuclear attack and for a specific point on the earth, we cannot predict quantitatively the materials which may be injected into the atmosphere, or how

they will react there. Consequently, for any major nuclear war, some decrease in temperature may occur over at least the northern mid-latitudes. But what this change will be, how long it will last, what its spatial distribution will be, and, of much more importance, whether it will lead to effects of equal or more significance than the horrific destruction associated with the short-term effects of a nuclear war, and the other long-term effects such as radioactivity, currently is beyond our ability to predict, even in gross terms. . . .

The Department of Defense recognizes the importance of improving our understanding of the technical underpinnings of the hypothesis which asserts, in its most rudimentary form, that if sufficient material, smoke, and dust are created by nuclear explosions, lofted to sufficient altitude, and were to remain at altitude for protracted periods, deleterious effects would occur with regard to the earth's climate.

We have very little confidence in the near-term ability to predict this phenomenon quantitatively, either in terms of the amount of sunlight obscured and the related temperature changes, the period of time such consequences may persist, or of the levels of nuclear attacks which might initiate such consequences. We do not know whether the long-term consequences of a nuclear war—of whatever magnitude—would be the often postulated months of subfreezing temperatures, or a considerably less severely perturbed atmosphere. Even with widely ranging and unpredictable weather, the destructiveness for human survival of the less severe climatic effects might be of a scale similar to the other horrors associated with nuclear war. As the Defense Science Board Task Force on Atmospheric Obscuration found in their interim report:

"The uncertainties here range, in our view, all the way between the two extremes, with the possibility that there are no long-term climatic effects no more excluded by what we know now than are the scenarios that predict months of sub-freezing temperatures."

These observations are consistent with the findings in the National Academy of Sciences (NAS) report, summarized earlier in this report. We believe the NAS report has been especially useful in highlighting the assumptions and the considerable uncertainty that dominate the calculations of atmospheric response to nuclear war. While other authors have mentioned these uncertainties, the NAS report has gone to considerable length to place them in a context which improves understanding of their impact.

We agree that considerable additional research needs to be done to understand better the effects of nuclear war on the atmosphere, and we support the IRP as a means of advancing that objective. However, we do not expect that reliable results will be rapidly forthcoming. As a consequence, we are faced with a high degree of uncertainty, which will persist for some time.

Finally, in view of the present and prospective uncertainties in these climatic predictions, we do not believe that it is possible at this time to draw competent conclusions on their biological consequences, beyond a general observation similar to that in the NAS report: if the climatic effect is severe, the impact on the surviving population and on the biosphere could be correspondingly severe. . . .

There are those who argue, in effect, that we no longer need to maintain deterrence as assiduously as we have, because the posited prospect of catastrophic climatic effects would themselves deter Soviet leadership from attack. We strongly disagree, and believe that we cannot lower our standards for deterrence because of any such hope. As summarized above, there is large uncertainty as to the extent of those effects; certainly today we cannot be confident that the Soviets would expect such effects to occur as a result of all possible Soviet attacks that we may need to deter. This entire area of consideration—the impact of possible climatic effects on the deterrence—is made more complex by the fact that it relates to what the Soviets understand about such climatic effects and how that understanding would influence their behavior in a crisis situation. We will probably never have certainty of either; indeed, we cannot know the latter before the event, and knowing

the former is made difficult by their behavior so far, which has been to mirror back to us our own technical analysis and to exploit the matter for propaganda. . . .

STRATEGIC MODERNIZATION PROGRAM

The President's Strategic Modernization Program is designed to maintain effective deterrence, and by doing so, is also an important measure in minimizing the risks of atmospheric or climatic effects. It is providing significantly enhanced command, control, communications and intelligence (C^3I) capabilities which, through their increased survivability and effectiveness, contribute immeasurably to our ability to control escalation. Survivable C^3I contributes to escalation control and thus, as explained above, to mitigation of damage levels (of whatever kind, including possible climatic effects) by reducing pressures for immediate or expanded use of nuclear weapons out of fear that capability for future release would be lost. The improvements to our sea-based, bomber and (with the Scowcroft modifications) land-based legs of our Triad—all intended also to improve survivability and effectiveness—are also essential to maintaining deterrence.

For nonstrategic weapons, our modernization programs have also resulted in increased discrimination through improved accuracy and reduced yield. Beyond that, we have a good beginning on a program to replace some types of nuclear weapons by highly effective, advanced conventional munitions. All of this would contribute to reduction in possible climatic and other global effects of nuclear war. The possibility of such effects, of course, adds urgency to the implementation of these programs. . . .

QUESTIONS FOR DISCUSSION

1. In what forms is energy released from a nuclear explosion? What are the effects—on human beings, buildings, and cities—of each of these forms of energy?

2. If the theoretical calculations predicting nuclear winter are correct, what policy changes, if any, do you think would be warranted?

3. Given the scientific uncertainty about the climatic effects of nuclear war, how should government officials make decisions about policy changes to cope with the threat of nuclear winter?

SUGGESTED READINGS

THE COMMITTEE FOR THE COMPILATION OF MATERIALS ON DAMAGE CAUSED BY THE ATOMIC BOMBS IN HIROSHIMA AND NAGASAKI. *Hiroshima and Nagasaki: The Physical, Medical, and Social Effects of the Atomic Bombings.* New York: Basic Books, 1981.

EHRLICH, P. R., et al. "The Long-Term Biological Consequences of Nuclear War." *Science* 222, no. 4630 (23 December 1983): 1293–1300.

GLASSTONE, SAMUEL, and PHILIP J. DOLAN. *The Effects of Nuclear War.* 3rd ed. U.S. Department of Defense, 1977.

KERR, THOMAS J. *Civil Defense in the U.S.: Bandaid for a Holocaust?* Boulder, Colo.: Westview Press, 1980.

SCHON, DONALD A. "Faith in the Rational Leap: Social Science Research and Crisis Relocation Planning." In Jennifer Leaning and Langley Keyes, *The Counterfeit Ark: Crisis Relocation for Nuclear War* (Cambridge: Ballinger, 1984), 26–47.

TURCO, R.P., et al. "Global Atmospheric Consequences of Nuclear War." *Science* 222, no. 4630 (23 December 1983): 1283–92.

PART TWO

The Weapons
of the Nuclear Age

The world was introduced to nuclear weapons on August 6, 1945, when the United States dropped an atomic bomb on the Japanese city of Hiroshima, killing more than 118,000 people. In a press statement issued the same day, President Harry Truman praised the scientists who developed the bomb, calling their accomplishment "the greatest achievement of organized science in history." "The battle of the laboratories held fateful risks for us. . . ," Truman declared, "and we have now won the battle of the laboratories as we have won the other battles."

Since the bombing of Hiroshima, the "battle of the laboratories" has continued, with scientists and engineers developing increasingly sophisticated nuclear weapons and delivery systems, such as the hydrogen bomb, the nuclear powered submarine, the intercontinental ballistic missile (ICBM), and the multiple independently targetable reentry vehicle (MIRV).

Part Two looks at "The Weapons of the Nuclear Age," examining the circumstances surrounding their development, the political choices made, and the growth of nuclear arsenals. Chapter III examines the politics of the atomic bomb project, the dilemmas of control that the bomb produced, and the development of the H-bomb. Chapter IV describes the nuclear arsenals of the superpowers and examines two space weapon systems currently under development: anti-satellite weapons (ASATs) and space-based missile defense (also known as "Star Wars").

Chapter III _____

The Development of the A-Bomb and H-Bomb

This chapter examines the development of nuclear weapons. The atomic bomb was developed during World War II by a secret research effort called the Manhattan Project. In the first reading, Martin J. Sherwin briefly discusses the secret debate that occurred among physicists and policy-makers over the implications of the new weapon. Many questions entered into this debate. How should this new invention be controlled in order to avoid a war that could mean the destruction of civilization? Should it be controlled by an international authority? Or should it be treated as just another new weapon? How should the Soviets be informed? Should the bomb be used on Japan? Or should it first be demonstrated on a deserted island? How could a post-war atomic arms race be averted? Sherwin's article provides a concise introduction to the debate over these issues.

The concept of a hydrogen bomb was proposed in 1942 by Edward Teller, who is popularly known as the "father" of the H-bomb, and the possibilities were studied by a number of physicists, including J. Robert Oppenheimer and Hans Bethe. Work on the hydrogen bomb was postponed, however, to allow Manhattan Project scientists to concentrate on the atomic bomb.

In 1949, following detection of the first successful Soviet test of an atomic bomb, the United States began a crash program to develop the hydrogen bomb. While many details about the U.S. H-bomb program have been kept secret, recently declassified documents have shed a new light on the H-bomb's history. In an article published in the journal *Science* in 1982, William J. Broad discusses a recently declassified account of the hydrogen bomb effort, originally written in 1954 by Hans Bethe. The final reading consists of a pair of letters, written by Edward Teller and Hans Bethe, in response to Broad's article.

50

10 How Well They Meant

Martin J. Sherwin

"History is a very important thing," I.I. Rabi told his audience of physicists at Los Alamos on the fortieth anniversary of that facility's founding, "because by perusal of history you see the greatness and the folly of humanity." And so it was with the Manhattan Project to which many of the finest minds in American physics dedicated themselves. Their first objective was "to save Western civilization" from fascism by building an atomic bomb ahead of the Germans; their second objective was "to save Western civilization" from the atomic bomb itself, by devising formulas to prevent a nuclear arms race.[1]

As Rabi and others are painfully aware, the ironies associated with those rescue efforts are numerous. But one that has gone almost unnoticed is particularly poignant: all of the ideas currently associated with nuclear weapons derive from those originally conceived by scientists during the war for the purpose of preventing a nuclear arms race afterward. Appropriately, the title of Rabi's 1983 Los Alamos speech was: "How Well We Meant."

The Strategic Arms Limitation Talks (SALT) were presaged by Niels Bohr and James Conant in 1944, and then officially proposed in 1946, in the State Department's Acheson-Lilienthal Report, the earliest nuclear arms control proposal. Nuclear intimidation, the psychological premise of nuclear containment, was anticipated in 1945 at the atomic bomb targeting committee meetings in Los Alamos. Limited nuclear war—an idea popularized in 1958 by Henry Kissinger's *Nuclear Weapons and American Foreign Policy*,

and then adopted in 1980 as Presidential Directive-59 by the Carter Administration—was discussed during the war as an integral part of plans for international control. Deterrence and even the "warning shot" strategy, if not the terms themselves, were implicit in the decisions that led to the destruction of Hiroshima and Nagasaki.

The concept of the atomic bomb as the final arbiter of war was recognized in 1939 with the publication of the discovery of nuclear fission. Every scientist familiar with the physics of this phenomenon understood that in theory a weapon of extraordinary power might be fashioned if the technical requirements could be mastered. To this end scientists enlisted the president's support; they formed committees to study the possibility of an atomic bomb; they lobbied the military; and they conducted experiments. But it was not until the summer of 1941, two-and-a-half years after fission was discovered in Germany, that scientists in England thought of a way to harness the theory to practical technology. In the fall of 1941 an Anglo-American scientific partnership was initiated. Its goal was to beat the Germans in a race for the atomic bomb.

The delay literally terrified the scientists associated with the bomb project. Aware of the weapon's potential and their own desultory start, they reasoned that the Anglo-American effort lagged behind Germany's, perhaps by as much as two-and-a-half years. In their minds the atomic bomb was the *ultimate weapon*; if the Germans developed it first, the Allied cause was lost. Arthur Compton, director of the atomic energy project at the University of Chicago, was so distressed at the slow rate of progress that, in June 1942, he urged a program for researching and developing "counter-measures" against a Ger-

Reprinted with permission from the *Bulletin of the Atomic Scientists*, August 1985, pp. 9–15. Copyright © 1985 by Educational Foundation for Nuclear Science.

man atomic bomb. In July J. Robert Oppenheimer wrote despairingly that the war could be lost before answers to the immediate problems under consideration could be found. "What Is Wrong with Us?" was the heading Leo Szilard chose for a memorandum in September criticizing the rate of progress.[2]

Despite the concern expressed at a high-level meeting at the White House in October 1941, the actual development of the bomb had not yet started at the beginning of 1943; and only limited progress had been made in constructing the many necessary facilities. General Leslie Groves was not appointed to head the project until September 17, 1942. The site for the uranium separation plant at Oak Ridge, Tennessee, was acquired only two days later. The land on which the bomb laboratory would be constructed outside Los Alamos, New Mexico, was not even purchased by the government until November; and it was December 1942 before Oppenheimer was appointed director. Enrico Fermi's critical experiment, the first controlled nuclear chain reaction, was completed that same month at the University of Chicago.

Thus, four years after fission was discovered, scientists were not confident that the United States was closing the lead the Germans were assumed to have. A feeling of desperate urgency grew with each passing month, and with it the conviction that once developed, the bomb would be a decisive factor in the war—a conviction that permeated the entire chain of command. Vannevar Bush and James Conant, the science administrators who oversaw the Manhattan Project, kept President Roosevelt informed of both their colleagues' progress and their fears.

The implications of Bush's ability to communicate directly with the president can hardly be exaggerated. Roosevelt came to accept the scientists' view that the Allies were involved in a two-front war. Not only were there hard enemies on the fields of battle, but in German laboratories there were enemies who posed an even greater danger: scientists who might be first to develop a weapon that could alter the course of the war. This view of the bomb assured that its importance would not be underestimated by policy-makers. Indeed, it assured that its value would be exaggerated, and that those responsible for the military security of the United States after the war would view it, as Secretary of War Henry L. Stimson did at the Potsdam Conference, as a "badly needed equalizer," as a

panacea for any real or imagined deficiencies of U.S. power.[3]

The atomic scientists' view that the bomb could win the war for Germany was easily converted by policy-makers to the idea that it could expedite the winning of the war for the United States. By the spring of 1944 the bomb's successful development appeared likely, but the timing of its completion remained uncertain. January 1945 was a possibility, but a later date—perhaps the summer of that year—appeared more probable.

Under the circumstances there is an irony in the decision to target Japan. Whatever other reasons may have contributed to that still incompletely understood decision, one element was the fear that an atomic attack on Germany might under certain conditions increase the possibility of a retaliatory attack in kind. This embryonic form of nuclear deterrence was expressed early. The May 5, 1943 minutes of a military policy committee meeting note that in a discussion of use of the first bomb "the general view appeared to be that its best point of use would be on a Japanese fleet concentration in the Harbor of Truk. General Styer suggested Tokio [sic], but it was pointed out that the bomb should be used where, if it failed to go off, it would land in water of sufficient depth to prevent easy salvage." The minutes went on to say: "The Japanese were selected as they would not be so apt to secure knowledge from it as would the Germans."[4]

Two years later, in the spring of 1945, with the Germans on the verge of defeat, confidence replaced caution and urban centers replaced military targets. While this shift in atomic bomb targets parallels an earlier shift in conventional bombing strategy, it also marks a new appreciation of the atomic bomb as a weapon of psychological intimidation. It was not expected that the destruction and havoc that two atomic bombs might wreak would suddenly break the back of Japan's war machine; but it was hoped that such attacks would shock the Japanese government into discontinuing their hopeless struggle. The selection of targets reflected this intention.

Guided by instructions from Groves, a target committee, composed of Manhattan Project scientists and ordnance specialists, studied the available options and developed criteria for their selection. The report of the committee's second and third meetings, held in Oppenheimer's office at Los Alamos in May 1945, suggests a major concern with the weapon's psychological impact.

The minutes record the committee's view that any small, strictly military target should be located in a much larger area subject to blast damage "to avoid undue risks of the weapon being lost due to bad placing of the bomb." The members of the committee agreed, too, that the psychological impression the bomb made was not just a matter of wartime interest. "Two aspects of this," the report states, "are 1) obtaining the greatest psychological effect against Japan and 2) making the initial use sufficiently spectacular *for the importance of the weapon to be internationally recognized* [emphasis added] when publicity on it is released."[5]

The Target Committee's concern that the full implications of the bomb be recognized internationally reflected a pervasive anxiety among those scientists who had begun to worry about the bomb's role in the postwar world. As an instrument of peace based on the international control of atomic energy, or as an instrument of diplomacy to be used in postwar negotiations, the influence of the weapon depended upon a general recognition that pre-atomic age calculations had to give way to new realities. If the Japanese did not accept this view, the war might continue; if the Soviets ignored it, the peace would be lost. In this sense the bomb became its own message, and within the context of the war the scientists who participated in the decision to bomb Japan were consumed by a single objective—to transmit in the most dramatic fashion possible the message that the new age required new forms of international organization.

Leo Szilard, who had composed Einstein's famous letter to Roosevelt warning of the military implications of the discovery of fission, was the first to suggest a resolution to the problem of the bomb in the postwar world. Writing to Bush in January 1944, he referred to the potential development of a bomb of even greater power (the hydrogen bomb), and commented that "this weapon will be so powerful that there can be no peace if it is simultaneously in the possession of any two powers unless these two powers are bound by an indissoluble political union." Some type of international control scheme had to be created, he argued, "if necessary by force," to prevent a war that would recreate the dark ages, or worse.[6]

This was not the last time a scientist would suggest the use of military force to achieve security against nuclear uncertainty. The overwhelming sense of hopelessness before the developing of an unprecedented power created an urge to seek assurance against that power being turned upon its inventors. Bound to their task by fear of German progress, and terrified by the consequences of their own success, men of sensibility, culture, and peace were driven to recommend policies that they would find abhorrent in other circumstances.

Like Kurt Vonnegut's Trafalmadorians in *Slaughterhouse Five*, the scientists could see into the future: a postwar nuclear arms race leading to circumstances that literally could bring about the end of the world. But no one with power to prevent such a catastrophe seemed to recognize that this problem existed. As they worked desperately to build the bomb, scientists who were alert to these issues grasped at schemes to keep its potential destructive force under control.

The first serious attempt to meet this challenge was offered by Niels Bohr, who escaped to England from Nazi-occupied Denmark in September 1943. "Officially and secretly he came to help the technical enterprise," Oppenheimer noted, but "most secretly of all . . . he came to advance his case and his cause." In the broadest sense, Bohr's cause was to ensure that atomic energy "is used to the benefit of all humanity and does not become a menace to civilization." More specifically, he warned that "quite apart from the question of how soon the weapon will be ready for use and what role it may play in the present war," some agreement had to be reached with the Soviet Union about the future control of atomic energy before the bomb was developed.[7]

Bohr's ideas on the international control of atomic energy remain significant today beyond any actual effect they might have had on Anglo-American policy. Arguing for a unilateral initiative, he insisted that the time to prepare for security in the nuclear age was before the bomb's development overwhelmed the possibility of international cooperation. If the bomb was born in secret in the United States, it would be conceived in secret by the Soviets. The only hope for avoiding a nuclear arms race after the war was to create an international-control arrangement before the war ended and before the bomb was tested. A nuclear arsenal was simply too big, in every sense, to be placed on any negotiating table; a weapon in the process of becoming was not.

As a scientist, Bohr apprehended the significance of the new weapon even before it was developed, and he had no doubt that Soviet scientists would also understand its profound implications for the postwar world. He was also certain that they would convey these implications to Stalin, just as scientists in the United States and Great Britain had explained them to Roosevelt and Churchill. Thus the diplomatic problem, as Bohr analyzed it, was not the need to convince Stalin that the atomic bomb was an unprecedented weapon that threatened the life of the world, but the need to assure the Soviet leader that he had nothing to fear from the circumstances of its development.

Roosevelt and Churchill shared neither Bohr's assumptions nor his vision, and perhaps it is too much to expect that they could. Harnessed to the yoke of war, without a scientist's intuitive understanding of the long-range implications of a weapon that did not yet exist, they accepted the bomb as it had been presented to them—as an ultimate weapon. "The suggestion that the world should be informed regarding [the atomic bomb], with a view to an international agreement regarding its control and use, is not accepted," they agreed in September 1944. "The matter should continue to be regarded as of the utmost secrecy."[8]

It was not only Bohr who tried to shed light on the dark shadow the bomb cast across the future. Scientists of a more politically conventional turn of mind, once alerted to the problem, turned to unconventional ideas. James Conant favored "the calculated risk," and to achieve a fair chance of success he was inclined "to talk in terms of concrete and limited objectives." Yet as early as May 1944, as James Hershberg has shown, Conant confronted the problem of the atomic bomb in the postwar world and came to the conclusion that limited objectives were dangerously inadequate. In the long run, he wrote to Bush, "the only hope for humanity is an international commission on atomic energy with free access to all information and right of inspection."[9]

In a memorandum entitled "Some Thoughts on International Control of Atomic Energy," Conant peered into the future and discerned only two alternatives: an atomic arms race and "in the next war destruction of civilization," or "a scheme to remove atomic energy from the field of conflict."[10] To achieve the second alternative Conant proposed 14 points. An association of nations specifically committed to control atomic energy had to be formed, and an international

commission on atomic energy, which would include Britain, the United States, the Soviet Union, and perhaps six other nations, had to control all atomic energy work.

The commission would license, finance, and control all research and development work, and all results would be published. Agents of the commission would police the system by frequent inspections of all laboratories, factories, or other relevant facilities, and even if two countries were at war, the inspectors would have the right of entry. The commission was to have its own international air force and an army of 10,000 men to prevent the seizure of supplies. If any nation refused to permit inspections, or interfered with the commission in any other important way, its actions would be "considered an act of war."

But, Conant asked, "what happens if a nation refuses entry of agents to factories etc. or disobeys [the] edicts of [the] commission?" His answer was "war," declared by the other members of the international organization who might, if the commission approved, *use atomic bombs* to bring the renegade nation to heel. This idea of a limited nuclear war to prevent a general conflagration was even extended to the "use of bombs by arsenal guards," if the United States, Canada, or Britain tried to seize the commission's atomic arsenal, which Conant had located in Canada.

By recommending the use of a limited number of atomic bombs to prevent a general nuclear war, Conant succumbed to the temptation that lies across the path of all nuclear arms control efforts. If the desire to rid the world of the potential danger of nuclear war stems from a fear of their destructive potential, then why not use that threat in the service of international security?

Conant believed not only that the bomb was an ideal weapon to shock Japan's leaders into surrender, but that its use was necessary to impress upon the world in general, and on the Soviet government in particular, his vision of the destruction that it could inflict. Assuming "that in another war atomic bombs will be used," he recommended to Stimson that in the present war "the bomb *must be used*" for that was "the only way to awaken the world to the necessity of abolishing war altogether. No technical demonstration . . . could take the place of the actual use with its horrible results." Nor was Conant the only scientist to hold this view. "If the bomb were not used in the present war," Arthur Compton wrote to Stimson in June 1945, "the world would have no adequate warning as to what was to be expected if war should break out again."[11]

A group of scientists at the University of Chicago reasoned quite differently, their analysis flowing from alternative assumptions formulated during the closing months of the war. Far removed from political pressures, and from considerations associated with the policy-making process, they broadcast a prescient warning to a deaf audience: the indiscriminate military use of the atomic bomb would undermine the possibility of achieving the international control of atomic energy.[12]

Early in June 1945, under the chairmanship of the distinguished emigre physicist James Franck, they assembled as the Committee on the Social and Political Implications of the Atomic Bomb. Their central concern was "the conditions under which international control is most probable," and their basic assumption was that the "manner in which this new weapon is introduced to the world will determine in large part the future course of events." They too saw the path from atomic bombs to superbombs with limitless destructive power. They too described the uncertain security that an attempt at monopoly would bring. And they too outlined methods of international control that might be feasible.

Their primary purpose, however, was less to enumerate the dangers of the atomic age than to recommend policies that might circumvent those dangers. The central argument of the report was that a surprise atomic attack against Japan was inadvisable—whether one was optimistic or pessimistic about the possibility of international control. "If we consider international agreement on total prevention of nuclear warfare as the paramount objective, and believe that it can be achieved," they argued, "this kind of introduction [surprise attack] of atomic weapons to the world may easily destroy all our chances of success. Russia, and even allied countries which bear less mistrust of our ways and intentions, as well as neutral countries may be deeply shocked."

They argued against dropping the bomb on a populated area to show its capacity for terror and annihilation. "It may be very difficult to persuade the world that a nation which was capable of secretly preparing and suddenly releasing a weapon as indiscriminate as the [German] rocket bomb and a million times more destructive, is to be trusted in its proclaimed desire to have such weapons abolished by international agreement."

The report also made the converse case for not using the atomic bomb, even "if one takes the pessimistic point of view and discounts the possibility of an effective international control over nuclear weapons at the present time . . . early use of nuclear bombs against Japan becomes even more doubtful—quite independently of any humanitarian considerations. If an international agreement is not concluded immediately after the first use," they reasoned, exhibiting Bohr's sense of timing that was elsewhere lacking, "this will mean a flying start toward an unlimited armaments race. If this race is inevitable, we have every reason to delay its beginning as long as possible in order to increase our head start still further."

The members of the Franck Committee shared a basic assumption with those who had a sanguine view of the results that would flow from using the bomb: an atomic attack against Japan would "shock" the Soviets as well as the Japanese. But their reasoning about the effect of such a shock was very different. Conant, Compton, Truman, Stimson, and Secretary of State James Byrnes shared the view that an undeveloped weapon was not a very useful bargaining counter, a concept that is all too familiar today. They believed that an actual combat demonstration would make a far greater impression on those who needed to be convinced to end the war, and on those who needed to be persuaded that postwar international control of the atomic bomb was in their long-range interest. It was this quest to make an *impression*—the psychological impact of a single bomb dropped from a lone aircraft causing damage equal to that caused by thousands of bombs dropped from hundreds of aircraft—that was the basis for the decisions that led to Hiroshima.

The Franck Committee, however, drew the diametrically opposite conclusion: the more awesome the bomb's demonstrated power, the more likely an arms race. The most important demonstration needed was some means of conveying to Moscow a U.S. commitment not to use the bomb, a commitment that might instill in the Soviets a measure of confidence that the Anglo-American monopoly would not be turned on them, a commitment that might persuade them that the objective of U.S. policy was the neutralization of the atomic bomb. Szilard made this point to Oppenheimer when they saw each other in Washington in June. "Don't you think," Oppenheimer rejoined, "if we tell the Russians what we intend to do and then use the bomb in Japan, the Russians will understand it?" "They'll understand it only too well," was Szilard's prescient reply.[13]

In a sense more complex than originally stated, P.M.S. Blackett's charge "that the dropping of the atomic bombs was not so much the last military act of the second World War, as the first major operation of the cold *diplomatic* war with Russia," contains an essential truth.[14] The scientists and policy-makers who promoted the international control of atomic energy and supported the use of the bomb against Japan never expected that good relations with the Soviet Union would be possible if diplomatic efforts to achieve a nuclear arms control pact were not successful. They never thought that achieving such an agreement would be easy, nor that tough negotiations and a measure of intimidation should be avoided. Hiroshima and Nagasaki were part of that diplomatic strategy. So were the postwar tests at Bikini, held in the summer of 1946, at the same time that Bernard Baruch was presenting the U.S. plan for the international control of atomic energy to the United Nations.

Following a line of reasoning that President Truman stated in January—that "unless Russia is faced with an iron fist and strong language another war is in the making"[15]—Conant believed that atomic diplomacy would serve a useful purpose in bringing about security from atomic war. Speaking at an off-the-record dinner sponsored by the Council on Foreign Relations in New York on April 12, 1946, Truman responded to a question about the relationship between the Bikini tests and the upcoming United Nations Organization's international control conference: "The Russians," he stated, "are more rather than less likely to come to an effective agreement for the control of atomic energy if we keep our strength and continue to produce bombs."[16]

Atomic testing was not the only arrow in Conant's atomic diplomacy quiver; history also had a role. The atomic bombings of Japan were supported by the majority of Americans, but in the aftermath of the war Conant discerned a "spreading accusation that it was entirely unnecessary to use the atomic bomb at all," particularly among those whom he described to Stimson as "verbal minded citizens not so generally influential as they were influential among the coming generations of whom they might be teachers or educators."[17] To combat that view he urged Stimson to write an article on "the decision to drop the bomb," which subsequently appeared under that title in the February 1947 issue of *Harper's* magazine.

If "the propaganda against the use of the atomic bomb had been allowed to grow unchecked," Conant wrote to Stimson after reading a prepublication version of the article, "the strength of our military position by virtue of having the bomb would have been correspondingly weakened," and the chances for international control undermined.[18] "Humanitarian considerations" that led citizens to oppose the strengthening of the U.S. atomic arsenal, in Conant's opinion, were likely to subvert the common effort to achieve an international atomic energy agreement. "I am firmly convinced," he told Stimson, "that the Russians will eventually agree to the American proposals for the establishment of an atomic energy authority of worldwide scope, *provided* they are convinced that we would have the bomb in quantity and would use it without hesitation in another war."[19]

That Conant and those who supported this view were wrong is less a criticism of their logic than of their fundamental assumptions about the nature of the forces underlying the atomic arms race. If the Americans viewed the bomb as an effective instrument of diplomacy, and as a weapon to be used "without hesitation in another war," the Soviets could hardly be expected to take a loftier view. Scientific greatness gave way to political folly with the view that the atomic bomb could be used to fashion a solution to its own existence. It is a folly that we continue to live with today. And, to paraphrase Rabi, how well we mean.

NOTES

1. I.I. Rabi, "How Well We Meant," transcript of Rabi's 1983 talk, Los Alamos National Laboratory Archives (no date).

2. Arthur Compton to Henry Wallace, June 23, 1942, F.D. Roosevelt, President's Secretary's File, Vannevar Bush folder, Roosevelt Library, Hyde Park, N.Y.; Robert Oppenheimer to John Manley, July 14, 1942, Oppenheimer Papers, Box 49, Library of Congress; Martin J. Sherwin, *A World Destroyed* (New York: Vintage Books, 1977), p. 47; Richard G. Hewlett and Oscar B. Anderson, Jr., *The New World, 1939/1946: A History of the United States Atomic Energy Commission, I* (University Park, Pa.: Pennsylvania State University Press, 1962), p. 179.

3. Henry L. Stimson and McGeorge Bundy, *On Active Service in Peace and War* (New York: Harpers, 1947), p. 617.

4. "Policy Meeting, 5/5/43," p. 2, Record Group 77, Manhattan Engineering District Records, Top Secret, folder 23A, National Archives.

5. Derry and Ramsey to Groves, May 12, 1945, MED–TS, Box 3, Target Committee Meetings, folder 5D.2.

6. Szilard to Bush, Jan. 14, 1944, in Gertrude Weiss Szilard and Spencer R. Weart, eds., *Leo Szilard: His Version of the Facts* (Cambridge, Mass.: MIT Press, 1978), p. 163.

7. J. Robert Oppenheimer, "Niels Bohr and Atomic Weapons," *The New York Review of Books*, 3 (Dec. 17, 1966), p. 7. Bohr memorandum, May 8, 1945, Oppenheimer Papers, box 34, Library of Congress; Bohr to Roosevelt, July 3, 1944, Oppenheimer Papers, box 34, LC.

8. Hyde Park Aide-Memoire, Sept. 18, 1944, President's Map Room papers, Naval Aide's File, box 172-General folder, Franklin Delano Roosevelt Library, reprinted in Sherwin, *A World Destroyed*, p. 284.

9. "The Tough-Minded Idealist," Sept. 23, 1946, *Harvard Alumni Bulletin*, 49, no. 2 (Oct. 12, 1946), quoted in James G. Hershberg, *Ends Versus Means: James B. Conant and American Atomic Policy, 1939–47.* Unpublished senior thesis, Harvard College, 1982), pp. 208–9. See also marginal comment by Conant on a memorandum, Bush to Conant, April 17, 1944, entitled "Shurcliff's Memo on Post-War Policies," Atomic Energy Commission Historical Document no. 180, Department of Energy Archives, Energy Research Collection.

10. James Conant, memo dated May 4, 1944, Bush-Conant files, box 9, folder 97, Office of Scientific Research and Development, S-1 Section files, National Archives; reprinted in Hershberg, *Ends Versus Means*, pp. 189–90.

11. James Conant to Grenville Clark, Nov. 8, 1945, Bush Papers, box 27, Conant folder, LC; Henry Stimson to Raymond Swing, quoting Conant, Feb. 4, 1947, Stimson Papers, Swing folder, Sterling Memorial Library, Yale University; Arthur Holly Compton, *Atomic Quest: A Personal Narrative* (New York: Oxford University Press, 1956), pp. 239–40.

12. The Franck Report is reproduced in Alice Kimball Smith, *A Peril and A Hope: The Atomic Scientists' Movement, 1945–1947* (Chicago: University of Chicago Press, 1965), Appendix B, pp. 560–72.

13. Leo Szilard, "Reminiscences," edited by Gertrude Weiss Szilard and Kathleen R. Winsor, in Donald Fleming and Bernard Bailyn, eds., *The Intellectual Migration: Europe and America, 1930–1960* (Cambridge, Mass.: Harvard University Press, 1969), p. 128.

14. P.M.S. Blackett, *Fear, War and the Bomb: Military and Political Consequences of Atomic Energy* (New York: Whittlesey House, 1948), p. 139.

15. Harry S. Truman, *Memoirs: Year of Decisions* (Garden City, N.Y.: Doubleday, 1955), pp. 551–52.

16. James Conant, "International Controls of Atomic Energy," April 12, 1946; *Records of Meetings*, vol. XII, July 1945-June 1947, Council on Foreign Relations Archives, New York, quoted in Hershberg, *Ends Versus Means*, p. 157.

17. Stimson to Felix Frankfurter, quoting Conant, Dec. 12, 1946, Stimson Papers, box 154, folder 14.

18. Conant to McGeorge Bundy, Nov. 30, 1946, Stimson Papers, box 154, folder 11.

19. Conant to Stimson, Jan. 22, 1947, Stimson Papers, box 154, folder 18.

11 Rewriting the History of the H-Bomb

William J. Broad ⎯⎯⎯⎯⎯⎯⎯⎯⎯⎯⎯⎯⎯⎯⎯⎯⎯⎯⎯⎯⎯⎯⎯⎯⎯

A once-secret history of the building of the hydrogen bomb takes issue with the popular notion that J. Robert Oppenheimer and Los Alamos Laboratory, the top-secret birthplace of the bomb in New Mexico, resisted for purely political reasons a crash program aimed at building an H-bomb. Instead it reveals long struggles with technical problems. Chief among these were faulty calculations that misled the U.S. nuclear weapons program between the years 1946 and 1950. The errors, according to the history, were the work of Edward Teller, "father" of the H-bomb.

The recently declassified account, written in 1954, also says the size and intensity of the H-bomb effort at Los Alamos meant there was no need for the founding of the Lawrence Livermore Laboratory in California, Teller's rival lab for the design of nuclear weapons.

The sweeping revision of H-bomb history was penned by Hans A. Bethe, a physicist at Cornell University who is widely respected in the weapons community. It appears in the current issue of *Los Alamos Science*, a quarterly publication of the laboratory.

Bethe's history "is the most revealing and authentic that I've ever seen in the open literature," says Richard L. Garwin, a physicist who worked on the development of the H-bomb and became a top Pentagon consultant. Its most striking revelation, he says, is that "Teller did a number of things wrong which were highly misleading to the laboratory."

Reprinted with permission from W.J. Broad, "Rewriting the History of the H-Bomb," *Science*, vol. 218, pp. 769–772, 19 November 1982. Copyright 1982 by the American Association for the Advancement of Science.

A pivotal figure in thermonuclear research, Bethe in 1938 deduced that fusion powers the sun and stars. That discovery, along with work on other nuclear puzzles, eventually won him the Nobel Prize. After the war Bethe helped with the development of fusion weapons, a project that culminated in 1952 with the 10-megaton rumble of the world's first hydrogen bomb. Bethe wrote his account in 1954 after a U.S. inquiry found that Oppenheimer had hindered a crash program on the "super." Oppenheimer, who directed Los Alamos and the building of the first atomic bomb, lost his security clearance and fell from power.

"My impression," says J. Carson Mark, head of the Los Alamos theoretical division between 1947 and 1973, "is that Bethe's article is factually accurate. And it's not badly colored, especially considering that Bethe was quite angry with Teller over his weasel-worded testimony in the Oppenheimer hearing."

At Teller's Hoover Institution office in California, an administrative assistant said Teller had not seen the article and could not comment.

In *Los Alamos Science*, Bethe says he had intended to put his 1954 account "into the Laboratory's archives and not to publish it, in order not to stir up old controversies." That he decided otherwise was due to the continued appearance of inaccurate articles and books, most recently *J. Robert Oppenheimer, Shatterer of Worlds*, published in connection with a recent PBS television series (Goodchild, 1981). "While this book is excellent in most respects," Bethe writes, "it gives a very wrong impression of the development of the H-bomb."

Popular history tends to stress Teller's positive role. It is true that Teller suggested the idea of an H-bomb early in 1942, and that Oppenheimer, Bethe, and others studied the possibility that summer. The work was soon interrupted by the Manhattan Project. After the war, atomic scientists argued over the wisdom of embarking on a high-priority program for the development of a super-bomb. Nobody knew if such a weapon was possible. Many hoped it was not. Teller, a foe of the Soviets, urged a crash program. Bethe, head of the Los Alamos theoretical division during the war and Teller's former boss, called for a more cautious approach, as did other physicists. Oppenheimer for one was deeply troubled by what he had wrought at Los Alamos, and was repulsed by the notion of bombs of unlimited power. The question is whether his personal aversion led to technical bias. Superficial histories hold that Teller overcame political resistance to the super and founded a rival laboratory at Livermore. The facts are more interesting.

Bethe divides the decade-long quest for thermonuclear weapons into the evolution of four distinct methods: A, B, C and D. Method A was the "classical super" proposed by Teller in 1942. After the war Teller also invented methods B and C. However, by 1947 it became clear that method B would fail and that method C would work only for weapons of small yield. Research at Los Alamos thus focused on method A. "New plans for calculations were made frequently," writes Bethe, "mostly by consultation between Teller and the senior staff of the theoretical division."

The calculations on the feasibility of method A were so complex that they quickly overpowered the crude computers then available. "Some greatly simplified calculations were done but it was realized that they left out many important factors and were quite unreliable. Work therefore concentrated on preparing full-scale calculations 'for the time when adequate fast computing machines become available'—a phrase which recurs in many of the theoretical reports of this period."

The calculations, given low priority, focused on what Bethe calls problem 1. However, the perceived stumbling block to the success of method A was seen to be problem 2. Teller came up with a possible solution, one that required a test. Plans were made for verification of Teller's idea at Eniwetok Atoll in the Pacific, a series of bursts known as Greenhouse.

Oppenheimer, chairman of the Atomic En-

ergy Commission's (AEC's) general advisory committee from 1947 to 1952, initially had successfully argued for a slow approach to the thermonuclear question. But early in 1950, President Truman, prompted by the detonation of the first Russian A-bomb and by the revelation that a spy had delivered H-bomb secrets to the Soviets, ordered the superbomb developed with all possible speed.

"While Teller and most of the Los Alamos Laboratory were busy preparing the Greenhouse tests," writes Bethe, "a number of persons in the theoretical division had continued to consider the various problems posed by Part 1. In particular Dr. Stanislaw Ulam on his own initiative had decided to check the feasibility of aspects of Part 1 without the aid of high-speed computing equipment. He, and Dr. Cornelius J. Everett who assisted him, soon found that the calculations of Teller's group of 1946 were wrong. Ulam's calculations showed that an extraordinarily large amount of tritium would be necessary." Tritium, a heavy form of hydrogen, does not occur in nature and is difficult to produce. Ulam's calculations of 1950 meant the cost of method A would be prohibitive. When Teller heard the news he went "pale with fury," according to Ulam (Hewlett and Duncan, 1969:440).

"That Ulam's calculations had to be done at all was proof," writes Bethe, "that the H-bomb was not ready for a 'crash' program when Teller first advocated such an idea in the fall of 1949. Nobody will blame Teller because the calculations of 1946 were wrong, especially because adequate computing machines were not then available. But he was blamed at Los Alamos for leading the laboratory, and indeed the whole country, into an adventurous program on the basis of calculations which he himself must have known to have been very incomplete. . . ."

"Teller himself was desperate between October 1950 and January 1951. He proposed a number of complicated schemes to save method A, none of which seemed to show much promise."

By early 1951, however, Teller and mathematician Ulam conceived an entirely new, ingenious method for a practical hydrogen bomb of unlimited power, a plan Bethe refers to as method D. After the *Progressive* case, in which the government tried and failed to keep a magazine from publishing H-bomb secrets, a key feature of method D was revealed to be the power of x-rays, traveling at the speed of light, to ignite thermonuclear fuel (De Volpi et al., 1981:82–

109). The whole idea was so "technically sweet," according to Oppenheimer, that he could no longer raise objections to a crash program.

"Concentrated work on Method A would never have led to Method D," writes Bethe. "By a misappraisal of the facts many persons not closely connected with the development have concluded that the scientists who had shown good judgment concerning the technical feasibility of Method A were now suddenly proved wrong, whereas Teller, who had been wrong in interpreting his own calculations, was suddenly right. The fact was that the new concept had created an entirely new technical situation. Such miracles do happen occasionally in scientific history but it would be folly to count on their occurrence. One of the dangerous consequences of the H-bomb history may well be that government administrators, and perhaps some scientists, too, will imagine that similar miracles should be expected in other developments."

Despite the tortuous path to the development of a superbomb, the scientists at Los Alamos worked enthusiastically on the project. Bethe estimates that between 1946 and 1949 the theoretical division worked about equally on the design of fission weapons and on the solution of the H-bomb problem. After Truman's call to arms in 1950, the effort expanded as more than a dozen scientists were added to the division's staff. Bethe's account is clearly at odds with popular history. In *Shatterer of Worlds*, author Peter Goodchild writes that "In spite of the President's directive, the work on the Super was given little priority and was overall at a low ebb."

In fact, ardor at Los Alamos was such that even the failure of method A did not dampen spirits. Bethe paid a visit in April 1950. "The entire Laboratory seemed enthusiastic about the project and was working at high speed," he writes. "That they continued to work with full energy on Teller's Greenhouse Test, even after Ulam's calculations had made the success of the whole program very doubtful, shows how far they were willing to go in following Teller's lead."

Atomic history from an insider's point of view, writes Bethe, not only refutes the notion that Los Alamos dragged its feet, but casts new light on reasons for the founding of Lawrence Livermore. "Certainly the events of the year 1950 would hardly seem to have given Teller any justification to ask the AEC, in the spring of 1951, to establish a second weapons laboratory."

Nonetheless, Teller continued to lobby passionately for a new lab. In December of that year he addressed the AEC advisory committee and cited the need for urgency because the Russians might already be ahead (Hewlett and Duncan, 1969:569–570). Los Alamos had not made good use of its limited resources, he said, and had been inflexible in its approach to the super.

In fact, as Los Alamos sped ahead with work on method D, relations between Teller and others on the staff cooled. Teller, among other demands, wanted the thermonuclear test moved up. Teller and Norris Bradbury, the postwar director of the lab, could not agree on who should direct the actual building of the bomb. "Bradbury had great experience in administrative matters like these," writes Bethe. "Teller had no experience and in the past had shown no talent for administration." Teller had abandoned programs in midstream. He had injected modifications into projects already under construction. "Everybody recognizes that Teller more than anyone else contributed ideas at every stage of the H-bomb program, and this fact should never be obscured," writes Bethe. However, as a journalistic profile of the period put it, "nine out of ten of Teller's ideas are useless. He needs men with more judgment, even if they be less gifted, to select the tenth idea which often is a stroke of genius."

Bethe's account adds up to a recasting of cold war history. The key issue in the 1954 inquiry was whether pure political pressure had slowed work on the super, although Oppenheimer was charged with additional indiscretions. As Teller told the inquiry: "If it is a question of wisdom and judgment, as demonstrated by actions since 1945, then I would say one would be wiser not to grant clearance."

What Bethe's revision of H-bomb history makes understandable is why atomic scientists of the inner circle often hold Teller in such contempt. In 1954, the laws of classification made it impossible for them to come to Oppenheimer's defense in public, to explain the technical reasons for a cautious approach to the super. They were barred from revealing the blind alleys, the mistaken calculations. Bethe tried, and his attempt was promptly seen as a potential breach of security, one that might jeopardize the U.S. lead in atomic weapons. After all, designs based on Teller's faulty calculations were among the H-bomb secrets that had been stolen by the Soviets. Why untangle the mess in public? Such restraint, moreover, may have been wise in some ways. The Soviets did not detonate an H-bomb built on the Teller-Ulam principle until late 1955, more than a year after the Oppenheimer inquiry and 3 years after the first such U.S. detonation (York, 1976:98–99). It has long been known that Oppenheimer urged a slow approach to the super. Bethe's account now reveals the extent to which Oppenheimer's opposition to a crash program was based on technical as well as political reasons. But in the fanaticism of the McCarthy era, any opposition was enough to ensure his demise.

REFERENCES

DeVolpi, A. et al. (1981). *Born Secret: The H-bomb, the Progressive Case, and National Security*. New York: Pergamon.

Goodchild, P. (1981). *J. Robert Oppenheimer: Shatterer of Worlds*. Boston: Houghton Mifflin.

Hewlett, R.G., and F. Duncan. (1969). *Atomic Shield 1947–1952*. University Park, PA: Pennsylvania State University Press.

York, H.F. (1976). *The Advisors: Oppenheimer, Teller and the Superbomb*. San Francisco: Freeman.

12   An Exchange of Letters on the Hydrogen Bomb History

Edward Teller and Hans A. Bethe

In the 19 November issue of *Science*, William J. Broad attempts "Rewriting the history of the hydrogen bomb," using as his starting point an article by my friend Hans Bethe, published in *Los Alamos Science*. Broad's article is not new, not accurate, and not constructive.

The valid parts of Broad's article are hardly novel. They were published in *Science* under the title "The work of many people."

The inaccurate parts of the argument are much harder to discuss. On the one hand, we are dealing with accusations based on partially declassified information. How can a scientific reader judge the connections and comparisons between methods A, B, C, and D, when none of these can be described? A general scientific judgment as to what contributed to and what obstructed progress on the hydrogen bomb must await the release of complete information. Furthermore, as a participant I am necessarily restrained from evaluating my own contribution.

The atmosphere in which work on the hydrogen bomb proceeded was characterized by the Atomic Energy Commission (AEC) General Advisory Committee meeting at Princeton on 16 June 1951, which Bethe describes incorrectly in his article. The meeting was arranged by Norris Bradbury, then director of Los Alamos. The report on the hydrogen bomb did not mention method D. When I asked to speak, Bradbury

denied me the opportunity. Although there were several people present who knew about method D, including Bethe and Oppenheimer, none chose to speak about it. However, AEC Commissioner Smythe, who believed that the other side of the argument should be heard, made my presentation possible. In the developments that immediately followed, this proved to be decisive.

While Bethe's article in *Los Alamos Science* primarily offered a criticism of Shepley and Blair's book, Broad neither mentions nor quotes these authors. Concerning that book, Bethe and I are in agreement. In fact, at our first meeting in 1958, Jack Kennedy offered a compliment on the basis of "the nice things said about me" by Shepley and Blair. I could find no better reply than to recite a Gilbert and Sullivan ditty which includes the phrase, "scarce a word of it is true."

There are two essential points on which I must comment. One is my advocacy of the hydrogen bomb. The result of our developing the hydrogen bomb was that we maintained our strength and could guarantee the stability of the world up to the mid-1970's. Herb York has argued [*The Advisors: Oppenheimer, Teller and the Superbomb* (Freeman, San Francisco, 1976)] that, had the Soviets developed the hydrogen bomb first, we would have matched them in a very short time. Recent events illustrate our capacity for self-delusion. Even when our President (disregarding his own political interests which would persuade him to offer an optimistic picture to the American people) was courageous enough to tell us the bitter truth—that Soviet military preparations have outstripped our own—a surprisingly large number of people (including York) are unwilling to acknowledge any danger.

Reprinted with permission from Edward Teller and H.A. Bethe, letters on the Hydrogen Bomb History, *Science*, vol. 218, p. 1270, 24 December 1982. Copyright 1982 by the American Association for the Advancement of Science.

The second point is that Broad calls into question the importance of the second weapons laboratory, which was established at Livermore. Actually Bethe in his article points out in a note added in 1982: "In the intervening 28 years, Livermore has contributed greatly to nuclear weapons development."

This is indeed true. Livermore led the way toward establishing a submarine-based nuclear force that today is considered the most secure aspect of our defense. At present, Livermore is spearheading the development of purely defensive weapons. Most fortunately—since the development of such weapons may replace the dubious security of the "balance of terror" with a more stable protective basis for peace, this trend has been generally adopted by both Los Alamos and Sandia Laboratory. Due to the variety in research made possible by the existence of several separate laboratories, such constructive plans receive emphasis.

Actually part of Bethe's intention in writing his comments was connected with a defense of Oppenheimer's role. Here, of course, our opinions are not in agreement, but perhaps we are less far apart than is generally assumed. I am submitting comments on the BBC television drama *J. Robert Oppenheimer* to the *Los Alamos Science*, and these should clarify this point.

In historic perspective, the Oppenheimer case, which is the underlying theme in both Bethe's and Broad's articles, was most unfortunate. It introduced a division in the scientific community that has weakened national defense and our ability to make peace secure.

Very recently Bethe wrote me a short, pleasant letter stating that he had wanted to present his opinion within a very limited community and was very unhappy about the broader use being made of his article. In this respect, Bethe and I again agree, but Broad does not. What we need is not to emphasize past disagreements but to bring about as much agreement as possible in order to face the future with its obviously great dangers.

EDWARD TELLER

Hoover Institution on War,
Revolution and Peace,
Stanford, California 94305

I agree with many points in Teller's letter, for example, with the statement that the Livermore laboratory contributed decisively to submarine-based nuclear weapons which today are the most secure components of our defense. But he brings in two points which were not in Broad's article, and with which I strongly disagree.

The first concerns the General Advisory Committee (GAC) meeting at Princeton on 16 June 1951. My recollection differs from Teller's. The main purpose of this meeting was to discuss method D, and I specially postponed a trip to Europe because method D was to be discussed. I had been informed of method D about a month earlier and was immediately persuaded that this was the correct solution to the problem. I was asked beforehand to participate with Teller in presenting the method to the GAC and the Atomic Energy Commission, and to the best of my recollection this was done after reports on the most recent test series had been given.

The second point concerns the development of "purely defensive" nuclear weapons at Livermore and other weapons laboratories. If reliable defensive weapons were feasible, I would welcome this escape from the balance of terror. But I remain convinced that, in the nuclear field, the offense will continue to have the advantage and can negate any defensive weapons with relatively little effort. Defensive nuclear weapons will at best remain wishful thinking.

HANS A. BETHE

Floyd R. Newman Laboratory
of Nuclear Studies, Cornell University,
Ithaca, New York 14853

QUESTIONS FOR DISCUSSION

1. During the spring and summer of 1945, policy makers and scientists debated whether the the U.S. should drop the A-bomb on Japan. Describe this debate and the positions taken by various groups.

2. Should the United States have developed the H-bomb? Discuss the pros and cons.

3. Many key decisions of the nuclear age have been made in the utmost secrecy. What implications does this fact have for the democratic process?

4. If you had an opportunity to talk with Bethe and Teller about the development of the H-bomb, what questions would you raise?

SUGGESTED READINGS

The Frank Report (A Report to the Secretary of War—June 11, 1945), Appendix B in Alice Kimball Smith. *A Peril and A Hope.* Chicago: University of Chicago Press, 1965.

GROVES, LESLIE R. *Now It Can Be Told.* New York: Harper & Row, 1962.

SHERWIN, MARTIN J. *A World Destroyed.* New York: Alfred A. Knopf, 1975.

SMITH, ALICE KIMBALL. *A Peril and A Hope: The Scientists' Movement in America, 1945–47.* Chicago: University of Chicago Press, 1965.

YORK, HERBERT F. *The Advisors: Oppenheimer, Teller, and the Superbomb.* New York: Freeman, 1976.

Chapter IV

The Growth of Nuclear Arsenals

The Manhattan Project scientists who feared a post-war atomic arms race have been proven right. Since 1945, nuclear arsenals around the world have grown in size and sophistication, and many types of nuclear weapons and delivery systems have been deployed. Between 49,000 and 59,000 nuclear weapons have been stockpiled worldwide. Nuclear weapons are deployed in land-based missiles, in aircraft, ships, submarines and cruise missiles, and in torpedos, depth charges, artillery shells, and demolition munitions. Increasingly accurate guidance systems now make it possible for intercontinental missiles to land within a few hundred feet of their targets.

This vast nuclear arsenal is the subject of this chapter. In the first reading, William M. Arkin and Richard W. Fieldhouse describe the nuclear arsenals of the United States, the Soviet Union, Britain, France and China, discussing the numbers, capabilities and missions of various types of weapons.

Next, Herbert Scoville gives a brief history of the growth of strategic nuclear forces, noting such developments as the post-World War II bomber build-up, the introduction of the intercontinental ballistic missile (ICBM), the placement of nuclear missiles on submarines, the debate over the anti-ballistic missile (ABM), and the deployment of the multiple independently targetable reentry vehicle (MIRV).

The last three readings address the current frontier of the arms race: space. Kurt Gottfried and Richard Ned Lebow describe the operation and probable political consequences of anti-satellite weapons (ASATs), which are now being developed and tested. They argue that the deployment of anti-satellite weapons would be very destabilizing, increasing the likelihood of escalation during a crisis.

The remaining readings address the U.S. Strategic Defense Initiative (SDI), popularly known as "Star Wars." First, we present an excerpt from a White House statement, prepared by the Reagan administration, that outlines the goals of the SDI. The final reading is an excerpt from a report by the Union of Concerned Scientists. The scientists who authored this report discuss critically the technologies for space-based missile defense and analyze possible political implications of a major "Star Wars" program.

13 The Growth of Strategic Forces

Herbert Scoville

Over the years strategic policies and the forces to support them have evolved as new weapons or new theories were developed. In some cases the weapons were procured in order to satisfy certain policy needs; yet far too frequently the weapons were developed and procured and then the policy modified to justify them. To some extent Presidential Directive 59 and the MX are an example of the latter case.

In the post–World War II years the United States produced large numbers of intercontinental bombers; the World War II B-29s were supplanted with B-36s, armed first with fission weapons and later hydrogen bombs. These planes were designed to give muscle to the policy of massive retaliation in the event of Soviet aggression anywhere in the world. The Soviet Union, starting considerably behind the United States, attempted to build a long-range bomber force of its own by procuring Bison jet and Bear turboprop bombers with intercontinental range. It also put a tremendous effort into building antiaircraft defenses in order to protect its cities from our bomber threat. In the mid-1950s the United States entered into a program for the procurement of more advanced B-47 bombers and then later the B-52s in order to eliminate the feared bomber gap from the Soviet buildup.

The Soviet Union, however, opted out of the race after building only about 200 Bison and Bear long-range bombers and instead turned its attention to ballistic missiles. Their initial ICBM, the very large and cumbersome SS-6, was first tested successfully in August 1957 and in the next two years went through a thorough testing

program so that it could have been operational by 1960, or perhaps even earlier. This same vehicle was used to launch the first Sputnik satellite on October 4, 1957, more than a year before the United States was ready to do so, and this caused great concern in American security circles.

Although ballistic missiles were given highest priority in the United States, there was no way that we could be in a position to deploy our first ICBMs by the time that the Soviets had demonstrated that the SS-6 could be ready for use (1959 or 1960). In view of the extensive Soviet testing program, which demonstrated the SS-6 to be a reliable missile, it was logically assumed that they were proceeding to deploy this ICBM, though it was not possible for us to locate any deployment sites. Our U-2 reconnaissance plane was capable of only limited photographic coverage of the Soviet Union, so the operational status of this missile could not be readily determined. Air force intelligence postulated widespread ICBM deployment by 1960, while the navy estimated the number of operational missiles to be very low or even nonexistent. CIA estimates were somewhere in between, but there were few people who did not subscribe to the existence of some missile gap even though its size and significance was uncertain. Fears of a Soviet surprise attack mounted as the decade ended. President Eisenhower, however, did not believe that the Soviet force was sufficient to threaten our very large force of bombers, many of which were kept on an alert status to avoid being caught by surprise on the ground.

Late in 1960, some months after the U-2 was shot down over the Soviet Union, the United States acquired the ability to photograph the Soviet Union from satellites. The first useful pictures were taken in November 1960, and gradually over the next six to nine months pictures of the entire Soviet Union were obtained. This new wide area coverage gradually showed during 1961 that the Soviet Union had never gone forward with the deployment of its first ICBM, probably because it was too big and unmanageable. At the most only a handful were deployed at Plesetsk, a site northwest of Moscow, which was also used for certain operational testing and space flights. Thus by the end of 1961 the missile gap had been imploded, and instead, because of the high priority given to the first-generation U.S. Atlas and Titan and the second-generation Minuteman ICBM and Polaris submarine missile programs, the Soviet Union ended up way behind.

Beginning in the early 1960s, the United States went rapidly ahead with a broad but orderly program to build up a balanced strategic deterrent force. Survivability was recognized as the most critical characteristic for such a force, and the vulnerable Atlas and Titan Is were replaced with a thousand Minuteman and fifty-four Titan II missiles in blast-hardened underground silos. The United States also built forty-one nuclear-powered submarines, each armed with sixteen strategic ballistic missiles; these are not considered to be vulnerable for the foreseeable future. The United States completed the procurement of about six hundred B-52 intercontinental bombers to provide the third leg of this strategic triad. By reliance on this three-pronged triad of strategic delivery vehicles, the United States was protected against any unforeseen technological or operational breakthroughs that could make the deterrent as a whole vulnerable.

Each part of the triad had strengths and weaknesses. The land-based ICBMs had the best command and control because of the simplicity of communications between the highest authority and the officers with access to the firing circuits. High accuracy is most easily achieved with fixed, land-based ICBMs. They can reach their targets within thirty minutes of launch and so provide for rapid response if required. But once they are out of their silos, they cannot be recalled, so a nuclear war could not be avoided. Because of their known, fixed location, they can be the target of accurate missile warheads.

The bombers have a slower reaction time (six to eight hours to reach their targets), but they do not have to be committed irrevocably to a nuclear attack when they take off from their airfields. Inflight refueling enables them to remain airborne for a long time, and until they cross the borders of the Soviet Union, they can always be recalled. Although they are quite vulnerable on the ground to a nuclear explosion, one-third of the force can be kept on fifteen-minute alert to prevent their being destroyed in a surprise ICBM attack. Once in the air, they are essentially invulnerable until they have to penetrate Soviet defenses. The extensive Soviet antiaircraft defenses could in the past be overcome by flying close to the ground to avoid radars and by bombing a path through the ground defenses. Since airborne radars for tracking low-flying planes are now greatly improved, it is planned in the future for the bombers to stay outside the perimeter of enemy defenses and to launch attacks through them with large numbers of small, low-flying, unmanned cruise missiles.

The submarine ballistic missile force is by far the most survivable of all elements of the triad, since there are no developments on the horizon that could make them vulnerable to a Soviet first strike. Although a single submarine might be sunk, there appears no way in which a fleet of about thirty submarines that would be at sea at any one time can be destroyed on short notice. The greatest disadvantage of the submarine force is the problem of maintaining two-way communications without disclosing the location of the ship. This difficulty creates problems for command and control. In order to remain undetected, submarines must stay below the surface of the water, which screens out all but extremely low-frequency radio waves. A number of redundant systems have been developed to provide safe communication, but none of these are ideal for use in very deep water.

Difficulties in knowing the precise location of the submarine and its relative motion at time of launch also make it harder for ballistic missiles launched from a submarine to be as accurate as those launched from a fixed presurveyed point on land. This is critical only if the warhead is aimed at a very blast-resistant target. Submarine missiles can easily destroy most other military targets. In the future when guidance corrections can be given to a warhead after it is well on its way to its target, even very hard targets can be destroyed by submarine missiles. The overall costs of a ballistic missile launched from a nuclear-powered submarine are high, but this is compensated for by its being virtually invulnerable to attack and even to being located.

By 1966 this well-balanced U.S. strategic deterrent force, consisting of 1,054 ICBMs, 656 submarine-launched ballistic missiles (SLBMs), and approximately 600 long-range B-52 bombers, was completely operational. The Soviets in the meantime were far behind. Their missile submarines were just beginning to become available, and their second-generation ICBMs were deployed in relatively limited numbers. Their 200 Bison and Bear intercontinental bombers had not been significantly improved since they were first deployed in the mid-1950s. In the late 1960s, the Russians struggled to catch up.

On the other hand, while the Soviet Union had lagged in offensive strategic systems, it had continued to concentrate on its defensive arsenal. Generation after generation of new radars dotted the Russian landscape. The 3,600 surface-to-air missiles deployed around Moscow in 1955 were replaced only a few years later by more modern defensive missiles, which were deployed in vast quantities throughout the Soviet Union. Interceptor aircraft were procured in large numbers. No expense was spared in order to satisfy the strong Soviet interest in defense.

Beginning in the late 1950s the Soviet Union began an extensive development and test program for ballistic missile defenses. When the United States was still in the stage of preliminary studies, the Soviet Union was testing concepts using intermediate-range ballistic missiles as their targets at their antiballistic missile (ABM) test site at Sary Shagan, near Lake Baikal in the southern Soviet Union. In the mid-1960s they started deployment of an ABM system around Moscow, and it was anticipated that defenses would be built around other Soviet cities. Satellite photographs picked up evidence of new construction in many places, but as the construction continued and intelligence became more extensive, it turned out that none of these other sites were ballistic missile defense installations. The only actual Soviet ABM deployment was around Moscow and about 1968 the construction on even this system was slowed to a crawl. About this time the Soviet Union first expressed an interest in the U.S. proposal to negotiate an arms control agreement to limit ABMs. Previously all Soviet officials and scientists had supported ballistic missile defenses and argued that only offensive systems should be limited. When the SALT I talks actually got underway in 1969, it was the Soviets who were soon pushing primarily for an ABM Treaty, while now the United

States was insisting on offensive systems being controlled as well. This was not the first or the last time that the two countries had exchanged their positions on an arms control issue.

In the 1960s the United States had put off any decision to deploy ballistic missile defenses. All of the U.S. designs, and the Soviet ones as well, appeared easy to penetrate and overcome. Although there were many debates on the virtues of various systems, Secretary of Defense McNamara managed to forestall any commitment of funds for deployment of ABMs. However, in September 1967 under strong political pressure, President Johnson authorized the deployment of the so-called Sentinel ABM, a limited but nationwide system designed to cope with an anticipated light Chinese ICBM threat. ABM enthusiasts viewed this as the opening wedge toward a full-scale anti-Soviet ABM, while skeptics accepted this as the best way of relieving political pressures until such time as an agreement could be reached with the Soviet Union to limit strategic arms. In 1969 the new Nixon administration scrapped the Sentinel anti-Chinese version, but after a strenuous public debate authorized the Safeguard ABM designed to protect missile sites, not cities. Again the proponents welcomed and opponents decried this as an opening wedge, since they did not believe that approval and funds could be obtained for a full-scale system.

Although the United States did not believe that ABMs could be made effective, it did carry out extensive development programs with its offensive missiles to ensure that any Soviet ABM system could be overcome and that our deterrent would not be degraded. The most important of these programs was the development and eventual deployment of MIRVs. The basic principle was to make the final stage of the missile, which contained in the U.S. case from three to fourteen warheads, a sort of "bus," which successively released its warheads on trajectories toward separate targets. The bus would be aimed on a path to a first target, drop off its warhead, then move to another trajectory toward a second target, and then unload a second warhead. This process was repeated until all warheads had been sent on their trajectories toward their separate targets. With large numbers of warheads on a single missile, it was possible to overwhelm an ABM system and guarantee that a warhead would reach the specific target.

Although this principle was ideal for ensuring that an ABM system would not undermine the deterrent, it had a corollary characteristic that is now profoundly destabilizing the arms race. Since each missile could fire several warheads at different targets, in theory a single missile with MIRVs could threaten several missiles of the other side. As long as there was only one warhead on each missile, there would never be any advantage for a missile to attack another. The exchange ratio between missiles destroyed and missiles used in an attack would always be less than one, an unfavorable position for the attacker because no missile with a single warhead could have complete assurance of destroying another missile in its silo. When a missile carries several warheads, however, this disadvantage for the attacker in theory could be reversed and turned into a gain. The exchange ratio could be greater than one, and thus favorable to the attacker, if the accuracy and reliability were sufficient to give each warhead a high probability of destroying a missile silo. Thus now there could be a real gain by launching a first strike against the opposing side's land-based ICBM force. MIRVs now created incentives to initiate a nuclear strike; nuclear war fighting would now seem a more attractive tactic; and

the dangers of a nuclear war would now be radically increased.

The U.S. first tested MIRVs in August 1968 and then went ahead with high-priority programs for their production for both the Minuteman III ICBM and the Poseidon submarine missile. Deployment of these new MIRVed missiles began in 1970 with three warheads on the Minuteman III and up to fourteen on the Poseidon (the average number of Poseidon warheads is reported to be ten). At this time a major debate arose in U.S. security circles over whether to seek an agreement to limit MIRVed missiles in SALT I before either side had deployed them. Rather than negotiate, however, the United States went ahead with its deployment programs. The Soviet Union, running about five years behind the United States in MIRV technology, tested its first MIRVed ICBM in the summer of 1973. Deployment of their ICBMs with MIRVs did not begin until late 1975. Submarine-launched MIRVed missiles were even further behind; they began to be extensively installed on Soviet submarines only in 1979. But by 1980 it was obvious that Soviet MIRVed missiles would soon threaten our land-based ICBMs.

14 Nuclear Arsenals

William M. Arkin and Richard W. Fieldhouse _____

Nothing in human experience can adequately describe the enormity of the nuclear weapons arsenals. More than 50,000 warheads, most smaller than suitcases, can each obliterate cities. Just a few can kill millions of people and destroy the environment for decades hence. The smallest nuclear warheads are ten times more powerful than the largest conventional weapons. The largest have the power of forty billion pounds of conventional explosives.

Why does the military stock such a huge arsenal of weapons? Warheads are bureaucratically and regionally categorized for seemingly specific and separate tasks. Half of the arsenals are "strategic" or long-range weapons for attacking enemy homelands: land-based missiles, submarine-launched missiles, and strategic bombers—all widely dispersed to increase their chances of surviving a surprise attack. Thousands of warheads from each category always sit at high readiness levels to meet the hair-trigger requirements of the nuclear infrastructure.

The remainder of the arsenals are nonstrategic forces. Their various labels indicate confusion or internal competition over roles: battlefield nuclear weapons, tactical nuclear weapons, theater nuclear weapons, intermediate-range nuclear weapons, and sea-control nuclear weapons. Unlike strategic weapons, most nonstrategic weapons are "dual capable," that is, their delivery systems or missiles can carry either nu-

clear or conventional (or chemical) warheads. Each military service and each geographic command—Europe, the Pacific, Middle East, or "reserve"—has its own nuclear weapons. Within the commands, the weapons are further divided and dispersed for different missions, flexibility, and survivability.

The 26,000 warheads of the United States form the most widespread arsenal in the world.[1] It was the first country to send nuclear weapons abroad (in 1952). Within the United States, nuclear warheads are permanently stored in twenty-eight states. . . . Overseas, they are in Guam and eight foreign countries: Belgium, Greece, Italy, the Netherlands, Turkey, South Korea, the United Kingdom, and West Germany. The armed forces of these foreign countries (except South Korea) also use U.S. warheads for their own nuclear delivery systems. The United States maintains about 5,800 warheads in Europe, another 580 in Asia (South Korea and Guam), and some 1,400 at sea. They are routinely present in the Atlantic, Pacific, and Indian Oceans and the Mediterranean Sea. About 13,000 warheads could strike targets in the Soviet Union, some 9,000 are intended for battlefield roles, and 1,900 are for nuclear warfare at sea.

The Soviet nuclear arsenal is thought to consist of some 22,000 to 33,000 warheads. Although the exact composition of the Soviet stockpile is unclear, particularly the nonstrategic warheads, roughly half of the Soviet arsenal is estimated to be long-range strategic weapons (just as in the U.S. arsenal).[2] Another 10,000 are available for theater attacks in Europe or Asia (and beyond), and 3,000 for naval warfare. Soviet nuclear weapons span the full range of delivery means and missions, from a single warhead 20-megaton SS-18 missile to nu-

From Arkin and Fieldhouse's _Nuclear Battlefields: Global Links in the Arms Race_ (pp. 37–39, 41–42, 44–47, 50–63). Copyright 1984 by William M. Arkin and Richard Fieldhouse. Reprinted with permission from Ballinger Publishing Company.

clear artillery. Like the United States, the Soviet Union has a "triad" of strategic weapons, and a full complement of "theater," "battlefield," and naval nuclear weapons.

Until recently, it was unclear whether the Soviet Union deployed nuclear warheads on foreign soil. It now appears that Czechoslovakia, East Germany, Hungary, and Poland host Soviet nuclear warheads. Unlike the United States, the Soviet Union does not share warheads with its Warsaw Pact allies. Nonetheless, the Soviet nuclear infrastructure is quite similar to the U.S. infrastructure in its balance between tactical dispersal and centralization. Strategic missiles are deployed at about twenty main bases, submarines operate from four bases, and long-range nuclear bombers fly from twenty airfields backed up by five Arctic "staging bases" where bombers can land en route to targets in North America. There are probably about thirty Soviet nuclear storage sites in Eastern Europe.

The only nuclear weapons aimed at America belong to the Soviet Union, but the Soviet Union faces the weapons not only of the United States but of Britain, France, and China who have a combined total of roughly 1,500 nuclear warheads, 900 of which could strike targets in the Soviet Union or other Warsaw Pact countries (and are called "strategic"). While Britain and France are often lumped together as the "other" western nuclear forces, their positions are quite different. Although each country has between 500 and 700 warheads, France has maintained its nuclear independence while Britain has chosen to integrate its weapons into U.S./NATO war plans, which makes them an adjunct of U.S. nuclear forces. Britain has a combination of British-made and U.S.-supplied warheads (controlled by the U.S.), thus requiring a smaller infrastructure for development and support than France.

Technological cooperation between Britain and the United States in nuclear matters is unique. Britain has access to a wide variety of technologies for the development or manufacture of warheads, missiles, and submarines. Britain relies on the United States for training assistance and testing. It tests its warheads in Nevada and fires its missiles on the U.S. Eastern Test Range. It also relies on the United States for a large portion of its targeting data. In the future, Britain's new Trident-equipped submarines will be serviced at the U.S. submarine base at Kings Bay, Georgia. In return, Britain incorporates its nuclear weapons into U.S. nuclear plans and provides the United States with support for its nuclear weapons, including a submarine base at Holy Loch in Scotland, major nuclear air bases, the Ballistic Missile Early Warning System (BMEWS) radar at Fylingdales, and key strategic communications and intelligence facilities.

Like America, Britain has a tradition of basing portions of its nuclear forces abroad. For twenty-two years, between 1954 and 1975, British nuclear aircraft and bombs were stationed in two overseas territories: Cyprus and Singapore. Today, Britain continues to base aircraft and nuclear bombs in West Germany, at Brüggen, and Laarbruch air bases. Britain also has the capacity, as demonstrated in the Falklands War, to bring nuclear weapons into the Third World.[3]

French nuclear forces exist for the same ostensible reason as Britain's (to have nuclear weapons independent of the U.S. and NATO) but have been independent since 1966, when France withdrew from NATO's military structure. The French forces consist of missile-carrying submarines, land-based long-range and short-range missiles, and nuclear-capable aircraft. . . . All French weapons are stationed in France; they are widely dispersed to ensure that only a massive preemptive attack could be successful. Of the 514 French warheads, about 270 can be delivered against targets in the Soviet Union, 204 are for battlefield purposes, and 40 are available for use in the Third World. The "survivable" French deterrent consists of three submarines (with 48 missiles) that are always at sea.

China is the newest and most mysterious nuclear power. It developed nuclear weapons for two reasons: to offset Soviet nuclear weapons and to attain the political advantages of a nuclear power. The Chinese, stressing the political status achieved by the nuclear nations, sought to "break the monopoly of the Superpowers." Little is known about the size or types of Chinese nuclear weapons. Like France, it possesses both land-based and submarine-launched missiles, in addition to several models of nuclear bombers. . . . Its deployment schemes (totally within China) include a high degree of mobility and dispersal to complicate the enemy's targeting. While a handful of full-range ICBMs could strike the United States and Europe, the weapons are thought to be aimed exclusively at targets in the Soviet Union.

Soviet technical, scientific, and military assistance in the 1950s helped China attain its nuclear status. Russia shared its aircraft, missile, and submarine designs with China and jointly developed "civilian" nuclear power resources. In return, the Soviets extracted Chinese uranium for their own nuclear weapons programs. The Soviets, however, never shared nuclear warhead technology with China, as they had initially promised.

STRATEGIC NUCLEAR FORCES

Strategic nuclear weapons are generally of intercontinental range, deliverable by land-based and sea-based missiles and bombers. These three categories of weapons form the so-called triad of U.S. and Soviet (and to a lesser extent French and Chinese) arsenals. The justification for the three types lies in differences of range, yield, accuracy, level of reliability, survivability, and readiness. Nearly all U.S. land-based missiles (over 95 percent), one-third of the bombers and half of the submarines—totaling some 5,000 warheads—are constantly ready to go to war. On the Soviet side, the readiness level is much lower. No bombers are kept on alert, and only about 15 percent of the submarine force is away from home waters on a regular basis. Nonetheless, some 5,000 Soviet warheads could be launched at any moment. Britain and France maintain one and three submarines, respectively, at sea at all times, and about 80 percent of France's eighteen land-based missiles could probably be launched immediately.

The United States maintains slightly over 1,000 intercontinental ballistic missiles (ICBMs), which carry a total of 2,100 nuclear warheads. . . . The ICBMs—550 Minuteman III, 450 Minuteman II, and about 30 Titan II missiles (now being retired)—are housed in hardened underground launchers (called silos) in ten states, covering an area of 80,000 square miles (roughly the size of the state of Minnesota). . . .

The Soviet Union has 1,398 ICBMs—550 SS-11s, 60 SS-13s, 150 SS-17s, 308 SS-18s, and 330 SS-19s—capable of carrying over 6,000 warheads (see Table). There are at least three modifications (or variations) of the three newest ICBMs, and the number of warheads varies accordingly. Soviet ICBMs are deployed in hardened underground silos at bases roughly following the route of the Trans-Siberian Railroad across the Soviet Union.

The United States and the Soviet Union are developing two and three new ICBM types, respectively. In the United States, the ten-warhead MX missile will first be deployed in late 1986, and a single-warhead small ICBM (SICBM or "Midgetman") is planned for the early 1990s. In the Soviet Union, the SS-X-24, SS-X-25, and SS-X-26 are under development.

China has also developed an ICBM capability, with a handful of CSS-3 (limited-range) and CSS-4 (full-range) missiles (perhaps ten and five each respectively) deployed in hardened underground silos. The full-range CSS-4 could strike targets throughout the Soviet Union, Europe, and North America.

SUBMARINE FORCES

All five nuclear powers deploy a major part of their missile forces on submarines because of advantages in mobility and survivability, and soon, missile accuracy equal to the best land-based missiles. At any time, seventeen to twenty U.S., ten Soviet, one to two British, and three French missile submarines are at sea, "on station," with some 3,100 nuclear warheads combined. Soviet long-range SLBMs and U.S. Trident I missiles can hit targets in each other's country from home waters.[4] China is the only nuclear power that does not yet regularly deploy submarines at sea, although it has two SSBNs that could probably go to sea during a crisis.

The U.S. submarine force consists of 36 missile-carrying submarines (SSBNs) with a total of 640 launch tubes containing over 5,500 nuclear warheads. Nineteen SSBNs carry the Poseidon C3 missile, and twelve carry the newer Trident I C4. The new Trident SSBNs (Ohio class) are also being armed with Trident I, which has a longer range and more than twice the yield of the Poseidon.

U.S. SSBNs are stationed at four bases, three in the Atlantic Ocean (at Kings Bay, Georgia; Charleston, South Carolina; and Holy Loch, Scotland) and one in the Pacific (at Bangor, Washington). Little is known about where U.S. submarines patrol, but they are thought to transit to "stations" well away from shipping lanes. They regularly operate in the Arctic, North Atlantic, and North Pacific Oceans and in the Mediterranean Sea. While about 30 percent of the total submarine force is "on station" on day-to-day alert, another 25 to 30 percent is at sea in transit or on training missions. U.S. submarines go to sea for about seventy days at a time, and because they are each assigned two crews they operate almost constantly.

TABLE 14–1 U.S. Strategic Nuclear Forces

| *Delivery Mode* | *WEAPON SYSTEM* | | *Year Deployed* | *Range (km)* | *Warheads/ Yield* | *Warhead Type* | *Number in Stockpile* |
	Number	*Type*					
Land-based	450	Minuteman II	1966	11,300	1 × 1.2 Mt	W56	480
missiles	550	Minuteman III	1970	13,000	3 × 170 kt/	W62	825
					3 × 335 kt	W78	1,000
	30	Titan II	1963	15,000	1 × 9 Mt	W53	50
Submarines	304	Poseidon	1971	4,600	10 × 40 kt	W68	3,300
(SLBMs)	288	Trident I	1979	7,400	8 × 100 kt	W76	3,000
Bombers	264	B-52G/H	1955	16,000	8–24 (a)	(a)	4,733
	60	FB-111	1969	4,700	6 (a)	(a)	360
Aerial Refuelers	615	KC-135	1957	—	—	—	—

(a) Bomber weapons include five different nuclear bomb designs with yields from 70 kt-9 Mt, air-launched cruise missiles (ALCMs) with yield of 200 kt and short-range attack missile (SRAM) with yield of 200 kt. FB-111s do not carry ALCMs or the 9 Mt bomb.

Sources: Thomas B. Cochran, William M. Arkin, Milton H. Hoenig, *Nuclear Weapons Databook, Volume 1: U.S. Forces and Capabilities* (Cambridge, Mass.: Ballinger, 1984); updated in *Bulletin of the Atomic Scientists* (Aug.–Sept. 1984).

In the Soviet fleet, 66 SSBNs and 14 SSBs (nuclear and non-nuclear powered missile-carrying submarines respectively) serve a combination of strategic and nonstrategic roles. There are ten classes of submarines armed with six different missiles, comprising 981 SLBMs with as many as 2,400 nuclear warheads. Soviet submarines tend to have much lower at-sea deployment rates than U.S. submarines. At any time some fifteen to twenty Soviet submarines are away from their home bases and about ten to twelve (15 percent) are on station within range of targets.[5] Soviet submarines, unlike their U.S. counterparts, have only one crew.

Since the mid-1970s the overall number of Soviet SSBNs has not increased, as new Delta III and Typhoon commissionings have been offset by Yankee and older submarine retirements. Soviet SSBNs spend most of their time in port, primarily assigned to four main bases in the Northern and Pacific Fleets: Petropavlovsk and Vladivostok in the Pacific and Polyarnyy and Severomorsk in the North. "Submarine tunnels" have reportedly been built for them.[6] While Delta-class submarines can strike U.S. targets from Soviet home waters, older submarines must go through "choke points" to Atlantic and Pacific stations to be within range.[7] Delta-class submarines patrol primarily east of Greenland, in the Norwegian and Barents Seas, and in the northern Pacific Ocean. Beginning in January 1984, some long-range Delta submarines have also been stationed "forward" in the Atlantic

Ocean as a Soviet reponse to deployment of U.S. Pershing II and ground-launched cruise missiles in Europe.

Some submarines with shorter-range missiles have European strike roles. Six Golf II-class submarines have been stationed in the Baltic since 1976, and four are assigned to the Northern Fleet. The United States, rather than using different submarine classes for European war plans, has allocated 400 Poseidon warheads for NATO targeting, carried on submarines operating out of Holy Loch, Scotland.

Britain has four Resolution-class SSBNs, each carrying sixteen Polaris A3 missiles with two or three MRVs (multiple reentry vehicles, not independently targeted). These submarines are routinely under the control of NATO and targeted in accordance with NATO plans, although British targeting plans are also thought to exist for possible unilateral use. The British submarines are based at Faslane on the Clyde Estuary in Scotland (near the U.S. base at Holy Loch). . . . One or two are on patrol at any time (one of the four boats is usually out of service undergoing maintenance at the Rosyth shipyard). Each SSBN has two crews, which rotate on twelve-week cycles: four weeks of trials and maintenance and eight weeks on patrol. Submarines transit north between Scotland and Ireland into the Atlantic Ocean to a specified "block" of water to the southwest of Ireland where they patrol.

The French Force Océanique Stratégique (FOST) consists of five Redoutable-class SSBNs, each armed with sixteen M20 missiles, and the first Inflexible-class SSBN carrying 16 MIRVed SLBMs, each of which carries 6 warheads—thus doubling the number of FOST warheads in one step. The submarines, based at Île Longue in Brest (on the Atlantic Ocean), go on two-month patrols in the eastern Atlantic off the coast of France and Portugal. Three French submarines are at sea at any time, and French policy is to have a fourth submarine available at all times for patrol.

China has one Golf-class SSB, which it built from Soviet parts. This submarine has two or three missile tubes in the conning tower, thought to be used only for testing and not normally loaded with operational missiles. China launched the first Chinese-designed SSBN, of the Xia-class, in April 1981 and a second in October 1982. Each has twelve launch tubes and carries the CSS-N-3 missile.[8] The Chinese have been working on national SLBM development since the late 1950s, but only recently developed a reliable solid fuel missile for the Xia. In October 1982 China announced a successful test flight of the CSS-N-3 SLBM from a submerged submarine.[9] Latest estimates of Chinese plans foresee a total of eight Xia class submarines with CSS-N-3 missiles. These submarines could begin patrol in 1985.[10]

The submarine forces of the nuclear powers are all undergoing major programs of modification and upgrade. The new U.S. Trident II missile will be loaded into the ninth Ohio-class submarine in 1989. Trident II will be as accurate as the most accurate land-based missiles and expand the missile range (and thereby the patrol area) of U.S. submarines to 4,000 miles. Each Trident II will probably carry eight 475 kiloton warheads so that each missile could destroy the "complete spectrum of targets in the Soviet Union."[11] Between twenty and twenty-five submarines will carry the Trident II.

The Soviet Union is also deploying new submarine and missile classes. Two large Typhoon submarines are already deployed with twenty solid fuel SS-N-20 missiles. The long-range SS-N-20 carries six to nine warheads and is the most accurate Soviet submarine missile in the water. There has also been speculation that the submarine's design is geared toward patrols under the Arctic ice cap.[12] Another new Soviet SLBM, the SS-NX-23, is also being tested for deployment aboard Delta submarines in 1985 or 1986.[13] The DOD has called it "a Trident II-equivalent" weapon.

In the mid-1990s, Britain will begin to deploy new submarines to replace its Polaris force and arm them with the U.S. Trident II missile (but with British nuclear warheads). A force of four or five new British submarines will carry some 512 to 640 multiple independently targetable reentry vehicles (MIRVs) (compared to 64 warheads today). Besides the huge increase in warheads, the Trident II's ability to destroy any targets (including "hardened" ones) will radically transform the British submarine force.

The French are upgrading too. In 1985 a sixth French submarine became operational with a new missile, the M4, which will carry six 150-kiloton warheads. By 1992 the French will load the M4 into four of the five existing Redoubtable-class SSBNs (one is too old and will be retired in 1995). The M4 program will expand the French submarine force from today's 80 warheads to 496 warheads. France will begin development of a fully MIRVed M5 missile in the late 1980s, and plans to build a seventh submarine, of a new design, to join the fleet in the mid-1990s.

BOMBER FORCES

Strategic bomber forces constitute a large and flexible element of the nuclear arsenals. Although bombers fly slowly, and are thus normally excluded from first-strike scenarios and computer-simulated war games, they are in many ways the "warfighting" arm of strategic forces. War planners endlessly construct complex bomber loading, routing, refueling, penetrating, targeting, and recovery plans. Bombers carry a variety of bombs and air-launched missiles and can fit into virtually any war plan. While missiles cannot be recalled or redirected once launched (and are thus "inflexible"), bombers can attack hardened, mobile, or previously unlocated targets and can be called back before reaching them. If they overcome air defenses and complete their mission, bombers can return to a "recovery" base and reload for more bombing missions.

The United States maintains a fleet of 264 B-52 and 61 FB-111 bombers, all assigned to the Strategic Air Command (SAC), with 615 KC-135 aerial-refueling tankers to support them. According to the JCS, "The primary role of this tanker force, which includes 125 aircraft operated by the Air National Guard and Air Force Reserve, is to support plans for nuclear retaliation."[14] The bombers are stationed at nineteen air bases in thirteen states and at Andersen AFB in Guam. The United States also maintains "dispersal" and "recovery" bases for the bombers. Overall, the force comprises some 5,000 nuclear warheads, including a variety of nuclear bombs, short-range attack missiles (SRAMs), and air-launched cruise missiles (ALCMs).

The Soviet bomber force includes 100 Bear and 45 Bison intercontinental bombers and 230 shorter range Backfire, Badger, and Blinder bombers. The 36th Air Army, the Soviet counterpart to SAC, controls long-range bombers. Some Backfires in the western Soviet Union and in the Far East are also assigned to long-range aviation. An Arctic Control Group maintains five northern staging and dispersal bases from which bombers can begin their attacks closer to U.S. targets.

Soviet bombers carry two types of gravity bombs and a variety of air-to-surface cruise missiles, including the AS-4 and AS-6 nuclear-capable missiles. As with U.S. bombers, in-flight refueling extends the range of properly equipped aircraft, particularly important in the case of the newest Backfire, which otherwise lacks the range for round-trip missions into the interior of the United States.

Britain, France, and China all have bombers that can strike the Soviet Union. Britain has retired the last of its Vulcan bombers but is reinforcing its nuclear air arm with Tornado strike aircraft, which are suitable for long-range bombing. By the end of the decade, Britain will have 220 nuclear-capable attack versions of the Tornado. France has four squadrons of about thirty-four Mirage IVA bombers in its Strategic Air Force (FAS), armed with 70-kiloton nuclear bombs. The squadrons are located at four bases in France supported by five additional dispersal bases. . . . They will be replaced by Mirage IVP aircraft with a new nuclear air-to-surface missile starting in 1986. Eleven C-135F tankers (purchased from the United States in the mid-1960s) can provide aerial refueling to allow the bombers to reach deep into Soviet territory.

China has one type of nuclear bomber, the B-6, modeled after the Soviet Badger design. Latest estimates put roughly ninety B-6 bombers into three regiments. Two older aircraft, the B-4 and B-5 (modeled after Soviet Tu-4 and Il-28 bombers respectively), are also believed nuclear-capable. China is estimated to have about 100 airfields that can accommodate these bombers, which are reportedly rotated randomly among them to complicate Soviet targeting.[15]

Both the U.S. and Soviet bomber forces are in the midst of significant change. The arma-ments of both forces will soon include long-range air-launched cruise missiles (ALCMs). The United States introduced its ALCMs in 1981, and the Soviet Union is expected to field its 2,000 mile range AS-X-15 in the near future. The U.S. is also developing a new air-to-surface missile for its bomber force and has introduced a new, more accurate bomb. Both countries are about to field new generations of bombers: the B-1B (U.S.) and the Blackjack A (Soviet). Currently, two Soviet bomber models are in production, the new Backfire, at the rate of some thirty per year (about half are for naval aviation), and the Bear-H, the latest configuration of the 1956 plane, which will carry the AS-X-15. The United States is developing an Advanced Technology Bomber (Stealth), which it could deploy in the mid-1990s.

The Soviet Union has an active, nuclear-armed anti-ballistic missile (ABM) system, based around Moscow and made up of thirty-two Galosh missiles armed with 3.5-megaton warheads. Two launch complexes each contain two launcher sites with eight missiles at each site. Work continues on designing and building new missile silos and installing new ABM radars and tracking equipment. The United States does not have an active ABM system, although two nuclear missile systems deployed in the mid-1970s—Sprint and Spartan—are still in storage and available for reactivation.

NONSTRATEGIC FORCES

Although they receive far less scrutiny, nonstrategic nuclear weapons are far more likely to be used before strategic nuclear weapons. Nonstrategic nuclear forces include numerous types of weapons for battlefield missions: nuclear bombs, atomic land mines, and weapons that resulted from nuclearizing an array of delivery systems since the 1950s: surface-to-surface, surface-to-air, and air-to-surface missiles as well as artillery shells. Developed before long-range weapons, these forces now augment strategic weapons.

Nonstrategic forces fall into many categories, representing geographic interests and dispersal of military forces, and competing military services and roles. Nonetheless, an increasing number of nonstrategic weapons are "crossover systems" (sometimes called "gray area" weapons), highly mobile and long-range, and usable in more than one "theater" of war or even for "strategic" strikes. Such systems include many types of naval nuclear weapons, as well as long-range cruise missiles and land-based aircraft.

The so-called long-range intermediate forces have received the most attention, particularly the highly mobile U.S. Pershing II ballistic missile and the ground-launched cruise missile (GLCM). Both weapons fall into the "gray area" category. The Pershing II is the first long-range terminally guided missile deployed anywhere; the GLCM is the first reliable long-range cruise missile deployed on land. Both weapons, with nuclear warheads of 80 and 150 kilotons maximum yield, respectively, are highly accurate and can destroy hardened military targets. By 1988 the United States will have deployed 108 Pershing II launchers and 464 GLCMs in five European countries. The entire force will be spread among thirteen bases in peacetime. In a crisis or during wartime the force would disperse in platoons of three launchers (for Pershings) or "flights" of four launchers (for GLCMs), for a total of thirty-six Pershing dispersal sites and twenty-nine GLCM dispersal sites.

Pershing and cruise have been touted as counters to Soviet intermediate-range missiles, particularly the triple-warhead SS-20, first deployed in 1977. From its bases in the Soviet Union, the SS-20 can hit targets throughout Asia, the Middle East, North Africa, and Europe. Two-thirds of the launchers are deployed in the western Soviet Union, and one-third are in the Far East. The 150-kiloton yield and moderate accuracy of the SS-20 make it suitable for striking virtually any target within range. In addition to the SS-20, the Soviets still deploy some older medium-range SS-4s, which were first deployed in 1958. About 224 SS-4s are in the western Soviet Union; all those in the Far East have been retired.

Another new class of weapon, as important as the Pershing II and SS-20, is the long-range sea-launched cruise missile (SLCM), entering service in the U.S. and Soviet navies. The U.S. Tomahawk SLCM is the same as the GLCM but configured for naval use. It was first deployed in June 1984 aboard attack submarines, battleships, and two destroyers. Out of 3,994 planned SLCMs, 758 will be the nuclear land-attack version (called the TLAM(N) for Tomahawk Land-Attack Missile–Nuclear). This nuclear missile will have three separate roles: "strategic reserve," theater strike, and tactical naval strike. It will be the first "strategic" platform not reserved specifically for that role. . . . By 1992, sixty-five ships and eighty-three submarines will be able to carry the nuclear SLCM, and by the end of deployment, 204 ships and submarines will have this capability.[16] In addition to the new Tomahawk, the secret Defense Guidance for 1984–1988 instructed the Navy to prepare an "advanced concepts study" for a new land-attack missile with a longer range and better targeting features.

The Soviet counterpart to the Tomahawk is the SS-NX-21 SLCM, which became operational in late 1984. This missile not only improves Soviet accuracy but extends the striking range of Soviet naval forces to 3,000 kilometers, giving them their first long-range nuclear capability at sea.[17] The SS-NX-21 is launched from standard 21-inch (533mm) torpedo tubes (which are on almost all the Soviet Navy's ships and submarines). A second long-range strategic land-attack SLCM is under development, as is a long-range GLCM, designated the SS-CX-4, which could be deployed in the next few years.[18]

Both France and China deploy land-based intermediate-range missiles (IRBMs). France has eighteen silo-based S-3 IRBMs on the Plateau d'Albion in southeastern France. With their 3,500-kilometer range, S-3s can reach targets throughout Eastern Europe and the western Soviet Union. A new mobile land-based missile, the S-X (designated "Danone"), is under development for deployment in the mid-1990s. As many as 100 S-X missiles and warheads could be deployed.[19]

Since 1972 China has deployed 85 to 125 CSS-2 IRBMs, with a range of 1,500 to 2,000 miles and a warhead of one to three megatons. The CSS-2s are mobile and are reported to be deployed in underground silos as well as in man-made caves.

BATTLEFIELD NUCLEAR FORCES

Tactical aircraft (of less than intercontinental range) are the most versatile arm of nuclear forces.[20] Nuclear-capable fighters and bombers afford greater control than missiles, are by far the most accurate means of delivering nuclear weapons, are capable of delivering a variety of nuclear weapons, and pilots can use their judgment to find and strike mobile or imprecisely located targets. All five nuclear powers maintain tactical aircraft. The Soviet Union has both a medium (capacity) bomber force and tactical nuclear aircraft. The United States has a wide variety of nuclear-certified fighters. . . . Britain and France both have nuclear fighters. It is unclear

TABLE 14–2 Soviet Strategic Nuclear Forces

Delivery Mode	WEAPON SYSTEM Number	Type	Year Deployed	Range (km)	Warheads/ Yield	Number in Stockpile (a)
Land-based	520	SS-11 Mod 1 (b)	1966	11,000	1 × 1 Mt	640–1,280
missiles		Mod 2/3	1973		3 × 250–350 kt (MRV)	
	60	SS-13 Mod 2	1972	9,400	1 × 600–750 kt	60–120
	150	SS-17 Mod 3 (c)	1979	10,000	4 × 750 kt	600–1,200
	308	SS-18 Mod 4	1979	11,000	10 × 550 kt	3,080–6,160
	360	SS-19 Mod 3 (d)	1979	10,000	6 × 550 kt	2,160–4,320
Submarines	42	SS-N-5	1963	1,400	1 × 1 Mt	42–60
(SLBMs)	368	SS-N-6 Mod 1/2	1967	2,400	1 × 1 Mt	368–736
		Mod 3	1973	3,000	2 × 200–350 kt (MRV)	
	292	SS-N-8	1973	7,800	1 × 800 kt–1 Mt	292–584
	12	SS-N-17	1977	3,900	1 × 1 Mt	12–24
	224	SS-N-18 Mod 1/3	1978	6,500	3–7 × 200–500 kt	672–2,510
		Mod 2	1978	8,000	1 × 450 kt–1 Mt	
	40	SS-N-20	1983	8,300	6–9 × 350–500 kt	240–288
Bombers	45	Mya-4 Bison	1956	8,000	2 × bombs	90–180
	125	Tu-95 Bear	1956	8,300	2 × bombs and ASMs	386–872
	130	Tu-22M Backfire	1974	5,500	2 × bombs and ASMs	390–780
	125	Tankers (e)	—	—	—	—
ABMs	32	Galosh	1964	750	1 × 3–5 Mt	32–64

(a) Warheads represent low and high estimates of possible force loadings (including reloads).

(b) Approximately 100 Mod 1 with 1 warhead, 360 Mod 2, and 60 Mod 3 are deployed.

(c) Some SS-17 Mod 2 missiles with one warhead may also be deployed.

(d) Some SS-19 Mod 2 missiles with one warhead may also be deployed.

(e) Includes Badger and Bison A bomber converted for aerial refueling

Sources: Authors estimates derived from: William M. Arkin and Jeffrey I. Sands, "The Soviet Nuclear Stockpile," *Arms Control Today* (June 1964), pp. 1–7; Department of Defense, *Soviet Military Power*, 1st, 2d, 3d eds.; NATO, "NATO-Warsaw Pact Force Comparisons, 1st, 2d eds.; Robert P. Berman and John C. Baker, *Soviet Strategic Forces: Requirements and Responses* (Washington, D.C.: Brookings, 1982); Defense Intelligence Agency, *Unclassified Communist Naval Orders of Battle*. DDB-1200-124-84. (May 1984).

how many nuclear bombs are allocated to the nuclear-capable planes of other countries, but in the United States, where the numbers are known, the percentage of warheads allocated for aircraft delivery is significant. For instance, of 5,800 forward-deployed U.S. warheads in Europe, about 1,700 (almost one-third) are bombs for aircraft delivery.

The Soviet medium-range bomber force is very large, consisting of 350 Badger, Blinder, and Backfire aircraft. These can carry nuclear bombs or air-to-surface missiles, but the precise number of warheads in the Soviet arsenal is unknown.[21] All of the bombers are assigned to bases within the Soviet Union, except for one Badger unit in Vietnam. The typical base has about forty-five aircraft, compared with a comparable U.S.

tactical fighter unit of seventy-two planes. The Soviet Union also has six different tactical fighters thought to have nuclear weapons roles. . . . The Fencer is the primary strike plane and has been deployed with nuclear weapons since 1981 in Czechoslovakia, East Germany, Hungary, and Poland.

The United States has a wide variety of tactical nuclear aircraft and nuclear bombs. Some 3,800 bombs arm these tactical aircraft: 1,700 in Europe, 130 in the Pacific, 720 aboard aircraft carriers at sea (on the average), and 1,250 in reserve. Although the United States does not have medium-range bombers, the F-111 is essentially equivalent to Soviet planes of that category. The United States has about 250 F-111s, with about 150 stationed at two forward bases

TABLE 14–3   U. S. Nonstrategic Nuclear Forces

Delivery Mode	WEAPON SYSTEM Number	WEAPON SYSTEM Type	Year Deployed	Range (km)	Warheads/ Yield	Warhead Type	Number in Stockpile
Nonstrategic							
Aircraft	2,000	(a)	—	1,060–2,400	1–3 × bombs	(a)	2,800
IRBMs/MRBMs	54	Pershing II	1983	1,790	1 × .3–80 kt	W85	63
	64	GLCM	1983	2,500	1 × .2–150 kt	W84	100
SRBMs	126	Pershing 1a	1962	740	1 × 60–400 kt	W50	280
	100	Lance	1972	125	1 × 1–100 kt	W70	1,282
	24	Honest John	1954	38	1 × 1–20 kt	W31	200
Land-based SAM	200	Nike Hercules	1958	160	1 × 1–20 kt	W31	500
Artillery (b)	4,300	(b)	1956	30	1 × .1–12 kt	(b)	2,422
ADMs	610	Medium/Special	1964	—	1 × .01–15 kt	W45/54	610
Naval							
Carrier aircraft	900	(c)	—	550–1,800	1–2 × bombs	(c)	1,000
Land attack cruise missile	50	Tomahawk	1984	2,500	1 × 5–150 kt	W80	50
ASW							
Ship-based	n.a.	ASROC	1961	10	1 × 5–10 kt	W44	574
Submarine-based	n.a.	SUBROC	1965	60	1 × 5–10 kt	W55	285
Air-delivered	630	P-3/S-3/SH-3	1964	Max 2,500	1 × sub–20 kt	B57	897
Ship-based SAM	n.a.	Terrier	1956	35	1 × 1 kt	W45	100

(a) Aircraft include Air Force F-4, F-16, and F-111 and NATO F-16, F-100, F-104, and Tornado. Bombs include four types with yields from sub kt–1.45 Mt.

(b) There are two types of nuclear artillery—155mm and 203mm—with three different warheads, a 0.1 kt W48 155mm shell, a 1–12 kt W33 203mm shell, and a 1 kt W79 enhanced radiation 203mm shell.

(c) Aircraft include Navy A-6, A-7, F/A-18, and Marine Corps A-4, A-6, and AV-8B. Bombs include three types with yields from 20 kt–1 Mt.

Sources: Thomas B. Cochran, William M. Arkin, and Milton H. Hoenig. *Nuclear Weapons Databook, Volume 1: U.S. Forces and Capabilities* (Cambridge, Mass.: Ballinger, 1984); updated in *Bulletin of the Atomic Scientists* (Aug./ Sept. 1984).

in Britain, and the other 100 in the United States. About 600 nuclear bombs are allocated to the forward force. Most U.S. aircraft intended for interdiction or close air-support missions, whether Air Force, Marine Corps, or Navy, have been nuclear-certified, including the AV-8B Harrier, F-16, and F/A-18s currently in production.

The U.S. Air Force's nuclear planes are stationed overseas in Britain, Italy, South Korea, Turkey, and West Germany. The U.S. Air Force keeps nuclear bombs at a dozen NATO air bases for the planes of the Belgian, Greek, Italian, Dutch, Turkish, and West German Air Force. At seventeen bases in Europe, U.S. and NATO planes stand on nuclear alert at all times. Five or six aircraft carriers at sea also carry various land-attack nuclear planes. Aboard these six forward-deployed aircraft carriers are over 700 nuclear bombs.

Some 300 British-made nuclear warheads are carried on about 200 nuclear-capable tactical aircraft of three types: Jaguar, Buccaneer, and Tornado. . . . These aircraft are stationed at four air bases in Britain and two in West Germany, Britain's only permanent overseas nuclear weapons bases. The new Tornado fighter bombers will replace the current Buccaneers and Jaguars. Eleven squadrons will be equipped with Tornado by 1987, three in Britain and eight in West Germany. Nuclear-armed Sea Harrier aircraft are stationed on three aircraft carriers.

An important element of the French military force is nuclear-capable aircraft. Nuclear-armed air units include two squadrons of thirty Mirage IIIEs and three squadrons of forty-five Jaguar aircraft. According to the Defense Intelligence Agency, these aircraft can deliver "a 6-to 8- or 30-kt tactical nuclear weapon."[22] The aircraft are stationed at three airbases in France, and will eventually be replaced by a new nuclear-strike aircraft, the Mirage 2000N, beginning in 1988. The French Navy's only tactical nuclear weapons equip thirty-six Super Étendard nuclear aircraft aboard two aircraft carriers based at Toulon

TABLE 14–4 Soviet Nonstrategic Nuclear Forces

Delivery Mode	WEAPON SYSTEM		Year Deployed	Range (km)	Warheads/ Yield	Number in Stockpile (a)
	Number	Type				
Nonstrategic Bombers	316	Tu-16 Badger	1955	4,800	2 × bombs and ASMs	632
	139	Tu-22 Blinder	1962	2,200	1 × bombs or ASMs	139
Tactical aircraft	2,545	(b)	—	700–1,800	1–2 × bombs	2,545
IRBMs/MRBMs	378	SS-20	1977	5,000	3 × 150 kt	2,268
	224	SS-4	1959	2,000	1 × 1 Mt	224
SRBMs	120	SS-12	1969	800	1 × 200 kt–1 Mt	120
	100	SS-22	1979	900	1 × 1 Mt	100
	570	SCUD-b	1965	280	1 × 100–500 kt	1,140
	48	SS-23	1982	350	1 × 100 kt	48
	620	FROG	1965	70	1 × 10–200 kt	2,480
	120	SS-21	1978	120	1 × 20–100 kt	480
Artillery	900	(c)	1974	10–30	1 × low kt	900
ADMs	n.a.	n.a.	n.a.	—	n.a.	n.a.
Land-based anti-ship	100	SS-C-1b	1962	450	1 × 50–200 kt	100
Land-based SAMs	n.a.	(d)	1956	40–300	1 × low kt	n.a.
Naval Aircraft	105	Tu-22M Backfire	1974	5,500	2 × bombs or ASMs	210
	240	Tu-16 Badger	1961	4,800	1–2 × bombs or ASMs	480
	35	Tu-22 Blinder	1962	2,200	1 × bombs	35
	200	ASW aircraft (e)			1 × depth bombs	200
Anti-ship cruise missiles	336	SS-N-3	1962	450	1 × 350 kt	336
	96	SS-N-7	1968	56	1 × 200 kt	96
	200	SS-N-9	1968	280	1 × 200 kt	200
	136	SS-N-12	1976	500	1 × 350 kt	136
	88	SS-N-19	1980	460	1 × 500 kt	88
	28	SS-N-22	1981	110	1 × unk kt	28
ASW missiles and torpedoes	310	SS-N-14	1968	50	1 × low kt	310
	76	SS-N-15	1972	40	1 × low kt	76
	10	SUW-N-1	1967	30	1 × 5 kt	10
	n.a.	torpedoes	1957	16	1 × low kt	n.a.
Ship-based SAMs	264	SA-N-6	1977	55	1 × low kt	264

(a) Estimates of total warheads are based upon minimal loadings of delivery systems.

(b) Nuclear-capable tactical aircraft models include Su-24 Fencer, Su-17 Fitter, Mig-27 Flogger, Mig-21 Fishbed, Yak-28 Brewer, Mig-25 Foxbat, and Su-25 Frogfoot.

(c) Artillery includes 152mm towed and self-propelled guns, and 180mm, 203mm, and 240mm calibers.

(d) Nuclear-capable SAMs probably include SA-1, SA-2, SA-5, and SA-10.

(e) Includes Bear, Mail, and May aircraft.

Sources: William M. Arkin and Jeffrey I. Sands, "The Soviet Nuclear Stockpile," *Arms Control Today* (June 1984), pp. 1–7; Norman Polmar, *Guide to the Soviet Navy*, 3d ed. (Annapolis, Md.: U.S. Naval Institute, 1983): Department of Defense, *Soviet Military Power*, 1st, 2d, 3d eds.; NATO, "NATO-Warsaw Pact Force Comparisons," 1st and 2d eds.: DIA, "A Guide to Foreign Tactical Nuclear Weapon Systems Under the Control of Ground Force Commanders," DST-1040S-541-83 (Secret, partially declassified) (Sept. 9, 1983).

in the Mediterranean. At any moment, one French carrier is in the Mediterranean Sea, and one periodically deploys to the Atlantic or Indian Oceans. France is also developing a 150-kiloton medium-range air-to-surface nuclear missile, the ASMP (Air-Sol Moyenne Portée), for the Mirage IVA, Mirage 2000N, and the naval Super Étendard.

The Soviet Union's large array of battlefield missiles includes short-range "division support missiles," Army support missiles, and longer range "Front support missiles." All three are being modernized. The FROG-7 (Free-Rocket-Over-Ground) (a division support missile with a range of forty miles) is being replaced by the longer range SS-21. Virtually all of the FROG-7 missiles in Soviet divisions in East Germany and Czechoslovakia (four launchers per division is the standard allocation) have been upgraded. The SCUD missile, allocated to the Army formations, is about to be replaced by the SS-23 (whose range is 300 miles, compared to the SCUD's 110). The SS-12 Scaleboard, currently assigned to the Front formations, is being replaced by the SS-22.

Most Soviet battlefield missiles have conventional and nuclear capabilities; only the SS-12 and SS-22 missiles are thought to lack conventional warheads. There is, in addition, evidence that the new SS-21 and SS-23 have primarily non-nuclear roles.[23] The SS-12 was never deployed outside of the Soviet Union, although FROG and SCUD missiles (and SS-21s) have been routinely based with Soviet forces in Czechoslovakia, East Germany, Hungary and Poland. The SS-22 has reportedly been deployed in East Germany, a significant departure from previous Soviet nuclear-basing practices.[24]

The medium-range Pershing 1a missile, deployed in West Germany, is assigned to the U.S. and West German militaries. The U.S. missiles and launchers are being replaced by the Pershing II, but the future status of the seventy-two West German launchers is still uncertain.[25] The mobile, dual-capable Lance missile, which has a maximum range of 125 kilometers, provides artillery support to numerous NATO armies. Some 692 Lance nuclear warheads are deployed in Europe (608 in West Germany), for Belgian, British, Italian, Dutch, U.S., and West German launchers. About 380 enhanced radiation warheads ("neutron bombs") for the Lance missiles were built in the United States between 1981 and 1983, but are stored in the United States pending European approval to station

them in Europe. A successor to the Lance, with a longer range and greater accuracy, is under development. Only the armies of Greece and Turkey continue to use the U.S. Honest John missile, first deployed in 1954.

The Chinese have one MRBM deployed, the CSS-1, its first missile fielded in 1966. The CSS-1 has a range of 600 to 700 miles. About forty to sixty missiles are deployed, each with one 20-kiloton warhead. From their bases in Shanxi province, these missile can strike Far Eastern Soviet targets.[26]

The United States and the Soviet Union both deploy nuclear artillery shells. In the U.S. military there are two sizes—155mm (6-inch) and 203mm (8-inch)—assigned to the Army and the Marines. About 920 155mm shells and 1,500 203mm shells are in the stockpile. The 155mm shell was introduced in 1967 and is slated to be replaced by a more versatile, higher yield, longer range shell in the next few years. The more numerous 203mm shell (the W-33) is one of the oldest nuclear warheads in the U.S. stockpile, but a replacement, the W-79, is in production (to be stockpiled in the United States while awaiting approval for storage in Europe). U.S. nuclear artillery shells are stored in five countries in Europe, in South Korea, and in Guam. Some 570 warheads are allocated for NATO use, by Belgium, Britain, Greece, Italy, the Netherlands, Turkey, and West Germany.

Soviet nuclear artillery has been in the field since the mid-1970s, but it is still unclear how important a role it will play in comparison to short-range missiles. For some time, there were U.S. government mentions of the existence of 180mm and 240mm Soviet nuclear guns, but it was not until 1981 that the Soviets' widespread adoption of nuclear artillery was confirmed. Now, DOD has concluded that the 152mm, 180mm, 203mm, and 240mm calibers are nuclear-capable, but large-scale production of four different nuclear warheads seems unlikely. A more important development in the Soviet Army is the conversion from towed to self-propelled artillery since the mid-1970s. (Self-propelled artillery is far more mobile and logistically sustainable than towed artillery.) Nuclear-capable self-propelled 152mm artillery guns are now assigned to Soviet divisions.[27]

The French Army maintains forty-two Pluton short-range ballistic missile launchers with reload missiles. The Pluton force is made up of five regiments, deployed in northeastern France. A new longer range missile, called Hadés, will be deployed beginning in 1992. France may decide to use an enhanced radiation warhead for the 350-kilometer range Hadés.

The two remaining battlefield nuclear weapons, comprising about 5 percent of the U.S. nuclear arsenal, are probably present in the Soviet arsenal as well: surface-to-air missiles (SAMs) and atomic demolition munitions (ADMs). Nuclear Nike Hercules SAMs are deployed in Europe, arming the United States, Belgium, Italy, Greece, West Germany, and the Netherlands. The U.S. and Belgian nuclear missiles are in the process of retirement (the U.S. missiles will be completely withdrawn by mid-1985), to be replaced by the conventionally armed Patriot. There are numerous reports of the existence of nuclear warheads for Soviet SAMs, particularly the SA-2 Mod 4 and SA-5 systems.[28]

Two types of ADMs are deployed in the U.S. military: Medium ADMs and Special ADMs. ADMs are intended for the destruction of physical features such as bridges, mountain passes, dams, and forests. The U.S. arsenal contains 608 ADMs, assigned to regular Army engineers, Marines, and "unconventional warfare forces." Some 372 are stored in Europe (351 in West Germany and 21 in Italy). Units of the British, Dutch, and West German armies also train with ADMs. ADMs are stored in South Korea and Guam, for Pacific nuclear "contingencies." There are reports of the existence of Soviet ADMs, but nothing is known about them.[29] The Defense Intelligence Agency has stated that ADMs "may also be used" by the Chinese.[30]

NAVAL NUCLEAR WEAPONS

The nuclear arsenals at sea include anti-submarine, anti-air and anti-ship weapons.[31] The nuclear-armed ships and submarines of the U.S. Navy comprise (as of early 1984): all of its 13 large aircraft carriers, all 5 helicopter and Marine Corps carriers, two recommissioned battleships, all 112 cruisers and destroyers, 64 nuclear attack submarines, and 61 of 86 frigates. Approximately 30 percent of these ships and submarines are at sea at any time. Soviet nuclear-capable ships consist of 69 of 281 surface ships (cruisers, destroyers, and frigates), and 119 of 268 attack and cruise-missile submarines. About 15 percent of Soviet ocean-going vessels are out of home waters at any time.

The West counters the large Soviet submarine force with a combined British and U.S. nuclear anti-submarine warfare (ASW) arsenal of 1,900 warheads (20 times the number of Soviet submarines). U.S. naval forces have 1,750 nuclear ASW warheads, stockpiled at sixteen bases in peacetime. Attack submarines carry nuclear-armed submarine rocket (SUBROC) missiles. A nuclear-capable weapon similar to SUBROC, the ASROC, is also deployed aboard 150 surface ships.

The U.S. Navy has 412 land-based P-3 Orion ASW patrol aircraft, which can carry B-57 nuclear depth bombs. They are organized into 37 squadrons of 9 aircraft, 24 active and 13 reserve. The planes rotate to numerous bases around the world: Bermuda, the Azores, Puerto Rico, Ascension Island, Spain, Italy, Iceland, Oman, Diego Garcia, the Philippines, Japan, Alaska, and Guam. The 187 carrier-based S-3A Viking aircraft and 104 SH-3 ASW helicopters can also deliver the nuclear depth bomb. Dutch P-3 Orion, Italian Atlantique, and British Nimrod ASW aircraft are all certified to carry U.S. B-57s, which are stored for their use on British and Italian soil. The British Navy also has three nuclear-capable aircraft carriers and fifty-nine ASW surface ships (which carry ASW helicopters). The carriers can operate with nuclear-capable Sea Harrier attack aircraft and Sea King helicopters. About 120 Lynx, Wasp, and Sea King nuclear-capable ASW helicopters operate from ships (Sea Kings also operate from shore). These helicopters can reportedly carry a British-made nuclear depth bomb, about which nothing is known. Britain's nuclear-capable naval aviation force is comprised of thirty Buccaneer and thirty Sea Harrier strike aircraft.

The Soviet Navy has approximately 1,200 ASW nuclear warheads, including rockets, torpedoes, and depth bombs. The Soviets deploy a nuclear-capable ASW rocket similar to SUBROC, the SS-N-15, which is estimated to be aboard about sixty-five submarines. A wide variety of ASW ships in the Soviet Navy carry either the SS-N-14 (a nuclear weapon similar to ASROC) or the SUW-N-1 nuclear depth charge. Both ships and submarines are thought capable of carrying nuclear-tipped 21-inch torpedoes. Two types of Soviet ASW aircraft, about fifty-one TU-142 Bear Fs and ninety-four BE-12 Mails, are nuclear-capable.

The U.S. Navy deploys the nuclear-armed Terrier surface-to-air missile (SAM), now in the process of being withdrawn and retired, on cruisers and destroyers. With the development of Soviet Backfire bombers and the increasing cruise missile threat to ships, nuclear-armed surface-to-air missiles have gained in importance to Naval planners who see them as last-ditch weapons to shoot down aircraft and nuclear missiles. Two warheads are now being developed for missiles that will replace the Terrier, one for the longer range Standard-2 SAM and one for the Phoenix air-to-air missile.

An important nuclear weapon in the Soviet naval arsenal is the sea-launched anti-ship cruise missile (ASCM) (the United States does not deploy anti-ship nuclear weapons). Seventy of 354 Soviet submarines are cruise missile launchers, all of them thought to be nuclear-capable. Most of the recently deployed cruise missile submarines (SSGNs) have short-range SS-N-7, SS-N-9, or supersonic SS-N-12 cruise missiles. In 1982 the Soviets deployed a new medium-range SS-N-19 cruise missile aboard the large, fast new Oscar-class submarines. The supersonic SS-N-19 has a range of around 460 km and can be launched from underwater. It is thus the most versatile Soviet ASCM to date.

An important component of the Soviet antiship nuclear force is its Naval aircraft force (called Soviet Naval Aviation or SNA), which is based on land since the Soviets have no aircraft carriers capable of carrying such nuclear-capable aircraft. Current Soviet "carriers" are equipped with helicopters and a few non-nuclear vertical take-off planes. SNA includes 423 land-based nuclear bombers: 105 Backfires, 279 Badgers, and 39 Blinders. All SNA bombers can carry nuclear bombs, and the Backfires and Badgers can carry AS-4 and AS-6 air-to-surface missiles (ASMs) as well.

Over the past decade, technological improvements have greatly reduced the number of weapons needed to destroy a given target. One logical consequence would be a reduction in the size of the nuclear arsenals. But as the nuclear powers build ever more effective weapons, they rarely reduce the number of weapons. And they never reduce their nuclear capabilities.

Forty years into the atomic age, there has not yet been a nuclear war: some therefore accept the vast nuclear arsenals; some even credit them with preventing nuclear war. But whatever the number of weapons, whatever the intentions of planners, the danger is ever greater. Technological advances and improvements in planning, command, and communications have seemingly shaved away uncertainties. Nuclear weapons have become more accurate, more reliable, more enduring—more usable.

NOTES

1. See e.g., Thomas B. Cochran, William M. Arkin, and Milton H. Hoenig, *Nuclear Weapons Databook: Vol. 1: U.S. Nuclear Forces and Capabilities* (Cambridge, Mass.: Ballinger, 1984); updated in *Bulletin of the Atomic Scientists* (August-September 1984).

2. See e.g., William M. Arkin and Jeffrey I. Sands, "The Soviet Nuclear Stockpile," *Arms Control Today* (June 1984), and Thomas B. Cochran, William M. Arkin, Jeffrey I. Sands, *Nuclear Weapons Databook, Vol.3: Soviet Nuclear Weapons* (Cambridge, Mass.: Ballinger, forthcoming).

3. The presence of British nuclear weapons in the Falklands is discussed in two unpublished papers: William M. Arkin and Andrew Burrows, "British Nuclear Weapons in the Falklands" (Washington, D.C.: Institute for Policy Studies, 1984), and George H. Quester, "Nuclear Implications of the South Atlantic War" (College Park, Md.: University of Maryland, 1984).

4. U.S., Joint Chiefs of Staff, Fiscal Year 1985, p. 25.

5. U.S., Joint Chiefs of Staff, Fiscal Year 1979, p. 28.

6. U.S., Strategic Air Command, "S. Con. Res. 26, A Resolution to Approve Funding for the MX Missile," *S. Hearing 98–444*, 98th Cong. 1st Sess. (1983), p. 260.

7. Five to six older Yankee I-class submarines with shorter range missiles patrol in the Atlantic and Pacific and "conduct lengthy transits in order to be within range of the targets in North America." Department of Defense, *Soviet Military Power, 3rd ed.* (Washington, D.C.: U.S. Government Printing Office, 1983) p. 23 (hereinafter DOD *Soviet Military Power*).

8. "China Launches First Nuclear-Missile Sub," *Baltimore Sun* (Nov. 29, 1981), p. 19; "The PLA Navy's Underwater Deterrent," *Jane's Defence Weekly* (April 28, 1984), pp. 659–60.

9. Lieutenant Commander David G. Muller, Jr., "China's SSBN in Perspective," *Proceedings* (March 1982), pp. 125–27.

10. Bradley Hahn, "China in the SLBM Club," *Pacific Defence Reporter* (Feb. 1984), p. 18.

11. U.S., Department of Defense, Fiscal Year 1984 RDA, p. V-7.

12. J.M. McConnell, "Possible Counterforce Role for the Typhoon," *Professional Papers 347* (Washington, D.C.: Center for Naval Analysis, March, 1982).

13. Rear Admiral John L. Butts, Director of Naval Intelligence, Statement on "The Naval Threat" before the Seapower and Strategic and Critical Materials Subcommittee of the House Armed Services Committee, 98th Cong., 2d Sess. (Feb. 28, 1984), p. 5.

14. U.S., Joint Chiefs of Staff, Fiscal Year 1984, p. 17.

15. Captain Thomas D. Washburn, "The People's Republic of China and Nuclear Weapons: Effects of China's Evolving Arsenal" (M.A. thesis, University of South Carolina, March 15, 1979).

16. U.S., Congress, House Appropriations Committee, Fiscal Year 1985 DOD, pt. 1, pp. 511–512.

17. DOD, *Soviet Military Power* (1983), p. 23.

18. Butts, "The Naval Threat," pp. 2, 6.

19. Charles Hernu, "France's Defense: Choices and Means," *Le Figaro*, Jan. 30–31, 1982 (reprinted by the Press and Information Service of the French Embassy, New York).

20. William M. Arkin, "Flying in the Face of Arms Control," *Bulletin of the Atomic Scientists* (Feb. 1984), pp. 5–6.

21. "Normally the majority of INF aircraft carry only one warhead but some types of aircraft, particularly those with longer ranges, can carry a second or third warhead." NATO, "NATO and the Warsaw Pact: Force Comparisons," 1st ed. (Brussels: NATO Information Service, 1982), p. 31.

22. Defense Intelligence Agency, *A Guide to the Foreign Tactical Nuclear Weapon Systems Under the Control of Ground Force Commanders*, No. DST-1040S-541-83-CHG1 (Aug. 17, 1984) (Secret, partially declassified), p. xviii.

23. U.S. Air Force Tactical Air Command, "Soviet Short Range Ballistic Missiles: New Generation," Slide 1, TAC Intelligence Briefing 79–10 (1979) (partially declassified).

24. *Jane's Defence Weekly* (June 2, 1984), p. 867.

25. William M. Arkin and Richard W. Fieldhouse, "Pershing and Cruise: No Room for Compromise," *ADIU Report* (March/April 1983), pp. 4–7.

26. S.K. Ghosh and Sreedhar, eds., *China's Nuclear and Political Strategy* (New Delhi: Young Asia Publications, 1975).

27. Defense Intelligence Agency, "Soviet Self-Propelled Artillery," No. DDI-1130–6–76 (May 1976) (Confidential, partially declassified).

28. DIA, *A Guide*, p. xii.

29. Ibid., pp. x, xii.

30. Defense Intelligence Agency, "Handbook on the Chinese Armed Forces,". No. DDI-2682–32–76 (July 1976), p. 3–15.

31. See William M. Arkin, Andrew Burrows, Richard Fieldhouse, Jeffrey I. Sands, "Nuclearization of the Oceans," Background paper presented at the Symposium on the Denuclearization of the Oceans, Norrtalje, Sweden, May 11–14, 1984.

15 Anti-Satellite Weapons: Weighing the Risks

Kurt Gottfried and Richard Ned Lebow

The mission of anti-satellite weapons (ASATs) is to destroy vital components of an adversary's network for intelligence gathering and for the command and control of his own forces. This raises a fundamental question: does the military usefulness of ASATs overshadow their capacity for exacerbating crises and conflicts? Any device that is able to destroy satellites has this dual nature; its targets' roles change dramatically as the world moves from peacetime, through crisis, to war. Satellites that can transmit images of military units electronically (in "real time") could be invaluable during negotiations to resolve a crisis and in building confidence that promises are being kept. Yet if diplomacy should fail, that same data could be used to optimize attack. A similar ambiguity characterizes satellites that give early warning of missile launches: in peacetime they provide reassurance, but in war they could be used to help target a retaliatory strike.

ASATs play a correspondingly complex role. On the one hand, they enhance a nation's military capability and thereby its ability to deter attack; on the other hand, the very fear of an ASAT attack on vital satellites could contribute to the escalation of a crisis or low-level conflict. An evaluation of ASATs must consider how they will affect this delicate balance between the somewhat contradictory goals of fighting a war, and preventing one.

This article will seek to strike that balance by examining the possible military and political roles of ASATs in a variety of crises and conflicts.

To do this, we shall have to distinguish between the near and long term, since ASAT technology is still in its infancy. Assessing future confrontations involving systems that do not yet exist is a speculative venture. Nevertheless, we still conclude that all the technological trends indicate that ASATs possess a considerably greater capacity for transforming a crisis into a war, and for enlarging wars, than they do for assisting in military missions or enhancing deterrence. Given this conclusion, we shall argue that our security would best be served by a comprehensive ASAT test-ban treaty, complemented by feasible satellite protective measures.

SATELLITES AND ASATS

ASATs do not currently pose a threat to all satellites, though by the next decade they might be able to. At the moment, the vulnerability of satellites is in large measure determined by their orbit. These orbits can be divided into four distinct categories. . . .

Low Orbits. Satellites in orbits below 5000 kilometers are the only ones vulnerable to the current generation of ASATs. Both superpowers use such orbits for photo-reconnaissance, electronic intelligence (ELINT), meteorology, geodesy, and manned spacecraft. The Soviets also use these vulnerable orbits for some communications satellites and for their radar ocean surveillance satellites.

Highly Elliptical, or Molniya Orbits. Satellites in Molniya orbits are used extensively by the Soviets for strategic early warning and for military and civil communication. Because these satellites remain in sight of ground stations at

Excerpted from Kurt Gottfried and Richard Ned Lebow, "Anti-Satellite Weapons: Weighing the Risks," Reprinted by permission of *Daedalus*, Journal of the American Academy of Arts and Sciences, Spring 1985, Cambridge, MA (pp. 147–148, 150–156, 160–169).

northern latitudes for about eight of their twelve-hour orbital periods, they would be potentially vulnerable to the forthcoming U.S. ASAT, if the United States should stage its attacks in the Southern Hemisphere where Molniya satellites dip to their lowest altitudes. To counter this threat, the Soviets could conceivably use geosynchronous satellites instead, and relay signals through semi-synchronous satellites to reach ground stations at high latitudes.

Semi-synchronous Orbits. Satellites in these orbits, at altitudes of about 20,000 kilometers, are beyond the range of ASATs expected to be operational in this decade. The U.S. Navstar system, which is expected to be fully operational by 1987, is now being placed in such orbits, as is the similar Soviet GLONASS system. These navigation satellites will enable military forces to determine their own location and deliver their weapons with remarkable accuracy.

Geosynchronous Orbits. Satellites in these orbits, at an altitude of 36,000 kilometers, circle the earth at the same rate as the earth's rotation and remain above a fixed point on the equator. Satellites in such high orbits are invulnerable to current ASAT systems. The United States exploits such orbits for strategic early warning, electronic intelligence, and military communication. At present, the Soviet Union has only communication satellites in such orbits, but by the next decade it is expected to have a wider array of geosynchronous satellites.[1]

CURRENT ANTI-SATELLITE WEAPONS

The current Soviet ASAT is a massive device weighing more than 2000 kilograms. It is lofted into orbit atop a liquid-fueled booster derived from the old SS-9 ICBM. In all past tests, the Soviets have launched the ASAT from two pads at the Tyuratam test range. After launch, the ASAT completes one or two trips around the earth, its orbit is changed to cross that of the target, the ASAT conducts final interception maneuvers under the guidance of an on-board homing device, and its warhead explodes into pellets directed towards the target. The U.S. Defense Department estimates that the Soviet ASAT is capable of intercepting satellites in orbits up to 5000 kilometers; the highest intercept ever attempted in a Soviet test has been only 1600 kilometers.

The first test of the Soviet ASAT took place in 1968, and the twenty tests since then can be classified according to the interception technique used.[2] In the first group, the ASAT intercepted targets on its second orbital pass, using an active radar homer. Out of ten such tests, seven succeeded. About three hours elapse between launch and interception in these second-orbit attacks; this gives a U.S. satellite opportunity for evasive maneuvering or jamming of the ASAT's radar homer. It was these considerations that presumably led the Soviets, in two other groups of tests, to attempt first-orbit intercepts with the radar homer, and second-orbit intercepts with an optical/infrared homer that detects the target's heat radiation and is not so easily foiled. In the first-orbit intercepts, four tests produced two successes; in the optical/IR homing tests, six tests yielded not a single success.

In addition to its poor test performance, the Soviet ASAT suffers from several inherent limitations. First, it can attack a satellite only when the target's ground track runs close to the ASAT launch site, which happens just twice a day; this means waiting an average of six hours to attack a given satellite. Second, the ASAT's heavy weight requires a massive booster; it can therefore only be launched from a few Soviet facilities. Third, it is difficult to fire such massive liquid-fuel boosters in rapid succession from a single launch site.

Taken together, these limitations lead informed observers in the U.S. to estimate that it would take the Soviet ASAT force a week or more to destroy those American low-altitude satellites that are theoretically within its reach, although it may take only several days to eliminate essential ELINT and photo-satellites. Attacking satellites at 20,000 kilometers or higher would require a much more massive booster rocket, and probably modifications and improvements to the interceptor as well. Futhermore, the ASAT would give ample warning of its attack, since it would take several hours to reach such altitudes.

An assessment of the threat posed by the Soviet ASAT was given several years ago by General Lew Allen, then Air Force chief of staff: "I think our general opinion is that we give it a very questionable operational capability for a few launches. In other words it is a threat we are worried about, but they have not had a test program that would cause us to believe it is a very credible threat."[3] Nothing that has happened in the Soviet test program since that assessment would suggest that the threat has increased.

The current U.S. ASAT program was begun by the Air Force in 1977. The ASAT's mission, as announced by the Carter administration, was to deter the Soviets from using their ASAT by threat of retaliation, to protect U.S. military units from observation by Soviet satellites, and to induce the Soviet Union to reach an ASAT arms-control agreement.

The U.S. Air Force ASAT weapon is launched by a two-stage rocket small enough to be carried to high altitude by an F-15 fighter. This rocket boosts a device known as a miniature homing vehicle into the path of the target satellite, using data on the target's path supplied by the ground-based satellite tracking network. The homing vehicle itself is a squat cylindrical object weighing about 15 kilograms. It has infrared sensors able to "see" the target against the cold background of space, and a set of small thrusters that can be fired to bring the cylinder into the path of its target. The resulting high-speed collision destroys the target. The maximum altitude of the U.S. ASAT has not been revealed, but the joint chiefs of staff have stated that the highest priority targets are Soviet satellites that can locate American forces—presumably photo-reconnaissance, ELINT, and ocean surveillance satellites at altitudes of 500 kilometers or less.

If it performs as it is supposed to, the U.S. ASAT will be more versatile and capable than its Soviet counterpart. In principle, any F-15 can be adapted to carry the ASAT. Furthermore, carrier-based aircraft, or mid-air refueled F-15s, can carry the ASAT to an attack position almost anywhere in the world. In contrast to the Soviet ASAT, the U.S. weapon does not go into orbit but ascends directly towards its quarry, thereby giving it little opportunity for evasion. If the United States were to invest in extensive tracking, control, and communication facilities, it could acquire an ASAT force able to destroy all Soviet low-orbit satellites in a matter of hours.

Although the Air Force is charged with the anti-satellite mission, the Army's Ballistic Missile Defense Program also contributes to the United States' ASAT capability. In the Army's Homing Overlay Experiment of 1984, an infrared-homing interceptor launched from Kwajalein destroyed a dummy ICBM warhead at an altitude of more than 150 kilometers. Since a satellite is much larger and more fragile than a warhead, there is no question but that this

weapon has an ASAT potential. Indeed, this experiment indicates that the United States and Soviet Union have now tested rather similar ASAT weapons. Both weapons have the handicap of being launched by ground-based ICBM boosters, though the U.S. homing overlay interceptor exploits an infrared homing device that the Soviets have not yet mastered.

FUTURE ANTI-SATELLITE WEAPONS

In addition to these existing weapons, other ASAT techniques have been proposed, including space mines and directed energy ASATs. A space mine would be a satellite containing explosives, placed in orbit well in advance of a conflict. When detonated by remote command (or on being tampered with), it would destroy its target. In principle, space mines could threaten satellites at all altitudes. However, if the target satellite had on-board sensors and could maneuver effectively, the space mine would have to be a sophisticated device, perhaps more complicated than current ASATs, in order to stay near its target. A possible drawback of the space mine is that its placement alongside another superpower's satellite could, in and of itself, trigger a confrontation.

There has also been much interest in anti-satellite weapons that exploit directed energy (laser or neutral particle) beams. Both the United States and the Soviet Union now have laser demonstration projects that could be turned to ASAT purposes. Directed energy concepts primarily intended for space-based ballistic missiles defense would, if pursued, also have a significant ASAT potential. Even though the energy deposited on a target by a directed energy weapon decreases sharply with distance, a laser or neutral particle BMD weapon able to destroy a missile in a matter of seconds could also deposit enough energy, at a high enough rate, to damage unprotected satellites in geosynchronous orbits. In this regard, it is essential to recognize that even an ineffective space-based BMD system could be a potent ASAT, while an effective BMD system would, as a matter of course, be an ASAT system par excellence.

SATELLITE PROTECTION

There are various ways of making satellites less vulnerable to ASATs. First, satellites could be promptly replaced when they are destroyed. At present, U.S. satellites are more sophisticated, reliable, and longer lasting than their Soviet counterparts. For example, the newest Soviet photo-satellites have a lifetime of six weeks, whereas that of the U.S. KH-11 exceeds two years. U.S. communications satellites have lifespans five to ten times longer than those of the Soviets. Hence, the Soviets need to replace satellites far more frequently, and this higher Soviet launch rate may grant them a potent wartime reconstitution capability. The United States has now begun to devote greater attention to satellite replacement: for instance, by placing spare satellites in orbit, to be activated when needed.

There are other ways, varying in efficacy and cost, to protect satellites. Attack by a homing ASAT could be frustrated by a satellite that can maneuver, or that can deceive the ASAT's homing device. If there is ample warning of attack, as is true with the current Soviet ASAT, evasion could be commanded from the ground. Against the swiftly approaching U.S. ASAT, evasion would be difficult if not impossible. Radar homing devices of the sort used by the Soviet ASAT could be foiled with jammers placed on board satellites. Infrared homing devices, such as the one on the U.S. ASAT, cannot readily be jammed but could be deceived by decoys deployed by the target satellite. With the exception of photo-satellites, most current satellites have little or no ability to maneuver. But manned spacecraft such as the space shuttle could be used to refuel low orbit satellites, if they were properly designed. This would allow the satellites to carry enough fuel for evasive maneuvering.

It is also possible to achieve some degree of protection against directed energy beams and radiation. Photo-satellites, for example, could be protected against blinding from low-intensity lasers by automated shutters. Electronics can also be hardened against neutral particle beams and nuclear explosions.

If the development of ASATs continues unrestrained, we can expect to see competition between techniques of destroying satellites, and methods of protecting them. Since satellites are inherently fragile and complex, they are virtually certain to lose this competition to simpler weapons whose sole mission is to destroy them. Satellites that have mission lifetimes of many years are particularly vulnerable since they must be equipped with defenses against future, unpredictable, ASAT threats.

THE MILITARY UTILITY OF ASATS

ASATs could be used by the superpowers in a variety of confrontations ranging from wars between their client states, to full-scale nuclear war. Various scenarios can be examined, but because of the number of unknown factors they are necessarily speculative. Indeed, the most serious threats to security are likely to arise from unexpected and unwise actions that may be taken simply because of the existence of an ASAT capability.

Our analysis will distinguish between possible near-term and more distant scenarios. This is a natural division to make because the current generation of ASATs does not threaten higher orbit strategic satellites, while those of the future are likely to do so.

Regional Conflicts

In the past, both superpowers have been very cautious about sharing intelligence data from satellites with even their closest allies, although they have occasionally provided allies with battlefield intelligence drawn from other sources. In 1973, for example, the Soviet Union gave Egypt aerial photographs of Israeli forces on the West Bank of the Suez Canal.[4] This superpower satellite reconnaissance of Third World battlefields is on its way to becoming a regular feature of international politics, however. Would either superpower deem it in its interest to use ASATs against the other's satellites?

The use of ASATs in such cases seems rather implausible because of the risks of escalation it would entail. Damaging or destroying the other superpower's satellite would almost certainly provoke a serious crisis. Moreover, there are less provocative, more direct, and long-accepted ways to show commitment and offer military assistance—increased logistics support, sending of advisers or even troops, intelligence support from aircraft or other traditional means—if it proved necessary to aid an ally or encourage caution in the other superpower. Unlike the destruction of a satellite, none of these actions involve a direct attack against a military asset of the other superpower.

Superpower War in Europe

That a major war between NATO and the Warsaw Pact would long remain conventional appears to us an illusion. Nevertheless, the superpowers devote the lion's share of their military budgets and training programs to preparations for conventional war. For this reason alone, we must consider the possible utility of ASATs in a conventional superpower war.

Our findings are disquieting. In the near term, neither side is likely to use ASATs because they offer no significant military advantage. In the long term, the temptation to use ASATs will be much greater. The combination of more capable ASATs with greater dependence upon satellites will create strong pressures to use these weapons. Attacks against satellites would significantly raise the nuclear alert level, producing new and complex interactions between the warning and response mechanisms of the two superpowers. They would also be likely to provoke retaliation in kind, an event that would aggravate the potential for loss of control. It seems that advanced ASATs are a military Pandora's box: at first glance, their use may be appealing, but the consequences may be disastrous. . . .

Nuclear War

Satellites would play a more important role in intercontinental nuclear war than in regional or conventional conflicts because they provide eyes and ears for early warning of nuclear attack, battle management of nuclear forces, and post-attack assessment of nuclear strikes.

American satellites that perform these functions are almost all in geosynchronous or semi-synchronous orbits where they cannot be attacked by the existing Soviet ASAT. Soviet satellites are now somewhat more vulnerable because the Molniya orbits of Soviet early-warning and many communications satellites are, in principle, within range of the current U.S. ASAT weapon. In the future, the development of directed energy ASATs, whether as part of ballistic missile defenses or as dedicated ASATs, could threaten satellites at all altitudes with prompt and simultaneous destruction, carried out at the same time as an offensive first strike.

To some extent, such an ASAT attack could impair the other side's ability to launch a coordinated counterforce strike in response. Nonetheless, our analysis persuades us that directed energy ASATs would not significantly affect the course of a nuclear war *once it has begun*. The real danger is that advanced ASATs would compound the difficulty of *terminating* a nuclear war, and in a crisis they would undoubtedly heighten the chance that nuclear war would break out.

Our judgment about the contribution ASATs would make in a nuclear war stems from several considerations. First, even advanced ASATs would, for the most part, only marginally degrade early-warning capabilities. For the United States, the increment of additional warning provided by satellites is important but insufficient to protect the national command authority, submarines in port, and bombers on the ground from destruction by Soviet missiles fired from off-shore submarines. The United States is more vulnerable in this regard than the Soviet Union because of its greater reliance on bombers and submarines as strategic launch platforms. It is nevertheless reasonable to assume that if an intercontinental nuclear war occurs, it will arise out of a serious crisis or war in Europe or elsewhere. American strategic forces would already be on alert and therefore less vulnerable. Contingency arrangements would also have been put into effect to shift the command center away from Washington, thus reducing the likelihood of strategic paralysis in the aftermath of an attack on command authorities.

Given the present situation, loss of early-warning satellites would be more easily borne by the Soviet Union, if only because their systems are less reliable and effective than their American counterparts. The Soviets continue to experience serious difficulties in maintaining an operational constellation of early warning satellites. Even if the Soviets established effective satellite coverage of North America, they would remain vulnerable to nuclear attacks by missiles deployed in Western Europe, and on submarines in the Mediterranean, Arctic Ocean, and, with the advent of the Trident submarine, the Indian Ocean as well. Submarine-launched Trident II missiles, when they become operational, will be accurate enough to destroy Soviet missile silos. Threats of this kind constitute a growing problem for the Soviets, as 75 percent of their MIRVed missiles are land-based, stationary, and increasingly vulnerable. Yet there is nothing to indicate that a U.S. ASAT attack on Soviet early-warning satellites or radars would significantly increase our ability to destroy their ICBMs. Destruction of these systems would in itself constitute early warning and could prompt Soviet leaders to launch their missiles.

In the aftermath of ASAT attacks, both superpowers would also lose important wartime communication capabilities. Here, the United States is probably more dependent on satellites because it uses them to communicate with submarines and airborne bombers. Although these functions could be assumed by ground stations and airborne relays, these systems are themselves highly vulnerable, and cannot be expected to endure very long in a nuclear war.

Both superpowers would presumably also use satellites for post-attack assessment. Since bombers and cruise missiles would reach their targets hours after warheads delivered by missiles, it would be most efficient to assess the result of a missile-delivered attack before following up with other forces. The U.S. government has placed great stress on post-attack assessment in recent years, in keeping with its overall notion of how an intercontinental nuclear war should be fought. The recent emphasis has been on developing the means to fight limited or protracted nuclear wars, despite the widespread conviction among strategists and senior military officers that such scenarios are unrealistic. The Soviets give every indication of sharing this skepticism and, for this reason, may judge post-attack assessment to be relatively unimportant. It also appears alien to their approach to nuclear combat, which emphasizes a massive initial strike, as opposed to a series of strikes, each followed by assessment.[5] In the case of full-scale nuclear war, both sides' satellites will, in any case, become useless after the first exchange, since satellite ground stations and launch pads will almost certainly be destroyed.

ASATs could both increase the likelihood of nuclear war and complicate its termination. Widespread destruction of communication satellites would make it difficult to restrain one's own forces or to transmit a cease-fire order, reducing still further the possibility of limiting a nuclear war once started. And if there were negotiations to end the war, it would be nearly impossible, without surveillance satellites, to monitor the adversary's behavior and gauge the extent of his compliance with any agreement.

Advanced ASATs could have a dramatic impact on crisis stability. Each side must anticipate that in the event of attack, it would have very little time to assess the threat and select an appropriate response. Laser ASATs, for example, could destroy an entire constellation of satellites almost instantly. Such an ASAT attack could coincide with a first-strike, increasing the risk and fear of "decapitation"—the destruction of a country's political-military leadership. A country could develop contingency procedures to be adopted during such crises, but even though this might reduce the probability of decapita-

tion, it would never eliminate the fears. Policy makers could be stampeded into making these fears of war self-fulfilling.

At high levels of strategic alert, advanced ASATs would exacerbate the inherent instability of the superpowers' command-and-control systems.[6] When the alert level of strategic forces is raised, it is necessary to diffuse nuclear launch authority within the military command structure as a precaution against decapitation. However, this heightened alert status would quickly be recognized by the early-warning and response system of the other superpower, which could be pressured into taking similar precautionary action. This feedback loop could progressively dilute centralized control and result in unauthorized actions and inadvertent war. This flaw in command-and-control structures would appear to be an inevitable consequence of the desire to deter a decapitating attack—a situation that would be aggravated by advanced anti-satellite weapons, whose very existence would require a very considerable acceleration of the response tempo.

ASAT ARMS CONTROL

The hazards of escalation or preemption posed by ASATs could be averted by constraining the growth of ASAT capabilities on both sides through negotiated arms control. Such a constraint would also close an important loophole in the ABM treaty.

Unfortunately, the record on ASAT negotiations thus far has been mixed. The United States induced the Soviets to join in several rounds of talks, beginning in 1978, but formal negotiations ceased in 1979 for reasons unrelated to ASAT. Since 1981, the Soviets have repeatedly asserted an interest in resuming negotiations, and from 1983, they have observed a test moratorium. The United States has recently shown interest in negotiating, but insists on continuing the development and testing of its ASAT.

The argument against ASAT arms control was set forth in a report to Congress from the Reagan administration in March 1984. The report contended that the large variety of space systems and activities that have some ASAT capability makes it very difficult to define the term "space weapon" for arms-control purposes; that a truly comprehensive ban on tests of all methods for countering satellites could not be verified; that test bans limited to weapons dedicated to ASAT activities, though perhaps verifiable, could induce the Soviets to develop covertly an ASAT capability that relies on other systems, such as ICBMs or maneuvering spacecraft; that cooperative verification measures might require the United States to divulge sensitive information; and that ASAT arms control would not provide protection for satellite ground stations and launch facilities.

The report also argued that there are compelling considerations in favor of a U.S. ASAT capability, quite apart from these arms-control problems. In particular, U.S. ASATs would deter use of Soviet ASATs, and prevent space from being a sanctuary for Soviet satellites that would enhance the capability of their military forces, especially in naval warfare. The report concluded that "no arrangements or agreements beyond those already governing military activities in outer space have been found to date that are judged to be in the overall interest of the United States and its Allies."[7]

We disagree. A viable ASAT arms-control regime that serves U.S. security interests can be identified. In principle, there are a number of forms that an ASAT agreement might take. The most rigorous would forbid the possession, testing, and use of all techniques that can threaten the functioning or survival of satellites. The least restrictive would not limit ASAT technology, but would only expand the rudimentary body of law that governs space activities. Among the latter are "rules of the road" that would restrict close encounters between space objects of one nation and that of another, or agreements that would outlaw the use of weapons against satellites— not unlike the laws that now apply on the high seas. While such constraints would still leave ASAT weapons deployed on both sides, they merit serious consideration for their ability to prevent inadvertent incidents that might otherwise trigger a crisis or conflict. These provisions could be negotiated in their own right or be included as articles in the treaties we shall discuss below.

A vexing problem for ASAT arms control is that a wide variety of space activities have some ASAT potential. For instance, manned or unmanned maneuvering spacecraft could approach an adversary's satellite and interfere with it or destroy it. But such "spin-off" ASAT techniques would not pose a prompt threat to a set of satellites dispersed in space, and approaching several satellites simultaneously would constitute warning in itself. From a military viewpoint, this

kind of "residual" ASAT capability is likely to be of marginal utility. Furthermore, whatever threat it poses could be reduced (though not eliminated) by formal "rules of the road," and by measures that allow satellites to assess such threats and evade them by maneuvering.

Another argument against ASAT arms control is that a very potent ASAT capability already exists in nuclear-armed ICBMs, SLBMs, and the Soviets' Galosh ABM interceptors. These, it is asserted, could be used to attack satellite ground stations and spacecraft at virtually any altitude with nuclear warheads. However, using nuclear warheads, even in outer space, is a risky and provocative act, and it is most unlikely that such acts would be committed unless a nuclear war were on the verge of breaking out, or had just done so. Treaties cannot offer protection once the nuclear threshold is crossed; ASAT arms control should seek to make that initial step less likely.

In sum, it is important to distinguish between *dedicated* ASAT systems that can promptly attack a whole set of satellites without resort to nuclear weapons, and *residual* ASAT capabilities in other weapons or systems. We therefore turn to possible restraints on dedicated ASATs.

A treaty that bans possession of all ASATs would be desirable, but compliance would be difficult to verify. The dismantling of readily visible facilities such as the launch sites used for the Soviet ASAT and the U.S. Army's Homing Overlay Experiment could, in principle, be verified. That would, however, be of limited utility, since ASATs could be launched from other Soviet space facilities, and Homing Overlay interceptors could presumably be launched from many U.S. ICBM silos. Even highly intrusive on-site inspection could fail to verify whether these ground-based interceptors were being covertly stockpiled, and possession of the very small F-15 ASAT would be especially difficult to establish.

A more realistic treaty would confine itself to those ASAT activities that are readily verified: ASAT tests and the development and deployment of new ASAT technologies. Such a treaty could still prevent the development of highly capable ASAT systems. An ASAT test ban treaty could be couched in a number of ways: it could forbid the testing of any technique that could prevent the functioning of a satellite, even if it caused no permanent damage. Or it could confine itself to techniques that actually damage the satellite, cause it to change its orbit, or destroy it. In the latter instance, the test ban could either cover all ASATs, regardless of their altitude capability, or only high altitude ASATs.

Activities that could hinder or prevent the proper functioning of a satellite, without causing any damage, are legion. Deception, camouflage, encryption, spoofing—all could prevent a satellite from "seeing" or "hearing" what it was intended to see or hear. These activities, however, could not be outlawed effectively. Jamming at an intensity that produced no damage could perhaps be forbidden, though it would be difficult to define unambiguously. Furthermore, jamming, encryption, spoofing, and so on are also benign and valuable countermeasures. For this reason, treaties restricted to acts that produce well defined damage or malfunctioning are to be preferred.

A high-altitude ASAT test ban treaty—one banning tests above 5000 kilometers, for example—at first glance appears very attractive. No dedicated ASAT weapons have yet been tested at such altitudes. The satellites essential to U.S. strategic forces are all at high altitudes, while the Soviet Union could presumably use a combination of geosynchronous and semisynchronous satellites for such purposes. It would therefore appear that a high-altitude ASAT test ban could "grandfather" the current Soviet and U.S. systems and start with a clean slate, while protecting the most essential military satellites. ASAT tests at high altitudes are also more amenable to verification since they are less likely to be confused with other space activities.

This case for a high-altitude treaty is undercut, though, by the movement toward directed energy weapons, whether for ASAT or ballistic missile defense. A variety of beam weapons could, once they had been tested against low altitude satellites or missile warheads, pose a grave and prompt threat to geosynchronous satellites *without* any testing against high-altitude targets. To be effective, a high-altitude ASAT test ban would therefore have to be accompanied by a ban on directed energy weapons at low altitudes.

An ASAT test ban that covers *all* altitudes therefore provides the most viable and valuable ASAT constraint. By including all ASAT weapons, such a ban would also close the most important loophole in the ABM treaty. The severe strictures on BMD development imposed by that treaty could be evaded by dressing the first phase of a BMD program in ASAT clothing. Indeed,

quite apart from any treaty, the kinship between ASAT and BMD techniques, and the great vulnerability of satellites as compared to missiles, make the ASAT route a natural path towards BMD. By the same token, a program that is only intended to produce an ASAT capability could, under many circumstances, be construed by the opponent as a budding and illegal BMD program. Since the ABM treaty is the foundation on which all strategic arms limitation rests, the prevention of further ASAT competition would strengthen the shaky arms-control edifice.

The Reagan administration has contended that an ASAT test ban treaty is not verifiable. Yet that judgment is disputed by a number of officials who have held high-level positions in intelligence and military space programs.[8] These officials stress that while verification cannot guarantee the total absence of covert testing of single weapons, it would be virtually impossible to test surreptiously a system of the complexity required for a prompt and reliable ASAT capability. Extensive experience in observing Soviet programs has convinced these experts that the Soviet military would have little confidence in a system that had not undergone realistic tests, and that such realistic tests could not escape detection. Their statements also underline a point that is not often appreciated outside the intelligence community, to wit, that a properly drawn treaty eases the task of intelligence assessment since it dramatically reduces the pace of technological change.

The Reagan administration's pessimism regarding ASAT verification stands in sharp contrast to its optimism over ballistic missile defense. The space surveillance complex that would mastermind the BMD system envisaged by the SDI is supposed to track vast numbers of space objects, discriminate among them, assign interceptors to each, assess the success of intercept, and reassign weapons—all in a matter of minutes. Moreover, it would have to perform these automated functions while itself under direct attack, and in the environment created by nuclear explosions. If such a formidable task can even be contemplated, it is presumably possible to develop a peacetime space surveillance system that would monitor the relatively infrequent and isolated events that are candidates for clandestine ASAT tests, especially as that system need not come to prompt decisions and would involve human beings.

A viable and adequately verifiable test ban

treaty *can* be constructed, provided it is focused on the objective of preventing the growth of a *prompt* and *dedicated* Soviet ASAT capability. If the objective is enlarged to encompass a host of secondary concerns raised by systems that have only *residual* ASAT capability, a viable treaty will no longer be possible. One should also recognize that ASAT arms control would be cost-effective. Under unrestrained ASAT arms competition, we would have to buy far more elaborate space surveillance facilities and satellite defenses—not to mention the ASATs themselves—than under ASAT treaty constraints.

CONCLUSION

Both superpowers are about to make fundamental decisions concerning the military uses of space, decisions that will have far-reaching implications for their security, in the widest sense of the term. Without doubt, their most fateful decision will be whether and how to pursue a space-based ballistic missile defense. Another critical choice they face is whether to continue placing ever greater reliance on military satellites. As satellites grow in military importance they also become more attractive targets. If, at the same time, space-based BMD is allowed to evolve, the capability for satellite destruction will increase dramatically. Unless these conflicting trends are resolved, the superpowers' unending quests for greater individual security will, once again, result instead in a mutual loss of security.

How are we to avoid this outcome, especially given the technologies that can be envisaged? We can do so only by maintaining and reinforcing the goals and stipulations of the ABM treaty. We should accompany this reinforcement with a comprehensive ban on the testing of space weapons, and more ambitious programs to protect satellites. As we have argued above, this is the prudent policy choice, for it recognizes that the space weapons technologies presently under consideration have a considerably greater potential for exacerbating tensions and enlarging conflicts, than they do for bolstering deterrence or improving actual military missions. Under such treaty constraints, the United States would

possess much more secure space-based intelligence, early-warning, and command-and-control facilities at considerably lower cost than it would in an environment in which both superpowers were continually refining their ability to destroy satellites.

It must be admitted that a side effect of these constraints would be the creation of a sanctuary in space that will be used to deploy satellites with ever greater military capabilities. Some would argue that such a development is intolerable and therefore unstable. But the alternative—unrestrained militarization of space—is far less tolerable. The superpowers must learn to live with the hazards posed by relatively secure satellites, for in the nuclear age the prevention of war must take precedence over the ability to wage it efficiently.

NOTES

1. See Nicholas L. Johnson, *The Soviet Year in Space: 1982* and *The Soviet Year in Space: 1983* (Colorado Springs, Co.: Teledyne Brown Engineering, 1983 and 1984); Stephen M. Meyer, "Soviet Military Programmes and the 'New High Ground,'" *Survival*, Sept.-Oct. 1983, pp. 204–15.

2. See Richard L. Garwin, Kurt Gottfried, and Donald L. Hafner, "Anti-Satellite Weapons," *Scientific American*, June 1984, pp. 45–55.

3. Testimony by Gen. Lew Allen, Senate Foreign Relations Committee, July 11, 1979.

4. Anwar L. Sadat, *In Search of Identity: An Autobiography* (New York: Harper & Row, 1977), p. 260; Mohammed Heikal, in *The Road to Ramadan* (New York: Ballantine Books, 1975), p. 241, insists that these were not satellite photographs.

5. Stephen M. Meyer, "Soviet Military Programs and the 'New High Ground,'" *Survival*, Sept.-Oct. 1983, pp. 204–15.

6. Paul Bracken, *The Command and Control of Nuclear Forces* (New Haven, Conn.: Yale University Press, 1983).

7. President's Report to Congress on U.S. Policy on ASAT Arms Control, March 31, 1984. See also Leslie H. Gelb in the *New York Times* (Aug. 3, 1984).

8. See R. Jeffrey Smith, *Science*, May 18, 1984, pp. 693–695.

16 The President's Strategic Defense Initiative

Office of the White House

"What if free people could live secure in the knowledge that their security did not rest upon the threat of instant U.S. retaliation to deter a Soviet attack, that we could intercept and destroy strategic ballistic missiles before they reached our own soil or that of our allies?"

from President Reagan's March 23, 1983 Speech

THE PRESIDENT'S VISION

In his March 23rd address to the nation, the President described his vision of a world free of its overwhelming dependence on nuclear weapons, a world free once and for all of the threat of nuclear war. The Strategic Defense Initiative, by itself, cannot fully realize this vision nor solve all the security challenges we and our allies will face in the future; for this we will need to seek many solutions—political as well as technological. A long road with much hard work lies ahead of us. The President believes we must begin now. The Strategic Defense Initiative takes a crucial first step.

The basic security of the United States and our allies rests upon our collective ability to deter aggression. Our nuclear retaliatory forces help achieve this security and have deterred war for nearly forty years. Since World War II, nuclear weapons have not been used; there has been no direct military conflict between the two largest world powers, and Europe has not seen such an extended period of peace since the last century. The fact is, however, that we have no defense against nuclear ballistic missile attack. And, as

the Soviet building program widens the imbalance in key offensive capabilities, introducing systems whose status and characteristics are more difficult to confirm, our vulnerability and that of our allies to blackmail becomes quite high. In the event deterrence failed, a President's only recourse would be to surrender or to retaliate. Nuclear retaliation, whether massive or limited, would result in the loss of millions of lives.

The President believes strongly that we must find a better way to assure credible deterrence. If we apply our great scientific and engineering talent to the problem of defending against ballistic missiles, there is a very real possibility that future Presidents will be able to deter war by means other than threatening devastation to any aggressor—and by a means which threatens no one.

The President's goal, and his challenge to our scientists and engineers, is to identify the technological problems and to find the technical solutions so that we have the option of using the potential of strategic defenses to provide a more effective, more stable means of keeping the United States and our allies secure from aggression and coercion. The Joint Chiefs of Staff, many respected scientists, and other experts believe that, with firm leadership and adequate funding, recent advances in defensive technologies could make such defenses achievable.

Excerpted from Office of the White House, "The President's Strategic Defense Initiative," January 1985, pp. 1–4.

WHAT IS THE PRESIDENT'S STRATEGIC DEFENSE INITIATIVE

The President announced his Strategic Defense Initiative (SDI) in his March 23, 1983, address to the nation. Its purpose is to identify ways to exploit recent advances in ballistic missile defense technologies that have potential for strengthening deterrence—and thereby increasing our security and that of our allies. The program is designed to answer a number of fundamental scientific and engineering questions that must be addressed before the promise of these new technologies can be fully assessed. The SDI research program will provide to a future President and a future Congress the technical knowledge necessary to support a decision in the early 1990s on whether to develop and deploy such advanced defensive systems.

As a broad research program, the SDI is not based on any single or preconceived notion of what an effective defense system would look like. A number of different concepts, involving a wide range of technologies, are being examined. No single concept or technology has been identified as the best or the most appropriate. A number of non-nuclear technologies hold promise for dealing effectively with ballistic missiles.

We do feel, however, that the technologies that are becoming available today may offer the possibility of providing a layered defense—a defense that uses various technologies to destroy attacking missiles during each phase of their flight.

- Some missiles could be destroyed shortly after they launch as they burn their engines and boost their warheads into space. By destroying a missile during this boost phase, we would also destroy all of the nuclear warheads it carries at the same time. In the case of ICBMs, they would probably be destroyed before leaving the territory of the aggressor.
- Next, we could destroy those nuclear warheads that survive the boost phase by attacking them during the post-boost phase. During this phase we would target the device that sits on top of the missile and is used to dispense its warheads while it is in the process of releasing its cargo. By destroying this device, the post-boost vehicle, we can destroy all the warheads not yet released.
- Those warheads that have been released and survive, travel for tens of minutes in the void of space on their ballistic trajectories towards

their targets. While we would now have to locate, identify, and destroy the individual nuclear warheads themselves, this relatively long mid-course phase of flight again offers us time to exploit advanced technologies to do just that.

- Finally, those warheads that survive the outer layers of defense, could be attacked during the terminal phase as they approach the end of their ballistic flight.

The concept of a layered defense could be extremely effective because the progressive layers would be able to work together to provide many opportunities to destroy attacking nuclear warheads well before they approach our territory or that of our allies. An opponent facing several separate layers of defenses would find it difficult to redesign his missiles and their nuclear warheads to penetrate all of the layers. Moreover, defenses during the boost, post-boost and mid-course phases of ballistic missile flight make no distinction in the targets of the attacking missiles—they simply destroy attacking nuclear warheads, and in the process protect people and our country. The combined effectiveness of the defense provided by the multiple layers need not provide 100% protection in order to enhance deterrence significantly. It need only create sufficient uncertainty in the mind of a potential aggressor concerning his ability to succeed in the purposes of his attack. The concept of a layered defense certainly will help do this.

There have been considerable advances in technology since U.S. ballistic missile defenses were first developed in the 1960's. At the time the ABM Treaty was signed (1972), ballistic missile defense prospects were largely confined to the attacking nuclear warheads during the terminal phase of their flight using nuclear-tipped interceptor missiles. Since that time, emerging technologies offer the possibility of non-nuclear options for destroying missiles and the nuclear warheads they carry in all phases of their flight. New technologies may be able to permit a layered defense by providing: sensors for identifying and tracking missiles and nuclear warheads; advanced ground and spaceborne interceptors and directed energy weapons to destroy both missiles and nuclear warheads; and, the technology to permit the command, control and communications necessary to operate a layered defense.

In the planning that went into the SDI research program, we consciously chose to look broadly at defense against ballistic missiles as it could be applied across all these phases of missile flight: boost, post-boost, mid-course, and terminal. Although it is too early to define fully those individual technologies or applications which will ultimately prove to be most effective, such a layered approach maximizes the application of emerging technology and holds out the possibility of destroying nuclear warheads well before they reach the territory of the United States or our allies.

As President Reagan made clear at the start of this effort, the SDI research program will be consistent with all U.S. treaty obligations, including the ABM Treaty. The Soviets, who have and are improving the world's only existing anti-ballistic missile system (deployed around Moscow), are continuing a program of research on both traditional and advanced anti-ballistic missile technologies that has been underway for many years. But while the President has directed that the United States effort be conducted in a manner that is consistent with the ABM Treaty, the Soviet Union almost certainly is violating that Treaty by constructing a large ballistic missile early warning radar in Siberia (at Krasnoyarsk) which is located and oriented in a manner prohibited by the Treaty. This radar could contribute significantly to the Soviet Union's considerable potential to rapidly expand its deployed ballistic missile defense capability.

The United States has offered to discuss with the Soviet Union the implications of defensive technologies being explored by both countries. Such a discussion would be useful in helping to clarify both sides' understanding of the relationship between offensive and defensive forces and in clarifying the purposes that underlie the United States and Soviet programs. Further, this dialogue could lead to agreement to work together toward a more stable strategic relationship than exists today.

WHY SDI?

SDI and Deterrence. The primary responsibility of a government is to provide for the security of its people. Deterrence of aggression is the most certain path to ensure that we and our allies survive as free and independent nations. Providing a better, more stable basis for enhanced deterrence is the central purpose of the SDI program.

Under the SDI program, we are conducting

intensive research focused on advanced defensive technologies with the aim of enhancing the basis of deterrence, strengthening stability, and thereby increasing the security of the United States and our allies. On many occasions, the President has stated his strong belief that "a nuclear war cannot be won and must never be fought." U.S. policy has always been one of deterring aggression and will remain so even if a decision is made in the future to deploy defensive systems. The purpose of SDI is to strengthen deterrence and lower the level of nuclear forces.

Defensive systems are consistent with a policy of deterrence both historically and theoretically. While today we rely almost exclusively on the threat of retaliation with offensive forces for our strategic deterrence, this has not always been the case. Throughout the 1950's and most of the 1960's, the United States maintained an extensive air defense network to protect North America from attack by Soviet bomber forces. At that time, this network formed an important part of our deterrent capability. It was allowed to decline only when the Soviet emphasis shifted to intercontinental ballistic missiles, a threat for which there was previously no effective defense. Recent advances in ballistic missile defense technologies, however, provide more than sufficient reason to believe that defensive systems could eventually provide a better and more stable basis for deterrence.

Effective defenses against ballistic missiles have potential for enhancing deterrence in the future in a number of ways. First, they could significantly increase an aggressor's uncertainties regarding whether his weapons would penetrate the defenses and destroy our missiles and other military targets. It would be very difficult for a potential aggressor to predict his own vulnerability in the face of such uncertainties. It would restore the condition that attacking could never leave him better off. An aggressor will be much less likely to contemplate initiating a nuclear conflict, even in crisis circumstances, while lacking confidence in his ability to succeed.

Such uncertainties also would serve to reduce or eliminate the incentive for first strike attack. Modern, accurate ICBM's carrying multiple nuclear warheads—if deployed in sufficiently large numbers relative to the size of an opponent's force structure, as the Soviets have done with their ICBM force—could be used in a rapid first strike to undercut an opponent's ability to retaliate effectively. By significantly reducing or eliminating the ability of ballistic missiles to attack military forces effectively, and thereby rendering them impotent and obsolete as a means of supporting aggression, advanced defenses could remove this potential major source of instability.

Finally, in conjunction with air defenses, very effective defenses against ballistic missiles could help reduce or eliminate the apparent military value of nuclear attack to an aggressor. By preventing an aggressor from destroying a significant portion of our country, an aggressor would have gained nothing by attacking in the first place. In this way, very effective defenses could reduce substantially the possibility of nuclear conflict.

If we take the prudent and necessary steps to maintain strong, credible military forces, there is every reason to believe that deterrence will continue to preserve the peace. However, even with the utmost vigilance, few things in this world are absolutely certain, and a responsible government must consider the remote possibility that deterrence could fail. Today, the United States and our allies have no defense against ballistic missile attack. We also have very limited capability to defend the United States against an attack by enemy bombers. If deterrence were to fail, without a shield of any kind, it could cause the death of most of our population and the destruction of our nation as we know it. The SDI program provides our only long-term hope to change this situation.

Defenses also could provide insurance against either accidental ballistic missile launches or launches by some future irrational leader in possession of a nuclear armed missile. While such events are improbable, they are not inconceivable. The United States and other nuclear-capable powers have instituted appropriate safeguards against inadvertent launches by their own forces and together have formulated policies to preclude the proliferation of nuclear weapons. Nonetheless, it is difficult to predict the future course of events. While we hope, and expect that our best efforts will continue to be successful, our national security interests will be well served by a vigorous SDI research program that could provide an additional safeguard against such potentially catastrophic events.

Today our retaliatory forces provide a strong sword to deter aggression. However, the President seeks a better way of maintaining deterrence. For the future, the SDI program strives to provide a defensive shield which will do more than simply make that deterrence stronger. It will allow us to build a better, more stable basis for deterrence. And, at the same time, that same shield will provide necessary protection should an aggressor not be deterred. . . .

17 Space-Based Missile Defense

Union of Concerned Scientists

> *I call upon the scientific community who gave us nuclear weapons to turn their great talents to the cause of mankind and world peace: to give us the means of rendering these nuclear weapons impotent and obsolete.*
>
> President Reagan, March 23, 1983

OVERVIEW

These words unveiled the President's Strategic Defense Initiative, a "comprehensive and intensive effort" with the "ultimate goal of eliminating the threat posed by strategic nuclear missiles." It proposes to rely on unborn generations of so-

---

This reading consists of excerpts from a report of the Union of Concerned Scientists on "Space-Based Missile Defense." The members of the panel that issued the report are: Kurt Gottfried (Professor of Physics and Nuclear Studies, Cornell University), Henry W. Kendall (Professor of Physics, Massachusetts Institute of Technology), Hans A. Bethe (Professor of Physics Emeritus, Cornell University; Nobel Laureate in Physics; Chief, Theoretical Division, Manhattan Project), Peter A. Clausen (Senior Arms Analyst, Union of Concerned Scientists; former fellow, Woodrow Wilson International Center for Scholars), Richard L. Garwin (IBM Fellow at the Thomas J. Watson Research Center), Noel Gayler (former Commander-in-Chief, US Forces in the Pacific), Richard Ned Lebow (Professor of Government and Director, Peace Studies Program, Cornell University), Carl Sagan (Professor of Astronomy and Space Sciences and Director, Laboratory for Planetary Studies, Cornell University), and Victor Weisskopf (Institute Professor Emeritus, Massachusetts Institute of Technology). Excerpts of the report were published in the *New York Review of Books*, April 26, 1984, and were later updated and reprinted in *The Fallacy of Star Wars: Why Space Weapons Can't Protect Us*. (New York: Vintage, 1984).

phisticated space weapons that the Secretary of Defense told *Meet the Press* would provide a "thoroughly reliable and total" defense. We shall adopt Mr. Weinberger's words, and refer to the President's goal as *total ballistic missile defense*, or *total BMD*—what in the vernacular is now called "Star Wars."

Every sane person yearns to escape from the specter of nuclear annihilation. But that consensus still leaves a host of unanswered questions: will these BMD systems, which still are just conceptual designs, provide a total defense of our civilization against the Soviet missile force? That force now carries 9,000 nuclear warheads, each far more powerful than the Hiroshima bomb, and able to arrive on US targets within thirty minutes. (The US arsenal is, of course, equally devastating.) If these defenses of the distant future could protect us totally against today's threat, could they cope with the Soviet strategic weapons of their own era?

What would the Soviets' response be? Would they devote themselves to a similar effort, and agree to reduce their offensive nuclear forces? Or would they perceive this new American program as an attempt to nullify Soviet nuclear forces—as a supplement to the emerging US capacity to destroy Soviet missiles in their silos? If so, would they not respond with a missile buildup and "countermeasures" to confound our defenses, so that they could still destroy the United States (just as the US can destroy the

USSR)? Or would the Soviets not have this option, because our defense would be truly total—robust enough to foil any offensive countermove? . . .

. . . There is general agreement that a defense of our population is impossible unless the vast majority of Soviet missiles can be intercepted in the first phase of their flight, while their booster engines emit a brilliant flame and before their multiple warheads are released. Otherwise, the subsequent layers of the BMD system will not be able to cope with the attack. We therefore devote the bulk of our attention to "boost phase" defense.

All boost phase interception must be carried out at long distance. Hence it is essential to transmit a blow to the enemy booster with a weapon that can travel quickly. The highest velocity attainable is the speed of light (186,000 miles per second). For that reason, laser beams which move at that speed, and beams of atoms or electrons which are nearly that fast, would be ideal if they could be made intense enough to cause damage at such large distances. Such devices are called directed energy weapons.

A laser is a device that emits a beam of light composed of rays that are almost perfectly parallel. We shall consider several types of lasers: chemical lasers that emit infrared light, excimer lasers that emit ultraviolet light, and a laser that is pumped by a nuclear explosion and emits X-rays.

In a weapon, the beam from an infrared or ultraviolet laser is concentrated on the target by adopting the familiar trick of lighting a fire with a magnifying glass that focuses the sun's rays. In a space weapon, the task of focusing and aiming the laser beam is carried out by a suitably oriented and shaped mirror or system of mirrors. The laser itself could be in space or on the ground, but the mirror must be in space if it is to send the beam toward the booster.

In assessing each BMD system, we first assume that it will perform as well as the constraints imposed by scientific law permit—that targets can be found instantly and aiming is perfect, that the battle management software is never in error, that all mirrors are optically perfect, that lasers with the required power output will become available, etc. Above all, we assume that the Soviets' forces remain static—that they do not build more missiles or install any countermeasures. Hence, our initial optimistic appraisal ignores the critical question of whether

BMD will eventually work as well as it possibly could, and does not depend on classified information.

Even in this utopian regime, our findings concerning the proposed BMD schemes are that:

- Chemical laser "battle stations" in low orbits, or "space trucks" carrying "kill vehicles," will have to number in the hundreds to give adequate coverage of the Soviet silo fields.

- Excimer lasers on the ground, whose beams would be reflected toward boosters by over a thousand orbiting mirrors, would require power plants which alone would cost some $40 billion.

- The atmosphere and the earth's magnetic field combine to make particle beam weapons implausible into the foreseeable future.

These cost estimates do not include research and development, or construction of space platforms, lasers, kill vehicles, mirrors, and command and control facilities. Just the R&D portion of this program has been described by Dr. Richard DeLauer, Under Secretary of Defense for Research and Engineering, as having at least eight components "every single one . . . equivalent to or greater than the Manhattan Project." Furthermore, all costs will climb rapidly should the mirrors be imperfect, the time for aiming exceed several seconds, redundancy be desired, etc. The full costs cannot even be estimated because the proposed technologies are still too immature, but it is clear that many hundreds of billions of dollars would be needed.

The proposal to launch X-ray lasers pumped by nuclear explosions at the time of an attack would require a new fleet of submarines, since there is no suitable base on land close enough to Soviet silos to allow interception in the time available. The laser's soft X-rays cannot penetrate the atmosphere, and they deliver a rather light blow from which the booster can readily be protected. These facts, when combined with the feasibility of shortening the boost so that it ends before the missile leaves the atmosphere, imply that the X-ray laser is not a viable BMD weapon.

These findings assume a minimal Soviet reaction to a US missile defense. But the Soviets have made it clear that they view the quest for a total BMD as an unacceptable threat. They fear that such a BMD system would give us the option to strike first—an understandable fear since Mr. Weinberger has said that he would view a similar Soviet system as "one of the most frightening prospects" imaginable. And they have heard Administration officials speak of space-based BMD as a lever for stressing the USSR's technologically less sophisticated economy.

In the real world we must therefore expect a determined Soviet reaction, unconstrained by all existing agreements, because the very testing of our defensive weapons would violate our obligations under the ratified Anti-Ballistic Missile (ABM) Treaty. The Soviet reaction is likely to include:

- Offensive missiles designed to circumvent BMD, such as cruise missiles that cannot be intercepted from space.
- Fitting ICBMs with more powerful engines so that the boosters would burn out quickly and inside the atmosphere, which would stress any BMD system, and eliminate interception by kill vehicles and X-ray lasers.
- Cheap decoy ICBMs—boosters without warheads in fake silos—to overwhelm boost phase interceptors.
- Weapons that would exploit the fact that even a battleship's armor could not protect a space station from quite primitive types of attack.
- A Pandora's box of largely developed countermeasures that would vastly complicate the problem of targeting boosters and warheads.

All these countermeasures would exploit off-the-shelf weapons and techniques that exist today, in contrast to the unproven and improbable technologies on which our proposed defenses would rely. Hence, the Soviet response will be cheaper and far more reliable than our defenses, and available as those defenses emerge.

While this quest for a total defense against nuclear missiles would be endless, the decision to embark would have immediate political repercussions. . . . The ABM Treaty could not survive the start of this endless journey, and with it all constraints on offensive forces would go overboard. The impact on NATO would be profound. Our allies in Europe would not be protected by an American BMD system, and this would inflame existing suspicion that the US intends to conduct nuclear operations in Europe without risk to itself. Alliance cohesion would erode because Europeans would hold the US responsible for exacerbating East-West tensions.

The risk to our survival would mount dramatically were we ever to begin erecting the BMD system. This budding system would be exceedingly vulnerable to attack. Nevertheless, its capabilities would be overvalued by our adversaries, and its installation could well be perceived as an attempt to disarm the Soviet Union. These circumstances could in themselves provoke open conflict.

If we get through this hazardous passage, will we have reached the promised land where nuclear weapons are "impotent and obsolete"? Obviously not. We would then have a defense of stupefying complexity, under the total control of a computer program whose proportions defy description, and whose performance will remain a deep mystery until the tragic moment when it would be called into action.

The President and his entourage occasionally argue that we must pursue this quest because the benefits of success outweigh the costs and risks. However, that is only an argument for a research program in strict conformity with the ABM Treaty. Such a program has always had our support. It is needed to protect us from Soviet surprises, and it might uncover concepts that could actually provide a viable defense. But there is an enormous gulf between such a program and a call from the ramparts for a national "experiment" to mount a defense based on untried technologies and provocative doctrines. We have delineated the costs and risks of such an "experiment." At best, the outcome would be a defense of precarious reliability, confronted by offensive nuclear forces designed to circumvent and overwhelm it, and a host of new "anti-BMD" weapons to attack our armada of space platforms which, in turn, would have to be defended by yet another fleet of anti-anti-BMD weapons.

It is difficult to imagine a more hazardous confrontation. And it is equally difficult to understand how anyone can believe that this is the path toward a less dangerous world. A direct and safe road is there for all to see—equitable and verifiable deep cuts in strategic offensive forces and immediate negotiations to ban all space weapons. If we are to take that road, we must abandon the misconception that nuclear explosives are military weapons, and the illusion that ever more sophisticated technology can, by itself, remove the perils that science and technology have created. We must, instead, recognize the overriding reality of the nuclear age—that we cannot regain safety by cleverly sawing off the thin, dry branch on which the Soviets are perched, for we cling to the same branch.

THE PROBLEM OF CRUISE MISSILES

A cruise missile is, in essence, a small ground-hugging pilotless airplane that can carry a nuclear warhead over distances of thousands of miles. It measures the altitude of the overflown terrain with an on-board radar and matches that altitude against a map stored in its computer's memory. An accuracy sufficient to threaten hard targets is therefore attainable, though the time from launch to impact is much greater than it is for ballistic missiles. Cruise missiles capable of penetrating into the Soviet Union are already on our B-52 strategic bombers and are being deployed on the ground by NATO. Both superpowers could develop cruise missiles for submarines that could strike both civilian and strategic targets far inside their adversary's borders from an unpredictable launch point.

None of the space-based defense systems that are under discussion can touch cruise missiles. That is not their purpose. But until a virtually perfect shield against cruise missiles is developed, there is no such thing as a *total* missile defense. . . . No one doubts that a significant number of US strategic bombers (*not* just their cruise missiles) could penetrate the highly touted Soviet air defense system to deliver their high-yield bombs on target; the experiences of two Korean airliners have shown that this is the case. Cruise missiles are far harder to detect with radar than much larger and higher-flying airplanes, and as the so-called STEALTH techniques develop, cruise missiles will become even more elusive. Since they are unmanned, a high attrition rate is quite acceptable. Given these facts, it is very difficult to envisage a shield against air- and sea-launched cruise missiles that would protect our population.

SYSTEMATIC PROBLEMS
AND VULNERABILITIES

Defense Suppression

One of the most effective tactics that can be employed against a Ballistic Missile Defense is to attack the ground and space assets on which it depends. Some of these assets are of surprising vulnerability while at the same time being crucial to the defense. Nuclear explosions in space . . . can blind infrared sensors and blackout radars. Detonated ahead of the flight of reentry vehicles, at altitudes of 60–80 km, a single precursor burst will ionize a region of space some tens of kilometers across, hiding the vehicles for several minutes. Anti-radiation homing vehicles may be used to destroy radars in space and on the ground. Space mines or inert objects, including sand, may be used against fragile space-based lasers and mirrors. A variety of measures can be taken to jam, spoof, and confuse the data transfer links of the battle management system.

Submarine-launched ballistic missile and cruise missile attacks can be a key factor in defense suppression in consequence of the immense damage that they would do to their targets. Submarine-launched missiles have short flight times, allowing as little as 3–5 minutes' warning for near-coastal targets. They have unpredictable launch points, which can make viewing angles poor for the defense. Moreover they can be launched on depressed trajectories, low enough to allow the missiles to evade most defenses. Cruise missiles are air-breathing, low-flying, and nearly invisible to optical and radar trackers. The BMD system cannot defend itself against such attacks. In the future, if an extensive missile defense moves toward deployment, increasing attention would have to be paid to submarine missile attacks.

Some improvements in sea-launched ballistic missile defense can be expected, but it is difficult to see what can be done to mitigate substantially the cruise missile threat. Targets would include ground facilities for battle management, rockets and basing facilities associated with pop-up sensors and weaponry, and communications and control stations. Successful pop-up launches from silos inside the United States which had survived the disarming strikes could be forestalled by nearby exoatmospheric explosions, or by bursts in the fringes of the atmosphere to destroy missiles in flight. Well-executed strikes of this sort, in advance of the main offensive missile launch, would in all likelihood disable the entire defense structure. There appears to be no way that this vulnerability can be adequately reduced.

Software and Algorithms

The battle management systems of a total BMD must deal with thousands to hundreds of thousands of objects. This requires computers with the capacity to carry out many hundreds of millions, if not billions, of arithmetic operations per second. Advances in computer technology suggest that the hardware to accomplish this monumental task may become available in the future. There are, however, several challenges whose solutions are doubtful. One is the problem of designing and writing the programs (software) required to guide the computers. Experience with earlier defense system software, as well as examples from nondefense experience, suggests that it will be exceedingly difficult, if not impossible, to construct software that would operate properly in the environment of a nuclear attack, for which it could never have been fully tested. . . .

Confidence

Suppose for a moment that a total missile defense system without obvious flaws had been developed and deployed. This defense, in a time of confrontation and nuclear attack, would represent the only prospect of avoiding overwhelming ruin. Could there be enough confidence in this defense that the US could safely reduce its nuclear forces unilaterally or that it could, during a crisis, ignore Soviet nuclear threats with impunity? The confidence that is needed is not just that each component of the myriad array of parts—the sensors, the weapons, the computers—would, individually, perform as expected. More important is the need for confidence that the entire assembly would operate as a harmonious machine and capably blunt the attack. Consider the nature of the defensive system: an enormous, intricate, and complex assemblage, novel in design, pushing the limits of technology, intended to provide a defense against a threat and, under circumstances which will be fully defined only when the attack comes, forced to meet an uncommonly high standard of performance. And, remarkably enough, it cannot ever have been adequately tested.

No amount of testing under simulated battle conditions could confidently explore the response of the defensive system to an actual nuclear attack. This is only in part because the nature of the attack and of the attacker's countermeasures cannot be known in advance. One simply cannot simulate the stress and the demands on the system of the circumstances of war.

The matter of testing is crucial. The performance of complex devices can rarely be confidently predicted before they are set in realistic operation even when their tasks are well defined. Complex designs breed complex problems. And this is also the case with computer software. All large programs contain "bugs," hidden flaws, and while their number dwindles over time as the programs are used, no one can ever be certain that the bugs are gone. The testing establishes a widening range of confident operation, no more. New circumstances can bring new flaws to light. There is no known way to get around this. We conclude that even if an apparently effective total defense could be prepared, it is highly unlikely much trust could be placed in its working properly when needed. . . .

POLITICAL AND STRATEGIC IMPLICATIONS

The political and strategic dangers raised by the "Star Wars" initiative are at least as important as its technical flaws. Indeed, these dangers would weigh heavily against development of ballistic missile defenses even if the technical prospects for such systems were much brighter than they are. A US commitment to BMD would precipitate Soviet responses and a chain of actions and reactions that would radically change the strategic environment to the detriment of both countries' security. The offensive arms race would be greatly accelerated, arms control treaties undermined, and the nuclear peace made more precarious.

Of course, the technical and political issues are not completely unconnected. If it were possible to put in place overnight a fully effective, invulnerable defense against nuclear weapons, there could hardly be serious objections to doing so. But, as the preceding analysis has shown, such a system cannot be built now or, in all likelihood, ever. In the real world, BMD systems will be imperfect. Even under very optimistic assumptions about their ultimate performance, the process of improvement would be incremental and prolonged. During this extended and highly unstable transition period the strategic and political implications of BMD become critical.

While the alleged benefits of BMD are distant and hypothetical, the dangers are near-term and predictable. The adverse consequences of a commitment to BMD would be felt long before the actual deployment of mature technological systems, and quite likely even while the ABM Treaty was still technically being observed. These consequences would follow the familiar anticipated reactions syndrome, driven by the highly threatening nature of BMD and the worst-case assumptions that would dominate nuclear planning amid large uncertainties about the effectiveness of BMD systems and ambiguities about the intentions behind them. Accordingly, the dangers posed by a US policy of ballistic missile defense would be virtually independent of the level of performance that BMD systems might, decades in the future, finally achieve.

Consequences for the Arms Race and Arms Control

A collapse of the ABM Treaty and the initiation of a BMD competition between the superpowers would have a devastating impact on the prospects for offensive arms control. Following an inevitable action-reaction pattern, the Soviets are certain to respond to an American BMD with new offensive measures. Both a quantitative and a qualitative escalation of the arms race would ensue. Adherence to the terms of the SALT II treaty—not ratified by the US but until now informally observed by both countries—would end, and hopes for new agreements would be undermined.

The enormously threatening character of the policy goal announced by President Reagan in his March 1983 speech guarantees a strong Soviet reaction. Despite presidential rhetoric that defenses might be in the mutual interest of the superpowers, the Soviet Union will certainly view a serious US commitment to BMD as an attempt to achieve military superiority by negating the Soviet deterrent. After all, it is Soviet weapons that would be rendered "impotent and obsolete" by an American BMD breakthrough.

The Soviets will interpret a US BMD program not in relation to some utopian future, but in the context of the ongoing US nuclear buildup, particularly the conversion of virtually all US strategic forces to a counterforce role, and the war-fighting doctrine that this buildup is meant to implement. From this standpoint, one can readily appreciate that the Soviet Union might view an American BMD as part of a larger US effort to acquire a first-strike capability—the ability to carry out an attack against Soviet nuclear forces and to defend effectively against a heavily degraded Soviet retaliatory strike. The Soviet Union is no more likely than the US to accept such a development.

In a world of BMD deployments, each superpower's first priority would be the maintenance of forces able to penetrate or circumvent the other's defenses. The resulting stimulus to the arms race would be aggravated by uncertainties about the effectiveness of defenses. Operating as usual on conservative, worst-case planning assumptions, each side would tend to exaggerate the effectiveness of the other's defense while discounting its own. As a result, offensive responses would tend to surpass the level actually needed to maintain second-strike or retaliatory capabilities. For example, US defenses assessed by American defense planners as 50 percent effective might elicit a Soviet buildup based on the assumption of 90 percent effectiveness, and vice versa. Each side would then perceive the other's reaction as excessive and threatening, and would respond in kind, creating a vicious cycle of escalation.

In these circumstances, the hope that BMD might improve the prospects for negotiated force reductions, as suggested by the Reagan Administration, is totally unrealistic. Even less plausible is the idea that a US BMD could be used as a lever, in the words of Dr. George Keyworth II, the President's Science Advisor, to "pressure the Soviets to take our arms reductions proposals more seriously than they do now."

Instead, BMD would be doubly fatal to the prospects for controlling offensive forces—raising fear and suspicion that would poison the political atmosphere for negotiations, and creating technical problems of comparison and verification far more complex than those associated with SALT or the Strategic Arms Reduction Talks (START). In effect, defenses function as a wild card, making the nuclear balance much less calculable than if only offensive forces need to be taken into account. Given the large uncertainties and controversy that already surround efforts to compare US and Soviet nuclear capabilities, the addition of BMD to the mix would place an unbearable strain on arms control. An arms control process healthy enough to support reductions in an environment of strategic defenses would be more than strong enough to produce such reductions in the absence of BMD systems. Conversely, an arms control process that is already faltering badly would be unlikely to survive at all in the face of BMD deployments by the two sides. . . .

Consequences for Deterrence and Crisis Stability

In addition to the arms race consequences discussed above, the administration's BMD proposal would have a profoundly destabilizing effect on the nuclear balance, increasing the risk of nuclear war at times of US-Soviet confrontation and reducing the chances of bringing hostilities under control if war did occur.

These consequences run directly counter to the arguments often made by BMD advocates that US defenses would strengthen deterrence and, in the event deterrence fails, play an important damage-limitation role. Such arguments, it should be emphasized, are attempts to construct strategic rationales for only modestly capable BMD systems. As such, they represent a very large retreat from President Reagan's vision of transcending (not reinforcing) the system of nuclear deterrence by making nuclear weapons "impotent and obsolete." Nevertheless, these justifications for imperfect BMD systems are important to address. As the President's original vision is increasingly understood to be illusory, a US BMD program is likely to be promoted primarily on grounds of deterrence and damage-limitation. Administration officials and supporters have already begun to argue in these terms during the year since President Reagan's speech. In this regard, a close link has often been noted between these more modest roles for BMD systems and the administration's nuclear warfighting strategy—a link that will not be overlooked by the Soviet Union.

The argument that BMD would strengthen nuclear deterrence rests mainly on the claim that it would reduce the vulnerability of US land-based missiles to preemptive attack. By protecting the US ability to retaliate, BMD would make a Soviet first strike less certain of success and therefore less likely. However, this is an argument for terminal, hard-point defense of US missile silos, not for the layered, area defenses being proposed by the administration. The administration's initiative is not only vastly more expensive and complex than is necessary for the protection of retaliatory forces, but it is provocative to the Soviet Union in a way that would reduce, not enhance, deterrent stability.

Area defenses undermine deterrence because they magnify the advantage of striking first. Indeed, the modest BMD systems likely to be attainable in the foreseeable future would be useful *only* to the attacker. They would be easily defeated by a well-executed first strike, but might perform with some effectiveness against a poorly coordinated and weakened retaliatory strike.

As a result, these systems are likely to be perceived as components of a first strike strategy rather than as deterrent weapons, and to create strong incentives for preemptive attacks during periods of high tension. At such times, the fact that a first strike would be complicated by the adversary's BMD would be judged less relevant than the fear that, if one fails to attack first, effective retaliation may be impossible.

BMD, then, would aggravate the dangerous "use them or lose them" pressures that are already increasing due to the trend toward offensive weapons designed for counterforce. The result would be a serious weakening of mutual deterrence precisely [when] it is most needed.

The damage-limitation rationale for BMD is as dubious as the deterrence argument. This rationale has two variants. First, in the event deterrence fails and nuclear war occurs, it is argued that defenses could save lives, reducing the threat of "assured destruction" that exists in the present offense-dominated system. Second, we are told, this damage-limitation effect would strengthen deterrence by making the threat of nuclear retaliation more credible. BMD advocates who emphasize these points generally subscribe to the theory that credible deterrence requires forces designed for actual warfighting, and capable of being used in a selective, flexible manner. In this context, the damage-limitation role of a BMD system is seen as useful not only to limit population fatalities but also to protect nuclear command and control systems.

These arguments are implausible in light of the size and destructive power of superpower nuclear arsenals and the adjustments in targeting and nuclear strategy the BMD deployments would bring about. The overkill capacity of both superpowers is such that only a near-perfect defense could hope to reduce fatalities appreciably in the event of major nuclear exchanges. For example, if the Soviet Union were to target its missiles to maximize damage to the US population—a likely response to a serious American attempt to protect cities—it would need only 5 percent of its *current* ballistic missile warheads to kill up to half of the US urban population immediately. . . . In other words, even a 95 percent effective BMD would leave the US with the prospect of tens of millions of prompt fatalities in a nuclear war, leaving aside all the subsequent deaths from fire, disease, and social disruption. Moreover, enough nuclear explosions would occur even in this very optimistic case to pose a serious danger of triggering a climatic catastrophe (the "nuclear winter" phenomenon).

The vulnerability of the US to destruction by Soviet nuclear forces, in short, cannot be mitigated by any foreseeable defensive shield as long as nuclear weapons exist in their current numbers. Only if offensive forces were radically reduced, to perhaps a tenth of their present size, could a moderately effective defense begin to make a dramatic difference in the vulnerability of populations to nuclear destruction. As we have seen, the prospect of negotiating such reductions would become virtually nonexistent amid a major US –Soviet BMD competition. . . .

Summary

The superficial attractions of a strategy of nuclear defense disappear when the overall consequences of BMD deployments are considered. More than any foreseeable offensive arms breakthrough, defenses would radically transform the context of US–Soviet nuclear relations, setting in motion a chain of events and reactions that would leave both superpowers much less secure. Deterrence would be weakened and crisis instability increased. Damage-limitation would be undermined by a greater emphasis on the targeting of cities and the increased vulnerability of command and control systems. And virtually the entire arms control process would be swept away by the abrogation of the ABM Treaty, the launching of a new offensive round of the arms race, and the extension of the arms race into space.

QUESTIONS FOR DISCUSSION

1. What are the differences between strategic, theater and tactical nuclear weapons systems? In capabilities? In missions?

2. Briefly discuss the growth of the nuclear forces of the superpowers and other members of the "nuclear club." Relate this discussion to the problem of nuclear proliferation addressed by Spector in Chapter I.

3. Why do Gottfried and Lebow conclude that antisatellite weapons (ASATs) could increase the risk of nuclear war?

4. What are some of the central issues in the debate over space-based missile defense? Which of these, in your opinion, can be resolved by research and which are a matter of conjecture?

SUGGESTED READINGS

BROWN, HAROLD. "Is SDI Technically Feasible?" *Foreign Affairs* 64, (1986): 435–545.
LONG, FRANKLIN A., DONALD HAFNER, and JEFFERY BOUTWELL, eds. *Weapons in Space.* New York: W.W. Norton, 1986.
PARNAS, DAVID LORGE. "Software Aspects of Strategic Defense Systems." *American Scientist* 73, no. 5 (September–October 1985): 432–440.
SCHROEER, DEITRICH. *Science, Technology and the Nuclear Arms Race.* New York: John Wiley, 1984.
STARES, PAUL B. *The Militarization of Space: U.S. Policy, 1945–1984.* Ithaca, N.Y.: Cornell University Press, 1985.
TSIPIS, KOSTA. *Arsenal: Understanding Weapons in the Nuclear Age.* New York: Simon and Schuster, 1983.
UNION OF CONCERNED SCIENTISTS. *The Fallacy of Star Wars: Why Space Weapons Can't Protect Us.* New York: Vintage, 1984.
U.S., CONGRESS, OFFICE OF TECHNOLOGY ASSESSMENT. *Ballistic Missile Defense Technologies: Summary.* September 1985.

PART THREE

The Dynamics
of the Nuclear Arms Race

In light of today's large and expanding nuclear arsenals, it is important to understand the dynamics of the nuclear arms race. What social forces have shaped nuclear policy? What policies and processes contribute to the continuation of the nuclear arms race?

We now turn to these questions, exploring some of the complex and interrelated factors—political, cultural, institutional, economic, and psychological—that influence the nuclear arms race. International conflict, domestic politics, economic processes, and the structure of military institutions are all involved. So too are the ideas and theories of academic analysts and military thinkers, whose strategic doctrines provide the intellectual underpinnings of policy. The interests of weapons manufacturers also play a role, as do the efforts of bureaucrats to expand their budgets. Many analysts believe that military policy and weapons procurement are affected by competition between branches of the armed services and by ongoing relationships between military contractors and government officials.

Theories of the causes of the arms race are often divided into two broad categories: external and internal. External theories emphasize international politics, military strategy, and responses to activities of perceived adversaries. Internal theories focus on domestic pressures for arms production, pressures that are rooted in the institutions of weapons building, and in the technological momentum of military research efforts.

The many interrelated factors that contribute to the nuclear arms race can best be understood through an interdisciplinary approach. Part Three examines the dynamics of the nuclear arms race from a number of perspectives. We begin with two chapters on nuclear strategy. The first, Chapter V, discusses nuclear deterrence, which has formed the backbone of U.S. nuclear policy. Chapter VI examines the strategic doctrine of "limited nuclear war."

Each of the remaining four chapters sheds light on a different aspect of the nuclear arms race. Chapter VII explores the politics of the relationship between the United States and the Soviet Union. Chapter VIII turns to economic aspects of the nuclear arms race, discussing the costs of nuclear weapons and the economics of military spending. Chapter IX looks at the role that bureaucratic structures play in shaping the arms race. Finally, Chapter X applies a psychological perspective to the arms race, examining the ways that perceptions and misperceptions can aggravate international tensions and impede efforts to prevent nuclear war.

Chapter V

Nuclear Deterrence

The centerpiece of American nuclear strategy is the doctrine of nuclear deterrence. As U.S. nuclear policy has evolved over the years, theories of deterrence have evolved as well, often changing in important ways. But despite the changes, the basic approach has remained the same. By threatening to retaliate with nuclear weapons, the United States seeks to deter the Soviet Union from attacking the U.S. and its allies. The Soviets use a similar strategy to deter U.S. aggression.

Advocates of the strategy of nuclear deterrence argue that as long as both sides have a nuclear arsenal sufficient to strike a devastating retaliatory blow, neither side will elect to strike first. Thus, they argue, the "balance of terror" can keep—and has kept—the peace.

Critics of nuclear deterrence are less comfortable with a strategy that is based on the threat of a nuclear holocaust. Some critics are concerned that deterrence might break down, that miscalculation, error, or overconfidence might lead one side to attempt a first strike. Others reject deterrence on ethical grounds, arguing that a system rooted in the threat to exterminate many millions of people is morally indefensible.

And so the debate is joined. The proponents of deterrence claim that "it works," and the critics counter "so far." Proponents say there is no alternative, and the critics charge that the alternatives have barely been explored.

This chapter provides a brief introduction to nuclear deterrence and the debate surrounding it. We begin with an excerpt from nuclear strategist Herman Kahn's 1962 book *Thinking About the Unthinkable*. Kahn discusses the use of nuclear weapons to pursue a number of different objectives, identifying several types of deterrence. Next, John Erickson surveys "The Soviet View of Deterrence," comparing it with the view of deterrence dominant in the West. Finally, Anatol Rapoport issues a moral and intellectual challenge to the assumptions that underlie the thought of deterrence strategists, arguing that conscience-based thinking provides an alternative to strategic thinking.

18   Thinking About the Unthinkable

Herman Kahn _____

U.S. military policy currently seeks to achieve at least six broad strategic objectives:

(1) *Type I Deterrence*—to deter a large attack on the military forces, population, or wealth of the United States, by threatening a high level of damage to the attacker in retaliation;

(2) *Type II Deterrence*—to deter extremely provocative actions short of large attack on the U.S. (for example, a nuclear or even all-out conventional strike against Western Europe) by the threat of an "all-out" U.S. nuclear reprisal against the Soviet Union;

(3) *Improved War Outcome*—to limit damage to U.S. (and allied) population and wealth, and to improve the military outcome for the U.S. should a war occur;

(4) *Stability*—to reduce the likelihood of an inadvertent thermonuclear war;

(5) *Comprehensive Arms Control*—to control and limit both the arms race and the use of force in settling disputes;

(6) *Type III Deterrence*—to deter provocations not covered by Type II Deterrence and provide support for the achievement of "peaceful" political objectives and for tactics such as Controlled Reprisal, other limited wars, mobilizations, negotiations, and so forth.

I do not propose to judge here the relative importance of these various objectives. During the past decade all of them have played major parts in the formation of United States defense policy. While they are to some extent competi-

tive and inconsistent so far as overall national security is concerned, they are also complementary; in most cases a catastrophic failure to achieve any one of them is unlikely to be rectified even by spectacular successes in the other five.

There are still other complications in designing and evaluating strategic forces. Not only may additional objectives come into being after a system has been built, but the balance among objectives may change. It is important, therefore, that our capability be flexible enough to accept efficiently increases, decreases, or major alterations in our objectives in reaction to changes in the technological, military, and political environment. Unless only a specialized question is being examined, studies of strategic forces must consider all six objectives jointly. Fortunately it often seems possible to design the components of our strategic forces to contribute to more than one of the objectives, and a well-designed strategic system will probably contribute a reasonable capability to all six.

Let us now consider each of these objectives and some of their implications in greater detail.

(1) TYPE I DETERRENCE

Probably the most essential mission of our strategic forces is to deter deliberate direct attack on the United States (whether aimed primarily at military forces or cities) by influencing the enemy's calculations as to the relative advantages to himself of attacking or not attacking. We want the enemy's calculations, whether explicitly or implicitly made, to indicate clearly that in all circumstances an attack on the United States would be a serious mistake. It must distinctly appear that any attack, however *care-*

fully designed or brilliantly executed will result in such a high probability of an unacceptable amount of damage being caused to some or all of the attacker's population, industry, or military forces, that our enemy must rule it out as a choice even if he is desperate or biased by wishful thinking.

Our ability to deter the Soviets depends on an estimate of what would be likely to happen if the Soviets were to strike *at a time and with tactics of their own choosing*, and we had to attempt to strike back with a *damaged* and perhaps *uncoordinated* force which must operate in the *post-attack environment*. The Soviets might attempt to follow up an attack with *threats to intimidate us into limiting our reprisal*. Not only would the Soviet active defenses be *completely alerted*, but if the strike had been preceded by a period of tension, they would probably have been *augmented* as well. Moreover, their cities might be at least *partially evacuated*. Each of these factors increases considerably the difficulty of guaranteeing retaliation adequate to deter.

For this reason, the problem of assuring retaliation must be viewed as a whole. It is not enough to have large numbers of nuclear weapon delivery systems before an attack, or even enough to insure the survival of an adequate number of them after an attack. We must, in a sense, also assume the survival of a whole retaliatory system. We must protect the legal (presidential) decision-making machinery, vital military personnel, enough military command and control to execute an appropriate operation, and finally the resolution to carry out this operation.

Type I Deterrence is in part a psychological matter. It rests principally upon an enemy's judgment of the likelihood of various possible outcomes of an attack on the U.S. Theoretically, if by some tricks we could convince the enemy that we had an invulnerable and overwhelming retaliatory power, we would not even need the hardware. Moreover, we might in at least one respect be better off since non-existent missiles will not go off accidentally. Unfortunately, in today's world we cannot rely on pulling off such a titanic bluff. We could not be certain or even very sure that the Soviets had not found us out. And unless we have faith in our deterrent we may be unwilling to so much as test it by standing firm in a crisis. Moreover, unless our own population was similarly fooled, internal pressures would prevent us from standing firm in any crisis. In all probability the only way to convince all those who have to be convinced that we have a deterrent is actually to have one.

Our Type I Deterrent must, of course, do more than deter the most cautious and responsible Soviet decision maker, who expects to wind up the cold war peacefully, from madly risking all in an attack launched suddenly in cold blood. Our deterrent must be powerful enough to withstand all of the stresses and strains of the cold war, of sudden and unexpected crises, of possible accidents and miscalculations, of satellite revolts, of limited wars, of fanciful calculations by optimistic gamblers or simple-minded theoreticians, and of the tense situations in which "reciprocal fear of surprise attack" might destabilize an inadequate deterrent. We want it to be clear even to less responsible Soviet decision makers that we have taken all of their most "optimistic" schemes into account.

Moreover we want to deter even the mad. It is sometimes stated that even an adequate Type I Deterrent would not deter an irrational enemy. This might be true if irrationality were an all-or-nothing proposition. Actually, irrationality is a matter of degree and if the irrationality is sufficiently bizarre, the irrational decision maker's subordinates are likely to step in. As a result, we should want a safety factor in Type I Deterrence systems so large as to impress even the irrational and irresponsible with the degree of their irrationality and therefore the need for caution. In short, a satisfactory Type I Deterrent for the United States must provide an objective basis for Soviet calculations that no matter how skillful, ingenious, or optimistic they are, and no matter how negatively they view their alternatives in a desperate crisis, an attack on the United States would entail a very high risk, indeed virtually guarantee an unacceptable large-scale destruction of Soviet civil society and military forces. As has been pointed out, such a Type I Deterrent may be difficult to achieve because there are many possible asymmetries in thermonuclear war that could favor a decision to attack in a paper calculation, and perhaps in the decision maker's mind.

(2) TYPE II DETERRENCE

One can distinguish at least three important deterrent situations, the first of which we have just described. The second, which we will call Type II Deterrence, is the deterrence of extremely provocative actions short of an attack upon the

United States itself by threat of a large attack on the Soviet Union. Although statements by the public officials are sometimes contradictory on this subject (e.g., nuclear war is unthinkable, but we will start one if the Soviets attack West Berlin), the United States does have solemn treaty obligations which, as these obligations are normally envisaged, could be honored in no other way. At some future date, the non-nuclear capability of NATO may be sufficient to repel a large but conventional attack on Western Europe. Until this time Western Europe will probably depend, at least in part, on Type II Deterrence (or Controlled Reprisal) to deter such attacks.

One basic distinction between Type I and Type II Deterrence is that Type I requires us to launch a counterattack after the enemy has launched an attack on our forces; Type II envisages a reprisal attack by our undamaged, and, at the moment, unthreatened forces. Although many people are willing to accept Type I Deterrence as being defensive, and therefore appropriate, they reject the Type II Deterrence objective as bellicose, aggressive, or tending to stimulate the arms race. They handle the problems of Type II Deterrence either by denying they can arise, by advocating various lesser and seemingly safer responses, or by redefining Type II Deterrence as a kind of Type I Deterrence. A typical attitude is, "The Soviets will never attack Europe without attacking the United States first, or at the same time. It would be too dangerous for them" (i.e., the Type II Deterrence they do not wish to discuss will deter the Soviets successfully). Let us consider some of the possibilities, however.

As the acquisition of relatively invulnerable strategic capabilities by both sides proceeds, the balance of terror grows firmer. The threat, or even the implied threat, of all-out war becomes less credible, hence less useful, as a deterrent. While it is by no means inevitable, one can easily imagine that by the late sixties or early seventies a reliable balance of terror between the Soviet Union and the United States could be achieved. Under these circumstances, the use by a rational (or at least rational-appearing) decision maker of Type II Deterrence will not be feasible.

Many people believe that the same can be said of the early and mid-'60s. Although we cannot now rely as much on the use of strategic threats as we could ten years ago, this does not mean there is no role for the strategic threat. All it means is that it plays a lesser role than it did in the recent past. This in turn means we must have more limited-war and other types of capabilities discussed under Type III Deterrence. But for the time being it is more a question of degree than of kind.

If we had no forces capable of Type II Deterrence and no possibility of an adequate level of Controlled Reprisal, the Soviets would know that they need not compromise in any crisis with one of our allies; they could achieve their goals merely by pressing hard enough. In such a case, we might take limited actions which would make their victory costly but not prohibitively so. It is easy to see what a bargaining advantage the Soviets would hold over our allies or neutrals. By pressing hard they might be able to achieve their goals painlessly. If, however, they guessed wrong and "went too far," they still would not suffer disaster since, by assumption, we would not use our SAC in reprisal. Our ally, however, would be risking total catastrophe at each step of the negotiations. The Soviets could even afford to be careless about getting into crises and staking a lot on "winning" them. In fact, a reputation for such carelessness would enhance their bargaining ability. In brief, then, if strategic forces are outmoded for Type II Deterrence objectives, we must develop new forces and policies until some more satisfactory and effective system of world order and security can be developed. Unsatisfactory and dangerous as Type II Deterrence may be, the interim measures may prove to be worse.

It is sometimes thought that the vulnerability of the U.S. forces is irrelevant to Type II Deterrence because in this case we would be attacking first. This is not correct. In order for Type II Deterrence to be effective, we would first have to possess a secure Type I Deterrent force. Otherwise an enemy might be tempted to preempt in any situation where he thought the use of our Type II Deterrence likely or possible. Moreover, in order to use our Type II Deterrence effectively, we must also have a reasonably strong position in Improved War Outcome. Only in such a case will our threat to attack be credible.

Another misconception concerning Type II Deterrence involves the distinction between active and passive deterrence. An active deterrent, as the name implies, requires an act of will on the part of the deterrer for the threat to be translated into action. In a passive deterrent the change from a contingent threat to an act is simply the result of an unthinking or unwilled response to the provocation. Many people regard Type I Deterrence as automatically passive and Type II Deterrence as necessarily active. Under current conditions, neither assumption may be completely valid.

In the first place, Type I Deterrence may not be so passive as is normally envisaged. If, for example, the Soviets destroyed a small number of initial strategic targets in the United States —let us say, a command and control headquarters—we would not know whether this had occurred by accident, through unauthorized behavior, as a Controlled Reprisal, or as a deliberate attempt to degrade our capability in order to pave the way for a full-scale attack. It would be difficult to imagine our reacting with an all-out attack. In this situation we might prefer to investigate, negotiate, or at most trade with the Soviets in some *quid pro quo* fashion, as in a Controlled Reprisal, and hope that this would discourage them from repeating their transgression. The handling of this type of situation should hardly be automatic.

Second, Type II Deterrence may exist in some degree even without an act of will. In some situations, it may be completely unthinking. The kinds of provocative actions which the Soviets would have to take in order to justify our use of Type II Deterrence would in themselves automatically entail some risk of war by escalation, by accident, by miscalculation, by unauthorized behavior, or by sheer anger, without a really deliberative decision having been made. Therefore, a considerable, perhaps even sufficient, degree of Type II Deterrence might be obtained through such "passive" mechanisms.

Although the case for the sufficiency of passive measures to achieve Type II Deterrence is plausible, it can be made too strongly; there are tactics available to the Soviets which they could explore and probe with relative safety if we had no military systems requiring an act of will on our part before they could be put into motion. The Soviets can teach us to be prudent. If our forces or our willingness to use them to achieve Type II Deterrence objectives were sufficiently weak, the Soviets could use tactics which would decrease the operable area of passive Type II Deterrence—perhaps to the vanishing point. For example, we cannot afford to let an enemy believe he can safely make multiple small limited attacks on our military forces either in or outside of the United States. Cumulatively, these attacks might degrade our military system to the point where it was but a precarious Type I Deterrent, while no particular attack was sufficiently provocative to touch off a mutual homicide reaction.

The distinction between Type I and Type II Deterrence has implications for suitable war plans. An attack keyed to Type II Deterrence objectives might well be all-out in the sense of using all the military resources we have. This, however, does not mean it should be uncontrolled or unlimited. All other things being equal, such an attacker should use a Counterforce or a Counterforce Plus Avoidance strategy. Such an attacker would not be trying to punish the defender, but to influence his behavior and reduce his military and political capability. The attacker can best achieve this goal by fighting as carefully controlled a war as possible. If the attacker avoids unnecessarily provoking the defender, the defender's rationality and his fear of reprisal might induce him to fight in a similiar manner. Such an attacker should simultaneously be making definite offers to terminate the war on a mutually advantageous (as compared to continuing war) basis. In a Type II Deterrence situation, these would most likely include an offer to return to the status quo which was disturbed by the initial provocation. Of course, in many situations a return to the status quo might not be sufficiently comforting to either side. At this point there may be hope for a more fundamental solution.

The relation of war plans to Type I Deterrence is far more complicated. Our response might depend upon both the military and civilian damage we had sustained. It might also be influenced by intra-war negotiations or blackmail. A rigid war plan which commits to Countervalue retaliation maximizes Type I Deterrence. However, even a flexible war plan which might easily result in a Counterforce Reprisal, could not be relied on by the enemy as being reliably and solely Counterforce.

The notion of Controlled Reprisal sees each side engaging in a series of tit-for-tat attacks (nuclear or non-nuclear) whose objective is not the destruction of the other side's military power but the destruction of his resolve. Each side attempts by threats and actual punishment to force the other side to compromise or back down. The Controlled Counterforce, on the other hand, visualizes reciprocal attacks on each other's military power with the object of destroying the opponent's Countervalue retaliatory capability to the point where it begins to be a doubtful Type I Deterrent. The Controlled Counterforce tries to extend deterrence to the intra-war period by using the threat of reprisal or escalation to induce the other side to avoid non-military bonus or collateral damage, perhaps even at the cost of handicapping military operations. If the intra-war deterrence does not break down completely, the war will end by negotiation (perhaps preceded by a period of Controlled Reprisal). The stakes in this negotiation will be the surviving people and resources; the cards will include the surviving offense, active defense, passive defense, Command and Control, and such imponderables as resolve, deception, and morale. If the intra-war deterrence does break down, then the failure of the restraints may result in much less destruction, since the controlled phase of the war may see a massive attrition or degradation of the forces available to one side or the other. If (or as) the balance of terror becomes more stable we can expect to see more study and discussion of the theory and practice of Controlled Reprisal and Controlled Counterforce.

(3) IMPROVED WAR OUTCOME

By Improved War Outcome, we do not restrict ourselves to making the military outcome better, though this is included. We also include lessening the destruction we suffer as well as remaining able to negotiate as beneficial a settlement as possible. Because war could come even if we had the most effective Type I Deterrence, it would be dangerous to rely completely on deterrence working. Our nation therefore must also have the ability to fight, survive, and terminate a war. The major argument for having such an ability is identical with the usual arguments for life insurance, safety belts, and lifeboats. . . .

A capability to survive and terminate wars may also be essential to the freedom of action necessary to Type II and Type III Deterrence. The objectives guiding our development of an Improved War Outcome capability will influence the kinds of systems we will procure.

The ability to survive and terminate wars requires more than the survival of adequate offensive and defensive forces during the enemy attack. Our forces must also have an effective endurance over days and perhaps weeks. Unfortunately, when one looks at many of the new weapons systems, this requirement seems to be much neglected in both design and operation. The most startling inadequacy, however, is not in the military weapons systems, but in our neglect of civil defense. . . .

(4) STABILITY

Almost everyone, expert and layman alike, worries about the possibility of war starting inadvertently, through mechanical or human error, false alarm, or unauthorized behavior, or as a result of some miscalculation in the process of the dangerous international analogue of the game of chicken. We must design our security system to lessen these possibilities. This can be done in two basic ways: First, we can reduce the probability that incidents of the above sort can occur; second, and even more important, we can reduce the probability that such incidents could actually lead to war. After all, it is decisions, not incidents that cause war.

The most important requirement of a stable strategic system is that it not be "trigger-happy." Its survival must not depend upon quick decisions in ambiguous circumstances. A well-protected system able to "ride out" an attack and respond later can provide commanders with the essential time for careful evaluations and decisions, thus improving stability.

The likelihood of accidents and wrong decisions will also be greater to the extent that we do not have centralized Command and Control of forces, together with confidence by local command in their ability to survive attack. Decentralized decision-making about whether we are at war, who the enemy is, or even which war plan should be executed, will increase the likelihood of unauthorized actions or wrong decisions. A vulnerable centralized system can be disastrous even if it is not in fact destroyed. So long as local commanders suspect its vulnerability, they will be encouraged to act on their own if unable to communicate with the central command even though it may turn out that the situation was due to a peacetime accident and not enemy action. The local commander who doesn't know may feel pressured to do something before he is destroyed. Thus a vulnerable Command and Control system may not only act improperly when an attack really has occurred, it may also act improperly if no attack occurs.

To summarize: If the strategic forces on both sides are well enough protected so that there is no necessity for either side to make any rushed decisions, and if the centralized Command and

Control systems are reliable, it is difficult to see how a war could start inadvertently.

(5) COMPREHENSIVE ARMS CONTROL

Many thoughtful and responsible students of the arms race believe that our present international order with its emphasis on unconditional national sovereignty, national egoism, nuclear deterrence, and national military forces is not going to last out the century, and perhaps not more than a decade or two. Many of those holding this belief do not deny that many successful adjustments have already been made to modern technology. They recognize the important, but often neglected fact, that the current arms race is not as uncontrolled as would be the case were narrow military, technological, and economic factors the exclusive determinants of military research, development, procurement and operations. Indeed, when compared to the inherent technological possibilities, the current arms race looks more like a walk rather than a race because it is so limited by political, social, moral, economic and doctrinal constraints on the participants. These constraints and adjustments doubtless "buy" time, but many believe that they do not buy enough time, under the given conditions, for the system to adjust itself satisfactorily by the usual processes of gradual evolution. It still seems likely that we will change the system "consciously" or, despite feasible shortrun safeguards, that it will "blow up." By "blow up," I mean a sudden and violent change in the system caused by cataclysmic events with little opportunity, in advance, to influence the shape of the new world which might result.

I will not discuss here any of the many proposals for achieving comprehensive arms control through negotiations or slow development. This is clearly the "natural" or preferred way for the system to develop. These changes can, however, also occur as a result of a war.

If the system does blow up in a war or a violent crisis, it is somewhat unlikely, perhaps most unlikely, that it will result in an "end of history." It is more likely to be a very serious crisis whose "solution" involves major structural changes in the international scene; it may be one of the "small" thermonuclear wars I have already discussed, followed by a viable peace; it may even be a large thermonuclear war but one which is not an Armageddon. It is difficult to

visualize—at least in the sixties—a likely sequence of events that would set back either the population or the wealth of the world by more than a generation or so. Catastrophic as this would be, it would not be an "end to history" or even an end to civilization. However great a misfortune it would be, we are not barred from noting that greater misfortunes could occur. The term comprehensive arms control should be taken not only as covering mutually desirable measures likely to decrease the probability of war, but similar measures that decrease the damage that is done if deterrence fails.

(6) TYPE III DETERRENCE

I place in this general category all the ways in which our strategic military capability can deter "provocative" and encourage "acceptable" behavior, other than by the threat of immediate "all-out" thermonuclear war. This includes the ordinary limited war, the use of all kinds of mobilizations and demonstration tactics, the show of force, and, finally, some types of controlled war as are envisaged in a Controlled Reprisal or a low-level Controlled Counterforce attack.

Type III Deterrence is a catch-all category, covering under one heading most of the important foreign policy and military problems that actually arise. It may seem strange to use one heading for all of these, and five others to cover the nuances of thermonuclear war. I feel it is valuable to direct attention to the many interactions between the more common and immediate problems and those more directly associated with strategic warfare. This approach may seem excessively narrow to many planners, but I suspect that this is partly because most of the intellectual effort in the United States and Europe has been concentrated in the areas of Type III Deterrence and on arms control, to the almost complete neglect of the problems of the use of strategic forces. Any formulation concerned mainly with strategic forces as something which might be used deliberately or inadvertently meets with resistance not so much because it is narrow (which it is), but because of the distasteful nature of the questions such possibilities raise.

My formulation does, however, obscure some important points. Some of these obscurities can be seen by examining the following chart [Table 18–1] illustrating a six-fold division of the range of deterrence situations.

TABLE 18–1   Different Deterrent Situations

	Provocation		
Reprisal	*Strike Against U.S.*	*Extreme Provocation*	*Other Provocation*
Some kind of "All-Out Attack"	I	II	Y
Other	α	β	III

I have talked much about deterrence Types I, II, and III. This automatically focused attention on these situations and shifted it away from what could be called deterrence Types α, β, and Y. Types α and β Deterrence would correspond to a unilateral renunciation of the all-out use of nuclear weapons in favor of action lower on the scale of violence. As already discussed, much current military thinking is concentrated on the area of Type β Deterrence—the use of Controlled Reprisal or Limited War to deter or correct even the most extreme provocation or attacks. As discussed in the next chapter this merges into Types I and II Deterrence as soon as Controlled Wars are considered. Types α and β Deterrence also include the non-nuclear responses to a Soviet attack that are recommended by many of the peace and unilateral disarmament groups. Type Y Deterrence would correspond to the usual interpretation of the Dulles massive retaliation philosophy. This concept was probably obsolete when it was formally promulgated in early 1954 and has, in effect, been replaced by giving Type III Deterrence an expanded role.

Type III Deterrence capability is and will probably remain most important for the foreseeable future. Even if we were to achieve a strategic superiority over the Soviets so that there was a relatively one-sided balance of terror, our freedom of action would not be greatly larger than it is today. Even a relatively small strategic force may be sufficiently destructive to make deterrence into a two-way street. Moreover, even if we could not be severely damaged, we would still be obliged to use self-restraint in the use of force. At the least, excessive amounts would not be appropriate; the punishment should fit the crime. Lastly, our use of thermonuclear threats, if it is to be consistent with our other policies, must look and be both prudent and rational. We cannot go around threatening to blow up a major portion of the world, or attempt to get our way by looking insane and dauntless. These strategies might be available to a totalitarian nation. They are not available to us, a democratic nation in a democratic alliance. Strategies overly dependent on resolve, on committing first, on extreme use of the rationality of irrationality, are not likely to succeed even if attempted by the West.

A more thoroughgoing discussion of the many kinds of deterrent situations would doubtless divide the row labeled "other" into many distinct categories: for example, limited nuclear strategic reprisal, limited nuclear tactical reprisal, use of conventional weapons, and then various non-military responses. At this point the discussion would get unwieldy. I chose the categorizations I did, because I wanted to emphasize the distinction between deterrence Types I, II, and III and because some of our major problems concern these situations. If and when we arrive at a firm balance of terror with the Soviets, then the many situations included in α and β are likely to become more important so far as policy discussions are concerned. In the still more confused situation when there are many countries with large nuclear weapon systems, a completely different terminology may need to be devised to focus on the, as yet unknown, major issues.

19   The Soviet View of Deterrence: A General Survey

John Erickson

In the course of some recent exchanges on Soviet military science and Soviet military organisation, my perceptive colleague Professor Roger Beaumont from Texas A & M University enjoined me to read (or rather, to reread) an article on Russian military development by Edward L. Katzenbach, erstwhile consultant to the United States Air Force.[1] This proved to be a most revealing exercise, for while the article pointedly referred to 'a serious lag in Soviet strategic thinking'—lag which amounted to three years at least by this calculation—the markedly condescending judgement was supplemented by a platitude which deserved more attention, namely, that Russians do not necessarily think like Americans. Both these observations merit some closer inspection, for their relevance persists to the present day. The disdain shown towards the quality (or lack of quality) in Soviet strategic thinking was a marked feature of the 1960s, rooted in the supposed intellectual superiority of American sophistication in matters of 'deterrent theory' and encouraging the notion that during the SALT I process the Americans would perforce initiate the Russians into the mysteries of deterrent theory and the complexities of nuclear war. To general discomfiture, it soon became apparent that the Russians needed no tutoring in matters pertaining to war in general and nuclear war in particular, that there was a singular cogency to Soviet strategic thinking and that Russians did not necessarily think like Americans. While Western specialists in stra-

tegic theory refined their concepts of 'deterrence' into ever more complex (and arcane) theorems, a kind of nuclear metaphysics, the Soviet command had worked much more closely within classically configured military concepts, inducing at once a much greater degree of military and political realism into what in American parlance is termed their 'mind-set'. Belated though this recognition of Soviet realism was, it had one unfortunate aspect, that Katzenbach's platitude went unremarked. Not only Western terminology but also Western preferences were frequently superimposed on the Soviet scene, even to the point of interpreting Soviet weapons programmes in terms of a *Western* rationale for such programmes, particularly the transposition of the notion of 'first strike'.

This process, long established though now subject to some limited change, has had damaging, not to say dangerous results; and paradoxically it could be said that this most abstract of items—let us call it 'doctrine' by way of intellectual shorthand—may well prove to be the most potent factor in the strategic equation. Indeed, it is becoming ever more apparent that improved mutual understanding of doctrine is a prerequisite of effective arms limitation and arms control as opposed to confining the matter to technicalities of weapons systems. True asymmetry may lie in doctrine (and perceptions) rather than in disparate numbers of weapons and characteristics of their presumed performance. By the same token, the dovish argument that there is actual convergence in doctrine (where no such convergence exists and where insufficient recognition is accorded to the factor of sheer military weight in Soviet priorities) can be misleading, while paradoxically the hawkish deprecation of American political will and the exaggeration of American vulnerabilities is yet another damaging distortion, leading in turn to crude over-simplifications of Soviet doctrine, all duly transmuted into a form of strategic demonology. While it would be mistaken to regard Soviet doctrine as an absolute master-plan prescribing all strategic objectives—including winning a nuclear war—it is equally feckless to be dismissive about (or ignorant of) doctrine as an indicator of *Soviet* perceptions of the deterrence process, of threat profiles, force structures and military precautions so involved (what I called 'deterring against what, with what') and, finally, of that military-operational provision relevant to the collapse of deterrence.[2]

That latter point is the nub of the matter. If Soviet realism and adherence to military orthodoxy has inculcated a persistent scepticism towards the metaphysics of deterrence, if Soviet political attitudes preclude placing any reliance on the goodwill (or rationality) of an adversary and if Soviet practice precludes any mutuality which would imply dependence on an adversary for even a particle of Soviet security, this is still some distance from postulating the rejection of deterrence as it might be generally understood in favour of viewing nuclear war as a rational instrument of policy and, moreover, as a process which is winnable. I am not suggesting that doctrine *tout court* will elucidate all problems inherent in Soviet strategic policies, but there is a case for some inspection of the more recent Soviet pronouncements and analyses. And therein lies a small irony, for if two decades ago Edward Katzenbach was pointing to the 'serious' lag in Soviet strategic thinking, at this juncture Soviet specialists point to the 'serious lag' in Western appreciation of Soviet doctrine; appreciation and evaluation which rely on sources which if not actually outmoded have become inevitably passé—for example, the stylised recourse to Marshal Sokolovskii's *Voennaya strategiya (Military Strategy).*[3] The convenient myth of Soviet nuclear troglodytes seemingly died hard, only to be replaced by the equally distorted simulacrum of Soviet nuclear supermen.

PEACE AND WAR, DETERRENCE AND DEFENCE

It is impossible to evaluate Soviet perceptions of 'deterrence' without some brief inspection of general Soviet theories of armed conflict, what might be called 'official doctrine' designed to suggest guidelines for weapons programmes in time of peace and rules for the use of such force in wartime. Such a sustained effort has produced a voluminous and complex literature (little of which is known in the West) and in which the *leitmotif* is the insistence that while nuclear weapons have clearly changed the character of any future war, they have in no way altered the essence (*sushchnost*) of war as a *political* phenomenon, to be understood as such. While it is frequently said that the Soviet view is 'Clausewitzian', in fact Lenin modified Clausewitz's dictum to read *'imperialist* wars are a violent extension of the politics of imperialism', where the essence of imperialism must generate chronic conflict. In this search for the 'laws of armed conflict' Soviet theory also departs from Clausewitz in refusing to regard wars as isolated phenomena: rather they have common features which inevitably involve 'the masses', as well as demonstrating various patterns in the relationship between war and politics.[4]

Further to this search for laws and predictability, Soviet military doctrine (*voennaya doktrina*) is concerned specifically with disclosing 'the nature of contemporary wars which may be unleashed by the imperialists', as well as formulating the missions of the Soviet armed forces, specifying military-operational methods involved and estimating what is required in the way of defence preparations: Soviet military science (*voennaya nauka*) contributes analyses drawn from past wars and present weapons performance, while military art (*voennoe iskusstvo*) develops operational, battlefield methods. Thus, to the political awareness which is fundamental to the Soviet outlook must be added the infusion of military ideas which have a strongly orthodox cast about them. Both elements fuse in the notion that the essence of war has not been changed by nuclear weapons, that the nuclear weapon is not an absolute which has made war unthinkable—on the contrary, the situation must be thought through, into the situation where deterrence could well fail, or where it could be undermined by the malevolence of the imperialist camp. The nuclear weapon has not made conventional weapons superfluous; on the contrary, a flexible composition of military force is essential, exemplified in the Soviet 'combined-arms' concept. Whether any future war be long or short, large standing armies are indispensable: in what could well be a nuclear battle in the accepted sense of battle, the Soviet forces cannot remain inert, committed to absorbing an enemy strike and then lashing out in some indiscriminate punitive response—deterrence by punishment. And after the near catastrophe of June 1941 when German armies were launched against the Soviet Union, it is inconceivable that any Soviet leadership will countenance absorbing any initial strike.

It follows, therefore, that this outlook places a premium on defence in the first instance, so that defence and deterrence must go hand in hand: the massive Soviet programme of defence (both active and passive) needs little or no advertising, though it has been the cause of misgiving and misunderstanding. Ironically, the Soviet interest in defence, including an extensive civil defence programme, fuelled American fears that here was indeed a major ingredient of a first-strike policy (with the Soviet Union taking major steps to protect itself), while Soviet opinion saw in the lack of a defence programme in the United States more than a hint that American policy was essentially one of first strike, surprise attack, an annihilating blow which would perforce elminate any retaliation, with the prime emphasis on offensive forces in a high state of alert.

It is here that Soviet reference to the possibility of 'victory' in the context of general nuclear war makes what to many is a disquieting, even alarming appearance. This is an issue which requires some careful consideration, beyond the rather simplistic assertion that such statements confirm absolute Soviet belief in surviving and winning a nuclear war, indeed might even encourage any Soviet leadership actually to think of nuclear war as a rational instrument of policy. Are we talking about 'victory' and 'survival' being synonymous, or as separate elements? It would seem that stereotyped statements affirming that in the event of an American/imperialist attack on the Socialist camp the latter system would prove superior and axiomatically survive, are little more than expressions of ideological conviction, or ideological rectitude. However, once the discussion closes more immediately on the operational features of any nuclear war, the tone changes.[5] Soviet professional military writing (as opposed to that of the political officers) proclaims a much more cautious line, eschewing the notion that capitalist society will collapse like a pack of cards and demonstrating a ready appreciation of American second-strike capability to inflict a horrendous scale of damage on the USSR. By the same token, there is implicit recognition that rapid and total escalation is the most likely contingency arising from any so-called 'limited'

war, speedily involving the full range of US strategic capabilities. This is the Soviet view.

Rhetoric and realism are obviously in conflict here. It is eminently understandable that political officers, responsible for moral and party-political education, should stress the superiority of the Socialist system and its potential for victory, but this is a far cry from asserting a military-operational reality. On the contrary, the military press stresses the unprecedented scale of damage following a nuclear attack, the huge volume of casualties and devastations of whole countries; observations supplemented very recently by the widespread publicity accorded to the exchanges between Soviet and American doctors on the effects of nuclear war, supplemented by the latest Ascot meeting.[6] While it is certainly impossible to specify just what 'unacceptable damage' would mean in the Soviet context (with one Western argument using the figure of Soviet losses in 1941–5 as evidence that the Soviet Union is somehow inured to a higher level of unacceptable damage), informed Soviet opinion seems inclined to the view that the scale of damage and loss would be unprecedented.

We should return, however, to the point of nuclear war as a means of politics, a rational instrument of policy. The possibility of nuclear war is recognised in terms of the Marxist-Leninist theory relating to the causes of war at large, namely, as a *political* product of a society composed of antagonistic classes pursuing competitive aims. Thus, the question of the essence of any future nuclear war must be kept separate from the other issue, the acceptability (or otherwise) of nuclear war as an *instrument* of policy.[7] On the whole, Soviet opinion seems to hold that nuclear war is not a rational instrument of policy, for means and ends lose any significance when the cost of destroying the enemy amounts to self-annihilation.

To take this logic a little further and returning to the fundamental tenet of the political essence of war, it is reasonable to infer that the sole contingency which could persuade any Soviet leadership of the 'rationality' of nuclear war in pursuit of policy would be the unassailable, incontrovertible, dire evidence that the United States was about to strike the Soviet Union: the political end would be the very survival of the Soviet Union through 'striking first in the last resort', to use Mr. Malcolm Mackintosh's succinct phrase. Yet this form of 'rationality' is almost too fearsome to contemplate, hence the specific form of Soviet deterrence—to prevent the very emergence of that cataclysmic contingency.

In general, the role of military power is seen from the Soviet side as a major instrument in impressing on the 'imperialist camp that military means cannot solve the historical struggle between the two opposing social systems, at the same time reducing (if not actually eliminating) the prospect of military gain at the expense of the Socialist camp. Putting this into the context of deterrent theory, while it might be said that the United States has embraced a concept of 'deterrence by punishment', the Soviet position is one of 'deterrence by denial'.[8] Obviously this is a somewhat simplified picture which must be developed in some detail, but it is worth noting that the terminology used in the Soviet Union to discuss deterrence tends to reflect this dichotomy. In the 1960s (and again in the 1980s) the Western deterrent concept has been defined as *ustrashenie* (which has a clear hint of threatening intimidation), while the Soviet stance is registered by the word *sderzhivanie* (conveying a sense of constraining and restraining an opponent, with even the word *oborona*—defence— used in a deterrence context).[9] As we shall shortly see, this is more than mere semantic hair-splitting.

Some qualifications: While it is true that the Soviet leadership regards the capability to wage nuclear war—in terms of military preparation —as a major element of a visible deterrent, this does not indicate any preference for or inclination towards regarding nuclear war as a rational instrument of policy: even more, Soviet deterrent policies are designed to minimise the incentives for attacking the USSR and, above all, are aimed at preventing the outbreak of hostilities. This is 'denial' in an absolute sense. Certainly, this does imply reliance on Soviet capabilities rather than on enemy rationality or goodwill, the supreme importance of retaining the initiative and a certain scepticism about 'crisis management' when the crisis is (or could be) so apocalyptic. Thus, we have here not a commitment to 'war-avoidance' but to 'war-denial' (if that phrase can be admitted): at the same time, this does suggest some reduction in the notion of 'mutuality', where the Soviet Union is not willing to be dependent on an adversary for any element of its security, but, even more important, sees in the notion of mutuality in assured destruction nothing less than a disguise of what is essentially a US counter force (and

first-strike) policy. Here we must return to the perception of the American notion of 'deterrence by punishment', which must be expanded to include 'compellence' which embraces 'escalation dominance' and connects military superiority with political, global dominance. Thus, the Soviet Union is to be 'deterred' into accepting this situation, where 'compellence' and 'extended deterrence' reflect an offensive military-political posture and commitment.

Mutuality is further diminished by the fact that while the Americans spoke of mutual assured destruction (MAD), in effect American policy was designed to increase counter-force capabilities: witness the MX missile programme, the Trident submarine-launched ballistic missile (SLBM) programme and the improvement in forward-based systems (FBS) which simply amounted to outflanking the SALT agreements. Even worse, Presidential Directive 59 (PD-59) allegedly reflected the real intent of US policy, reinforced and supported by the release of previously secret US documents such as the operational plan Dropshot.[10] US policy is designed to legitimise nuclear war by making the idea of limited nuclear war more feasible and thus more acceptable, resulting in a lowering of the nuclear threshold. A Eurostrategic nuclear war might then be pursued, leaving the USSR open to attack but giving sanctuary to the United States. Behind all this lies the intent of establishing (or re-establishing) escalation dominance and thus intimidating the USSR, or so the Soviet leadership reads the present situation.

While admitting the unremitting hostility of the adversary, Soviet military planners must take account in their deterrent calculations of the NATO theatre nuclear forces (TNF) modernization, which is seen as nothing less than a larger US design to regain military superiority. The idea is to tie NATO ever more closely into US strategic planning, to divert or to deflect Soviet counter-action towards Europe (rather than against the United States itself) and to adjust the overall strategic balance in American favour. More pertinently, the new weapons—above all, the Pershing II—can only be regarded as a first-strike counter force weapon, improving by a factor of ten the capabilities of Pershing I and capable of destroying not only inter-continental ballistic missile (ICBM) silos but also command and control centres[11]. What must impress Soviet military specialists is that the Pershing II has a flight time to target of only 4–6 minutes (as opposed to an ICBM which takes up to 30 minutes to reach its target): thus, with such a short flight time to target, the Pershing II nullifies any Soviet resort to launch under warning and even launch under attack. Apparently the Soviet General Staff is prepared to regard the Pershing II range of 1500 miles (up to 2600 kms) as the truly effective range of the new missile, a figure which would mean much wider target coverage.

If we add the cruise missile, the Soviet sense of vulnerability can only deepen, leading to a denial concept without any measure of adequacy since it depends crucially on over-insurance—hence the preoccupation, not to say the obsession, with numbers and some numerical hedge of advantage. It is fair to comment here that this is not only a doctrinal requirement but one which also represents a number of bureaucratic and institutional interests (the Soviet equivalent of the military-industrial complex); yet by a fierce irony it is precisely this numerical fixation which will provide the coming crisis for Soviet deterrence policies. At the moment, the Soviet interpretation is that PD-59 plus NATO's TNF deployment plans amount to nothing less than an American push for superiority *tout court*, together with an attempt to implement a Eurostrategic variant for limited nuclear war.

The Soviet rejection of the idea of limited nuclear war is axiomatic, based as it is in the political notion that *political* objectives—not the performance of particular weapons—decree the essence or scope of war: it follows, therefore, that if American objectives are unlimited in the sense of regaining military superiority and escalation dominance over the USSR, then any war operation cannot be limited, whatever the technicalities of the weaponry involved. At the same time Soviet attention is concentrated on the offensive nature of US 'deterrent forces', where counter force targeting was—and has remained—a prime US interest, bringing Soviet nuclear delivery systems into the tight focus of such a targeting philosophy. 'Punishment' was allegedly only part of the story: American lack of interest in defence (active and passive) pointed to a singular approach to deterrence, with important destabilising implications, while American emphasis on mutual assured destruction seemed to be in sharp contradiction to the development of a counter force capability.[12] The critical point for Soviet deterrence comes with the recognition that US counter force capability is not only expanding but will continue to expand in excess of a comparable Soviet capability.

Deterrence modes. We have already seen that the Soviet concept of deterrence is rooted in 'denial', designed to prevent the United States from the actual initiation of hostilities, to reduce the prospect of making military gains at the expense of the Socialist camp (a commitment which has steadily committed the Soviet Union to a global role), to assure the survival of the Soviet system (hence the priority accorded to strategic defence) and, through the development of actual military (war-fighting) capability, to minimise the incentives for attacking the USSR by guaranteeing counter-strike—hence the mix of pre-emptive and secondary retaliatory forces. What has certainly become increasingly prominent in Soviet military-political thinking is the idea of a more protracted war—should it come to war—with consequent emphasis on survivability and sustainability, including wartime force reconstitution. (One recent effect of Soviet command reorganization has been to blur the previous sharp distinction between strategic and tactical force elements, presumably in an effort to provide greater flexibility: a visible manifestation of this process is the greater autonomy now allowed to Soviet theatre commanders.)

On the other hand, for all the augmentation of military capability, Soviet military opinion cautions against any 'adventurist strategy' which might prematurely initiate a total struggle when the requisite 'correlation of forces' (*soot-noshenie sil*) cannot assure a favourable outcome (even 'victory') in such a struggle: as for the notion of a *blitzkrieg*, one Soviet general emphasized that 'blitz war can only lead to a blitz collapse'. *Blitzkrieg* for its own sake can only mean assuming unacceptable (and uncontrollable) risk: though the surprise factor has been enormously enhanced, the blitz solution does not seem to recommend itself to Soviet military planners, who have argued that the effect of modern weapons has been to extend the duration of war, as well as increasing its intensity, so that the interconnection of strategy, economics and the morale factor has assumed a correspondingly greater significance.

While eschewing any adventurist blitz strategy, Soviet military doctrine draws on its own established orthodoxy in linking military principles—speed, surprise, shock, fire-power the winning of the initiative—with what might be called the Soviet nuclear outlook. It is easy enough to label this after Western styles, such as 'pre-emption' or 'first strike', but I think this is better described as a preference for a strategic 'disruptive strike', not unlike Soviet artillery practice in World War II when the artillery *kontrpodgotovka* fired off its delicately-timed fire blow designed to disrupt enemy preparations for attack (it is worth noting that the Soviet missile forces were first developed by officers who had an artillery background). Equally, the Soviet principle of 'a succession of fires' (developed by military theorists in the 1930s) is also applied to the nuclear battle; hence we see Soviet strategic missile forces not only organized into 'missile armies' (with divisions, regiments, battalions and batteries) but also with first and second echelons, plus reserves. Yet the strategic disruptive strike may not succeed entirely, thus precipitating more protracted war and the utilisation of the 'combined-arms' forces; nuclear, conventional and chemical all interacting in land, sea and air operations with ICBM support.

Much confusion arises from over-simplification relating to the Soviet mode of simultaneously working to prevent nuclear war and also preparing to wage such a war, should it occur. The Soviet leadership with its military and political segments has no wish to embark on nuclear war, an outlook which seems to have wide popular support; and in this sense war-avoidance is fundamental to Soviet policies. But that immediate transposition of a Western term is somewhat misleading. The essence of Soviet deterrence is not the avoidance of war but the prevention of war—thus giving Soviet deterrence a positive, active cast. Here actual military capability has a prominent role—Soviet deterrence as restraint of the imperialists. There is mutuality of deterrence in recognizing that both sides have overwhelming capability to inflict unacceptable damage if nuclear war were to be initiated by any act of rational (or supposedly rational) calculation, but this cannot be construed as accepting the posture of hostage and thus denying any initiative to the Soviet Union, even to the point of forcing surrender upon it. A natural and inevitable scepticism pervaded the Soviet view of mutual assured destruction, not only because this ran counter to the principle of any dependence on a potential adversary for Soviet security, but more importantly because Soviet specialists perceived that the real issue was not MAD as such but rather that mutual deterrence in broad terms was being modified as the Americans moved away from deterrence via punishment and into greater emphasis on 'compellance', all with the aim of ensuring that 'US deterrence of the Soviet Union [will be] "more

efficient" than Soviet deterrence of the United States'.

'Deterring against what, with what': Threat profiles, force structures: In the United States and the 'imperialist camp' at large, the Soviet Union faces a formidable adversary, whose real purposes arguably are not disclosed by declaratory doctrinal positions (such as 'assured destruction' or even 'mutual assured destruction'). The reality in Soviet eyes lies in the American pursuit of war-waging counterforce capabilities with offensive strategic forces eminently capable of first strike: the 'punishment' concept has steadily given way to coercion and constraint, with counterforce capability growing constantly. American programmes, according to Professor Trofimenko (and others) are aimed at regaining unilateral deterrence, to which end the United States works to realign the balance in its own favour and to outflank the SALT agreements. As for counterforce capabilities and options, the Soviet side insists that their own recourse to such capabilities was a reaction to American initiatives and weapons programmes. In particular, the Schlesinger doctrine and more recently PD-59 are viewed as the development of a 'strategy of victory in a nuclear way through build-up of counterforce potential'.

In this counterforce context it is also important to recognize significant Soviet-American differences over what exactly comprises 'the balance': while Western sources evaluate the 'net balance' (ICBMs, SLBMs and long-range bombers as strategic weapons systems) Soviet reckoning perforce includes the Pershing II medium-range ballistic missile and the ground-launched cruise missile—due for deployment in Europe—as strategic components (if only because of the Soviet definition that any weapon which can strike the USSR is 'strategic', irrespective of its geographical basing). The same criterion is applied to the whole nexus of forward based systems (FBS), including land- and carrier-based aircraft. More pertinently, Pershing II with its high accuracy and extended range, is perceived not as a counterpart to restoring imbalance in theatre nuclear forces,[13] but expressly as a high-precision first-strike counterforce weapon: witness the 4–6 minute flight time of Pershing II to target, which effectively rules out launch on warning (assuming even rapid launch detection); and with strikes against Soviet missile silos and command and control centres, launch under attack will be hazardous if not actually impossible. In brief, the Soviet command sees itself facing the development of nothing less than a Eurostrategic nuclear capability associated with existing (and expanding) American offensive first-strike weaponry.

If such are Soviet preoccupations and perceptions (let me add the proviso here that these observations have been drawn almost exclusively from Soviet materials), it is worth examining briefly the present Soviet view of the 'correlation of forces', the strategic equation and Soviet effectiveness in terms of missions. In other words, what explains the Soviet military build-up? On the current count, Soviet strategic forces consist of 1398 ICBM launchers, 950 SLBM launchers and 156 inter-continental bombers (without Backfire), encompassing some 7000 nuclear warheads. The ICBM force is made up of 580 SS-11s, 60 SS-13s, 150 SS-17s, 308 SS-18s (the largest ICBM in the world) and 300 SS-19s, with the latter group (17s, 18s and 19s) carrying multiple warheads; while the submarine-launched missile, the SS-N-18, is the first Soviet SLBM to carry multiple warheads. The primary mission of the Soviet strategic missile forces is to destroy enemy means of nuclear attack (including command and control systems). Thus, while numbers are important, the progression of improvement in the Soviet ICBM force must be related to greater effectiveness against given target arrays. While concentrating on effectiveness against 'time-urgent hard targets', Soviet planners can now envisage attacking the entire hard and soft target array in the United States with a mix of Soviet systems. Also, the addition of heavy bombers and Soviet cruise missiles can at least provide some compensation for the growing vulnerability of land-based missiles, though the Soviet deterrent has not yet put to sea on anything like the American scale.

If there is any measure of sufficiency in Soviet force planning, then it must be reckoned against the requirement to cover the entire hard/soft target array with mixes of Soviet weapons, plus a survivable reserve—a position which is being steadily attained with the modernization of Soviet strategic forces. While launch on warning has been and remains part of the Soviet operational repertoire, the development of a survivable reserve force could have tempered this option. Refire and reload for Soviet ICBMs using the 'cold-launch' mode also provides a possible hedge for more protracted nuclear war, with a Soviet exercise in the autumn of 1980 rehearsing the reloading of 25–40 SS-18 silos over a period of 2–5 days (technically no breach of SALT, for this was not 'rapid reload' but tending to confirm the notion of the echeloning of missile armies).

The heart of the Soviet strategic system is the heavy bombardment force of 308 SS-18s (in two versions, MOD-1 with a single warhead, MOD-2 with 8-10 multiple warheads). While there is much talk about missile accuracy, the problem of reliability has recently come to the fore and must be introduced into projections of any attack mode. Discounting the reliability aspect, it can be made to seem that a relatively few Soviet ICBMs could wreak havoc on US silos, but this is to assume well nigh perfect performance: 125 SS-18s each with eight 1.5 megaton warheads could theoretically take out 1000 US silos, but Soviet prudence would dictate some insurance against equipment failure and assigning more war-heads (and more missiles) to wave attacks, each of diminished effectiveness.[14] 'High-confidence first-strike capability' (to use Dr. Schlesinger's phrase) is demonstrably an elusive animal, a point not lost on the Soviet command.

The Soviet ICBM structure, both present and planned, could well be seen as the best approach to the real world of the nuclear battle, with a high numerical ceiling for the heavy bombardment force and a recognition that multiple (wave) attacks on ICBM silos could be less effective than one-on-one attacks with heavy megatonnage; with the multiple warhead (MIRV) arsenal available for dealing with soft targets and also for cross-targeting Minuteman silos; and with MOD-2 (single warhead SS-17s and SS-19s) also assigned to the hard target array including command and control centres. Thus, the Soviet command will continue to have at least two heavy ICBM systems committed against the hard-target array, while SLBM systems will be improved and developed as a survivable reserve force.

There are, however, some disturbing problems which face Soviet planners. While there is undoubted Soviet advantage in 'time-urgent hard target kill capability', this is matched—some would say outweighed—by US 'discretionary force potential' (the capacity to meet its overall targeting plan). Here we come to the US MX missile, which poses a major threat to Soviet land-based ICBMs (where a large segment of the Soviet deterrent is housed; much larger than US land-based systems). The net result of deploying the MX would be the massive degradation of Soviet counter force/counter-strike forces, in which contingency the Soviet command would be forced to redeploy its submarine missiles to cover soft targets and thus deplete its crucial survivable reserve. In sum, the advent of MX must impose more severe dilemmas on Soviet planners than present Soviet 'time-urgent hard-target potential' poses to the Americans. Equally, the development of the B-1 bomber, the 'stealth bomber' and the loadings of air-launched cruise missiles (ALCMS) means urgent and necessary refurbishing of air defence systems, indeed of the entire Soviet system of strategic defence. Add to this the programme involved in modernizing the Soviet SLBM force (in terms of missile performance), and the modernizing of Soviet theatre nuclear systems, and the outlook is dispiriting, to say the least.

SUMMARY

To sum up, Soviet opinion from the outset was not inclined to accept what might be called the metaphysics of deterrence, or any arcane system of scholasticism which merely screened the American policy of containment: the Soviet Union was deterred and was intended to remain in that condition, all in the age of *ustrashenie* (the West's concept of deterrence). In the Soviet view, though American declaratory statements ostensibly committed US policy to concepts of nuclear sufficiency, in the real world—in the world of military procurement—the American build-up belied the notion of 'sufficiency' and American capabilities were being developed beyond those which could be identified with 'deterrence through punishment'. It was impossible, therefore, for the Soviet Union to subscribe to the mutuality of 'assured destruction' when military reality appeared to suggest further expansion of US counterforce capability: it was no part of Soviet policy to increase Soviet vulnerability nor to pinion the Soviet Union in a 'hostage' concept. As for mutual deterrence, it had to be a mutuality stripped of American attempts at coercion (compellance) and without resort to the reimposition of 'unilateral deterrence'. Yet another contradiction was that certain American attitudes professed war-avoidance and the 'unthinkability' of nuclear war, while the Soviet Union determined on war-prevention coupled with the acceptance of the possibility of nuclear war, an admixture which produced no small degree of confusion, acrimony and accusation in Western circles, certain of which insisted on the implacability of Soviet intentions in a quest for unchallenged military superi-

ority—thus demolishing deterrence and undermining any mutuality.

It is too easy to dismiss deterrence as some kind of word-game or a form of nuclear mumbo-jumbo meant to obscure the significance of nuclear weaponry, a form of academic-intellectual conspiracy on the part of 'strategists' against humanity. But if there is a fault, it may well be not that we have paid too much attention to this phenomenon but too little, particularly in the matter of perceptions and, specifically, Soviet perceptions. These require at the very least close inspection, fair evaluation and due application of mutuality: as a very senior Soviet official put it in the course of our 'Edinburgh Conversations on Survival in the Nuclear Age' (a meeting held at Edinburgh in October 1981), what is sauce for the goose should be sauce for the gander. Whatever the dispute over Soviet intentions and capabilities, whatever the disparagement of deterrence as a moral or metaphysical hoax, it is nevertheless fair to state unequivocally that it is no part of rational Soviet design to see our collective goose cooked.

NOTES

1. Edward L. Katzenbach Jr, 'Russian Military Development', *Current History*, November 1960, pp. 262–6.
2. See Benjamin Lambeth under 'Key Themes in Soviet Doctrine'. Pp. 108–9 in *Soviet Strategy*, John Baylis and Gerald Segal, eds. (Croom Helm, 1981).
3. See interview with Lt Gen. M. Milshtein, 'Moscow Expert Says US is Mistaken on Soviet War Strategy', *International Herald Tribune*, August 28, 1980. See also Professor Henry Trofimenko's study *Changing Attitudes towards Deterrence*, University of California ACIS Working Paper No. 25 (July 1980), Note No. 32 (p. 54).
4. See e.g. *Marksizm-leninizm o voine i armii* 5th edition (Moscow, Voenizdat, 1968), *Filosofskie nasledie V.I. Lenina i problemy sovremennoi voine* (Moscow, Voenizdat, 1972); M.V. Popov, *Sushchnost zakonov vooruzhennoi bor'by* (Moscow, Voenizdat, 1964); K.V. Tarakanov, *Matematika i vooruzhennaya bor'ba* (Mathematics and the Laws of Armed Combat) (Moscow, Voenizdat, 1974); *Metodologiya voenno-nauchnogo poznaniya* (Moscow, Voenizdat 1977) and I.A. Korotkov, *Istoraya sovetskoi vennoi mysli* (Moscow, Nauka, 1980).
5. See Robert L. Arnett, 'Soviet Attitudes Towards Nuclear War: Do they really think they can win?', *Journal of Strategic Studies*, Vol. 2, No. 2, September 1979, pp. 172–91.
6. See *The Guardian* report, 'Brezhnev's Doctor is

Anti-Bomb', 6 October, 1981: conference of Russian, American and European doctors.

7. For an elaboration, see Colonel T. Kondratkov, 'War as a Continuation of Policy' in *Soviet Military Review* (English version published in Moscow), No. 2, 1974, pp. 7–9.

8. See Glenn Snyder, *Deterrence and Defense*, (Princeton U.P., 1961).

9. See note 29 (pp. 53–4) in Professor Trofimenko, *loc. cit.*

10. See Anthony Cave Brown, *Dropshot: The United States Plan for War with the Soviet Union in 1957*, (New York, Dial Press, 1978).

11. See Doug Richardson, 'Pershing II—NATO's Small Ballistic Missile', *Flight International*, 8 August 1981, pp. 431–4.

12. See A.G. Arbatov, 'Strategicheskii paritet i politika administratsii Karteva', *SShA: Ekonomika, politika, ideologiya* (Journal), 1980, No. 11, pp. 29–40. See also A. Arbatov, *Bezopasnost v yadernyi vek i politika Vashingtona* (Moscow, Politizdat, 1980) and *SShA: Voenno-strategicheskie kontseptsii* edited by R.G. Bogdanov, M.A. Milshtein and L.S. Semeiko (Moscow Nauka, 1980).

13. See 'Russians deny the missile gap', *The Observer*, 11 October 1981.

14. See 'Panel Reexamines ICBM Vulnerability', *Aviation Week and Space Technology*, July 13, 1981, pp. 141–8.

20 Strategy and Conscience

Anatol Rapoport _____

WHO ARE THE STRATEGISTS?

The ills plaguing the world have frequently been blamed on identifiable groups of people, nations, minority groups, adherents of assorted creeds, professions, etc. In my references to "the strategists," I may have given the impression that I have singled out a group of people who are exerting a pernicious influence on United States foreign policy. My intent, however, was to examine a way of thinking, not a group of people.

When I say "strategists," I mean someone who at the moment conceives international problems in strategic terms. At other times, he may think about the same problems in other terms, and so the same person may at times be a "strategist" and at other times may not. Therefore, the fact that strategists are "like everybody else," i.e., share their psychological make-up with a broad spectrum of the population, are motivated or constrained by the same impulses and norms—this fact is irrelevant in the matter of identifying "the strategists." The strategists constitute not a sector of the population but a sector of social roles. They are strategists when they are playing out their roles, i.e., when they are thinking strategically.

Another misunderstanding which should be forestalled lurks in the temptation to link the strategists with certain political views. There are people in the United States who nurture deep hatreds against the Enemy. Such hatreds lead those people to advocate courses of action which can hardly be supported by "rational" con-

siderations, however rationality is defined. These people call for immediate cessation of negotiations with the Enemy, a declaration that a state of war already exists, and similar histrionics. There are few, if any, strategists, among the "total victory" enthusiasts or among compulsive flag wavers. Indeed, many strategists express considerable contempt for these gentry.

THE ABSTRACTIONISTS

I believe there are two types of strategists in the United States. One type I shall call the abstractionists. The abstractionists have at times been called the "cool young men." Their habitat is the research factories which service the armed forces. Their mode of thought is largely apolitical. That is to say, in formulating strategic problems, the abstractionist would feel quite comfortable if the players were relabeled. In fact, he is used to labeling them "A" and "B" in the first place. It is among the abstractionists that the impact of game-theoretical formulations is most strongly felt, and it is to them that the motto is addressed which is said to adorn an office at the Rand Corporation: "Don't think—compute!"

The abstractionists' contribution to the present conduct of international conflict is largely in the fields of operations research and logistics. Military problems, given certain norms, have "optimal" answers. For example, on the basis of known effects of nuclear blasts and thermal effects, calculations can be made concerning the number of bombers which are able to wreak a given level of destruction. On the basis of attrition rates which can be reasonably expected, assuming a certain effectiveness of the enemy's defenses, one can calculate the number of bombers which should be sent in order for the required number to get through. In replacing bombers by missiles, one calculates what one is exchanging for what: to what extent the heavier development effort is compensated by cheaper production, to what extent the "capabilities" derived from missiles will be matched by the opponent's efforts, etc., etc. (U.S. Senate, 1956).

On the defense side, one must know what to expect from ground-to-air defenses and air-to-air defenses against bombers; what one can hope for in the way of antimissile missiles and, if one really wants to think ahead, in the way of anti-antimissile missiles. One must know how much concrete can withstand how much blast pressure and how much heat, and one must translate this knowledge into designs of "hardened" missile sites, or "shelters" for civilians. These are clearly the same old problems of war "economics." Only the content has changed. Where one hundred years ago it was necessary to think about how much hay a calvary regiment would require, fifty years ago about how many railroad cars (40 *hommes*—8 *chevaux*) were optimal for an echelon, twenty-five years ago about the fire power of a Sherman tank, one has now graduated to the mathematics of missile guidance and overkill factors. The technical knowledge required for the really advanced problems of this sort is enormous. Specialization is, of course, mandatory, and the joints between the specialities must also be welded, which requires still another class of "integrating specialities."

Into this picture, the game-theoretical orientation fits most naturally. For the logistic efforts of one side are, of course, opposed at all times by corresponding efforts of the enemy. No doubt this feature has always been present in strategic formulation. But game theory seems to have given the formulations of logistic problems a new, exciting luster and a rigor comparable to that conferred by advanced methods of mathematics upon the physical sciences.

Game-theoretical models are not confined to military tactics and strategy. As an example consider the following situation. Assume that an agreement has been concluded between Country A and Country B on some method of arms control or a disarmament procedure or, perhaps, on a ban against testing nuclear weapons. Suppose the agreement provides for a maximum number of inspections per year by either party on the territory of the other. The timing and the places of inspections are to be at the discretion of the inspecting party. Here is an opportunity to for-

mulate a genuine two-person game involving mixed strategies. For clearly, secrecy about when and where an inspection is to be made is of central importance if (1) the inspected party is to be discouraged from attempting evasions and (2) if the chances for discovering evasions are to be maximized. Accordingly, a game can be formulated between two parties, one called Inspectors, the other Evaders. The payoffs accruing to the Inspectors are of two kinds, namely: (1) negative payoffs associated with the extent of undiscovered violations perpetrated by the Evaders and (2) positive payoffs associated with the number of violations discovered. For the Evaders, naturally, these payoffs have the opposite sign: It is in their interest to get away with as many violations as possible.

The game calls for mixed strategies. For example, if a violation is the possession of mobile missile-firing installations, the idea is to keep moving them around to minimize the chances of their being discovered. (If the missile launchers stay in one place, then the Inspectors, having failed to find a launcher at one site, can safely choose a different site on their next inspection and eventually close in on their prize.) The Inspectors, on the other hand, must also randomize their inspections geographically and possibly in time so as to minimize the number of launchers which the Evaders can hope to get away with and/or to maximize their chances of discovering one.

The theory of the two-person zero-sum game states that there exists an optimum strategy for the Evaders, namely, a maximum number of illegal missile launchers (or nuclear test explosions or whatever) and a certain randomization pattern in space and, perhaps, in time. Also for the Inspectors there is an "optimal" mixed strategy of randomized inspections.

The challenge offered by problems of this sort is formidable and understandably intriguing to the specialist. There is practically no limit to the complexities that can be introduced. For instance, in the case of mobile missile launchers, not all locations may be equally valuable as launching sites. Therefore, the payoffs necessary to the Evaders involve the number of undetected launchers weighted by the frequencies with which they can be placed in the tactically preferable locations. If the relative "values" of the locations are also known to the Inspectors, they must weight their inspections accordingly with frequencies.

One cannot hope to solve the problem in all

of its complexity at once, but as in the case of any mathematicized science, one can begin with some drastically simplified models and work one's way up to more and more realistic ones. In doing so, one follows the tested methods of applied mathematics: One brings to bear the greatest intellectual prowess on man's most excellent mode of thought—problem solving. In this mode, it is irrelevant to ask who are the Evaders and who the Inspectors and why the ones are so anxious to cheat and the others to catch them at cheating. In fact, the "solution" of the game reveals an optimal strategy *both* to the ones and to the others. The services of the same mathematician are available to both sides (as once were the services of the Prussian military specialists). There is even no point to keeping research of this sort classified; for the same solution can be obtained independently by the other side.

In short, the abstractionist works in a context devoid of content. It is in this sense that the abstractionist is characteristically apolitical.

THE NEO-TRADITIONALISTS

Strategists of another type, whom I shall call the neo-traditionalists, think in somewhat more political terms. Unlike the abstractionists, who are likely to have received their training in mathematics or in the physical sciences, the neo-traditionalists are more likely to have a background in political science, occasionally in history or economics. To them the participants in the present conflict are not interchangeable players A and B, but specific nations, the great powers, their allies, and their satellites. The powers also play a game, but theirs is the real game of indentifiable "interests" instead of hypothetical parries, thrusts, and "nuclear exchanges." I call these writers neo-traditionalists because the most conspicuous feature of their mode of thought is the revival of traditional views of international politics.

This trend is most clearly discernible in the writings of Henry A. Kissinger. It is epitomized in a tribute to Clausewitz.

War, argued Clausewitz, can never be an act of pure violence because it grows out of the existing relations of states, their level of civilization, the nature of their alliances, and the objectives in dispute. War would reach its ultimate form only if it became an end in itself, a condition which is realized only among

savages and probably not even among them. For war to rage with absolute violence and without interruption until the enemy is completely defenseless is to reduce an idea to absurdity (Kissinger, 1958:65).

This paraphrase of Clausewitz occurs in the context of attributing Clausewitzian ideals to the Communists. In fact, the immediately succeeding paragraph Kissinger quotes a Soviet military authority: "If war is a continuation of politics, only by other means, so also peace is a continuation of struggle, only by other means" (Shaposhnikov, 1929). I came across this statement after I started to write this book and was startled with its striking similarity to my own opening sentence. However, as the reader must have gathered by now, this book is a polemic *against* the view that politics ought to be equated to a struggle for power, while the views of Kissinger, as those of Shaposhnikov (the Soviet strategist, whom he quotes) and of Clausewitz amount to an acceptance of the power-struggle definitions of both war and peace.

At this point some of the neo-traditionalists may well point out the distinction between what ought to be and what is. There may be some among them who will readily admit that the perpetual struggle among the powers is not a desirable state of affairs. But they will insist that it is an actual one, and that therefore a theory of international relations ought to be predicated on this actuality. This is the traditional position of *realpolitik*. Later we shall inquire into the nature of the difference between the two senses of the word "accept," the sense of recognition and that of approval. For the present we shall confine ourselves to the non-controversial meaning of "acceptance," with which the strategists will readily agree. They accept (in the sense of recognizing as real, perhaps as inevitable) the power struggle as a normal relation among sovereign states and see international political "reality" rooted essentially in the issues of that struggle.

Why, then, one might ask, if the reality of the power struggle is axiomatic, and if the "rational" use of force is an obvious desideratum, is it necessary to reiterate this with so much emphasis, as is done in the writings of the neo-traditionalists?

The answer to this question is quite clear in the writings of Kissinger. Since World War I, we have been witnessing a *perversion* of the rational power principle, he says. War has ceased to be a tool by means of which rational participants in the power game pursue their "interests." A particularly vicious symptom of this degeneration of war as a rational pursuit, according to Kissinger, is found in American thought about war. There is a reason for this in our recent experience with war. He writes:

> The literalness of our notion of power made it impossible to conceive of an effective relationship between force and diplomacy. A war which started as a surprise attack on us had of necessity to be conducted in a fit of righteous indignation, and the proper strategy for waging it was one of maximum destructiveness. By the same token now that the risks of war had grown so fearsome, the task of diplomacy was to attempt to settle disputes by the process of negotiation, and this, in turn, was conceived as a legal process in which force played a small role, if any. The objective of war was conceived to be victory, that of diplomacy peace. Neither could reinforce the other, and each began where the other left off. (Kissinger, 1958:29)

Observe what is being said. Diplomacy and war have become separated. They ought to be reintegrated. This is exactly what Clausewitz was saying in his famous dictum. His magnum opus *On War* was written shortly after the Napoleonic Wars. These wars had departed from the accustomed patterns of the eighteenth century. The objectives of pre-Napoleonic wars were not "total." No state sought to deprive another state of its sovereignty. A war was simply one way of conducting disputes. For example, if the crowned heads had an argument as to who should succeed to the throne of Spain, they sent their armies on marches. After some maneuvers and perhaps a pitched battle or two, the monarchs would have a family reunion (most of them were cousins) and settle the business. This was *not* Napoleon's way. He was not anybody's cousin, and he played for keeps. An upstart corporal wearing an emperor's crown had no use for the niceties of the European "system."

The system was restored (or was thought to have been restored) in 1815, and for a century Europe reverted to the old game called the balance of power. It is of this game that the neotraditionalists write with sometimes undisguised nostalgia. The rules of the balance-of-power game are spelled out by Morton Kaplan (Kaplan, 1957:23).

1. Act to increase capabilities but negotiate rather than fight.
2. Fight rather than pass up an opportunity to increase capabilities.
3. Stop fighting rather than eliminate an essential national actor.
4. Act to oppose any coalitions or single actor which tends to assume a position of predominance with respect to the rest of the system.
5. Act to constrain actors who subscribe to supranational organizing principles.
6. Permit defeated or constrained essential national actors to re-enter the system as acceptable role partners or act to bring some previously inessential actor within the essential actor classification. Treat all essential actors as acceptable role partners.

The over-all objective of the balance-of-power game, then (the objective of all the players as distinguished from their individual objectives) was not the preservation of peace but the preservation of the system. The victor must make sure that the defeated participant is reintegrated into the system, so that he can fight another time; for, who knows, next time he may be an ally.

The strategists are seldom so naive as to believe that the European system can be restored in its entirety, and they note the features of our era which make this impossible.

First and foremost of these is the destructiveness of modern weapons. Nowadays, the decision to "fight" rather than allow this or that is a decision to stake "national survival" on the outcome. Indeed as even many of the strategists admit, a decision to employ all the existing technical capacity in a war may be tantamount to a decision to commit national suicide *regardless* of the outcome.

Second, specifically with regard to the United States, the all-or-none conception of war and peace is incompatible with the rules of the balance-of-power game. The United States has never been a member of the system. Consequently, the Clausewitzian conception of war as a rational pursuit of national interest has never been internalized in our way of thinking. We still harbor the illusion (or so it appears to the strategists) that war is a dirty business and that the goal of diplomacy is peace.

Finally, there have appeared on the scene other powers to be reckoned with who have no use for the "system," namely, the U.S.S.R. and China.

Kissinger calls them revolutionary powers (analogous to France of 1794). Kaufmann calls them aggressive powers: "It has long been a basic assumption of American foreign policy that both the Soviet Union and Red China are aggressive powers, that they assign a very high priority to expansion in the hierarchy of their goals, and are likely to use any and all means, including violence to attain their ends" (Kaufmann, 1956a:1).

In view of the acceptance of the power struggle principle by the neo-traditionalists, it seems strange that any power would be singled out as an "aggressive" power simply because it is likely to "use violence to attain its ends." What is meant here (it should be understood, in fairness to the author) is that there are no apparent limits to *how much* power the U.S.S.R. and China will try to attain. In other words, they will not, according to this view, play the game according to the rules set up by the old established members of the club.

What, then, is to be done? Time was when the United States Secretary of State could announce that any encroachment by the revolutionary powers on the status quo would be likely to be countered with a nuclear attack on their homelands. But this did not work. For one thing, "public opinion" is to be reckoned with in a democracy. Kaufmann writes:

> . . . a policy of deterrence will seem credible only to the extent that important segments of public opinion in domestic [sic] and allied countries support it. . . . This consideration suggests a rather crucial and specific requirement that a policy of deterrence must fulfill. Its potential costs must seem worth incurring. In other words, there must be some relationship between the value of the objective sought and the costs involved in its attainment. A policy of deterrence which does not fulfill this requirement is likely to result only in deterring the deterrer. (Kaufmann, 1956b:20)

The central idea in the writings of the neo-traditionalists is the Gilbertian notion that the punishment ought to fit the crime. The trouble with the doctrine of massive retaliation is that the magnitude of the threat mitigates against our willingness to use it. A threat of massive retaliation which is not believed by the threatened party can have disastrous consequences for the would-be retaliator. For if the threat is not believed, the bluff can be called. And if the bluff

is called, the fist-shaking party faces a choice between nasty alternatives—to unleash a nuclear war or to back down and so reduce the credibility of future threats. The massive retaliator appears, then, to be talking loudly and carrying a stick so big that he may not be able to lift it.

The prudent thing, according to the neo-traditionalist, is to have a range of both decibels and sticks at one's disposal and *to use* either or both as the situation warrants: small transgressions—small punishments; big transgressions—big punishments. And the important thing is to keep the *capability* of the biggest punishment which technology allows and also the determination to use it "if necessary."

This is the gist of the limited war theory, the neo-traditionalists' answer to the threat of mutual annihilation. To their credit, it must be stressed that both the "need" for the theory and its aim are spelled out in the clearest terms. The "need" arose from the bankruptcy of the massive retaliation doctrine. It was impractical to bomb Moscow every time a riot occured in Caracas. The Communists, knowing this, could proceed to "nibble away at the edges of the Free World." The aim of the theory was to restore war to its rightful and honorable place in international affairs.

". . . the problem is this: How can the United States utilize its military power as a rational and effective instrument of national policy?" (Osgood, 1957:ix).

If limited war was to become a rational and respectable substitute for total war, its strategic theory ought to occupy more of the strategists' attention; consequently, all-out war became a topic to be avoided, and so it is, in most of the writings of the neo-traditionalists.

Herman Kahn played the part of the *enfant terrible* when he broke through the tacit taboos and plunged into the "extended" theory, into the oh, so evermore exciting challenges and potentialities of thermo-nuclear war.

The neo-traditionalists had stopped at the edge, because it seemed to them that "the pursuit of national policy by thermo-nuclear war" was a contradiction in terms. Kahn's greatest achievement was to show, at least to his own satisfaction, that this was not necessarily the case, first, because there were untapped potentialities in the art of blackmail against the background of thermonuclear annihilation; second, because if nuclear war were to be fought after all, the strategist should not shirk his duty—he should work out (well in advance) the best way of fighting such a war if only to "prevail" (since "victory" in the accepted sense was difficult to define); third, because there was a public relations job to be done: What sort of impression do we make if we keep sniveling about the horrors of war?

Kahn became the loudest and clearest spokesman of the "cool young men."

WHO ARE THE OTHERS?

I have now identified the strategists and have presented their framework of thought. As the reader may have gathered from the title of this book, I juxtapose to the mode of thinking in which strategy is central another mode in which conscience is central. My task is now to describe this other mode and the camp to which people who think in it belong.

I do not know what to call those people, and I will not bother. The designing of strategies is a profession; an appeal to conscience is not. At least the professionalization of this activity tends to degrade it, as the history of organized religions has shown. Therefore, one cannot always recognize members of the conscience camp by what they do publicly. To be sure, many of them engage in agitation and in organization of community and political action, just as the strategists are frequently found among consultants to military agencies. But just as the way of thinking of the strategist is spread far beyond the circle of professionals, so the other way of thinking is not confined to the "professional" peace worker. It will be useful, therefore, to mention some other divisions of views which are correlated with the division between the strategic thinkers and the others, but do not quite coincide with it.

In the press, the dichotomy "warhawks vs. peace doves" was coined. This dichotomy implies commitments to war and to peace respectively and is not useful, since the coldest blooded of the cold warriors can protest his devotion to peace. One cannot challenge this protestation without questioning its sincerity, and this will not be done in this book.

Another dichotomy, proposed by Singer, (Singer and Rapoport, 1963) is between the "armers" and the "disarmers." On this scale, positions are clearly discernible, and the distinction coincides more closely with the one we are concerned with. Also, the individuals who line

up along the armers-disarmers axis line up pretty much the same way on the strategy-conscience axis. Yet the armers-disarmers division makes for a confrontation on matters of *policy*, not modes of thought. It is possible to arrive at a position favoring disarmament without leaving the strategic mode of reasoning. There are disarmers who write effectively on this issue entirely in the strategic mode. (See Etzioni, 1962; Waskow, 1962; Waskow, 1964.)

A dialogue on the level of a policy debate is certainly possible. Such a dialogue between, say, the armers and the disarmers might be fruitful if in its course the underlying assumptions made by both parties were brought out, provided some agreement could be reached at the outset about desirable goals. One such agreement appears plausible. Many of the armers are firmly convinced that their program is most likely to prevent the outbreak of a nuclear war (if not of "small" limited wars). Whatever the disarmers may feel about the feasibility or the morality of limited wars, most of them would agree that the prevention of nuclear war is a desirable goal under any circumstances. The two camps can thus agree on at least one goal. Since the disarmers are equally convinced that only disarmament can ultimately prevent nuclear war, the disagreement is seen to be about means. This sort of disagreement can be fruitfully discussed. It is, in fact, easy to take the next step, that is, to state the fundamental assumptions of both sides with regard to some proposed policy, say the policy of deterrence. The armers, it seems, believe:

1. That the capacity to destroy the opponent is *necessary* to prevent him from destroying you. (In other words, if it were not for our retaliatory capacity, we would have been destroyed by now);

2. That the capacity to destroy the opponent is *sufficient* to prevent him from destroying you. (In other words, deterrence is a workable safeguard).

Most disarmers deny both of these assumptions. The debate, therefore, is joined at the very base of the two positions.

If a debate crystallized around the choice of a policy (e.g., a "hard" versus a "soft" policy on a specific issue), the armers and the disarmers could also formulate their respective positions in terms of possible outcomes, their estimated probabilities, and utilities assigned to them. They would then find that the disarmers assign greater probabilities and larger negative utilities to escalation and war; the armers, on the contrary, assign higher probabilities and greater utilities to the other side's backing down. In this sense both positions are seen to be based on "rational" considerations. Their differences are traceable to different subjective estimates and values which are unavoidable in decision problems.

It will thus be found that up *to a point* disagreements arising in the pursuit of strategic analysis can, in principle, be resolved, not in the sense of effecting agreements but in the "optical" sense of being resolved into components, so that the analysis can proceed to the next stage. Ultimately, no further resolution will be possible, because the basic values will have been reached. Polite dialogue must stop at this point: One can only agree to disagree on subjective estimates of unique future events and on preferences. Beyond this point, attempts to continue the discussion in the same mode will either get nowhere or will explode into hostile exchanges.

But the dialogue could continue if the mode of discourse were changed. It could continue if one allowed introspection, insight, and conscience to guide the discussion. Therefore, whether a dialogue is possible beyond the point of the "irreducible" clash of values depends on whether the strategist is able and willing to talk in another language and to think in another mode.

What, then, is the way of thinking of those who are concerned primarily with conscience, and how does it differ from the strategic mode?

First, whereas the strategic thinker conceives of each choice of action primarily (perhaps exclusively) in terms of its effects on the environment, the conscience-driven thinker conceives actions primarily with regard to their effects on the actor.

Second, whereas the strategist can begin his work only when values (utilities) are given or assumed, the conscience-driven thinker considers the determination of these values to be the principal problem. He rejects the relativist notion that all values are matters of preference like brands of cigarettes. To be sure, one cannot "prove" the superiority of one set of values over another if one confines one's self to methods of proof appropriate to other inquiries. Nor can one prove by rational analysis that *King Lear* is a more profound work than *Tarzan of the Apes*. The conscience-driven thinker will not relinquish the problem of discerning human values simply because the problem does not yield to

rational analysis; nor will he divorce any important sphere of human activity from this problem.

Third, while the strategist frequently recognizes the importance of self-fulfilling assumptions, their role is hardly ever actually taken into account in strategic analysis. The strategist assumes not only that the values are given but also that the "state of the world" at a given moment (including the values and the thinking processes of the enemy) is an objective fact to be ascertained. The critic of strategic thinking, on the contrary, while admitting that the state of the non-human environment may be considered as an "objective fact" at a given time, denies that values and predispositions are "objective facts." What they "are," in his way of thinking, is to a significant degree determined by what we think of them. Therefore in this area the aphorism of Henry Margenau is especially appropriate: "All of man's facts have become acts."

It is extremely difficult for one who subscribes to this orientation to join in a dialogue with a strategist, even with the best intentions. The basic question in the strategist's mind is this: "In a conflict how can I gain an advantage over him?" The critic cannot disregard the question, "If I gain an advantage over him, what sort of person will I become?" For example, he might ask what kind of a nation the United States might become if we succeeded in crushing all revolutions as easily as in Guatemala. With regard to deterrence, the critic might ask not "What if deterrence fails?" (everyone worries about *that*) but, on the contrary, "What if deterrence works?" Erich Fromm asks just this question: He inquires into the kind of *reality* behind the strategist's prescriptions of security:

> . . . the biggest and most pervasive reality in any man's life if deterrence should 'work' is the poised missile, the humming data processor connected to it, the waiting radiation counters and seismographs, the overall technocratic perfection (overlying the nagging but impotent fear of its imperfection) of the mechanism of holocaust. (Fromm, 1960:1015–1028)

The critic is convinced of the corrupting effect of power, especially of unimpeded power. And this, for him, is not simply "something to think about" in off moments, but a fundamental insight. Moreover, he is convinced that this insight is not a symptom of softheadedness. It stems from looking at the facts of history, not ignoring them. If Stalin's Russia is to be used as an example of pure despotism (as the rationalizers of the Cold War frequently insist), it ought to be an object lesson on the results of power unimpeded by conscience. Moreover, conscience is silent when the wielders of power are convinced that it is being used to achieve good ends.

The neo-traditionalists' acceptance of international relations as a power game seems self-defeating to one who questions the value of power. Here the strategist will, of course, argue that his "acceptance" of the power game is not predicated on approval, that he merely takes the world "as it is." But the strategists' conclusions are not mere descriptions. They are frankly recommendations, predominantly recommendations to try to get more power in the power struggle, and so are predicated on the tacit assumption that power is a "pure good." The conscience-driven thinker challenges this assumption.

In my grandmother's time, body weight was considered a "pure good." I remember a passage from one of her letters written long ago from the Old Country. "Your aunt Rose, glory be, has added to her health (knock on wood). She has gained 16 kilograms since the birth of her baby and now tips the scales at 102." Similarly, financial standing is considered a "pure good" in our society, certainly as it applies to firms and often to individuals. Yet it seems as reasonable to question this assumption and even to deny it, as it is to question the assumption that health is reflected in obesity. With regard to power, we also have weighty reasons to question its value and to inquire into the mentality that considers the power game among nations as a normal, civilized state of affairs. For that is what Clausewitz implied when he said that only savages fight wars for the sake of fighting. We may forgive Clausewitz, writing before Victoria's accession, this cavalier distinction between civilization and savagery. But after what the descendants of Clausewitz brought about in Europe, it seems odd that this distinction is still made by the new traditionalists, who seek to restore respectability to war by making it "an instrument of policy."

In spite of occasional protestations on the part of strategists that their job is rational analysis, not value judgments, value judgments are unavoidably included in their analyses, because the end results of these analyses are policy recommendations. For example, some strategists pride themselves on having broken through the inhibitions which delayed a strategic analysis of thermonuclear war. In assuming the posture of staring this eventuality in the face, they liken themselves to the surgeon who does not permit himself to be swayed either by the horror of what he sees or even by empathy with the patient (for he needs detachment to cut human flesh.) This comparison may be valid if thermonuclear war is viewed as a disaster to be guarded against and coped with, if, in spite of precautions, it does occur. However, thermonuclear war is not a natural disaster. It is being carefully planned and prepared by the strategists themselves. It could not occur if the strategists of both sides did not put forward convincing arguments about the necessity of possessing "nuclear capabilities" and the "will to use them." In this context, the "detachment" of the strategist resembles not so much that of the surgeon as that of a butcher or still more that of all the other organizers of mass exterminations. Those technicians too were for the most part "detached" in the sense that their work was not charged with affect. German chemists were detached when they prepared the poison gas; German engineers were detached when they built the gas chambers; German transportation experts were detached and efficient as they kept the trains moving, carrying people to the slaughter sites; German bookkeepers were detached while keeping tallies of the despatched, etc. Doubtless many of those responsible for this activity took a certain pride in having overcome any inhibitions they might have had in this matter. They might have been sincerely convinced that the "Jewish question" was a problem to be solved in a detached and definitive manner, possibly for the good of humanity. In other words, the charge of depravity, sadism, etc., can be made convincingly only against certain isolated individuals. It cannot be made against the entire corps of specialists who planned, designed, and carried out the exterminations of the 1940's. These people did not go berserk. They were carrying out their duties methodically and systematically. They were "normally functioning" human beings.

Our strategists are also exactly like other people of their social class, education, and background. They enjoy the same sort of personal relations as the rest of us, appreciate the same gifts that life bestows, suffer from the same griefs and misfortunes. The monstrosity of their work carries little or no emotional meaning for them, not because they are mentally ill, but because they share with the rest of us or perhaps are more richly endowed than the rest of us with the most creative of human faculties, which becomes also the most dangerous one when coupled with a lack of extensional imagination— the faculty of abstraction.

To the mathematicians among them equations on the blackboard are just equations. Mathematics is a great leveler. When a problem is mathematically formulated, its *content* has disappeared and only the form has remained. To the strategists "targets" are indeed only circles on maps; overkill is a coefficient; nuclear capacity a concept akin to heat capacity or electric potential or the credit standing of a concern. The logic of abstract reasoning applies in the same way to all problems which are logically isomorphic.

The logician, the mathematician, the statistician, and the strategist all derive their competence (and so their social status) from an ability to handle abstract chains of reasoning detached from content. This, rather than freedom from preconceived notions and from the bias of vested interest, is the true meaning of their detachment.

If a dialogue is to take place between strategy and conscience, these are the things that must be said.

Given the etiquette of civilized discussion, especially in the English-speaking world, it is difficult to bring such matters up without eliciting accusations of foul play. The strategists accuse the moralists of prudery, of refusing to face certain facts of life. But the moralists can claim with equal, I would say with much greater, conviction that it is the strategists and their supporting hosts of bureaucrats who refuse to look facts in the face.

At a recent trial of a group of British pacifists (who engaged in a sit-down protest at Wethersfield Air Base on December 1, 1961), one of the defendants, acting as his own counsel, was cross-examining a government witness, an air force officer. The following is an excerpt from the cross-examination.

Q: So actually there is no order which you would not accept?
A: It is my duty to carry out any order that is given to me.
Q: Would you press the button that you know is going to annihilate millions of people?
A: If the circumstances demanded it, I would.

Q: Would you slit the throats of all the two-year-old children in this country, Air Commodore?
Mr. Justice Havers: I think you must stop all that. (Garst, 1962)

This line of questioning was forbidden by the judge as irrelevant. But from the point of view of the defendants, the picture evoked by the questions was far more relevant to the issue tried (whether the war resisters acted against the interests of the United Kingdom) than are the concepts in which the military thinks. The military concepts of defense have only a "logical" relevance to the country's national interests. That is, they are connected to the conventional ideas of "national interest" by the force of our thinking habits, but by hardly anything else. On the other hand, the horrible deaths of a nation's two-year-olds has a *direct* relevance to the country's "national interest." These deaths are expected as *actual*, not merely logical, consequences of nuclear war. Nevertheless, the demand for "rational argument" is a demand that the moral aspect of genocide be dismissed as "irrelevant."

I heard this attitude stated quite frankly by an official of our Department of Defense, a man not only of superlative intelligence but also easy to talk to, in the sense that he listened carefully, got the central point of what was said, and replied directly to it.

"You keep worrying what is going to happen to the two-year-olds," he said, when I kept harping on the subject, following the example of the British defendant, "but what I want to know is who is going to get West Berlin, if we do what you propose."

And again, "No, I don't see them [the Communists] as fiends or criminals. To me the whole thing looks more like a basketball game between Pekin, Illinois, and Peoria, Illinois."

The moral issues are beyond the scope of military and political decisions. Moral convictions are private and so should not be injected into the formulation of public policy. But more effective than any explicit arguments against bringing in the moral issue is the functional deafness developed by the strategists to any discourse in other than strategic mode. Consequently, if someone wants to *reach* the strategists, to induce them to listen seriously, he must either gloss over the moral issues or lay them aside altogether. Someone with a facile knowledge of weaponry and logistics has an excellent chance of catching the strategist's ear. Someone moved by a passionate concern for human values but with no understanding of the intricate strategic issues and their highly proliferated ramifications may as well be speaking a dead language.

The emphasis by the critic of strategic thinking on the vital importance of the self-predictive assumption is, perhaps, the crucial stumbling block to the dialogue. For the strategist's deeply internalized conviction is that he takes the world "as it is." To the critic, however, the world looks somewhat as it does to the wisest of the three umpires. The first umpire, who was a "realist" remarked, "Some is strikes and some is balls, and I calls them as they is." Another, with less faith in the infallibility of the profession, countered with, "Some is strikes and some is balls, and I calls them as I sees them." But the wisest umpire said, "Some is strikes and some is balls, but they ain't nothing till I calls them."

A value is not a fact. The act of choosing a value and the act of guessing the other's values are facts. It is, therefore, by no means a matter of indifference what values one puts into one's own matrix and what values one will assign to the payoffs of the other. The game one will play depends vitally (sometimes irrevocably) on the values one has put in. But in real life it is the way the game is played that reveals the values. How "objective," then, are the strategists' estimates if there is good reason to suppose that the strategists themselves have made the game what it is? In no laboratory would the results of observations be taken seriously if there was reason to suspect that the methods of observation had influenced the results. Nevertheless it is precisely in their claims to "scientific objectivity" that the defenders of strategic analysis are most vociferous when confronted with questions of value. On the basis of their "objectivity" they accuse of muddleheadedness and naiveté anyone who asks embarrassing questions about whether their games are worth playing, or whether one ought to identify with actors whose moral code resembles that of Louis XIV, Frederick the Great, and Catherine II at its best and that of Attila, Genghis Khan, and Hitler at its worst.

If dialogue becomes impossible on these matters, it is because neither side can really listen to the other. In most cases, such blocks to communication are unfortunate. The improvement of communication is one of the crucial problems of our time, and brave efforts go into this enterprise. Books are written and courses taught on this subject; innumerable techniques are proposed, ranging from forensics to semantics. I often wonder whether it is worthwhile to try to bridge the chasm between strategic and conscience-inspired thinking. It may be feasible and advisable to broaden the views of both management and labor: The industrial process must keep functioning, and both sides may stand to gain from increased mutual understanding. It is imperative to establish avenues of communication between Blacks and Whites and between East and West, because they all must either learn to live with each other or perish. In the case of strategy and conscience, I am not sure. Here, I believe, is essential incompatibility, not merely a result of misunderstanding. I do not believe one can bring both into focus. One cannot play chess if one becomes aware of the pieces as living souls and of the fact that the Whites and the Blacks have more in common with each other than with the players. Suddenly one loses all interest in who will be champion.

REFERENCES

ETZIONI, A. (1962) The Hard Way to Peace, A New Strategy. New York: Collier Books.

FROMM, E. (1960) "The case for unilateral disarmament." Daedalus 89: 1015–1028.

GARST, J.D. (1962) "Conscience on trial." Nation, March 24.

KAPLAN, M.A. (1957) System and Process in International Politics. New York: John Wiley & Sons.

KAUFMANN, W.W. (ed.) (1965a) Military Policy and National Security. Princeton, N.J.: Princeton University Press.

KAUFMANN, W.W. (1965b) "The requirements of deterrence." In W.W. Kaufmann, ed., 1965a.

KISSINGER, H.A. (1958) Nuclear Weapons and Foreign Policy (abridged edition). Garden City, N.Y.: Doubleday.

OSGOOD, R.E. (1957) Limited War. The Challenge to American Strategy. Chicago: University of Chicago Press.

SHAPOSHNIKOV, B.M. (1929) Mozg Armii. Moscow-Leningrad: Gosizdat.

SINGER, J.D. and A. RAPAPORT (1963) "The armers and the disarmers." Nation, March 2.

U.S. Senate (1956) Study of Airpower. Hearings before the Subcommittee on the Air Force of the Committee on Armed Services, 84th Cong., 2d sess. Washington, D.C.: Government Printing Office.

WASKOW, A. (1962) The Limits of Defense. New York: Doubleday.

WASKOW, A. (1964) "Non-lethal equivalents of war." In R. Fisher (ed.), International Conflict and Behavorial Science, "The Craigville Papers." New York: Basic Books.

QUESTIONS FOR DISCUSSION

1. How do the types of deterrence discussed by Kahn differ?

2. What, according to Erickson, are the differences between U.S. and Soviet concepts of nuclear deterrence?

3. How, according to Rapoport, do abstractionists differ from traditionalists? How do both differ from what he calls the conscience-motivated approach?

4. Discuss the relationship between the strategy of nuclear deterrence and the nuclear arms race.

SUGGESTED READINGS

JERVIS, ROBERT. *The Illogic of American Nuclear Strategy*. Ithaca, N.Y.: Cornell University Press, 1984.

KAHN, HERMAN. *Thinking about the Unthinkable in the 1980s*. New York: Simon and Schuster, 1984.

PORRO, J. D. "The Policy War: Brodie vs. Kahn," *Bulletin of the Atomic Scientists* (June 1982): 16–19.

POWELL, ROBERT. "The Theoretical Foundations of Strategic Nuclear Deterrence," *Political Science Quarterly* 100, (1985): 75–96.

SCHELLING, THOMAS C. *Arms and Influence*. New Haven, Conn.: Yale University Press, 1966.

Chapter VI

Limited Nuclear War

The strategic doctrine of limited nuclear war holds that nuclear weapons can be used to fight "small" wars: in a limited geographic area, with a limited number of nuclear weapons used, in pursuit of limited objectives. This doctrine developed out of two impulses on the part of military strategists. First, some strategists sought to make nuclear weapons more usable. By developing a doctrine stating that nuclear weapons could be used to fight "limited" wars, military planners sought to turn nuclear weapons into useful instruments of policy. Second, some strategists believed that the ability to fight limited nuclear wars would strengthen nuclear deterrence. They sought to provide national leaders with nuclear "options" that lay somewhere between a "total" war of mutually assured destruction and a policy of "no use" of nuclear weapons. The existence of limited nuclear options would make the threat to use nuclear weapons during a crisis more "credible," thus encouraging the other side to exercise restraint.

During the last decade, the United States has placed increasing emphasis on limited nuclear war as a basis for its nuclear strategy. Such a policy was articulated by the Carter administration in Presidential Directive 59 (PD–59). The Reagan administration continued this trend by developing doctrine for fighting "protracted" nuclear war. The emphasis on limited nuclear war is reflected in strategic doctrine, in official statements, and in military procurement patterns. Meanwhile, debate has raged over the concept of limited nuclear war, with critics charging that Pentagon planners are engaging in collective self-delusion.

These critics maintain that a limited nuclear war is unlikely to remain limited, arguing that it would probably expand into a total nuclear war. They point out that it is easier to control nuclear war in theory than in practice, arguing that the emotions, confusion and time pressures of a real nuclear conflict would increase the likelihood of rapid escalation. How, they ask, would limits be set and enforced? How would control be maintained during the chaos that would result from even a few nuclear explosions? How would the hostilities be terminated? How much damage would have occurred by the time the last shot was fired? Would the destruction—on a densely populated continent, such as Europe—be "limited" in any meaningful sense of the word?

This chapter provides an introduction to the debate over limited nuclear war. We begin with an excerpt from Lawrence Freedman's famous book *The Evolution of Nuclear Strategy*. Freedman traces the roots of the theory of limited nuclear war, discussing such theorists as Liddell Hart and Henry Kissinger. Next, an article by Richard Halloran describes a recent Pentagon plan for fighting a "protracted" nuclear war. In the third reading, Desmond Ball asks "Can Nuclear War Be Controlled?" Finally, Ian Clark discusses three distinct models of war limitation that have appeared throughout history. His analysis sheds light on today's dilemmas.

21 The Evolution of Nuclear Strategy

Lawrence Freedman ⸻

THE CONCEPT OF LIMITED WAR

The intellectual father of contemporary theories of limited war was Captain Basil Liddell Hart. Liddell Hart's advocacy of this approach to war stemmed from his whole philosophy. It was not, as it was with many of the 1950s adherents, a pragmatic response to the exigencies of the moment. To Liddell Hart it was axiomatic that, because of the suffering and the disruption of normal relations between nation states caused by war, wars should be limited.

Liddell Hart's achievement was to develop an alternative to the prevailing strategies of total war based on sound principles rather than simply an emotional response to the horror of it all. Since the late nineteenth century, at a series of international conferences, there had been attempts to agree on means of containing war as a social institution and to maintain a sharp distinction, through bans on indiscriminate weapons and prohibitions on attacks on commerce and cities, between the military and the civilian spheres.[1] The attempt had been to preserve the traditional forms of warfare in response to the steady progress of military technology. It had been to little or no avail.

Liddell Hart sought to remind his audience that wars were but an unpleasant episode in relations between nations, and were usually avoidable. The country that you now called an enemy might be needed as a friend in the future.

War should therefore be a controlled affair, conducted with the minimum of fuss and bother and without the barbarous excesses to which the most civilized democracies seemed capable once their ire had been raised, the result of which was to inflict superfluous suffering, encourage reprisals and lower all standards.

The development of airpower had introduced a source of tension into Liddell Hart's theories. At first he saw the ability to move right to the heart, and the brain, of the enemy without the painful necessity of proceeding through battlefields as a logical development. It seemed to fit in with his own preference for an 'indirect strategy', that is one aimed at the 'dislocation of the enemy's psychological and physical balance', rather than a predictable struggle 'along the line of natural expectation'.[2] However, though a method of paralysing the enemy's will, airpower was a blunt instrument. It resulted in brutal attacks on civilians which would increase the hostility between the two sides and render the objective of a moderate, negotiated peace more distant. The bluntness of the air instrument also offended against Liddell Hart's sense of the military art. By the start of World War II he had come round to a view, that became quite prevalent after the war, namely that airpower did not constitute a means of delivering a decisive, paralysing blow but was merely another means of attrition—but one that pushed the dehumanizing trend of modern warfare a stage further.

Thus Liddell Hart's critique of total war predated the atomic bomb and had indeed been articulated throughout World War II. The atomic bomb served to confirm his worst fears. Writing just after Hiroshima, he did not look to the immediate future but anticipated the age of large nuclear stockpiles and rocket carriers available to both sides in a war. In such circumstances nothing of benefit to anybody could result from a war:

> When both sides possess atomic power, 'total warfare' makes nonsense. Total warfare implies that the aim, the effort, and the degree of violence are unlimited. Victory is pursued without regard to the consequences. . . . Any unlimited war waged with atomic power would be worse than nonsense; it would be mutually suicidal.

He further argued, almost uniquely at the time and in contrast to the strong belief that atomic bombs would make *all* warfare unthinkable, that it was by no means certain that 'warfare will completely disappear. But, unless the belligerent leaders are crazy, it is likely that any future war will be less unrestrained and more subject to mutually agreed rules. Within such limits it may develop new forms'. For instance, aggressors might avoid direct confrontations but prefer subtle means of 'infiltration' that would 'check the employment of atomic bombing in retort'.[3]

Liddell Hart's views on limited war were not readily accepted in the 1940s. However preferable in principle, in practice such wars were hard to arrange. War appeared to many as an activity limited only by the quantity and quality of military capabilities. It might be best to understand the enemy in human terms, unless, as in the last war, the enemy was so genuinely barbarous that compromise was impossible. For restraints on weapons and targets to hold, a modicum of trust was needed, and this tended to be in short supply in war. When the issues were the survival of whole civilizations, a way of life or a national identity, there was little inclination to admit defeat, or to show mercy, or to miss any opportunity to bring it all to a satisfactory conclusion, even if that meant the employment of distasteful methods. Perhaps the strongest charge against Liddell Hart was that he was out of touch with his time. The distinguished American strategist Edward Mead Earle accused him of being 'nostalgic'. 'Wars are an inherent part of the societies within which they are fought', which meant that they were now 'primarily battles of production and logistics'. 'No nation possessed of sea power has ever abandoned the blockade; it is unlikely that any nation possessed of air power will abandon bombing as a means of immobilizing the enemy'.[4]

Liddell Hart found no reason to change his views. The stupendous accretions of destructive power represented by H-bombs underlined his arguments. Not long after Dulles' 'massive retaliation' speech, he repeated his earlier arguments.

> Would any responsible government, when it came to the point, dare to *use* the H-bomb as an answer to local and limited aggression? . . . To the extent that the H-bomb reduces the likelihood of full-scale war, it *increases* the possibilities of limited war pursued by widespread local aggression: . . . the value of strategic bombing forces has largely disappeared—except as the last resort.[5]

By now Liddell Hart was not alone. The approach of a thermonuclear stalemate had alerted many to the danger of assuming the inevitability of total war. Bernard Brodie wrote to Liddell Hart how 'I became in effect a follower of yours early in 1952, when I learned . . . that a thermonuclear weapon would be tested in the following autumn and would probably be successful'.[6]

In 1954 Brodie, who had always recognized the role of nuclear threats as a source of restraint, argued that 'The availability of this threat as a deterrent will be increasingly limited to only the most outrageous kind of direct aggression'. A prudent regard for the suicidal character of nuclear exchanges, when the West seemed to be relying on a threat of total war, would create a 'diplomacy straight-jacketed by fear'. It was therefore necessary to 'explore ways of consciously limiting those conflicts we may be unable entirely to avoid'.[7]

This message was frequently repeated over the next two years. In 1956 a collection of essays edited by William Kaufmann, entitled *Military Policy and National Security* appeared, providing a forum for a number of critics of 'massive retaliation'. In his introductory essay, which had been distributed as a monograph in 1954, Kaufmann stressed the importance of 'credibility'. In assessing the risk of an American response to any aggression, the enemy would use three sources of information: the statements and behaviour of the US government; the attitudes of public opinion; and also the 'government's performance in comparable contingencies'. He then noted, with justice, that the up-to-date evidence of East—West confrontations would suggest that it would be 'out of character' for the US to retaliate massively. In fact, it would suggest 'rather strongly that the United States is willing—and, it should be added, able—to meet [Soviet efforts at expansion] successfully on the grounds and according to the rules set by the opponent'. If the United States was unable to respond in this way, because of the communists' own ability to retaliate on a massive scale, then any threats it cared to make with regard to less-than-total provocations would not be taken seriously.

> If the Communists should challenge our sincerity and they would have good reasons for daring to do so, we would either have to put up or shut up. If we put up, we would plunge into all the immeasurable horrors of atomic war. If we shut up, we would suffer a serious loss of prestige and damage our capacity to establish deterrents against further Communist expansion.[8]

The same message—that the choice was between having to put up or shut up—was repeated in different forms throughout the 1950s. It would be 'holocaust or humiliation'; 'suicide or surrender', 'sudden destruction or slow defeat'.

In 1957 Robert Osgood published a book which sought to establish the theoretical and historical credentials of limited war. He stressed that the 'principal justification of limited war lies in the fact that it maximises the opportunities for the effective use of military force as a rational instrument of policy', and then argued that America's experience in the twentieth century had proved to be so unsatisfactory because of a failure to establish this link between military power and national policy. Recognition had been forced upon her since 1945, but the process of adaptation had been partial and *ad hoc*. The Korean War, fought according to the right principles, especially that of the primacy of politics, had proved to be so traumatic for the American people because these principles had been inadequately explained. It was now necessary, to achieve success in the cold war, to confront this problem in an organized and systematic manner. If there was to be a strategy of deterrence it had to be credible, and 'credibility, in turn, requires that the means of deterrence be proportionate to the objectives at stake'.[9] This was the essential principle of the limited war theorists.

The most stimulating book of the mid-1950s, bringing this debate to a wider public, was Henry Kissinger's *Nuclear Weapons and Foreign Policy*, also published in 1957. Kissinger was acting as rapporteur for a Council on Foreign Relations study group which included a number of Democrats and supporters of the army. Though not original in its basic formulations, it was written in a challenging, confident, and assertive style. Kissinger too attacked the propensity of the Americans to think in total, absolute categories, in which war and peace, the military and politics, were seen as separate and opposite. The only available doctrine was one concerned with the repulsion of overt aggression. Atomic bombs had been seen as 'merely another tool in a concept of warfare which knew no goal save total victory and no mode of war except all-out war'. But now the problem of limited war had 'forced itself on American strategic thought despite itself'. With the end of the atomic monopoly 'it is no longer possible to impose unconditional surrender at an acceptable cost' nor could one 'combine a deterrent based on a threat of maximum destructiveness with a strategy of minimum risk'.

This problem of limited war could not be understood in purely military terms. To stop when ahead but not triumphant, or when behind but not defeated, was against military logic. 'The prerequisite for a policy of limited war is to reintroduce the political element into our concept of warfare and to discard the notion that policy ends when war begins or that war can have goals distinct from those of national policy'.[10] . . .

LIMITED NUCLEAR WAR

Henry Kissinger wrote that 'The more moderate the objective, the less violent war is likely to be', as if the choice of weapons and the manner of their use would be governed by the war-aims of the contestants. Yet the choice of means had to be decided on the basis of those available, and the problem faced by the proponents of limited war was that the means most appropriate for limited objectives—strong, local conventional forces—were by far the most expensive. However strong the argument for conventional forces in terms of military logic, it would not carry the day if there were no funds available from hard-pressed and restricted national budgets (paradoxically, limited budgets did not make for limited war). In consequence many, but not all, of the proponents opted for 'tactical' nuclear weapons. This was not with great reluctance for, it should be remembered, there had long been an interest in the use of small nuclear weapons in a tactical mode amongst those who had been seeking an alternative to strategic bombardment as the centre-piece of Western defence.

Therefore, what many were writing about was limited *nuclear* war. Bernard Brodie wrote:

> Whether or not we can relinquish strategic bombing as a way of war, we can hardly afford to abjure tactical use of such weapons without dooming ourselves and allies to a permanent inferiority to the Soviet and satellite armies in Europe.

Robert Osgood said much the same:

> With the Communist superiority in trained manpower, magnified by our own reductions in ground troops, these weapons may be virtually the only effective means the West possesses for checking local Communist advances, short of massive strategic retaliation.[11]

It was believed that this was likely to be an area of overwhelming Western superiority for some time to come, at least until the end of the 1950s. Soviet nuclear technology was still in its infancy. Not only were the Russians some way from refining small fission bombs for tactical use, but they were still building up their stockpile for strategic use and could not spare any for battlefield operations.

The argument in favour of tactical nuclear weapons was not simply that this was an area of Western superiority. It was felt that these were weapons that favoured the defender of territory—the position the West expected to be in when facing communist aggression. The proposition was that offensive action required the concentration of forces, and that once so concentrated these forces would provide an attractive target for nuclear weapons. Furthermore, with a quantum jump in available firepower per man, a smaller army would suffice. As Denis Healey noted in Britain: 'An army equipped with tactical nuclear weapons should be able to hold up an enemy many times its own size.' Blackett, his compatriot, gave a qualified endorsement of this view, which adding that 'it may prove false': 'Highly trained and heavily equipped land forces might exploit tactical atomic weapons for effective offence.'[12]

Others also noted this possibility. Could not the offence use the extra firepower to breach a hole in the defence through which it could then move? In these circumstances the defence would have to remain dispersed, making it harder to concentrate its firepower and hold a line. All that this indicated was that, in preparing to fight war in which *both* sides would be armed with nuclear weapons, new tactical doctrines would have to be developed.

The most celebrated effort to develop a doctrine for limited nuclear war was that of Henry Kissinger. He insisted on the need to be rid of the concepts of old-fashioned land warfare, taking sea warfare as a more appropriate model, 'in which self-contained units with great firepower gradually gain the upper hand by destroying their enemy counterparts without physically occupying territory or establishing a front-line'. Thus the units for tactical nuclear warfare should be small so as not to provide a worthwhile target for the enemy. Because nuclear firepower would not depend on numbers these small units should be mobile (to avoid detection and thus easy destruction) and self-contained 'because the supply system of World War II is far too vulnerable to interdiction'. The ability of these units to carry their own supplies and maintain their own equipment was important in Kissinger's scheme of things. Forces would be much less dependent upon lines of supply. The lines of supply therefore, which usually passed through centres of population, would be less attractive as targets. In an age of nuclear plenty, forces in being at the start of hostilities would suffice. Future wars would be less 'wars of production' and there would be less interest in attacking cities as centres of production. Cities might therefore be spared completely the horror of bombardment, so keeping the war limited. 'With cities no longer serving as key elements in the communications system of the military forces, the risks of initiating city bombing may outweigh the gains which can be achieved.'[13]

It was not, as Kissinger himself eventually came to realize, quite as easy as that. Certainly the US Army had already by 1957 come to the conclusion, which it was not too unhappy to reach, that nuclear weapons could not be relied upon to reduce manpower requirements. Once involved with large ground forces, a support organization was needed. Large forces were required because the rates of attrition must be expected to be high and because, presumably, there would still be an advantage in having superior numbers of nuclear delivery systems and warheads. Furthermore, these would constitute a prize for the other side. Nuclear weapons were useful mainly against fixed targets rather than moving 'targets of opportunity'. In consequence, so as to be less vulnerable to the other side, the units were to be mobile. But could they not be attacked by mobile *conventional* forces? To guard against this eventuality conventional forces of some size would be needed, not only to beat off a conventional attack but also to protect the nuclear delivery systems—and then it would be necessary to provide a logistics organization to support them, and once any form of logistics organization is set up this too has to be protected.

Kissinger's arguments on how to do away with such an organization were the least satisfactory aspect of his case, depending on futile hopes of technological advances. As tactical nuclear weapons were considered particularly suitable for interdiction, lines of communication would soon be under attack. Once this began to happen the consequences for the society playing host to the battle would be horrific. As James King, who developed these arguments in one of the most penetrating critiques of the Kissinger strategy, observed, there could be no promise of 'immunity to society and its facilities'.

On the contrary, sizeable opposing forces nervously trying to get in the first effective nuclear blow will use far more nuclear weapons than the one-per-battle unit theoretically necessary to do the job if all hit their marks, and civilian facilities and centers will be used because using them will enable both sides to increase their forces.[14]

William Kaufmann, reviewing Kissinger's work, emphasized the implausibility of civilians surviving a limited nuclear war with as much ease as in a conventional war. 'In his version of warfare, airmen do not get panicky and jettison their bombs, or hit the wrong targets, missiles do not go astray, and heavily populated areas—whether rural or urban—do not suffer thereby. Surely this is wishful thinking.'[15]

All the practical exercises with simulated tactical nuclear weapons also suggested that it was wishful thinking. This would be a war in which the 'fog of war' would be even murkier than usual. With both sides dispersed, one's own troops would be hard to identify and communication would be extremely difficult. These would be battles of great confusion; the casualties would be high; troops would be left isolated and leaderless; and morale would be hard to maintain. It would be difficult to ensure uncontaminated supplies of food and water or even of spare parts. The Army found it extremely difficult to work out how to

prepare soldiers for this sort of battle and to fight it with confidence.[16]

A more alarming conclusion was that there seemed little hope of protecting civilians from the worst effects of nuclear explosions. Two exercises became notorious: Operation Sage Brush, a war game in Louisiana (the size of Greece and Portugal) in which, after some seventy bombs, each of not more than 40 kilotons yield, had been dropped on military targets, the umpires ruled that all life in the state had 'ceased to exist'. In an exercise called Carte Blanche in West Germany in the same year tactical weapons were 'used' only by the NATO Allies. The results showed that the German people would be devastated in this sort of nuclear war through the effects of blast and fallout. Over two days, 355 devices were exploded, mostly over West German territory. Even without the effects of residual radiation, this would have left up to 1.7 million West Germans dead and 3.5 million wounded— more than five times the number of German civilian casualties in World War II. West German public opinion was alarmed. This could hardly be considered to be either a 'tactical' or a 'limited' matter.

The recognition that tactical nuclear weapons could not be used in such a precise, discriminating manner as to spare civilians had two consequences. First, it meant that if they were to be used it was best that they were used early on in a conflict and before the invading forces had captured much territory. If it were true that nuclear weapons favoured the defence, then they would be of little use in regaining lost ground and a forward defence would avoid too much of Germany becoming a nuclear battleground. Some felt that the results of these exercises did no more than preclude defending Europe with tactical nuclear weapons. Elsewhere, where the population was less dense and there were large open spaces, their use might still be appropriate. This view was criticized as rendering the West vulnerable to the charge that it only considered nuclear weapons appropriate for use against Asians.

The second consequence of appreciating the local consequences of limited nuclear war was to cast grave doubts on the notion that tactical nuclear weapons could be considered virtually conventional in nature. Many nations, especially those whose allegiance to the West was wavering, would not be pleased to be defended with these weapons. There would therefore be strong grounds for holding back on their use. If not quite 'weapons of last resort' they would be of 'penultimate resort'. But any employment after defeats in conventional battles would be over friendly territory, accentuating the problem of inflicting nuclear devastation on people whose rights to self-determination justified the fighting in the first place. What was certain was that the use of nuclear weapons could never be a purely 'tactical' decision, taken by the local commander according to the state of battle. It would be a strategic decision to be taken at the highest level and with reference to the prevailing, overall political and military situation.

NOTES

1. Michael Howard, *Restraints in War: Studies in the Limitation of Armed Conflict* (Oxford University, 1979).
2. Liddell Hart, *Strategy: The Indirect Approach*, p. 25. On Liddell Hart's theories see Brian Bond, *Liddell Hart: A Study of His Military Thought* (London: Cassell, 1977).
3. Liddell Hart, *The Revolution in Warfare* (New Haven: Yale University Press, 1947).
4. Edward Meade Earle, 'The Influence of Air Power upon History,' *Yale Review* 25 (June 1946) pp. 577–593.
5. Taken from a piece written in April 1954 that was later reprinted in B. H. Liddell Hart, *Deterrent or Defence* (London: Stevens & Sons, 1960), p. 23.
6. Letter of 26 April 1957: 'You led all the rest of us in advocating the principle of limited war'. Quoted in Bond, *op. cit.*, p. 196.
7. Bernard Brodie, 'Unlimited Weapons and Limited War', *The Reporter* (1 November 1954).
8. William Kaufmann (ed.), *Military Policy and National Security* (Princeton: Princeton University Press, 1956), pp. 21, 24–5.
9. Robert Endicott Osgood, *Limited War: The Challenge to American Strategy* (The University of Chicago Press, 1957), pp. 26, 242.
10. Henry Kissinger, *Nuclear Weapons and Foreign Policy* (New York: Harper, 1957).
11. Bernard Brodie, 'Strategy hits a dead end', *Harpers* (October 1955); Osgood, *Limited War*, p. 230.
12. Denis Healey, 'The bomb that didn't go off', *Encounter* (July 1955); Blackett, *Atomic Weapons and East-West Relations*, p. 8.
13. Kissinger, *Nuclear Weapons and Foreign Policy*, pp. 174–83.
14. James E. King, 'Nuclear weapons and foreign policy. II—Limited annihilation', *The New Republic* (15 July 1957), p. 18.
15. William Kaufmann, 'The crisis in military affairs', *World Politics*, x:4 (July 1958), p. 594.
16. For a devastating critique of the Army's attempts to do so, see T. N. Dupuy, 'Can America fight a limited nuclear war?', *Orbis*, v:1 (Spring 1961).

22 Pentagon Draws Up First Strategy for Fighting a Long Nuclear War

Richard Halloran

Washington, May 29—Defense Department policy-makers, in a new five-year defense plan, have accepted the premise that nuclear conflict with the Soviet Union could be protracted and have drawn up their first strategy for fighting such a war.

In what Pentagon officials term the "first complete defense guidance of this Administration," drafted for Secretary of Defense Caspar W. Weinberger's signature, the armed forces are ordered to prepare for nuclear counterattacks against the Soviet Union "over a protracted period."

The guidance document, drawn up in the Pentagon and reflecting its views, will form the basis for the Defense Department's budget requests for the next five fiscal years. The document was also a basic source for a recent strategic study done by the National Security Council, according to Defense Department officials. That study is the foundation of the Administration's overall strategic position.

DEBATE ON NUCLEAR WAR

The nature of nuclear war has been a subject of intense debate among political leaders, defense specialists and military officers. Some assert that there would be only one all-out mutually destructive exchange. Others argue that a nuclear war with many exchanges could be fought over days and weeks.

The outcome of the debate will shape the weapons, communications and strategy for nu-

clear forces. The civilian and military planners, having decided that protracted war is possible, say that American nuclear forces "must prevail and be able to force the Soviet Union to seek earliest termination of hostilities on terms favorable to the United States." The Pentagon considers a "protracted" war anything beyond a single exchange of nuclear weapons.

Those views on nuclear war are expressed in a 125-page unpublished document that outlines the Pentagon's military strategy in detail for the next five years and generally for the next decade. Providing the most authoritative insight to date into the military thinking of the Reagan Administration's senior defense strategists, it instructs the armed forces to devise plans for defeating the Soviet Union at any level of conflict from insurgencies to nuclear war.

OTHER MAIN POINTS

The document makes explicit a strategy under which the military forces would be prepared to strike the Soviet homeland and Soviet allies such as Cuba, Vietnam and North Korea in the event of a long conventional war with the Soviet Union.

The guidance document makes these other main points:

¶Nuclear war strategy would be based on what is known as decapitation, meaning strikes at Soviet political and military leadership and communications lines. . . .

¶Special operations, meaning guerrilla warfare, sabotage and psychological warfare, would have to be improved. Space would have to be exploited for American military needs.

¶Readiness of existing forces and building ammunition and other stockpiles to sustain those forces in battle would be given priority over buying new weapons and equipment. The American defense industry would have to be modernized. . . .

As a peacetime complément to military strategy, the guidance document asserts that the United States and its allies should, in effect, declare economic and technical war on the Soviet Union.

It says that the United States should develop weapons that "are difficult for the Soviets to counter, impose disproportionate costs, open up new areas of major military competition and obsolesce previous Soviet investment."

A MORE DETAILED PLAN

Despite its sometimes arcane language, the document, called "Fiscal Year 1984–1988 Defense Guidance," provides a better understanding of the thinking of military planners in the Reagan Administration than earlier documents, which were either routine public statements or revisions of the Carter Administration's strategy.

In many parts of this document, the Reagan military planners started with a blank sheet of paper. Their views on the possibility of protracted nuclear war differ from those of the Carter Administration's military thinkers, as do their views on global conventional war and particularly on putting economic pressure on the Soviet Union.

The guidance paper represents the basic views of Mr. Weinberger and his deputy, Frank C. Carlucci, as well as those of the Joint Chiefs of Staff, senior field commanders, civilian policy planners and technical specialists.

The document was a basic source for the recent strategic study done by the National Security Council, according to Defense Department officials. The study was the foundation of the Administration's overall strategy as described by Mr. Clark in a speech May 21. But the tone of his address was more restrained than the guidance document.

HOW PAPER WILL BE USED

In the Defense Department, the document will provide the overall strategy for proposed programs in the military budget, such as procurement of weapons, operations and maintenance

and the size of the armed services for the five years beginning Oct. 1, 1984.

Those programs will be scrutinized by the Office of Management and Budget, then by the President before they are sent to Congress for debate and appropriation of funds. The President, of course, could reduce any of them if the United States negotiated an arms reduction agreement with the Soviet Union.

The wide-ranging document directs the armed forces to open up new areas of weaponry, particularly in space, where it proposes the "prototype development of space-based weapons systems," including weapons to destroy Soviet satellites. . . .

A LONG NUCLEAR WAR

In developing a strategy for fighting a protracted nuclear war, Mr. Weinberger's policy planners went beyond President Carter's Presidential Directive 59, which focused American nuclear strategy on attacks on specific military and political targets.

The new nuclear strategy calls on American forces to be able to "render ineffective the total Soviet (and Soviet-allied) military and political power structure." But it goes on to require the assured destruction of "nuclear and conventional military forces and industry critical to military power." Those forces must be able to maintain, "through a protracted conflict period and afterward, the capability to inflict very high levels of damage" on Soviet industry.

The nuclear strategy emphasizes communications, so the President and his senior military advisers could control a nuclear exchange and not be limited to one all-out response to Soviet attack.

Communications systems "must provide the capability to execute ad hoc plans, even subsequent to repeated attacks," the document says. "In particular, these systems should support the reconstitution and execution of strategic reserve forces, specifically full communications with our strategic submarines." Communications with submarines today are considered slow and cumbersome.

CONCERNS ABOUT THE SEA

The guidance plan provides refinements in nuclear doctrine. It says that nuclear weapons intended for strategic strikes at the Soviet homeland might be used for attacking targets, such as military bases, in areas such as Eastern Europe. That appears to be an allusion to cruise missiles launched from submarines.

Moreover, the document says, the Soviet Union might be tempted to start a nuclear attack on the United States Navy in the belief that the conflict could be limited to the sea. "Therefore," it says, "it will be United States policy that a nuclear war beginning with Soviet attacks at sea will not necessarily remain limited to the sea."

The military plan says that development of ballistic missile defense systems to defend the United States against Soviet nuclear attack would be accelerated. It also says that the United States might seek a revision in the antiballistic missile treaty if deployment of the MX intercontinental missile required it. . . .

23 Can Nuclear War Be Controlled?

Desmond Ball

For the greater part of the nuclear age, Western strategic thought focused on deterrence and other means of avoiding strategic nuclear war. The principal concerns of the strategic studies community were the conditions of viable mutual deterrence and crisis stability, the prevention of accidental nuclear war, and the promotion of nuclear non-proliferation to limit the danger of catalytic war. Virtually no consideration was given to the conduct of nuclear war in the event that deterrence failed or that, for whatever the reason, nuclear strikes were initiated. It was assumed, at least implicitly, that any significant use of nuclear weapons by either the United States or the Soviet Union against the territory or military forces of the other would inevitably develop into an all-out nuclear exchange limited only by the size of their respective nuclear arsenals.

During the last decade, however, there has been a radical shift in this thinking. Today, the principal concerns of the strategic studies community relate to the period *following* the initiation of a strategic nuclear exchange—i.e. to questions of nuclear war-fighting, such as targeting plans and policies, the dynamics of escalation during a strategic nuclear exchange, and the termination of any such exchange.

Controlled Escalation has become the central operational concept in current US strategic doctrine. This concept requires the US to be able to conduct very selective military operations, initially focussing on the protection of vital American interests immediately threatened, but also aimed at foreclosing opportunities for further enemy aggression; the intention is to deter escalation and coerce the enemy into negotiating a war termination acceptable to the United States by maintaining our capability to effectively withhold attacks from additional hostage targets highly valued [or] vital to enemy leaders, thus limiting the level and scope of violence by threatening subsequent destruction.[1] Controlling escalation requires *both* adversaries to exercise restraint, and current US policy is to offer a combination of measures involving a mixture of self-interest and coercion.

The capabilities for command and control, and the conditions which enable control to be exercised throughout a strategic nuclear exchange are critical to the viability of the current US strategic doctrine. Without survivable command, control and communication C[3] systems, for example, any limited nuclear operations involving control, selectivity, discrimination and precision would rapidly become infeasible.

Concern with the command and control of the US strategic nuclear forces is of course not entirely novel. In 1961–2, for example, much official attention was devoted specifically to this issue. In April 1961, a task force was established within the Pentagon to study the whole field of command and control, and in November 1961 a major report was completed which contained plans for a national command-and-control system designed to survive nuclear attack and provide the President of the US with instantaneous command over vital American military forces.[2] Implementation of these plans over the following years produced the underground SAC and NORAD headquarters at Omaha, Nebraska and

Excerpted with permission from Desmond Ball, "Can Nuclear War Be Controlled?" in James A. Schear, ed., *Nuclear Weapons Proliferation and Nuclear Risk* (pp. 3–4). (New York: St. Martin's Press, 1984). Copyright 1984 by International Institute for Strategic Studies.

Cheyenne Mountain, Colorado; alternative command posts at sea and in the air; and redundant communications links to all elements of the US strategic force. In fact, over the past two decades some $40 billion has been spent on C³ systems for the US strategic nuclear forces.[3] However, this expenditure was directed towards a variety of ends, such as improving the safety of strategic weapons or simply taking advantage of new technological developments, not all of which served to enhance the prospects for controlling nuclear escalation. . . .

Three particular (though closely related) aspects of the current interest in strategic command and control are especially noteworthy. First, the concern with command and control is now at the centre of US strategic planning. Previous consideration of nuclear war-fighting focussed essentially on two variables: the targets to be attacked in any nuclear exchange (counterforce or countervalue), and the rate at which the attack was to proceed (massively or slowly and selectively).[4] Of course, various aspects of control were important to both these variables. At least in some formulations, counterforce strategies were closely associated with damage limitation and 'city avoidance', and required the exercise of discrimination and restraint for successful implementation. And demands on capabilities to control rates of fire would be particularly great if the decision was to conduct the exchange slowly and selectively, holding forces in reserve rather than launching the entire nuclear stockpile simultaneously. Both variables —targets and rate of fire—were to be essentially determined before the outbreak of war, and little change would have been possible during the actual exchange. Now, however, the concern is much more with the dynamics of escalation and the capabilities and conditions for managing the exchange as it progresses. Command and control are obviously central to this.

Second, the concern with command and control now has a new dimension—that of endurance. As the Nuclear Targeting Policy Review (NTPR) concluded in 1978, the US command, control, communications and intelligence (C³I) system 'should have much greater endurance than the present system".[5] At least since 1961–2, substantial resources have been devoted to improving the survivability of US command and control systems. Most particularly, command centres were hardened and alternative systems deployed to ensure that command capabilities would survive a Soviet nuclear attack and that

the order for a retaliatory strike could be given and executed. But endurance was not required of command and control systems beyond perhaps a few days or a week, whereas the current requirement is measured in terms of weeks and even months.

Third, there has been a significant shift in the prevailing rationale for the continued (and increasing) allocation of resources to command-and-control systems. The rationales that dominated command-and-control programmes in the 1950s and 1960s were to prevent accidental or unauthorized nuclear war and to enhance deterrence by maintaining a survivable capability for ensuring retaliation; only infrequently did concern emerge for a serious ability to conduct nuclear strikes other than massive and indiscriminate ones. The notion of deterrence is still invoked, but it is now seen as involving much more than simply maintaining an unambiguous second-strike assured destruction capability. Greater attention is now given to the requirements for deterring both quite limited attacks (such as a strike against some ICBM silos), against which the threat of massive destructive responses might be incredible, and also theatre nuclear conflict, particularly on the NATO/Warsaw Pact front. More fundamentally, however, as the spectrum of contingencies to be deterred has widened, so has the nature of the concept itself. Whereas in the 1960s, for example, the concept of deterrence was starkly contrasted with that of defence, both are now seen as integral parts of a continuum; the capacity for nuclear war-fighting is now regarded as an essential ingredient of a successful deterrent. Insofar as this reformulation depends on maintaining survivable and endurable C³, the new rationales are extremely sensitive to the vulnerabilities of strategic command-and-control.

The recognition that the command-and-control network is the most vulnerable component of the US strategic forces has generated an extensive effort to correct some particular deficiencies. However, many C³ systems are inherently susceptible to a wide range of physical and electronic threats, and certain critical nodal points are inevitable. . . . These vulnerabilities impose very severe physical limits to the extent to which a nuclear war could be controlled.

Various operational strategic, military and political considerations also work against the possibility of controlling a nuclear war. . . . For example, the collateral damage involved in even quite controlled, precise and discriminating nuclear strikes is likely to be both substantial and somewhat unpredictable; there must be great doubt as to whether nuclear weapons can be designed and employed in ways that constitute an unambiguous and fully coherent signalling mechanism—at least when more than a handful are involved. In any case, the control of escalation requires that all participants in the conflict have both the capabilities and the willingness to exercise restraint, and, although the Soviet capabilities for control improved markedly during the 1970s, there is still a very real question mark over whether Soviet strategic doctrine can accommodate the requisite restraint. . . .

Moreover, the dynamics of a nuclear exchange are likely to generate military and political pressures for the relaxation of restraints, even where both adversaries agreed at the outset that it was in their mutual interest to avoid unwanted escalation. There are compelling military arguments both against the highly graduated application of force and for attacking the command-and-control infrastructure of the adversary's strategic nuclear forces. Differences in interests and perspectives among the various groups and individuals that comprise the respective national leaderships (as well as between those leaderships) would make intra-war bargaining and conciliation extremely difficult exercises.

It does not follow that all limited or selective nuclear operations would necessarily lead to an all-out nuclear exchange. Small, carefully conducted attacks designed to demonstrate political resolve could well have a salutary effect. However, it is difficult to envisage the maintenance of control in situations beyond the detonation of several tens of nuclear weapons.

NOTES

1. Dr. William J. Perry, Under Secretary for Defense for Research and Engineering, in Hearings before the Senate Armed Services Committee, *Department of Defense Authorization for Appropriations for Fiscal Year 1980* Part 3. March–May, 1979, p. 1437.

2. Desmond Ball, *Politics and Force Levels: Strategic Missile Program of the Kennedy Administration* (Berkeley: University of California Press, 1980).

3. Harold Brown, *Department of Defense Annual Report Fiscal Year 1981*, U.S. Government Printing Office, 1980, p. 71.

4. Michael D. Intriligator, "The Debate Over Missile Strategy," *Orbis* 11, Winter 1968, pp. 1138–59.

5. Senate Armed Services Committee, *Department of Defense Authorization for Appropriations for Fiscal Year 1980* January–February, 1979, p. 298.

24 Limited Nuclear War

Ian Clark

At least one of the world's present superpowers, the United States, officially adheres to a strategic doctrine in accordance with which a future nuclear war could be conducted in a limited manner: the other power, the Soviet Union, officially denounces such a posture but is thought, by some analysts, to be likely to limit its own operations if once it found itself in a nuclear exchange with the United States. Whereas once we were assured of mutual destruction in a nuclear war, officialdom now encourages us to believe in the possibility of limited nuclear survival: the war that was deemed to be the ultimate form of total war is increasingly presented as a rational and controllable instrument of national policy. What has made it seem such is the growing belief that wars, even intercontinental nuclear ones, might be fought within tacitly agreed limits.

This perspective has emerged as a major one in the 1970s and appears set to dominate strategic thinking in the 1980s. It entails a substantial change of emphasis. As against the realist attitude, which regards war's only problem to be that of discovering how best to win it, and as against the utopian attitude which conceives of war's problem as being one of effective abolition, the limitationist occupies the middle ground: he shares the realist assumption that wars will occur and that they have a purpose, while going part-way with the utopian denial of egoistic national self-assertion and hence accepting the need for restraint in war, if not its prohibition. All

Ian Clark, *Limited Nuclear War: Political Theory and War Conventions*. Copyright © 1982 by Ian Clark. Excerpts, pp. 1–2, 103–104, 106–107, 116–120, 133–137, and 223–237, reprinted by permission of Princeton University Press.

the fundamental paradoxes of war-limitation derive from this initial position because the limitationist is, in a sense, attempting to square the circle. The realist describes war in zero-sum terms whereas the utopian insists on a harmony of human interests, in the context of which war can be no more than an absurdity: the limitationist has the unenviable task of explaining why belligerents have interests in common at that very moment when they attempt, by violent means, to prevail over each other. It is this uneasy juxtaposition, of a sophisticated perception of mutuality with the crass physical realities of combat, which provides the teasing paradoxes and contradictions in which the limitation of warfare abounds, especially when it is recalled that limitation requires a level of co-operation with the enemy in war that proved unattainable in averting recourse to hostilities.

It is also apparent what has prompted the reorientation of nuclear strategic theory towards concepts of limited usage. Given the attainment of some degree of strategic parity between the superpowers by the early 1970s, and given the consequent diminution in the credibility of massive nuclear exchanges, and of the deterrence based thereon, theorists were driven once again to the task of constructing an intellectual framework within which nuclear force and political ends might be brought into meaningful relationship. In the most general terms, the recent attraction of strategic theory to the creation of limited nuclear options has been stimulated by the perceived erosion of the Clausewitzian paradigm of politically-instrumental war. Limitation has been the chosen means by which strategists have sought to put the policy back into the usage of nuclear weapons.

At no time in history has a proper under-

149

standing of limits to war been more pressing than it is now. We live in an age of uncomfortable choices and even when the alternative seems to be one of all-out nuclear holocaust, there is nothing like a consensus in favour of opting for the path of limited war. As *The Economist* was to express the view a quarter of a century ago, but in words as germane today: 'logic says that the most unutterably horrible war that does not

happen is preferable to the most humane war that does.' (Groom, 1974:74) There are those, therefore, who regard the adoption of limited nuclear alternatives with the utmost trepidation. But for these same people, insensate Armageddon is no more attractive a prospect. Neither side in this strategic debate has a monopoly on virtue and it is this fact which lends the issue its special poignancy. . . .

Models of War-Limitation: Champions, Charity and City-Swapping

THE CHAMPION

The settlement of a conflict by means of a combat between champions representing the opposing sides is an extension of some of the principles we have already encountered. For instance, it formalizes observance of the rule of equal advantage, the combat being between equal numbers with identical equipment or, at least, with weaponry of the contestants' own choosing. It epitomizes also the invitation to battle, whereby the time and place of the combat are specified. It delineates who, from amongst the enemy, is a legitimate target and, to be effective, it requires an agreed procedure for determining who is the victor. It should already be apparent that combat by champions is an extremely complex social institution. But is it warfare? Is combat by champions a highly sophisticated and elaborate set of conventions for setting limits to war? Or does it turn war into something else?

To some analysts, combat by champions is a microcosm of warfare, but warfare nonetheless: it is nothing but a manifestation of war in miniature. This is the line taken by Ayala (1912:29) when he describes the combat between the two sets of triplets, the Horatii and the Curiatii, representing Tullus Hostilius, King of the Romans and Mettius Suffetius, King of the Albans, as simply 'an abridged form of the war' that they were already fighting and which was proving too costly. It is a view to which Schelling also appears to subscribe when he is discussing restraints in war and the collaboration between enemies which is necessary for such restraints to be observed. He provides as an example of this 'the duel, *as a method of war*' (Schelling, 1966:144). Clearly Schelling recognizes the championship duel as a legitimate and genuine mode of warfare.

Other analysts would demur from such an interpretation and have variously described combat by champions as a form of game, sport or recreation, but certainly not as a form of warfare. The instances of championship contests in medieval Europe have, accordingly, been dismissed as examples of chivalric display with no serious purpose to them, other than as a means of demonstrating the courage, prowess and honour of the knight. The problem here is that precisely the same comment has been made about the battles of that period, which were ironically little more than champion duels on a larger scale. This is how some of these battles have been described:

> Many of the battles of this period were no more than shock skirmishes between small bodies of armoured knights, in which individual combats were sought, to prove rather the worth of the fighter than his destructive capabilities. The object was to unhorse one's opponent rather than to slay him. In short, battles were frequently little more than sharp-weapon tourneys. (Fuller, 1946:63)

Presumably, on this reasoning, such battles would also have to be dismissed as instances of some other form of activity and not of warfare itself.

A concise statement of the view that combat by individual champions is not genuine warfare, can be found in one description of the champion practice in the ancient Greek epics. According to this account, the champion combat is a form of theatre:

> . . . a certain artistic ideal was applied in the institution of single combats between chiefs and distinguished warriors, who thus played

the part, as it was, of the protagonists of a tragedy, whilst their respective nations filled that of the spectators and judges of fair play. Thus was fought the duel between Paris and Menelaus. (Phillipson, 1911:209)

More strikingly than any other form of war-limitation, then, the champion confronts us with the question, how far can war be limited while remaining war? . . .

Whatever its historical or theoretical origins, the practice of resolving disputes by single combat has been a transcultural phenomenon. . . .

Some of the better known champion episodes are to be found in the Greek epics and histories. Champions were apparently employed in the wars against the Persians as well as between the city states themselves. Herodotos mentions the instance where 'Hyllus made proclamation, that it would be better not to run the hazard of engaging army with army; but that from the Peloponnesian camp, the man amongst them who they judge to be the best, should fight singly with him. . . .' (Phillipson, 1911:209–210)

The most frequently cited instance, again narrated by Herodotos, dates from the mid-sixth century BC and refers to a perennial dispute between Argos and Sparta over the territory of Thyreae. It is an interesting case because, although an example of combat by champions, it was not a contest between single champions:

The Argives . . . agreed in conference with the Spartans that three hundred picked men a side should fight it out, and that Thyreae should belong to the victors; the rest of the two armies were to go home without staying to watch the fight, lest either side, seeing its champions getting the worst of it, might be tempted to intervene. On these terms they parted, leaving behind the men chosen to represent them, and the battle began. . . . (Garlan, 1975:27)

. . . .

The problems surrounding victory in a championship duel can be found at two distinct levels. The first group concerns the problem of recognizing who has actually won the contest; the second concerns the vulnerability of a victory that is conventional and rests, therefore, upon mutual observance. These two situations may be treated separately.

The first problem is likely to arise when ground rules specifying the constituents of victory have not been elaborated in advance. The previously mentioned contest between Sparta and Argos is the most memorable case in point:

So closely was it contested that of the six hundred men only three were left alive—two Argives, Alcenor and Chromios, and one Spartan, Othryadas—and even these would have been killed had not darkness put an end to the fighting. The two Argives claimed the victory and hurried back to Argos; but the Spartan, Othryadas remained under arms and, having stripped the bodies of the Argive dead, carried their equipment to his own camp. . . . The two armies met again on the following day, to learn the result of the battle. For a while both Argives and Spartans maintained that they had won, the former because they had the greater number of survivors, the latter because the two Argives had run away, whereas their own man had remained on the battlefield and stripped the bodies of the dead. The argument ended in blows, and a fresh battle began. . . . (Garlan, 1975:27)

The other problem is a more fundamental one, not one of recognizing victory but of preserving it: the task is to ensure compliance with the outcome of the combat on the part of an army that has been 'defeated' symbolically, but which still exists as a physical reality. Why should the vanquished party abide by the decision when, having already 'lost', it has no more to 'lose'. . . ?

CHARITY

Charity, as a model of war-limitation, is mostly associated with varieties of just war theories. Although such theories have differed both in content and in motivation, we might accept the general formulation that 'the just war stops short of countenancing the utter destruction of the adversaries and tends to limit the incidence of violence by codes of right conduct, of noncombatant immunity and by other humanitarian restraints. . .' (Russell, 1975:2). Regardless of the specific moral content of the doctrine, there is a general insistence that charity constitutes a limitation beyond which it is not possible to go even in the prosecution of a war with just ends. Vattel (Vattel, 1916:289–290) was to make the point succinctly and his observation can stand as a general depiction of charity as a form of limitation: 'let us never forget that our enemies are men. Although we may be under the unfortunate necessity of prosecuting our right by force of arms, let us never put aside the ties of charity which bind us to the whole human race'. . . .

The principle of charity urges us to refrain from doing certain things to the enemy during war. We must be clear about the reasons why we should so refrain and this can best be done by contrasting charity with alternative motivations.

Firstly, we could refrain from certain military actions out of prudential or utilitarian considerations. In this case, the principal consideration, inducing restraint on our part, is the prospect that it might induce reciprocal restraint by the enemy: the restraint becomes an attribute of our relationship with the enemy rather than an attribute of the action that we are refraining from doing.

Secondly, we may refrain from doing something to the enemy in order that we might be able to threaten to do it in the future. Here again we have a form of war-limitation which is, in principle, different from that derived from charity. This second motivation for restraint is most clearly expressed in Schelling (1966:24) when he argues that 'each might feel the sheer destruction of enemy people and cities would serve no decisive military purpose but that a continued *threat* to destroy them might serve a purpose. The continued threat would depend on their not being destroyed yet.' What induces restraint in this case is neither the intrinsic moral repugnance of the act, nor the prospect of reciprocity, but simply the utility of not doing now what we may wish to do, or threaten to do, in the future. As Schelling (p.193) again says: 'the reason for not destroying the cities is to keep them at our mercy'. Objectively, the restraint is similar in both cases but the motivation which leads to the restraint is fundamentally different. The principle of charity accordingly asserts itself by limiting war neither for reasons of reciprocity nor for reasons of mounting a future threat.

As previously indicated, charity may find its source in a multitude of philosophical and metaphysical considerations—moral, humanitarian, religious and natural law amongst them. . . .

CITY-SWAPPING

In this section, a third distinctive conception of war-limitation will be outlined. Firstly, we will describe its general characteristics and then, as with the previous two models, we can move on to examine it in greater detail in terms of the analytic categories already established. What we are concerned with in this section is a generalized notion of what constitutes limited war, as it emerges from the analyses of the nuclear strategists. The strategists have, of course, developed a mind-boggling array of escalatory stages, each of which is limited in relation to the next rung on the escalation ladder, and there are therefore as many accounts of what constitutes limited war as there are gradations in the threat and exercise of military force. The nomenclature 'city-swapping' should not be taken literally to mean only a countervalue strategy in which cities are taken out alternately but rather as a generic term referring to a type of relationship between limitation and bargaining before and during warfare.

What, then, are the general characteristics of this third model? What we are dealing with here is a form of limited war in which the limits are as much an outcome of the bargaining between belligerents as they are conventions about how the bargaining shall be conducted: chronologically, the limits cannot actually be known until the conflict is resolved. In a very important sense, therefore, we are confronted here with a model of limited war which has no intrinsic limits.

In its essentials, this model of limitation is equivalent to Halperin's strategy of 'limited retaliation' of which he states that 'this strategy involves severe quantitative restraint. Both sides fire few missiles, perhaps one at a time, increasing to larger numbers if one side does not back down after the initial exchanges' (Halperin, 1963:96). As such, this form of warfare shares the characteristics of two of Schelling's models being both a war of 'risk' and a war of 'pain and destruction' (1966:166–167). As will be seen shortly, this warfare is a competition in risk-taking and the risk is of increasingly greater quantities of pain and destruction. Despite all this, city-swapping has to be regarded as a principal model for the limitation of contemporary warfare.

There is debate in the literature as to the novelty of this form of limitation, with its proponents seeing it as a model elaborated systematically only during the nuclear age. The argument seems to be that this model of limitation is predicated upon collaboration, which is conscious, even if tacit, between enemies in wartime itself; such collaboration is deemed to be a development of the theory of limited war in the nuclear era. . . .

What, then, might induce enemies to enter into tacit cooperation with each other? Why, if they are both trying to win, should either of them withhold forces that it has available to it. What is the incentive that will induce 'a deliberate hobbling of a tremendous power that is already mobilized' (Brodie, 1959:311)? The recurrent answer to this question is that the belligerents will agree to restrain their available forces only if they perceive it to be in their respective self-interests to do so. As Brodie (1954:19) was to point out in an early contribution to the theory of limited war in the nuclear age: 'the reciprocity of restraint, whether openly or tacitly recognized, will have to be on the basis of mutual self-interest'.

We must now briefly consider the sense in which city-swapping constitutes a limited form of warfare, as well as some of the restrictions upon such a usage. If two belligerents are engaged in war, and if their convention is to destroy targets on either side slowly, selectively and alternately, in what sense does this represent a limited form of warfare?

Ramsey (1963:20), in the very act of disparaging such a model of limitation, implicitly concedes that it may nonetheless limit the destruction of warfare:

> This is the secret meaning of the statement that countervalue warfare can, as a test of wills, have only *quantitative* limitations. This really means that there are no limits, except that quantity of destruction which will cause one side to give up first. If there had been more resolution to continue fighting . . . the quantity would have been higher.

Evidently, however, despite Ramsey's protestations, if the punishment inflicted in the initial stages of war is sufficient to diminish the resolution of one of the parties, the war will be limited, in the sense that the quantity of damage wrought will be less: two cities destroyed on either side is a limitation in comparison with ten cities destroyed on either side. City-swapping may, therefore, be described as a model of warfare which is quantitatively limited.

Or, at least, it *may* be so limited. The problem with this form of limitation is that it is impossible to know beforehand at what point the war will, in fact, be limited. What appear as limitations, as terminations to the war, may be no more than breathing spaces or breaks in the sequence of action. We do not know in advance where the limits, if any, will be found. It is for

this reason that Ramsey (1963:23) denounced the 'abyss of infinitude and illimitability into which strategic city exchange has already plunged'. His specific argument is that 'to this there are no real boundaries: and to speak of "quantitative" limitations is misleading and dangerous language. Even the understandings reached during the fighting will be arbitrary ones, maintained only by encounters of resolve.' On this issue, Ramsey's reasoning is supported by that of Schelling, even if otherwise the two have little in common. The problem with all limitations which are purely quantitative is, as Schelling would argue, that they are not salient: there is no logical reason for stopping at one quantity rather than another. As Schelling (1966:164) noted: 'to argue that one can as readily stop after the third city, or the thirteenth, or the thirtieth, detracts from the more promising boundary at zero'.

It might, therefore, be suggested that city-swapping, as a form of warfare, is an all-out fight (potentially) with the significant qualification that it is in slow motion and that its sequential nature allows the action to be broken into. This permits the action to be broken off but does not in itself guarantee that it will be. . . .

City-swapping and War-limitation

The structure of this model is most vividly captured in Schelling's account of San Franciscan duels: 'in early days, wealthy San Franciscans, it is said, conducted their "duels" by throwing gold coins one by one into the Bay until one or the other called it quits' (Knorr and Read, 1962:243–244). We might call such a conflict limited in two distinct senses. Firstly, the two contestants are not trying to throw each other into the Bay, which is to say that neither is seeking to eliminate his opponent physically. Secondly, the two contestants do not simultaneously throw into the Bay their entire holdings of gold coins. In some sense, therefore, we are confronted with a limited contest and yet, equally, we have no way of knowing beforehand at which limit the contest will stop: the coin-swapping may conceivably continue until all coins have been expended on both sides (assuming they have equal amounts); conceivably, also, when this has happened, one party might, in exasperation, throw the other into the Bay. The likelihood of the latter outcome is dependent upon the strength of the conventions of the contest but clearly the former outcome is not equally proscribed. . . .

NUCLEAR WAR AND UNCERTAIN LIMITS

Apart from this entire issue of the likelihood of Soviet reciprocity in limiting a nuclear war, the main point of contention in discussions of limited nuclear warfare has been the technical one of determining whether, even if a war were fought by agreed conventions of limitation, its effects could in any meaningful sense be considered to be limited (see Drell and Hippel, 1976). The present author does not have the technical competence to pass judgment on these arguments. Nonetheless, one thing is abundantly clear. While it is one of the main premises of all the theories of limited nuclear war that such wars can be sufficiently contained to produce specific effects and to reduce other effects substantially, the fact remains that the most impressive characteristic of all the scientific study of the impact of nuclear war, is its marked uncertainty about the extent of the resulting damage. The main finding of the Office of Technology Assessment's report on *The Effects of Nuclear War*, published in 1979, was accordingly that 'the effects of a nuclear war that cannot be calculated are at least as important as those for which calculations are attempted'. The report also suggested that the 'impact of even a "small" or "limited" nuclear attack would be enormous'. . . . Thus one well-informed observer, in reviewing the OTA report, concluded that the certitudes of limited nuclear option programmes were based on dangerously shifting foundations:

> The effects of any nuclear operation are therefore essentially unpredictable. . . . And all the limited and selective options that have now been incorporated in the SIOP notwithstanding, the possibility of conducting limited and controlled nuclear exchanges in which damage is a matter only of policy choice remains no less unreal than it was before the re-thinking of the mid-1970s. (Ball, 1980:234)

Above all, one cannot fail to gain an impression that many of the forms of limitation proposed in these theories are, in principle, as quaint as many of the ancient and medieval practices which would, no doubt, be dismissed as irrelevant to the conditions of contemporary warfare. Codes of military etiquette and chivalry which depend for their sustenance upon cosmopolitan norms, perceived mutuality and coordination with the enemy would be thought inapplicable to present-day conditions. Nonetheless, in their place, the theorists of limited nuclear war have attempted to create a new code of nuclear chivalry, every bit as colourful and fanciful as the medieval chivalric displays. Could there be anything more quixotic than the following scenario, recommended by Halperin, (1963:107) for American conduct during a nuclear confrontation:

> . . . limiting a central war may depend on both sides' believing that limitation is possible and that the other is likely to reciprocate restraint. The United States should continue to emphasize that the changes it is making in its strategic posture are relevant to the limitation of central war: for example, its increased control over its strategic forces, the location of these forces away from population centres, and its programme for the construction of fallout shelters. The United States might also suggest that the Soviets take similar action. . . . The United States might spell out even more explicitly its commitment to particular kinds of limitations by stating more clearly than was done in the McNamara speech that we would not target cities unless the Soviets did so, and we might privately suggest to the Soviets that they separate these two types of targets so that city destruction would not become necessary.

Of all the stylized conflicts that can be found in history, this is surely as contrived and theatrical as any.

Even more so is the case where the theorists envisage a negotiated termination of the war after a few limited nuclear exchanges between the parties. Again we might ask whether there is any fundamental difference between artificial limitations before the event, as in the form of an agreement to hold a single combat, and premature termination of the war after it has begun? Is there not a deficiency in the logic which argues that it is absurd to do before the outbreak of war what it is reasonable to do—indeed is the *only* objective—once war has broken out? It is surely naive to believe that the mutuality of interests necessary for war-limitation is unattainable before war but to expect it to emerge when the positions of the antagonists are, *a fortiori*, polarized by hostilities?

Apart from these general observations, there are a number of specific criticisms, or requests for greater clarification, which might be addressed to the contemporary theorists of limited nuclear war. The remainder of this [reading] . . . will outline a number of these issues.

Firstly, as to that most intractable of all arguments about limits to war, whether a diminution of its horrors increases the likelihood of its occurrence, the recent official pronouncements on limited nuclear war have little of value to contribute. Carter's Defense Secretary, Harold Brown, resolved the problem to his own satisfaction by insisting that it simply did not exist. 'There is no contradiction,' Brown reiterated, 'between this focus on how a war would be fought and what its results would be, and our purpose of insuring continued peace through mutual deterrence' (see *Survival*, November-December, 1980:268). The claim, however, was patently disingenuous and less than respectful to those critics who had deployed the argument. For instance, on 17 August 1980, only a few days before Brown's remarks, the *New York Times* had quoted the opinion of P. Warnke, former Director of the Arms Control and Disarmament Agency, to the effect that 'deterrence is always weakened by any strategy that seems to contemplate a limited nuclear war'. It was less than charitable to respond to the argument by simply denying that there was anything to it.

Not only was it uncharitable, it was logically perverse, because in a very fundamental sense all strategies of deterrence are predicated upon the intentional manipulation of the risk of war. An editorial in *The Times* of 4 September 1980 was perfectly correct when it commented upon criticisms of Presidential Directive 59 that 'the most familiar one is that by making the United States' nuclear force easier to use it makes it more likely to be used. But it is just this likelihood that is the essence of deterrence.' Viewed in this light, the conclusion that limited nuclear war doctrines strive to increase the threat of war breaking out is undeniable, as otherwise the argument that they possess greater deterrent power would be equally invalid. We might, therefore, observe with greater precision that selective nuclear options, as presented in recent American programmes, are designed to reduce the *risk* of war by increasing the *threat* of it: whether that greater threat is sufficient to deter war's occurrence is the central dilemma of all deterrence theory and, accordingly, to assert that the dilemma does not exist is completely untenable.

Secondly, it deserves to be repeated that whatever selectivity the new doctrines intend to introduce into nuclear targeting, the revisions do not entail any conscious and irreversible decision to switch the nuclear threat away from civilian populations. Schlesinger was unequivocal on this point in one of his early press con-

ferences on the topic of counterforce. 'The shift in targeting strategy,' he clarified, '. . . does not mean that we are pointing missiles away from city targets to military targets . . . we must continue to target cities . . .' (*Official Text*, U.S. Embassy, London, 25 January 1974:2). The question asked by Bruce Russett was, therefore, a moot one. Reserving judgment on the 1974 revisions of strategic targeting, Russett wanted to know 'to what degree will the targeting of Soviet military installations replace, rather than merely supplement, the targeting of cities?' (Letter to *The Times*, 15 January 1974).

In this context, Schlesinger's clarifications in testimony before the Senate Armed Services Committee on 5 February 1974 are of interest. Schlesinger's remarks were as follows:

> . . . if a nuclear clash should occur . . . in order to protect American cities and the cities of our allies, we shall rely into the wartime period, upon our assured destruction force and persuading through intra-war deterrence any potential foe not to attack cities. (*Official Text*, US Embassy, London, 15 February 1974, p. 2)

The statement is highly revealing: it indicates not the abandonment of mutual assured destruction, but its displacement in time. What Schlesinger's new strategy seems to do, on his own description of it, is to postpone MAD and to reinstate it as the orthodoxy of a war-time rather than of a peace-time strategy. From being the reprisal held in reserve to preserve the peace, MAD under the Schlesinger innovations would become the reprisal held in reserve to preserve nuclear war's limitations.

Thirdly, in any listing of the pressures to devise new strategic policies in the 1970s and 1980s, it would be remiss not to highlight the momentum of technological development and the brute facts of weapon system acquisition. As a consequence of MIRV technology and the acquisition of large numbers of theatre nuclear devices, the actual number of available nuclear warheads expanded dramatically in the course of the 1970s. This fact alone impinged upon targeting policy because, to put it in its crudest terms, there simply were not enough soft civilian targets to go round. As G. Treverton had suggested: 'with more and more nuclear warheads, the United States reached the point in 1974 where even the all-out "assured destruction" retaliation would have sent some 70 per cent of the war heads against military, not civilian or economic targets' (*Observer News Service*, 5 September 1980). Similarly, it was not the quantity alone of nuclear weapons, but also their improving quality, which was to precipitate new thinking on their use. It was suggested above that limited-war theory has, to some extent, been prisoner to a technological imperative, as a consequence of which strategic doctrine has followed design achievements as much as it has dictated them. The force of this argument had in no way diminished during the 1970s. There is, therefore, unconscious irony in the defence, put forward by Robert Ellsworth, of the Schlesinger proposals of 1974. Taking exception to an earlier *New York Times'* editorial, Ellsworth contended that 'it is not a "new Nixon strategy" which . . . requires enormous numbers of new, highly accurate warheads. The contrary is the case: it is the enormous numbers of new, highly accurate warheads which require a new strategy' (letter to *New York Times*, 25 January 1974). Ellsworth was right but for the wrong reasons. As an explanation of the pressures leading to a reassessment of strategic targeting, Ellsworth's analysis had much to commend it: as a vindication of that new policy, it was less than persuasive, because surely no administration could claim virtue for a strategic policy seen to be hostage to technological fortune.

Fourthly, and following from the previous account of Soviet attitudes to limited nuclear war, it is necessary to record the uniformly hostile Soviet response to Carter's Presidential Directive 59. What we are to conclude from this negative response as to future Soviet intentions is far from clear, but at the very least it is necessary to recognize ostensible Soviet opposition to the content of the strategic doctrine given official sanction in the United States in July 1980. While public Soviet declarations on this issue may not reflect the totality of Soviet thinking, nor even its dominant features, they must at least be acknowledged and efforts made to come to terms with them. We can distinguish at least three grounds on which Soviet spokesmen took exception to the enunciated American policy. The first was the articulation, as in *Pravda* of 7 August 1980, of fears that the underlying American intention was to develop a first-strike capability. Secondly, Soviet commentaries alluded to the theme of the increased likelihood of war concomitant with erroneous thinking about the possibilities of fighting limited wars. A *Tass* report by A. Krasikov on 8 August 1980 developed this objection:

The White House is trying to instill in Americans and people of other countries the idea that it is possible to wage a nuclear-missile war dealing blows only against troops and command posts while the civilian population escapes suffering or suffers only minimally. This is a very dangerous doctrine whose aim is to lull the people's vigilance and to bring closer the destruction of civilization.

The final theme was an assertion of Soviet autonomy and a refusal to be seen to be bound by American-devised prescriptions for the conduct of nuclear war. This might be thought the least serious of the Soviet objections, centring as it does upon Soviet *amour propre* rather than upon the actual substance of the American policy. At any rate, G. Trofimenko of the USSR's Institute for the Study of the USA and Canada, rebutted the expectations of US policy makers that they 'could hope to impose upon the other side their own "rules of the game" in a military conflict' (*New York Times*, 22 September 1980).

Fifthly, we need to be aware that scepticism about the new posture was not confined to the Soviet Union but was expressed also within Carter's own administration. Defense Secretary Harold Brown, during his Senate confirmation hearings, had said he thought it unlikely that a limited nuclear exchange would remain limited and, while he was to defend the posture affirmed in PD 59, he continued to express reservations about the prospects for successful limitation. During an interview on an ABC news programme on 17 August 1980, Brown maintained his belief that 'nuclear strikes, a nuclear strike on the United States, even though we retaliated initially in a limited way, would probably escalate ultimately to an all-out nuclear war' (*Official Text*, US Embassy, London, 19 August 1980). The replacement Secretary of State, Edmund Muskie, was similarly to tell a Senate hearing on Carter's directive that 'I do not want anyone to wrongly conclude that we suddenly have become confident about our ability to orchestrate nuclear exchanges and control escalation. . .' (*Official Text*, US Embassy, London, 17 September 1980).

Sixthly, although there are general similarities between Schlesinger's selective options and Brown's countervailing strategy, there are nonetheless some apparent differences that must not be allowed to escape our notice. Curiously, the public relations' claims made on behalf of the two strategic postures to some extent belie the novelty of their respective substances. On the one hand, during the Ford administration, Schlesinger was happy to draw attention to the new look of his strategic offerings whereas, as previously illustrated, there were marked continuities between the 1960s and early 1970s: limited counterforce options were part of American strategic practice long before they became part of declared strategic policy. As regards PD 59, we can perhaps arrive at the reverse judgment, that the administration's emphasis upon continuity distracts attention from some original features. Whilst the Schlesinger doctrine might fairly be regarded as old wine in new bottles, there is a specific sense in which Carter's strategic decisions represent new wine in old bottles.

What are the reasons for this claim? Ostensibly, as administration spokesmen were at pains to demonstrate, PD 59 is no more than the culmination of a decade's strategic development. '. . . PD 59 is not,' in Brown's words, 'a new strategic doctrine; it is not a radical departure from US strategic policy over the past decade or so' (address reproduced in *Survival*, November-December 1980, p. 268). Nonetheless, some of the emphases of PD 59 had not been as apparent in earlier policy statements. Above all, one feature of PD 59 which had not previously been given prominence, if stated at all, was the one pertaining to the targeting of the enemy's political and military control centres. Numerous official and background statements suggested that such Soviet centres featured high on the list of target priorities. One official, for instance, argued that the emphasis in the new policy would be upon threatening the targets most valued by the Soviet leadership amongst which he included 'its own ability to maintain control after a war starts' (*New York Times*, 6 August 1980). Brown, himself, cited as a more credible deterrent one which threatened 'the military and political command systems' (*Official Text*, US Embassy, London, 19 August 1980).

Various analysts noted this new emphasis of PD 59 and were puzzled as to its implications, and one inspired *New York Times* report of 17 August 1980 suggested that the puzzlement was felt also in official circles. It quoted a spokesman as saying that: 'this policy seems to assume that both sides could engage in selective nuclear strikes without blowing each other up. . . . But how will the Soviet leaders be able to control what their generals do during war if the Kremlin is going to be the first place that's taken out?'

Flora Lewis likewise drew attention to both the novelty and the dangers of this aspect of the recently stated nuclear strategy:

> A policy question raised by the latest White House directive is the inclusion of 'command and control' targets. One constant of nuclear strategy has been the understanding that contrary to conventional doctrine, the enemy's command should be left intact so that there is still someone capable of stopping action with whom to negotiate before escalation becomes automatic and unconditional for humankind. Is this axiom being abandoned? Some American officials say not necessarily, that the US President should have the choice of liquidating the enemy's leadership if he thinks there is someone more amenable around to take charge. That is an intensely risky notion (*New York Times*, 15 August 1980).

What added to the seeming inappropriateness of such a measure in the context of the conduct of a limited nuclear war, was the almost simultaneous issuance of Presidential Directive 58, a series of measures designed to ensure greater survivability for America's own command structure in event of war. Such measures accorded well with the requirements of a limited nuclear strategy, but made the targeting of the enemy control systems seem even more out of phase with the general tenor of the new doctrine.

A seventh point which can be made refers to the crucial question of termination of a war that has begun. Regrettably, on this score, PD 59 and its accompanying exegeses offer no enlightenment. In a discussion of the ingredients of a countervailing strategy, Harold Brown remarked that 'in our planning we have not ignored the problem of ending the war, nor would we ignore it in the event of war' (*New York Times*, 21 August 1980). However, he did not elaborate on the nature of these plans for terminating the war. We are left to ponder, as with the city-swapping model, at which limit it would all end. When we recall Brown's other cautions that a limited nuclear war is likely to go all the way, the precise content of such plans for ending a war becomes even more elusive and our faith in its efficacy cannot but be shaken. If the Secretary of Defense knew the details of these plans for terminating war but could still fear that limited war in the beginning would become all-out war in the end, we can be forgiven for harbouring an occasional doubt.

An eighth and final observation is in order. What underlies the various strategic rethinkings of the 1970s, and is articulated in PD 59, is the need to think through, in a serious and comprehensive fashion, the realities of preparing for and, if need be, of actually conducting a nuclear engagement. It is this which the limited nuclear warriors of the past decade claim to have achieved—that they have faced up to, and come to terms with, the conduct of nuclear war in a limited form. Given this context, it is more than a little confusing to have the authors of the programme tell us also that 'nothing in PD 59 contemplates that nuclear war can be a deliberate instrument for achieving our national security goals, because it cannot be' (*Official Text*, US Embassy, London, 19 September 1980). How realistic has been the rethink about fighting a limited nuclear war is called fundamentally into question by this statement. Either fighting a nuclear war cannot serve strategic interests, or the administration is not serious in its intention to acquire the capacity to fight such a war. In the light of Brown's statement, the limited nuclear warriors cannot have it both ways.

One summary and general point remains to be made. This study has been concerned with conventions mitigating warfare, but the recurrent question has been how far war can be convention-governed without alteration to its fundamental nature. In other words, we are back to the possibility that rules governing the character of war may be such as to transmute warfare into some game-like activity. Paskins and Dockrill (1979:105–106) make this point obliquely by reference to an extreme convention designed to prevent fatality:

> ... it makes sense to think of wrestling matches and even duels as surrounded with rules designed to guard against fatalities. With war it is different. There are many instances in military history of the evolution of practices aimed to limit fatalities, but fighting whose rules were aimed to preclude fatality would not be war.

Let us examine this proposition in the light of one famous wartime suggestion—the proposal that, instead of employing the atomic bomb against Japanese cities, the surrender of Japan be induced by a harmless demonstration of the bomb's military capabilities. Would such a course of action, intended to terminate the war without fatalities, have been a normal act of war, or must it be dismissed as a frivolity inconsistent with war's deadly serious purpose? Certainly the scientific committee charged with the task of examining the technical feasibility of such a demonstration claimed to have taken the proposal seriously and to have carefully examined its possibilities. 'We were determined,' Arthur Compton, a senior scientific adviser, was to record, 'to find, if we could, some effective way of demonstrating the power of an atomic bomb without loss of life that would impress Japan's warlords' (Compton, 1956:239). Even Edward Teller was subsequently to regret that such a demonstration was not attempted:

> I believe that we should have demonstrated it to the Japanese before using it. Had we succeeded, had the Japanese surrendered after such a demonstration, then a new age would have started in which the power of human knowledge had stopped a war without killing a single individual. (Quoted in Giovannitti and Freed, 1967:329)

Would such a contrived and artificial termination of the war have been a humane limitation on war? Or would it have been a social nicety in complete contradiction to the stated aims for which the United States was engaged in war with Japan?

The capacity of stylized conventions to limit killing in war could not be thought encouraging in the light of earlier precedents in the course of the Second World War. As is well known, the precision bombing with which Britain prepared to conduct the war rapidly took the form of indiscriminate area bombardment as Bomber Command groped for an operational policy which was consistent with its role as an independent force and with the technical limitations of its bomber fleet. It is difficult to conceive that the very Bomber Command which was to devise the saturation bombings of Berlin, Hamburg and of Dresden had but a few short years before prevented its aircraft from bombing German naval vessels at Wilhelmshaven, as they were considered too close to the shore to be attacked without collateral civilian damage (Hastings, 1981:28). The conventions of aerial bombardment were, therefore, to be the most spectacular casualties of the war. Likewise, although the United States Air Force had a slightly cleaner record in its offensive against Germany, by early 1945 it was heavily engaged in fire-bombing of Japan with massive civilian loss of life.

It was against this background that the decision on use of the new atomic weapon had to be taken. The politico-strategic problem was how to end the war while minimizing loss of life in securing that objective and, of course, it is history that the view which prevailed was the one which argued that these objectives could best be realized by military employment of the atomic bomb, without warning, against Japanese cities.

What, then, are we to make of the abortive proposal to demonstrate the bomb's destructive potential? It has been argued above that, as a result of a set combat between champions, a conventional or artificial notion of victory is substituted for victory as a brute physical fact: the enemy, although defeated, is still in existence as a military force. The champion is accordingly the supremely stylized form of resolution of conflict by military encounter. From this perspective, if in a less extreme form, the proposal that the United States demonstrate the bomb, rather than employ it as a weapon of war, can be seen as a suggestion for an equally stylized termination of the conflict with Japan. War is thought to require killing, and yet this was a proposal to conduct the final stages of the war in such a manner that any further killing could be averted. As with the champion, the intent of the proposal was that a conventional notion of victory (based on the awe of a demonstrated effect) be substituted for the bloody but 'real' victory which would flow from invasion, or from repeated poundings of Japan by atomic weapons. In other words, if adopted, this initiative would have led to a convention of limitation whereby the United States agreed not to destroy Japan (actually) if Japan agreed not to resist further. The demonstrated detonation of the nuclear device would constitute a symbolic victory for the Americans, just as if their appointed champion had carried the day: the Japanese would be defeated (symbolically) although still capable of resistance (physically).

The proposal to demonstrate the bomb never gained much support in the highest échelons of the American decision-making apparatus. The writings of Truman, Stimson and Byrnes convey the impression that no decision was needed to use the bomb in a military capacity: it would have required a decision *not* to use it, and this possibility was not seriously entertained. This conforms with Compton's impression of the discussions at the decisive Interim Committee meeting of 31 May 1945 to the effect that 'it seemed to be a foregone conclusion that the bomb would be used' (1956:238) and with Oppenheimer's intuitive judgment that 'the decision was

implicit in the project. I don't know whether it could have been stopped' (quoted in Giovannitti and Freed, 1967:328). Nonetheless, the proposal for a demonstration was repeatedly made and was persistent over time even if most of its adherents were to be found within the scientific community, rather than amongst those in political authority (See Smith, 1965:26). Scientific advisers Bush and Conant had made a suggestion for a demonstration of the bomb in a memorandum to Stimson on 30 September 1944, and Alexander Sachs had reported that President Roosevelt was favourably impressed by a similar suggestion made by him in December 1944 (Schoenberger, 1969:45). The proposal was reiterated in the Franck report of June 1945 which favoured a 'demonstration in an appropriately selected uninhabited area' (Smith, 1965:45). The possibilities of a demonstration had already, by this time, been mooted during a lunch-time discussion at the 31 May meeting of the Interim Committee.

Perhaps the fullest, and most colourful, suggestion for a demonstration of the bomb, as an alternative to its direct employment against Japanese cities, was that put forward by Lewis Strauss, Special Assistant to Navy Secretary, Forrestal:

> . . . I proposed to Secretary Forrestal that the weapon should be demonstrated before it was used. Primarily it was because it was clear to a number of people, myself among them, that the war was very nearly over . . . My proposal to the Secretary was that the weapon should be demonstrated over some area accessible to Japanese observers and where its effects would be dramatic. I remember suggesting that a satisfactory place for such a demonstration would be a large forest of cryptomeria trees not far from Tokyo . . . I anticipated that a bomb detonated at a suitable height above such a forest . . . would lay the trees out in windrows from the center of the explosion in all directions as though they were matchsticks, and, of course, set them afire in the center. . . . (Quoted in Giovannitti and Freed, 1967:145)

In fact, Ralph Bard, Under Secretary of the Navy, was to resign over the issue. He argued that the Japanese should at least be given some preliminary warning of the dropping of the bomb and, in support of this, appealed to the humanitarianism and the 'fair play attitude' of the United States (p. 146).

Many reasons were given for the non-adoption of the demonstration proposal. Interestingly, however, they all related to the technicalities of the operation or to other practical difficulties. Oppenheimer recalled that 'we did say that we did not think exploding one of these things as a firecracker over a desert was likely to be very impressive', (quoted in Feis, 1966:55) and fears of malfunction, or Japanese interference, were widely expressed. At any rate, the scientific committee reported that 'we can propose no technical demonstration likely to bring an end to the war; we can see no acceptable alternative to direct military use' (Schoenberger, 1969:143). No one seemed to question, in principle, whether this was a proper thing to do *in time of war* when American lives were at stake. Or, perhaps, the judgment that such gentlemanly etiquette had no place in war did not have to be expressed: it was already embodied in the irresistibility with which the use of the bomb became policy, and in the unspoken consensus that employment of the bomb was a legitimate act of war requiring no particular justification nor special gestures of chivalry towards the enemy.

Mercifully, we have very little experience of the manner of employment of nuclear weapons in war. The bombings of Hiroshima and Nagasaki constitute the totality of our direct experience. While it would be rash to draw general conclusions, or to base prescriptions, on that single experience in what might have been a unique situation (if for no other reason than that possession of the bomb was unilateral), we can at least make the comment that the saving of lives by the adoption of stylized conventions of combat has no firm precedent in the nuclear age. Whether the demonstrations of intent, outlined in the recent theories of limited nuclear war, will have more appeal than did the idea of an atomic demonstration in 1945, or whether symbolic acts of war will have a greater capacity for inducing limitation now than then, remains to be seen.

REFERENCES

AYALA, B. (1912). *De Jure et Officiis Bellicis et Disciplina Militari Libri III*. Washington: Carnegie Institute.

BALL, D. (1980). "Review of 'The effects of nuclear war.'" *Survival* (September-October).

BRODIE, B. (1954a). "Nuclear weapons: strategic or tactical." *Foreign Affairs 32* (January).

BRODIE, B. (1954b). "Unlimited weapons and limited war." *The Reporter* (18 November).

BRODIE, B. (1959). *Strategy in the Missile Age*. Princeton: Princeton University Press.

COMPTON, A.H. (1956). *Atomic Quest*. London: Oxford University Press.

DRELL, S.D., and F. von HIPPEL (1976). "Limited nuclear war." *Scientific American* (November).

FEIS, H. (1966). *The Atomic Bomb and the End of World War II*. Princeton: Princeton University Press.

FULLER, J.F.C. (1946). *Armament and History*. London: Eyre and Spottiswood.

GARLAN, Y. (1975). *War in the Ancient World*. London: Chatto and Windus.

GIOVANNITTI, L., and F. FREED (1967). *The Decision to Drop the Bomb*. London: Methuen.

GROOM, A.J.R. (1974). *British Thinking About Nuclear Weapons*. London: Frances Pinter.

HALPERIN, M.H. (1963). *Limited War in the Nuclear Age*. New York: Wiley and Sons.

HASTINGS, M. (1981). *Bomber Command*. London: Pan Books.

KNORR, K. and T. READ (Eds.). (1962) *Limited Strategic War*. London: Pall Mall.

PASKINS, B., and M. DOCKRILL (1979). *The Ethics of War*. London: Duckworth.

PHILLIPSON, C. (1911). *The International Law and Custom of Ancient Greece and Rome* (2 vols). London: Macmillan.

RAMSEY, P. (1963). *The Limits of Nuclear War*. New York: Council on Religion and International Affairs.

RUSSELL, F.H. (1975). *The Just War in the Middle Ages*. Cambridge: Cambridge University Press.

SCHELLING, T. (1966). *Arms and Influence*. New Haven: Yale University Press.

SCHOENBERGER, W.S. (1969). *Decision of Destiny*. Ohio: Ohio University Press.

SMITH, A.K. (1965). *A Peril and a Hope: The Scientists' Movement in America 1945–7*. Chicago: University of Chicago Press.

VATTEL, E. de (1916). *The Law of Nations or the Principles of Natural Law*. Washington: Carnegie Institute.

QUESTIONS FOR DISCUSSION

1. What are some of the features of current policies for fighting a nuclear war?

2. What factors might contribute to the expansion of a limited nuclear war? To its containment?

3. Describe the three models of war limitation identified by Clark. How do they relate to the issue of limited nuclear war?

4. Discuss the relevance of C³I to strategies for waging limited nuclear war.

SUGGESTED READINGS

BRACKEN, PAUL. *The Command and Control of Nuclear Forces*. New Haven Conn.: Yale University Press, 1983.

BREWER, GARRY D., and PAUL BRACKEN. "Some Missing Pieces in the C³I Puzzle," *Journal of Conflict Resolution*, vol. 28, no. 3, September 1984.

GRAY, COLIN S. "Warfighting for Deterrence." *Journal of Strategic Studies*, vol. 7, March 1984: 5–28.

GRAY, COLIN S. "Strategic Defense, Deterrence, and the Prospects for Peace." *Ethics*, vol. 95, April 1985: 659–672.

KAHN, HERMAN. *On Escalation: Metaphors and Scenarios*. New York: Praeger, 1965.

KISSINGER, HENRY A. *Nuclear Weapons and Foreign Policy*. Council on Foreign Relations, 1957.

SCHELLING, THOMAS C. *The Strategy of Conflict*. New York: Oxford University Press, 1963.

Chapter VII

Politics of the Arms Race

Any attempt to understand the dynamics of the nuclear arms race must consider the politics of the relationship between the United States and the Soviet Union. In the bipolar world system that emerged after World War II, competition between the U.S. and the Soviet Union became a dominant force. Rivalry between the two superpowers has been a constant feature of post-World War II international relations, although the level of tension has varied. The bitter cold war of the late 1940s and the 1950s eventually gave way to the détente of the 1970s, an era of increased cooperation. But détente was short-lived; since the end of the 1970s, U.S.–Soviet relations have deteriorated markedly. Hostilities have reached such intensity that the current state of affairs has been dubbed the "new cold war."

The new cold war has profound implications for the nuclear arms race. High levels of hostility and suspicion encourage weapons build-ups and hinder arms control and disarmament negotiations. Such tensions also raise the risk of international crises that could precipitate war.

This chapter on the Politics of the Nuclear Arms Race focuses on current U.S.–Soviet relations. In the first reading, Alexander L. George briefly discusses the management of international crises involving the U.S. and the Soviet Union. Next, Fred Halliday compares today's hostile superpower relationship with the earlier cold war, commenting on the political, economic, military and ideological dimensions of the rivalry between East and West.

Raymond L. Garthoff then examines the dilemmas in the U.S.–Soviet relationship that arise from the "imperative of coexistence and the reality of competition." He discusses confrontation and détente, concentrating on three key policy areas: national security, geopolitical conduct and economic relations.

The final reading returns to the issue of nuclear deterrence, which is covered in Chapter V. Michael MccGwire examines the role of deterrence policy in U.S.–Soviet relations. He argues that America's unquestioning acceptance of what he dubs "deterrence dogma" has aggravated U.S. misperceptions of the Soviet Union, thus contributing to the nuclear arms race and obstructing serious steps toward peace and international security.

25 Political Crises

Alexander L. George

Competition for power and influence has always been inherent in the "anarchic" system of sovereign states. In the European balance-of-power system of the nineteenth century, competition was regulated and moderated by a shared commitment on the part of the great powers to maintain that system, by the cultural homogeneity of their elites, and by various norms and practices for moderating rivalry and preserving the balance. It will be useful to recall the diplomatic options employed by the great powers from time to time to regulate their global rivalry, since this will provide a benchmark for discussing possibilities for moderating U.S.–Soviet competition in the post-World War II era. These options included: (1) spheres of influence; (2) the principle of compensation whereby any significant augmentation of power by one great power had to be accompanied by appropriate increases in territory, population, and resources for the other great powers in the interest of preserving the balance; (3) arrangements for mutual and collective decision-making in matters affecting or threatening the balance; (4) careful delineation and definition by the great powers of their interests and/or areas of involvement in third areas; (5) agreements for communication and advance notification of unilateral actions to be taken in third areas; (6) agreements to avoid unilateral action in third areas and, if necessary, to intervene only via multilateral action by several great powers; (7) arrangements for localizing and restricting regional conflicts; (8) agreements to limit the flow of weapons to third areas; (9) arrange-

ments for pacific settlement of disputes; (10) the creation of buffer states between great powers; (11) establishment of neutral states and zones and of demilitarized areas.

One may regard these diplomatic practices for moderating great-power rivalry as constituting a complex regime for avoidance of dangerous crises and war. The nineteenth-century European model worked imperfectly, of course, and collapsed during World War I; but our purpose here is not to evaluate the performance of the nineteenth-century model or to explain its demise. Rather, we wish to identify some of the changes in the international system and in conditions affecting world politics since World Wars I and II that have accentuated great-power competition. It proved impossible after the breakdown of the European system during World War I to recreate a stable multipolar balance of power; abortive efforts to do so gave way after World War II to a bipolar configuration dominated by the United States and the Soviet Union. The emergence of powerful rival ideologies and new elites shattered the cultural homogeneity of the European ruling classes that had underpinned the balance-of-power system. Whereas the European great powers had attempted to base foreign policy on the criterion of national interest, detached as much as possible from sentimental or ideological considerations, the outlook on foreign policy and world politics of the two superpowers—the Soviet Union and the United States—that confronted each other after World War II was heavily influenced by their ideological differences.

The new bipolar configuration of power after World War II combined with sharpened ideological conflict to accentuate U.S.–Soviet rivalry in third areas and to handicap efforts to moderate

Excerpted with permission from Alexander L. George, "Political Crises," in Joseph S. Nye, Jr., ed., *The Making of America's Soviet Policy* (pp. 129–132) (New Haven: Yale University Press, 1984). Copyright © 1984 it. The search for stability during these years has been further prejudiced by the process of worldwide decolonization that vastly expanded the number of states in the international system. These new states often experienced internal instability and rivalries of their own that interlaced with and exacerbated the global rivalry of the superpowers. Further complicating the search for regional and local stability in the post-World War II era has been the revolution in weapons technology and easy access to conventional arms. An additional dimension to the already difficult task the United States and the Soviet Union were experiencing in efforts to control the risks of their competition in third areas emerged when, after the Sino-Soviet split, the Soviet Union and the People's Republic of China began to compete with each other for influence with "national liberation" movements in third areas.

The emergence of new states from the colonies of the former imperialist powers, their vigorous assertion of nationalism and sovereign independence, their voice in international forums such as the United Nations, and the universal condemnation of anything that smacks of imperialism have meant that the two superpowers cannot employ some of the modalities available to the great powers in the nineteenth century for moderating their competition in third areas. Explicit spheres of influence that played an important role in regulating the global rivalry of the great imperial powers of the nineteenth century are not acceptable in the modern era. Even collaborative efforts by the two superpowers to settle regional conflicts (such as in the Middle East from time to time) or to map out ground rules for moderating their competition in third areas, even when undertaken to reduce the likelihood of possibly dangerous U.S.–Soviet confrontations, trigger fears elsewhere in the international community of a superpower condominium harmful to the interests of other states.

Counterbalancing these various changes in the international arena that exacerbate superpower rivalry is another historical development —the emergence of nuclear weapons—that has powerfully reinforced the incentives of the two superpowers to prevent their conflicts of interest and rivalry from leading to a possibly disastrous war. The fear of a thermonuclear holocaust is undoubtedly the major factor that accounts for the success which the two superpowers have achieved in managing a series of diplomatic crises and tense confrontations since the beginning of the Cold War. On the other hand, while the danger of such a war has undoubtedly contributed to dampening the escalation potential inherent in U.S.–Soviet competition, it has not prevented the occurrence of dangerous confrontations and lesser crises that have damaged the overall Soviet–American relationship.

The success of the two superpowers thus far in managing their crises without war cannot be explained solely with reference to their shared fear of thermonuclear war. The United States and the Soviet Union quickly grasped the requirements for managing crises. Fortunately these requirements are more easily recognized and applied than the principles for crisis prevention. To be sure, crisis management requirements must be operationalized and tailored to the special configuration of any particular situation, but these requirements remain the same, generally speaking, from one situation to another. Not only is crisis management easier to learn than crisis prevention, but the learning experiences are more easily accumulated and transferred to management of subsequent crises. Then, too, domestic politics generally are less intrusive in the management of existing crises than they are in policymakers' efforts to avoid them.

In contrast to crisis management, crisis prevention is a more amorphous objective and is not one that both superpowers are equally committed to in every situation. There are different kinds of crises in U.S.–Soviet relations, some more dangerous than others. Not only are some crises more acceptable (to one side if not both) because they are thought to carry with them a lesser, controllable risk of war; in the era of thermonuclear weapons some crises have become a substitute for war. That is, crises may be deliberately initiated or tolerated by one side in the hope of catalyzing desired changes in the status quo. Viewed in this way, crises offer opportunities for achieving foreign policy goals even though they may represent threats to important values.

Crisis prevention is more complicated than crisis management also because there is no single, prototypical set of requirements or strategy for preventing U.S.–Soviet competition in third areas from developing into a confrontation. Thus, crises can be avoided by a variety of *unilateral* policies undertaken by either superpower—for example, deterrence; economic, military, or political assistance to reduce instability in a third country or region that might otherwise provide tempting opportunities for encroachments by the other superpower or its proxies; decisions by one superpower not to compete with the other superpower in a given third area.

Crises can also be avoided through *initiatives by third parties* (e.g., the United Nations, the Organization of American States, the Organization of African Unity, or other regional actors) to mediate or resolve local disputes.

Finally, there are various ways in which the United States and the Soviet Union can *cooperate*, or coordinate their policies, in order to moderate competition and avoid being plunged into a crisis. I shall discuss in detail later in this chapter several different modalities for U.S.–Soviet cooperation in crisis prevention.

Given these important differences between crisis management and crisis prevention, it should not be surprising to learn that the United States (indeed, the Soviet Union, too) quickly learned how to manage crises with its major cold war opponent and that developments during the era of détente reinforced and further strengthened crisis-management capabilities. The principles of crisis management and the operational requirements that go with them are now not only well understood but are much more explicitly formulated than they were during the early cold war. There can be no guarantee, however, that crisis management will be successful in confrontations with the Soviet Union that may occur in the present era of renewed hostility. Not only is the danger of a fateful misperception and miscalculation, by one or both sides, ever present in a crisis; one or another of the requirements for crisis management may be inadvertently or deliberately ignored and a direct military clash—such as has not yet occurred—between U.S. and Soviet military forces may take place which, on however limited a scale initially, may generate pressure for escalation that may be difficult to control. . . .

26　The New Cold War

Fred Halliday ────────────────────────────────

1. THE MILITARY, POLITICAL, IDEOLOGICAL AND ECONOMIC DIMENSIONS

Since the middle of 1979, east-west relations have been in a period of cold war, a new or second cold war comparable to the first cold war of the late 1940s and early 1950s. One index of this is the intensified pace of the arms race and the accompanying emphasis in both camps on the need for military preparedness. The initiative in this new round of armaments production lies with the USA, but the USSR has pledged itself to match US advances and to maintain what it terms the 'rough parity' that it achieved in the early 1970s.

Yet the cold war is more than just the arms race, convenient and urgent as it may be to focus on this dimension of international relations. Cold war also involves a political conflict between east and west, a stress on the values that unite each side and an assertion of the need to struggle against the opposing camp. This is evident in the speeches which President Reagan has been making, calling for a new crusade against communism, and in the preparations drawn up by the US Administration for a comprehensive economic campaign against the USSR and its allies.

This cold war, like its predecessor, also involves intensified conflict in the Third World, whilst the 'Central Front' of Europe remains calm, frozen in entrenched confrontation, no such truce prevails in El Salvador, the Middle East, or Southeast Asia. The US administration has stressed the need for more active US involvement in the Third World, and much of the current US mil-

itary build-up is directed towards possible intervention in the South. Indeed the strategic and conventional-interventionist build-ups are seen as linked; strategic superiority acts as an umbrella for conventional interventions, whilst the repression of Third World challenge is a necessary part of controlling the spread of Soviet influence. Cold war is therefore a comprehensive conflict, one that focusses upon the nuclear arms race but involves political, ideological, economic and conventional military dimensions as well.

2. RIVALRY BETWEEN EAST AND WEST

The intensification of conflict between east and west is, of course, linked with increased conflict within the blocs. The disputes within NATO and, more generally, between the advanced capitalist countries over trade, finance, and defense grew through the 1970s and had reached by the beginning of 1982 the stage of a major trade war. The U.S. pressure for increased defense expenditures on the part of NATO states and the attempt to enforce boycotts of the Soviet Union on European firms are prime examples of this linking of the East-West conflict to the inter-capitalist one. The Soviet Union's hostility to the USA and its anxiety about developments in Afghanistan and Indochina were accentuated by the growing alliance between Washington and Peking in the late 1970s. It is obvious that the rhetoric of cold war, which calls for unity against an external enemy, is used by the dominant powers within each bloc to impose or re-impose discipline on the junior partners in the alliance.

Yet important as the dimension of inter-capitalist conflict is, it cannot be said that the real focus of the cold war is conflict within the west-

Excerpted with permission from the *Bulletin of Peace Proposals*, vol. 14, no. 2, 1983, pp. 125–128. Copyright © 1983 by International Peace Research Institute, Oslo.

ern bloc rather than conflict between east and west. It is intellectually tempting to argue this since these inter-capitalist conflicts are of such force that they could, on their own, be thought to account for major shifts in world politics. Politically it is even more tempting to argue this, since it serves to avoid the difficult issues of the Soviet role in world affairs, and the problems involved in arresting and reversing the arms race. The recession, trade conflicts, currency wars and the growing strategic divergences of the major capitalist states have all played their part in bringing on the new cold war. But they do not alone constitute it. The central issue remains that of the rivalry between east and west, and, more particularly, between the USA and the USSR.

had it refused to help the Angolas, Cubas, Vietnams and Ethiopias, and had abandoned the communist regime in Afghanistan, then the cold war would have been much less likely.

But the ability of the west to launch this cold war has also been based upon a *third* contribution of the USSR and of the communist camp more generally, namely the increasing discredit in which communism as a political and economic system is regarded. Despite the marked decline in repression as compared to the Stalin period, and the real improvement in living standards over the past two decades throughout the USSR and Comecon, neither freedom nor prosperity are seen in the West as represented by the USSR even to the extent to which this was the case, however misguidedly, during the first cold war.

3. THE QUESTION OF RESPONSIBILITY

In the literature on the first cold war much of the debate has centered on the question of responsibility: who started the cold war. Established opinion in the West was that the USSR initiated it. The 'revisionists' argued that it was the West. It does, however, seem most reasonable to argue that responsibility was shared, but differentiated: i.e. that both the USA and the USSR contributed to the onset of the first cold war, although they did so in distinct ways. Had the USA not sought to impose a new world order dominated by Washington there would have been no cold war; had the Soviet Union accepted this, and forced its communist allies in China, Korea and Vietnam to accept it too, then cold war would also have been avoided.

A similar responsibility, joint but differentiated, applies in the second cold war. Much of the peace movement has sought to argue not only that responsibility is shared, but that it is equally and similarly shared. Those who espouse theories of the two superpowers argue a similar position. Yet the historical record does not bear out such an argument. The USSR has contributed to the new cold war in three major respects: *first*, by refusing to accept its subordinate position in the world and building up its military arsenal to a position of parity in some respects with the USA; and *secondly*, by continuing to provide assistance to revolutionary forces in the Third World that are challenging western domination and which look to the USSR for assistance. Had the Soviet Union simply accepted the inferiority of the 1950s and early 1960s, and

4. SOVIET AND U.S. POLICY

Yet the contribution of the internal political changes in the USSR and USA to the second cold war is quite different. The situation inside the USSR has not led to sharp changes in foreign policy, to the kind of uncertainty and adventurism characteristic of the latter period of the Carter administration and of the Reagan period. Soviet policy has, rather, been markedly consistent through the almost two decades since Khruschev's fall. It is this very steadiness which has so unnerved the West and led to the current counter-attack. For the real initiators of the cold war, those who have decided to abandon detente in favor of a period of greater confrontation, are those who hold power in Washington and in the allied capitals of the western alliance. The cold war is a response on their part to the increase in Soviet strength and to the successes which revolutionary forces aided in some degree by the USSR have won in the 1970s.

The instigators of this cold war campaign are well enough known not to require lengthy analysis. First, President Reagan is engaged in an unprecedented build-up of the US military arsenal. In strategic nuclear terms, this is designed to give the USA a significant margin of superiority over the USSR in nuclear weapons, comparable to that which it enjoyed in the early 1960s. Reagan officials publicly deny that they are seeking 'superiority', but the words they use, 'the need to prevail', a 'war-winning capacity', indicate that this is regarded as a practical gain. Not only will this, it is believed, give the USA the kind of edge it enjoyed when it faced the

Russians in the Cuba Missile Crisis of 1962, but it will also use the great technical advances in missile accuracy and detection of enemy weapons of the 1970s to prepare a capacity for a successful first strike against Soviet forces. The build-up in the conventional field is designed to restore to the USA that Third World intervention capability which was eroded by the Vietnam war and then by the Nixon Doctrine of delegating responsibility to other Third World powers. 25% of the military budget is believed to go on Third World intervention forces, as opposed to under 10% on strategic nuclear forces; the political logic of such expenditure is obvious.

At the same time, Reagan has launched a new ideological and economic offensive against the USSR, one begun by Carter with his particular interpretation of the human rights policy and with the boycotts after Afghanistan, but taken to new heights of systematic application and intensity under Reagan. The belief of the U.S. Administration is that the burden of competition in the arms race, combined with sanctions, will serve to undermine the Soviet Union, limit its foreign policy and foster discontent at home. This was a belief held at the time of the first cold war and equally mistaken at that time.

5. 1979—THE TURNING POINT

Cold wars do not have beginnings as easily identifiable as hot wars, but it is plausible to argue that this second cold war began in the latter part of 1979. Many of the events that contributed to it long preceded 1979, but as late as June of that year Carter met Brezhnev in Vienna to sign the SALT-II agreement. It was the refusal of the US Senate to ratify that agreement, in the summer and autumn of 1979, which really marked the full onset of the new cold war, and this was confirmed by a bunch of significant events at the end of that year: the NATO decision to install Cruise and Pershing missiles in Europe, the Soviet intervention in Afghanistan, and the US upgrading of its military ties to China.

The particular issue which occasioned the Senate revolt was a trival and contrived one, the 'discovery' of a 3,000-man Soviet combat brigade in Cuba. In fact, the existence of this Soviet force had been known for years, it hardly comprised a major threat to the security of the continental United States, and it was blown up out of proportion by Congressmen trying to fend off right-wing attacks from within their own constituen-

cies. As Carter reveals in his memoirs, the level of Soviet forces in Cuba had gone down substantially since the 1960s. But the Senatorial rejection of SALT-II reflected much deeper concerns which are central to the new cold war—the refusal to accept strategic nuclear parity with the USSR, a delayed reaction to the spate of revolutions in the Third World, from Vietnam to Nicaragua, and the rise of a belligerent populist sentiment within the USA itself.

6. COMPARISONS BETWEEN THE FIRST AND THE SECOND COLD WARS

Despite the obvious worsening of international relations, those who argue that we are now living through a new cold war are often faced with an apparently cogent objection, namely that, whilst East-West relations have certainly deteriorated since the detente of the early 1970s, the current world situation is still not as bad as that which prevailed during the first cold war of the late 1940s and early 1950s. The difference is said to lie in three main respects.

First, whilst Soviet-US relations are bad, there are still negotiations and contacts between them—in contrast to the almost total breakdown in bilateral links in the earlier period. *Secondly*, there is little of the ideological fervour that marked the first cold war: Soviet communism and American capitalism have both lost their allure. This is far more a conflict between equally voracious superpowers. *Thirdly*, there is little of the internal repression of dissent that marked the first confrontation. Titoists or their equivalent are not being shot in the East. There is no McCarthyist witch hunt in the West.

Each of these qualifications has some force. There are Geneva talks on strategic and European nuclear missiles. The Hot Line remains in place. But few expect anything serious to emerge from Geneva, and the Hot Line or its equivalents are being used by Reagan to send aggressive notes to the USSR. The US Administration seems bent not upon finding common ground with the USSR for solving world problems, but on using these problems to press its advantage against the USSR.

The decline of ideological fervour is certainly the case, abetted as it is by the support given to the USA by many who consider themselves communists or socialists, from Peking to Paris. But this point too can be overstated; the Soviet and American blocs are not isomorphic. They are organized in accordance with different and conflicting political and social principles, and their responsibility and role in the new cold war, whilst shared, is not identical. Ideological fervour may be less, but ideological and systemic differences remain.

As for the lower level of repression, this is undoubtedly true, but again the degree of tolerance should not be overstated. The onset of the cold war in the USA has been accompanied by a wide-ranging counter-offensive by conservative groups against the social changes of the early 1970s, a counter-offensive directed at women, gays, blacks, atheists and all who dissent from orthodox Judeo-Christian culture. Thatcherism has initiated a similar campaign in Britain. The tightening of controls on the dissident movement in the USSR dates from the early 1970s, and is more a contributory cause of the new cold war than a contemporary component of it. But this policy has been maintained through the last few years in the USSR, and the development of the cold war has been accompanied by new acts of repression, such as the exiling of Sakharov and the reduction of contacts with the West, as well as by the crackdown on Solidarity in Poland. The repression and vilification directed against the independent peace group in the USSR are indices of a refusal to tolerate dissent on such issues.

7. INCREASING RISKS

However, the real contrasts between the first and second world wars lie not so much here as in other dimensions, ones suggesting that, if anything, the second cold war is more ominous than the first. During the first cold war there was a danger of war, and, after 1949, both sides had nuclear weapons. But the arsenals of both sides, and the long-range means of delivery were, by to-day's standards, insignificant. With the ability to destroy the whole human race twenty times over now in the hands of the nuclear powers, we are at a far more perilous point in international relations than was the case during the Berlin Blockade or the Korean War. At the same time, the spread of nuclear weapons to the Third World and the growing incidence of wars between Third World states suggest that, whatever the agreements or disagreements of the great powers, the risk of major conflict is increasing, with the possibility of nuclear exchanges and of major outside involvement. . . .

27 Détente and Confrontation

Raymond L. Garthoff

American-Soviet relations stand in need of a re-definition of goals and means. Anyone who in the heyday of détente a decade ago may have forgotten or misjudged the continuation of competition and of an adversarial relationship has been sharply reminded of it since Afghanistan. The fragility of the structure of cooperation erected early in the 1970s was evident in its collapse at the end of the decade. The absence of mutual trust is, in the mid-1980s, stark and clear. Dispelling illusions about détente can be useful. What is not useful—indeed is dangerous—is to resurrect in their place cold war myths and misperceptions. A misreading by one side of the motivation and intentions of the other, and action on that basis, is akin to Don Quixote's charge against windmills of imagined threatening and evil strength. But the danger is much greater than misapplied chivalry and energy. It is the risk of giving substance to a sharper and deeper conflict than would have been justified by a sound understanding and sober evaluation of real conflicts of interest and the real requirements for competition—and, equally important, of the opportunities still available to realize areas of cooperation in serving mutual interests, including, above all, survival in a nuclear world.

The imperative of coexistence and the reality of competition remain. So do the problems of reconciling them. Thoughtful study of the experience of the 1970s is of the highest importance in order to learn as much as possible about the requirements and conditions for—and limitations on—cooperation, and about the nature and forms of competition. That knowledge can contribute to the design of policies and a policy process for the future that can help to work toward a world order that, while short of the ideal or preference of any one ideology or nation, will nevertheless preserve the essential peace. Without that peace, no idea or people in our day can survive.

Some proponents have mistakenly suggested that détente provides the only alternative to war. What needs to be carefully weighed is what course of action, among many, best serves peace and security. Some opponents of détente, on the other hand, have attempted to counterpose it to security. But détente is one possible (and, under favorable circumstances, preferable) means of contributing to security. Again, what is needed is a sober consideration of the range of possible combinations of political strategies, defense programs, arms control, and other policy measures. The true antipode to détente is not security or hardheaded national interest, but tension. And tension serves neither of those objectives. Critics of détente, arms control, negotiation, engagement, and contact should recognize that the antipodes are tension, an uncontrolled arms race, confrontation, containment, and isolation. While confrontation may seem a better course of action, that judgment is counterintuitive, and the burden of proof rests on its proponents. Opponents of détente, who ascribe to the Soviet leaders hardheaded pursuit of their interests and a very high degree of success and skill, do not explain why, if détente, arms control, negotiation, engagement, and contact are necessarily soft policies, a hardheaded Soviet Union pursues them. They do not adequately explain why they

Excerpted with permission from Raymond L. Garthoff, *Detente and Confrontation: American-Soviet Relations from Nixon to Reagan* (pp. 1090–1096, 1100–1102, 1114–1118, 1123–1124). Copyright 1985 by Brookings Institution, Washington D.C.

believe the United States cannot pursue such a policy while the Soviet Union can. There are, to be sure, systemic differences that do make at least some tactics of manipulation much easier for Soviet leaders to pursue. And there may be more of a tendency in American opinion to build excessive expectations. But there are also fundamental systemic strengths in an open society.

The experiment with punitive containment within a policy of nominal suspended détente, pursued in the last year of the Carter administration, and the avowed repudiation of détente and pursuit of a more confrontational policy in the first three years of the Reagan administration, both proved ineffective and counterproductive. A confrontational approach, designed and intended to place pressure on the Soviet Union, results in reduced support, in particular from U.S. allies, for American policies and provides the Soviet Union with enhanced opportunities. Even at home, the American public, while wary of détente, is not eager to assume the avoidable additional burdens and risks of choosing confrontation. . . .

In framing U.S. policy toward the Soviet Union, it is necessary not only to examine both U.S. and Soviet objectives and courses of action, but also what may be termed courses of interaction. Reactions of the other side to any U.S. action obviously should be considered, although in reality they are not always weighed. But far too little attention is paid to a further chain of interactions. Similarly, effects on others, including unintended effects, should be anticipated to the extent possible. The perceptions of the other side (and of others) should be part of such evaluations. Finally, the extent of unity and consistency of one's own objectives and policy course, and of the course of interaction with the other side, should be calculated.

As this study has made clear, the interactions of U.S. and Soviet policy have overlapped with complex interactions in East-West European relations, in the triangle of relations involving China, and in many situations and some conflicts born of local developments around the world. In short, it is necessary to think in terms of developing a strategy of U.S. policy in terms of the interplay of U.S. and Soviet strategies in a broad context of world politics.

Regrettably, the record indicates a progressive decline in such strategic policymaking in the United States from the early 1970s to the mid-1980s. While the Nixon-Kissinger leadership showed lamentable miscalculation in a number of cases, it did proceed from an understanding of the need for a strategy of policy. It exaggerated its own ability to control and manage events, but at least it sought to do so in pursuit of a purposeful strategy. While the Reagan administration certainly has had aims, it has had a much less coherent strategy. Moreover, by misconstruing many aspects of both Soviet policy and world politics, it has had much less success in meeting its own aims than it could otherwise have had, to say nothing of failing to set and reach other aims that would have been in the interest of the United States.

One necessary condition is to discard illusory aims of either a comprehensive settlement of differences and achievement of a complete accommodation of U.S. and Soviet interests on the one hand, a goal sometimes misattributed to détente, or a U.S. victory in a contest with the Soviet Union, an aspiration of proponents of confrontation. The real question is how best to manage the relationship of mixed competition and cooperation between rivals.

It is not easy to deal with the dialectical relationship between competition and cooperation. This relationship is a reality, but it is difficult to articulate in terms that command the necessary public support. It is also, for that and other reasons, very difficult to manage without competition getting out of hand and leading to confrontation. Yet that undesirable outcome is not necessary.

American relations with the Soviet Union cover many areas. Three principal areas of specific policy are of salient importance: *national security, geopolitical conduct*, and *economic relations*. . . .

NATIONAL SECURITY

National security is at the core of the interests and concerns of every country and is salient in both American and Soviet policy. While readily understood by Americans as applying to the United States, it is less often made explicit in American discussion of the Soviet Union.

Soviet policy is made on the basis of Soviet interests, of which security is preeminent. In their pronouncements, and in their actions, the Soviet leaders recognize national security as fundamental. It underlies such basic lines of policy as the prevention of nuclear war. At the same time, the Soviet leaders are not pacifists; they believe they must be prepared to defend their vital interests if those interests are attacked—just as the leaders of the United States do.

Deterrence of attack by the other side is a principal aim of both sides. The role of deterrence in American thinking has been enlarged to such an extent that it tends to dominate both defense and foreign policy. While it is a necessary element of policy, it is not central; that is, it does not deal with the main range of problems involved in managing relations with an adversary. It does not even deal with the main lines of Soviet efforts to expand its influence and reduce that of the United States. More broadly, while the role of military power is essential, it is not central to most of the action of world politics. The shadow of military power influences a great deal of political maneuvering, but it is not its only source.

Deterrence provides insurance and reinforcement of other disincentives against attack by the other side. It is, if only because of its value as reassurance, an essential continuing element in both Western and Soviet policy. Indeed, the main *real* role of most military programs and deployments seen as buttressing deterrence may have been reassurance rather than deterrence of temptations to attack. But deterrence does not prevent and need not impede collaborative military détente, to use the Soviet-coined term.

Each side influences the definition of the security requirements as seen by the other. In many cases such influence makes itself felt in ways not intended or controlled or even recognized. Moreover, the effects of one of the superpower's actions or policies on the other side are often not those sought or desired—they may result in consequences opposite to those intended. For example, the reciprocal failures to recognize the intentions involved in the deployments of intermediate-range missiles in Europe in the latter 1970s led to an arms race and political confrontation not intended or desired by either side. Ultimately it did not serve the security interests of either side, although both *perceived* their decisions and actions as necessary for security reasons.

The fact that deterrence is designed above all to influence the perceptions of the other side is generally recognized, but the implications of the fact are not adequately appreciated. Particularly in the United States, this question, *essentially* one of political perception, has come to be addressed almost exclusively in military-technical terms. Excruciatingly antiseptic computations of residual theoretical force capabilities after *n* number of strategic "exchanges" are substituted for the commonsense thinking of political leaders evaluating national interests. Moreover, even in dealing with the human element of the equation, failure to consider the perceptions of the other side leads to grave political error. Intended displays of firm resolve for defensive deterrence may be (and, alas, often are) seen by leaders on the other side as offensive intimidation requiring a reciprocal display of firm resolve. If a fraction of the effort given to calculating technical deterrence requirements were devoted to raising political awareness of the perceptions of the other side, there might be a substantial increase in security for both sides.

Deterrence is predicated on denying or reducing the expected *gains* to a putative attacker from a premeditated attack. In more sophisticated calculations it may be intended to reduce the chance of choice of war in a crisis situation. But by far the greatest risk of war lies not in decisions by one side or the other in which it sees a choice and possible gain, but from action under circumstances in which it sees no real choice except whether to seize the initiative before an expected imminent attack by the other side. Military programs and actions intended to enhance deterrence by reducing assumed enemy "incentives" to attack not only may be irrelevant, but may in fact increase risks rather than reduce them. Finally, the prevention of nuclear war requires a much wider range of political efforts than deterrence alone, to say nothing of the still wider range of actions to manage and mitigate the political and geopolitical competition.

During the late 1960s and early 1970s security concerns on both sides initially gave impetus to arms control negotiations. Wariness and caution on both sides led to only modest achievements in this area. Later, increasing security concerns led to decreased use of cooperative security approaches and increased reliance on unilateral pursuit of military security, spurring the arms race and raising fears. Paradoxically, the shortcomings of arms control measures such as the SALT I Interim Agreement and the SALT II Treaty in meeting perceived security requirements tended to be blamed on the process of negotiated arms limitations. The real blame stemmed from the fact that both sides had been too reluctant to give up promising military "options," and too cautious to agree on more effective and far-reaching constraints. In addition, the fact that the Soviet Union, still overcoming its inferiority, continued to build its strategic forces (in accordance with the provisions of the SALT agreements and, at least from the Soviet perspective, also consistent with maintaining parity) was widely perceived in the United States as either violation or circumvention of the agreements. What it really contravened was the expectation the agreements had created in American eyes.

Arms control is never an end in itself. It is a tool of policy, and in particular of security policy, as are unilateral military programs (or "arms uncontrolled"). Both the Soviet Union and the United States always judge possible negotiated arms control limitations and reductions from this perspective. Arms control may provide specific constraints designed to enhance stability and reduce the risk of war. Arms control agreements (or the mere pursuit or conduct of arms control negotiations) may also, or alternately, be intended to serve broader political and public relations effects. Finally, arms control limitations may be sought to reduce requirements for resource allocations in an unlimited arms competition. For arms control to have more than modest impact, it must be seen by the parties as making a contribution to security that outweighs the constraints it imposes on military tools of policy.

This analysis points to two lessons that must be applied in the future:

1. *Arms control can play an important part in stabilizing a strategic military balance, and can contribute to improved political relations as well, only if it is given the chance to do so.* The experience of SALT does not demonstrate the limitations of arms control or its failure, but rather the failure of the United States and the Soviet Union in the 1970s to give arms limitation a chance to do more.

2. *A stable strategic balance under negotiated arms control must be defined in sufficiently concrete terms to provide a common framework for permitted unilateral military programs for the two sides.* SALT defined clear constraints on strategic arms, and those limits were adhered to. But they were so excessively permissive that new unilateral strategic programs pursued by both sides, as allowed by the agreements, were perceived by the other side as threatening the balance. There must be stronger limitations—at whatever level—

and an agreed conception of what constitutes the balance. . . .

GEOPOLITICAL CONDUCT

Concern over the strategic balance was important in raising American suspicions and fears of the Soviet Union, as was, to a much lesser extent, unease over the continuation of repressive internal Soviet activities. Probably the chief cause of U.S. public and political disillusionment with détente, however, was the growing impression that the Soviets were pursuing an expansionist policy in the world that involved both actions and objectives not consistent with détente—or at least not consistent with American expectations of Soviet behavior under détente, a significant but little appreciated difference. The widespread impression of an energetic Soviet pursuit of a policy of aggrandizement was perceived in the United States as standing in contrast to a much more restrained American policy. Americans saw the vigorous Soviet intervention or support for the successful expansion of communist rule in Angola, Ethiopia, South Yemen, Afghanistan, and Kampuchea as taking advantage both of American restraint and of a decline in American power, and as reflecting both a growing Soviet strength and a growing readiness to use that strength in ways that advanced Soviet interests and contravened American interests. Empirical evidence and logical arguments in support of this view were powerfully reinforced by psychological considerations. The United States seemed to be increasingly impotent—from the fall of Vietnam in 1975 through the humiliating failure for over a year to obtain the release of the hostage embassy staff in Iran. That neither of these (or many other) developments was due to Moscow's machinations was given little weight. Many Americans simply felt the United States was being pushed around. The fact that changes in the strategic nuclear balance were irrelevant not only to those events, but also to the Soviet advances in Africa and Afghanistan, did not prevent a gut feeling that the United States was becoming weaker and the Soviet Union stronger. And these changes were associated with the period of détente.

Many in the United States quickly seized upon these and other developments to argue that the American administrations of the 1970s, and the policy of détente and of arms control negotiations, were to blame, along with the Soviet Union, for this sorry state of affairs. The Soviet Union was depicted as taking advantage of détente and of American military and political restraint to build its own military and political power and more boldly to advance in the world.

This American (and, to a much lesser extent, more general Western) image of Soviet behavior is far removed from the picture the Soviet leaders hold of their own actions, and of those of the United States. Not only do the Soviets see their moves as justified and restrained, but from their perspective their geopolitical gains were much less. Indeed, gains were more than offset by a chain of geopolitical losses (Soviet influence in Egypt, Sudan, Somalia, Guinea, and Chile), to say nothing of the growing American-Chinese politico-military tie and potential encirclement of the USSR by the United States, NATO, China, and Japan. From the Soviet standpoint, while Angola and Ethiopia were carefully selected cases of local situations permitting legal and limited Soviet involvement and expanded influence, Afghanistan (like Poland) was not an opportunity for advance, but a reluctantly accepted necessity to hold a critical defensive line. Finally, the Soviets saw the decline and fall of Soviet-American détente as engineered by cold warrior opponents of détente in the United States, abetted by China and Israel. While claiming that their purpose was to stop Soviet expansion, these cold warriors manipulated both events and their interpretation in order to effect a return to a confrontational line and to gain public support for a major arms buildup aimed at reacquiring strategic military superiority. Their purpose was to conduct a more far-reaching political offensive against the Soviet Union and the socialist community (Soviet bloc) not only on its periphery, but even within the socialist countries.

In the United States, the general impression has been one of Soviet activism, indeed adventurism, in pursuing an expansionist course. In fact, Soviet policy has been active, but selective and cautious, not adventuristic. While the general impression has been exaggerated, it is less in error in seeing an active Soviet role than in failing also to recognize an active U.S. role. There is also a tendency to give much more attention to alarming developments than to favorable ones. Soviet advances are given a great deal of attention; Soviet reverses are scarcely noted. The result is a very skewed picture in the minds not only of the public but of many American political leaders as well. The image of Soviet expansion

of influence in the third world in the 1970s was blown up out of all proportion. Moreover, this situation has then often been ascribed to weakness of U.S. resolution or military capabilities. One consequence has been to misdirect American countermeasures to military programs rather than to diplomacy in the third world. Another consequence was to make the détente in American-Soviet relations appear to be responsible for a trend that was not only overstated, but not caused by that policy. Détente clearly did not prevent continuing competition, but it did not create it. Nor did it disarm or disable the United States from pursuing the competition very actively and much more successfully than has been generally recognized. Ironically, a U.S. course of policy that seemed weak to most Americans has seemed excessively strong to the Soviet leaders.

Rivalry and competition for influence and power have characterized American-Soviet relations since 1945. What was unique in the détente of the 1970s was the first attempt to devise basic principles to govern the conduct of the two powers. The purpose was, ostensibly, to constrain and limit the risks of competition—to establish a code of conduct or rules of the game. These two unofficial slogans, however, encapsulate two somewhat different aspects of the experiment. A code of conduct (especially one formulated in appropriately idealized terms) implies acceptance of a common high standard of behavior. Rules of the game, on the other hand, implies a common set of guidelines for carrying out a competitive exercise such as a sport—hitting below the belt may be banned, but other continuing blows and parries are expected and accepted.

As has been seen, from the outset it was relatively easy to agree on broad guidelines—partly because they were not examined closely to determine if there was *real* acceptance of a common standard or even of agreed rules for regulating the competition. Indeed, it was quite evident to those involved that there was no common standard or agreed rules. But the leaders on both sides believed they would be able to justify their *own* behavior by their unilateral interpretation of the rules, and that they could use the rules to constrain the other side marginally. In addition, in adopting high rhetorical standards, both leaderships were playing for popular support from their own domestic political constituencies, as well as from the world's peoples. This tactic was in keeping with long-standing practice in world public diplomacy. The first effect, however, was to create excessively high public expectations about the behavior of the other side, especially in the United States. Leaders who themselves assumed *Realpolitik* as the prevailing political reality failed, especially in the United States, to recognize their inability to control popular expectations that they themselves did not for the most part share. Moreover, the Soviet leaders seriously underestimated the way in which these nominal rhetorical commitments, especially the Helsinki Final Act, could be held against them by both domestic dissidents and Western opponents of close relations with the Soviet Union. And the American leaders failed to recognize that while they could manage their own interpretations of and applications to Soviet behavior, they could not control more far-reaching applications by domestic political opponents, in particular those opposed to close American relations with the Soviet Union. Adopting rhetoric with excessively demanding ideal standards of conduct did not curb either side's actions, but it did disorient those who accepted the rhetoric at face value. And it gave a weapon to those who wanted to strike at the less-than-ideal reality of relations under détente. . . .

The subsequent failure of the code of conduct stemmed more from the failure of this détente strategy of Nixon and Kissinger to do what they expected than from Soviet violation of the code. Kissinger, with some justification (although less than he claims), blames this failure on congressional refusal to provide key carrots (such as most-favored-nation trade status) and key sticks (banning further covert aid in Angola, or, unconvincingly, renewed arms supply to South Vietnam in 1975).

While U.S. attention was focused on the several cases of clear Soviet and Cuban direct or indirect military intervention (in Angola, Ethiopia, and Afghanistan), Americans have been oblivious to the much longer list of local crises and conflicts in which Western powers or other associates of the United States became involved and in which the Soviet Union and its allies chose not to be involved—the Katangan incursions into Zaire; the continuing conflict in the Western Sahara; the Rhodesian internal conflict; Namibia; the externally aided changes of regime in Equatorial Guinea, the Central African Republic, Uganda, and Chad; the Indonesian occupation and bloody suppression of East Timor; the division of Cyprus; and many others. The Soviets, for their part, see these and many other Western interventions as inspired and

supported by the United States and its allies, along with such other cases of direct and indirect U.S. intervention as the reversal of unwanted progressive change by the overthrow of Allende in Chile in 1973, the counterrevolution in Portugal in 1975, the invasion of Grenada in 1983, and the attempt since 1981 to destabilize Nicaragua.

There is a strong tendency on each side to draw attention only to those situations in which it wants to criticize the other side, and to interpret the facts as well as justifications from its own perspective, as well as to manipulate facts and arguments for propaganda and political justification of its own preferences and actions and to discredit the arguments and actions of its adversary. Both sides apply double standards.

Americans are well enough aware of the Soviet uses of a double standard (and vice versa). Sometimes American critics of administration policies recognize its application. But generally Americans are little inclined to see matters from other perspectives. The Soviets also not only see things from a different perspective, but tend to see and interpret (and still more to present) matters from a completely one-sided standpoint. Unless one seeks the facts and reviews the history in some detail, one is often not even aware of the bases for other viewpoints.

Leaders (and publics) on both sides apply double standards of judgment not only because this approach is self-serving, but also because it stems from one-sided perceptions of reality.[1] Such discrepant perception, and in part also biased depiction, is not conscious and is therefore extremely difficult to change. And it affects not only how particular events and developments are perceived but also the whole frame of reference and selection of events. Thus while, as noted, Americans have tended to look only at Soviet and Cuban involvements in Angola, Ethiopia, South Yemen, and Afghanistan, and the

---

[1]In theoretical terms, there are two alternative standards, either of which may be applied. They may be termed the "realist-geopolitical" and the "moral-ideological." The behavior of the United States and the Soviet Union may be judged by either standard, but it is not proper (or wise) to judge one's own actions by one standard and the other side's by the other. In practice, each side usually judges the other with a slanted moral-ideological standard, while accepting only for itself the justification of realist motivations (reconciled with its own subjective moral assumptions). This practice makes for lively propaganda but ill serves the policy and diplomatic processes.

Vietnamese in Kampuchea, the Soviets have seen the American efforts to exclude the Soviet Union from the Middle East (to "expel" them, to use Kissinger's apt statement of the U.S. objective), including Egypt, the Sudan, Somalia, and to a degree Iraq; the playing of the China card against the Soviet Union; and U.S. involvements in a wide series of third world situations, also including Angola, Somalia, North Yemen, Oman, Zaire, Chile, El Salvador, Grenada, and Nicaragua. The Soviets also see as related the many interventions by American allies or proxies noted earlier. . . .

It is not easy for either power to accept the norms of behavior it sets for the other. Yet "restraint and reciprocity," given political realities, must indeed apply to both sides. If the United States wishes to draw the Soviet Union into accepting norms of behavior and an existing international order, it too must observe those norms itself. The Soviet leaders are naturally more influenced by what Americans do than by what they say, especially when the two diverge. Yet the United States, under all administrations, has routinely acted on the Eurasian periphery of the Soviet Union in ways that it would not accept in Soviet behavior in the Western Hemisphere. And the Soviet leaders have to give up the idea that support for "progressive" revolutions is acceptable while support for "reactionary" counterrevolutions is not. The fact is that most guerrilla insurrections in the mid-1980s are in communist or other leftist-ruled countries aligned with the Soviet Union: Afghanistan, Cambodia, Angola, Ethiopia, Mozambique, and Nicaragua. All were the scene of leftist accession to power in the 1970s, but the wheel has turned.

This discussion of geopolitical conduct has concentrated on the roles of the Soviet Union and the United States in the third world. That focus takes as its point of departure that perceived American concern over Soviet actions in the third world poses a serious problem for relations between the two countries, and then considers as well the Soviet perspective and the need in the future to take both perspectives into account. The geopolitical arena has two other highly important elements that affect American-Soviet relations: Europe and China.

The European-centered East-West détente that began in the latter 1960s, somewhat earlier than the American-Soviet one, was assumed by many during most of the 1970s to be concomitant with the American-Soviet détente of that period. The fact that it had different roots and

a different impact on the political relationship was not evident to many until the sharp decline and collapse of American-Soviet détente by the end of the decade. The disjunction between American and Western European attitudes toward détente in relations with the Soviet Union has become most evident in American-European friction over economic relations, but it has extended to other aspects of policy as well. To be sure, there is no identity of view among or within the Western countries, but as a whole Western and Eastern Europe have maintained a détente relationship that underlies the differences between the United States and its Western allies (including Japan). While the Soviet Union has preferred détente with both Western Europe and the United States, when that has no longer been possible, it has sought to play upon internal Western differences to its own benefit.

In conducting its relations with the Soviet Union—and with the Western Europeans—the United States should not exacerbate Western differences and thereby serve Soviet interests. To the extent that the United States and its NATO allies do not agree on aspects of their relations with the East, the United States should not seek to compel its allies to follow its preferred course of action. It is better to recognize and accept differences on some issues than to enlarge or deepen the areas of divergence in the name of demanding unity. More broadly, the United States must consider the whole range of East-West European relations on their own merits, as well as in conjunction with American-Soviet relations.

The other major element has been, and will be, the triangular relationship among the United States, China, and the Soviet Union. The American rapprochement with China that paralleled the development of American-Soviet détente in the early 1970s significantly boosted the U.S. role. Later in the decade, when the United States moved into an alignment with China against the Soviet Union, a shift that was made at a time of sharp deterioration in American-Soviet relations, the U.S. role was seriously reduced. The Chinese naturally sought to improve their own position. By the early 1980s they no longer needed to curry American favor to ensure against a Soviet-American détente and could afford to improve their relations with the Soviet Union. Both countries, especially China, thus increased their leverage in the triangle vis-à-vis the United States.

In the future, the United States should return to seeking more of a balancing role, above all by not committing itself to alignment with either China or the Soviet Union in a way that inhibits improving relations with the other.

ECONOMIC RELATIONS

In view of the adversarial relationship between the United States and the Soviet Union, the long-standing American and general Western refusal to export weaponry and strategic goods to the Soviet Union and its allies has not been at issue and will no doubt continue. Questions have arisen over the strategic significance of some high-technology items, such as certain computers and high-precision drilling tools. These questions on the margin will continue to be resolved on a practical basis after case-by-case review. Although opinions on individual decisions may vary, the purpose and the process will remain. The range of economic policies and strategies that the United States (and the Western European countries) may consider would all incorporate this element.

What has become a political issue in the United States, and to some extent between the United States and its European (and Japanese) allies, is whether the West should seek not only to deny advanced technology directly useful for Soviet military industry, but also to deny access to a much wider range of goods important to the Soviet economy. The question of terms of trade, in particular credits (and especially at concessional rates), is a related issue.

Advocacy of a broad policy of economic denial by the Reagan administration met widespread Western disagreement, highlighted by the ill-starred attempt by the United States in 1982 to impose sanctions on European subsidiaries of American firms and on European licensees (and even to apply those sanctions retroactively to prevent deliveries of goods under signed contracts). There was something ironic in the argument that the United States must impose economic pressures and sanctions on Western Europe in order to protect it from growing dependence and possible future imposition of economic pressures and sanctions by the Soviet Union. It also went against the grain for the United States to insist that Europe make economic sacrifices involving the gas pipeline, while the United States permitted, indeed encouraged, the Soviets to purchase its grain.

A policy of confrontation, consistently pros-

ecuted, would include as one element in its strategy far-reaching constraints on trade intended to increase economic—and political—tensions within the Soviet bloc and the Soviet Union itself. That approach would involve a much longer-term American policy of sharp competition than would economic sanctions related to particular Soviet behavior with respect, say, to Afghanistan or Poland. A challenge to the Soviet system presumes either a preference for, or prejudgment of the inevitability of, a continuing and intensifying cold war.

An alternative range of economic strategies would use trade constraints to affect particular Soviet *policies*, rather than to wage economic war as a way to challenge the Soviet economic and political *system*. A "hard headed detente," as advocated recently by former President Nixon and as favored by Kissinger, Brzezinski, and Haig, would relate economic constraints to Soviet foreign political behavior. The key difference with a confrontational strategy is the readiness to lift trade constraints if Soviet actions eschewed the particular behavior to which the United States objected. In most variants such a strategy of manipulated trade relations also offers inducements—carrots—as well as sanctions—sticks—to help move Soviet policy in the preferred directions.

Throughout the 1970s American trade relations were gradually expanded and developed, with limited use of economic incentives. But the ability to pursue this strategy was severely limited when in 1974 Congress linked trade normalization and credits to changes in internal Soviet policy. This move and the use of economic sanctions by the Carter and Reagan administrations have cut U.S.–Soviet trade sharply. But the sanctions have not achieved their political purposes. By the mid-1980s the Reagan administration had reduced its use of economic sanctions, but had not developed a new economic policy.

In looking to the future, the United States must first of all seek to develop whatever policy it adopts on economic relations as an integral part of its broader overall policy toward the Soviet Union. This policy may include encouraging trade with minimal strategic constraints and maximum normalization (for example, granting most-favored-nation status and eliminating predetermined credit limits). Or the United States may seek to tie some steps in the development of economic relations to improvement in political relations (as was the general design in the 1970s).

Particularly if an understanding is reached on reciprocal restraints in global competition, that could be accompanied by agreements on more open economic ties.

Decisions on economic policy toward the Soviet Union should remain a subject of serious consultation among the Western allies, even when they cannot reach full agreement. This approach should apply above all to any consideration of sanctions. On the whole, sanctions appear to be of limited economic or political efficacy. On the one hand they should be considered only in serious situations, but on the other hand they are not likely to be effective in moving the Soviet Union in such situations. Perhaps the most that can be said is that economic sanctions are not a useful tool in most cases, although they are a possible resort if an appropriate situation arises. And the effectiveness of sanctions is highly dependent on substantial Western unity—but should not in turn be permitted to become a cause of increasing Western disunity. . . .

CONCLUSIONS

This look at the future has pointed to three salient areas of bilateral U.S.-Soviet relations: national security, global geopolitical competition, and economic relations. American interest in Soviet internal affairs was omitted not because developments in that sphere are not important to the United States, or ultimately relevant to its policy, but because they are not intrinsically a matter of American relations with the Soviet Union. The conflicts in ideological worldviews and values between the Soviet Union and the United States are profound, but they are a reality to which policy must be geared. The problems, and potential dangers, in relations between the two states make the containment of competition a sine qua non. Global competition involves risks of precipitating direct conflict between the two powers, as well as many limited shifts in power relationships. Efforts to contain the continuing competition are difficult enough to manage, and important enough on their own merits, not to be further weighted by other matters. Economic relations are, for the United States, more open to unilateral management. But experience confirms that manipulating economic relations has very limited potential for influencing Soviet behavior. To the contrary, direct attempts to wield an economic stick are more likely to reduce than to increase U.S. influence on Soviet internal practices.

Successive American administrations, through détente and confrontation, have had to address the way to handle human rights practices in the Soviet Union. A confrontational policy prescribes a confrontational approach to this subject. But any policy of mixed competition and cooperation, whether the mix leans toward détente or containment, poses a question of how to deal with a problem of concern to Americans but one that involves Soviet internal affairs. Basically, there are three possible approaches. One is to make clear the American viewpoint and do nothing more. Some critics have accused the Nixon and Ford administrations of taking this course. The second course is not only to make the American view clear but also to seek to persuade the Soviet leaders to alleviate the situation. This approach can include incentives, but not punitive sanctions. The third approach is to vilify the Soviet system and place pressure on the Soviet leaders in an attempt to compel changes in their internal practices or at least penalize them for not making them. It seeks to do so by establishing linkage with other aspects of American-Soviet relations of interest to the Soviet leaders, for example, trade or arms control, for leverage to effect such internal changes. The record strongly supports the conclusion that while the Soviet leaders object even to any American expression of judgment on such matters, they are prepared to take that consideration into account and make some accommodation. If, on the other hand, they are faced with attempts at intimidation and coercion, they will react strongly and not yield. Above all, attempts to link demands for internal changes with important arms control or trade agreements are likely only to sacrifice those security or economic interests and worsen political relations without moderating Soviet internal practices. The real "linkage" is often a matter of internal *American* political gamesmanship rather than one that affects positively internal Soviet affairs. The case of the Jackson-Vanik amendment is a prime example; by 1984 Jewish emigration from the Soviet Union was down to 896, the lowest figure since 1970 and more than 50,000 below the peak reached in 1979 when the Carter administration had promised to seek cancellation of the amendment. Ultimately, while the American people and their government are not indifferent to human rights and other aspects of internal affairs in the Soviet Union (and other states), those concerns should not be made central to state relations. . . .

28 Deterrence: The Problem Not the Solution

Michael MccGwire

The thesis of this essay is that many of the problems that now assail the West stem from the adoption in the early 1950s of "nuclear deterrence" as the basis of defense and foreign policy. The complaint is not against generic deterrence, a simple concept that applies at most levels of human interaction, but against the body of theory that grew up around nuclear weapons in the 1950s.

There was, of course, no one theory, doctrine, or policy of nuclear deterrence, but a whole series of them that differed between countries and between government departments within countries. There was also a wealth of difference between the sophisticated approach of the more thoughtful deterrence theorists and the bowdlerized and homogenized version of their theories that was passed down to the rest of us. Nevertheless, there was a central dogma concerning the requirements of deterrence and, more important, there was a mindset that went with the dogma. It is the mindset that is at the root of the problem.

This body of attitudes and ideas that I am labeling "deterrence dogma" was being taught at service colleges and universities throughout the 1950s and 1960s under the rubric of "nuclear deterrence theory." The dogma was the basis of innumerable and repetitive articles in service journals, and underlay most discussion of defense and foreign policy matters in the daily press and in the weekly and monthly magazines. And it appeared continually in NATO policy statements and national defense white papers. This deterrence dogma came to crowd out other long-established ideas, becoming at times a virtual substitute for both foreign and defense policy.

The usual rebuttal to this type of criticism is that "nuclear deterrence has kept the peace for thirty-five years," peace being defined as the avoidance of East-West conflict, particularly in Europe. A more thoughtful rebuttal acknowledges that although we cannot be sure that it was deterrence that preserved the peace, "it is better to be safe than sorry." An implication of that caveat is that while nuclear deterrence may not have been responsible for keeping the peace, neither did we suffer any harm through adopting such a policy. It is this comforting and widely held assumption—that deterrence has caused no harm—that is the focus of the argument. Only when the costs of nuclear deterrence are clearly established can one refute with clarity the more extravagant claims that this same deterrence has kept the peace for thirty-five years.

In the wake of World War I, war was seen as too important to leave to generals, and it was taken over by the politicians. They, having done little better in World War II, left the field to the academics, who moved in to address the new conundrums that came with the atomic bomb. There was a peculiar quality to this subdiscipline of "strategic studies" as it emerged in the 1950s: It focused almost entirely on the problems of nuclear weapons, deterrence doctrine, and, in due course, theories of limited nuclear war. With a few notable exceptions such as Bernard Brodie, the field became dominated by academics from axiomatic disciplines such as mathematics, physics, and economics, who took over from the military and diplomatic historians that had traditionally presided over the study of international politics.

Reprinted with permission from *SAIS Review*, vol. 15., no. 2, Summer-Fall, 1985, pp. 105–124. Copyright © 1985 by The Johns Hopkins Foreign Policy Institute, School of Advanced International Studies (SAIS).

To all these theorists, the Soviet "threat" was a given. The Soviet Union was assumed to have a relentless drive for territorial conquest, and the reality of a monolithic communist bloc went unquestioned. The governing concept of deterrence assumed a Soviet urge above all to seize Europe, and it was this assumption that provided the basis for most strategic theorizing. The field developed a new breed of self-styled "tough-minded" strategic analysts, who like to think through problems abstractly and in a political vacuum. To this new breed, the opponent was not "Soviet man"—not even "political man"—but an abstract "strategic man," who thought, as they did, in game theoretical terms.

The original concept of nuclear deterrence derived from a belief that the only practical way of restraining Soviet aggression was to threaten unacceptable punishment. Initially, the theorists concentrated on how to keep the threat of U.S. nuclear retaliation "credible," which required that the United States be seen to have both the capability to inflict unacceptable punishment and the will to do so. Capability, in turn, required that the means of inflicting the punishment be made invulnerable to Soviet surprise attack, with the possibility of technological breakthroughs adding a further dimension to the problem. This need for invulnerability introduced a new factor into the offense-defense calculus and gave full rein to an extreme form of worst-case analysis. Imaginative strategic theorists worked hard to discern chinks in the armor of assured response, which a determined opponent might hope to exploit with a bolt-from-the-blue attack or in some other way.

The perception that the Soviets could only be held in check by the threat of nuclear devastation persisted, but by the second half of the 1950s another danger had become apparent: the temptation to preempt, a by-product of the emerging Soviet capability to strike directly at the United States with nuclear weapons. The advantages of getting in the first blow were so overwhelming that a prudent leader could be expected to launch a nuclear strike if it were suspected that the other side were contemplating war. This assumed pressure to preempt introduced a new concern for the "stability" of the strategic balance, and the simple requirement that Soviet aggression be *deterred*, came to be qualified by the somewhat contradictory requirement that the Soviet Union be *reassured* that the United States would not initiate a nuclear war, lest the

Soviets be driven to launch a preemptive attack.

Two main requirements had to be met for strategic stability to be achieved. One was that enough weapons should be able to survive a first strike in order to inflict unacceptable punishment on the initiator—an assured second strike (or, more properly, strike second) capability. And since, in theory at least, both sides had to meet this requirement, they each had to eschew weapon systems and offensive or defensive deployments that might deprive the other of such a second-strike capability. These requirements were the underpinnings of "assured destruction," a doctrine that was adopted by the arms control community in the 1960s, although it never became official U.S. policy.

Deterrence theory and its reassurance corollary both assumed the Soviet threat, and to the extent there was disagreement on this point, it focused on which element was more likely to prompt a Soviet attack: expansionist urge or reciprocal fear. Both theories shared the common premise of an assured second-strike capability, but the theoretical requirements that had to be met to ensure stability were more demanding than those for credibility. For an assured response to be credible, it was only necessary to be able to launch on warning or under attack. For stability purposes, even a launch-under-attack capability was insufficient to meet the requirement. Stability required that a sufficient number of weapons be able to suffer and survive a deliberate surprise attack, and then inflict the unacceptable punishment required by deterrence doctrine.

Deterrence theory and its reassurance corollary evolved over time. The ramifications of both theories were spun out to their logical ends, and deterrence moved away from the concept of massive retaliation to greater discrimination in the use of nuclear weapons. While the idea was to increase credibility and the options available to the president, it also provided persuasive reasons for increasing the size of weapons inventories, and did not reduce the overall scale of nuclear devastation. But those developments are peripheral to the main argument. The four aspects that are central to understanding the effects of deterrence dogma need to be highlighted.

One point was the abstract style of reasoning and the axiomatic nature of the underlying theories. This led to a definition of rational behavior that in political terms was at best arational and more often irrational, and favored mathematical models like the "prisoners' dilemma" over studies in the political psychology of opponents and allies.

Another was the absence of serious Sovietologists from the theoretical debate, even though theories of limited war and escalation depended on assumptions about how the Soviets would react under given circumstances. This inadequacy was partly the result of the abstract nature of the debate, but it was also because Soviet intentions were taken as given, and only their capabilities were of analytical interest.

When combined with the catastrophic consequences of nuclear surprise, these two aspects encouraged an extreme form of worst case analysis, where a course of enemy action had only to be "conceivable" for it to be included in the calculus of threat. Strategic studies thus came to be dominated by "tough-minded" theorists.

A third aspect was the fundamentally punitive thrust of nuclear deterrence as formulated in the West—not just a passive matter of locking the door and barring the windows to avoid tempting a light-fingered neighbor. Rather, it was an active policy that asserted a hostile Soviet intent and threatened wholesale devastation. The policy relied on the capability and the will to inflict such punishment, and a prerequisite for making this posture credible was a sustained perception of high threat among the electorate.

Fourth was the fact that the reassurance corollary stemmed from the same roots as nuclear deterrence and shared most of its underlying assumptions. Reassurance was designed to suppress certain unpleasant side effects of deterrence, and was preoccupied with a narrowly defined concept of stability rather than with limiting the buildup of arms.

With these salient characteristics in mind, the way in which deterrence dogma has affected our policies over the years becomes clearer. In order to sharpen the argument, the terms "deterrers" and "reassurers" have been used as if they were two clearly defined schools of thought. There was, of course, no such definition. Rather, there existed a spectrum of opinion with individuals emphasizing different aspects at different times. However the use of such a heuristic device highlights the important role of the two theories and their shared assumptions in shaping defence and foreign policy.

People of great intelligence and considerable good will formulated these theories as they sought to grapple with the complexities of the nuclear era. The only hindsight available to them was the events of the 1930s and 1940s. Their judgments about Soviet intentions were shaped by the Greek civil war, the Berlin blockade, the emergence of communist China, and the Korean war. They believed that World War III would come about through Soviet aggression and they were determined not to repeat the mistakes of the 1930s; Soviet aggression had to be deterred. They were unusually perspicacious in their appreciation that nuclear weapons were qualitatively different, and they were convinced that the implications needed to be thought out.

All of this is understandable and even admirable, but it does not explain why much the same perceptions persist in the 1980s. Deterrence dogma does. It imposed a rigid framework on our thinking that prevented our view of the world from evolving with new information and more relevant hindsight and yet also became a form of intellectual Valium, its sophisticated logic imparting a sense of false certainty and inhibiting attempts to challenge the underlying assumptions.

Soviet theory, which was "innocent of the higher calculus of deterrence,"[1] did not ossify in the same way. In the period from 1948 to 1953, the Soviet perception of threat was the mirror image of our own, with equally good reason. But by 1959 the Soviets had concluded that the primary threat to their well-being was nuclear war (from whatever the cause) rather than deliberate aggression by the West.[2] The primary objective, therefore, was to avoid war rather than to deter aggression. This same dichotomy, as we shall see, underlies the current debate in the West.

The peculiar characteristics of deterrence dogma acted differently on foreign policy, arms control theory, and military doctrine. In some cases the effect was indirect, providing a rationale for policies, attitudes, and actions toward which the American polity was already predisposed, which raises the question whether deterrence dogma shaped U.S. policy or whether its adoption reflected the innate preferences of American society. The question cannot be answered, but the dogma certainly played to the American habit of viewing the world in black and white, and the tendency to believe that problems should (and can) be solved—rather than managed or even avoided.

Deterrence dogma's overall effect on foreign policy has been to narrow the policy's focus and to limit unnecessarily the range of policy options. In the wake of World War II, it was to be expected that initially the "colonel's fallacy" in threat analysis would prevail, but deterrence dogma perpetuated it. At the military-tactical— or "colonel's"—level, the focus of threat analysis is properly on the enemy's capabilities, with the assumption of hostile intentions. Worst-case analysis of this sort is appropriate to contingency planning, but it is wholly inappropriate at the political-strategic or "ministerial" level of analysis that should underlie foreign policy.

At this level our primary concern is with the most likely course of events, the assessment of which must take into account four factors. Two of them are linked: the opponent's military capabilities and his "legitimate" requirements. The two are compared in order to establish whether there is the kind of surplus that would indicate aggressive intentions. This kind of assessment is necessary if one is not to rely on the untested assertion that "the Soviets have more than they need," the persistent claim of the last thirty-five years.[3] The other two elements of threat analysis are interests and intentions. It is difficult to determine any country's interests (even one's own), but it is relatively easy to identify what is not in a nation's interest. The concept of negative interests is central to avoiding the pitfall of assuming that what is bad for us must be good for our opponent.

Soviet intentions must be addressed directly. To claim that they should be ignored because they can change overnight is to fall into the colonel's fallacy and impute worst-case intentions without doing the analysis. At the national level, intentions are remarkable consistent; they change radically only as the result of political shifts of a kind that have not occurred in the Soviet Union since the Bolshevik revolution. We now have more than sixty-five years of Soviet actions and pronouncements, and when this is combined with an analysis of Soviet interests and placed within the historical constraints of geography and social inertia, a fairly clear picture of Soviet intentions emerges, particularly regarding such fundamental matters as peace and war.

Just as deterrence dogma predisposed the threat analyst to focus on the worst rather than the most likely case, so did the dogma predispose the foreign policy specialist to focus on the containment of Soviet power rather than to pursue an objective of a higher order that would allow a wider range of policies in support. If containment is the primary objective, policies are inevitably negative; a broader objective, however, such as "securing cooperative Soviet behavior," opens up more constructive policy options.

At this higher level, containment continues to be an important mission, but it can be flanked by positive missions such as increasing trade interdependence, fostering institutional links, and even encouraging rising expectations by improving the Soviet standard of living. Such policies would be incompatible with containment as the main objective, but an objective of a higher order could even accommodate a cooperative policy such as joining with the Soviet Union to stifle dangerous developments before they become unmanageable.

During the period of détente in the early 1970s, the United States did adopt a higher level objective and this did allow a broader range of initiatives. These brought benefits that extended beyond the Soviet-American relationship and helped to bridge the East-West divide in Europe. But the assumptions that deterrence dogma makes about Soviet intentions are incompatible with the assumptions that underlie a policy of détente. The deterrent calculus was manipulated to expose a "window of vulnerability," and was then used to justify a return to more restrictive policies.

While deterrence dogma worked to narrow the focus, and unnecessarily limited the range of policy options, it also encouraged a particular style of foreign policy. Central to the dogma is the question of credibility, with the will to inflict punishment as important as the capability to do so. There are two dimensions to this will: the willingness to see the enemy suffer what is (by definition) "unacceptable" punishment, and one's own willingness to endure whatever retaliation the enemy can muster. Even in the days of the U.S. atomic monopoly, for the electorate to support a policy of nuclear deterrence required that the American people see the Soviets as enemies who deserved such a fate. And as the United States was brought within range of Soviet nuclear delivery systems, its people had to be persuaded that they were ready to suffer massive devastation and perhaps commit national suicide. Bluster and bravery are inversely correlated, and the more improbable this American response became, the more important it was to reaffirm the will to take such action, and to paint the issues at stake in stark, moral terms.

In other words, a policy of nuclear deterrence

tends to encourage exaggerated and moralistic rhetoric directed at domestic constituents as well as the opponent, and it becomes hard to distinguish between the two. In a populist democracy such as the United States, it is easier to inflame hostility than to assuage it, and a leadership can become a prisoner of past rhetoric. Add to this potential the need to make the threat credible to one's opponent, and a policy of deterrence favoring intransigence becomes almost inevitable, discouraging serious negotiations and the search for compromise.

The effects of deterrence dogma on U.S. arms control policy and on NATO military doctrine are intertwined. An assured second-strike capability is a premise shared by deterrence and its reassurance corollary, and concern for the capability has always been at the center of U.S. arms control policy. That policy however, has had to reconcile the differing perceptions of the "deterrers" and the "reassurers" on this straightforward issue.

The deterrers concentrate on ensuring that the U.S. second-strike capability is not eroded. To this end they hypothesize a malevolent Soviet Union anxious to seize any chance to destroy the United States; they assume an American president easily blackmailed into inaction; they then conceive of every possible scenario, now and in the future, in order to reach their assessment of what is needed to ensure an adequate U.S. capability; and the answer is always more.

The reassurers, however, are concerned that both sides have an assured second-strike capability. The assumptions they make about how the Soviets perceive their interests and how Moscow would assess the chances of Soviet success and U.S. inaction are more carefully grounded in reality, and in that respect their assessment of U.S. requirements is more moderate. On the other hand, the reassurers' definition of an assured second strike justifies a significantly larger weapons inventory, since stability requires the U.S. force to be able to survive an attack. For credibility purposes it would only need to be able to launch under attack, a capability that is related to warning time and not the size of the initial inventory. The deterrers do not dispute the reassurers' more demanding definition of force requirements.

An assured second-strike capability is, however, only part of reassurance doctrine. There is also the presumption that each side will eschew weapon systems that might deprive the other of that capability. However, one should not suppose that the Soviets have adopted a self-denying ordinance, nor does the accumulated evidence suggest that the United States is serious about such restraint. And in the absence of any self-denying ordinance, reassurance theory becomes a recipe for arms racing, as each side seeks to ensure that it can absorb a first strike and still retaliate.

While mutual reassurance provides the basis of Western arms control theory, it does not determine U.S. arms control policy. An inherent tension exists between the requirement of credibility and stability, and experience shows that when push comes to shove, deterrence invariably wins out over reassurance. When one then adds the reassurers' second-strike capability to the deterrers' assumptions about the Soviets' current cost-benefit calculi and possible future capabilities, the resultant military requirements become hard to distinguish from a specification for U.S. superiority, including a first-strike capability.

But even U.S. military superiority would cover only one aspect of deterrence, since official criteria for credibility have evolved far beyond the simple requirement for an assured second-strike capability. For almost a decade people have argued that the Soviet military doctrine recognizes the need to be able to fight and win a nuclear war and that the only way to deter the Soviets is with a comparable capability. The argument is logically flawed, but that is not really important. The new criteria have nothing to do with the original concept of being able to inflict unacceptable damage on the Soviet Union (a capability that is manifest), and everything to do with a U.S. reluctance to take such action in defense of Europe, knowing that to do so would invite the nuclear devastation of North America.

The argument does, however, illustrate some of the problems that are being discussed. The Soviet Union has finally been brought into the calculus, but only in terms of its military doctrine for the contingency of world war. Avoiding such a war is one of the Soviets' first objectives, but should it prove inescapable, the Soviets hope not to lose, and plan accordingly. So, of course, do we, which says nothing about our broader intentions toward Russia. But in assessing Soviet intentions, we take their operational concepts at face value and persist in the colonel's fallacy. Nor do we offer any explanation of how Soviet interests would be served by the military seizure of Europe. We sidestep that issue by ignoring the principle that deterrence can only be directed against certain kinds of action, and talk instead of deterring an activity, war, or the Soviet Union.

"Deterring the Soviet Union" is a marvelous slogan that is used to justify almost anything, from a new weapons system to all kinds of military deployment. It is also almost meaningless, because it ignores the factor of temptation, which makes up the other half of the deterrence equation. For deterrence to have any meaning, somebody must be tempted to take the action being deterred. Temptation is made up of opportunity and urge, and while military capabilities may tell us something about the opportunity to act, they tell us little about the important matter of urge.

Evidence of an increased Soviet urge to take over Europe was absent from the rationale advanced in 1980 to support a more extensive U.S. deterrent capability, and this absence was one of its logical flaws. But taking temptation for granted had more far-reaching consequences in the case of flexible response, a concept accepted in Washington in 1961 and formally adopted by NATO in 1967. By replacing the policy of automatic resort to nuclear weapons with one in which NATO would initially use conventional weapons to check a Soviet assault on Europe, flexible response was ostensibly intended to increase the credibility of the Western nuclear deterrent. The conventional phase would serve the double purpose of allowing NATO to be certain that it was facing a major attack while giving the Soviets the opportunity to see the error of their ways, and withdraw.

Whatever one may think of this argument (the French were not persuaded and the rest of NATO went along with varying degrees of reluctance) it only began to make sense if the Soviet Union had an inherent urge to take over Western Europe, which is the assumption that underlies NATO's defense plans. This assumption is not, however, supported by the evidence. The evidence does indicate that, in the event of a world war, if the Soviets are not ultimately to lose, they must take over NATO Europe and deny its use as a bridgehead by the United States.[4] The problem that would face the Soviets would be how to achieve this without precipitating nuclear war in Europe, which would most probably escalate to an intercontinental exchange and result in the nuclear devastation of Russia. The conventional phase envisaged by flexible response offered the Soviets a way out of this impasse. It provided the opportunity for neutralizing NATO's theater nuclear delivery systems with conventional means, thereby removing the first rung of the escalation ladder. It also opened up the possibility of a conventional blitzkrieg to knock out NATO forces in Europe, thereby rendering moot the question of escalation. A combination of both operations would increase the chances of success, and it was this kind of Soviet capability that we saw emerging in the late 1970s.

Two points can be drawn from this. One is that a Soviet drive into Western Europe would be responding to a strategic imperative where war was imposed, not to the temptation to go to war for territorial gain. This means that the Soviet offensive would be a byproduct of the much more momentous decision that world war was unavoidable, and the offensive could not be prevented by simple threats of punishment, which would already have been taken into account. The other point is that this new possibility of finessing nuclear escalation in the European theater reduces the constraints on launching a preemptive conventional attack. Thus, in the event of an East-West crisis that seemed inescapably headed for war, a NATO policy of imposing a conventional phase and foregoing the first use of nuclear weapons would make it that much more likely that the Soviet Union would cross the threshold from peace to war.

These paradoxical and unintended results of flexible response illustrate the limitations of a theory built on the 1950s' assumption that the cause of World War III would be Soviet aggression. But the effect of that outdated assumption on contemporary foreign policy behavior is even more distorting. Drawing on the experience of the 1930s, the major corollary was that war could be prevented by deterring such aggression with the threat of punishment. The shorthand for such a policy was "deterring war," a term that has become a cornerstone of Western policy pronouncements, and permeates our thinking on peace and war. Besides falling into the fallacy of claiming to deter an activity rather than an action, the honorific overtones of the term obscure the radical nature of the underlying principle. U.S. policies are now based on the idea of deterring or *preventing* war by the threat of force, rather than the time-honored principle of averting or *avoiding* war through negotiation and diplomacy.

While deterrence dogma worked to undermine diplomacy, its moralistic quality worked to distort sound strategic analysis. An example of this was the 1960 expectation that since it was the Soviets who were threatening world peace, they would recognize the logic of deterrence theory and the nonthreatening nature of U.S. nuclear capabilities. The Soviets' persistence in thinking in traditional terms of matching an opponent's capabilities was interpreted at best as an indication of strategic backwardness, and more generally as confirming their aggressive intentions.

More dangerous was the pseudo-moral argument that was based on the theoretical distinction between counterforce and countervalue targeting. This ignored the practical realities of target interspersion and the effects of fallout, but provided a moral justification for moving away from relying on mutual assured destruction as a deterrent to war, and adopting a warfighting strategy. Once introduced into the debate, the "moral" factor became a powerful argument, since the arms control community had made itself vulnerable by talking of mutually assured destruction as a policy, rather than as a description of the objective situation. The arms controllers lost their political constituency on the left, who charged that high theory had resulted in higher force levels, and the situation was ripe for an attack from the right on established policies. The concept of mutual assured destruction was ridiculed, and a space-based defense system was offered as a panacea to the problems that beset us, and one that was moral to boot.

The increasingly obvious flaws in accepted strategic theory and its inability to solve these problems thus opened the way for a simplistic concept. The Strategic Defense Initiative (SDI) launched in March 1983 looks to some unspecified future where America and the Soviet Union sit snug beneath their space-based shields. A wish more than a theory, as a means of addressing the problems of nuclear weapons it is flawed more fundamentally than the doctrine it seeks to replace. But while it makes little sense in the terms in which it is being peddled to the public, it has quite different implications in the terms of classical military strategy. Were the United States to be successful in developing its space-based defense system, it will have regained the position of relative military advantage that it enjoyed for twenty years after the war. Experience suggests that the Soviets will make every effort to prevent this advantage from coming about.

While deterrence dogma has provided the necessary rationale for exotic weapons programs, it has also undermined the cooperative potential of arms control where there were significant prospects for Soviet-American collaboration in reducing the danger of nuclear war. Traditionally, the objectives of arms control have been twofold. At the political level the negotiations can be a means of making war less likely, the process being as important as the specifics. At the military level the concern is with the contingency of war and maximizing one's relative advantage. There is an obvious tension between the two, but to the extent that the negotiating process is successful in reducing the danger of war, so does the military objective become less important and, of course, vice versa.

The arms control policy that stemmed from deterrence dogma was nominally interested in the same objectives, but there was a crucial difference in the approach to making war less likely. Deterrence dogma decreed that one *prevented* war by the threat of punishment, embodied in a second-strike capability. The primary concern of the deterrers was that the means of retribution should be able to survive a surprise attack. The concern of the reassurers was to counteract the pressure to preemption by denying such action any advantage. Both focused on the dangers of sudden attack, so that U.S. efforts toward reducing the likelihood of war were concentrated on developing measures to prevent crises from getting out of control.

The obvious objection to this approach is that by the time a crisis arises serious enough to engender thoughts of nuclear preemption, it is almost certainly too late. It is a technical and theoretical approach to a problem that is fundamentally political. For a period from the late 1960s through the first half of the 1970s, when the reassurers had the dominant voice in formulating policy, the U.S. approach to arms control did manage to balance the technical with the political, and this equilibrium fostered fruitful negotiations and contributed to the relaxation in international tension. But then push came to shove, the deterrers regained their natural dominance of national security matters, and technical factors became paramount. The United States focused on enhancing its military capability to prevent war, and arms control became a field of ascerbic confrontation.

As President Reagan has said, "it takes two to tango" and it is therefore relevant that the Soviets have a traditional approach to arms control that is political and practical rather than technical and theoretical. They consider war something to be avoided through negotiation and compromise rather than prevented by threat of dire punishment. A primary objective of the arms control process is therefore to help create a political climate that makes war less likely—ostensibly one of the major accomplishments of the SALT negotiations. The Soviets consider that the U.S. obsession with the pressure to preempt obscures the greater danger that comes from the dynamic of events over which there can be no control. Priority should therefore be given to avoiding situations that lead to crises rather than devising ways to manage crises that may well be inherently uncontrollable.[5]

The costs of a policy based on nuclear deterrence can be summarized under six general indictments. Some of them reflect deep-rooted tendencies in American society, but deterrence dogma at the very least encouraged these attitudes, and it often provided the moral and intellectual justification that allowed such policies to flourish.

The first indictment concerns the intellectual framework of the theories of nuclear deterrence. At a very early stage the question of how one handled the awesome new capability got entangled with the question of how one handles the Soviets. With hindsight one can see that the broader problem was addressed at too low a level of generality; that of "nuclear weapons" and "deterring the Soviets" rather than the higher order of "avoiding world war," a mistake that Bernard Brodie appears to have sensed, if not articulated.

Defining the Soviet threat in worst-case terms meant that concern for the innate dangers of nuclear weaponry yielded precedence to deterring the Russians. With the Soviet threat as a given, intellectual effort focused on developing a technical solution to what was essentially a political problem. As the analysts' scenarios were embroidered, the simple principle of deterrence was obscured by theoretical ramifications, and the strategic debate increasingly became the preserve of specialists who had the time and inclination to master the minutiae of nuclear theology.

These high priests acquired significant authority in Western councils and could silence disagreement by noting the dissenter's inability to grasp the finer points of sophisticated theory. Deterrence theory soon became an intellectual tranquilizer. It was so tortuous that it could be used to support the opposite sides of the same argument. It could also be transmuted into sim-

ple objectives like preserving peace and deterring war that were as unobjectionable as baseball and apple pie. A combination of its simple and complex forms provided the intellectual and moral authority of a state religion, and the effect was just as stultifying.

The second indictment concerns the impact of deterrence theory on domestic attitudes; here the effects have probably been most pernicious. The persistent assumption of a high level of Soviet threat despite a balance in military capabilities that favored the West for most of the postwar period played to a visceral anticommunism organic in many sectors of the community. The threat of punishment central to deterrence fostered the impression of America the magistrate and Russia the law breaker, reinforcing the belief that the problem was one of good and evil, rather than conflicting ideologies and interests.

The credibility of deterrence required that political will be reasserted at frequent intervals, and for forty years the American people have been propagandized as assiduously as their Soviet counterparts.[6] Meanwhile the irrefutable slogans of "deterring war" and "deterring the Soviets" persuaded Congress to invest in massive inventories of strategic nuclear weapons, which the Russians duly matched. However amicable the objective state of Soviet-American relations, the level of armaments denied the reality of the situation and, following the dictates of cognitive dissonance, threat perceptions moved back into line with the weapon inventories.

The third indictment relates to U.S. foreign policy. Because deterrence and its corollary containment have remained the dominating concepts in foreign and defense policy, popular threat perceptions have remained frozen in the mold of the 1947–53 period. The theory has provided the intellectual casing that makes this world view impervious to contradictory evidence and analyses, even for some of the decision-making elites. The emphasis on containment and deterrence results in policy toward the Soviet Union limited to a narrow range of mainly negative objectives. The theory fosters an assertive, apolitical style that favors preventive and punitive instruments, is distrustful of negotiations, and sees compromise as weakness. The possibility that U.S. interests might be served by cooperating with the Soviets in dealing with problems around the world is excluded from consideration, and long-term objectives regarding future Soviet policies simply are not addressed.

The fourth indictment is that theory has fueled the arms race, rather than checked it. The belief that a sudden buildup in U.S. strategic weapons in the early 1960s would "improve the stability of deterrence" fostered the unwarranted assumption that the Soviets would accept it as being in the interests of peace.[7] The reassurers, meanwhile, were concerned with relative rather than aggregate levels of weapons and, in any case, large inventories were theoretically more stable than small ones.

The deterrers focused attention on numbers when they saw that the Soviets would not only match the U.S. buildup but surpass it. Arms control policy moved to cap the number of Soviet missiles, while the deterrers tried to regain their original advantage by multiplying the number of U.S. warheads. As the Soviets moved to catch up in that field, too, the deterrers sought relative advantage in added diversity, and their arguments could be summed up as "more is better." They redefined the requirements for stability, and by using carefully selected units of account, they were able to exploit reassurance theory to discredit arms control and to demonstrate an urgent requirement for new offensive weapons programs. And since it was mutual assured destruction that had justified the treaty banning antiballistic missiles, once that concept was discredited, the theoretical constraints on ballistic missile defense systems were weakened. The temptation to open the Pandora's Box of space-based systems became irresistible to many.

The fifth indictment is that military strategy itself was driven from the so-called strategic debate. It was replaced in part by more tangible concepts like force exchange rations, damage expectancies, and kill probabilities, which were amenable to mathematical permutation. But the debate also focused on the theoretical elaboration of deterrence and reassurance, and pondered the rationality of irrationality and the potential for compellance. The mathematical models were excellent for generating hard numbers, and anchored the debate at the level where Americans are most comfortable: the technical and budgetary aspects of force requirements. The theoretical elaborations applied Cartesian logic to complex problems of political psychology, which resulted in bad politics and bad strategy, as we found in Vietnam.

In Europe questions of deterrence, escalation, firebreaks, coupling, and decoupling came to dominate the debate, with military strategy largely a side issue. The NATO concept of flexible response adopted in 1967 may have made sense within deterrence theory, but it offered the Soviets a strategic opportunity that contributed to their adoption of a new set of military objectives, and justified a radical restructuring of the Soviet armed forces and the introduction of fundamentally new concepts of operation.[8] The politically divisive deployment of Euromissiles that was decided in 1979 and initially implemented in 1983 was seen by the Europeans as strengthening coupling, viewed by the Soviets as dangerously destabilizing, and interpreted by the Americans as a test of loyalty to the alliance.

The sixth indictment is that deterrence dogma encouraged an unwarranted complacency, and diverted public attention and intellectual resources from more fundamental problems. By defining crisis stability as the critical aspect of the nuclear problem, it diverted attention from the *avoidance* of crises, and hence the central importance of the Soviet-American political relationship as the source of global war. By focusing exclusively on the possibility of Soviet aggression, the theory obscured the fact that war itself was the greatest danger, and could be made more likely by the measures being taken to deter aggression.

By claiming to have solved the problem of nuclear weapons, deterrence dogma dissipated the sudden urgency that this devastating capability had brought to the search for new ways of managing interstate relations. The pressure for a new approach had been building up for fifty years and more, with World Wars I and II demonstrating the inherent limits of the existing system. But the steam was let out of the movement by the promise of deterrence, and the abstract style of reasoning and tough-minded thinking basic to the dogma were inhospitable to radical ideas about conflict and cooperation.

While the scope of the indictment may be broader than some can accept, the comforting belief that deterrence dogma has done no harm is clearly untenable. What, then, were the benefits that justified these significant costs? In particular, what of the claim that deterrence has kept the peace since World War II? This persistent claim cannot be disproved, but neither can the opposing claim that nuclear deterrence was not responsible for keeping the peace. As the policy of nuclear deterrence imposes significant costs, the conclusion "better safe than sorry" no longer holds, and the opposing assertions must be dissected and their probable validity weighed against each other.

One must start with the original purpose of the policy, which was based on the assumption that the Soviets were set on military aggression that would lead to world war, unless it were deterred. There are, of course, a number of cases where communist aggression was not deterred by the U.S. nuclear capability: Korea, Vietnam, Hungary, Czechoslovakia, and Afghanistan. Compellence is quite different from deterrence, so the two cases where the nuclear threat was used in that role in the 1950s are irrelevant to this argument. One is left, then, with the narrow claim that were it not for the nuclear deterrent, the Soviets would have invaded NATO Europe, precipitating World War III.

For that to be true one must prove that nothing less than nuclear punishment could have deterred such Soviet aggression. Given the devastation of Russia and its people in World War II, would the prize of a vanquished Europe have been worth the costs of another conventional war? And what of the effect on other Soviet objectives, such as the attempt to build up the power and prosperity of the Russian homeland, the progress of the world communist movement, and Soviet standing in the competition for world influence? The assumptions that underlie the claim reflect the war-clouded perceptions of 1947–50 rather than a realistic appraisal of Soviet costs and benefits.

The claim is a classic example of the colonel's fallacy and assumes a simple Soviet objective of territorial conquest without explaining how such a conquest would serve their interests. Nor is such an objective supported by historical analyses of Soviet behavior over the last sixty years, or by their doctrine. In the wake of World War II they withdrew from Arctic Norway, Finland, Czechoslovakia, Yugoslavia, Bulgaria, Azerbaijan, and Manchuria. Roughly ten years later they withdrew from Austria and gave up their bases at Porkala and Port Arthur.

This is not to suggest that the Soviets are benevolently inclined, however. They are certainly preoccupied with maintaining control in their national security zone, as they showed in Hungary, Czechoslovakia, and Afghanistan. But even as those cases (to say nothing of others where the Soviets did not resort to direct military intervention)[9] demonstrated, the military instrument is not the first one they reach for, and the record argues that they are not possessed by a Napoleonic or Hitlerite urge for military expansion.

Many now accept that the threat of Soviet aggression has been overblown, but insist that there is still a role for nuclear deterrence in preventing war. They postulate a situation in which the Soviet Union finds itself in some complex crisis that makes resorting to war perhaps a lesser evil, were there not a high probability of its escalating to an intercontinental exchange.

The argument is irrefutable with calculations that might be made in a narrow set of circumstances, isolated in space and time. But crises are not isolated in that way, and the argument exemplifies what is being criticized in this paper. By focusing on a hypothetical worst case where war would be a lesser evil, it ignores the possibility that a different U.S. policy might encourage a less restrictive range of Soviet options. The argument concentrates on managing a crisis rather than on creating the circumstances that would make such crises less likely. And above all it ignores the effect that a deterrence-based policy has on Soviet-American relations and the likelihood of war.

This point is a nub of the argument. The advocates of nuclear deterrence implicitly assume that war can only come about as the result of Soviet initiative. Originally, this initiative was seen as deliberate military aggression, but now it may involve a resort to war as the lesser evil. It is also assumed that any such resort to war can be deterred by the threat of nuclear escalation.

Those who do not share those two assumptions argue that it is precisely this obsession with the remote possibility of extreme cases (that may, in any case, be inherently uncontrollable) that increases the danger of war. The steady buildup of nuclear weapons to deter these possible Soviet initiatives actually makes war more likely through accident, miscalculation, or the increased tension and tougher political posturing that go with such policies.

The deterrent advocates talk of necessary insurance. Their opponents can counter with the analogy of the person who is obsessed with the danger of a meteor strike, and who steadily increases the thickness of the roof of the house until the entire thing collapses.

The final defense of the deterrent dogmatist is to ask: "What would you put in its place?" The short answer is "nothing." The immediate objective is to reduce the salience of deterrence dogma in the formulation of policy and allow its place to be taken by traditional approaches to foreign and defense policy. Certainly these approaches will be enriched by a more subtle understanding of classic concepts such as deterrence and reassurance, and by a deeper awareness of human frailty under stress in crises.

The situation is, however, more complex than that, because the problem lies as much in the attitudes that are engendered by the dogma as in the dogma itself. This way of thinking now pervades the Western political-military establishment, and one has to ask what kind of ideas can take the place of these attitudes that have proven so counterproductive. It will not be easy to change a mindset that is congenial to our way of thinking, panders to our prejudices, and reflects the conventional wisdom of forty years. But we might start with four general principles.

We should pay less attention to developing the military means to deter the onset of war, and concentrate more on developing the political means to avert those situations that make war more likely.

We should recognize that for all except the most extreme circumstances (which are probably inherently uncontrollable) mutual deterrence is an objective fact. We should also recognize that cognitive dissonance inhibits improved Soviet-American relations as long as large weapons inventories remain in place. We should therefore approach arms control with the objective of significantly reducing the existing number of nuclear weapons and blocking new avenues for arms racing rather than seeking to shape the arsenals to deter, or, if necessary, control nuclear war.

We should recognize that it is world war, however it starts, and not Soviet aggression, that poses the greatest threat to all our people. When devising the means to counter the Soviets' offensive capability, we must be sensitive to whether these will increase the tendency to war, in the long run as well as the short.

We should recognize that the danger of war stems from the adversarial nature of the Soviet-American relationship, and not from their nuclear arsenals. Worst-case scenarios masquerading as analyses of Soviet intentions reinforce the conflictual tendencies in the relationship, and stifle the cooperative ones, increasing the likelihood of war. The state of the relationship bears directly on the peace of the world, and we must recognize that it is too important to be manipulated for tactical advantage in the superpower competition or for domestic political gain.

NOTES

1. Arthur A. Schlesinger, *A Thousand Days: John F. Kennedy in the White House* (Boston: Houghton Mifflin, 1965), 301, describing a discussion between Walt Rostow and Deputy Foreign Minister Vasily Kuznetsov in December 1960.

2. Michael MccGwire, *Soviet Military Objectives* (Washington, D.C.: Brookings, forthcoming), chapter 2.

3. For a preliminary attempt, see Michael MccGwire, "Soviet Military Requirements" in *Soviet Military Economic Relations: Proceedings of a Workshop on 7–8 July 1982*, Joint Economic Committee of Congress, U.S. GPO, 1983. See also my *Soviet Military Objectives*. The short answer is that the Soviets have enough to cause us justifiable concern, but they do not have "more than they need."

4. *Soviet Military Objectives*, chapters 2 and 4.

5. *Soviet Military Objectives*, chapter 10.

6. Cora M. Bell talks of "the Cold War image of Russian society, constructed with some deliberation in the West" in *Negotiating from Strength* (New York: Alfred A. Knopf, 1963), 239.

7. Schlesinger citing Walt Rostow in *A Thousand Days*. See also Raymond L. Garthoff, *Intelligence Assessment and Policymaking: A Decision Point in the Kennedy Administration* (The Brookings Institution: 1984), 24–26.

8. This process started in 1968 and was largely complete by 1975. *Soviet Military Objectives*, chapters 2 and 3.

9. Examples are Yugoslavia from 1949 on, Poland in 1956, Albania from 1960 on, Rumania from 1963 on, and Poland in 1980–81. See also Ken Booth, *The Military Instrument in Soviet Foreign Policy 1917–72* (London: Royal United Services Institute, 1973).

QUESTIONS FOR DISCUSSION

1. Briefly compare and contrast the cold war of the 1940s and 1950s with the "new cold war" of the 1980s.

2. Discuss the three arenas of détente and confrontation described by Garthoff.

3. According to MccGwire, how has "deterrence dogma" adversely affected U.S.–Soviet relations?

4. Discuss the implications of George's distinction between crisis prevention and crisis management.

SUGGESTED READINGS

BARNET, RICHARD. *Real Security: Restoring American Power in a Dangerous Decade,* New York: Simon and Schuster, 1981.

HALLIDAY, FRED. *The Making of the Second Cold War.* London: Verso, 1983.

HOLLOWAY, DAVID. *The Soviet Union and the Arms Race.* New Haven: Yale University Press, 1983.

HOLLOWAY, DAVID and JANE M.O. SHARP. *The Warsaw Pact: Alliance in Transition.* Ithaca, N.Y.: Cornell University Press, 1984.

KENNEDY, ROBERT and JOHN M. WEINSTEIN, eds. *The Defense of the West.* Boulder, Colo.: Westview Press, 1984.

KEOHANE, ROBERT O. and JOSEPH S. NYE. *Power and Interdependence: World Politics in Transition.* Boston: Little, Brown and Company, 1977.

CHAPTER VIII

ECONOMICS
OF THE NUCLEAR ARMS RACE

Many analysts believe that economic factors are an important stimulus of the nuclear arms race. First, military strategists have often made economic arguments in favor of nuclear buildups, pointing out that nuclear weapons are far cheaper per unit of destructive power than conventional arms. Nuclear weapons provide a "bigger bang for the buck" than conventional explosives; they also require fewer troops to operate and maintain. Such arguments have been important in motivating NATO's choice to rely heavily on nuclear weapons for the defense of Europe.

Second, many analysts believe that economic factors provide a major domestic impetus for the arms race. A relatively small fraction (roughly 15 to 22 percent) of the military budget is spent on programs associated with nuclear weapons and nuclear defense. Though this percentage is not very large, the amount of money reaches into the tens of billions of dollars. Moreover, the beneficial economic effects of this spending—jobs and profits—are concentrated among certain corporations and communities, creating a constituency that is strongly committed to building more nuclear weapons. Thus, some analysts argue, much political support for the development of new nuclear weapons stems from domestic pressures for profitable, job-producing arms contracts. Firms and communities initially seek the economic boon of military contracts; eventually, they become dependent upon them.

This chapter addresses the economics of the nuclear arms race. We begin with an article by Randall Forsberg that discusses the economic costs of the nuclear arms race. Forsberg describes the extent of expenditures on nuclear weapons around the world, and then she explores the value of these resources for alternative uses.

The remainder of the chapter addresses the debate about the economic effects of overall military spending. Some economists believe that high levels of military spending are damaging to the economy. This argument is presented by Roger W. DeGrasse, Jr. in the second reading, an excerpt from his book *Military Expansion, Economic Decline*. Other economists argue that the U.S. is sufficiently rich to afford whatever level of military spending is required. Charles L. Schultze presents this view in the chapter's final reading.

Despite the fact that the bulk of military spending is for conventional forces, arguments about the economic effects of total defense spending are a recurring theme in the debate about the nuclear arms race. The reason: many nuclear policies and policy proposals have implications for total military spending. For example, some analysts think that NATO should defend Western Europe with conventional—not nuclear—forces. Thus, they propose replacing nuclear weapons with increased deployments of conventional forces, a move that would increase both costs and troop requirements. Nevertheless, these analysts argue that the economy can afford such an expenditure to reduce the risk of nuclear war. Opponents of this approach counter that a conventional defense for Europe would be too expensive.

Economic issues arise in other policy disputes as well. Still another group of analysts, for example, propose that negotiations seek parallel cuts in nuclear and conventional forces, arguing that both impose unacceptable economic costs and risks to security. And the economic impact of proposed nuclear weapons systems is inevitably the subject of debate as decisions are made about whether to develop and deploy it. For all of these reasons, an appreciation of the debate over the economic effects of military spending is essential to an understanding of the nuclear arms race.

29   The Economic and Social Costs of the Nuclear Arms Race

Randall Forsberg ———————————————————————————

This paper surveys the economic and social costs of the nuclear arms race. It concentrates on the direct economic costs, which are easiest to define and identify. These are analyzed in the first part. The second part looks at the "opportunity costs" of the arms race: the conversion value or alternative use of nuclear-weapon related resources, assuming that nuclear forces were sharply curtailed or eliminated. . . .

I. THE ECONOMIC COSTS AND MANPOWER REQUIREMENTS OF THE NUCLEAR ARMS RACE

Total Financial Cost

Spending associated directly with nuclear forces and with warning and defense against nuclear attack comes to only about 20 percent of the US military budget and a comparable fraction for the USSR. On a worldwide basis, the share of military resources allocated to nuclear arms is probably only 10–15 percent.

The programs included in these relatively low shares of military spending are development, production and deployment of the following:

1. Long-range offensive "strategic" nuclear forces:
- Bomber aircraft, bomber-launched missiles and aerial-refueling tanker aircraft;
- Land-based intercontinental ballistic missiles (ICBMs);
- Submarines with long-range submarine-launched ballistic missiles (SLBMs); and
- Intermediate-range ground- and sea-launched cruise missiles (GLCMs and SLCMs).

2. Shorter-range "tactical" nuclear weapon systems which carry nuclear warheads as their sole munition, including surface-to-surface, anti-aircraft and antisubmarine weapons and atomic demolition mines.

3. Nuclear warheads.

4. "Strategic" defense forces, including systems for surveillance and warning of nuclear attack, interceptor aircraft, antiballistic missiles and civil defense.

5. Strategic and defense-wide intelligence and communications forces.

6. A pro-rated share of basic military support activities, such as supply and maintenance of equipment; basic training, medical care and other personnel costs; administration; and technology development activities.

The bulk of military spending—about 80 percent for the USA and USSR and 85–90 percent for the world as a whole—goes not to the nuclear arms race but to conventional (non-nuclear) military forces. These are ground troops, tactical air forces and naval forces of the type used in World War II, Vietnam, the Middle East or Afghanistan.

While US and Soviet conventional military forces are trained and equipped primarily to use conventional high-explosive munitions, many of their weapon systems are "dual-purpose": that is, they can deliver nuclear warheads (bombs) in place of conventional. This is true of most US and Soviet tactical aircraft, and most US and many Soviet naval ships. The ground forces can

Excerpted with permission from Randall Forsberg, "The Economic and Social Costs of the Nuclear Arms Race," Institute for Defense and Disarmament Studies Occasional Paper 2, March 1981, pp. 1–8. Copyright © 1981 by Institute for Defense and Disarmament Studies.

be deployed with or without their tactical nuclear surface-to-surface weapons.

In combat situations which involve only one superpower, its conventional forces are likely to be used—and have been used—with conventional munitions only. However, if there were a major conventional war involving large-scale use of both US and Soviet conventional forces, the chance that some or all of these forces would employ their alternative nuclear munitions would be much greater. In that case, these forces would be nuclear rather than conventional. Thus, as an option, most US and Soviet military forces and spending can be considered part of the nuclear arms race.

The US military budget for the next fiscal year (FY 1982) is about $200 billion (slightly under in the Carter version, over in the Reagan version). Of this amount, about $45 billion is associated with nuclear forces, excluding dual-purpose systems. This is about 1.5 percent of the US GNP (gross national product) and about 6 percent of Federal spending. An effort of comparable scale ($40 billion at US prices) is apparent in the USSR.

The nuclear forces of other countries with announced nuclear-weapon programs—the United Kingdom, France and China—are much smaller. Their total military budgets come to a few tens of billions of dollars each, and the nuclear share probably averages no more than $2–3 billion a year. In the case of countries believed but not announced to have nuclear-weapon programs or a developing capability to make nuclear weapons—India, Israel, South Africa, Pakistan and Iraq—total military spending is currently estimated at $5 billion a year or below each; and nuclear-weapon related costs probably come to less than $1 billion annually.

This brings worldwide spending for nuclear arms-related programs to roughly $100 billion, out of world military spending for 1982 currently projected at $700 billion. If all US and Soviet dual-purpose, nuclear-capable forces were included, the nuclear arms bill would be substantially higher: in the range of $300–$350 billion.

Manpower Requirements, and Operating vs. Investment Costs

Nuclear forces are less "manpower-intensive" and more capital- or equipment-intensive to maintain and operate than conventional military forces.

Out of the approximately 2 million military personnel in the US active duty armed forces (about 1 million Army and Marines, 550,000 Air Force and 500,000 Navy), less than 150,000 are directly employed with the strategic nuclear forces. These include the following:

- 60,000 Air Force personnel with strategic bomber forces
- 25,000 Air Force personnel with ICBMs
- 20,000 Navy personnel with strategic submarines
- 5,000 Air Force personnel with air defense interceptors
- 35,000 Air Force personnel with strategic command and control, surveillance and warning.

In addition, about 20,000 members of the Air National Guard support the strategic forces by flying aerial refueling tankers for the bombers and by manning most of the current US strategic interceptor aircraft.

Of the 1 million civilian employees of the Department of Defense, it is estimated that less than 30,000 are employed with the strategic combat forces, mainly in maintenance and office work. A comparable number may be employed in strategic and defensewide intelligence and communications. The single largest operating cost of existing nuclear forces, paid for along with the salaries of civilian employees out of Operation and Maintenance appropriations, is the cost of fuel for the training and patrol missions of bomber, tanker, interceptor and control aircraft operated by the Air Force. This cost and large military personnel requirements make strategic bomber forces about twice as costly to maintain and operate than either ICBMs or strategic submarines.

The investment costs—both development and production—of nuclear forces and related intelligence, command, control and communications (C^3) are considerably higher in relation to operating costs than is the case for conventional forces. Operating costs and investment costs are about evenly divided for the conventional forces, whereas the ratio is one-third to two-thirds for the nuclear forces. The difference between the two types of forces is most marked in the area of research and development (R&D, or, in Department of Defense terminology, research, development, test and evaluation, RDT&E). While strategic and related intelligence and C^3 components account for only 18 percent of total current operating costs, they account for 43 percent of the R&D budget. Taking into account the nuclear-weapon R&D activities of the Department of Energy, which develops and produces the nuclear warheads that are fitted on nuclear aircraft and missiles, the nuclear arms race probably accounts for about half of all US military R&D.

Most military R&D and production is performed not in government laboratories or factories but by private industry. Total private employment on Defense Department contracts is estimated by the Department of Defense at 2.1 million. This figure is not broken down by weapon system or area of warfare. However, an estimate based on spending ratios suggests that about 550,000 individuals are employed in the development and production of nuclear-weapon systems and related equipment. Of these, roughly 150,000 are engaged in R&D and 400,000 in production.

Individual nuclear weapon systems tend to be much more expensive to produce than conventional weapons. However, the nuclear warhead generally constitutes only a small fraction of the production cost. Most of the cost goes into the delivery vehicle and the onboard or ground-based electronic and other equipment used to operate and support it. The larger the delivery vehicle and the more costly the electronic and other associated equipment produced for it, the higher will be the unit cost. Aircraft carriers are the single most expensive item produced for the military ($2.5 billion each), followed by strategic submarines ($1.3 billion) and other combat ships, which cost $0.5–1.0 billion each. Large, heavily-armed aircraft, equipped with a great deal of advanced electronic equipment, can now cost $50–100 million each, as is the case for the proposed new US strategic bomber or the P-3C anti-submarine patrol plane. Missiles are cheaper: $10–20 million each for large, long-range strategic missiles, $2–5 million for medium-range missiles; and less for short-range ones. The price of the actual nuclear warheads is not published, but is probably less than $1 million each.

II. THE OPPORTUNITY COST OF THE NUCLEAR ARMS RACE

Opportunity cost is an economic concept that refers to the alternative uses of particular resources that might be made if they were allocated differently. It is intended to be a more accurate measure of the economic and social burden of a particular activity than might be indicated merely by a straightforward citing of financial cost or manpower requirements.

There are five types of valued or scarce resources employed in the nuclear arms race that might be used differently: government funds, total manpower, skilled manpower, creative scientific and engineering talent, and natural resources.

The alternative use of these resources is traditionally measured in economics by calculating the elasticity of demand in other sectors. However, in a period of high inflation, high unemployment and fluctuating growth rates, predictions about the effects of lowered government spending and government-funded employment are notoriously difficult and controversial.

It is likely that the US government could balance the budget, and hold down or reduce taxes without cutting social programs if all of the funds devoted to the nuclear arms race were cut out of the Department of Defense and Energy budgets and diverted instead to civilian uses. However, this move, if not cushioned by a transitional, government-subsidized conversion program that used most of the released funds for several years, would create large-scale unemployment, raising the rate of unemployment by almost a full percentage point.

Many people believe that if nuclear forces were substantially reduced or eliminated, spending on conventional forces would rise, or should rise, because nuclear weapons act as a deterrent to conventional warfare, particularly between East and West. While in my view there is neither a lack of adequate conventional forces nor a significant risk or incentive for a major conventional war between East and West, there is no doubt in my mind that, if nuclear forces were substantially reduced over a short period of time, there would be heavy pressure to divert the savings to increased conventional strength rather than to civilian uses. Since nuclear forces constitute a relatively small part of total military spending and an integral part of mixed, nuclear-conventional military strategies, careful consideration of the cost and functions of conventional forces would have to be included in any attempt to win civilian economic benefits from nuclear force reductions.

The question of the opportunity cost of the R&D side of the nuclear arms race involves three imponderable, "what-if" issues. First, government support of nuclear-weapon related R&D has clearly acted as a subsidy or jumping off point for related areas of civilian technology and production. This is true of jet aircraft engines and engine technology generally; materials; fuels; precision measurement; miniaturization; electronics; computers; and, obviously, nuclear power. Some people believe that the rate of change in civilian technology, the increase in productivity and the resulting economic growth in the United States in the 1950s and 1960s was enhanced by the indirect subsidy to civilian technology provided by military R&D, and mainly by the high-technology areas associated with the nuclear arms race. The lowering of US investment in strategic weapon R&D in the 1970s and the renewed spurt that is occurring today are argued to be associated with the decline in productivity and an expected renewal. According to this view, a cutback in nuclear-weapon R&D might produce a decline rather than an increase in civilian benefits. There is a second view that contradicts the first. This is that, over the long term, the concentration of US economic activity in military production and, particularly, military R&D has been responsible for declining productivity and the worsening of the US competitive position in international trade. Those with this view point to the relative economic success of West Germany and Japan—two large industrialized countries with relatively low rates of military spending and, because they import their advanced weapon systems from the USA rather than designing and developing them indigenously, particularly low rates of investment in military R&D. These two countries, it is argued, have slowly but surely laid a better foundation in civilian capital investment, civilian technology and civilian R&D than the United States and gradually overtaken the United States in productivity in many industries.

The analysis of relative Japanese and West German advantage in industrial production rests in part on unrelated aspects of economic activity, such as protective tariffs or import quotas; in part on macro-economic trade-offs, such as a possible trade-off between private investment in plant and equipment and government spending, particularly military spending; and in part on a presumed trade-off between military R&D and civilian R&D. This brings us to the third issue concerning the opportunity cost of military R&D: whether R&D spending or, more accurately, R&D manpower constitutes a cohesive, identifiable and limited "resource" which, if employed in the military area, will reduce activity in the civilian area. The case against this view is that the pool of scientists, engineers and technicians who might perform research and development includes many more than those actually employed in R&D: individuals engaged in production, maintenance, quality control and other activities. In addition, the pool is not fixed but can be expanded relatively quickly by increased college and graduate education in relevant areas, which will result from increased job opportunity. The case in favor of a limited R&D pool and a trade-off in invention between military and civilian areas rests on the view that, while the R&D manpower pool is not fixed, it is limited by the special skills, talents, interests and job-style of those who can and want to work creatively with invention, discovery and technical change. The argument is that some of the most creative and powerful minds are siphoned off from productive activity to do military work. Clearly, whether or not there is a direct trade-off between personnel in military R&D and civilian R&D, there is a drain of highly capable and motivated individuals in the military sector, particularly in R&D, who could benefit society more by employment in other areas. . . .

30 Military Expansion, Economic Decline

Robert W. DeGrasse, Jr. ─────────────────────────────────────

> *. . .we must remember that at least 350,000 jobs are at stake and will be lost if there are drastic cuts [in military spending].*
>
> Secretary of Defense Caspar Weinberger, before the National Press Club,
> March 8, 1982

The economic aspects of arms spending have often dominated questions of national security. Considering the amount of public funds spent on the military, this is hardly surprising. In fiscal year 1983 [FY 83], the national defense budget will be $214.8 billion, which is 26.7 percent of the total federal budget and 6.7 percent of the expected gross national product (GNP).[1] Expenditures of this magnitude can have substantial impacts. For example, cuts in military procurement as the Vietnam war wound down left many people unemployed in heavily defense-dependent areas such as Seattle, Santa Clara County in California, and the Route 128 area around Boston. Yet during the war, rapidly increasing arms spending produced an inflationary surge that hurt the entire nation.

Decisions regarding which weapon to build or where to locate a military base should be determined by our security needs. Very often, however, these choices are strongly influenced by economics. Four recent occurrences illustrate this point. Item one: During a campaign trip to Columbus, Ohio, last fall, President Reagan warned that support for the nuclear freeze could hurt the local economy because it would mean cancelling the B-1B bomber, which is partly manufactured in that area.[2] Item two: At the same time, highly visible Democratic Congressional candidates were calling for cuts in the military budget because they believed that rapid growth in Pentagon spending hurts the economy. Item three: Not long before the 1982 elections, Congress was the scene of a pitched battle over who should supply the Air Force with new transport planes. Members of Congress from Washington state fought to have Seattle's Boeing Co. awarded the contract, while members from Georgia worked to keep the project in their state at Lockheed.[3] Item four: During the December 1982 Congressional debate over cutting one of the two nuclear aircraft carriers from the Pentagon's budget, numerous members defended the program because it would create employment in America's industrial heartland. One member went so far as to call the aircraft carrier program a "jobs bill."[4] . . .

The employment created by military spending has a powerful influence on our defense policy. Despite the fact that numerous members of Congress were calling for deep cuts in the administration's military buildup during the fall of 1982, the proposed FY 1983 Department of Defense budget was cut by only a token amount. Analysts for Prudential-Bache Securities suggest that two economic factors prevented deeper cuts. First, they believe that the broad geo-

Excerpted with permission from Robert W. DeGrasse, Jr., *Military Expansion, Economic Decline* (pp. 17–18, 23–33, 73). Copyright © 1983 by Council on Economic Priorities. Tables and charts that were referenced in the original are not reprinted here.

graphic distribution of Pentagon spending gives even the Congressional "doves" good reason for voting for arms increases. Second, they note that pressure to vote for military programs is greater during a period of high unemployment. Therefore, these Wall Street analysts predict that military spending will continue to grow rapidly and recommend that investors purchase defense stocks.[5]

It is hard to argue with their logic. The pervasive influence of military contracting makes it difficult for our elected representatives to vote against major weapons systems, even when the weapons are of questionable military value. During the 1981 debate over the B-1B bomber, for example, the plane's prime contractor, Rockwell International, informed Congress that components for the system would be purchased from companies in 48 of the 50 states.[6] Although the plane probably will be obsolete by the late 1980s,[7] it was approved by Congress with the support of liberals such as Senators Alan Cranston (D-Cal.) and Howard Metzenbaum (D-Ohio), whose states stand to gain thousands of jobs from the program.

In times of recession, military spending has also gained support as a "Keynesian" mechanism for stimulating the economy. During 1974, in the midst of the last prolonged recession, the Ford administration added over $1 billion to the Defense Department's budget at the last minute as a tactic to pump more money into the lagging economy.[8] As early as 1950, an article in *U.S. News and World Report* summed up the benefit of using military spending in this way:

> Government planners figure that they have found the magic formula for almost endless good times. They are now beginning to wonder if there may not be something to perpetual motion after all. Cold War is the catalyst. Cold War is an automatic pump primer. Turn the spigot, and the public clamors for more arms spending. Turn another, the clamor ceases.[9]

Support for this tactic clearly derives from the fact that arms production during World War II helped jolt the nation out of the Great Depression.

This pump priming tactic can become addictive, however. During the early years of the Cold War, some observers worried that large cuts in military spending might allow the economy to lapse back into a depression. In 1953, for example, James Reston went so far as to suggest in a front page story in *The New York Times* that the Soviet Union's friendlier attitude toward the United States was a ploy to bring about a slump in the West:

> So long as the Kremlin was waging war in Asia and crying havoc all over the world, the Western nations were able to achieve full employment . . . now, as the experts here see it, one of their objectives seems to be to smile us into disarmament, deflation, unemployment and depression.[10]

Throughout the recent recession, Reagan administration officials have reminded the American people of the economic benefits of higher arms spending.[11] Yet thorough examination of its immediate impact shows that the benefits are dwarfed by the opportunity costs. Moreover, as we discuss later, the real question Congress should be asking is whether the military value of a given program is greater than its long-term economic costs.

This chapter examines the direct effects of military spending in two parts. First, we broadly map the Pentagon's influence in the overall economy. How extensive is the military's impact? Where is it concentrated? Second, we compare the employment created by military spending with employment that would be created by other uses of the same funds. Does the military create as many jobs? Does it help those most in need of employment? We conclude by assessing the role of military spending as an economic stabilizer. Is military spending an effective buffer against depression? Or can we influence the course of the economy more effectively by other means?

MEASURING THE MILITARY'S IMPACT

The Pentagon is the largest single purchaser of goods and services in the economy. During 1981, national defense purchases by the federal government totalled $153.3 billion.[12] In comparison, the business expenses of Exxon, the largest corporation in America, were 33 percent less during the same year. The cost of operating the nation's second largest corporation, Mobil, was 60 percent less.[13]

The military has been the largest single source of demand in the economy throughout the last three decades. After adjusting for inflation, there has been little variation in the substantial size of the Defense Department's budget since the early 1950s. Excluding the dramatic increases during the Korean and Vietnam wars, military spending has remained high at about $170 billion (in 1983 dollars).

Although Pentagon spending has been a major factor in the economy, the military's proportionate share has declined as the overall economy has grown. While the military budget stayed the same, the gross national product (GNP) has almost tripled in real terms during the past three decades. As a result, the military's share of the GNP dropped from an average of 10 percent during the 1950s to an average of six percent during the 1970s.

The military's share of government spending has also fallen, but by a smaller amount. Of the goods and services directly purchased by the federal government during the 1970s, the military consumed 70 percent. In the 1950s, the Pentagon's share averaged 85 percent. The military's portion stayed so high because much of the growth in civilian government spending has been in transfer payments, which are not direct government purchases.

While transfer payments do affect the economy, their impact is usually more geographically diffuse than direct purchases. For example, unemployment benefits are paid to anyone who qualifies, no matter where they live. On the other hand, contracting for a tank, or building a hydroelectric dam, directly affects a specific area. The difference is politically important. Members of Congress can demonstrate their political effectiveness back home by steering federal purchases into their states. The responsibility that any one Senator or Representative can claim for additional transfer payments is usually less clear.

Since military spending is by far the largest category of federal purchases, it is an extremely important source of political power. Two examples illustrate this point. First, as chairman of the Senate Subcommittee on Defense Preparedness during the 1950s, Lyndon Johnson built his political career calling for a larger Air Force and helping direct aircraft contracts into his home state.[14] Second, in 1969, toward the end of Mendel Rivers' (D-SC) long tenure as chairman of the House Armed Services Committee, there were *nine* military installations located in his district. A Lockheed plant was located there because, as Rep. Rivers explained, "I asked them to put a li'l old plant here."[15]

REGIONAL AND INDUSTRIAL IMPACT

The military spends its money on a variety of different programs. The four most important categories—military personnel, operations and maintenance (O&M), procurement, and research and development (R&D)—make up over 85 percent of the expenditures.

Broadly, the Defense Department keeps track of the regional distributions of these expenditures in two ways. One is the state-by-state listing of prime contract awards made by the Pentagon. The other is the Defense Department's estimate of expenditures by state, excluding prime contracts.

Prime contract awards cover purchases from the private sector for a wide variety of goods, ranging from missiles and spare parts to fuel and food. In FY 1981, military prime contracts (above $10,000) with private firms in the 50 states and the District of Columbia totaled $87.8 billion. Over 68.0 percent of the total went for weapons and communications equipment. Fuel was the biggest non-hardware category.

In FY 1981, 29 states and the District of Columbia received more than $500 million in prime contract awards. However, almost 65 percent of the prime contracts went to firms in 10 states. Corporations in the top five states received 45 percent of all contract awards. From the limited data available on the subcontract awards of prime contractors, it appears that the second tier of military contracting is more geographically concentrated than the first. Almost three-quarters of the subcontracts that the Pentagon could trace were performed in 10 states during FY 1979, the only year in which these data were collected. Another 5.8 percent of the subcontracting went to companies in foreign countries.[16]

Defense Department expenditures, excluding major procurement awards, totalled $74.0 billion in FY 1981. These expenditures covered virtually all payroll expenses for both civilian and military personnel, about 50 percent of the operations and maintenance budget, 55 percent of research and development expenses, and 75 percent of the military construction budget. Nonprocurement Pentagon expenditures are similarly concentrated in only a few states. While 31 states and the District of Columbia received more than $500 million in FY 1981, 56 percent of nonprocurement spending occurred in just 10 states. The top five states received 41 percent of the total.

States come in all sizes, however the raw data do not take size into account, preventing us from comparing the relative impact of military spending among the states. They also do not take into account the fact that individuals and corporations pay taxes to the government for military programs. Therefore, we adjusted the total amount of Pentagon spending each state received in FY 1981 for the number of people in the work force and calculated each state's net Pentagon tax.

After these adjustments, we found that 23 states received less money from the Defense Department in FY 1981 than they paid in taxes. Another 10 states received less than $500 more per worker than they paid to the Pentagon. Only 17 states and the District of Columbia received a substantial amount of net expenditures per worker from the Defense Department.

The net impact of military spending is also unevenly distributed by region. None of the seven midwest states received more money from the Pentagon than they paid in taxes. Five of the 11 states in the northeast also experienced a net loss. On the other hand, seven of the 14 southern states and the District of Columbia received a significant amount of net military expenditures per worker. Eight of the 18 western states also experienced a substantial net gain.

In addition to being distributed unevenly across regions, Pentagon spending is concentrated in a few industries. The distribution of military purchases among industries can be traced using the detailed input-output table of the economy compiled by the Commerce Department. A breakdown of Defense Department purchases for 1979 shows that the bulk of military purchases—85 percent—was obtained from only twenty industries. Ten industries accounted for almost 70 percent of the Defense Department's purchases. The top five industries —aircraft, communications equipment, missiles, ordnance, and ships—accounted for 55 percent alone. Military purchases are also concentrated in the manufacturing sector: 74 percent of all military purchases came from manufacturing industries in 1979. The top ten manufacturing industries provided the Pentagon with 65 percent of all military purchases during that year.

Few industries would be hurt significantly by a major decrease in military purchases. Of the top 20 industries selling to the Pentagon in 1979, only eight depended on the Defense Department for more than 10 percent of all final sales. Only a handful of the over 100 other industries in the economy gained more than five percent of final sales from military purchases.[17] However, four of the top five industries selling to the military depended on the Pentagon for over half of their sales in 1979. The fifth, aircraft, relied on the military for almost 40 percent of its final sales. Many of the companies in these top five industries are heavily dependent on the Pentagon.[18] As a result, defense-dependent companies and industries have a significant interest in preventing reductions in the Defense Department budget. They pursue this interest vigorously through special-interest lobbying and large campaign contributions.[19]

In summary, the economic benefits of military spending are strongly felt only in a few regions and a few industries. During the 1970s, the military also became a smaller part of the overall economy, reducing the role of the Pentagon as a source of demand. However, since the military remains the federal government's single most important fiscal mechanism for directly stimulating the economy, the benefits of military spending still remain a significant political factor. Indeed, because the Pentagon's spending pattern is highly concentrated, the constituencies supporting specific Defense Department programs are probably better organized than if the distribution of expenditures were diffuse.

MILITARY EMPLOYMENT VS. THE ALTERNATIVES

Just as with any other form of spending, whether it be by an individual, a corporation, or the government, military spending also creates jobs. The Defense Department alone directly employed more than three million people in FY 1981— over two million on active duty in the armed forces and another million in civil service jobs. At least two million more people were employed in FY 1981 by private corporations with military contracts and by other institutions, such as universities.[20]

While military spending clearly creates jobs, a meaningful assessment of the Pentagon's employment impact must include an accounting of the jobs forgone by using our resources to produce weapons. Any form of spending creates jobs, the key question is: How does military spending compare with other uses of the same money? Does it create as many jobs per dollar spent as do other options? Does it provide employment in the occupational categories with high unemployment?

We will focus on the jobs created in the private sector by Pentagon purchases because government employment created by military spending is quite similar to other types of federal employment. Money for civil service workers creates approximately the same number of jobs whether it is spent by the Defense Department or the Department of Health and Human Services. Funds covering the personnel costs of soldiers and sailors would create roughly the same number of jobs if they were spent instead on CETA (Comprehensive Employment Training Act) programs. However, if money for the civil service or military personnel were transferred to the private sector, it would probably not create as much employment. Government jobs, like those in many service industries, require little capital equipment and tend to pay lower wages, particularly in the case of soldiers and sailors. As a result, more people can be hired per dollar spent on the armed forces and the civil service than if the money were spent on subway cars.

Fewer Jobs: However, the comparison between the number of jobs created by military purchases from the private sector and the number created by other forms of private spending is quite different. Most industries selling to the Pentagon create fewer jobs per dollar spent than the average industry in the American economy. Seven of the 11 manufacturing industries selling the greatest volume of goods to the military create fewer jobs per dollar than the median manufacturing industry. Seven of the nine largest military suppliers create fewer jobs per dollar than the median non-manufacturing industry. More importantly, the three largest manufacturing industries—those accounting for over 40 percent of the Pentagon's total purchases from the private sector—create fewer jobs per dollar than the median manufacturing industry.

Those comparisons, based on data from the Labor Department's employment requirements table, include both direct and indirect employment. Direct jobs are those created in the industry that provides the final product to the Defense Department. Indirect jobs are those created by the final producer's requirements for goods and services. For example, the aircraft industry requires structural forgings, communications equipment, titanium and numerous other intermediate goods to produce jet fighters. Aircraft firms also use outside services such as

air transportation and accountants. Such purchases indirectly create employment.

One factor that the lower job-creating manufacturing industries which serve the Pentagon share is a high level of technical sophistication. The aircraft, communications equipment, missile and computer industries all produce very specialized, highly complex products. In each case, the production process requires particularly expensive skilled labor, raw materials and intermediate products. The other three manufacturing industries that create fewer jobs than the average—autos, chemicals, and petroleum products—produce more general goods; however, the production process in each of these industries requires a larger amount of sophisticated capital equipment than is used by the average manufacturing firm. In both cases, the technical sophistication of the industries limits the number and types of jobs created.

The concentration of military purchases in a small number of lower job-yielding industries helps explain why various economic analyses have found that transferring military expenditures to other sectors of the economy creates more jobs. Three econometric simulations of a compensated reduction in military spending done during the 1970s all show that the alternatives—whether greater civilian government spending or a tax cut—create higher employment.[21] More recently, the Employment Research Associates used the Labor Department's employment requirements table to test the impact of shifting $62.9 billion in 1981 from military purchases to personal consumption expenditures.[22] This scenario showed a net gain of some 1.5 million jobs after the shift. The funds created a total of 3.3 million jobs if spent on private consumption, but only 1.8 million jobs if spent on military purchases.

The Employment Research Associates' study indicates that military contracting creates roughly 28,000 jobs per billion dollars of spending (in 1981 dollars). This is slightly less than the 30,000 jobs created by the median industry in the Bureau of Labor Statistics' input-output model. Military contracting also provides fewer jobs than public works projects such as new transit construction. It creates significantly fewer jobs than personal consumption and educational services. However, military contracting does create more jobs than industries such as oil refining and car manufacturing.

While military purchases create fewer jobs than most alternative expenditures, they still represent a significant source of demand in the economy for goods and services. The importance of providing an alternative source of demand when arms expenditures are reduced is underscored by the results of econometric simulations that do not compensate for lower levels of military spending by either cutting taxes or increasing other types of spending. For example, a recent simulation by Data Resources, Inc., comparing the Reagan administration's arms buildup to a much slower one, found that the smaller buildup resulted in almost one percentage point more unemployment.[23]

Highly Skilled Work Force: Military purchases also create a very different mix of jobs than other expenditures.[24] Military contractors generally employ a larger portion of technically skilled workers than does the average manufacturing firm. In 11 of the top 15 manufacturing industries producing output for the Pentagon, the percentage of the industry's work force accounted for by production workers is lower than the average for all manufacturing.

The extent of the reliance on highly skilled employees is illustrated by more detailed data from the Labor Department on the top five military-oriented industries. In four of the five industries producing the most for the Pentagon, the percentage of professional and technical workers is significantly higher than the average in manufacturing. Engineers make up the bulk of this category in three of the four. The share of managers in military-related industries is also slightly higher than in the average manufacturing firm. Finally, all five of the top military industries require a smaller than average share of semi-skilled machine operators ("operatives" in Labor Department parlance).

According to Labor Department economists, their figures may understate the percentage of technically skilled employees working in military-serving aircraft and communications equipment firms.[25] Much of the military output produced by those two industries is highly specialized and produced in small batches. As a result their development usually requires more engineering than needed for commercial products. For example, in the guided missile industry, which produces mainly for the government, engineers make up 31.1 percent of the work force. Production of military goods also requires a greater number of machinists and technical workers to create and assemble specialized parts. In the civilian sector of the aircraft and communications industries, larger production runs

and greater standardization probably reduce the need for specialized labor. Thus, the skill distribution on the military side of these two industries is probably higher, as in the guided missile industry.

The high cost of technically-skilled labor is also a major reason why the manufacturing industries receiving most of the Pentagon's contracts create fewer jobs than the median. While some have speculated that military spending creates fewer jobs because the production process is capital-intensive,[26] this speculation is only true for a small number of industries serving the Pentagon, such as oil refining. In the major suppliers, including the aircraft, communications equipment and missile industries, large parts of the assembly process are often performed by skilled technicians and engineers. Moreover, much of the capital equipment used by large defense firms is very old because there is little incentive to make new investments.

Normally, a firm invests to increase production efficiency and reduce costs in order to increase sales and profits. In the defense sector, however, lower cost seldom increases the market for a product and cost overruns are regularly reimbursed.[27] Capital purchases by military contractors are not ordinarily subsidized by the Defense Department. Therefore, there is little incentive to invest. Indeed, numerous reports identify lower productivity growth, resulting from less investment, as a major reason for cost overruns in the defense sector.[28]

On the other hand, Pentagon procurement practices encourage greater use of highly skilled workers. Defense Department officials value high performance above cost.[29] Thus, to gain the edge in selling to the Pentagon, military contractors often hire additional engineers. Moreover, the highly demanding specifications of military components often cannot be met by off-the-shelf items. As a result, many parts must be produced in small batches by subcontracting firms like machine shops and specialty semiconductor producers. These firms use much more skilled labor than firms that mass-produce standard components.

The specialized nature of military employment reduces its economic usefulness. Much of the new employment generated by a military buildup goes to people who need it least. Professional and technical workers have the lowest unemployment rate of any occupational category in the economy. Even during December 1982, when overall unemployment was 10.8 percent, unemployment for professional and technical workers was only 3.7 percent. Demand for engineers was so great during the 1980 recession that salaries continued to rise dramatically. Indeed, during that recession, increased military spending fueled inflationary pressures in the high-technology sector while the rest of the economy faltered.[30]

At the other end of the spectrum, military spending creates very few jobs for those most in need of work. Meanwhile, unemployment among laborers and machine operators was above 20 percent in December 1982. And, although the present buildup will increase the need for skilled workers, programs to help train the groups with the highest unemployment rates—young people and minorities—have been cut severely.

Clearly, military spending is a limited counter-cyclical aid. It creates fewer jobs than most other industries. It employs highly skilled people who would have relatively little trouble finding jobs elsewhere. Military expenditures are highly concentrated in only a few regions and industries. Moreover, even though military spending creates a substantial demand for goods and services, cutting military spending would not make us more prone to depression. Increasing civilian government programs and/or reducing taxes could replace the purchasing power lost by cutting the arms budget. While large reductions in the current level of military spending would create adjustment problems in selected regions and industries,[31] many of these difficulties could be overcome with planning and specific assistance programs.[32]

When the economy requires federal assistance, programs should be developed to fill the nation's greatest needs, not simply the most convenient pork barrel. The construction industry, hard-hit during the recent recession, will receive a shot in the arm from the recently-approved government program to rebuild the nation's deteriorating roads and bridges. Yet the sad state of America's infrastructure leaves us with many other public works options.[33] Instead of creating greater competition for skilled labor by increasing military spending, the federal government might also institute training programs to help those currently unemployed to develop technical skills that will be heavily in demand during the 1980s. If the federal government were to develop a comprehensive mass transit program, we could revive an industry that would employ production workers laid off by the auto makers, and

create a hedge against future increases in energy prices.[34] These options clearly indicate that we should not spend money on the military just because it creates jobs.

Some might still wonder if it is possible to create enough public support for civilian government programs to replace military spending as a source of demand.[35] However, we would rephrase the question: Can the U.S. government afford to continue relying on the military budget as the largest public mechanism for stimulating the economy? . . . Military expenditures draw wealth from the civilian economy. While we might have been able to "afford" a substantial military burden during the 1950s and 1960s, the loss of skilled labor and investment from the private economy during the 1980s could cost us dearly in export potential. Many American industries could continue to lose markets to foreign producers if U.S. firms do not modernize their factories, and America's technological leadership could continue to slip away if we ask too many of our brightest engineers and scientists to solve military-related problems instead of creating better civilian products. These considerations indicate that, instead of relying on military spending as a source of jobs, we should avoid any military expenditure that is not necessary for our security. . . .

While numerous factors influence economic performance, America's heavier military burden seems to have stifled investment, and reduced our economic and productivity growth over the last few decades. During the 1950s and 1960s, higher arms expenditures in the United States probably allowed other industrial nations to close the economic gap separating America from the rest of the world more quickly than if we had spent less on the military. While more industrialized nations tend to grow more slowly, our economy probably would have performed significantly better if the United States had reallocated a portion of the resources used by the military. For example, if the government had more heavily subsidized the development and repair of mass-transit systems in major metropolitan areas throughout the United States, we could have sustained and expanded the now-failing American mass-transit vehicle industry, reducing the need to import subway cars from Europe, Canada and Japan to fill the needs of New York, Boston and Philadelphia. If the government had not spent so much on high technology military products, the engineers doing military work might have developed commercial electronics products to compete more effectively with the Japanese. Our highly skilled people might also have worked on developing renewable energy resources. Moreover, we also could have used part of the "peace dividend" to assist sound economic progress in some of the world's poorest nations,[36] thereby helping open up new markets for our goods and services. Surely, given the wide array of possible alternatives, we would have found productive jobs for the thousands of engineers, scientists and skilled workers who were building weapons for the "electronic battlefield."

Military spending also slowed economic performance during the 1970s. While the rising cost of energy clearly damaged performance across the board in the industrial world, military spending continued to draw away resources that could have been used to develop energy self-sufficiency. Moreover, if more engineers and greater investment had been available to the private sector after 1973, American business might have been able to offset part of the higher cost of energy by expanding exports of U.S. manufactured goods.

Increased arms expenditures during the Reagan administration could have the opposite effect on the economy that they had during the Second World War. As the "arsenal of democracy" during that war, America built its industrial base while other nations saw their industrial power consumed by the fires of war. Yet during the next decade, if we increase arms expenditures in the United States while most other advanced nations concentrate on expanding their industrial strength, we could be left watching our economic health continue to slip away. . . .

NOTES

1. *Budget of the United States Government, FY 1984* (Washington, DC: U.S. GPO, 1983), pp. 9–4, 9–53.

2. Herbert Denton, "Reagan Coolly Received on Midwest Swing," *Washington Post*, October 5, 1982.

3. Richard Halloran, "Expansion of Military Air Transport Fleet is Stalled by Dispute in Congress," *The New York Times*, June 20, 1982.

4. U.S. Congress, House of Representatives, *Congressional Record*, December 8, 1982, pp. H 9123–H 9129.

5. Paul H. Nisbet and Richard L. Whittington, "Defense: Increase Spending or Cut Jobs," *Industry Outlook: Aerospace/Defense*, Prudential-Bache Securities, Inc., December 8, 1982.

6. Frank Grove, "Military Cuts Hard to Find in '84 Budget," *Philadelphia Inquirer*, January 10, 1983, p. 5A.

7. Gordon Adams, "The B-1: Bomber for All Seasons?," *Council on Economic Priorities Newsletter*, February 1982.

8. John W. Finney, "Military Budget Spurs Economy," *The New York Times*, February 27, 1974.

9. Fred J. Cook, *The Warfare State* (New York: Collier Books, 1964), p. 183.

10. James Reston, "Soviet Tactics Give U.S. Problem of Avoiding Slump if Peace Comes," *The New York Times*, April 8, 1953, p. 1.

11. Herbert H. Denton, "Reagan Coolly Received on Midwest Swing," *The Washington Post*, October 5, 1982.
    George Wilson, "Senators Urge Defense Spending Cut," *The Washington Post*, February 2, 1983, pp. A1, A10.
    "Cutting Defense Won't Solve Job Problem, Weinberger Says," *The Washington Post*, November 9, 1982, p. 16.
    Caspar Weinberger, "Address to the National Press Club," *News Release*, Office of the Assistant Secretary of Defense (Public Affairs), March 8, 1982, p. 3.
    "Weinberger Says Military Spending Rise Won't Spur Inflation or Disrupt Economy," *Wall Street Journal*, July 29, 1981, p. 12.
    Peter Meredith, "Shipyard Jobs Tied to Defense Votes," *The Baltimore Sun*, March 6, 1982.

12. *Economic Report of the President* (Washington, D.C.: U.S. GPO, February 1983), p. 163.

13. "Fortune 500," *Fortune Magazine*, May 3, 1982, p. 260.

14. Richard Kaufman, *War Profiteers* (New York: Doubleday, 1972), pp. 32–36.

15. Peter H. Prugh, "The War Business, Mendel Rivers' Defense of Armed Forces Helps His Hometown Prosper," *Wall Street Journal*, June 17, 1969.

16. U.S. Department of Defense, Washington Headquarters Service, "Geographic Distribution of Subcontract Awards, Fiscal Year 1979," p. 9.

17. U.S. Department of Commerce, Bureau of Industrial Economics, "Sectoral Implications of Defense Expenditures," August 1982.

18. David Gold with David Brooks, Paul Murphy and Mary Shea, "The Defense Department's Top 100," *Council on Economic Priorities Newsletter*, August 1982.

19. Gordon Adams, *The Iron Triangle: The Policies of Defense Contracting* (New York: Council of Economic Priorities, 1981).

20. U.S. Department of Defense, Office of the Assistant Secretary of Defense (Comptroller), "National Defense Estimates, Fiscal Year 1983," p. 82. This publication estimates that Pentagon con-

tracts with private industry employed 2,230,000 people in 1981. This figure is probably overstated, given the results of input-output analysis performed by Marion Anderson, Jeb Brugmann and George Erickcek, "The Price of the Pentagon: The Industrial and Commercial Impact of the 1981 Military Budget" (Lansing, Mich.: Employment Research Associates, 1982).

21. Roger H. Bezdek, "The 1980 Impact—Regional and Occupational—of Compensated Shifts in Defense Spending," *Journal of Regional Science*, February, 1965.
Chase-Econometrics Associates, *Economic Impact of the B-1 Program on the U.S. Economy and Comparative Case Studies* (Cynwyd, Pennsylvania: Chase Econometric Associates, 1975).
Norman J. Glickman, *Econometric Analysis of Regional Systems* (New York: Academic Press, 1977). Each of the above is discussed in Michael Edelstein, "The Economic Impact of Military Spending" (New York: Council on Economic Priorities, 1977).

22. Marion Anderson *et al., op. cit.*

23. Data Resources, Inc., *Defense Economics Research Report*, August 1982, p. 5.

24. Bezdek, *op. cit.*, p. 195.

25. Richard Dempsey and Douglas Schmude, "Occupational Impact of Defense Expenditures," *Monthly Labor Review*, December 1971, p. 12.

26. Marion Anderson, *et al., op. cit.*, p. 2.

27. Jacques S. Gansler, *The Defense Industry* (Cambridge, Mass.: The MIT Press, 1980), Chapter 3.

28. U.S. General Accounting Office, Comptroller General, "Appendix I—General Accounting Office Draft Report on Defense Industry Profit Study, Dated December 22, 1970" (Washington D.C.: U.S. GAO, January 1971), p. 51.
U.S. General Accounting Office, Comptroller General, "Impediments to Reducing the Costs of Weapons Systems, Report to Congress" (Washington, D.C.: U.S. GAO November 8, 1979), p. 31. (Hereafter, "Impediments. . . .")
U.S. Congress, Senate Committee on Banking, Housing and Urban Affairs, jointly with the Subcommittee on Priorities and Economy in Government of the Joint Economic Committee, "Department of Defense Contract Profit Policy" (Washington, D.C.: U.S. GPO, March 21, 1979), pp. 1–2.

29. Gansler, *op. cit.*, p. 83.
U.S. General Accounting Office, "Impediments. . .," *op. cit.*, p. 23.
Morton J. Peck and Frederic M. Scherer, *The Weapons Acquisition Process: An Economic Analysis* (Boston: Harvard Graduate School of Business Administration, 1962), p. 594.

30. U.S. Congress, House Committee on Armed Services, "The Ailing Defense Industrial Base: Unready for Crisis," a report of the Defense Industrial Base Panel (Washington, D.C.: U.S. GPO, December 31, 1980), p. 13.

31. Wassily Leontieff, Alison Morgan, Karen Polenske, David Simpson, Edward Tower, "The Economic Impact—Industrial and Regional—of an Arms Cut," *The Review of Economics and Statistics*, Volume XLVII, Number 3, August 1965.
Bezdek, *op. cit.*, pp. 188–196.

32. Seymour Melman, "Planning for Conversion of Military-Industrial and Military Base Facilities" (Washington, D.C.: U.S. Department of Commerce, August 1972), draft.
Bernard Udis, ed., *The Economic Consequences of Reduced Military Spending* (Lexington, Mass.: Lexington Books, 1973), Chapters 4 through 7.
Charles L. Shultze, statement before the U.S. Congress, Joint Economic Committee, "Economic Effects of Vietnam Spending," hearings (Washington, D.C.: U.S. GPO, April 24, 1967) pp. 30–67.
U.S. Congress, Senate Committee on Labor and Public Welfare, "Postwar Economic Conversion," hearings, (Washington, D.C.: U.S. GPO, December 1969), Part 1.

33. Pat Choate and Susan Walter, *America in Ruins: Beyond the Public Works Pork Barrel* (Washington, D.C.: The Council of State Planning Agencies, 1981).

34. Philip Webre, *Jobs to People* (Washington, D.C.: Exploratory Project for Economic Alternatives, 1979), unpublished.

35. Richard DuBoff, "Converting Military Spending to Social Welfare: The Real Obstacles," *Quarterly Review of Economics and Business*, Vol. 12, Spring 1972.

36. Wassily Leontieff and Faye Duchin, *Military Spending: Facts and Figures, Worldwide Implications, and Future Outlook* (New York: Oxford University Press, 1983), Chapters 6 and 7.

31 Economic Effects of the Defense Budget

Charles L. Schultze

The United States is fortunate in having an economy that, with proper policies, can adjust to about as high or as low a level of defense spending as the nation and its leaders think is appropriate. We need not shrink from an increase or a decrease in defense spending on grounds that we cannot afford the increase or productively reemploy the resources freed by a decrease.

While decisions about the proper long-run level of defense spending should not be determined principally by economic considerations, the nation nevertheless needs to understand the economic effects of defense spending—first, because we need to adjust our tax, monetary, and other policies to absorb the effects of a higher or lower level of defense spending; second, because we need to pay attention to the *speed* at which we change the level of defense spending. Although the economy's ability to adjust is very large in the long run, its ability to make large changes quickly is far from unlimited. . . .

SOME GENERAL PRINCIPLES

Let me begin by getting one often repeated fallacy out of the way. Defense spending is sometimes alleged to be inherently inflationary compared to other forms of governmental spending because the products the defense establishment buys are "wasteful" or "nonproductive" and do not add to the supply of useful goods, presumably like food, automobiles, or toothpicks.

Excerpted with permission from Charles L. Schultze, "Economic Effects of the Defense Budget," *The Brookings Bulletin* (vol. 18, no. 2, Fall 1981) pp. 1–3. Copyright © 1981 by Brookings Institution, Washington, D.C.

In fact the economic effect of defense purchases has nothing whatever to do with one's judgment about the usefulness of the products bought.

In a private market, two things happen when goods are produced: income is paid to the producers, and an equivalent amount of income is removed from those who buy the goods. The creation of purchasing power is matched by the sale of goods, the receipts from which absorb the purchasing power. But a government purchase, civilian or military, completes only half of the two-way transaction. The government indeed pays income to the producers, but the government doesn't turn around and sell those goods in the marketplace, thereby absorbing an equivalent amount of income and purchasing power. Because the extra income earned in production is not absorbed by the sale of an added supply of goods on the market, the government must levy taxes to soak up the added purchasing power created when goods are produced for it. While government need not cover every dollar of its purchases by taxes, large-scale failure to absorb the added purchasing power—that is, large-scale budget deficits—can cause inflation and high interest rates. Purchasing power has been added to the system but not reabsorbed.

In sum, government purchases do not add to market supply in the economic sense of the term. Hence taxes must be levied. But the military nature of the goods is absolutely irrelevant. If government bought massive amounts of food, clothing, and houses and distributed them free of charge, it would add nothing to the *economic* supply of goods in the country. Inflation would result, no matter how "useful" the goods in question.

Another frequently heard proposition is that the lower share of defense spending in the economy of Japan (and to a lesser extent Germany) compared to the United States is an important reason for Japan's higher rate of productivity growth. A variant of this argument holds that the Japanese have gained a competitive edge on the United States in world markets because of their low defense spending. Both propositions are essentially wrong. If the U.S. defense share of GNP came at the expense of investment rather than consumption, the reduction of investment might indeed lower our productivity and competitiveness. But there is no reason in principle why we cannot design the taxes needed to support defense spending so as to depress consumption rather than investment. If we do otherwise, the resulting fall in investment is our own choice and not something inherent in defense spending. In any event, in the post-war period there is little evidence that the share of business investment spending in GNP moved up and down in tandem with changes in the defense share of GNP, which ranged between 5 and 10 percent.

It might be argued that the heavy call of a large defense budget on skilled manpower, scientific talent, and R&D facilities would impair the technological capabilities of civilian industries. There is probably something to this argument. But against it must be set the spillover of defense-financed technology into the civilian sector. A large defense budget for procurement and R&D in all likelihood works to the advantage of some civilian industries and to the detriment of others. It is probably no accident that Japanese competitiveness and exports are particularly strong in consumer goods, while the United States is a strong world competitor in fields more closely related to defense, such as aircraft, computers, large communications equipment, and the like.

So there is nothing inherently inflationary or productivity-lowering about defense spending that should prevent the United States from having the *level* of spending it believes is required for its national security, so long as it is willing to pay for increased defense through lower spending on consumption. But some special characteristics of the defense budget give rise to economic problems when attempts are made to *change* that budget rapidly.

For most of the finished goods and their components that are sold to the defense establishment, there is only one market: the military. While many nonspecialized parts, materials, and skills are bought by military prime contractors,

government business constitutes a large fraction of the sales of many of those contractors. With some exceptions (space, nuclear energy), this is not true of most other large components of the federal budget. A $20 billion increase in defense and R&D procurement, for example, represents less than 1 percent of GNP, but a very large increase in the output of the major industries supplying defense—10 to 20 percent for industries manufacturing ordnance, aircraft, and communications equipment. On the other hand, a $20 billion increase in government transfer payments for such things as social security and unemployment compensation will be spent by the recipients on the whole gamut of goods and services that Americans normally buy. It is unlikely that any one industry would be faced with an increase of more than about 2 percent in its output and sales.

Thus, in contrast to other areas of the budget, a rapid increase in military spending requires an abnormally large expansion in the output of a particular group of firms or industries. This in turn is likely to lead to "bottleneck" cost increases as defense firms scramble to increase output more rapidly than can be efficiently managed, and as prices are bid up for the particular materials, components, and labor skills needed in defense production.

Consequently the Pentagon ends up with substantial cost overruns, and civilian industries face rising costs to the extent they use the scarce materials and labor whose prices have been bid up. Almost by definition, however, those specialized materials and labor skills that are subject to bottleneck price increases are unlikely to bulk so large in the costs of other firms as to be a major inflationary factor for the economy as a whole. The principal problem that arises from an attempt to expand the defense budget too rapidly is the harmful effect of the resulting cost overruns on the military establishment and on the nation's security.

Because rapid changes in defense spending have large impacts on a well defined group of industries, the defense budget has other special characteristics. When large increases are enacted, and even before contracts are bid on or let, managers of defense firms can begin to respond to the prospects of substantially enlarged markets. Initial decisions about R&D and personnel expansion can be made. Inventories can be stockpiled and financing tentatively arranged. An equivalent dollar expansion of civilian government spending, on the other hand, is diffused so widely among civilian industries that, however large the national impact, it usually is both small and unpredictable for the individual firm. Increases in defense business expected to flow from a rapid expansion of defense spending are often large enough to require individual defense firms to invest in capacity expansion. A similar advance impact of government spending on investment is much less likely to arise from

a corresponding increase in civilian government spending.

Although the very long lead times typical of defense contracts are often thought to slow and moderate the economic impact of large changes in the defense budget, the paradoxical fact is that the relatively narrow industrial base of defense procurement brings about some of these economic effects rather quickly.

QUESTIONS FOR DISCUSSION

1. Briefly discuss the economic costs of nuclear weapons. According to Forsberg, what are some alternative uses of these resources?

2. What, according to DeGrasse, is the overall impact of military spending on the economy?

3. In what respects does Schultze differ with Degrasse about the economic effects of military spending?

SUGGESTED READINGS

ANGELOPOULOS, ANGELOS TH. *Global Plan for Employment: A New Marshall Plan*. New York: Praeger, 1983.

BALL, NICOLE, and MILTON LEITENBERG. *The Structure of the Defense Industry*. London: Croom Helm, 1983.

BOULDING, KENNETH E. *Conflict and Defense: A General Theory*. New York, Harper, 1962.

LEONTIEF, WASSILY, and FAYE DUCHIN. *Military Spending*. New York: Oxford University Press, 1983.

MELMAN, SEYMOUR. *Pentagon Capitalism: The Political Economy of War*. New York: McGraw Hill, 1970.

Chapter IX

Bureaucratic Aspects
of the Nuclear Arms Race

Military organizations are large institutions, and many analysts argue that the bureaucratic structure of the armed forces contributes to the nuclear arms race. They argue that in both superpowers bureaucratic factors often stimulate unnecessary weapons production. For example, many observers believe that the division of the U.S. military into separate services—the Army, Navy, and Air Force—promotes both inefficiency of operations and the purchase of unneeded arms. These analysts contend that "interservice rivalry" causes each branch of the armed forces to seek new weapons of its own; by acquiring new weapons, each service can expand its mission, budget and prestige. As new weapons technologies are developed, each service tries to get a piece of the action, causing duplication and leading to inflated arsenals. Such purchases are also in the interest of the defense industries, which profit from military contracts. Thus, the structure of the "military-industrial complex" may lead to the deployment of weapons that are not needed. While such bureaucratic factors may apply to weapons of all kinds, many believe they have an important bearing on the nuclear arms race.

This chapter considers the bureaucratic aspects of the arms race. The first reading is President Dwight D. Eisenhower's farewell address to the nation. Eisenhower, a decorated general and former Army Chief of Staff, warns of the danger that a growing "military-industrial complex" could gain too much power over national affairs. Next, David C. Jones, the former Chairman of the Joint Chiefs of Staff, briefly discusses some problems with the structure of the military establishment.

In the third reading, Marek Thee addresses the large and organized military research and development (R&D) efforts that continually produce new weapons. Thee suggests that certain bureaucratic features of military research have an important impact on the pace and direction of the arms race.

The final reading is an excerpt from Gordon Adams's systematic study of the politics of defense contracting. Adams argues that weapons funding is controlled by a triangular network of Pentagon officials, military contractors, and members of Congressional committees that handle the armed forces. This "iron triangle" makes decisions in its own interest and with only limited public input.

32   Farewell Address to the Nation

Dwight D. Eisenhower

My fellow Americans: Three days from now, after half a century in the service of our country, I shall lay down the responsibilities of office as, in traditional and solemn ceremony, the authority of the Presidency is vested in my successor.

This evening I come to you with a message of leavetaking and farewell and to share a few final thoughts with you, my countrymen.

Like every other citizen, I wish the new President and all who will labor with him Godspeed. I pray that the coming years will be blessed with peace and prosperity for all.

Our people expect their President and the Congress to find essential agreement on issues of great moment, the wise resolution of which will better shape the future of the Nation.

My own relations with the Congress, which began on a remote and tenuous basis, when long ago a member of the Senate appointed me to West Point, have since ranged to the intimate during the war and immediate postwar period and, finally, to the mutually interdependent during these past 8 years.

In this final relationship the Congress and the administration have, on most vital issues, cooperated well to serve the national good rather than mere partisanship and so have assured that the business of the Nation should go forward. So my official relationship with the Congress ends in a feeling on my part of gratitude that we have been able to do so much together.

Delivered January 17, 1961. Reprinted from United States, Department of State, *Bulletin*, vol. 44, February 6, 1985.

II

We now stand 10 years past the midpoint of a century that has witnessed four major wars among great nations. Three of these involved our own country. Despite these holocausts, America is today the strongest, the most influential, and most productive nation in the world. Understandably proud of this preeminence, we yet realize that America's leadership and prestige depend not merely upon our unmatched material progress, riches, and military strength but on how we use our power in the interests of world peace and human betterment.

III

Throughout America's adventure in free government our basic purposes have been to keep the peace, to foster progress in human achievement, and to enhance liberty, dignity, and integrity among people and among nations. To strive for less would be unworthy of a free and religious people. Any failure traceable to arrogance or our lack of comprehension or readiness to sacrifice would inflict upon us grievous hurt both at home and abroad.

Progress toward these noble goals is persistently threatened by the conflict now engulfing the world. It commands our whole attention, absorbs our very beings. We face a hostile ideology—global in scope, atheistic in character, ruthless in purpose, and insidious in method. Unhappily the danger it poses promises to be of indefinite duration. To meet it successfully there is called for not so much the emotional and transitory sacrifices of crisis but rather those which enable us to carry forward steadily, surely, and without complaint the burdens of a prolonged and complex struggle—with liberty the stake. Only thus shall we remain, despite every provocation, on our charted course toward permanent peace and human betterment.

Crises there will continue to be. In meeting them, whether foreign or domestic, great or small, there is a recurring temptation to feel that some spectacular and costly action could become the miraculous solution to all current difficulties. A huge increase in newer elements of our defense, development of unrealistic programs to cure every ill in agriculture, a dramatic expansion in basic and applied research—these and many other possibilities, each possibly promising in itself, may be suggested as the only way to the road we wish to travel.

But each proposal must be weighed in the light of a broader consideration: the need to maintain balance in and among national programs—balance between the private and the public economy, balance between cost and hoped-for advantage, balance between the clearly necessary and the comfortably desirable, balance between our essential requirements as a nation and the duties imposed by the Nation upon the individual, balance between actions of the moment and the national welfare of the future. Good judgment seeks balance and progress; lack of it eventually finds imbalance and frustration.

The record of many decades stands as proof that our people and their Government have, in the main, understood these truths and have responded to them well in the face of stress and threat. But threats, new in kind or degree, constantly arise. I mention two only.

IV

A vital element in keeping the peace is our Military Establishment. Our arms must be mighty, ready for instant action, so that no potential aggressor may be tempted to risk his own destruction.

Our military organization today bears little relation to that known by any of my predecessors in peacetime, or indeed by the fighting men of World War II and Korea.

Until the latest of our world conflicts, the United States had no armaments industry. American makers of plowshares could, with time and as required, make swords as well. But now we can no longer risk emergency improvisation of national defense; we have been compelled to create a permanent armaments industry of vast proportions. Added to this, 3½ million men and women are directly engaged in the Defense Establishment. We annually spend on military security more than the net income of all United States corporations.

This conjunction of an immense Military Establishment and a large arms industry is new in the American experience. The total influence—economic, political, even spiritual—is felt in every city, every statehouse, every office of the Federal Government. We recognize the imperative need for this development. Yet we must not fail to comprehend its grave implications. Our toil, resources, and livelihood are all involved; so is the very structure of our society.

In the councils of government we must guard against the acquisition of unwarranted influence whether sought or unsought, by the military-industrial complex. The potential for the disastrous rise of misplaced power exists and will persist.

We must never let the weight of this combination endanger our liberties or democratic processes. We should take nothing for granted. Only an alert and knowledgeable citizenry can compel the proper meshing of the huge industrial and military machinery of defense with our peaceful methods and goals so that security and liberty may prosper together.

Akin to and largely responsible for the sweeping changes in our industrial-military posture has been the technological revolution during recent decades. In this revolution research has become central; it also becomes more formalized, complex, and costly. A steadily increasing share is conducted for, by, or at the direction of the Federal Government.

Today the solitary inventor, tinkering in his shop, has been overshadowed by task forces of scientists in laboratories and testing fields. In the same fashion the free university, historically the fountainhead of free ideas and scientific discovery, has experienced a revolution in the conduct of research. Partly because of the huge costs involved, a Government contract becomes virtually a substitute for intellectual curiosity. For every old blackboard there are now hundreds of new electronic computers.

The prospect of domination of the Nation's scholars by Federal employment, project allocations, and the power of money is ever present and is gravely to be regarded.

Yet, in holding scientific research and discovery in respect, as we should, we must also be alert to the equal and opposite danger that public policy could itself become the captive of a scientific technological elite.

It is the task of statesmanship to mold, to balance, and to integrate these and other forces, new and old, within the principles of our democratic system—ever aiming toward the supreme goals of our free society.

V

Another factor in maintaining balance involves the element of time. As we peer into society's future, we—you and I, and our Government—must avoid the impulse to live only for today, plundering for our own ease and convenience the precious resources of tomorrow. We cannot mortgage the material assets of our grandchildren without risking the loss also of their political and spiritual heritage. We want democracy to survive for all generations to come, not to become the insolvent phantom of tomorrow.

VI

Down the long lane of the history yet to be written, America knows that this world of ours, ever growing smaller, must avoid becoming a community of dreadful fear and hate and be, instead, a proud confederation of mutual trust and respect.

Such a confederation must be one of equals. The weakest must come to the conference table with the same confidence as do we, protected as we are by our moral, economic, and military strength. That table, though scarred by many past frustrations, cannot be abandoned for the certain agony of the battlefield.

Disarmament, with mutual honor and confidence, is a continuing imperative. Together we must learn how to compose differences, not with arms but with intellect and decent purpose. Because this need is so sharp and apparent I confess that I lay down my official responsibilities in this field with a definite sense of disappointment. As one who has witnessed the horror and the lingering sadness of war, as one who knows that another war could utterly destroy this civilization which has been so slowly and painfully built over thousands of years, I wish I could say tonight that a lasting peace is in sight.

Happily I can say that war has been avoided. Steady progress toward our ultimate goal has been made. But so much remains to be done. As a private citizen I shall never cease to do what little I can to help the world advance along that road.

VII

So, in this my last good night to you as your President, I thank you for the many opportunities you have given me for public service in war and peace. I trust that in that service you find some things worthy; as for the rest of it, I know you will find ways to improve performance in the future.

You and I, my fellow citizens, need to be strong in our faith that all nations, under God, will reach the goal of peace with justice. May we be ever unswerving in devotion to principle, confident but humble with power, diligent in pursuit of the Nation's great goals.

To all the peoples of the world, I once more give expression to America's prayerful and continuing aspiration:

We pray that peoples of all faith, all races, all nations, may have their great human needs satisfied; that those now denied opportunity shall come to enjoy it to the full; that all who yearn for freedom may experience its spiritual blessings; that those who have freedom will understand, also, its heavy responsibilities; that all who are insensitive to the needs of others will learn charity; that the scourges of poverty, disease, and ignorance will be made to disappear from the earth; and that, in the goodness of time, all peoples will come to live together in a peace guaranteed by the binding force of mutual respect and love.

33 What's Wrong with Our Defense Establishment?

David C. Jones

At a late-afternoon meeting at the White House a few months ago, President Reagan, who had just returned from horseback riding at Quantico, turned to me in jest, but with a touch of nostalgia, and asked, "Isn't there some way we can bring back the horse cavalry?" My reply was: "Just wait, Mr. President. We are starting by resurrecting battleships."

Below the surface of this lighthearted exchange lie two pervasive problems within defense:

- We are too comfortable with the past.
- We do not make a sufficiently rigorous examination of defense requirements and alternatives.

By their very nature, large organizations have a built-in resistance to change. As the largest organization in the free world, our defense establishment—the Department of Defense—has most of the problems of a large corporation but lacks an easily calculated "bottom line" to force needed change. At the core are the Army, Navy, Air Force and Marine Corps: institutions that find it difficult to adapt to changing conditions because of understandable attachments to the past. The very foundation of each service rests on imbuing its members with pride in its mission, its doctrine and its customs and discipline—all of which are steeped in traditions. While these deep-seated service distinctions are important in fostering a fighting spirit, cultivating them engenders tendencies to look inward and to insulate the institutions against outside challenges.

Excerpted from David C. Jones, "What's Wrong with Our Defense Establishment?" *New York Times Magazine*, November 7, 1982. Copyright © 1982 by The New York Times Company. Reprinted by permission.

The history of our services includes striking examples of ideas and inventions whose time had come, but which were resisted because they did not fit into existing service concepts. The Navy kept building sailing ships long after the advent of steam power. Machine guns and tanks were developed in the United States, but our Army rejected them until long after they were accepted in Europe. The horse cavalry survived essentially unchanged right up until World War II despite evidence that its utility was greatly diminished decades earlier. Even Army Air Corps officers were required to wear spurs until the late 1930's.

But the armed services are only part of the problem. The Defense Department has evolved into a grouping of large, rigid bureaucracies—services, agencies, staffs, boards and committees—which embrace the past and adapt new technology to fit traditional missions and methods. There is no doubt that the cavalry leaders would have quickly adopted a horse which went farther and faster—a high-technology stallion. The result of this rigidity has been an ever-widening gap between the need to adapt to changing conditions and our ability to do so. Over the last two to three years the American public has become increasingly concerned over our deteriorating position in military power and convinced that we must devote more to our defenses than we did in the 1960's and 1970's. But after serving on the Joint Chiefs of Staff longer than anyone else in history and under more Presidents and Secretaries of Defense (four of each), and being a student of military history and organizations, I am convinced that fundamental defense deficiencies cannot be solved with dollars alone—no matter how much they are needed.

34 Military Research and Development

Marek Thee _____

Nuclear deterrence is one of the essential driving forces behind the contemporary arms race. But nuclear doctrine is not developed in a vacuum. It is a function of the advancements in military technology. It draws its inspiration and has its material foundation in the operation of military R and D [research and development], the engine of armaments innovation and modernization. There is a mutual stimulation between the doctrine of nuclear deterrence and the feats of military R & D.

Among a number of economic and socio-political factors, as well as structural phenomena in state internal and external relations which fuel the arms race—such as systemic and imperial rivalry, the role and influence of vested interests of the military, the military industry and state bureaucracy—military R & D stands out today as one of the prime movers of armaments. The very fact that on a global scale military R & D today employs approximately half a million of the best qualified scientists and engineers with a budget in the neighborhood of 70–80 billion US dollars annually must have a dramatic effect on the arms race.[1]

It is not only the magnitude of the endeavor which confers special power on military R & D. Even more important are the structural features, the institutional set-up and mode of operation of military R & D. Before touching on these traits, however, let me present a few general remarks about the impact of technology on the arms race.

Excerpted from Marek Thee, "The State of the Globe: Rethinking Problems of the Nuclear Arms Race," *Bulletin of Peace Proposals*, vol. 5, no. 4, 1984, pp. 371–372. Copyright © 1984, International Peace Research Institute, Oslo *Bulletin of Peace Proposals*.

Today's arms race is basically different from similar competitions in the past. It is no longer a rivalry in quantities only; predominantly it is a race in military technology, in product improvement, modernization and new technological breakthroughs. We should note, for example, that in sheer numbers of missiles and warheads the world stockpile of nuclear weapons has not increased substantially in recent years—indeed, it has in certain instances even been reduced as, for instance, in tactical nuclear munitions. At the same time its efficiency and destructive power have grown immensely.[2] In the process, also older, obsolete types of nuclear weapons have been withdrawn, to be replaced by more sophisticated new ones. Herein lies partly the arms control game, which advances the limitation in numbers while keeping the gates wide open for renewal and modernization.

Thus, the arms race today focuses less on the number of missiles and more on their technical excellence and such indices as accuracy, speed, range, guidance, penetrability or yield against the weight ratio. The mix of these characteristics knows no limit. Improvements in some of them may have a basic impact on nuclear war-fighting capabilities. Thus, for instance, a ten fold increase in accuracy of missiles, assuming the same yield, will produce a 100 times greater lethality to a hardened missile silo.[3] The general trend has been to reduce size and yield of warheads, while increasing their maneuverability and precision instead.

This shift from quantity to quality has significant implications for the dynamics of the arms race. As attention turns to technological advances and possible future technological breakthroughs, so also traditional restraints stemming from the high costs of the race or the saturation of arsenals are being subdued, and are losing their power. Moreover, as long as we lack exact knowledge about the advances of the adversary abroad or competing institutions within the national military R & D establishment, the prevailing tendency, in line with worst case planning, is not only to react to imaginary achievements of the competitors but to overreact, running ahead of any real challenges or real needs. There is less restraint and more aggressive verve in the contemporary arms race.

This touches on the mode of operation of military R & D. Predetermined in this mode are the long lead-times required for the conceptualization, prototype production, repeated testing, development and production of new weapons. This takes on the average 10–15 years. Once a decision has been taken to initiate a new weapon system, the effort will continue uninterrupted for years without regard to possible outside political developments, be it change of administration or arms control negotiations. This invests the arms race with continuity and perseverance.

The regularity of these long cycles is compounded by another fundamental operational law of military R & D: the follow-on imperative. Each new discovery in defense or offense has to be followed up as a matter of professional routine by research and development on counterdevices. The assumption here is that the adversary is at par or ahead of one's achievements. But this means that the contest turns into a race against one's own achievements. Innate in the style and method of military R & D is the compulsion for a chain-reaction spiralling pursuit of ever new frontiers of military capability. This naturally perpetuates the race still more. A Frankenstein-like self-propelling process is set in motion.

We need not go into greater detail regarding the institutional set-up and operational compulsions of military R & D to realize the enor-

mous impact which R & D has on the arms race. Arms race theories distinguish between external and internal determinants of armaments. Military R & D belongs par excellence to the internal determinants. It is also the crucial factor which has since World War II generated a shift in the center of gravity of the arms race, from the external to the internal domain. Internal determinants of a technological and doctrinal nature affect the dynamics of armaments far stronger than do pressures from the international environment.

Thus in thinking about arms control and disarmament we need to pay much greater attention to the domestic scene. Especially we must look for ways to bring the technological momentum of military science under control. We need to heed the prophetic advice of President Eisenhower, who in his farewell address warned against the 'danger that public policy could itself become the captive of a scientific-technological elite.'. . .

NOTES

1. Cf. Mary Acland-Hood, 'Military Research and Development: Some Aspects of its Resource Use in the USA and USSR', *SIPRI Yearbook 1983*, London and New York: Taylor and Francis Ltd., 1983, and Marek Thee, 'Military Research and Development: Its Impact on Society', in Kåre Berg and Knut Erik Tranøy (Eds.), *Research Ethics*, New York: Alan R. Liss, Inc., 1983.

2. Cf. Frank Barnaby and Malvern Lumsden. World Nuclear Weapon Stockpiles', *SIPRI Yearbook* 1983, op. cit., and Richard Halloran. '29 000 US Warheads foreseen for 1990', *International Herald Tribune*, January 9, 1984.

3. Cf. Kosta Tsipis, 'Offensive Missiles'. In Marek Thee (Ed.), *Armaments and Disarmament in the Nuclear Age*, op.cit., p. 74.

35   The Making of an Iron Triangle

Gordon Adams

For over a century, the private sector of the U.S. economy has been organized into companies which have grown in size, become more concentrated and are increasingly self-conscious about their impact on the federal government. This surge of corporate concern with and involvement in government policy has resulted in the development of corporate policies, practices and structures which enable a firm to follow government policy developments and to intervene in the policy process to make it more responsive to its needs.

THE IRON TRIANGLE

The government relations practices of defense contractors, far from being unique, are typical of business/government interactions generally. Defense firms have, in fact, been trend-setters in developing techniques to influence government behavior because their intimacy and dependence on federal policy has such a long history. Many defense contractors depend directly on government procurement for corporate survival, while the government maintains close ties to the industry in order to ensure a steady supply of weapons and supplies.

The Department of Defense has developed a substantial bureaucracy to design, help produce, maintain and use weapons. Although some crit-

Excerpted from Gordon Adams, "Corporate Political Influence and Government Relations Practices: The Making of an Iron Triangle," *ICCR Brief*, February 1981, pp. 3A–3. Copyright © 1981 by Interfaith Center on Corporate Responsibility, taken from *The Politics of Defense Contracting: The Iron Triangle*, Council on Economic Priorities, 1982. Reprinted with permission.

ics, notably Seymour Melman, have argued that the "military industrial complex" involves government control over industry, it is clear that defense firms draw substantial advantages from doing military business and have a significant, even major impact on defense procurement policies.[1] Richard Kaufman, counsel to the congressional joint economic committee, describes these "hidden profits":

> Padded costs, the use of government-owned equipment for commercial activities, the cash flow advantages of progress payments, the privilege of making late delivery of products that do not meet original specifications, bailouts and get-well devices for contractors with cost overruns, executive salaries and fringe benefits and the personal career opportunities for those who oscillate between the Pentagon and the defense industry and who operate within those two powerful publicly-supported institutions.[2]

The interrelationship of government and business in this sector of policy has given birth to the "iron triangle" of defense policy and defense procurement. The iron triangle has four characteristic features. First, it involves a close working relationship in a fairly clearly delineated area of policy between the three key participants in the policy-making process: the federal bureaucracy, key committees and members of Congress tied into this policy area, and the industry that benefits from government policy. The triangle in this, as well as other policy areas, appears as a slightly separate piece of government dealing with specific questions. In defense, the key participants are the Defense Department (plus NASA and the nuclear weapons branch of the Department of Energy); the House and Senate Armed Services Committees and Defense Appropriations Sub-Committees, key Congress members from defense-related districts and states; and the companies, labs, research institutes, trade associations and trade unions in the industry itself.

Second, there is a powerful and intimate interpenetration between the industry and the federal bureaucracy in an iron triangle. Policy makers and administrators move freely between the two and policy issues are generally discussed and resolved among participants who develop and begin to share common values, interests and perceptions.[3] This interpenetration leads to an actual sharing of decision-making power; industry officials become policy makers and administrators even without entering public service. Government power and private power become the same thing.

Third, an iron triangle emerges over time, through continuous interaction among the participants. Government bureaucrats and private industry officials, alike, actively pursue policies and procedures to maintain the triangle. The interests of bureaucrats (self-preservation, measurable results) and industry (profit, growth) are repeatedly reconciled over time through such constant interaction.

Fourth, the triangle becomes "iron", that is, it is strengthened and becomes increasingly isolated from other policy arenas. Private interests, bureaucrats and key members of Congress all strive to keep their policy arena isolated and protected from outside interference. As a result, perspectives on policy alternatives narrow and proposals for alternative policies from outside the triangle have no credibility inside. Policy makers and industry begin to share the assumption that they act not only in their own interests, but in the "public interest" generally. As Ziegler and Peak describe the result:

> On the day-to-day performance of their tasks, administrators see very little of the more general public support which accompanied the establishment of the agency. The only people who are likely to come to the attention of administrators are those whose problems are uniquely a part of the administrative environment. . . . Under such circumstances it is not surprising that the administrator's perception of the public interest is in reality defined by the interests of the regulated parties.[4]

THE MEANING OF DEFENSE DEPENDENCE

Companies in the iron triangle develop government relations practices because they want governmental policies or need to prevent governmental decisions that counter corporate interests. For the eight defense contractors in our study a significant part of corporate business, in some cases corporate survival itself, depends on maintaining a steady flow of defense contracts to the firm. All are, in other words, defense dependent. Boeing, General Dynamics, Grumman, Lockheed, McDonnell Douglas, Northrop, Rockwell International and United Technologies have been consistently important contractors with the Department of Defense and with NASA. These eight have received 25 percent of all DoD contracts (in $ value) between 1970 and 1979 and have appeared sixty-six times among the top ten DoD contractors (out of a possible total of one hundred positions, ten in each of those years). Lockheed has been the Pentagon's number one contractor five of those nine years, General Dynamics three times and McDonnell Douglas twice. Northrop is the only company which has not regularly ranked among the top ten.

These eight companies also depend, to a significant extent, on the Department of Defense and NASA for their business. Computing total government sales as a proportion of total corporate sales, as disclosed (unevenly) by the companies shows that Grumman received 82 percent of its sales from the government, while Boeing (31 percent) ranked lowest in such dependency. [See Table 35–1.]

As defense spending stabilized in the early 1970's, following the end of the Vietnam War, these firms both sought to diversify from their dependency on defense contracts and kept up an active government relations effort—at home and abroad—to maintain their defense business. Sales of military and commercial products overseas made up the gap in domestic sales. The foreign alternative was especially significant for several companies in the study, including Northrop and McDonnell Douglas. Grumman might have had to close many of its doors without the large F-14 sale to the government of Iran in 1974 and lending provided by Iran's Melli Bank to help finance the sale. Lockheed, McDonnell Douglas and Boeing all pushed overseas sales of their wide-bodied transports in the 1970's.

TABLE 35–1   ($ M)

	Company Sales (1970–79)	Government Sales (Yrs. as Indicated)	Govt. as % of Sales	Years in Top 10 DoD Contractor (1970–79)
Boeing	41,402.6	8,954.4 (1974 on)	30.9	9
General Dynamics	24,121.5	11,854.5 (1973 on)	64.1	10
Grumman	12,015.8	7,838.2 (1973 on)	82.2	9
Lockheed	31,355.6	20,938.3	66.8	10
McDonnell Douglas	32,713.6	20,237.0	61.9	10
Northrop	10,593.6	6,741.5 (1972 on)	71.8	2
Rockwell	42,060.3	15,865.5 (1971 on)	40.2	8
United Technologies	42,003.3	13,716.3	32.7	10
Total	236,266.3	106,145.7	50.1%*	

*Calculated as % of relevant sales years. Total for relevant years is 211,952.8.

GOVERNMENT RELATIONS PRACTICES

The companies in our study have innovated in the creation of a wide variety of government relations practices to maintain their defense business. All of them have among their top management and board members, individuals with substantial knowledge of and experience in the defense sector (both government and industry). Added to these resources, each company has hired a significant number of former military and civilian employees of the Defense Department and a surprisingly high number of company employees have spent time working in DoD. From such interchanges of personnel, a company acquires close knowledge of and access to defense policy processes. A significant proportion of civilian transfers of personnel between the companies and the government involve individuals with technical knowledge moving into or out of critical R & D offices in DoD.

In the defense business, access at the level of research and development decisions is crucially important for a firm to stay in the defense contracting business. Research and development lies at the heart of the relationship between the defense industry and the government. Through the R & D process, the next generation of weapons systems is defined often long before the Congress or general public becomes aware of the effort. If both the contractor and DoD have an early investment in a project, pressure builds down the line for a favorable production decision. The defense industry has a strong impact on the definition of DoD R & D policies.

As Morton Peck and Frederick Scherer noted in a study done in the 1960's:

> . . . Defense firms are not only major sources of new weapons program ideas, but they also provide information on the technological feasibility of new concepts and on estimated development costs and schedules. In addition, by the late 1950's practically every major weapons systems prime contractor had an operations analysis group which studied the relative military value of new weapons possibilities.[5]

Successful contractors don't wait until the Pentagon defines its needs, for at that point they are out of the competition for an R & D contract. Contractors focus on the need for constant, early interaction with the DoD offices defining future needs. G.A. Busch, Lockheed's Director of Corporate Planning has defined this interest well:

> We recognize it is the government agency that must prepare the "Mission Element Need Statement," but we feel that industry may be able to provide valuable inputs to the agency as it defines its mission needs. In our company, we tried our hand at drafting MENS ourselves.[6]

Other contractor representatives describe their effort clearly:

> The day is past when the military requirement for a major weapons system is set up by the military and passed on to industry to build the hardware. Today it is more likely that the military requirement is the result of joint participation of military and industrial personnel, and it is not unusual for industry's contribution to be a key factor. Indeed, there are highly placed military men who sincerely feel that industry currently is setting the pace in the research and development of new weapons systems.[7]

GOVERNMENT RELATIONS TOOLS

The defense contractors in the study use a wide variety of government relations tools to influence defense policy making both in Congress and in the executive branch.

- Each company maintains a sizeable Washington office, expending considerable sums to maintain close contact with the executive branch and to lobby members of Congress. The staff of these offices both seek information and generate pressure to obtain federal policies which meet corporate needs.
- All eight firms participate in trade association activities. Through regular conferences and discussions, these associations provide a vehicle for close interaction between company and government officials, generating further information and opportunities for influence over federal policies.
- Personnel of each company are members of advisory committees to DoD and NASA. Here, in closed-door sessions, companies obtain advance information on government plans and have the opportunity to influence future weapons systems.
- Especially in the 1970's, defense contractors have begun to mobilize their constituencies at the grass roots to support company objectives. Defense contractors, like most large corporations have a wide range of constituents: employees, stockholders, communities and regions where they do business, subcontractors and suppliers. In the 1970's, at least two major defense contractors made full-scale appeals to their grass roots for political support in Congress—Rockwell on behalf of its

B-1 program and Grumman for its F-14. Since the constitutents also depend on defense spending, they too, become active lobbyists for the company's contracts.

TAKING AIM AT CONGRESS: POLITICAL ACTION COMMITTEES (PACs)

Campaign contributions aimed at cementing close ties between the industry and the congressional corner of the iron triangle are one of the most controversial and complicated elements of government relations strategies. The contributions of corporations, unions, trade associations and political groups have always been controversial, especially because of the amounts involved and revelations of illegal corporate political giving during the Watergate era. The 1907 Tillman Act prohibited direct corporate contributions to federal candidates. This prohibition was repeated in the 1925 Federal Corrupt Practices Act and was extended to include giving a candidate "anything of value." A similar prohibition was applied to the use of union dues in the Smith-Connally Act of 1943 and the Taft-Hartley Act of 1947.

By 1971, reformers had become concerned about the apparent high volume of unregulated, under-the-table corporate political giving. It was clear that the prohibitions of the 1925 Act were being systematically evaded, both legally and illegally. Trade unions which had had PACs since the 1930's had also become concerned about possible restrictions on their PAC activities. These pressures led to the Federal Elections Campaign Act (FECA) of 1971, which was the first wedge in the 1970's corporate PAC explosion. The 1971 Act permitted a corporation, union or association to use funds to create a separate, segregated fund for political activity (PAC). This activity, funded by soliciting the PAC's members, could include communications with members, stockholders and employees, registration and polling efforts, fund-raising solicitations as well as campaign contributions. The 1971 Act also included a requirement that campaign contributions be disclosed.

In 1974, the FECA was amended limiting individual contributions to each candidate, placing ceilings on PAC contributions and regularizing the reporting of campaign contributions. Subsequent interpretations and amendments to the FECA further opened the door to even greater PAC creation and activity by clarifying what PACs might do, where they could solicit funds, and how they should disclose data. One significant element of the Supreme Court's *Buckley et al. v. Valeo* decision of January 1976 permitted PACs to make unlimited "independent" expenditures (spending for or against a particular candidate, uncoordinated with any individual's campaign committee).

The defense industry leaped into PAC activity, creating what are, by 1981, some of the largest PACs in the corporate sector. Moreover, further reinforcing the iron triangle, the scope of PAC activity has developed enormously since 1976. PACs are increasingly becoming involved with internal corporate political education (communications with managers, supervisors and employees), with grass roots lobbying and state and local electoral activities. Some PACs have become planning groups for coordinating all these corporate political efforts and linking them into the company's government relations activity in Washington, D.C. The *Wall Street Journal* described Political Action Committees as "a fundamental vehicle for the business community's growing political zest," and quoted Joseph Fanelli, director of the Business-Industry PAC, as saying: "Business is on the verge of a political renaissance."[8]

PACS AND THE IMPORTANCE OF ACCESS

Increasingly, companies coordinate their PAC contributions with their overall government relations strategy. A contribution, even small, provides access to the office of a member of Congress as virtually every student of campaign contributions confirms. Fred Wertheirmer of Common Cause which urged the PAC reforms, now has stated:

> It's not a question of buying (votes), it's a question of relationships that get built, obligations and dependencies that get established . . . It puts PACs at the head of the line as opposed to the great bulk of a Congressman's constituents.[9]

In a *New York Times* article, Steven Roberts argues:

> There are probably few cases where campaign cash actually purchases a vote. But many Congressmen say that taking a contribution creates a feeling of obligation and sympathy, a debt that must eventually be paid.

In one sense, power in Washington can be equated with access—the quicker your phone call gets returned, the more influence you have. And when a lobbyist calls a lawmaker who has taken his money, the return time is reduced considerably.[10]

Corporate executives also underline the importance of access. The Conference Board quoted one executive as saying: "The PAC is not designed to influence elections, but to open the doors."[11]

Through many contributions appear small and may not influence a specific vote, members of Congress tend to keep them in mind in the Congressional process. At least one member of the House, Congresswomen Patricia Schroeder (D-Colorado), has explicitly linked the two:

> I've had people on my committee ask how many tickets a company bought to a fundraiser, while we're trying to decide what planes to buy.[12]

The impact of a contribution grows, moreover, if companies in industry and their trade association aggregate their contributions. Campaign funds then become one of the most significant tools in strengthening the relationship between industry and Congress in the iron triangle.

CONCLUSION

National security is an issue of central concern to all citizens. Because of the resources they can muster for their government relations, defense contractors have unusual access to and influence over the definition of national security policy, especially over weapons research and development and procurement decisions. Issues of intense public interest—the size and content of the defense budget, the definition of a conflict of interest and standards of conduct, whether lobbying costs should be charged to contracts—tend to be defined within the iron triangle, with limits on public access. The criteria used to make these decisions are largely defined by actors within the iron triangle. The preconceptions shared by actors in the triangle are codified as "legal" or "correct". The public can attempt to change the standards from the outside but access to the policy apparatus is difficult. The public interest in national security policy, defense contracting policy and the manner in which defense contracting companies create and maintain their relationship with Congress and the executive branch needs to be clarified.

The first element of such a public interest standard is information. The disclosure of contractor-government relations practices needs to be expanded and the reporting requirements tightened and more rigorously enforced. Current disclosure makes it difficult to estimate the magnitude of a contractor's overall government relations effort. More strict disclosure of lobbying and campaign expenditures at all levels of government would be a useful change in this area.

The second element in defining public standards in these areas is greater public participation in the process—opening up the iron triangle. Stockholders who seek greater disclosure of corporate campaign contributions and government relations practices, public representatives on federal advisory groups, wider congressional debate on defense budgets—these and other measures would expand participation in the debate over the meaning of national security.

NOTES

1. See Seymour Melman, *Pentagon Capitalism* (New York: McGraw-Hill, 1970) and Melman, *The Permanent War Economy* (New York: Simon & Schuster, 1974).

2. Richard Kaufman, *The War Profiteers* (Garden City, N.Y.: Doubleday Anchor, 1972) p.xciii.

3. See, e.g., Harmon Zeigler and Wayne Peak, *Interest Groups in American Society*, 2nd edition (Englewood Cliffs, N.J.: Prentice-Hall, 1972) p. 172, 180.

4. *Ibid.*, p. 172.

5. Morton Peck and Frederick Scherer, *The Weapons Acquisition Process: An Economic Analysis* (Boston: Harvard Graduate School of Business Administration, Division of Research, 1962) p. 242.

6. Christopher Paine and Gordon Adams, "The R & D Slush Fund," *The Nation*, 26 January 1980, p. 75.

7. Peter Schenck of Raytheon Corporation as quoted in David Sims, "Spoon Feeding the Military: How New Weapons Come to Be," Leonard Rodberg and Derek Sherer (eds.), *The Pentagon Watchers* (Garden City, N.Y.: Doubleday 1970) p. 248.

8. *Wall Street Journal*, 11 September 1978.

9. *National Journal*, 17 May 1980.

10. *New York Times*, 19 October 1979.

11. Phillis S. McGrath, *Redefining Corporate Federal Relations* (New York: Conference Board, 1979) p. 50.

12. *New York Times*, 26 September 1979.

QUESTIONS FOR DISCUSSION

1. In what ways may the structure of the military bureacracy contribute to the arms race?

2. What are the three parts of the "iron triangle" described by Adams? How do they operate together?

3. How, according to Thee, does the institutional structure of military research and development contribute to the nuclear arms race?

4. Are you convinced by former President Eisenhower's warning about the dangers of a military-industrial complex? Why or why not?

SUGGESTED READINGS

HOLLOWAY, DAVID. *The Soviet Union and the Arms Race*, New Haven, Conn.: Yale University Press, 1983.

KOISTINEN, PAUL A. C. *The Military-Industrial Complex: An Historical Perspective*, New York: Praeger, 1980.

KORB, L. J. "The Budget Process in the Department of Defense, 1947–1977," *Public Administration Review*, July/August 1977.

LONG FRANKLIN A., and JUDITH REPPY, eds. *The Genesis of New Weapons: Decision Making for Military R&D*, Elmsford, N.Y.: Pergamon Press, 1980.

RASOR, DINA. *The Pentagon Underground,* New York: Times Books, 1985.

ROSEN, STEVEN. *Testing the Theory of the Military-Industrial Complex* Lexington, Mass.: Lexington, 1973.

SARKESIAN, SAM C. ed., *The Military-Industrial Complex: A Reassessment,* Beverly Hills, Calif.: Sage, 1972.

Chapter X

Psychology
and the Nuclear Arms Race

Psychologists—like political scientists, sociologists and economists—have much to contribute to our understanding of the nuclear arms race. A variety of psychological mechanisms can mediate our relationship with nuclear weapons, affecting our attitudes, perceptions and behavior. This chapter briefly examines some of these psychological mechanisms.

In the first reading, Robert Jay Lifton discusses our fear of nuclear weapons, the mystery surrounding them, and our sense of helplessness in the face of the nuclear threat. He argues that our anxieties cause us to be quite vulnerable to illusions about nuclear war. These illusions are rooted in the psychological mechanisms of denial of the threat of nuclear war and of resistance to acknowledging its reality. Such illusions can influence policy—with potentially disastrous consequences.

Robert S. Moyer's article, "The Enemy Within," explores the role of a variety of defense mechanisms, such as denial, projection, and dehumanization, in shaping our perceptions of nuclear war. He also discusses some ways in which assumptions, preconceptions and mental images contribute to misunderstandings between the United States and the Soviet Union.

36 Nuclear Illusions

Robert J. Lifton

Nothing lends itself more to illusion than our perceptions of nuclear weapons. This is so because of the quality of fear they inspire, their special mystery, their relationship to the infinite, and our sense of profound helplessness before them.

Our *fear* of them is amorphous, but contains Hiroshima-like images of extraordinary destruction and of extraordinarily grotesque forms of collective dying. Our fear is heightened by the invisibility of the added lethal component, the radiation.

This invisibility is part of the weapons' *mystery*. But the mystery also is importantly associated with our sense that we do not know, and cannot ever know, exactly what the weapons will do. Their action—above all their destructiveness—is beyond our grasp. Hence the weapons are readily perceived as a kind of revenge of nature on us for our tampering; or as being outside of nature in the sense of possessing more-than-natural (supernatural) destructive power.

This sense of mystery is bound up with the weapons' relationship to the *infinite*. We sense we are tapping an ultimate force of destructive energy—from atomic nuclei, from the sun itself. We sense their destructive power to be equally infinite. Again there are Hiroshima images: a single object from a single plane destroying a whole city; poisonous effects from radiation remaining throughout one's life and extending *endlessly* over subsequent generations. And that first "tiny bomb," we know, is the progenitor—

the direct ancestor—of a "doomsday machine" —a nuclear weapons structure, or set of structures, that could literally destroy the earth.

In the face of such perceptions we feel immediately, excruciatingly, overwhelmingly *helpless*. Compared to the bomb's infinite, mysterious killing power, we feel ourselves to be nothing— to be vulnerable creatures whose lives and very humanity can be snuffed out instantaneously. We feel ourselves unable to break out of the death-trap we know to be of our own making.

Now I would stress that these are not "irrational" or "pathological" reactions. With the exception of viewing the bomb as supernatural, all of the perceptions I have described can be considered more or less appropriate mental formations or symbolizations of a particular entity.

There is first, then, the overriding *illusion of limit and control*. Virtually all false assumptions about the bomb are related to this most fundamental of nuclear illusions. But here let us look at the militarized version of it: the concept of "tactical" or "limited nuclear war." One could say that the United States fought such a war during the final days of World War II but that nuclear war could stay limited because the enemy had no atomic weapons and because no one had thermonuclear weapons. During the 1950s, nuclear scenarios bandied about very frequently assumed "rational" decisions of limitation—you destroyed Moscow so we must destroy New York, but let us stop there (Why? Because we are gentlemen!)—made in the midst of nuclear conflict. The leading nuclear scenarists of the time were Herman Kahn and Edward Teller, each of whom published books in the early 1960s advocating readiness for limited nuclear war. Teller in particular provides psychologically astounding scenarios demonstrating the thesis.[1] In one sequence, for instance, there are two outcomes. The scenario includes a Communist uprising in a small, fictitious democratic country with whom the United States has a mutual defense treaty. American indecisiveness and oversensitivity to Soviet nuclear threat combine to prevent the United States from making a declaration of war or taking effective action of any kind. The Communists win, and the war becomes "the beginning of the end of world leadership for the United States," following which "the Near East [is] abandoned," and "three months later. . ."

But in the second scenario, when there is a similar Communist revolution and the Soviet Union sends paratroopers, the United States acts swiftly, making effective use of small nuclear weapons, and when the U.S.S.R. threatens a nuclear attack on the U.S., this is met with a "nationwide atomic alert" and immediate second-strike readiness, which quickly aborts the Soviet threat. The U.S.S.R. withdraws its forces, free elections are held under United Nations auspices, and the Loyalist officials are returned to office. The clear moral is that nuclear restraint will lead to our downfall, while limited nuclear war brings complete success. But the psychological key is the assumption that a preplanned combination of bold, limited nuclear action and equally bold, more or less *unlimited* nuclear threat can enable us to *control* the situation and keep it *limited*. That assumption defies virtually all psychological experience. Having nuclear weapons dropped on one or even on a close ally can readily be perceived as threatening to a nation's overall existence. A response to that kind of threat is likely to include full expression of one's potential for violence,[2] which means full use of one's available nuclear arsenal.

Hence a number of careful studies over the years, even when posed in essentially military and political terms, have expressed grave doubts about limited nuclear war. One of the most recent, reported by the International Institute for Strategic Studies in London in November 1981, concluded that it would be "most unrealistic" to expect "a relatively smooth and controlled progression from limited and selective strikes to major counterforce exchanges or a breaking off of the war prior to large-scale attacks on urban-industrial areas." Controlled nuclear war is described as a "chimera,"[3] that is, an illusion.

But the concept, while frequently out of favor, has persisted, at least among some American and presumably Soviet strategists. In the late 1970s and early 1980s it has even had a bit of a revival. President Jimmy Carter, after first rejecting the concept, somehow embraced it toward the end of his administration. And it has been still more belligerently articulated by President Ronald Reagan and his military advisors. But a closer look at Reagan's statements reveal much of the way in which the illusion is maintained. On October 16, 1981, the president told a group of visiting editors at the White House that a nuclear exchange could occur "without it bringing either one of the major powers to pushing the button." When asked twenty-five days later at a press conference whether he still held to that belief, he became uncomfortable, made a long rambling response, concluding with the statement that limited nuclear exchange was a "possibility" that "could take place" and adding: "You could have a pessimistic outlook on it or an optimistic. I always tend to be optimistic."[4]

We get the sense here that Reagan is not willing to insist that a nuclear exchange can *with certainty* be kept limited, but rather that it was a "possibility" one could believe in by staying "optimistic" (leaving aside the grotesquery of considering millions of deaths an "optimistic" outcome). Nor would one *with certainty* contest that statement, for it is at least conceivable that a nuclear war, as Reagan says, *could* stay limited. The overwhelming psychological—as well as military and political—likelihood is that it would *not*. Yet not only Reagan but many strategists cling to the remote possibility of a limited nuclear war and build a vast set of policies around it. Various motivations, including the need to *feel* in control, as well as specific deep-seated attitudes toward nuclear weapons (which we will discuss later) are at issue here. What results is a reassertion, in the face of all evidence, of the illusion of control and limitation.

The second great nuclear deception is the *illusion of foreknowledge*. At Hiroshima we know that people were deeply confused and had no idea of what had hit them or (with the occurrence of acute radiation effects) what was happening to them. Now we know what the bombs are and do, it is argued, so that we can teach people what to expect. The model here is the known value of such knowledge for helping people to withstand ordinary disasters, such as a tornado, a flood, or, in wartime, an air raid with conventional bombs. But if people who had been told the truth about current nuclear weapons—their radius of destructiveness and the consequences of radiation fallout—would they, as survivors of the initial blast, be strengthened by that knowledge? I think not. Indeed the reverse is probably true. Knowledge of what the weapons really are and do is likely to evoke in the survivor an appropriate sense of doom. Genuine knowledge of the weapons is essentially incompatible with belief in the efficacy of any kind of preparation for attack.

The third deception, then, is the *illusion of preparation*. Preparation consists of such things as evacuation plans, extensive shelter systems, and assignment of particular people to carry out various responsibilities in a nuclear attack. These "preparations" presuppose that the attack will be "limited," but the extent and destructive power of current nuclear arsenals render the idea of preparation something on the order of a psychotic fantasy. That is, each assumption logically follows upon the other, but each is at the same time patently absurd (people would not gather at the gathering places because they would either be dead or preoccupied with finding family members; the cars, buses, or trains designated to transport them to rural areas would hardly be functional, etc.), and the entire constellation is radically divorced from actuality. When such a fantasy structure becomes fixed, we call it a delusion. This fantasy or delusion is a product not of individual but of *social madness*. We thus encounter the kind of situation in which individual people who are psychologically "normal" (in the sense of being functional in a given society) can collude in forms of thought structure that are unreal in the extreme, in this case based on assumptions relevant to prenuclear crises and insisting—against all evidence—on their implementation as a way of managing—again controlling—nuclear destruction.

Closely related is the *illusion of protection*. This is the idea that something we call "shelters" will live up to their name, again in willful disregard of such truths that, in a large-scale nuclear war, very few people would have the time or capacity to arrive at such shelters; once there most would be incinerated in them; and those few who were still alive would emerge into a "dead world" of lethal radiation fallout.

It is often said that the Soviets must be planning for a nuclear war because they have built an extensive fallout system. To the extent that they have, we may say that they are as contradictory as we. But I can vividly remember a full delegation of Soviet doctors at a recent convocation of International Physicians for the Prevention of Nuclear War joining American and European delegations in rejecting shelters or any other "protection" against nuclear war and insisting on a perspective of "preventive medicine" in approaching the overall problem of nuclear war.

Next is the *illusion of stoic behavior under nuclear attack*. Herman Kahn has here provided us with a classic illustration. Kahn is concerned with minimizing fear of radiation, hypochondriacal behavior, and psychological contagion ("If one man vomits, everyone vomits") during a thermonuclear attack. That is why he recommends individual radiation meters and boy-scout stoicism. ("You have only received ten roentgens, why are you vomiting? Pull yourself together and get to work!"). But contrast that picture with what I consider a much truer one, as portrayed in a short paper by Kai Erikson and myself. . . . We anticipate in survivors psychic numbing so extreme that the mind would be shut down altogether.

One's answer to Kahn, then, is that nuclear weapons make either corpses or, at best, hypochondriacs of us all. Kahn's absurd image is again based on other, more genuinely manageable disasters, where accurate estimates of physical capacity can combine with discipline to produce genuinely stoic and constructive behavior. But the image has nothing to do with the kind of destruction and lethal radiation effects that would occur in nuclear war, and little to do with the way people react to radiation fears in general.

There is also the related *illusion of recovery*. The supposition behind this illusion is that there will be an outside world to come in and help. Again the projection Kai Erikson and I made is relevant. We anticipate the most extreme form of collective trauma stemming from a rupture of the patterns of social existence, with no possibility of outside help.

The international doctors antinuclear movement has devoted itself to dispelling the medical side of the illusion. In our systematic presentations of the overwhelming medical consequences of nuclear war, we have rejected outright the concept of medical contribution to recovery. The concept itself is more a product of prenuclear times and wars: the injured would be treated by doctors, who would do their duty and stay at their posts, healing all those who could be healed. Our message in the doctors' movement is, in effect: In a nuclear war, don't expect us to patch you up. You'll be dead and we'll be dead too. And whatever tiny bands of survivors might exist will, at least for a while, be at a stone-age level of struggle for the means of maintaining life, with little capacity either to heal or to be healed.

Not surprisingly, these various illusions tend to accompany one another, as again illustrated in the convictions of Edward Teller and Herman Kahn. Teller informs us that "rational behavior" consists of "courage," "readiness," and being "prepared to survive an all-out nuclear attack." For this we must "have adequate shelters for our entire population" as well as "plans and stockpiles [food and equipment] so that after an all-out attack, we could recover"; and also maintain "secure retaliatory forces to make sure that any all-out attack against our nation could be answered with a crushing counter-blow." And he reassures us:

> . . . this much is certain: Properly defended, we can survive a nuclear attack; we can dig out of the ruins; we can recover from the catastrophe. . . . As a nation, we shall survive, and our democratic ideals and institutions will survive with us, if we make adequate preparations for survival now—and adequate preparations are within our reach and our capabilities.[5]

Kahn also tells us that a "reasonable" individual (by which he means nonhypochondriac) who survives a future nuclear war "should be willing to accept, *almost with equanimity* [italics added], somewhat larger risks than those to which we subject our industrial workers in peace time. We should not magnify our view of the costs of the war inordinately because such postwar risks added to the wartime casualties"[6] (emphasis added).

One could claim that these strange words were written twenty years ago, but in 1980 Colin S. Gray and Keith Payne wrote an article entitled "Victory Is Possible," in which they insist that "If American nuclear power is to support U.S. foreign policy objectives, the United States must possess the ability to wage nuclear war rationally." That means that "The United States should plan to defeat the Soviet Union and to do so at a cost that would not prohibit U.S. recovery . . .

[and] identify war aims that in the last resort would contemplate the destruction of Soviet political authority and the emergence of a postwar world order compatible with Western values."[7]

In these three stated attitudes we encounter another fundamental deception, the *illusion of rationality*. In these last three statements we encounter assumptions about the "reasonable individual," and we are urged toward "rational behavior" and told (by Gray and Payne) to be ready to "wage nuclear war rationally." The illusion is of a "systems rationality"—of a whole structure of elements, each in "logical" relation to the other components and to the whole. We are dealing here with nothing less than the logic of madness—of the social madness and collective "mad fantasy" we spoke of earlier.

In all nuclear weapons' discourse we must be on guard for such bootlegging of claims to reason and rationality. For the builders of such "rational systems"—of weapons and ideas—are, like the rest of us, confronted by an image they really do not know how to cope with, and seek desperately to call forth, however erroneously, the modern virtue of reason. . . .

NOTES

1. Edward Teller with Allen Brown, *The Legacy of Hiroshima* (Garden City: Doubleday, 1962), pp. 244ff.
2. Robert Jay Lifton, *The Broken Connection: On Death and the Continuity of Life* (New York: Touchstone Books, 1979), pp. 147–62, 330–334. See also, Jerome D. Frank, *Sanity and Survival* (New York: Vintage, 1968).
3. Desmond Ball, "Can Nuclear War be Controlled?" in Adelphi Paper no. 169, The International Institute for Strategic Studies, London (Autumn, 1981).
4. *Boston Globe*, 11 November 1981, p. 1.
5. Teller, *Legacy of Hiroshima*, p. 244.
6. Herman Kahn, *On Thermonuclear War* (Princeton: Princeton University Press, 1961), pp. 42, 71.
7. Colin S. Gray and Keith Payne, "Victory is Possible," *Foreign Policy*, (Summer 1980): 14–27.

37 The Enemy Within

Robert S. Moyer ───────────────────────────────────

Everyone who hasn't slept through the 20th century knows about the Soviet threat, and we do well to take it seriously.

But there are internal threats as well: powerful psychological mechanisms that jeopardize the national security of the United States and the Soviet Union as surely as do missiles and bombers. They include inner defenses that seem to shield us from anxiety over nuclear war but actually increase its dangers; preconceptions that exacerbate old antagonisms by filtering and distorting new information; and inaccurate assumptions and inconsistencies in policy that undermine our strategy of nuclear deterrence.

Since the dawn of the nuclear age some 40 years ago, neither the United States nor the Soviet Union has done much to quell these internal threats. Perhaps by exposing the enemy within, catching it in the act on the world stage, we can curtail the escalation of tension without.

INNER DEFENSES

Nuclear weapons threaten our very existence, and threat produces anxiety. Since there is as yet no physical defense against nuclear attack, many of us seek protection against the anxiety produced by guilt, inner conflict and external stress through defense mechanisms such as denial, dehumanization and projection.

Denial. Faced with an unpleasant reality, many people refuse to acknowledge its existence. Some people consider nuclear war "unthinkable" and

Excerpted from Robert S. Moyer, "The Enemy Within," *Psychology Today*, vol. 19, January, 1985, pp. 31–35. Reprinted with permission from Psychology Today magazine. Copyright © 1985 American Psychological Association.

steer conversation away from the topic. Others protect themselves against anxiety by denying that a nuclear war would have terrible consequences. T. K. Jones, Deputy Under Secretary of Defense, has apparently worked out the details for avoiding extermination: "Dig a hole, cover it with a couple of doors and then throw three feet of dirt on top. . . . If there are enough shovels to go around, everybody's going to make it." The Federal Emergency Management Agency (FEMA), though not as sanguine about cheating nuclear death entirely, maintains that with adequate civil-defense measures, "performance in a large-scale, mid 1980s attack would be on the order of 80 percent survival of the U.S. population if the bulk of the risk-area population had been evacuated to host areas prior to attack and if fallout protection had been developed and other crisis actions taken."

Even those who acknowledge the horror of a nuclear war allay their fear by denying the possibility that one could occur. In an interview immediately following the ABC-TV broadcast of *The Day After*, which simulated the effects of a nuclear attack, Secretary of State George Shultz agreed that the program "dramatizes the unacceptability" of nuclear war, but reassured everyone that the film doesn't represent "the future at all." Secretary of Defense Caspar Weinberger has similarly maintained, "Our entire strategic program . . . has been developed with the express intention of assuring that a nuclear war will never be fought."

Others who acknowledge danger intellectually deny the feelings appropriate to it. Former Secretary of State Henry Kissinger denounced *The Day After* and asked: "Are we supposed to make policy by scaring ourselves to death?" Stanford biologist Paul Ehrlich countered this rhetorical question with one of his own: "If one should not get emotional about the possibility of the horrible deaths of one's self, one's family and friends, and of the end of civilization, what should one get emotional about?"

Dehumanization. This defense mechanism, a popular propaganda tool, leads people to regard or portray others as subhuman. If we view our enemies as beasts we don't feel so guilty about killing them. As Joseph Goebbels, Hitler's minister of propaganda, said in a 1938 radio broadcast, "I keep on hearing voices that assert that Jews are also humans. To this I can only reply that bedbugs are also animals, but extremely disagreeable ones."

We and the Soviets don't go quite this far to make ourselves more comfortable, but we do denigrate each other's attitudes and ethics. The Soviet press in July 1982 implied that President Reagan is a "pygmy," saying, "Pygmies have often tried to cast aspersions on the immortal name of V.I. Lenin." Reagan, for his part, dehumanizes the Soviets when he says things like ". . . we have a different regard for human life than those monsters do."

Projection. We tend to attribute our undesirable characteristics to others. If we have aggressive impulses, or if our group has done terrible things, we can allay our anxiety by believing that our enemies are guilty of the same offenses. Our enemies, naturally, purify themselves by attributing their misdeeds to us.

Pravda, for example, announced in July 1982 that "it is against the Afghan people that an undeclared war is being waged, the main inspirer and organizer of which is, once again, Washington." And it asked, "How many million dollars have been spent in an attempt to use counter-revolutionary forces to crush the socialist system in Poland?" But it was the Soviets who sent troops to Afghanistan and the Soviets who have been the prime manipulators of events in Poland. The United States may make mischief in Afghanistan and Poland, but it hardly measures up to the level of Soviet meddling.

We, too, practice projection, as Reagan did in a May 1982 speech: "The Soviet Union continues to support Vietnam in its occupation of Kampuchea and its massive military presence in Laos. . . . The Soviet Union has provided toxins to the Laotians and Vietnamese for use against defenseless villagers in Southeast Asia." We attack them for the kind of intervention we took in Vietnam years before.

Dehumanization and projection work together. Evil actions can be more readily projected onto subhumans, and people already cloaked with undesirable qualities are easier to dehumanize. Further, since projection often produces a response in kind, a spiral of insults and defamation results, simultaneously widening the gulf between adversaries and aggravating existing tensions.

Once we have reduced our adversaries to subhumans and projected many of our evils onto them, it is easy to see ourselves as good, peace-loving and self-defense-oriented, and portray our enemies as evil, aggressive and warlike. Our adversaries' view, naturally, is a mirror image of our own. Almost any Soviet or American foreign-policy statement will illustrate this point. Reagan, for example, remarked in March 1983, "We will never stop searching for a genuine peace. . . . [the Soviets] are the focus of evil in the modern world." He also warned the United States not to "ignore the facts of history and the aggressive impulses of an evil empire, to simply call the arms race a giant misunderstanding and thereby remove yourself from the struggle between right and wrong, good and evil."

The Soviets, of course, have a different view. As Yuri Andropov explained in September 1983, "The course that the present U.S. administration is pursuing . . . is a militarist course, one that poses a serious threat to peace. . . . The U.S.S.R. wishes to live in peace with all countries, including the U.S. It does not nurture aggressive plans, does not impose the arms race on anyone and does not impose its social system on anyone."

PRECONCEPTIONS

New evidence is rarely regarded strictly on its merits. Rather, what we already know and believe significantly influences how we interpret any new information.

Images. With a firmly held idea of the enemy as evil, people tend to remember evidence that confirms the image and ignore evidence that might contradict it. In the United States, we notice and remember good things about ourselves—our free press—and bad things about the Soviets—their political prisoners. The Soviets notice and remember good things about themselves—they signed SALT II, which the Senate failed to ratify—and bad things about us—we invaded their country in 1918.

Even when the two sides address the same problems, they can bolster their own images by focusing their attention on different aspects of the same issue. In his September 1983 speech to the United Nations General Assembly, Reagan said, "Evidence abounds that we cannot simply assume that agreements negotiated with the Soviet Union will be fulfilled. We negotiated the Helsinki Final Act, but the promised freedoms have not been provided. . . . We negotiated a biological-weapons convention, but deadly yellow rain and other toxic agents fall on Hmong villages and Afghan encampments. We have negotiated arms agreements, but the high level of Soviet encoding hides the information needed for their verification."

Andropov gave the Soviet side in April 1983: "The American administration behaves as if the centuries-old history of international relations and the practice of agreements and treaties does not exist. As is known, the U.S. scuttled the SALT II Treaty and withdrew from a whole series of talks that were making progress or nearing a successful conclusion. I might remind you that the U.S. broke off, and is still avoiding the resumption of, the talks on the general and complete prohibition of nuclear weapons tests, on anti-satellite systems, on the deliveries and sales of conventional arms and on the limitation of military activity in the Indian Ocean. I will add to this the treaties with the Soviet Union on the limitation of the underground testing of nuclear weapons and on nuclear explosions for peaceful purposes, which the United States has not ratified to this day."

Theories of Behavior. Foreign policy and national-security posture also flow from preconceived theories of behavior. In his 1982 State of the Union address Reagan outlined his administration's guiding theory of Soviet behavior: "Winston Churchill, in negotiating with the Soviets, observed that they respect only strength and resolve in their dealings with other nations. That's why we've moved to reconstruct our national defenses." There is certainly nothing wrong with theory-guided foreign policy. The danger to our security arises when theory becomes impervious to contradictory evidence, when predictions about how the adversary should behave overshadow observations of how the adversary does in fact behave.

The Geneva medium-range missile talks, which began November 30, 1981, and ended with a Soviet walkout November 23, 1983, provide an example of preconceived behavior. At Geneva, we thought the Soviets would negotiate seriously because we displayed strength and resolve by developing the MX and threatening to deploy Pershing II and cruise missiles in Europe. In his 1982 State of the Union address Reagan said, "In those talks it is essential that we negotiate from a position of strength. There must be a real incentive for the Soviets to take these talks seriously. This requires that we rebuild our defenses."

The Soviets, however, claimed that the deployment of medium-range missiles in Europe would make it impossible for them to continue negotiating in Geneva. They made this known repeatedly for almost two years. Administration officials stuck with their theory. A failure to deploy the Pershing II, Weinberger said in April 1983, "would reduce the incentive for serious Soviet negotiation." On the day the first Pershing II missiles arrived in West Germany, the Soviets, true to their word, walked out of the Geneva talks.

What happened when the American theories and prophecies failed? Paul Nitze, the chief American negotiator at the talks, said, "As you know, the Soviets did not say they were breaking off the talks absolutely." Reagan added the same day, "They'll come back. . . . I can't believe that it's going to be permanent." Weinberger, in an uncharacteristic burst of enthusiasm, announced one week later that the prospects for negotiation were "better than ever."

The United States and the Soviet Union no doubt will eventually resume negotiations. But, at this writing, more than a year of vital negotiating time has been lost, mainly because of a failure to consider Soviet words and actions as evidence relevant to our theory of Soviet behavior.

The problem for policymakers is to distinguish accurate theories and impressions from faulty ones. Thinking that is guided chiefly by rigid preconceptions is poorly suited to this task. Far from helping us to understand and predict an adversary's behavior, preconceptions perpetuate misunderstanding, make miscalculation more likely and often increase the risks of conflict. . . .

QUESTIONS FOR DISCUSSION

1. What are the "nuclear illusions" described by Lifton? In his view, why are nuclear weapons often the subject of illusions?

2. How would you relate Lifton's analysis of nuclear illusions to evidence of widespread anxiety about nuclear war?

3. According to Moyer, what psychological mechanisms contribute to international misunderstandings? How do they operate?

4. Discuss some possible policy implications of Lifton's and Moyer's analyses.

SUGGESTED READINGS

EINSTEIN, ALBERT and SIGMUND FREUD. "An Exchange of Letters on the Prevention of War." In *Einstein on Peace*, edited by Otto Nathan and Heinz Norden, 188–203. New York: Simon and Schuster, 1960.

FORNARI, FRANCO. *The Psychoanalysis of War*. Bloomington, Ind.: Indiana University Press, 1975.

GIVENS, R. DALE and MARTIN A. NETTLESHIP, eds. *A Discussion on War and Human Aggression*. Hawthorne, N.Y.: Mouton Publishers, 1976.

HILGARTNER, STEPHEN, RICHARD C. BELL, and RORY O'CONNOR. *Nukespeak*. New York: Penguin Books, 1983.

JERVIS, ROBERT. *Perceptions and Misperceptions in International Politics*. Princeton: Princeton University Press, 1976.

LIFTON, ROBERT JAY. *Death in Life: Survivors of Hiroshima*. New York: Touchstone Books, 1976.

WHITE, RALPH K., ed. *Psychology and the Prevention of Nuclear War*. New York: New York University Press, 1986.

Strategies for Preventing Nuclear War

How can nuclear war be prevented? What can be done to reduce the risk that it will occur? What policies and programs could lead to a safer world? These questions are among the most controversial ones in the whole area of nuclear policy. They are also the most important.

Part Four examines strategies for preventing nuclear war, exploring some of the proposals made by participants in the nuclear debate. Chapter XI takes a look at the contemporary peace movement, examining some of its founding statements. The next two chapters examine policies that national governments could take to reduce the risk of nuclear war. Chapter XII looks at negotiated arms control and disarmament agreements, treaties that two or more nations can reach through a process of diplomacy and bargaining. Chapter XIII explores "Unilateral Initiatives for Peace," policies for reducing the risk of nuclear war that a government could adopt unilaterally, without waiting for complicated and time-consuming negotiations. Chapter XIV discusses the strategy of the economic conversion of military facilities to peaceful purposes, a measure that some analysts believe could reduce the domestic pressures for arms production. The final chapter considers international law and international organizations.

Chapter XI

Contemporary Peace Movements

Since the bombing of Hiroshima and Nagasaki, there have been occasional episodes of widespread public concern and activism about nuclear weapons. Following World War II, there was an extensive debate about the proper institutional mechanisms for controlling atomic energy. In the late 1950s and early 1960s, nuclear fallout became an international issue, with worldwide protest against nuclear weapons testing culminating in the Limited Test Ban Treaty, which banned atmospheric tests. At the beginning of the 1980s, nuclear war again emerged as a major political issue, as antinuclear weapons movements burgeoned in the United States and Europe.

Whether the contemporary peace movements will have a lasting political effect remains an open question. But these movements have grown rapidly and have involved many millions of people. Broadly-based grassroots organizations have been joined by groups of professionals—physicians, lawyers, computer specialists, and business executives—in the campaign against the nuclear arms race. It is possible that this trend may increase the ability of peace movements to influence policy. Moreover, in addition to the traditional "peace churches," such as the Quakers, a number of religious organizations, in Europe and the U.S., have issued statements calling for policies that will prevent nuclear war.

This chapter takes a look at contemporary peace movements. We begin with an article by Nigel Young on the European peace movement. The second reading is the "Call for a Nuclear Freeze," the founding document of the "nuclear freeze" campaign in the U.S. Next, we include a resolution passed at the first congress of the International Physicians for the Prevention of Nuclear War, an organization founded in 1980 by American and Soviet physicians. Finally, we include a sampling of statements by religious organizations, such as the Pastoral Letter on War and Peace of the U.S. Catholic Bishops, and statements by several American Protestant bodies.

38 The Contemporary European Anti-Nuclear Movement

Nigel Young ────────────────────────────────

Spontaneously coordinated mass demonstrations in twelve European capitals and several other major cities in 1981, more than any other single event, seemed to have had an effect on political negotiators East and West and given new life to the American peace movement. With between two and three million people taking part, an upsurge of antinuclear weapon activity between October and December 1981, in Bonn, Brussels, Paris, Athens, London, Bucarest, Rome, Madrid, Amsterdam, Helsinki, Oslo, Berlin (Potsdam), Stockholm, and Copenhagen created a sense of transnational unity and a vision of success. These demonstrations revealed a sense of political purpose that rarely had been seen before; indeed, some observers looked back as far as 1848 for such a trans-European movement.

The peace movement fanned out from Holland to Germany and Britain, to Belgium and Italy; it elicited the first signs of an independent peace mood in Eastern Europe; it steadily expanded through Scandinavia and the Mediterranean; it reached the United States; and, last of all, France. These campaigns had their decisive catalyst in the December 1979 NATO decisions to deploy a new generation of missiles in the context of what appeared to many as a new cold war, and of the abandoning of serious disarmament negotiation after SALT 2 was left unratified.

The arms race seemed to be accelerating: there was a feeling that neither the superpowers nor the independent nuclear powers of Europe had

Reprinted with permission from *Peace and Change: A Journal of Peace Research*, Vol. IX, no. 1, Spring 1983, pp. 1–11. Kent State University. Copyright © 1983 by Nigel J. Young.

any will to initiate serious efforts at disarmament or nuclear disengagement. A number of things contributed in Britain at least to a new sense of international tension and potential escalation of the kind we had experienced in the years 1960–63: the debate over the Moscow Olympic boycott, the propaganda use of the Afghan occupation, fears over American adventures in Iran and tensions in the Middle East, the war-fighting rhetoric of some Western leaders, and governmental civil defense preparations. The brash assertiveness of Thatcher and Reagan merely confirmed existing fears, as did the nuclear alerts and accidents of 1980–81, and lent impetus to the groundswell of public opinion throughout Europe.

This was a more transnational and massive protest than anything in the sixties, and it also involved a broader political coalition with new elements contributed during the period of the Vietnam war and by the women's, environmental and antinuclear power movements. These gave a transnational as well as international dimension to the protest, together with new forms of political organizing, less reliance on formal structure and leadership, and a greater political awareness.

The churches were also more centrally involved than they had been in the nuclear disarmament campaigns twenty years earlier. Following the example of the Dutch churches, the Church of England, often called the Tory party at prayer, produced a commission report advocating a non-nuclear Britain. Yet a further new dimension, particularly apparent in Britain, is a grassroots movement for peace education in and out of schools, organized from the bottom by parents, pupils, teachers, local counselors, and churches. This was of such strength that the British Secretary of State attacked it publicly as "appeasement" education and the Government widely circulated its own counter-propaganda. In response, the Labour Party Shadow Education Secretary called for peace studies in every school.

Three elements are particularly important in understanding the re-emergence of widespread militant opposition to nuclear weapons in Europe after sixteen years: the revival of unilateralism as an idea; the prior strength of the antinuclear power movement and the acceptance of direct action; and the grassroots character of the new movement, rooted in local communities. The second and third elements were not present in the antinuclear weapons campaigns of the late 1950s when the movement was much more sponsored and created from the top down, where direct action was more controversial, and where opposition to civil nuclear energy was lacking.

A GATHERING MOVEMENT

The Dutch were undeniably first in both their political campaigns (No to the Neutron Bomb, 1976) and the broader mass appeal led by the Dutch Interchurch Peace Council (IKV).[1] The former came from the World Peace Council initiative, and was undoubtedly an aligned movement opposing Western militarism but not the Soviet Union's arsenal. Despite this, and unlike most Communist peace fronts since the fifties (a notable exception was the 1950 Stockholm appeal), it did gain a mass following and with it a shift of political emphasis away from its origins. It naturally took up the next unifying single issue, the Cruise Missiles and their deployment, in 1979–80. But it was the strength and determination of the unilateralist, church-based IKV which took the peace movement to the heart and center of Dutch politics and made it a potentially majority campaign, thus swinging the left *and* center against deployment, indeed, transcending political boundaries in raising the moral issue of first strike weapons or genocidal threats of nuclear annihilation.

The IKV started in 1967 with annual peace weeks and later introduced the slogan, "let us rid the world of nuclear arms—starting with the Netherlands," dramatized by the symbol of a group of people pushing back a giant missile. Hundreds of local groups based on broad religious, political, and class coalitions have created

a swing in Dutch opinion against deployment of NATO missiles and against even budgetary contributions to deployment elsewhere. Somewhat over sixty percent of public opinion supports this policy. This extension of the campaign shows the way in which the movement's unilateralism has been internationalized across Dutch frontiers. The campaign was echoed both in Flanders (the VAK) and French-speaking Belgium (the CNARD). Both Brussels and Amsterdam have seen massive demonstrations as well as major conferences and conventions (1981–82). The Dutch campaign has been cited to illustrate that it was the effectiveness of *unilateral* nuclear disarmament (i.e. initiatives) policy as a platform which re-generated in Holland and then throughout Europe, protests of the scale of the global movements of 1957–63 and 1966–70 (Vietnam) periods and contributed to the growth of a transnational peace movement.

In Britain, meanwhile, the unilateralist Campaign for Nuclear Disarmament (CND) founded in 1958, and the Committee of 100, had faded into insignificance during the mid-sixties when they were overshadowed by the growing protests against the Indo-China wars.

An organizational rump remained, but it was completely dominated by the old style British Communist Party and there were real questions in 1979 about whether CND should be revived in light of a slowly growing membership or should be succeeded by an entirely new, nonaligned, and internationalist organization. Probably the key factor in salvaging CND was the secretaryship of Bruce Kent, a Catholic Monsignor seconded to peace work who helped steer it through a sea of political difficulties to become the largest single peace coalition in Britain. However, and unlike the fifties or sixties, a multitude of other local peace groups, women's peace programs, peace action groups, peace camps, anti-Cruise missile campaigns, European disarmament (END), World Disarmament, and other groups have arisen in each locality. Sometimes they paralleled CND groups, and sometimes they took the place of CND groups but were, often, affiliated with CND. As a result, CND's membership grew from under 3,000 in 1979 to over 50,000 in 1982, increasing by 35,000 in 1980–81 alone.

There also exists in Britain the World Disarmament Campaign (WDC) created in relation to the first United Nations Special Session on Disarmament (SSDI) in 1978 by Philip Noel Baker (deceased) and Fenner Brockway in order to campaign for nongovernmental, and largely multilateralist, initiatives through the UN Special Session on Disarmament II in New York, in June 1982. Most local peace groups used its petition, and it continues in a limited form despite the setback of disarmament efforts in the second UN session.

Probably the most significant new strategic ingredient in Europe is END, the European Nuclear Disarmament movement, which stemmed from Britain. An appeal drafted by historian E. P. Thompson and edited by Ken Coates was circulated in 1980 by the Bertrand Russell Peace Foundation in Nottingham with support from other Europeans. From the appeal sprang an inchoate END organization of signatories and subscribers with a shadow organization in London which produced a newsletter and organized collateral groups. The Russell group in Nottingham publishes a European bulletin, helps organize the European liaison committee, and publishes END papers. It helped the Brussels convention out of which a more representative European steering group emerged in July 1982, which, in turn, is organizing the major convention in Berlin scheduled for May 1983. The London and Nottingham units cooperate closely, and Russell or END groups exist all over Western and Northern Europe and to some extent in Eastern Europe.

This adds a new dimension to the nuclear disarmament movement: an emphasis on transnational linkage and nonalignment, END campaigns for a nuclear free Europe or a nuclear free zone or zones in Europe (e.g. Nordic,[2] Balkan, Central European). Based on these demands it tries to link the national unilateralist and multilateralist groups into a common third force crossing national boundaries and bridging East and West. Its slogans, "No Cruise, No SS20s" or "an end to NATO and the Warsaw Pact," a nuclear free zone "from Poland to Portugal" (or "Atlantic to the Urals") have been accused of being a crude attempt at even-handedness, naive about the possibilities of unfreezing the cold war or generating an independent peace movement in the East.

In response, END argues that such a political shakeup is an essential part of any strategy to disarm Europe: forcing both the superpowers back into their national fortresses of mutual assured destruction is utopics with a strong dash of strategic realism. This analysis can be applied also to the political situation within each country, for each has become politically frozen. For decades, the social democratic, labor, and communist parties have been part of the cold war freeze, inhibiting new breakthroughs, and especially in northern Europe, END has had to work outside them as an autonomous and extraparliamentary force (although some left-wing socialists, and others, especially in Germany, have responded to the new initiatives with flexibility).

END recognizes that greater Europe is a key sector if theatre nuclear weapons are to be deployed alongside the battlefield ones already in place. The paralysis of Europe represented by Communist party government in the East, and even the Social-Democratic governments in the West, can be alleviated only by a cross-national and nongovernmental campaign built from within the regions and communities which challenges the hegemony of the nuclear monoliths and lesser "independent" nuclear powers of France and Britain.

The major debates in the British peace movement remain, as in the sixties, the issue of alignment, NATO membership, the role of British peace activity vis-a-vis Europe, and, the relationship with the British Labour Party (where the unions and the left-wing retain somewhat fragile control through Michael Foot, but have taken decisive votes against nuclear weapons). Civil disobedience has been a much less divisive issue than in 1960–61 when it split CND. The overwhelming consensus accepts massive direct, nonviolent action and training for it as necessary to obstruct deployment. This shift in opinion is partly because of civil disobedience campaigns of 1959–63 and the direct actions against Polaris and US bases and partly, in the seventies, because of those against nuclear power plants. Not least, civil disobedience has new respect because of admiration for the symbolic witness of the strongly feminist camps at Greenham Common (scheduled with Comiso in Sicily as one of the first sites for Cruise missiles) and Molesworth: these are among at least ten peace camps now in Britain and there are others in Germany, Italy, and Holland.

END undoubtedly has been a significant ingredient in all this. Its influence owes much to the writings and speeches of its leading figures: E. P. Thompson, radical historian; Mary Kaldor, writer on the arms race; Bruce Kent and Dan Smith, also active in CND; Ken Coates and others from the Russell Peace Foundation; the late Peggy Duff, formerly secretary of both CND and the International Confederation for Disarmament and Peace; and Stuart Holland and a number of individual Labour MP's. One effect of END in Britain has been to create pressure on CND to be clearly nonaligned between East and West, to broaden to an internationalist and European approach, and also to open up dialogue between unilateralists and multilateralists around the ideas of reciprocal initiatives and regional nuclear free zones.

In this debate, movements like CND question whether "multilateral" approaches or calls for "general and complete disarmament" by negotiation, or bilateral arms control or limitation, are either sincere or effective campaigning platforms.

It is often not appreciated in countries like the USA where the peace movements are not significantly unilateralist, how crucial this debate has been in Europe. CND, IKV or Svenske Freds (Sweden), each of whom call for major action by each country *regardless* of what others do, tend to be polarized from those who argue for conditional steps relating to bilateral or multilateral negotiation (e.g. missile trade-offs). It can be argued that "unilateralism" alone has been the necessary but not sufficient factor in the rise of the European peace movement. What is also necessary is building a pattern of such unilateral, graduated steps across Europe—East and West—as a program and strategy that becomes multilateral at the level of the movement *as well as* in talks between political leaders.

In each country and region there has been an aspiration to direct the European movement. In Holland the IKV, in Germany the Greens, in Britain CND/END, and elsewhere the Eurocommunists (Italy). END offers the best hope of a synthesis of all of these, while recognizing the special role—theoretically and practically—of movements like the German and the Dutch. END also gave to the local grassroots movements the idea that they could create their own *local* nuclear free zones by winning 130 British local authorities (including the whole of Wales) to the idea, creating community nuclear free zones, and then pairing them with nuclear free municipalities on the European continent.[3] Through END many British peace activists have also been brought into contact with the grassroots activism and ideas of the European movement. This has been a critical factor in internationalizing movements like the British, which were narrowly insular and inward looking, broadening their programs and outlooks.

The movement in West Germany especially illustrates the community basis of opposition to nuclear power which has so powerfully fed the nuclear weapons protest there. Because Germany, East and West, is the likely first victim and atomic battlefield of any theater nuclear war, protest there has special significance, and it is to Berlin that peace activists will go in May 1983 for the major European Nuclear Disarmament convention. The movement in the Federal Republic has made some inroads into the Social Democratic Party (SDP), and many deputies opposed Cruise and Pershing deployment and supported the large demonstrations of 1981. Out of them came the Krefeld appeal, a manifesto backed by hundreds of local groups and millions of signatures. A similar appeal was circulated in Denmark and Norway with similar impact.

The political alignments in the Federal Republic are somewhat similar to those in Britain and Holland, except that the state's political harassment is far more severe, the antinuclear power movement was stronger and more militant and, as a result the Greens (Die Grönen) have emerged as the third political force in German electoral contests, gaining 8% in the Hessen state elections and 9% in Hamburg.[4]

Die Grönen represent a freshly programmatic approach to peace politics with a synthesis of antimilitarism, ecology, feminism, local and worker democracy, and political decentralism. Such syntheses are now emerging more strongly in other parts of Northern Europe and especially Scandinavia. Petra Kelly's emergence as a key spokesperson and the writings and speeches of the emigre Rudolf Bahro are symptomatic of this tendency. Countercultural politics run stronger in Germany than anywhere else, and the influence of the extraparliamentary New Left of the sixties and seventies remains more noticeable. Being so close to military, political, and psychological frontiers, the ideological problems of East/West alignment and nonalignment, of reunification or separate development, are complex and fraught, the dangers of escalation closer to reality. In response, the demonstrations in Germany have been some of the largest and most dramatic.

Thus, the emergence of the "ploughshares" movement in East Germany and the Berlin Appeal is especially significant. Initially based on Protestant and youth opposition to military service (opposition that is also widespread in West Germany) and support for conscientious objection, its base is in the largely evangelical Lutheran churches in the East, but the movement has also shown support for the END position favoring military disengagement and denuclearization of Central Europe, including both Germanies and possibly Czechoslovakia.

More than in any other European country, one of the bases of the peace movement in Germany is its conscientious objectors who constitute a movement with their own organization. Applications for conscientious objector status have run at a massive rate since the Vietnam war, reaching over 50,000 a year (between 12 and 15% of those eligible for military service). In the East, 4,000 young Germans have written to ask for similar status, although none exists. In the Netherlands, and to a lesser degree in Belgium and Germany one has seen a spread of peace ideas into the armed forces, where there is even a group of dissident generals. Soldiers and officers in uniform appeared in demonstrations in Brussels, Amsterdam and elsewhere.

In France, the so-called peace movement has been dominated by the Moscow-oriented "Mouvement de la Paix" which accepts the French independent "deterrent" as the price for a distance from NATO. However, a new and genuinely nonaligned coalition CODENE (Committee pour le Desarmament Nucleaire) has been formed which links pacifists, independent socialists like the Parti Socialists Unifie (Claude Bourdet), radical Catholic activists, and those who fought the nonviolent campaign against military control on the Larzac plateau. These people demand a nuclear free Europe, an end to the French nuclear role, and an East-West peace movement on a nonaligned basis. They have drawn also on the strong green element in France: the radical ecologists who opposed nuclear power.

In Southern Europe—France, Spain, Italy, and Greece—the existing political formations, socialists and communists, play a far more determining and central role than in Central and Northern Europe and Britain. But the Italian Euro-Communists have been genuinely nonaligned in supporting the peace movement, which coincides with a grassroots upsurge in Sicily, Umbria and elsewhere. Although the Italians were crucial in agreeing to deployment in 1979, they may yet prove to be one of the weakest links in the chain. They also have a central European perspective (from Sicily to Finland) as opposed to a simple East-West one, and support the idea of a Mediterranean "sea of peace." But there are real problems in the Italian movement. Unless it achieves the autonomy of Northern Europe, it will not prevent cruise missiles coming to Comiso. Much depends on the strength of the noncommunists in the broad peace coalition, the Radical party and the pacifists, in sustaining a more spontaneous response.

In Spain, the election of the socialists under Gonzales means a nonnuclear policy whether in or out of NATO. The election of Papandreiou and PASOK in Greece meant that a campaign for the ending of American nuclear military bases had come to power, although the exact timetable and terms of change remain unclear. In both cases the nonaligned orientation of the governments coincides with a similar thrust in nongovernmental circles.

This more assertive autonomy and independence of the movements in Germany, Britain, and the Netherlands vis-a-vis NATO and the Warsaw Pact coincides with the somewhat quiescent official nonaligned positions of Yugoslavia, Austria, Finland, and Sweden, and the gradually more active neutralism of the Irish Republic. Ceaucescu's independent nonnuclear policy for Roumania, while strongly autocratic and nationalist, gives greater credibility to the Balkan's nuclear free zones proposal. The Bulgarian churches also have supported a strongly worded anti-nuclear statement. In Eastern Europe there are, of course, official and government-linked peace committees affiliated with the World Peace Council. But outside Roumania these have little popular support. However, unofficial "independent" peace movements in East Germany, Hungary and Russia have surfaced, and in Poland representatives of "Solidarity" discussed the relationship of human rights to détente and disarmament before and after its repression.

Finally there is the movement in the Nordic area, an interesting and distinct case both in the variety and homogeneity of its responses to the East-West bloc-confrontation from which, even within those countries like Norway and Denmark in NATO, people feel detached. The Norwegian and Danish *No to Atomic Weapons* movements, while largely single issue pressure group campaigns like CND in the sixties, are given wider significance by the Scandinavian historical nonnuclear or nonaligned tradition (as expressed in Swedish neutrality), Norwegian rejection of the EEC, Finland's special but not subservient relation with the Russians, and the Danish relation with other small countries in Europe. The Nordic nuclear free zone, the Swedish third party intervention, Finnish entrepreneurship on Human Rights, confidence building and disengagement, make them both symbolically and really a source of political innovation and détente in Central Europe. An example of this is the Palme proposal for a battlefield nuclear free strip linking a Nordic nuclear free zone with a similar zone in the Balkans. Since 1979 the Norwegian and Danish campaigns have shown a significant challenge to NATO deployment policies and nuclear budgets, renouncing the stationing of nuclear warheads in crisis.[5] Also in the Nordic countries the women's peace movement plays a special and important transnational role. The women's marches from Scandinavia, first to Paris and then to Moscow, have played a key part in spreading the movement symbolically and in establishing cross border links. They have helped to give the women's movement a major role in the peace movement and, like the human arm-chain linking the US and Russian embassies in Stockholm, have made this *transnationalism* more real, inspiring groups elsewhere, as at Greenham.

It is probably clear from this brief survey that the new peace movement in Europe is so complex and varied that a short article cannot do it justice. It certainly is better informed, more plural, probably larger, clearly ready to move towards a more political and militant strategy than was the movement of the sixties. It also appears that nonviolence is taken a great deal more seriously by the current movements, both in relation to their own actions and as a potential alternative form of resistance to aggression, than by previous ones. The new activism is distinguished also by the re-emergence of unilateralism as a departure point for nonalignment, by the prior strength of the antinuclear power effort and its organizational experience, and by a relatively stronger base in local communities.

On the other hand, to talk of a "new" peace movement is only to say that this one is a coalition of new and old elements. It includes in fact the various prophetic minorities, the full range of accumulated peace traditions of the past with a rich historical experience: liberal and socialist internationalists, Communist internationalists, religious and radical pacifists, nonviolent (Gandhian) revolutionaries, independent Marxists, anarchists, and antimilitarists, together with groups largely new to the antinuclear weapons campaigns—ecologists, feminists, and the antinuclear power groups. To all of these one must add a new generation of activists, many of them young and new to protests or resistance politics, and an active women's peace movement.[6]

CURRENT CHALLENGES

The key problems, not only in Britian but above all in France and even in Holland and Scandinavia, are with a residual tendency to narrow down the campaigns to purely national and single issue movements focusing on one party (usually the Labour, or in Italy, Communist Party), one weapon system (Cruise, the Neutron bomb or Trident), and one national political arena (i.e. "little englandism"). To "refuse Cruise" is simple and emotive, but it is problematic both tactically and ideologically.

It is here that the new consciousness raising and peace educational work is most critical in sustaining a transnational and indeed global consciousness, a sense of the larger Europe and not just NATO or the EEC, but including the neutral and nonaligned strip (Finland, Sweden, Switzerland, Austria, Yugoslavia, as well as Ireland) and the Eastern European countries and European Russia. It is here that third party intervention and initiatives for disengagement and detente become crucial ideas enlarging the strategic vision of more parochial peace groups, and force them to confront the cultural and political and underpinnings of a unified and nonnuclear "greater Europe." The Italian campaign for the Mediterranean as a sea of peace is a further complement to this, involving nuclear free initiatives (Sicily, Malta, Greece, etc.). Comiso is its symbol.

The peace movements between 1958 and 1963 lacked (and this is where END's nonaligned populism is so relevant) a practical neutralism that had an activist, and nongovernmental underpinning. Thus when the Rapacki plan emerged in the fifties, it could not easily be linked to ideas of campaigns of "positive neutralism" or popular protest; it was a plan for political negotiators, and when CND tried to adopt such a proposal in 1963 (Steps Towards Peace), it lost touch with its own rank and file.[7] But now the situation is different: such plans can be linked to a grassroots upsurge of protest and pressure. The idea of a Europe free of the nuclear giants now has great unifying appeal. The potential for linking different national movements exists in an entirely new way because since 1963, the world has seen the Vietnam war, the experiences of the New Left (e.g. of 1968), and the Russian incursions in Czechoslovakia and later the repression of "Solidarity." The nuclear free zone idea is no longer remote from popular understandings and movements, and the transnationalism is much more solidly based, as the women's peace marches across Europe and various international gatherings have demonstrated.

Of course the difficulties are immense; the struggle over nonalignment is not yet won. And the movement by sections of the traditional left to an anti-NATO position might prove premature and divisive as well as tactically disastrous unless a policy of opposing the Warsaw Pact is pursued equally vigorously. The denuclearization of NATO would have a profound effect, if it did not actually result in dismantling the alliance. Accordingly, it appears to many ENDers (however much they dislike NATO politically) tactically stupid and publicly alienating to call for withdrawal from NATO alone when the peace movement appears to be winning a majority public opinion on the nuclear weapons issue in many or most Western European (NATO) countries, when the clear majority in these countries also still identifies with the Western alliance as long as the Warsaw Pact exists intact. Once the lobbying within NATO to denuclearize it fails then there must of course be second thoughts. There are other crucial obstacles: the problems of the repression of the peace movements in Germany (East and West), in Russia, and in Czechoslovakia, and in Turkey. The problem of Poland; the issues of human rights in all these and other countries; the tentative survival of the unofficial peace movement in GDR and now in Hungary; and the top down character of the officially sponsored peace movement in Roumania: the lack, until recently, of a significant peace movement in France. Then there are old fears of a reunified (if denuclearized) Germany felt by French and Russians alike.

All these make transitional strategies and linkages at times look like utopian dreams; certainly the Falklands war temporarily ruptured the internationalism of the British and European movements, just as the repression in Poland dashed many peace movement hopes of a massive political thaw in the East. Both these events, and the militaristic speeches of Western defense spokesmen and women at the SSDII, confirmed the continuation of cold war hostility, tension, and the lesser national chauvinisms. But the signs are that the peace movement has survived those blows and is recovering its momentum.

As defense expenditure, inflation, and unemployment rise together in Britain and elsewhere, right wing governments like Thatcher's who defy such moves are seeing a slow but sure erosion in their popular support. It is not impossible that in 1983–84, a new parliament with a minority Labour unilateralist party in opposition, probably with Liberal support, (a Liberal Party that is on paper opposed to Cruise missiles, Trident, and US nuclear bases) the British Social Democratic Party (SDP) itself may be pressured to go along with its alliance partner. It also is now moving towards a less bellicose posture, but towards conventional rearmament —but has not gained seats. Even moderate conservatives are now rethinking issues of first strike, and battlefield nuclear weapons, as well as the combat role of tactical weapons in Europe. Inspired by the Myrdals and Olaf Palme, Sweden, under its new government, is moving towards playing a more critical and catalytic role in Europe, not only in Nordic areas, but with other (Southern) neutrals in pressuring for Central European détente—a strip of disengagement.

Thus the position is almost unrecognizable from two years ago. The center of gravity has lurched towards the peace movement's platform, as is shown by the dramatic move in moderate opinion from 40% to 56–58% against "Cruise" and Trident, between 1981 and 1982.[8] Such a shift gives much greater legitimacy to civil disobedience and direct action. When the Church of England came out with its commission report recommending a nonnuclear Britain, it was accused of being the peace movement at prayer, and Mrs. Thatcher criticized it after the Falklands memorial in St. Paul's Cathedral for praying for the Argentinian dead. To some extent this rebounded.

Nevertheless there does exist a somewhat unholy peace alliance between religious pacifists, nuclear pacifists and pro-Moscow peace fronts and old style communists, which fails to grasp the real political nettles. The crucial danger is that simple, emotive, single issue national campaigns (like those on Cruise) which have attainable objectives could produce (in the UK), all the mistakes of the sixties. The campaign could founder on Michael Foot's leadership or on the success or failure of the Cruise campaign. Above all it could lose its nonaligned internationalism on a simple anti-American "out-of-NATO" isolationist platform, easily outmaneuvered and co-opted or defeated, especially if founded on opposition to one or two weapons systems. The pressures against Foot going it alone will be massive (internally and, from the US, externally), even if 58% of the electorate is behind such a decision. Only a broad internationalist stance, with an alternative *foreign* and *defense* policy, can sustain such a move, an alternative defense commission and other groups have worked feverishly to provide such policies and to help educate public opinion for such alternatives.

These problems are paralleled in Holland, Belgium, Norway, and Denmark, and only in Germany does the peace movement seem potentially able to surmount them. The civil disobedience campaigns of the coming months will, however, shift the focus back from elite negotiations back to communal grassroots action from where the longer term vision and strategy may spring. At Comiso and Greenham, in international camps and mass confrontations, at Berlin and in transnational debate and dialogue the peace movement may make this final strategic leap from its communal base to a global strategy.

This inevitably raises the issues of the American movement. The Nuclear Freeze Campaign is difficult to integrate into the European movement because, like zero option, it would be a substantial step back for almost every peace group except the vaguest multilateralist ones, reducing dramatically their present demands. But there is much to be done in the US on NFZ's and MX, on first strike or first use, on deployment, and on preventing financial pressures on unilateralist governments in Europe, that will be complementary to the European movement. The two movements need to understand each other and the different contexts in which they both operate. Tactical differences in the short term do not disguise the fundamental solidarity of the long term vision. Certainly isolationism is the very last thing that either peace movement needs or wants, which is why the principle of reciprocity and the echo in Eastern Europe is so essential, both officially and unofficially. The US movement has been more advanced in peace education and information than the European since

the sixties, but it has to educate itself about the European movement and also to communicate with it. To articulate its own strategies in relation to a transcontinental demand for a nuclear free Europe, for disengagement, for an end to political and cultural polarities: that could be, but need not be, a traumatic period in transatlantic politics. There are potential dangers there, but that is no reason to cease the effort when so many new possibilities and hopes are being realized.

NOTES

1. See Jim Forest and Peter Herby, "Hollanditis: Europe's Plague of Peace," *IFFOR Report* (Jan. 1982): 1–15; Mient Jan Farber, "The Peace Movement in Europe," *Gandhi Marg* 4 (May/June 1982) :288–97.

2. See "A Nuclear Weapons Free Zone in the Nordic Countries" by Erik Alfsen and others in *Bulletin of Peace Proposals* 13 (1982) :2–10, and J. Grepstead, "Norway and the Struggle for Nuclear Disarmament," paper presented at the World Conference on Atomic Weapons, Tokyo, Hiroshima, and Nagasaki, 3–9 August 1981. (Duplicated.) See also S. Lodgard, "A Nuclear Free Zone in the North," *Bulletin of Peace Proposals* 1 (1980) :33–39, and an article in 1982 Stockholm International Peace Research Institute *Yearbook*.

3. See Ken Coate's article in *END Spring Papers* 2 (1982), "Nuclear Free Zones in Britain."

4. For an impression of the "Green's" attitudes, see the interview with one of their main spokespersons, Petra Kelly, in *Newsweek*, July 12, 1982, p. 56.

5. See articles by Gripstead, Barthe, Lodgard, and Alfsen in *Bulletin of Peace Proposals*.

6. See R. Steinke, "Is the Peace Movement a Single Issue Movement?," in *END Papers* 3 (Autumn 1982); and also Fred Singleton, "Comment," *West Yorkshire END, Newsletter* (July/August 1982).

7. See Young, *An Infantile Disorder?* ch. 4; and also John Minnion and Philip Bolsover, eds. *The CND Story*; and R. Taylor and C. Pritchard, *The Protest Makers* (London: Pergamon, 1981).

8. These findings were published by *Sanity*, the journal of CND in October 1982.

39 Proposal for a Mutual U.S.–Soviet Nuclear-Weapon Freeze

Randall Forsberg

To improve national and international security, the United States and the Soviet Union should stop the nuclear arms race. Specifically, they should adopt a mutual freeze on the testing, production and deployment of nuclear weapons and of missiles and new aircraft designed primarily to deliver nuclear weapons. This is an essential, verifiable first step toward lessening the risk of nuclear war and reducing the nuclear arsenals.

The horror of a nuclear holocaust is universally acknowledged. Today, the United States and the Soviet Union possess 50,000 nuclear weapons. In half an hour, a fraction of these weapons can destroy all cities in the northern hemisphere. Yet over the next decade, the USA and USSR plan to build over 20,000 more nuclear warheads, along with a new generation of nuclear missiles and aircraft.

The weapon programs of the next decade, if not stopped, will pull the nuclear tripwire tighter. Counterforce and other "nuclear warfighting" systems will improve the ability of the USA and USSR to attack the opponent's nuclear forces and other military targets. This will increase the pressure on both sides to use their nuclear weapons in a crisis, rather than risk losing them in a first strike.

Such developments will increase hairtrigger readiness for a massive nuclear exchange at a time when economic difficulties, political dissension, revolution and competition for energy supplies may be rising worldwide. At the same time, more countries may acquire nuclear weapons. Unless we change this combination of trends, the danger of nuclear war will be greater in the late 1980s and 1990s than ever before.

Rather than permit this dangerous future to evolve, the United States and the Soviet Union should stop the nuclear arms race.

A freeze on nuclear missiles and aircraft can be verified by existing national means. A total freeze can be verified more easily than the complex SALT I and II agreements. The freeze on warhead production could be verified by the Safeguards of the International Atomic Energy Agency. Stopping the production of nuclear weapons and weapon-grade material and applying the Safeguards to US and Soviet nuclear programs would increase the incentive of other countries to adhere to the Nonproliferation Treaty, renouncing acquisition of their own nuclear weapons, and to accept the same Safeguards.

A freeze would hold constant the existing nuclear parity between the United States and the Soviet Union. By precluding production of counterforce weaponry on either side, it would eliminate excuses for further arming on both sides. Later, following the immediate adoption of the freeze, its terms should be negotiated into the more durable form of a treaty.

A nuclear-weapon freeze, accompanied by government-aided conversion of nuclear industries, would save at least $100 billion each in US and Soviet military spending (at today's prices) in 1981–1990. This would reduce inflation. The savings could be applied to balance the budget, reduce taxes, improve services, subsidize renewable energy, or increase aid to poverty-stricken third world regions. By shifting personnel to more labor-intensive civilian jobs, a nuclear-weapon freeze would also raise employment.

Stopping the US-Soviet nuclear arms race is the single most useful step that can be taken

Originally published by the Nuclear Freeze Campaign, 1980.

now to reduce the likelihood of nuclear war and to prevent the spread of nuclear weapons to more countries. This step is a necessary prelude to creating international conditions in which:

- further steps can be taken toward a stable, peaceful international order;
- the threat of first use of nuclear weaponry can be ended;
- the freeze can be extended to other nations; and
- the nuclear arsenals on all sides can be drastically reduced or eliminated, making the world truly safe from nuclear destruction.

STATEMENT ON THE NUCLEAR-WEAPON FREEZE PROPOSAL

Scope of the Freeze

(1) Underground nuclear tests should be suspended, pending final agreement on a comprehensive test ban treaty.

(2) There should be a freeze on testing, production and deployment of all missiles and new aircraft which have nuclear weapons as their sole or main payload. This includes:

U.S. Delivery Vehicles	Soviet Delivery Vehicles
In Production:	*In Production:*
Improved Minuteman ICBM	SS-19 ICBM
Trident I SLBM	SS-N-18 SLBM
Air-launched cruise missile	SS-20 IRBM
(ALCM)	Backfire Bomber
In Development:	*In Development:*
MX ICBM	SS-17, SS-18, SS-19
Trident II SLBM	ICBM improvements
Long-range ground- and	New ICBM
sea-launched cruise	New SLBM (SS-N-20)
missiles (GLCM, SLCM)	
Pershing II IRBM	
New bomber	

(3) The number of land- and submarine-based launch tubes for nuclear missiles should be frozen. Replacement subs could be built to keep the force constant, but with no net increase in SLBM tubes and no new missiles.

(4) No further MIRVing or other changes to existing missiles or bomber loads would be permitted.

All of the above measures can be verified by existing national means of verification with high confidence.

The following measures cannot be verified nationally with the same confidence, but an effort should be made to include them:

(5) Production of fissionable material (enriched uranium and plutonium) for weapon purposes should be halted.

(6) Production of nuclear weapons (bombs) should be halted.

There are two arguments for attempting to include these somewhat less verifiable steps. First, with a halt to additional and new delivery vehicles, there will be no need for additional bombs. Thus, production of weapon-grade fissionable material and bombs would probably stop in any event. Second, the establishment of a *universal* ban on production of weapon-grade fissionable material and nuclear bombs, verified by international inspection as established now for non-nuclear-weapon states under the Non-proliferation Treaty and the International Atomic Energy Agency, would greatly strengthen that Treaty and improve the prospects for halting the spread of nuclear weapons.

The Agreement to Freeze

The US and Soviet governments should announce a moratorium on all further testing, production and deployment of nuclear weapons and nuclear delivery vehicles, to be verified by national means. The freeze would be followed by negotiations to incorporate the moratorium in a treaty. The negotiations would cover supplementary verification measures, such as IAEA inspections; and possible desirable exceptions from the freeze, such as an occasional confidence test.

This procedure follows the precedent of the 1958–61 nuclear-weapon test moratorium, in which testing was suspended while the USA, USSR and UK negotiated a partial test ban treaty.

Relation to SALT Negotiations

The bilateral freeze is aimed at being introduced in the early 1980s, as soon as sufficient popular and political support is developed to move the governments toward its adoption.

The freeze would prevent dangerous developments in the absence of a SALT treaty. It would preclude exploitation of loopholes in past treaties and, at the same time, satisfy critics who are concerned that the SALT process may not succeed in stopping the arms race.

The freeze does not replace the SALT negotiating process, but should supplement and strengthen it. The freeze could be adopted as a replacement for SALT II or as an immediate follow-on, with the task of putting the moratorium into treaty language the job of SALT III.

The Case for a Nuclear-Weapon Freeze

There are many reasons to support a halt to the nuclear arms race at this time:

Parity —There is widespread agreement that parity exists between US and Soviet nuclear forces at present.

Avoiding "Nuclear Warfighting" Developments —The next generation US and Soviet nuclear weapons improve "nuclear warfighting" capabilities—that is, they improve the ability to knock out the enemy's forces in what is termed a "limited" nuclear exchange. Having such capabilities will undermine the sense of parity, spur further weapon developments and increase the likelihood of nuclear war in a crisis, especially if conflict with conventional weapons has started. It is of overriding importance to stop these developments.

Stopping the MX and New Soviet ICBMs — Specifically, a freeze would prevent the deployment of new and improved Soviet ICBMs, which are expected to render US ICBMs vulnerable to preemptive attack. This would obviate the need for the costly and environmentally-destructive US mobile MX ICBM, with its counterforce capability against Soviet ICBMs. That, in turn, would avoid the pressure for the USSR to deploy its own mobile ICBMs in the 1990s.

Stopping the Cruise Missile —The new US cruise missile, just entering production in an air-launched version and still in development in ground- and sea-launched versions, threatens to make negotiated, nationally-verified nuclear arms control far more difficult. Modern, low-flying, terrain-guided cruise missiles are relatively small and cheap and can be deployed in large numbers on virtually any launching platform: not only bombers, but also tactical aircraft, surface ships, tactical submarines, and various ground vehicles. They are easy to conceal and, unlike ICBMs, their numbers cannot be observed from satellites. If the United States con-

tinues the development and production of cruise missiles, the USSR will be likely to follow suit in 5–10 years; and quantitative limits on the two sides will be impossible to verify. A freeze would preclude this development.

Preserving European Security —A freeze would also prevent a worsening of the nuclear balance in Europe. To date, the USSR has replaced less than half of its medium-range nuclear missiles and bombers with the new SS-20 missile and Backfire bomber. The United States is planning to add hundreds of Pershing II and ground-launched cruise missiles to the forward-based nuclear systems in Europe, capable of reaching the USSR. Negotiations conducted *after* additional Soviet medium-range weapons are deployed are likely to leave Europe with more nuclear arms on both sides and with less security than it has today. It is important to freeze before the Soviet weapons grow to large numbers, increasing pressure for a US response and committing both sides to permanently higher nuclear force levels.

Stopping the Spread of Nuclear Arms — There is a slim chance of stopping the spread of nuclear weapons if the two superpowers stop their major nuclear arms race. The freeze would help the USA and USSR meet their legal and political obligations under the Nonproliferation Treaty. It would make the renunciation of nuclear weapons by other countries somewhat more equitable and politically feasible. In addition, a US—Soviet freeze would encourage a halt in the nuclear weapon programs of other countries which are known or believed to have nuclear weapons or nuclear-weapon technology. These are Britain, France and China, with publicly acknowledged nuclear weapon programs, and India, Israel and South Africa, without acknowledged programs.

Timing —There is a unique opportunity to freeze US and Soviet nuclear arms in the early 1980s. The planned new US and Soviet ICBMs and the US Pershing II and ground-launched cruise missile are not scheduled to enter production until 1982 or later. The Soviets have offered to negotiate the further deployment of their medium-range nuclear forces and submarine-based forces. Given the pressure to respond to new weapons on both sides and the existing nuclear parity, an equally opportune time for a freeze may not recur for many years.

Popular Appeal —Campaigns to stop individual weapon systems are sometimes treated as unilateral disarmament or circumvented by the development of alternative systems. The pros and cons of the SALT II Treaty are too technical for the patience of the average person. In contrast, an effort to stop the development and production of all US and Soviet nuclear weapons is simple, straightforward, effective and mutual; and for all these reasons it is likely to have great popular appeal. This is essential for creating the scale of popular support that is needed to make nuclear arms control efforts successful.

Economic Benefits —Although nuclear forces take only a small part of US and Soviet military spending, they do cost some tens of billions of dollars annually. About half of these funds go to existing nuclear forces, while half are budgeted for the testing, production and deployment of new warheads and delivery systems. A nuclear-weapon freeze, accompanied by government-aided conversion of nuclear industries to civilian production, would yield several important economic benefits:

- About $100 billion each (at 1981 prices) would be saved by the United States and the Soviet Union over the period from 1981 to 1990 in unnecessary military spending.
- The savings could be applied to balance the budget; reduce taxes; improve services now being cut back; subsidize home and commercial conversion to safe, renewable energy resources; or increase economic aid to poverty-stricken third world regions, thereby defusing some of the tinderboxes of international conflict.
- With the shift of personnel to more labor-intensive civilian jobs, employment would rise. At the same time, the highly inflationary pressure of military spending would be mitigated.

Verification

The comprehensive nature of a total freeze on nuclear weapon testing, production and deployment (and, by implication, development) would facilitate verification.

Long-range bomber and missile production would be proscribed. The letter of assurance attached to the draft SALT II Treaty that the USSR will not increase its rate of production of Backfire bombers indicates not only *deployment* but also *production* of the relatively large aircraft and missiles in question can be observed with considerable confidence. While concealed production and stockpiling of aircraft and missiles is theoretically possible, it would be extraordinarily difficult to accomplish with no telltale construction or supply. Any attempt would require the building or modification of plants and the development of new transport lines that are not operational at present. It would also involve high risks of detection and high penalties in worsening relations without offering any significant strategic advantage.

Verification of a ban on *tests* of missiles designed to carry nuclear weapons can be provided with high confidence by existing satellite and other detections systems. Here, too, a comprehensive approach is easier to verify than a partial or limited one.

Verification of aircraft, missile and submarine *deployments*, by specific quantity, is already provided under the terms of the SALT II and SALT I Treaty language. Verifying *no* additional deployments or major modifications will be considerably easier, in fact, than checking compliance with specific numerical ceilings in a continually changing environment.

Verification of a comprehensive nuclear *weapon test* ban, the subject of study and negotiation for many years, has been determined to be possible within the terms of the existing draft comprehensive test ban treaty.

40 Statement of the International Physicians for the Prevention of Nuclear War

It is difficult for us, as physicians, to describe adequately the human suffering that would ensue a nuclear war. Hundreds of thousands would suffer third-degree burns, multiple crushing injuries and fractures, hemorrhage, secondary infection, and combinations of all of these. When we contemplate disasters, we often assume that abundant medical resources and personnel will be available. But contemporary nuclear war would inevitably destroy hospitals and other medical facilities, kill and disable most medical personnel, and prevent surviving physicians from coming to the aid of the injured because of widespread radiation dangers. The hundreds of thousands of burned and otherwise wounded people would not have any medical care as we now conceive of it: no morphine for pain, no intravenous fluids, no emergency surgery, no antibiotics, no dressings, no skilled nursing, and little or no food or water. The survivors will envy the dead.

It is known from the Japanese experience that in the immediate aftermath of an explosion, and for many months thereafter, the survivors suffer not only from their physical injuries—radiation sickness, burns, and other trauma—but also from profound psychological shock caused by their exposure to such overwhelming destruction and mass death. The problem is social as well as individual. The social fabric upon which human existence depends would be irreparably damaged.

Those who did not perish during the initial attack would face serious—even lifelong—dangers. Many exposed persons would be at increased risk, throughout the remainder of their lives, of leukemia and a variety of malignant tumors. The risk is emotional as well as physical. Tens of thousands would live with the fear of developing cancer or of transmitting genetic defects, for they would understand that nuclear weapons, unlike conventional weapons, have memories—long, radioactive memories. Children are known to be particularly susceptible to most of these effects. Exposure of fetuses would result in the birth of children with small head size, mental retardation, and impaired growth and development. Many exposed persons would develop radiation cataracts and chromosomal aberrations. . . .

Nuclear war would be the ultimate human and environmental disaster. The immediate and long-term destruction of human life and health would be on an unprecedented scale, threatening the very survival of civilization.

The threat of its occurrence is at a dangerous level and is steadily increasing. But even in the absence of nuclear war, invaluable and limited resources are being diverted unproductively to the nuclear arms race, leaving essential human, social, medical, and economic needs unmet.

For these reasons, physicians in all countries must work toward the prevention of nuclear war and for the elimination of all nuclear weapons. Physicians can play a particularly effective role because they are dedicated to the prevention of illness, care of the sick and protection of human life; they have special knowledge of the problems of medical response in nuclear war; they can work together with their colleagues without regard to national boundaries; and they are edu-

From Ruth Adams and Susan Cullen, eds., *The Final Epidemic: Physicians and Scientists on Nuclear War.* Reprinted by permission of *The Bulletin of the Atomic Scientists*, a magazine of science and world affairs. Copyright © 1981 by the Educational Foundation for Nuclear Science, Chicago, IL 60637.

cators who have the opportunity to inform themselves, their colleagues in the health professions, and the general public.

WHAT PHYSICIANS CAN DO TO PREVENT NUCLEAR WAR:

- Review available information on the medical implications of nuclear weapons, nuclear war and related subjects.
- Provide information by lectures, publications and other means to the medical and related professions and to the public on the subject of nuclear war.
- Bring to the attention of all concerned with public policy the medical implications of nuclear weapons.
- Seek the cooperation of the medical and related professions in all countries for these aims.

- Develop a resource center for education on the dangers of nuclear weapons and nuclear war.
- Encourage studies of the psychological obstacles created by the unprecedented destructive power of nuclear weapons which prevent realistic appraisal of their dangers.
- Initiate discussion of development of an international law banning the use of nuclear weapons similar to the laws which outlaw the use of chemical and biological weapons.
- Encourage the formation in all countries of groups of physicians and committees within established medical societies to pursue the aims of education and information on the medical effects of nuclear weapons.
- Establish an international organization to coordinate the activities of the various national medical groups working for the prevention of nuclear war.

41 The Pastoral Letter of the U.S. Catholic Bishops on War and Peace

Apprehension about nuclear war is almost tangible and visible today. Nuclear war threatens the existence of our planet; this is a more menacing threat than any the world has known. It is neither tolerable nor necessary that human beings live under this threat.

As Pope John Paul II said at Hiroshima: "From now on it is only through a conscious choice and through a deliberate policy that humanity can survive." As Americans, citizens of the nation which was first to produce atomic weapons, which has been the only one to use them and which today is one of the handful of nations capable of decisively influencing the course of the nuclear age, we have grave human, moral and political responsibilities to see that a "conscious choice" is made to save humanity.

A CHURCH AT THE SERVICE OF PEACE

The Catholic tradition on war and peace is a long and complex one, reaching from the Sermon on the Mount to the statements of Pope John Paul II. At the center of the Church's teaching on peace and at the center of all Catholic social teaching are the transcendence of God and the dignity of the human person. The human person is the clearest reflection of God's presence in the world; all of the Church's work in pursuit of both justice and peace is designed to protect and promote the dignity of every person. For each per-

This condensed version of the U.S. Catholic Bishops' Pastoral Letter on War and Peace was published in *Catholic Update* in 1983. Copyright © 1983 by the United States Catholic Conference.

son not only reflects God, but is the expression of God's creative work and the meaning of Christ's redemptive ministry.

Christians approach the problem of war and peace with fear and reverence. God is the Lord of life, and so each human life is sacred; modern warfare threatens the obliteration of human life on a previously unimaginable scale. The sense of awe and "fear of the Lord" which former generations felt in approaching these issues weighs upon us with new urgency.

We believe that the Church, as a community of faith and social institution, has a proper, necessary and distinctive part to play in the pursuit of peace. Because peace, like the Kingdom of God itself, is both a divine gift and a human work, the Church should continually pray for the gift and share in the work. We are called to be a Church at the service of peace.

WHAT THE BIBLE TELLS US ABOUT PEACEMAKING

For us as believers, the sacred Scriptures provide the foundation for confronting the dilemma of war and peace today. In the Old Testament, all notions of peace must be understood in light of Israel's relation to God. Peace is always seen as a gift from God and as fruit of God's saving activity. Peace is a special characteristic of the covenant; when the prophet Ezekiel looked to the establishment of the new, truer covenant, he declared that God would establish an everlasting covenant of peace with the people (Ezekiel 37:26).

As Christians we believe that Jesus is the

Messiah or Christ so long awaited. And as the one in whom the fullness of God was pleased to dwell—through whom all things in heaven and on earth were reconciled to God—Jesus made peace by the blood of the cross (Colossians 1:19–20). Jesus proclaimed the reign of God in his words and made it present in his actions. In God's reign the poor are given the Kingdom, . . . the meek inherit the earth, . . . and peacemakers are called the children of God (Matthew 5:3–10).

All who hear Jesus are repeatedly called to forgive one another. The forgiveness of God, which is the beginning of salvation, is manifested in communal forgiveness and mercy. Jesus also described God's reign as one in which love is an active, life-giving, inclusive force. He called for a love which went beyond family ties and bonds of friendship to reach even those who were enemies (Matthew 5: 44–48; Luke 6:27–28).

Jesus Christ, then, is our peace, and in his death-resurrection he gives God's peace to our world. In him God has indeed reconciled the world, made it one, and has manifested definitively that his will is this reconciliation, this unity between God and all peoples, and among the people themselves. The way to union has been opened, the covenant of peace established.

Because we have been gifted with God's peace in the risen Christ, we are called to our own peace and to the making of peace in our world. As disciples and as children of God it is our task to seek for ways in which to make the forgiveness, justice and mercy, and love of God visible in a world where violence and enmity are too often the norm.

THE RIGHT TO LEGITIMATE DEFENSE

The protection of human rights and the preservation of peace are tasks to be accomplished in a world marked by sin and conflict of various kinds. The Church's teaching on war and peace establishes a strong presumption against war which is binding on all: it then examines when this presumption may be overridden, precisely in the name of preserving the kind of peace which protects human dignity and human rights.

As Vatican II made clear, "Certainly war has not been rooted out of human affairs. As long as the danger of war remains and there is no competent and sufficiently powerful authority at the international level, governments cannot be denied the right to legitimate defense once every means of peaceful settlement has been exhausted. Therefore, government authorities and others who share public responsibility have the duty to protect the welfare of the people entrusted to their care and to conduct such grave matters soberly.

"But it is one thing to undertake military action for the just defense of the people, and something else again to seek the subjugation of other nations. Nor does the possession of war potential make every military or political use of it lawful. Neither does the mere fact that war has unhappily begun mean that all is fair between the warring parties" (*Pastoral Constitution on the Church in the Modern World. #79*).

The Christian has no choice but to defend peace, properly understood, against aggression. This is an inalienable obligation. It is the *how* of defending peace which offers moral options.

THOSE WHO BEAR ARMS AND THOSE WHO DON'T

We stress this principle because we observe so much misunderstanding about both those who resist bearing arms and those who bear them. Great numbers from both traditions provide examples of exceptional courage, examples the world continues to need.

Of the millions of men and women who have served with integrity in the armed forces, many have laid down their lives. Many others serve today throughout the world in the difficult and demanding task of helping to preserve the "peace of a sort" of which the Council speaks.

We see many deeply sincere individuals who, far from being indifferent or apathetic to world evils, believe strongly in conscience that they are best defending true peace by refusing to bear arms. In some cases they are motivated by their understanding of the gospel and the life and death of Jesus as forbidding all violence. No government, and certainly no Christian, may simply assume that such individuals are mere pawns of conspiratorial forces or guilty of cowardice.

Catholic teaching sees these two distinct moral responses as having a complementary relationship in the sense that both seek to serve the common good. They differ in their perception of how the common good is to be defended most effectively, but both responses testify to the Christian conviction that peace must be pursued and rights defended within moral restraints and in the context of defining other basic human values.

HOW THE 'JUST-WAR' THEORY LIMITS WAR

The moral theory of the "just-war" or "limited-war" doctrine begins with the presumption which binds all Christians: We should do no harm to our neighbors. Just-war teaching has evolved as an effort to prevent war. Only if war cannot be rationally avoided does the teaching then seek to restrict and reduce its horrors. It does this by establishing a set of rigorous conditions which must be met if the decision to go to war is to be morally permissible. Such a decision, especially today, requires extraordinarily strong reasons for overriding the presumption *in favor of peace* and *against* war. The conditions for a just war are as follows:

1. *Just cause.* War is permissible only to confront "a real and certain danger," i.e., to protect innocent life, to preserve conditions necessary for decent human existence and to secure basic human rights.
2. *Competent authority.* War must be declared by those with responsibility for public order, not by private groups or individuals.
3. *Comparative justice.* In essence: Which side is sufficiently "right" in a dispute, and are the values at stake critical enough to override the presumption against war? Do the rights and values involved justify killing? Given techniques of propaganda and the ease with which nations and individuals either assume or delude themselves into believing that God or right is clearly on their side, the test of comparative justice may be extremely difficult to apply.
4. *Right intention.* War can be legitimately intended only for the reasons set forth above as a just cause.
5. *Last resort.* For resort to war to be justified, all peaceful alternatives must have been exhausted.
6. *Probability of success.* This is a difficult criterion to apply, but its purpose is to prevent irrational resort to force or hopeless resistance when the outcome of either will clearly be disproportionate or futile.
7. *Proportionality.* This means that the damage to be inflicted and the costs incurred by war must be proportionate to the good expected by taking up arms.

Because of the destructive capability of modern technological warfare, the principle of proportionality (and that of discrimination) takes on special significance. Today it becomes increasingly difficult to make a decision to use any kind of armed force, however limited initially in intention and in the destructive power of the weapons employed, without facing at least the possibility of escalation to broader, or even total, war and to the use of weapons of horrendous destructive potential.

"Indeed, if the kind of weapons now stocked in the arsenals of the great powers were to be employed to the fullest, the result would be the almost complete reciprocal slaughter of one side by the other, not to speak of the widespread devastation that would follow in the world and the deadly after-effects resulting from the use of such weapons" (*Pastoral Constitution*, #80). To destroy civilization as we know it by waging such a "total war" as today it *could* be waged would be a monstrously disproportionate response to aggression on the part of any nation.

Just response to aggression must also be *discriminate*: it must be directed against unjust aggressors, not against innocent people caught up in a war not of their making. The Council therefore issued its memorable declaration: "Any act of war aimed indiscriminately at the destruction of entire cities or of extensive areas along with their population is a crime against God and man himself. It merits unequivocal and unhesitating condemnation."

Side by side with the just-war theory throughout Christian history has been the tradition of nonviolence. One of the great nonviolent figures was St. Francis of Assisi.

While the just-war teaching has clearly been in possession for the past 1,500 years of Catholic thought, the "new moment" in which we find ourselves sees the just-war teaching and nonviolence as distinct but interdependent methods of evaluating warfare. They diverge on some specific conclusions, but they share a common presumption against the use of force as a means of settling disputes. Both find their roots in the Christian theological tradition: each contributes to the full moral vision we need in pursuit of a human peace. We believe the two perspectives support and complement one another, each preserving the other from distortion.

NEW MORAL QUESTIONS

Nuclear weapons particularly and nuclear warfare as it is planned today raise new moral questions. As indicated in a statement from the Holy See to the United Nations in 1976, the arms race is to be condemned as a danger, an act of aggression against the poor and a folly which does not provide the security it promises. And according to a study of the Pontifical Academy of Sciences commissioned by Pope John Paul II, "Recent talk about winning or even surviving a nuclear war must reflect a failure to appreciate a medical reality: Any nuclear war would inevitably cause death, disease and suffering of pandemonic proportions and without the possibility of effective medical intervention. That reality leads to the same conclusion physicians have reached for life-threatening epidemics throughout history: Prevention is essential for control."

We believe it is necessary for the sake of prevention to build a barrier against the concept of nuclear war as a viable strategy for defense. There should be a clear public resistance to the rhetoric of "winnable" nuclear wars, or unrealistic expectations of "surviving" nuclear exchanges and strategies of "protracted nuclear war." We oppose such rhetoric. We seek to encourage a public attitude which sets stringent limits on the kind of actions our own government and other governments will take on nuclear policy.

SOME PRINCIPLES ON THE USE OF NUCLEAR WEAPONS

1. *Counterpopulation warfare.* Under no circumstances may nuclear weapons or other instruments of mass slaughter be used for the purpose of destroying population centers or other predominantly civilian targets. Retaliatory action, whether nuclear or conventional, which would indiscriminately take many wholly innocent lives, lives of people who are in no way responsible for reckless actions of their government, must also be condemned.

2. *The initiation of nuclear war.* We do not perceive any situation in which the deliberate initiation of nuclear warfare on however restricted a scale can be morally justified. Nonnuclear attacks by another state must be resisted by other than nuclear means. Therefore, a serious moral obligation exists to develop non-nuclear defensive strategies as rapidly as possible.

3. *Limited nuclear war.* Unless certain questions (namely, those challenging the ability of military leaders to keep a nuclear exchange limited) can be answered satisfactorily, we will continue to be highly skeptical about the real meaning of "limited." One of the criteria of the just-war tradition is a reasonable hope of success in bringing about justice and peace. We must ask whether such a reasonable hope can exist once nuclear weapons have been exchanged. The burden of proof remains on those who assert that meaningful limitation is possible.

On deterrence. Essentially deterrence means dissuasion of a potential adversary from initiating an attack or conflict, often by the threat of unacceptable retaliatory damage. Pope John Paul II makes this statement about the morality of deterrence: "In current conditions 'deterrence' based on balance, certainly not as an end in itself but as a step on the way toward a progressive disarmament, may still be judged morally acceptable. Nonetheless, in order to ensure peace, it is indispensable not to be satisfied with this minimum, which is always susceptible to the real danger of explosion."

In concert with the evaluation provided by Pope John Paul II, we have arrived at a strictly conditional moral acceptance of deterrence. We cannot consider such a policy adequate as a long-term basis for peace.

SOME SPECIFIC RECOMMENDATIONS

In light of the present size and composition of both the U.S. and Soviet strategic arsenals, *we recommend*:

1. Support for immediate, bilateral, verifiable agreements to halt the testing, production and deployment of new nuclear weapons systems.

2. Support for negotiated bilateral deep cuts in the arsenals of both superpowers, particularly those weapons systems which have destabilizing characteristics.

3. Support for early and successful conclusion of negotiations of a comprehensive test ban treaty.

A BETTER SYSTEM OF GLOBAL INTERDEPENDENCE

We are now entering an era of new, global interdependencies requiring global systems of governance to manage the resulting conflicts and ensure our common security. We live in a global age with problems and conflicts on a global scale. Either we shall learn to resolve these problems together or we shall destroy one another. Mutual security and survival require a new vision of the world as one interdependent planet. We call for the establishment of some form of global authority adequate to the needs of the international common good.

Papal teaching of the last four decades has not only supported international institutions in principle, it has supported the United Nations specifically. Pope Paul VI said to the U.N. General Assembly: "The edifice which you have constructed must never fail; it must be perfected and made equal to the needs which world history will present. You mark a stage in the development of mankind from which retreat must never be admitted, but from which it is necessary that advance be made."

THE CHALLENGE BEFORE US

To be a Christian, according to the New Testament, is not simply to believe with one's mind, but also to become a doer of the Word, a wayfarer with and a witness to Jesus. These comments about the meaning of being a disciple or a follower of Jesus today are especially relevant to the quest for genuine peace in our time.

We urge every diocese and parish to implement balanced and objective educational programs to help people of all age levels to understand better the issues of war and peace. We reject criticism of the Church's concern with these issues on the ground that it "should not become involved in politics." We are called to move from discussion to witness and action.

Reverence for life. No society can live in peace with itself or with the world without a full awareness of the worth and dignity of every human person and of the sacredness of all human life (James 4:1–2). Violence has many faces: oppression of the poor, deprivation of basic human rights, economic exploitation, sexual exploitation and pornography, neglect or abuse of the aged and the helpless, and innumerable other acts of inhumanity. Abortion in particular blunts a sense of the sacredness of human life. In a society where the innocent unborn are killed wantonly, how can we expect people to feel righteous revulsion at the act or threat of killing noncombatants in war?

The arms race presents questions of conscience we may not evade. As American Catholics we are called to express our loyalty to the deepest values we cherish: peace, justice and security for the entire human family. National goals and policies must be measured against that standard. Given the growth in our understanding of the evergrowing horror of nuclear war, we must shape the climate of opinion which will make it possible for our country to express profound sorrow over the atomic bombing in 1945. Without that sorrow, there is no possibility of finding a way to repudiate future use of nuclear weapons.

In a democracy the responsibility of the nation and that of its citizens coincide. Nuclear weapons pose especially acute questions of conscience for American Catholics. The virtue of patriotism means that as citizens we respect and honor our country, but our very love and loyalty make us examine carefully and regularly its role in world affairs, asking that it live up to its full potential as an agent of peace with justice for all people.

We reaffirm our desire to participate in a common public effort with all men and women of goodwill who seek to reverse the arms race and secure the peace of the world.

CALLED TO BE BUILDERS OF PEACE

We are the first generation since Genesis with the power to virtually destroy God's creation. We cannot remain silent in the face of such danger. Peacemaking is not an optional commitment. It is a requirement of our faith. We are called to be peacemakers, not by some movement of the moment, but by our Lord Jesus.

It is our belief in the risen Christ which sustains us in confronting the awesome challenge of the nuclear arms race. Respecting our freedom, he does not solve our problems, but sustains us as we take responsibility for his work of creation and try to shape it in the ways of the Kingdom. We believe his grace will never fail us.

42 Pronouncements on Nuclear Arms by Four American Protestant Bodies

A. UNITED PRESBYTERIAN CHURCH

The "Call to Halt the Nuclear Arms Race," approved in May 1981 by the General Assembly of the United Presbyterian Church in the U.S.A., supports a nuclear freeze, a drastic reduction in nuclear arms, and a reallocation of resources to help the poor in the Third World. It is reprinted here in full.

To improve national and international security, the United States and the Soviet Union should stop the nuclear arms race. Specifically, they should adopt a mutual freeze on the testing, production, and deployment of nuclear weapons and of missiles and new aircraft designed primarily to deliver nuclear weapons. This is an essential, verifiable first step toward lessening the risk of nuclear war and reducing the nuclear arsenals.

The horror of a nuclear holocaust is universally acknowledged. Today, the United States and the Soviet Union possess 50,000 nuclear weapons. In half an hour, a fraction of these weapons can destroy all cities in the northern hemisphere. Yet over the next decade, the United States and the U.S.S.R. plan to build over 20,000 more nuclear warheads, along with a new generation of nuclear missiles and aircraft.

The weapon programs of the next decade, if not stopped, will pull the nuclear tripwire tighter. Counterforce and other "nuclear warfighting" systems will improve the ability of the United States and the U.S.S.R. to attack the opponent's nuclear forces and other military targets. This will increase the pressure on both sides to use

their nuclear weapons in a crisis, rather than risk losing them in a first strike.

Such developments will increase hairtrigger readiness for massive nuclear exchange at a time when economic difficulties, political dissension, revolution, and competition for energy supplies may be rising worldwide. At the same time, more countries may acquire nuclear weapons. Unless we change this combination of trends, the danger of nuclear war will be greater in the late 1980s and 1990s than ever before.

Rather than permit this dangerous future to evolve, the United States and the Soviet Union should stop the nuclear arms race.

A freeze on nuclear missiles and aircraft can be verified by existing national means. A total freeze can be verified more easily than the complex SALT I and II agreements. The freeze on warhead production could be verified by the Safeguards of the International Atomic Energy Agency. Stopping the production of nuclear weapons and weapon-grade material and applying the Safeguards to U.S. and Soviet nuclear programs would increase the incentive of other countries to adhere to the Nonproliferation Treaty, renouncing acquisition of their own nuclear weapons, and to accept the same Safeguards.

A freeze would hold constant the existing nuclear parity between the United States and Soviet Union. By precluding production of counterforce weaponry on either side, it would eliminate excuses for further arming on both sides. Later, following the immediate adoption of the freeze, its terms should be negotiated into the more durable form of a treaty.

A nuclear weapons freeze, accompanied by government-aided conversion of nuclear industries, would save at least $100 billion each in

From Ernest W. Lefever and E. Stephen Hunt, eds., *The Apocalyptic Premise* (pp. 341–348). Italic introductions © 1982 by Ethics and Public Policy Center, Washington D.C. Reprinted by permission.

U.S. and Soviet military spending (at today's prices) in 1981–1990. This would reduce inflation. The savings could be applied to balance the budget, reduce taxes, improve services, subsidize renewable energy, or increase aid to poverty-stricken Third World regions. By shifting personnel to more labor-intensive civilian jobs, a nuclear weapons freeze could also raise employment.

Stopping the U.S.–Soviet nuclear arms race is the single most useful step that can be taken now to reduce the likelihood of nuclear war and to prevent the spread of nuclear weapons to more countries. This step is a necessary prelude to creating international conditions in which:

- further steps can be taken toward a stable, peaceful international order;
- the threat of first use of nuclear weaponry can be ended;
- the freeze can be extended to other nations; and
- the nuclear arsenals on all sides can be drastically reduced or eliminated, making the world truly safe from nuclear destruction.

B. EPISCOPAL CHURCH

In a pastoral letter entitled "Identity, Pilgrimage, and Peace," the Episcopal House of Bishops in September 1982 calls the "arms race" a "strange insanity that grips the governments of the great nations." The bishops say that a U.S. "policy of deterrence that intends the use of nuclear weapons in a massive first strike against whole cities" is evil, that U.S. spending on nuclear arms is "an act of aggression" against starving children, and that the "American fever to match the Soviet Union weapon for weapon appears to be damaging the personality structure of a whole generation." A major portion of the "Peace" section of the letter follows.

Your bishops perceive the nuclear arms race as the most compelling issue in the world public order. The arms race summons all morally serious people to action. Christians and Jews and all religious people are joined by multitudes of no religious allegiance.

Thus the voice we raise in this Pastoral Letter mingles with a chorus across the earth, in and out of the churches. The chorus mounts each precious day of life on the planet, warning against the strange insanity that grips the governments of the great nations.

We take seriously the lament of the former American ambassador to the Soviet Union, George Kennan, who writes, "We are losing rational control of weapons. . . . We are becoming victims of the monster we have created. I see it taking possession of our imagination and behavior, becoming a force in its own right, detaching itself from the political differences that inspired it, and leading both parties inexorably to the war they no longer know how to avoid."

Most of the passion for arms in America appears to rise from fear of a predatory power. If Russia would slow down, we would slow down. If Russia would stop, we would stop. Who is free? Who is hostage to whom? From whence shall come the moral freedom to break the spiraling thrall of seeking security in instruments that only purchase a diminished safety for both countries and a mounting insecurity for the entire world?

Does any Episcopalian seriously wish at this perilous moment for a muted Church, unready to risk the corrective clarity of a heavenly citizenship? This citizenship transcends in prophetic judgment all political systems. All human freedom finally depends on the value of human life and the freedom from paralyzing fear that a transcendent allegiance bestows.

We urge upon our people the detachment of penitence and forgiveness. Such detachment quiets our worldly fevers. It reveals our true identity. We are pilgrims with first fealty to the crucified and risen Christ. Holding that identity clearly and firmly, Christians may still disagree on the means of peace. We need not disagree, however, on our need for a dedicated military. We recognize that devoted Christians serve in our armed forces, which forces we need lest the United States signal irresolution. Still, we assert that a morally serious people must consider three aspects of American policy.

First, it is our understanding that the United States has never disavowed a policy of deterrence that intends the use of nuclear weapons in a massive first-strike against whole cities and land areas should it serve the national interest in warfare. Two hundred population centers are now targeted for such a strike. We ask, how can this policy be squared with a free nation's commitment to justice when it intends the calculated killing of millions of human beings who themselves are not on trial? We hold such an intention to be evil.

Second, the undiminished production and deployment of nuclear weapons, even if never used, consume economic, technical, and natural resources of astronomically rising proportions. The squandering of such resources constitutes an act of aggression against the thirty children who die every sixty seconds of starvation in the world. It is a callous act of indifference to the 500 million people of the world who are underfed. We declare this to be immoral and unjust.

Third, American fever to match the Soviet Union weapon for weapon appears to be damaging the personality structure of a whole generation. Current studies show that our children are growing up with a pervasive sense of fear, menace, cynicism, sadness, and helplessness. The effect of these eroding inner sensations is to impair the ability to form stable values, a sense of continuity and purpose, and a readiness for responsibility. Insofar as a belligerent nuclear arms policy distorts the spiritual and moral formation of children, such a policy defeats the free nations from within. The decadence that marks our culture may be of our own making. We believe it can only worsen without a tide of peacemaking witness, especially the steady protest of Christian people who claim their first allegiance, declare their true identity, and recover the bravery of pilgrim people.

We believe it to be the responsibility of the United States to take the bold initiative in nuclear disarmament, and to keep on taking it. The United States was the first to possess a nuclear weapon. The United States is the only nation to have used the weapon in war. If it comes to pass that these weapons, which the United States continues to refine and aim and stockpile, are used in war again, it is difficult to believe that any history a surviving neutral nation might record would fail to fix the blame on the United States.

C. UNITED METHODIST CHURCH

The "Pastoral Letter to a People Called United Methodist" approved by the United Methodist Council of Bishops in May 1982 deals in part with nuclear arms. Like the Presbyterian call, it supports a nuclear freeze, deep cuts in nuclear stockpiles, and a reallocation of resources for civilian purposes. It refers to the U.S.–U.S.S.R. "arms race" as "madness." Portions of the letter are reprinted here.

In 1945 two atomic bombs initiated our current nightmarish dilemma. Today there are 50,000 nuclear weapons deployed or stockpiled. Thousands of these weapons have more than fifty times the lethal power of the bombs dropped on Hiroshima and Nagasaki. Even arguments concerning parity have become irrelevant because of the frightening overkill capacities of both the United States and the Soviet Union.

With military budgets skyrocketing and Cold War rhetoric escalating, the possibility of a nuclear holocaust becomes more and more real. The people of the world, both East and West, are awakening to the fact that we are on the verge of blowing ourselves up. The leaders of the superpowers, with the push of a button, could provide a "final solution" to the human story. Hundreds of millions of people would be burned to death or blown away or reduced to subhuman levels of existence. Networks of transportation and communication would be destroyed. The fabric of the social order would be torn to shreds. Life as we know it would cease to exist. It would be "annihilation without representation."

Because the threat of nuclear destruction looms ever larger and is qualitatively different from any other challenge confronting the human family, the Council of Bishops of the United Methodist Church endorses the Joint Resolution on Nuclear Freeze and Arms Reduction, now sponsored by more than 190 U.S. Senators and members of the House of Representatives. Governments must stop manufacturing nuclear weapons. Deployed weapons must be removed. Stockpiles must be reduced and dismantled. Verification procedures must be agreed upon. Eventual nuclear disarmament is necessary if the human race, as we know it, is to survive.

The Nuclear Freeze Resolution does not call for unilateral disarmament. Rather, it calls upon both the U.S.S.R. and the U.S.A. to halt the manufacture of nuclear weapons, reduce current supplies of nuclear arms, and agree upon verification procedures. Realizing that the superpowers do not trust one another, the serious negotiations called for should be based on mutual self-interest and a commitment to a global future.

Your Council of Bishops calls upon every United Methodist to pray for and work for peace with justice and freedom. Let your voice be heard in your own community. Let your convictions be shared with your state and national lawmakers. Write the President of the United States. We urge United Methodists outside the United States to work in their own communities and with their leaders and governments, as we join together in seeking an end to the arms race.

We must reverse the madness of our present course for the sake of your children, grandchildren, and generations yet unborn.

D. NATIONAL COUNCIL OF CHURCHES

The National Council of Churches of Christ in the U.S.A. is composed of some thirty Protestant and Orthodox denominations, including most of America's mainline bodies. Reprinted below is the "Resolution on a Nuclear Weapons Freeze" adopted by the Governing Board of the Council in May 1981. . . .

The 1981 statement urges "the United States and the Soviet Union to halt the nuclear arms race now by adopting promptly a mutual freeze on all further testing, production, and deployment of weapons and aircraft designed primarily to deliver nuclear weapons." It also supports unilateral initiatives on either side to make such a freeze more likely. . . .

Whereas, the Strategic Arms Limitation Talks (SALT) between the Soviet Union and the United States are in abeyance as a result of events of the last two years; and

Whereas, heightened international tension is leading to sharp increases in the armament programs of the Soviet Union and the United States as well as other nations with a consequent increase in the danger of war; and

Whereas, the National Council of Churches has long held that all the earth's resources are gifts of God, the Lord of Creation, and that men and women have a responsibility to preserve and enhance the created order, not to abuse and destroy it; and

Whereas, the National Council of Churches has consistently stressed the value of human life and God's activity in creation through the reconciling act in Christ whereby we are called to be agents of reconciliation, and

Whereas, representatives of the Orthodox and Protestant Churches of the Soviet Union and of the National Council of Churches, in a joint statement on March 27–29, 1979, entitled "Choose Life," "confessed that seeking our security through arms is, in fact, a false and idolatrous hope, and that true security can be found only in relationships of trust";

Therefore be it resolved that the Governing Board of the National Council of the Churches of Christ in the United States of America:

1. Urges both the United States and the Soviet Union to halt the nuclear arms race now by adopting promptly a mutual freeze on all further testing, production, and deployment of weapons and aircraft designed primarily to deliver nuclear weapons;

2. Until such time as a nuclear freeze by the United States and the Soviet Union may be agreed upon, supports initiatives by either or both that would demonstrate good faith and make it easier for the other to take similar steps; and

3. Encourages all program units of the National Council of Churches to examine their responsibilities and opportunities in providing educational materials and other resources regarding the nuclear freeze to constituent communions; and

4. Calls upon affiliated denominations, their judicatories and congregations, and related councils of churches to consider supporting this call for a nuclear freeze by:

   a. Making available to their membership speeches, printed resources, and audiovisual materials that inform Christians about the reasons for and the importance of such a freeze;

   b. Supporting financially and by direct involvement the movement for a nuclear freeze;

   c. Calling upon their senators and representatives to provide congressional support for implementing such a freeze; and

   d. Urging the President and the Department of State to pursue initiatives leading toward a mutual freeze on the testing, production, and deployment of all nuclear weapons and delivery vehicles.

QUESTIONS FOR DISCUSSION

1. Describe some characteristics of contemporary peace movements. What are their strengths and weaknesses?

2. How would you explain the failure of the nuclear freeze movement to achieve major changes in United States policy?

3. Describe the positions on nuclear issues taken by religious and professional organizations whose statements are reprinted above. In what respects do you agree and disagree with these statements?

4. What, in your opinion, lies ahead for the contemporary movements against the nuclear arms race?

SUGGESTED READINGS

ALBERT, MICHAEL and DAVID DELLINGER, eds. *Beyond Survival: New Directions for the Disarmament Movement*. Boston: South End Press, 1984.

BRIGHT, CHARLES and SUSAN HARDING, eds. *Statemaking and Social Movements: Essays in History and Theory*. Ann Arbor, Mich.: University of Michigan Press, 1984.

DOUGHERTY, JANE E. and ROBERT L. PFLATZGRAFF, JR., eds. *Shattering Europe's Defense Consensus: The Antinuclear Protest Movement and the Future of NATO*. New York: Pergamon-Brassey's, 1985.

McCARTHY, JOHN D. and MAYER N. ZALD. "Resource Mobilization and Social Movements: A Partial Theory," *American Journal of Sociology* 82, no. 6, (May 1977): 1212–1241.

OBERSCHALL, ANTHONY. *Social Conflict and Social Movements*. Englewood Cliffs, N.J.: Prentice-Hall, 1973.

Chapter XII

Negotiating Arms Control and Disarmament

Negotiation between national governments has been an important strategy for reducing the risk of nuclear war. The goal of such negotiations has been to formulate mutually beneficial treaties for nuclear arms control and disarmament.

The term nuclear *disarmament* refers to efforts to reduce the number of nuclear weapons or ban them completely. In contrast, nuclear *arms control* agreements seek to reduce the risk of nuclear war by adjusting the number, types, deployment and testing of nuclear weapons, or by taking steps designed to control crisis situations. While nuclear disarmament efforts have so far made little progress, a number of arms control treaties have been passed. Some of these are bilateral treaties between the United States and the Soviet Union. Others are multilateral treaties, involving a number of nations.

Nuclear arms control treaties now in effect include: the Limited Test Ban Treaty of 1963, which bans testing nuclear weapons in the atmosphere, in outer space and underwater; the Nonproliferation Treaty of 1968, which seeks to control the spread of nuclear weapons; the Antiballistic Missile Treaty of 1972, which places numerical and geographical restrictions on ABM systems; and the Antarctic, Outer-Space and Seabeds treaties, which ban the deployment of nuclear weapons in these locations.

To what extent have previous arms control negotiations been successful? What are the reasons for their successes and failures? What opportunities exist today for arms control and disarmament? What issues should be the focus of negotiations? How can negotiated agreements and international initiatives help prevent nuclear war?

These questions remain the subject of heated debate. This chapter introduces the reader to some of the issues surrounding arms control and disarmament negotiations. The chapter begins by examining the record of arms control and disarmament negotiations, ending with a series of proposals for international initiatives for peace.

The first reading, by Roger Fisher and William Ury, addresses the process of negotiation. They present an approach to negotiation that leads to agreements that resolve conflicting interests fairly, that are durable and efficient, and that tend to improve relations between the parties.

Next, Herbert F. York, a physicist and arms control expert, gives an historical overview of arms-limitation strategies, focusing on treaties and negotiations.

The remaining readings make proposals for bilateral or multilateral initiatives for peace. George Kennan suggests that the United States and Soviet Union each make a 50 percent cut in their nuclear arsenals. Scientists Richard Garwin and Carl Sagan call for a ban on space weapons. William Langer Ury and Richard Smoke propose the establishment of a "nuclear crisis control center," a facility that they believe could help reduce the risk of unintentional nuclear war. And William M. Evan calls for the creation of an international peace research program with an operating budget, derived from contributions from the U.S. and Soviet Union, equal to one-half of one percent of their respective military budgets.

43 Getting to YES

Roger Fisher and William Ury ——————————————

DON'T BARGAIN OVER POSITIONS

Whether a negotiation concerns a contract, a family quarrel, or a peace settlement among nations, people routinely engage in positional bargaining. Each side takes a position, argues for it, and makes concessions to reach a compromise. The classic example of this negotiating minuet is the haggling that takes place between a customer and the proprietor of a secondhand store [see table].

And so it goes, on and on. Perhaps they will reach agreement; perhaps not.

Any method of negotiation may be fairly judged by three criteria: It should produce a wise agreement if agreement is possible. It should be efficient. And it should improve or at least not damage the relationship between the parties. (A wise agreement can be defined as one which meets the legitimate interests of each side to the extent possible, resolves conflicting interests fairly, is durable, and takes community interests into account.)

The most common form of negotiation, illustrated by the above example, depends upon

Customer	*Shopkeeper*
How much do you want for this brass dish?	
	That is a beautiful antique, isn't it? I guess I could let it go for $75.
Oh come on, it's dented. I'll give you $15.	
	Really! I might consider a serious offer, but $15 certainly isn't serious.
Well, I could go to $20, but I would never pay anything like $75. Quote me a realistic price.	
	You drive a hard bargain, young lady. $60 cash, right now.
$25.	
	It cost me a great deal more than that. Make me a *serious* offer.
$37.50. That's the highest I will go.	
	Have you noticed the engraving on that dish? Next year pieces like that will be worth twice what you pay today.

Excerpted from *Getting to Yes: Negotiating Agreement Without Giving In* (pp. 3–14, 45–57), by Roger Fisher and William Ury (Boston: Houghton Mifflin, 1981). Reprinted by permission of Houghton Mifflin Company.

successively taking—and then giving up—a sequence of positions.

Taking positions, as the customer and storekeeper do, serves some useful purposes in a negotiation. It tells the other side what you want; it provides an anchor in an uncertain and pressured situation; and it can eventually produce the terms of an acceptable agreement. But those purposes can be served in other ways. And positional bargaining fails to meet the basic criteria of producing a wise agreement, efficiently and amicably.

Arguing over positions produces unwise agreements

When negotiators bargain over positions, they tend to lock themselves into those positions. The more you clarify your position and defend it against attack, the more committed you become to it. The more you try to convince the other side of the impossibility of changing your opening position, the more difficult it becomes to do so. Your ego becomes identified with your position. You now have a new interest in "saving face"—in reconciling future action with past positions—making it less and less likely that any agreement will wisely reconcile the parties' original interests.

The danger that positional bargaining will impede a negotiation was well illustrated by the breakdown of the talks under President Kennedy for a comprehensive ban on nuclear testing. A critical question arose: How many on-site inspections per year should the Soviet Union and the United States be permitted to make within the other's territory to investigate suspicious seismic events? The Soviet Union finally agreed to three inspections. The United States insisted on no less than ten. And there the talks broke down—over positions—despite the fact that no one understood whether an "inspection" would involve one person looking around for one day, or a hundred people prying indiscriminately for a month. The parties had made little attempt to design an inspection procedure that would reconcile the United States's interest in verification with the desire of both countries for minimal intrusion.

As more attention is paid to positions, less attention is devoted to meeting the underlying concerns of the parties. Agreement becomes less likely. Any agreement reached may reflect a mechanical splitting of the difference between final positions rather than a solution carefully crafted

to meet the legitimate interests of the parties. The result is frequently an agreement less satisfactory to each side than it could have been.

Arguing over positions is inefficient

The standard method of negotiation may produce either agreement, as with the price of a brass dish, or breakdown, as with the number of on-site inspections. In either event, the process takes a lot of time.

Bargaining over positions creates incentives that stall settlement. In positional bargaining you try to improve the chance that any settlement reached is favorable to you by starting with an extreme position, by stubbornly holding to it, by deceiving the other party as to your true views, and by making small concessions only as necessary to keep the negotiation going. The same is true for the other side. Each of those factors tends to interfere with reaching a settlement promptly. The more extreme the opening positions and the smaller the concessions, the more time and effort it will take to discover whether or not agreement is possible.

The standard minuet also requires a large number of individual decisions as each negotiator decides what to offer, what to reject, and how much of a concession to make. Decision-making is difficult and time-consuming at best. Where each decision not only involves yielding to the other side but will likely produce pressure to yield further, a negotiator has little incentive to move quickly. Dragging one's feet, threatening to walk out, stonewalling, and other such tactics become commonplace. They all increase the time and costs of reaching agreement as well as the risk that no agreement will be reached at all.

Arguing over positions endangers an ongoing relationship

Positional bargaining becomes a contest of will. Each negotiator asserts what he will and won't do. The task of jointly devising an acceptable solution tends to become a battle. Each side tries through sheer will power to force the other to change its position. "I'm not going to give in. If you want to go to the movies with me, it's *The Maltese Falcon* or nothing." Anger and resentment often result as one side sees itself bending to the rigid will of the other while its own legitimate concerns go unaddressed. Positional bargaining thus strains and sometimes shatters the relationship between the parties. Commercial enterprises that have been doing business together for years may part company. Neighbors may stop speaking to each other. Bitter feelings generated by one such encounter may last a lifetime.

When there are many parties, positional bargaining is even worse

Although it is convenient to discuss negotiation in terms of two persons, you and "the other side," in fact, almost every negotiation involves more than two persons. Several different parties may sit at the table, or each side may have constituents, higher-ups, boards of directors, or committees with whom they must deal. The more people involved in a negotiation, the more serious the drawbacks to positional bargaining.

If some 150 countries are negotiating, as in various United Nations conferences, positional bargaining is next to impossible. It may take all to say yes, but only one to say no. Reciprocal concessions are difficult: to whom do you make a concession? Yet even thousands of bilateral deals would still fall short of a multilateral agreement. In such situations, positional bargaining leads to the formation of coalitions among parties whose shared interests are often more symbolic than substantive. At the United Nations, such coalitions produce negotiations between "the" North and "the" South, or between "the" East and "the" West. Because there are many members in a group, it becomes more dif-

ficult to develop a common position. What is worse, once they have painfully developed and agreed upon a position, it becomes much harder to change it. Altering a position proves equally difficult when additional participants are higher authorities who, while absent from the table, must nevertheless give their approval.

Being nice is no answer

Many people recognize the high costs of hard positional bargaining, particularly on the parties and their relationship. They hope to avoid them by following a more gentle style of negotiation. Instead of seeing the other side as adversaries, they prefer to see them as friends. Rather than emphasizing a goal of victory, they emphasize the necessity of reaching agreement. In a soft negotiating game the standard moves are to make offers and concessions, to trust the other side, to be friendly, and to yield as necessary to avoid confrontation.

The following table [Table 43–1] illustrates two styles of positional bargaining, soft and hard. Most people see their choice of negotiating strategies as between these two styles. Looking at the table as presenting a choice, should you be a soft or a hard positional bargainer? Or should you perhaps follow a strategy somewhere in between?

The soft negotiating game emphasizes the importance of building and maintaining a relationship. Within families and among friends much negotiation takes place in this way. The

TABLE 43–1

PROBLEM Positional Bargaining: Which Game Should You Play?

Soft	*Hard*
Participants are friends.	Participants are adversaries.
The goal is agreement.	The goal is victory
Make concessions to cultivate the relationship.	Demand concessions as a condition of the relationship.
Be soft on the people and the problem.	Be hard on the problem and the people.
Trust others.	Distrust others.
Change your position easily.	Dig in to your position.
Make offers.	Make threats.
Disclose your bottom line.	Mislead as to your bottom line.
Accept one-sided losses to reach agreement.	Demand one-sided gains as the price of agreement.
Search for the single answer: the one *they* will accept.	Search for the single answer: the one *you* will accept.
Insist on agreement.	Insist on your position.
Try to avoid a contest of will.	Try to win a contest of will.
Yield to pressure.	Apply pressure.

process tends to be efficient, at least to the extent of producing results quickly. As each party competes with the other in being more generous and more forthcoming, an agreement becomes highly likely. But it may not be a wise one. The results may not be as tragic as in the O. Henry story about an impoverished couple in which the loving wife sells her hair in order to buy a handsome chain for her husband's watch, and the unknowing husband sells his watch in order to buy beautiful combs for his wife's hair. However, any negotiation primarily concerned with the relationship runs the risk of producing a sloppy agreement.

More seriously, pursuing a soft and friendly form of positional bargaining makes you vulnerable to someone who plays a hard game of positional bargaining. In positional bargaining, a hard game dominates a soft one. If the hard bargainer insists on concessions and makes threats while the soft bargainer yields in order to avoid confrontation and insists on agreement, the negotiating game is biased in favor of the hard player. The process will produce an agreement, although it may not be a wise one. It will certainly be more favorable to the hard positional bargainer than to the soft one. If your response to sustained, hard positional bargaining is soft positional bargaining, you will probably lose your shirt.

There is an alternative

If you do not like the choice between hard and soft positional bargaining, you can change the game.

The game of negotiation takes place at two levels. At one level, negotiation addresses the substance; at another, it focuses—usually implicitly—on the procedure for dealing with the substance. The first negotiation may concern your salary, the terms of a lease, or a price to be paid. The second negotiation concerns how you will negotiate the substantive question: by soft positional bargaining, by hard positional bargaining, or by some other method. This second negotiation is a game about a game—a "metagame." Each move you make within a negotiation is not only a move that deals with rent, salary, or other substantive questions; it also helps structure the rules of the game you are playing. Your move may serve to keep the negotiations within an ongoing mode, or it may constitute a game-changing move.

This second negotiation by and large escapes notice because it seems to occur without conscious decision. Only when dealing with someone from another country, particularly someone with a markedly different cultural background, are you likely to see the necessity of establishing some accepted process for the substantive negotiations. But whether consciously or not, you are negotiating procedural rules with every move you make, even if those moves appear exclusively concerned with substance.

The answer to the question of whether to use soft positional bargaining or hard is "neither." Change the game. At the Harvard Negotiation Project we have been developing an alternative to positional bargaining: a method of negotiation explicitly designed to produce wise outcomes efficiently and amicably. This method, called *principled negotiation or negotiation on the merits*, can be boiled down to four basic points.

These four points define a straightforward method of negotiation that can be used under almost any circumstance. Each point deals with a basic element of negotiation, and suggests what you should do about it.

PEOPLE: Separate the people from the problem.

INTERESTS: Focus on interests, not positions.

OPTIONS: Generate a variety of possibilities before deciding what to do.

CRITERIA: Insist that the result be based on some objective standard.

The first point responds to the fact that human beings are not computers. We are creatures of strong emotions who often have radically different perceptions and have difficulty communicating clearly. Emotions typically become entangled with the objective merits of the problem. Taking positions just makes this worse because people's egos become identified with their positions. Hence, before working on the substantive problem, the "people problem" should be disentangled from it and dealt with separately. Figuratively if not literally, the participants should come to see themselves as working side by side, attacking the problem, not each other. Hence the first proposition: *Separate the people from the problem.*

The second point is designed to overcome the drawback of focusing on people's stated positions when the object of a negotiation is to satisfy their underlying interests. A negotiating position often obscures what you really want. Compromising between positions is not likely to produce an agreement which will effectively take care of the human needs that led people to adopt those positions. The second basic element of the method is: *Focus on interests, not positions.*

The third point responds to the difficulty of designing optimal solutions while under pressure. Trying to decide in the presence of an adversary narrows your vision. Having a lot at stake inhibits creativity. So does searching for the one right solution. You can offset these constraints by setting aside a designated time within which to think up a wide range of possible solutions that advance shared interests and creatively reconcile differing interests. Hence the third basic point: Before trying to reach agreement, *invent options for mutual gain.*

Where interests are directly opposed, a negotiator may be able to obtain a favorable result simply by being stubborn. That method tends to reward intransigence and produce arbitrary results. However, you can counter such a negotiator by insisting that his single say-so is not enough and that the agreement must reflect some fair standard independent of the naked will of either side. This does not mean insisting that the terms be based on the standard you select, but only that some fair standard such as market value, expert opinion, custom, or law determine the outcome. By discussing such criteria rather than what the parties are willing or unwilling to do, neither party need give in to the other; both can defer to a fair solution. Hence the fourth basic point: *Insist on objective criteria.*

The method of principled negotiation is contrasted with hard and soft positional bargaining in the table below [Table 43-2], which shows the four basic points of the method in boldface type.

The four basic propositions of principled ne-

TABLE 43-2

PROBLEM Positional Bargaining: Which Game Should You Play?		**SOLUTION** Change the Game —Negotiate on the Merits.
Soft	*Hard*	*Principled*
Participants are friends.	Participants are adversaries.	Participants are problem-solvers.
The goal is agreement.	The goal is victory.	The goal is a wise outcome reached efficiently and amicably.
Make concessions to cultivate the relationship.	Demand concessions as a condition of the relationship.	**Separate the people from the problem.**
Be soft on the people and the problem.	Be hard on the problem and the people.	Be soft on the people, hard on the problem.
Trust others.	Distrust others.	Proceed independent of trust.
Change your position easily.	Dig in to your position.	**Focus on interests, not positions.**
Make offers.	Make threats.	Explore interests.
Disclose your bottom line.	Mislead as to your bottom line.	Avoid having a bottom line.
Accept one-sided losses to reach agreement.	Demand one-sided gains as the price of agreement.	**Invent options for mutual gain.**
Search for the single answer: the one *they* will accept.	Search for the single answer: the one *you* will accept.	Develop multiple options to choose from; decide later.
Insist on agreement.	Insist on your position.	**Insist on objective criteria.**
Try to avoid a contest of will.	Try to win a contest of will.	Try to reach a result based on standards independent of will.
Yield to pressure.	Apply pressure.	Reason and be open to reasons; yield to principle, not pressure.

gotiation are relevant from the time you begin to think about negotiating until the time either an agreement is reached or you decide to break off the effort. That period can be divided into three stages: analysis, planning, and discussion.

During the *analysis* stage you are simply trying to diagnose the situation—to gather information, organize it, and think about it. You will want to consider the people problems of partisan perceptions, hostile emotions, and unclear communication, as well as to identify your interests and those of the other side. You will want to note options already on the table and identify any criteria already suggested as a basis for agreement.

During the *planning* stage you deal with the same four elements a second time, both generating ideas and deciding what to do. How do you propose to handle the people problems? Of your interests, which are most important? And what are some realistic objectives? You will want to generate additional options and additional criteria for deciding among them.

Again during the *discussion* stage, when the parties communicate back and forth, looking toward agreement, the same four elements are the best subjects to discuss. Differences in perception, feelings of frustration and anger, and difficulties in communication can be acknowledged and addressed. Each side should come to understand the interests of the other. Both can then jointly generate options that are mutually advantageous and seek agreement on objective standards for resolving opposed interests.

To sum up, in contrast to positional bargaining, the principled negotiation method of focusing on basic interests, mutually satisfying options, and fair standards typically results in a *wise* agreement. The method permits you to reach a gradual consensus on a joint decision *efficiently* without all the transactional costs of digging in to positions only to have to dig yourself out of them. And separating the people from the problem allows you to deal directly and empathetically with the other negotiator as a human being, thus making possible an *amicable* agreement. . . .

FOCUS ON INTERESTS, NOT POSITIONS

How do you identify interests?

The benefit of looking behind positions for interests is clear. How to go about it is less clear. A position is likely to be concrete and explicit; the interests underlying it may well be unexpressed, intangible, and perhaps inconsistent. How do you go about understanding the interests involved in a negotiation, remembering that figuring out *their* interests will be at least as important as figuring out *yours*?

Ask "Why?" One basic technique is to put yourself in their shoes. Examine each position they take, and ask yourself "Why?" Why, for instance, does your landlord prefer to fix the rent—in a five-year lease—year by year? The answer you may come up with, to be protected against increasing costs, is probably one of his interests. You can also ask the landlord himself why he takes a particular position. If you do, make clear that you are asking not for justification of this position, but for an understanding of the needs, hopes, fears, or desires that it serves. "What's your basic concern, Mr. Jones, in wanting the lease to run for no more than three years?"

Ask "Why not?" Think about their choice. One of the most useful ways to uncover interests is first to identify the basic decision that those on the other side probably see you asking them for, and then to ask yourself why they have not made that decision. What interests of theirs stand in the way? If you are trying to change their minds, the starting point is to figure out where their minds are now.

Consider, for example, the negotiations between the United States and Iran in 1980 over the release of the fifty-two U.S. diplomats and embassy personnel held hostage in Tehran by student militants. While there were a host of serious obstacles to a resolution of this dispute, the problem is illuminated simply by looking at the choice of a typical student leader. The demand of the United States was clear: "Release the hostages." During much of 1980 each student leader's choice must have looked something like that illustrated by the balance sheet below [Table 43–3].

If a typical student leader's choice did look even approximately like this, it is understandable why the militant students held the hostages so long: As outrageous and illegal as the original seizure was, once the hostages had been seized it was not irrational for the students to *keep* holding them from one day to the next, waiting for a more promising time to release them.

In constructing the other side's presently perceived choice the first question to ask is "Whose decision do I want to affect?" The second question is what decision people on the other side

TABLE 43–3

AS OF Spring 1980

Presently Perceived Choice of: An Iranian student leader

Question Faced: "Shall I press for immediate release of the American hostages?"

If I Say Yes	*If I Say No*
− I sell out the Revolution.	+ I uphold the Revolution.
− I will be criticized as pro-American.	+ I will be praised for defending Islam.
− The others will probably not agree with me; if they do and we release the hostages, then:	+ We will probably all stick together.
	+ We get fantastic TV coverage to tell the world about our grievances.
− Iran looks weak.	+ Iran looks strong.
− We back down to the U.S.	+ We stand up to the U.S.
− We get nothing (no Shah, no money).	+ We have a chance of getting something (at least our money back).
− We do not know what the U.S. will do.	+ The hostages provide some protection against U.S. intervention.
But:	*But:*
+ There is a chance that economic sanctions might end.	− Economic sanctions will no doubt continue.
+ Our relations with other nations, especially in Europe, may improve.	− Our relations with other nations, especially in Europe, will suffer.
	− Inflation and economic problems will continue.
	− There is a risk that the U.S. might take military action (but a martyr's death is the most glorious).
	However:
	+ The U.S. may make further commitments about our money, nonintervention, ending sanctions, etc.
	+ We can always release the hostages later.

now see you asking them to make. If *you* have no idea what they think they are being called on to do, *they* may not either. That alone may explain why they are not deciding as you would like.

Now analyze the consequences, as the other side would probably see them, of agreeing or refusing to make the decision you are asking for. You may find a checklist of consequences such as the following helpful in this task:

Impact on my interests
• Will I lose or gain political support?

• Will colleagues criticize or praise me?

Impact on the group's interests
• What will be the short-term consequences? The long-term consequences?
• What will be the economic consequences (political, legal, psychological, military, etc.)?
• What will be the effect on outside supporters and public opinion?
• Will the precedent be good or bad?
• Will making this decision prevent doing something better?

- Is the action consistent with our principles? Is it "right"?
- Can I do it later if I want?

In this entire process it would be a mistake to try for great precision. Only rarely will you deal with a decision-maker who writes down and weighs the pros and cons. You are trying to understand a very human choice, not making a mathematical calculation.

Realize that each side has multiple interests. In almost every negotiation each side will have many interests, not just one. As a tenant negotiating a lease, for example, you may want to obtain a favorable rental agreement, to reach it quickly with little effort, and to maintain a good working relationship with your landlord. You will have not only a strong interest in *affecting* any agreement you reach, but also one in *effecting* an agreement. You will be simultaneously pursuing both your independent and your shared interests.

A common error in diagnosing a negotiating situation is to assume that each person on the other side has the same interests. This is almost never the case. During the Vietnam war, President Johnson was in the habit of lumping together all the different members of the government of North Vietnam, the Vietcong in the south, and their Soviet and Chinese advisers and calling them collectively "he." "The enemy has to learn that *he* can't cross the United States with impunity. *He* is going to have to learn that aggression doesn't pay." It will be difficult to influence any such "him" (or even "them") to agree to anything if you fail to appreciate the differing interests of the various people and factions involved.

Thinking of negotiation as a two-person, two-sided affair can be illuminating, but it should not blind you to the usual presence of other persons, other sides, and other influences. In one baseball salary negotiation the general manager kept insisting that $200,000 was simply too much for a particular player, although other teams were paying at least that much to similarly talented players. In fact the manager felt his position was unjustifiable, but he had strict instructions from the club's owners to hold firm without explaining why, because they were in financial difficulties that they did not want the public to hear about.

Whether it is his employer, his client, his employees, his colleagues, his family, or his wife, every negotiator has a constituency to whose interests he is sensitive. To understand that negotiator's interests means to understand the variety of somewhat differing interests that he needs to take into account. . . .

44 Arms-Limitation Strategies

Herbert F. York ⎯⎯⎯⎯⎯⎯⎯⎯⎯⎯⎯⎯⎯⎯⎯⎯⎯⎯⎯⎯⎯⎯⎯⎯⎯⎯⎯

In 1934, when the Nazi terror was just beginning, and artificial radioactivity and the neutron had just been discovered, Leo Szilard invented the idea of a neutron chain reaction. He believed there must be some atomic nucleus that would, upon absorbing one neutron, emit two neutrons and energy, and that these two neutrons would lead to four, and so on. He did not know what nuclear process would be involved or what element would support that process. Nevertheless, he quickly went on to sketch two distinct devices based on such a neutron chain reaction.

One of these devices would release energy in a steady and controlled fashion, resembling in principle today's nuclear reactors; the other would release energy suddenly and in an uncontrolled fashion, similar in principle to today's nuclear bombs. Szilard's intuition told him that the former would be a boon to mankind, and that the latter would constitute a most serious threat. His views concerning this threat were strongly influenced by the rise of Nazi terror and his projection of how the political situation would develop. (Szilard had only recently arrived in England as one of the very first of what was to become a flood of refugees.) His solution to the dilemma inherent in all this was classic: He took out a public patent on the reactor-like device and he managed, with some difficulty, to obtain a secret patent on the bomb-like device.

Thus, one might say secrecy was the first nuclear-arms limitation strategy. Indeed, governments still consider secrecy useful, although the approach to arms control they now favor most is the treaty. But because treaties to date have

Reprinted with permission from *Physics Today*, Vol. 36, No. 3, 1983, pp. 24–30. © 1983 American Institute of Physics.

fallen far short of eliminating nuclear weapons or removing nuclear weapons from the realm of national sovereignty, they are, at best, only partial measures against the threat that Szilard foresaw. Nevertheless, these partial measures may buy time, so it is important that physicists who wish to participate in research and education concerning the prevention of nuclear war know about the measures that have been taken, and about those being proposed or negotiated. My goal in this article is to present some of this information, emphasizing international agreements that bear on arms control. Some readers will probably be surprised to find that there are quite a few relevant treaties in force or in various stages of development (U.S. Arms Control and Disarmament Agency, 1982).

Ever since Szilard's secret patent, governments have used secrecy to attempt to separate the development and promotion of nuclear power from the development and acquisition of nuclear weapons. In particular, they have used secrecy to prevent the spread of nuclear weapons to other powers and, more recently, even to subnational groups. Among governments, secrecy is not only a highly regarded means to this end, it is the only universally agreed-upon means. Obviously, secrecy does not "work" in the absolute sense—weapons have already spread to other countries and it seems certain that they will continue do so. However, secrecy does inhibit the whole process by sharply limiting the total number of people—scientists and inventors—who can engage in the kind of personal interaction that speeds the development of this or any technology, and it cuts off the interaction between groups of such people in different countries. Indeed, Edward Teller's well-known advocacy of reduction in the secrecy barrier is based in part on his belief that with less secrecy qualitative improvements in weaponry would come at a faster pace, and that would be a net benefit to the United States. In the early years, the American and Soviet programs did, in fact, unavoidably trade information by providing each other with radioactive fallout to analyze; but since the atmospheric test ban of 1963, that channel of communication has been closed.

PERIL ANTICIPATED

In December of 1938, Otto Hahn and Fritz Strassman in Germany discovered that neutrons induced in uranium what was soon named the fission process. Other experiments and theoretical elucidations quickly followed, and it was immediately and widely recognized that here was the process that would make the neutron chain reaction possible in both its controlled and violent forms.

Programs to explore and, if possible, exploit these new discoveries started in at least six countries. However, only the American program was to succeed. Only in America was it possible, given the violent circumstances then prevailing most everywhere else, to marshal the intellectual and material resources necessary to produce an atomic bomb.

But, even before the Manhattan Project achieved its goal, many among its leadership were able to find some time to contemplate the future they were striving to bring about. They again took it as almost axiomatic that nuclear power would be a boon to mankind, and that nuclear research in general had an exciting and fruitful future before it. Many of them also believed that no matter what short-term benefits their work might bring, in the long run the advent of nuclear weapons, and the nuclear arms race that they feared would build up around them, constituted a most serious peril for the future of man and his civilization. President Harry Truman, and many other knowledgeable statesmen soon came to share similar views.

Immediately after the war, as one of its responses to these growing concerns, the government established a special committee to explore means and generate proposals for coping with this great problem. David Lilienthal chaired the committee, which reported to the highest levels of government. Members included Robert Oppenheimer, Chester Barnard, Charles Thomas and Harry Winne. Because of his knowledge and intellect, Oppenheimer was the committee's central figure, just as he was in other similar instances at the time.

THE RADICAL SOLUTION

The Lilienthal committee considered the general situation to be unprecedented both in its seriousness and its substance and they proposed what they held to be an appropriately novel and radical solution. They proposed to create an international agency that would "conduct all intrinsically dangerous operations in the nuclear field, with individual nations and their citizens free also to conduct, under license and a minimum of inspection, all non-dangerous, or safe, operations." They also proposed to eliminate nuclear weapons—eventually—saying that nothing less would suffice. In sum, they said the rules and customs that derive from the concept of national sovereignty must not be allowed to prevail in the realm of nuclear fission and all the processes and activities that derive from it.

It was not to be. The American plan, which was presented to the United Nations in 1946 by Bernard Baruch, and whose central substance consisted of the proposals of the Lilienthal Committee, was promptly rejected by the Soviets. Also, it seems unlikely that the American body politic would have accepted it in the end, even though it had the full blessing of the President himself.

Historians and analysts have often questioned the sincerity of Oppenheimer and Lilienthal, Truman and Dean Acheson, and Baruch. Surely, it has been said, they must have known the plan was too radical to succeed. In fact, the authors of the plan anticipated just such a reaction. In the report itself they wrote:

> The program we propose will undoubtedly arouse skepticism when it is first considered. It did among us, but thought and discussion have converted us.
>
> It may seem too idealistic. It seems time we endeavor to bring some of our expressed ideals into being.
>
> It may seem too radical, too advanced, too much beyond human experience. All these terms apply with peculiar fitness to the atomic bomb.
>
> In considering the plan, as inevitable doubts arise as to its acceptability, one should ask oneself, "What are the alternatives?" We have, and we find no tolerable answer.

I believe Oppenheimer and the others were right: There are no alternative solutions to the problems created by the advent of nuclear weapons. The other approaches discussed in the remainder of this article are all palliatives, means for moderating or delaying the nuclear holocaust, but inadequate for preventing it altogether. Of course, in a situation as dreadful as the one in which we find ourselves, it is very definitely worthwhile to pursue and promote palliative and partial measures in the hope that they will both buy time and eventually lead to a real solution. But while we are pursuing such measures, we should bear in mind their true nature.

During the first decade following World War II, no progress toward arms control was possible, but in the mid-fifties the outlook improved. A number of factors contributed importantly, including the achievement of the atomic bomb by the Soviets, a development that made it possible for them to deal with the West at least nominally from a position of equality. In addition, Stalin died and was replaced by leaders more open to dealing with the outside world. At about the same time, the international dialog, which had never totally ceased, changed from one with a strong rhetorical emphasis on total measures—"general and complete disarmament"—to a more serious search for partial measures that could be taken up individually and in a serious manner more likely to lead to success in each case.

Since then, governments have proposed and attempted many such partial measures, and some have been achieved. These measures have come in several quite different formats and have involved a wide variety of substantive issues. The formats have included bilateral treaties such as SALT, multilateral treaties such as the Nonproliferation Treaty, United Nations Conventions such as the Convention on Biological Warfare, carefully matched unilateral actions such as the test moratorium of 1958–61, simple unilateral actions such as the 20 years of US restraint in the development of antisatellite weapons, and the establishment of special international regimes such as the International Atomic Energy Agency. The substance of these measures has varied even more widely, and has included a variety of limitations on nuclear testing, restrictions on providing assistance to others, prohibitions on the misuse of assistance from others, the denuclearization of specific regions such as Latin America and outer space, numerical ceilings on specific deployments, the legitim-

ization of certain unilateral intelligence-gathering techniques and the establishment of some cooperative means of verification.

TREATIES NOW IN FORCE

The arms-limitation format most favored by governments, statesmen and diplomats is the treaty. The principal advantage of a treaty over, say, paired unilateral actions, is that is spells out in detail all the limitations and restrictions that are to be undertaken, the means to be used for verifying compliance, the duration, and the conditions under which it may be terminated. Only by providing such details is it possible to avoid the misunderstanding (which often seem deliberate) that so commonly characterize relations between states with strongly differing political systems. Moreover, treaties between the US and the USSR are developed step by step and in detail by the superpowers themselves. As a result, all of their provisions are carefully tailored to be in the mutual interest of both parties, thus ensuring a higher probability of compliance than in the case of UN conventions and other very broadly international arrangements.

Conversely, the principal disadvantage of the treaty approach is that negotiation and ratification often take a very long time, during which external events can take place that cause the process to abort. One recent case in point is SALT II, which was slowed and delayed by a series of such events—Deng Xiao-Ping's visit to Washington, the controversy over the brigade of Soviet troops in Cuba, the Teheran embassy capture—and finally aborted by the invasion of Afghanistan. Another case is that of the Comprehensive Test Ban Treaty negotiations during the Carter Administration. Internal opponents of the treaty were able to search out and use bureaucratic maneuvers to slow the negotiating process until it too was finally aborted by the same events that killed SALT II.

Let us take a quick look at some of the arms-control treaties now in force.

- The Antarctic Treaty of 1959 in essence demilitarizes Antarctia. It was signed by all the parties having territorial claims or other special interests in the region. A special feature is its provision for on-site inspections of the various research bases maintained in the region to assure that they are not conducting banned activities. The United States has frequently exercised its rights under this provision.

- The Limited Test Ban Treaty of 1963 prohibits nuclear testing in the atmosphere, outer space and under water. The original intent was to ban nuclear tests altogether, but in the end the US view was that no adequate means were available for verifying a ban on underground tests so these could not be included in the treaty. Numerically speaking, most of the public support for this treaty came from those whose principal stated concern was the health problem posed by radioactive fallout, and their concern was, of course, satisfied by the limited test ban.

- The Outer-Space Treaty of 1967 and the Seabeds Treaty of 1972 ban the placement of "weapons of mass destruction" in those two locations.

- The Nonproliferation Treaty of 1968, which went into force in 1970, is designed principally to bar the nuclear-weapons states from helping other states to get or build nuclear weapons, and to bar the non-nuclear weapons states from seeking to obtain or build such weapons. The treaty contains several additional provisions designed specifically to make it more palatable to the nuclear have-nots. One such provision calls for the nuclear-weapons states to "pursue negotiations in good faith on effective measures relative to cessation of the nuclear arms race." Others call for the nuclear-weapons states to help the non-nuclear-weapons states acquire the benefits of nuclear energy, including benefits deriving from the so-called "peaceful uses" of nuclear explosives. The treaty calls for a review of the nonproliferation regime at five-year intervals. In the past two such reviews, there have been widespread charges that the superpowers have not lived up to their obligations under all of the additional provisions.

- The Latin American Nuclear Free Zone Treaty of 1968 is designed to eliminate all nuclear weapons from Latin America. It has been ratified by most but not all of the states of the region. It also includes protocols placing certain consistent requirements on states outside the region when those states own Latin American territories or possess nuclear weapons. This treaty has served as a model for as yet unfulfilled proposals for "nuclear-free zones" in several other parts of the world.

- The Antiballistic Missile Treaty was ratified in 1972. Together with its later amendments, this treaty defines an ABM system and places numerical and geographical limits on its deployment. It contains provisions designed to limit certain characteristics of ABM subsystems and to inhibit, but not prevent, the development of new types of ABMs. In addition, it contains provisions legitimizing and protecting so-called "national technical means" of verification and restricts practices that would confound such systems. The treaty is of indefinite duration, but it is to be reviewed every five years. It also calls for the establishment of a "Standing Consultative Commission," which would meet in private and consider complaints and questions raised by either side. This commission has met as required and has reported that all questions raised have been resolved satisfactorily.

- The Executive Agreement Covering Certain Offensive Systems, also ratified in 1972, places limits on the numbers and sizes of specific offensive systems, including ICBMs and sea-launched ballistic missiles. This agreement was in essence a "freeze," because the limits were set at the numbers of systems already deployed or in the process of being deployed. It restated the provisions dealing with national technical means of verification. It was to run for five years, at which time it was to be replaced by a treaty that would be broader and more far reaching in scope. The United States and the Soviet Union have not achieved this, but through a continuing series of understandings they have kept the executive agreement in force.

UNCOMPLETED TREATIES

The SALT II Treaty was negotiated and signed during the Carter Administration. It was called for in the executive agreement of SALT I, and was based in large part on certain general "guidelines" presented in the Vladivostok agreement worked out by Presidents Ford and Brezhnev in 1974. It sets numerical limits on all the major types of strategic offensive systems, and it sets sublimits that restrain the total number of warheads by limiting the "MIRVing" of delivery vehicles. The treaty contains a data base and numerous working definitions, all of which are designed to make it easier to achieve further agreements, which the treaty tacitly assumes will follow, and which would eventually lead to a real reduction in numbers. The SALT II treaty was finally signed and submitted to the Senate in late 1979 after several long delays. But before it could be ratified, the events mentioned above intervened and put the necessary two-thirds majority in the Senate beyond reach.

The Threshold Treaty of 1974 and the Peaceful Nuclear Explosions Treaty of 1976 were worked out and signed in the Nixon and Ford Administrations respectively. The first was designed to prohibit tests of nuclear weapons exceeding 150 kilotons in yield, and the latter was designed to allow multiple nuclear explosions conducted for peaceful purposes to exceed this limit in the aggregate but not individually. Two very important features of these treaties are that they provide for an exchange of geophysical data concerning the test site, and that they call for onsite observations and measurements by personnel of the other principal in certain special circumstances. This was the first instance in which the Soviets ratified a treaty allowing such intrusive procedures to take place on their home territory, but these treaties have not been ratified by the United States, so these special provisions are not in force. Both states, however, have said they would for now comply with the 150-kt limit, and both appear to be doing so.

Treaties attempted or proposed. A Comprehensive Test Ban, which would prohibit all nuclear weapons tests everywhere, has been a stated goal of both the US and the USSR since 1958. The pursuit of this goal has led to several partial measures—the Limited Test Ban and Nonproliferation treaties, and the signed-but-not-ratified Threshold and Peaceful Nuclear Explosions treaties—but the goal itself remains elusive. Negotiations during the Carter Administration did achieve several advances of fundamental importance in the area of verification. The US and USSR reached agreement in principle on a system of voluntary onsite inspections. These would be based on a series of challenges and required responses and the deployment of national seismic stations (the "black boxes" of earlier years), which would be placed on each other's territory and which would be constructed and operated so as to provide a continuous, unadulterated, stream of data in near real time. In addition, the Soviets agreed to forego at least temporarily their program to develop and use so-called "economic nuclear explosions," analogous to our "peaceful nuclear explosions." After some important early progress, this negotiation encoun-

tered a steadily and seriously deteriorating political climate (Teheran, Kabul, the 1980 US elections), and was eventually stalled by the bureaucratic maneuvers of its opponents. As a result, the details underlying these agreements-in-principle were never fully elaborated. When President Reagan took office in 1981, the negotiations were cancelled.

The anti-satellite, or ASAT, negotiations of 1978–79 were intended to forestall the construction of anti-satellite weapons systems and the eventual preparation to conduct warfare of various novel kinds in space. Three negotiating sessions took place during the early Carter years, but it eventually became evident they were leading nowhere and they were abandoned even before the international scene seriously deteriorated. In my view, this happened largely because neither side was able to develop a clear and generally internally acceptable view of its objectives.

During the last quarter century, several proposals to limit certain nuclear-weapons activities have been put forward but never seriously negotiated. These included proposals to cut off production of the special materials needed to construct nuclear weapons, to limit seriously launches of large rockets so as to inhibit greatly their further development, and to nip in the bud the MIRV development program. In addition, there have been proposals for many other "nuclear-free zones," as well as proposals for making certain parts of the ocean safe "havens" for nuclear submarines as a means of supporting the so-called mutually assured destruction, or "MAD," doctrine.

Conventions and the like. United Nations conventions have the advantage of being universal, or nearly so. And, to the extent that they work and exercise a positive influence, they tend to reinforce other peacekeeping and peace-supporting activities of the UN. The corresponding disadvantage, as compared to bilateral treaties between states of roughly equal size and power (or multilateral treaties involving two distinct sides or two dominant parties), is that they are not taken quite so seriously. Thus, while the record of compliance with arms-control treaties is generally quite good, the record in the case of these more broadly based arrangements is quite different, as evidenced by the many apparent violations of the Chemical Protocol and the Biological Convention, and the cavalier way in which many states, the US and USSR included, fail to live up fully to the purposes and regulations of the International Atomic Energy Agency. The reason for this difference, I believe, lies in the fact that the superpowers have much less control over the details of universal conventions, and they frequently end up facing a "take it or leave it" situation. They often choose to "take it," but then are less likely comply with the detailed provisions than when they are in full control of the details. I believe Soviet behavior in connection with the Chemical and Biological Conventions is a case in point. Both are broadly multilateral conventions produced by an international organization, not by direct principal-to-principal negotiations, and the latter in fact contains no provisions for verification.

The 1925 Geneva Protocol on Chemical Weapons and the 1977 Biological Weapons Convention were sponsored by the League of Nations and the United Nations, respectively. The former seeks to prohibit the use of poisonous gases and "bacteriological methods" of warfare, and the latter seeks to prohibit the development, production and stockpiling of bacteriological and toxic weapons as well. The Geneva Protocol went into effect in 1928, but the United States did not ratify it until 1975, when it also ratified the Biological Weapons Convention. The parties to the latter also agreed to destroy such stocks as then existed within nine months after it went into force.

The International Atomic Energy Agency, which was created under the aegis of the UN, grew out of President Eisenhower's "Atoms for Peace" speech of 1953. Its twin purposes were to promote the spread of nuclear energy throughout the world and at the same time prevent the spread of nuclear weapons technology along with it. While the system of inspections and other procedures cannot prevent the spread of nuclear weapons—as those knowledgeable of but hostile to the Agency like to repeat—this system can and does greatly inhibit the process. Similar but more limited arrangements with the same objective have also been carried out in other contexts. For instance, the European Atomic Energy Community has similar purposes within Europe.

UNILATERAL ACTIONS

The defense programs of all countries involve a continuous stream of unilateral actions, many of which have the effect of moderating the nuclear arms race. But nearly all of the moderating actions are the result of fiscal, not political, restraints. Occasionally, however, a unilateral restraint is imposed for the sole or principal purpose of moderating the military confrontation or avoiding some particular exacerbation of it.

A particularly interesting and important example was the 20-year period of restraint imposed by US presidents on the development of anti-satellite weapons. The United States, almost from the very beginning of the space age, has used its military space assets—reconnaissance satellites, for example—for a variety of very important national-security purposes. From Eisenhower onward, our Presidents have concluded that we would derive a net benefit from a situation in which no state had any anti-satellite capability. The US, therefore, was willing to forego a program to develop such weapons, in the hope that the Soviets would follow suit. As a result, proposals arising in the US Air Force and aerospace industry to develop a general-purpose anti-satellite weapon were continually rejected.

In the meantime, and despite US restraint, the Soviets launched their first anti-satellite experiment in 1968, and they have continued since then to conduct further tests in an on-again off-again fashion. Finally, in 1977 President Carter decided to make a three-pronged response to those Soviet actions: first, to initiate the development of a US anti-satellite weapon; second, to explore means for defending satellites against attack; and third, to begin negotiations with the Soviets to forestall all such developments. Beginning at Helsinki in 1978, three negotiating sessions took place, and, as I mentioned above, they got nowhere. Now both the US and the Soviets have anti-satellites programs underway.

Another important unilateral action took place in October 1958 when, after a succession of slowly converging unilateral statements by Eisenhower and Khrushchev, the US and the Soviet Union both suspended nuclear tests. This moratorium, as it was called, was in essence based on a matched set of unilateral statements in which each party pledged not to test if the other party did not test. The purpose was to create an atmosphere suitable for working out a formal treaty on the subject, and Eisenhower estimated that one year should suffice. The negotiations did not work out, however, and after fourteen months, on 29 December 1959, Eisenhower denounced the moratorium, saying the US was no longer bound by it, but would not begin testing without giving notice. Three days later, the Soviets denounced it also, but said they would not test unless the "Western powers" did so first.

When France tested its first nuclear weapon three months later, Khrushchev took formal and public note of it. Hence, as of that time there was no longer any *de jure* basis for a nuclear moratorium, but testing did not in fact resume until 18 months later, when an extensive Soviet series put a final end to the then purely *de facto* moratorium. Although there were no external legal restraints—formal or informal—on such testing by any party at that time, US official opinion has always held that we were in an important sense entrapped by the Russians. In the words of one current high-level White House official, "they used the moratorium to gain a full lap on us" in the cycle of nuclear testing and development. Ever since then, unverifiable moratoria, whether bilateral or not, have found little support in US government circles.

In recent years, the Chinese and the Soviets have made unilateral pledges to the effect that they would not be the first to use nuclear weapons, and many have urged that the United States also make such a "no first use" pledge. United States policy has always been to reserve the right to initiate the use of nuclear weapons, particularly in situations where the conventional balance may be very heavily weighted against us, and so we have always declined to join in such a pledge, whether on a unilateral or a multilateral basis. Another basic argument has been that such a pledge, if unaccompanied by any further, more concrete actions that might really make first use more difficult or less desirable, would be too easily reversed or disregarded.

More recently, a number of Europeans and Americans have proposed that we unilaterally and as a "first step" either eliminate all so-called "battlefield nuclear weapons" (such as nuclear artillery) or at least remove them from close proximity to the inter-German border. They argue that the actual use of such weapons for resisting an armed attack would not be to our net advantage, that we can successfully develop and deploy conventional means for resisting such an attack, and that removing such battlefield "nukes" would substantially reduce the probability of nuclear war in Europe. They argue further that the longer-range nuclear systems, which would presumably still remain available after such a "first-step," would be fully adequate for continuing the state of nuclear deterrence that has persisted the last 35 years.

THE FREEZE MOVEMENT

The people behind the current wave of "nuclear freeze" proposals have two distinct purposes. One is to provide a simple, easily understandable focus for public opinion; the other is to outline the substance for an international agreement to stop the nuclear arms race in its tracks.

In their first role, the proposals have taken the form of resolutions placed before the Congress and before the voters in many state and even local elections. In their second role, the goal is usually said to be a "bilateral and verifiable" freeze in the development, production and deployment of all nuclear weapons systems. Only through the treaty-writing process discussed above would it be possible to elaborate and negotiate the details necessary to achieve and sustain such a goal. A number of treaties encompassing partial freezes have, in fact, already been fully or partially negotiated—SALT I, SALT II, the Comprehensive Test Ban—so there are some precedents for such an action. However, some of the experts who commonly advocate nuclear restraints in general have argued that the freeze proposals include too many elements that are too widely disparate to serve as the basis for a unitary bilateral or multilateral negotiation.

It is clear that in its first purpose, the freeze movement is succeeding. In November 1982, in eight of the nine states where a freeze resolution appeared on the ballot, the electorate favored it. I believe these and similar actions will stimulate some real progress by governments in moderating the nuclear confrontation and achieving formal agreements further limiting the development and deployment of nuclear weapons, especially in Europe. However, it is not at all clear to me at this time precisely what final and formal form these new limitations will take. Nor is it clear whether any such progress can happen soon, or whether it must await the arrival of an administration in Washington (and perhaps in Moscow) more closely attuned to the public's concerns in this vital matter.

REFERENCE

United States Arms Control and Disarmament Agency. (1982). *Arms Control and Disarmament Agreements*, 1982 edition. Washington, D.C.

45   A Proposal for International Disarmament

George F. Kennan

Adequate words are lacking to express the full seriousness of our present situation. It is not just that we are for the moment on a collision course politically with the Soviet Union, and that the process of rational communication between the two governments seems to have broken down completely; it is also—and even more importantly—the fact that the ultimate sanction behind the conflicting policies of these two governments is a type and volume of weaponry which could not possibly be used without utter disaster for us all. . . .

What is it then, if not our own will, and if not the supposed wickedness of our opponents, that has brought us to this pass?

The answer, I think, is clear. It is primarily the inner momentum, the independent momentum, of the weapons race itself—the compulsions that arise and take charge of great powers when they enter upon a competition with each other in the building up of major armaments of any sort.

This is nothing new. I am a diplomatic historian. I see this same phenomenon playing its fateful part in the relations among the great European powers as much as a century ago. I see this competitive buildup of armaments conceived initially as a means to an end but soon becoming the end itself. I see it taking possession of men's imagination and behavior, becoming a force in its own right, detaching itself from the political differences that intially inspired it,

Excerpts from a speech delivered on receipt of the Albert Einstein Peace Prize, May 19, 1981. The full speech appeared in *The Nuclear Delusion* by George F. Kennan, copyright 1982 by Pantheon Books, a Division of Random House, Inc. Reprinted with permission.

and then leading both parties, invariably and inexorably, to the war they no longer know how to avoid.

This is a species of fixation, brewed out of many components. There are fears, resentments, national pride, personal pride. There are misreadings of the adversary's intentions—sometimes even the refusal to consider them at all. There is the tendency of national communities to idealize themselves and to dehumanize the opponent. There is the blinkered, narrow vision of the professional military planner, and his tendency to make war inevitable by assuming its inevitability.

Tossed together, these components form a powerful brew. They guide the fears and the ambitions of men. They seize the policies of governments and whip them around like trees before the tempest.

Is it possible to break out of this charmed and vicious circle? It is sobering to recognize that no one, at least to my knowledge, has yet done so. But no one, for that matter, has ever been faced with such great catastrophe, such inalterable catastrophe, at the end of the line. Others, in earlier decades, could befuddle themselves with dreams of something called "victory." We, perhaps fortunately, are denied this seductive prospect. We have to break out of the circle. We have no other choice.

How are we to do it?

I must confess that I see no possibility of doing this by means of discussions along the lines of the negotiations that have been in progress, off and on, over this past decade, under the acronym of SALT. I regret, to be sure, that the most recent SALT agreement has not been ratified. I regret it, because if the benefits to be expected from that agreement were slight, its disadvantages were even slighter; and it had a symbolic value which should not have been so lightly sacrificed.

But I have, I repeat, no illusion that negotiations on the SALT pattern—negotiations, that is, in which each side is obsessed with the chimera of relative advantage and strives only to retain a maximum of the weaponry for itself while putting its opponent to the maximum disadvantage—I have no illusion that such negotiations could ever be adequate to get us out of this hole. They are not a way of escape from the weapons race; they are an integral part of it.

Whoever does not understand that when it comes to nuclear weapons the whole concept of relative advantage is illusory—whoever does not understand that when you are talking about absurd and preposterous quantities of overkill the relative sizes of arsenals have no serious meaning—whoever does not understand that the danger lies, not in the possibility that someone else might have more missiles and warheads than we do, but in the very existence of these unconscionable quantities of highly poisonous explosives, and their existence, above all, in hands as weak and shaky and undependable as those of ourselves or our adversaries or any other mere human beings: whoever does not understand these things is never going to guide us out of this increasingly dark and menacing forest of bewilderments into which we have all wandered.

I can see no way out of this dilemma other than by a bold and sweeping departure, a departure that would cut surgically through the exaggerated anxieties, the self-engendered nightmares, and the sophisticated mathematics of destruction in which we have all been entangled over these recent years, and would permit us to move, with courage and decision, to the heart of the problem.

President Reagan recently said, and I think very wisely, that he would "negotiate as long as necessary to reduce the numbers of nuclear weapons to a point where neither side threatens the survival of the other."

Now that is, of course, precisely the thought to which these present observations of mine are addressed. But I wonder whether the negotiations would really have to be at such great length. What I would like to see the president do, after due consultation with the Congress, would be to propose to the Soviet government an immediate across-the-board reduction by 50 percent of the nuclear arsenals now being maintained by the two superpowers; a reduction affecting in equal measure all forms of the weapon, strategic, medium-range, and tactical, as well as all means of their delivery: all this to be implemented at once and without further wrangling among the experts, and to be subject to such national means of verification as now lie at the disposal of the two powers.

Whether the balance of reduction would be precisely even—whether it could be construed to favor statistically one side or the other—would not be the question. Once we start thinking that way, we would be back on the same old fateful track that has brought us where we are today. Whatever the precise results of such a reduction, there would still be plenty of overkill left—so much so that if this first operation were successful, I would then like to see a second one put in hand to rid us of at least two-thirds of what would be left. . . .

It will be said this proposal, whatever its merits, deals with only a part of the problem. This is perfectly true. Behind it there would still lurk the serious political differences that now divide us from the Soviet government. Behind it would still lie the problems recently treated, and still to be treated, in the SALT forum. Behind it would still lie the great question of the acceptability of war itself, any war, even a conventional one, as a means of solving problems among great industrial powers in this age of high technology.

What has been suggested here would not prejudice the continued treatment of these questions just as they might be treated today, in whatever forums and under whatever safeguards the two powers find necessary. The conflicts and arguments over these questions could all still proceed to the heart's content of all those who view them with such passionate commitment. The stakes would simply be smaller; and that would be a great relief to all of us.

What I have suggested is, of course, only a beginning. But a beginning has to be made somewhere; and if it has to be made, is it not best that it should be made where the dangers are the greatest, and their necessity the least? If a step of this nature could be successfully taken, people might find the heart to tackle with greater confidence and determination the many problems that would still remain. . . .

46 Ban Space Weapons

Richard Garwin and Carl Sagan

In the quarter century since the first artificial Earth satellite was launched, on October 4, 1957, humans have used their new spacefaring capability wisely—for global communications; navigation; weather observations; monitoring Earth resources; for reconnaissance, which tends to moderate destabilizing world political and military trends; and for verifying the compliance of nations with their treaty obligations. The exploration of space by men and women, and particularly the scientific results of planetary missions and observations from space platforms, have changed our view of the universe. They have made it possible for us to understand our environment in ways which may be critical in the solution of major world problems. These developments have been almost wholly benign, have significantly benefitted the peoples of the Earth and represent an important aperture to a hopeful future for the human species.

After American nuclear explosions in space inadvertently damaged satellites of the United States and other nations in 1962, most countries of the world, including the United States and the Soviet Union, agreed in the Limited Test Ban Treaty of 1963 never to explode nuclear weapons in space, in the oceans or in the atmosphere. In 20 years no signatory nation has violated this agreement. Most nations, including the United States and the Soviet Union, also adhere to the Outer Space Treaty of 1967 banning from space all weapons of mass destruction, and, specifically, all nuclear weapons. But fic-

tion writers and military strategists have for about a century romanticized the purported inevitability of warfare in space. The use of non-nuclear weapons of more limited lethality than "mass destruction," while forbidden on other celestial bodies by the 1967 treaty, is still permitted in Earth orbit, and in cislunar, circumplanetary and interplanetary space.

We believe that the testing or deployment of any weapons in space—in part by threatening vital satellite assets—significantly increases the likelihood of warfare on Earth. The Soviet Union has tested a rudimentary anti-satellite weapons system beginning in the early 1970s, but in 1981 formally presented a draft treaty banning all space weapons and prohibiting damage to or destruction of satellites by any means. The United States will soon begin testing a much more sophisticated anti-satellite system. Once such weapons systems are established in national arsenals they become very difficult to displace. Proposals, for example, to ban MIRVs before their deployment were rejected; today these destabilizing weapons systems are generally distributed and threaten the security of all nations. Failure to limit their deployment is now widely regretted. If space weapons are ever to be banned, this may be close to the last moment in which it can be done.

Richard L. Garwin
IBM Thomas J. Watson Research Center
Yorktown Heights, New York 10598

Carl Sagan
Professor of Astronomy and Space Sciences
Director, Laboratory for Planetary Studies
Cornell University
Ithaca, New York 14853

From *The Bulletin of the Atomic Scientists*, November 1983, pp. 2–3. Reprinted by permission of *The Bulletin of the Atomic Scientists*, a magazine of science and world affairs. Copyright © by the Educational Foundation for Nuclear Science, Chicago, IL 60637.

We join in urging the United States, the Soviet Union and other space-faring nations to negotiate, for their benefit and for the benefit of the human species, a treaty to ban weapons of any kind from space, and to prohibit damage to or destruction of satellites of any nation.

Hans A. Bethe, professor of physics emeritus, Cornell University; Nobel Laureate in physics; head, Theoretical Division, Manhattan Project; consultant, Los Alamos Scientific Laboratory

E. Margaret Burbidge, professor of astronomy and director, Center for Astrophysics and Space Sciences, University of California at San Diego; president, American Association for the Advancement of Science

Clark R. Chapman, senior scientist, Planetary Science Institute, Science Applications Inc., Tucson; chairman, Division for Planetary Sciences, American Astronomical Society

Thomas M. Donahue, professor of atmospheric science, University of Michigan: chairman, Space Science Board, National Academy of Sciences/National Research Council

Sidney D. Drell, professor of physics, Stanford University; consultant to the Senate Select Committee on Intelligence and, formerly, to the National Security Council

Lee A. DuBridge, president emeritus, California Institute of Technology; science advisor to former President Nixon

Herbert Friedman, former superintendent, Space Science Division, Naval Research Laboratory, Washington; former chairman, Committee on Solar-Terrestrial Research and Geophysics Research Board. National Academy of Sciences/National Research Council

Admiral Noel Gayler (U.S. Navy, Retired), former director, National Security Agency; former commander-in-chief, U.S. Forces in the Pacific; former deputy chief of naval operations

Donald M. Hunten, professor of planetary sciences, University of Arizona

Christopher C. Kraft, former director, Flight Operations, Apollo missions to the moon; former director, NASA Johnson Space Center

Vice-Admiral John Marshall Lee (U.S. Navy, Retired), former assistant director, U.S. Arms Control and Disarmament Agency

Franklin A. Long, professor of chemistry emeritus, Cornell University; former associate director, U.S. Arms Control and Disarmament Agency

Carson Mark, former head, Theoretical Division, Los Alamos Scientific Laboratory

James S. Martin, Jr., former vice president and general manager, Martin Marietta Corporation; project manager, Viking mission to Mars, NASA

David Morrison, professor of astronomy, University of Hawaii

Philip Morrison, group leader, Manhattan Project; professor of physics, Massachusetts Institute of Technology

Bruce C. Murray, professor of planetary sciences, California Institute of Technology; former director, Jet Propulsion Laboratory, NASA

Gerry Neugebauer, professor of physics, California Institute of Technology; director, Mount Palomar Observatory

Tobias Owen, professor of astrophysics program, State University of New York at Stony Brook

Wolfgang K.H. Panofsky, director, Stanford Linear Accelerator Center; former member, General Advisory Committee, U.S. Arms Control and Disarmament Agency

Gordon H. Pettengill, professor of planetary physics, Massachusetts Institute of Technology

William Pickering, professor of electrical engineering emeritus, California Institute of Technology; former director, Jet Propulsion Laboratory, NASA

Edward M. Purcell, professor of physics emeritus, Harvard University; Nobel Laureate in physics

I.I. Rabi, professor of physics emeritus, Columbia University; Nobel Laureate in physics

George W. Rathjens, professor of political science, Massachusetts Institute of Technology; former chief scientist, Advanced Research Projects Agency, Department of Defense

Glenn T. Seaborg, professor of chemistry, University of California at Berkeley; former chairman, Atomic Energy Commission; Nobel Laureate in chemistry

Eugene M. Shoemaker, research geologist, United States Geological Survey; professor of geology and planetary science, California Institute of Technology

John A. Simpson, professor of physics, Enrico Fermi Institute, University of Chicago; chairman, Steering Committee, Space Science

Working Group, Association of American Universities

Edward C. Stone, professor of physics, California Institute of Technology; chief project scientist, Voyager mission to the outer solar system, NASA

James Van Allen, professor of physics, University of Iowa; president, American Geophysical Union

Victor F. Weisskopf, professor of physics emeritus, Massachusetts Institute of Technology; former director, European Center for Nuclear Research; member, Pontifical Academy of Sciences, Rome

Jerome B. Wiesner, president emeritus, Massachusetts Institute of Technology; science advisor to former Presidents Kennedy and Johnson

Robert R. Wilson, professor of physics, Columbia University; head, Research Division, Manhattan Project; former director, Fermi National Accelerator Laboratory; president-elect, American Physical Society

Herbert F. York, professor of physics, University of California at San Diego; former chief scientist, Advanced Research Projects Agency, Department of Defense; former director, Defense Research and Engineering, Department of Defense; former director, Lawrence Livermore Laboratory, University of California

The preceding is a partial list of signatories. Affiliations are for identification purposes only.

47 Nuclear Crisis Control Center

William Langer Ury and Richard Smoke

BACKGROUND

If a nuclear detonation suddenly occurred on American territory and its source were not yet known, uncertainty would be at an extreme among U.S. decision-makers. If the detonation were actually the work of a terrorist group or a third nation unconnected with the Soviet Union, the United States would want to know this as quickly and surely as possible. If a Soviet missile had been fired by accident or without authorization, the United States would also want to have this information verified immediately. In either case it would be greatly in the Soviet interest to assist in providing and authenticating relevant information.

Mere exchange of information or even consulting on the Hotline may not be enough to avoid stumbling into an unintended war. The tasks of interpreting and authenticating information and determining how to cope with such an extremely dangerous and delicate situation might be helped by the existence of a joint U.S.–Soviet facility with highly trained military officers and diplomats from both sides who had prepared for just such contingencies.

Such a facility could move quickly to control a crisis, but it would be most useful if it were able to prevent the crisis in the first place. The U.S. and the USSR might conceivably pool intelligence and cooperate to prevent an act of nuclear terrorism, or a nuclear attack from a third country. A precedent for such cooperation in a less critical situation exists in the Soviet Union's

Excerpted from William Langer Ury and Richard Smoke, *Beyond the Hotline: Controlling a Nuclear Crisis*, A Report to the U.S. Arms Control and Disarmament Agency, 1984.

tip-off to the U.S. in 1977 that the South Africans might be about to test a nuclear device.

Another example may be suggested by the Korean Air Lines Flight 007 incident. The center's staff might have analyzed similar scenarios beforehand, recalling the unfortunate intrusion of a Korean airliner into Soviet airspace in 1978, and formulated standard procedures to prevent such accidental intrusions and to deal with them peaceably if they occurred.

By now there has been considerable discussion of creating some kind of joint U.S.–Soviet crisis control center. Public suggestion of the idea by Senators Jackson and Nunn dates back . . . to 1981. The idea has been given attention within the Defense Department, and has been discussed in a number of arms control seminars held by universities and private groups as well as at a conference held in February 1983 in Austin, Texas. It has been the subject of at least two unclassified working papers by defense experts, and of a report by the Nunn-Warner working group on nuclear risk reduction.[1]

The idea of a crisis control center has received so much attention in part because at first glance it seems quite plausible and attractive. On more careful consideration, however, it is not at all obvious exactly what a center would do. Most of the time there is no crisis; how could one attract personnel of the highest caliber to sit and wait for a crisis? And during a severe crisis, when decisions are forced to the very top, a center would run a high risk of being ignored altogether. At the other extreme, there seems to be a myriad of subjects to work on, including terrorism, proliferation, accidents, nuclear doctrine, and notifications of military exercises and launches. A small staff might be badly overloaded; and indeed the tasks may be best handled by various agencies which work on many of them already. After a first glance at the idea, one is led to under take a more thorough analysis and ask whether a center is a workable concept.

Presented here is a suggestion for a center with a number of potential functions. The "nuclear crisis control center," as it is termed here, is intended not as a final proposal but . . . as an illustration of how the stabilization approach presented in this report could be applied to the question of a superpower crisis institution. This analysis discusses the functions of the nuclear risk reduction center both *before* and *during* crises, analyzes the benefits and problems, explores whether one center or two is preferable, and suggests the value of an incremental strategy in moving toward a joint superpower institution.

BEFORE A CRISIS: A PROFESSIONAL WORKING GROUP

During normal times, the center's experts could serve as a professional working group examining scenarios for superpower crises and devising possible measures to prevent them or, if they occurred, to help resolve them short of nuclear war. The focus on the information exchange functions of a center should not lead us to overlook the opportunities for joint problem-solving ahead of time for certain kinds of crises. In spite of the difficulties of American and Soviet diplomatic and military officers sitting down together, they can—as was proved in developing the INCSEA Agreement—discuss and analyze technical problems, develop options for coping with them, and even agree on solutions to narrow issues once the principles for agreement have been established at a higher level.

This process needs to start with those problems where the interests are almost entirely shared by the two sides. These are typically crises that neither side starts partially or entirely by its own initiative, but which arise inadvertently (from the perspective of Washington and Moscow). Possible cases to start with might be the *agent provocateur* scenario or the detonation of unknown origin outside the two superpowers' territories. As the center's personnel build up positive experience with this kind of joint problem-

solving, they can gradually extend this practice to a wider class of problems, possibly including, as time passes, some problems where interests are by no means entirely congruent. Even in the most inadvertent kinds of crises, both superpowers might place limits on how far the problem-solving exploration could go without some higher-level understandings about permissible outcomes.

In this problem-solving process, the center's personnel would generate options, not make decisions. The discussions would be informal and each government would understand that no suggestion could be taken as an official proposal. This procedure is not new; it was apparently employed productively, for instance, by certain U.S. and Soviet delegates during the SALT I negotiations.

Decisions on crisis prevention and control measures would of course need to be made by high-level policy-makers. Some or all of the center's personnel might serve as briefers or staff support for those policy makers. . . . Incidentally, this kind of staff work associated with high-level policy-makers, quite apart from its substantive value, would ensure that personnel of the highest caliber would be attracted to the job and be well utilized.

In normal times the joint working group might study possible procedures both for controlling crises that might occur and for helping to prevent them. Among the former are:

1) Joint study of the problem of how one side could validate for the other that a launch was accidental or unauthorized.

2) Designing and testing technical capabilities and SOPs for the investigation of detonations of unknown origin.

3) Developing a set of procedural options for each side's decision-makers to consider in other kinds of crises. Agreement might not be necessary in all cases; it may be helpful simply to have developed the options long beforehand and to have discussed them so that they are clearly understood by both sides. This process may also help develop some common understandings about managing nuclear crises.

4) Developing possible negotiating procedures in the event of designated hypothetical crises.

5) Analyzing how to bring about a rapid cease-fire.

6) Doing scenario analysis of a range of hypothetical escalation scenarios posing the danger of superpower confrontation; conducting simulations and exercises with hypothetical scenarios and national actors. The purpose would be to discover and to suggest contingencies where standard procedures would be useful.

7) Briefing appropriate military and diplomatic officials about crisis prevention and contact.

8) Raising questions regarding explicit and implicit crisis control implementation (in a fashion analogous to some work done in the Standing Consultative Commission).

Possible crisis *prevention* tasks are more numerous and more diffuse. Some possibilities are:

1) Exchanging information about potential nuclear terrorism, missing nuclear weapons or material, or proliferation to the extent that it might trigger a superpower crisis.

2) Giving notifications of strategic (and nonstrategic) tests and exercises.

3) Raising queries regarding disturbing military activity by the other side.

4) Devising "nuclear codes of conduct" to reduce the possibility of either side's engaging in practices the other sees as threatening.

5) Discussing nuclear doctrines relevant to controlling nuclear crises.

As the list of tasks expands, it becomes clear that the staff could not handle even half the work. A larger center is not the answer: it would probably detract from the original purpose of informal, professional communication and problem-solving. Much of the work is probably most easily and effectively done not jointly, but unilaterally by each side in parallel with each other. The center might come to serve as a point of exchange and communication between the various agencies on the two sides concerned with terrorism, proliferation, and so on. The discussions at the center could highlight problems which in turn might inspire needed parallel work.

Finally, the working relationships that would develop between the American and Soviet experts at the center should not be overlooked. If and when the center were used in time of crisis, these relationships might prove invaluable for the delicate exchange and authentication of technical information and for technical problem-solving.

DURING A CRISIS: A CRISIS CENTER WITH EXPERTS ON CALL

Should a superpower crisis occur, the center as an institution and as a group of experts would be ready to help in inhibiting it in its early stages, in containing it later, and even in helping to terminate hostilities should they break out.

The center could serve as a conduit for information that, for technical reasons or reasons of interpretation, is better communicated personally than by Hotline or data link. It could also be a place for each side to express concerns and query information regarding military moves and alerts. At the height of the Cuban Missile Crisis, the Americans thought, apparently mistakenly, that they detected a speed-up in Soviet work on the Cuban missile sites. The center could be a place to help correct such a dangerous misperception. Concerns could be raised, and in reply each side could provide information. The center staff might help interpret it and, where possible, authenticate it. Thus the superpowers could clarify their intentions and the limits of their military moves. . . .

In some kinds of crises, the center could carry out previously agreed-upon procedures. If, for instance, there had been a detonation of unknown origin, a previously designated joint team might be dispatched from the center to help identify it. If there had been an accidental launch, one or more staff officers of the nation from which the launch originated might be sent to the detonation area to confirm that a nuclear explosion had indeed occurred and to verify the extent of the damage. Conceivably, staff officers of the nation struck might be sent to the launch site to investigate and to interview the military personnel responsible, in an effort to confirm that it was indeed an accident.

It is impossible to design procedures in advance for all the kinds of crises that could arise. In many crises the center might serve the limited but important function of being an ad hoc resource. For instance, center personnel might jointly explore and help develop the details—not the main political lines—of a disengagement agreement, such as procedures for verifying mutual compliance with it.

In focusing on what role the institution could play, it is vital not to overlook the individuals involved, for they might prove to be the chief resource in a crisis. When the drawbridge is raised and only a tiny number of leaders are making decisions, there is a good chance that some of the specialists from the center might be tapped for their expertise even if the institution itself is not used in that particular crisis. The center's experts would have spent much of their time studying the art and science of crisis prevention and control; from the study of past cases and current leadership styles, they would become highly knowledgeable about the ways their own nation and the opposing superpower make decisions in crises. They would serve, in a sense, as a human repository of the accumulated wisdom from past crises and expertise for handling future ones.

If some or all of the center's staff were also to serve as briefers or staff for decision-makers on each side during normal times, those same decision-makers might be more likely to tap them for their expertise in time of crisis. A working relationship and an appreciation of their knowledge would already exist. Americans familiar with Soviet crisis decision-making might be asked to help interpret Soviet actions or to design American actions so that they convey the message intended. Alternatively, perhaps more daringly, an expert from the other side might be called in by decision-makers to help explain his government's decision-making processes.

In summary, the proposed Nuclear Crisis Control Center would consist of a small group of American and Soviet defense and diplomatic experts. In normal times they would work as a professional working group devising possible crisis prevention and control measures for a range (listed above) of possible contingencies. Some or all center personnel might also serve as a joint staff for regular talks between top policy-makers from each side.

In time of crisis, the center could facilitate the exchange and authentication of information, might help implement some agreed-upon procedures, and would be an ad hoc resource for operational problem-solving. Its personnel, moreover, would be on call as individual experts to aid decision-makers in controlling the crisis.

As with the Standing Consultative Commission (SCC), the center's workings would be confidential and professional, fostering effective working relations between American and Soviet personnel. . . .

CONCLUSION

A joint Soviet-American crisis control center, probably most feasible in the form of twin centers in the two capitals linked by teleconferencing, can help control crises in a variety of ways. Carefully designed functions can help to reduce uncertainty, can increase the number of available options, and through its symbolic role can help reduce expectations of hostility. Made permanent, such a center could also become a focus and repository for learning from past crises.

Against these benefits need to be weighed the possible problems of added bureaucracy, foreign perceptions of condominium, intelligence leaks, disinformation, and the opportunities for troublemaking in crises.

In weighing the risks against the potential benefits, one should recognize the tendency to presuppose that the kinds of crises we are likely to experience are ones on the model of the Cuban Missile Crisis, the Middle East War of 1973, or perhaps the various Berlin crises. Crises of these types may indeed recur. But there is also a likelihood, increasing over time, of crises in which genuine U.S.–Soviet shared interests could dominate the competitive interests. *Agent provocateur* and many kinds of Third World nuclear war crises are examples. When the planning context is shifted to embrace nuclear crises in which the shared superpower interest dominates the competitive interest, a joint crisis control center seems more plausible.

NOTE

1. The papers, by Barry Blechman (February 1983) and Richard Betts (unpublished, March 1983), were produced for the Nunn-Warner Commission based at the Roosevelt Center for American Policy Studies in Washington, D.C. Blechman's paper has since been published in H. Roderick (ed.) *Avoiding Inadvertent War* (LBJ School of Public Affairs, Austin, 1984). This treatment of the concept, although different in several respects, is indebted to both papers.

48   One-half of One Percent for Peace

William M. Evan _____

In his "star wars" speech of March 23, 1983, President Reagan addressed the following challenge to scientists and technologists:

> I call upon the scientific community in our country, those who gave us nuclear weapons, to turn their great talents now to the cause of mankind and world peace; to give us the means of rendering these nuclear weapons impotent and obsolete.

This proposal—which is currently being seriously explored by a Pentagon task force—epitomizes America's faith in technological panaceas. Now that we have finally acknowledged that we are in a spiraling nuclear arms race with the Soviet Union, why bother to search for imaginative social, political, economic and legal inventions to stop it when a new technological "break-through" will do the trick? One such social invention to promote world peace would cost a mere one-half of one percent of the annual military budgets of the United States and the Soviet Union.

The addiction to *technological* solutions to the neglect of creative *social* solutions results in what the late sociologist William F. Ogburn called "cultural lag," which tends to result in major dislocations in our economic, social and political life. This technological addiction is prevalent in both the United States and the Soviet Union. In each country the doctrine of strategic deterrence has provided the justification for feverishly conducting research and development in order to

deploy and stockpile ever more destructive nuclear weapons.

Especially ominous in recent years are policies articulated in both the White House and the Kremlin providing for a "protracted limited nuclear war." Almost imperceptibly, the strategy of nuclear deterrence is being replaced with a strategy of limited nuclear war-fighting in the vain hope that it is possible to wage, win and survive a nuclear war.

Outstanding U.S. physical scientists have repeatedly warned that the existing nuclear warheads in the U.S. and Soviet arsenals are much more than enough to guarantee "mutual assured destruction" in the event either side resorts to a first strike.

Still, since the arms race began over 30 years ago, hundreds of thousands of U.S. and Soviet scientists and engineers have worked on the problems of applying science and technology to the designing of additional lethal weapons. A rough estimate of the total military expenditures on the arms race by the two superpowers from, say, 1953 to the present is about $10 trillion. By contrast, a minuscule amount of time and treasure has been devoted by social scientists and other scientists to such problems as:

- how to conduct disarmament negotiations between parties harboring mutual distrust and who have deep ideological conflicts;
- how to achieve industrial conversion from military to civilian uses;
- how to forecast the effects that reversing the arms race would have on the world economy;
- how to design new information and communications systems to help manage international crises and thus reduce the chances of a nuclear war that neither side wishes.

An international institution already exists that is capable of coordinating this type of research in the service of world peace. It is the United Nations University, headquartered in Tokyo and operating on a very modest budget. The general purpose envisioned in establishing this unique university in 1973 was to grapple with global problems and thus promote world order. To date, neither the United States nor the Soviet Union has contributed *any* funds for the operations of this University.

If the United States and the Soviet Union were willing to allocate just *one-half of one per-cent* of their annual military budgets to the U.N. University, a substantial amount of money would become available for peace-promoting and peace-keeping research by U.S. and Soviet scientists and by scientists from other countries as well.

According to the Stockholm International Peace Research Institute's 1982 *Yearbook*, the U.S. military budget in constant dollars in 1981 was $134,390 million, and the estimated Soviet military budget for 1981 was $118,800 million. One-half of one percent of these two budgets would have yielded roughly $1.25 billion to the University.

The arms race, to quote Herbert York, is a "race to oblivion." Unless we expeditiously invest in the development of new social, political, economic and legal inventions to stop it—and thus discover how to eliminate the fateful "cultural lag" between the rapidly accumulating arsenals of nuclear weapons and our feeble institutions of world order—no one, neither Americans nor Soviets, may be around to witness the dawn of the twenty-first century.

QUESTIONS FOR DISCUSSION

1. What are some of the differences between positional bargaining and bargaining based on interests, as advocated by Fisher and Ury?

2. How can arms control address the problem of controlling international crises?

3. In what ways have arms control and disarmament negotiations succeeded? In what ways have they failed?

4. Describe several international treaties concerning nuclear weapons that are currently in force.

5. Discuss the pros and cons of Garwin and Sagan's argument for banning space weapons.

6. If Evan's proposal for a U.N. University peace research program were implemented, what should be the main priorities for research?

SUGGESTED READINGS

BARTON, JOHN H. *The Politics of Peace: An Evaluation of Arms Control.* Stanford, Calif.: Stanford University Press, 1981.

BLECHMAN, BARRY M. and JANNE E. NOLAN. "Reorganizing for More Effective Arms Control Negotiations." *Foreign Affairs* 61 (Summer 1983): 1157–1182.

CLARKE, ARTHUR C. *1984: Spring: A Choice of Futures.* New York: Ballantine, 1984.

EVAN, WILLIAM M. and J. A. MacDOUGALL. "Interorganizational Conflict: A Labor-Management Bargaining Experiment." *Journal of Conflict Resolution* 11 (December, 1967): 398–413.

FORSBERG, RANDALL. "Parallel cuts in nuclear and conventional forces." *Bulletin of the Atomic Scientists* (August 1985): 152–56.

GOLDMAN, RALPH M. *Arms Control and Peacekeeping.* New York: Random House, 1982.

RAPOPORT, ANATOL. *Fights, Games and Debates.* Ann Arbor, Mich.: University of Michigan Press, 1960.

RUBIN, JEFFERY Z. and BERT R. BROWN. *The Social Psychology of Bargaining.* New York: Academic Press, 1975.

SCHELLING, THOMAS C. "What Went Wrong With Arms Control." *Foreign Affairs* 64 (Winter 1985/86): 219–233.

Chapter XIII

Unilateral Initiatives for Peace

Historically, progress toward arms control and disarmament agreements has been slow. Negotiations are laborious and time-consuming. Agreements are hard to reach. And while bilateral or multilateral talks drag on, weapons technology continues to advance, creating new issues that must be addressed in the next round of negotiations.

The limitations of bilateral and multilateral initiatives have led many analysts to look for steps that nations can take unilaterally to reduce the risk of nuclear war. Though some peacekeeping measures can only be achieved through negotiation, there are also many possibilities for unilateral actions that could lower the likelihood of nuclear war. Analysts have proposed a wide range of innovations—both technological and social—that could be adopted unilaterally and that their advocates say would promote peace. (Such unilateral initiatives should not be confused with unilateral disarmament, though this step has from time to time been advocated by some peace activists.)

This chapter introduces the concept of unilateral initiatives as a strategy for preventing nuclear war and describes some of the proposals people have made for unilateral action. The authors we have chosen often disagree about specific unilateral initiatives, though they all believe that such initiatives can play an important role in keeping the peace.

We begin with an excerpt from Charles Osgood's essay on "graduated unilateral initiatives for peace." Osgood argues that a cycle of small unilateral actions, taken by one side and then reciprocated, could gradually wind down international tensions and promote peace.

Next, Albert Carnesale, Joseph S. Nye, Jr., and Graham Allison propose an "Agenda for Action" that the U.S. could follow to help prevent nuclear war. Most of the ideas they suggest are unilateral initiatives, though they make several proposals that would require international efforts.

In the third reading, former Secretary of Defense Robert McNamara outlines eighteen steps that the U.S. could take to prevent nuclear war. Thirteen of McNamara's proposals involve unilateral actions.

Finally, Kurt Gottfried, Henry Kendall and John E. Lee argue that the North Atlantic Treaty Organization (NATO) should pledge never to be the first to use nuclear weapons during a conflict. They maintain that taking such a step could markedly lower the risk of nuclear war breaking out in Europe.

49   Graduated Unilateral Initiatives for Peace

Charles E. Osgood

ARMS CONTROL AND TENSION CONTROL

The combination of nationalism, cold-war thinking, and the paradoxes of the nuclear age—particularly the imbalance between offensive and defensive capabilities—is forcing nations inexorably toward the policy of mutual nuclear deterrence. This combination of factors has simultaneously been forcing policy-makers toward serious consideration of the stability of such deterrence. Just because we have a phrase, "stabilized deterrence," which seems to imply that there must be some solid, protective technological system, does not mean that such a referent really exists.

Deterrence is more a psychological question than a technological answer. An opponent is assumed to be deterred from initiating a nuclear attack by his expectation of unacceptable retaliation. But if the opponent is not deterred, if he makes a wrong decision—whether due to fear, to overconfidence, to misinformation, or even to some accident—then the invulnerability of one's retaliatory capacity and the certainty of its delivery does nothing whatsoever to defend one's own civilian population. This is why discussions of stabilized deterrence inevitably involve matters like the "credibility" of retaliation and the "rationality" of human decisions, which are also psychological problems. So let us now confront some of the assumptions of stabilized deterrence

Excerpted from Charles E. Osgood, "Graduated Unilateral Initiatives for Peace," *Preventing World War III: Some Proposals* (pp. 168–177), copyright © 1962 by Quincy Wright, William M. Evan, and Morton Deutsch. Reprinted by permission of Simon & Schuster, Inc.

with some of the facts of human decision-making under stress that we have just been analyzing.

The credibility of deterrence assumes full appreciation of the dangers of nuclear war on all sides; but the mechanism of denial, the perverse attractiveness of denied dangers, and the essential meaninglessness of the words with which we talk about it all prevent such full appreciation. Stability of deterrence assumes objective evaluation of the intentions of an opponent and objective interpretation of world events; but both psycho-logic and the relativity of social judgment hinder such objectivity and transform the complexities of international relations into an oversimplified contest between the Good Guys and the Bad Guys. Stability requires that decisions be based on accurate determination of probabilities rather than emotional reaction to mere possibilities; but the wishful-fearful thinking characteristic of schizophrenics also affects the decisions of normals under stress, and they become prone to deciding in terms of their wishes (overconfidence) or their fears (underconfidence). Maintaining stable deterrence in a world where situations change with bewildering speed and complexity demands great flexibility of means yet consistency of ends; but cognitive stereotypy both restricts the range of alternatives and shortens perspective, substituting blind reactions to immediate pressures for long-range persistence toward ultimate goals.

It is true that men can be rational, and often are, but it is also true that they can be nonrational, and these are merely some of the mechanisms of nonrationality. These are some of the ways in which humans reach decisions without the benefit of logic and without even maximizing their own self-interest in the game-theoretic sense, and yet these ways of thinking are lawful in that they conform to and are predictable from the principles of human behavior. In a situation where the consequences of wrong decisions are so awesome, where a single bit of irrationality can set a whole chain of traumatic events in motion, I do not think that we can be satisfied with the assurance that "most people behave rationally most of the time."

What are the conditions that strengthen and exaggerate these nonrational mechanisms in human decision-making? What conditions make normal people appear irrational? And we must add, what conditions make truly irrational people appear normal, because under analysis it seems that the same conditions which make normals seem irrational make irrationals seem normal: To a population driven into nonrationality, a fanatic may seem not only normal but ideal. There are two general sets of conditions that magnify nonrationality: The first concerns *information*—its availability, bias, and overload in the human decision system; the second, and the one I wish to emphasize here, is *tension-level*.

We have already seen that, beyond some optimal level, further increases in tension serve to restrict the range of perceived alternatives, thereby limiting the flexibility and creativity of human problem-solving. It is also certainly true that increases in tension, beyond some optimal level, serve to magnify the ratio of nonrational to rational alternatives. Under stress men are more likely to act irrationally, to strike out blindly or even to freeze into stupid immobility. In other words, both flexibility and rationality "ride on the back" of tension-level.

World events may have either a tension-increasing or a tension-decreasing impact upon the international system. *The real stability of the system depends upon its capacity to absorb such event-shocks, and this in turn depends upon the absolute level of tension.* If the system is at a relatively low level of tension, it can absorb a succession of event-shocks, such as a revolution in Latin America, the demonstration of a new weapon, or the accidental explosion of an old one, without being moved far from an optimum level of flexibility and rationality. But if the system is already functioning at a relatively high level of tension, then the same set of event-shocks may push it over into the region of rigidity and irrationality.

It is important to realize that while tension cumulates across various sources, its effect upon flexibility and rationality is independent of source.

Equally important for the remainder of my argument is the fact that reduction in tension-level is independent of its sources. In other words, tension is something like money in a bank account; its amount can be increased by "deposits" from a variety of sources and decreased by "withdrawals" for a variety of uses.

If my analysis of the relation between what is called "stability of the military environment" and tension-level is valid, then it puts a premium on the development and application of *techniques of tension control*. Stability is a dynamic concept, not a static one, and we need to create and maintain a dynamic, shock-absorbing "cushion" for the international system. But tension control cannot be entirely a unilateral affair, so we must look for techniques which are likely to induce reciprocation.

The traditional, if seldom successful, method of reducing international tensions is through mutual-disarmament negotiations. We have behind us a long and dismal history of unsuccessful negotiations. It is perhaps another paradox that the greater the need for negotiated agreements, the more difficult they are to obtain. It is easy for each side to blame these failures on the intractability and insincerity of the other, but the same mechanisms operate on both sides. One is what I call *biased perception of the equable*: Given their quite different national life-histories, both sides approach negotiations with different sets of meanings; "inspection" means espionage for one but elimination of secrecy for the other, "The United Nations" means a biased tool to one but an unbiased international body to the other, "overseas bases" mean aggressive intent to one but defensive intent to the other, and so on. Another mechanism is *the self-fulfilling prophecy*: Prior to any negotiation, the press on each side predicts that the other is insincere and merely using the discussions for propaganda purposes; each side then behaves in such a way as to counteract what it expects of the other; nothing is accomplished, and both sides go away saying, "I told you so!" And then there is the plain, ordinary matter of *mutual distrust*: Under the impetus of psycho-logic, each side expects the other to cheat, and one even hears it said that treaties with THEM are not worth the paper they're written on.

The conclusion we seem driven to is this: *Negotiated agreements require commitment prior to action, and under the conditions of the cold war mentality commitments of any significance are difficult to obtain; thus neither side is able to take the initiative as long as it remains chained to the requirement of prior commitment by the other.* Clearly, some other approach is needed if we are ever to break out of this impasse.

INITIATIVE THROUGH UNILATERAL ACTION

In the remainder of this paper I would like to explore with you the possibilities that may lie in unilateral action of a particular type. For several years I have been trying to develop and justify an approach to international relations which I call *Graduated Reciprocation in Tension-Reduction.* The essence of the idea is that the tensions/arms-race spiral may provide the model for its own reversal. As a type of international behavior, *the arms race is a case of graduated and reciprocated unilateral action.* It is unilateral in that the nation developing a new weapon, increasing its stockpile, or setting up a new military base does not make its action contingent upon any prior agreement with the other side. It is reciprocal, however, because each increment in military power by one side provides the stimulus for the other to try to catch up and get ahead. It is necessarily graduated, first by the irregular and somewhat unpredictable occurrences of technological break-through and second by the oscillating nature of the threat stimulus itself.

But the arms race is obviously a *tension-increasing* system. One can readily conceive of a graduated and reciprocated, unilaterally initiated system that is *tension-reducing* in nature. The question is whether or not it is feasible under present conditions. I will try to demonstrate that, given anything like the dedication and energy now being thrown into the arms race, it would be feasible, even though by no means magically simple.

This approach must be sharply distinguished from the kind of abject and complete unilateral disarmament sponsored by pacifist groups. To the contrary, what I am proposing is a flexible, self-regulating procedure in which the participants continually monitor their own actions on the basis of their evaluation of the reciprocating actions taken by the other side. It involves some risk, to be sure, but the risk is limited; merely going on doing what we are now doing involves infinitely greater risk! It is broader than disarmament, or even disengagement as usually conceived, since it would include programs of graduated unilateral actions of a tension-reducing nature in the areas of science and secrecy, social, economic, and cultural exchange, Communist China and the United Nations, controls and inspection, and so forth, as well as actual military and disarmament steps. It may be viewed as a kind of international (rather than interpersonal) communicating and learning situation, where the communication is more by deeds than by words and where what is learned is mutual understanding and trust.

However, being both unconventional and conciliatory in nature, this procedure is liable to suspicion abroad and resistance at home, particularly under conditions of the cold war mentality. Therefore it needs to be spelled out in detail, critically evaluated, and even tried out under both laboratory and field conditions. Specifically, it is necessary to indicate the characteristics that unilateral actions in such a program should have in order to maintain adequate felt security while nevertheless inducing reciprocation from an opponent; furthermore, we need to clarify the criteria for both determining the substance of unilateral initiatives and evaluating the bonafideness and significance of unilateral reciprocations. In other words, while admittedly idealistic in purpose, this rather novel approach must be shown to be realistic and feasible within the existing situation of competing sovereign states.

In the following analysis I will be speaking from the viewpoint of a nation which initiates such a policy of graduated reciprocation in tension-reduction. This is necessary to maintain a consistent orientation. But I want it understood that I have no particular nation in mind as the initiator—it could be either of the two polar nuclear powers, the United States or the USSR, or it could very well be some other nation or group of nations, present or future. Furthermore, just as with an arms race, once this kind of international behavior were underway, the distinction between initiation and reciprocation would become as meaningless as the distinction between stimulus and response within the central nervous system.

MAINTAINING SECURITY

1. *Unilateral actions should not reduce a nation's capacity to inflict unacceptable nuclear retaliation on an opponent should it be attacked.* I would be the first to agree that nu-

clear deterrence does not provide any real security over the long haul, but on the other hand, highly invulnerable second-strike forces will exist in the near future, if not already, and under present levels of tension they are not likely to be given up. Particularly if their retaliatory nature is made explicit, and moral prohibition against their first use is accepted by all sides, nuclear weapons can be viewed not only as a deterrent *but also as a security base from which limited risks can be taken.* I am assuming that since there is no necessary correlation between the tension-reducing impacts of actions and their military significance, a program of graduated reciprocation in tension-reduction could produce an atmosphere of mutual trust in which the nuclear deterrents themselves could ultimately be eliminated by negotiated agreement.

2. *Unilateral actions should be graduated in risk potential according to the degree of reciprocation obtained.* This is the essential self-regulating characteristic of the proposal. The magnitude of a unilateral step taken at a particular time would depend upon that nation's evaluation of the reciprocative behavior of the other. The process can be slowed down or speeded up, as conditions require, but it should be kept going.

3. *Unilateral actions should be diversified in nature so as not to weaken a nation progressively in any one sphere.* Diversity in areas of action both provides an essential flexibility of approach and prevents the unstabilizing effect of too large steps in a single sphere. The only common property of the actions envisaged in this proposal is their tension-reducing nature. This, as I pointed out earlier, can be cumulative over a highly diversified range of actions, e.g., student exchanges, sharing of scientific information, reducing trade barriers, diplomatic recognition, elimination of bases, and so on.

4. *Prior to announcement, unilateral actions should be unpredictable by an opponent as to their nature, locus, and time of execution.* This is to minimize the likelihood of encroachment. I submit that, psychologically, an opponent is much less likely to encroach aggressively in an area after public announcement of intent by another than prior to it, and he is certainly less likely to gain world support if he does. However, if encroachments do occur they must be resisted

just as firmly as if this policy were not in operation. Yet, this resistance should be pinpointed to the area of encroachment and the program of tension-reducing moves continued flexibly in other areas. This is clearly a different approach than the traditional, monolithic reaction of nations to tension-increasing events, but it is an approach that seems necessary in a nuclear age. Under conditions of nuclear deterrence, encroachments are likely to be tentative and probing in nature, and therefore can constitute a learning experience on all sides—learning that graduated reciprocation in reducing tensions is not synonymous with surrender.

INDUCING RECIPROCATION

1. *Unilateral actions should be announced publicly at some reasonable interval prior to their execution and indentified as part of a deliberate policy of reducing tensions.* Announcement prior to action is suggested as a means of augmenting pressure toward reciprocation, of avoiding the unstabilizing effect of unexpected moves, of providing time for preparing reciprocation, and, particularly, of influencing the interpretation of the action when it comes. Public announcement makes it possible to enlist pressures of world opinion toward reciprocation, and identification of each act as part of a deliberate policy is designed to make the pressures toward reciprocation cumulative.

2. *In their announcement, unilateral actions should include explicit invitation to reciprocation in some form.* Initiation and reciprocation need not be the same in kind nor even equal in quantity. There are some unilateral actions that could not be reciprocated in kind (e.g., if the United States were to denuclearize some Pacific base, the Chinese Communists could not reciprocate in kind) and the burden of the same rule may be quite different in two countries (e.g., absolute amounts of inspection permitted). On the other hand, the fact that reciprocation in some form is expected must be made explicit. The isolated unilateral gestures that have occasionally been made in the past have been largely abortive, in part because they did not call for reciprocation.

3. *Unilateral actions that have been announced must be executed on schedule regardless of*

prior commitment by the opponent to recip-rocate. This is the characteristic that distinguishes this policy from traditional bargaining and negotiating procedures; it is the characteristic that provides an increased degree of freedom on all sides for taking the initiative. Of course, if no reciprocation is forthcoming, or attempts are made to take advantage of the initiator, then the process slows down or stops. In this sense, reciprocation can be viewed as a kind of postcommitment that enables the policy to continue.

4. *Unilateral actions should be planned in graded series and continued over a considerable period regardless of immediate reciprocation or police action elsewhere.* Given the tense atmosphere in which such a strategy must begin, it is likely that initial actions would be greeted by cries of "cold war trick!"; but the bonafideness of the intent becomes more and more difficult to deny and rationalize as action follows announced action. Furthermore, the pressure toward reciprocation should cumulate over such a period of continued action. Here again we have a kind of international learning situation—in this case, unlearning the bogeyman image of the opponent, since the psycho-logic expectations and prophesies being made about him are being repeatedly denied.

5. *As far as possible, unilateral actions should be overt deeds rather than either positive or negative sanctions and should be as unambiguous and as susceptible to verification as possible.* Overt acts have the obvious advantage of bonafideness, particularly if the announced action includes invitation to observe and inspect. Sanctions, on the other hand, have no visible execution or test until their failure—the unilaterally imposed bans on nuclear testing are a case in point. This emphasizes another difference between this kind of policy and ordinary negotiations, a difference well expressed by the homely saying, "actions speak louder than words."

What about the problem of *evaluating reciprocations* (and, for that matter, the problem an opponent has in evaluating one's unilateral initiations)? There are two rather different questions here: One concerns the bonafideness of actions, which seems to come down to the adequacy of intelligence in the military sense; the other concerns the significance of actions, and this seems to be a matter for strategic analysis.

To enhance *bonafideness*, both the initiator's unilateral acts and the reciprocations requested should be as unambiguous and susceptible to verification as possible; provisions for adequate inspection may be included in both initiations and requested reciprocations. As a matter of fact, it might be possible to get around the apparent deadlock on inspection by introducing it in small, manageable and perhaps palatable packages under such a program as this; if one side accepts an invitation to unilaterally inspect some specific action of the other, it becomes psychologically difficult to deny him the same privilege. As to the *significance* of reciprocations, two criteria would have to be kept in mind: first, that the risk potential in the unilateral actions by one party should be roughly balanced by the increased security gained through the reciprocations of the other party; second, that tension-decreasing steps in one area must be balanced against the total level of tension-increasing and tension-decreasing events in all areas. I realize that these estimations are not easy, but they involve the sort of strategic analysis that is going on all the time anyhow.

Finally, there are some additional criteria for selecting actions that should be mentioned. First, it is probably wisest to begin such a program with actions in areas other than the critical military and disarmament spheres, moving in toward these matters only when the general level of tension has been sufficiently reduced. Second, particularly in the early phases, unilateral initiatives should involve areas in which both parties in the conflict are known to be ready to move, in which restraints may already have been reciprocally self-imposed, and in which both are likely to see issues of human welfare rather than national security. Again, we have here a kind of learning situation on all sides, and it is important that the probabilities of reinforcement be high at first. And since we would wish the substance of our actions to be consistent with our long-term goals as well as our immediate needs to control tensions, they should be designed to gradually shape the world of tomorrow; therefore, unilateral initiatives and reciprocations should involve gradual transfer of sovereignty from national to international auspices, gradual lessening of the imbalance between "have" and "have not" countries, and gradual shifting of scientific research onto an international basis on the model of the IGY, particularly research having military implications where scientific breakthroughs have an unstabilizing impact.

Despite the unilateral initiative which characterizes this proposal, it should be apparent that the two parties in conflict are really dependent on each other for its success. This is because on each side there are competing factions spread over the spectrum of policy alternatives. If President Kennedy, exercising administrative initiative, were to announce and execute a carefully planned series of tension-reducing moves, opposition groups in the United States government, in its mass media, and in its public would become increasingly critical. The only way to quiet this opposition and keep the policy moving, in the long run, would be to receive reciprocation from the opponent. I am sure that much the same situation would hold in the case of Soviet initiation. Now it is true that the leadership of a nation would be risking its position by initiating such a policy and that an opponent might assist in the demise by withholding reciprocation—*but in doing so the opponent should be fully aware of the fact that he is strengthening forces more violently antagonistic to him and more likely to act inflexibly and irrationally in future relations*. Thus it would be to the advantage of both sides to be on the alert for tension-reducing probes from the other and to be prepared for reciprocations that will allow the process to continue.

Could the initiator of such a policy expect to obtain bonafide and significant reciprocation under present conditions? I cannot give an unqualified "yes" to this question. Here, obviously, lies the risk—but as I pointed out earlier, merely going on as we are involves even greater risk. And surely it would be cause for cosmic irony if two human groups in conflict were to bring their world down in destruction because of their threatening images of each other without ever testing the validity of these images. Despite the differences between us, there are many things we share; we share common modes of thinking and feeling, we share a common technology that is rapidly transforming us into one world whether we like it or not, and above all we share a common desire to get out of this dangerous situation and go on living. If my basic assumption about the contemporary motivation of international behavior is right—that it is based more on fear

and insecurity than on any urge toward national aggrandizement—then I think reciprocation would be forthcoming, if not for reasons of good will then for reasons of good sense. And here another psychological principle applies: If two people are forced to keep on behaving *as if* they trusted each other, their beliefs and attitudes tend to fall in line with their behaviors. I think the same applies to nations.

CONCLUSION

The preservation of peace is the biggest problem of our time, and I have no illusions about my own capacity to comprehend it all. Although the problem has important psychological components, much more than psychology is involved —political science, economics, international law, communications, nuclear and space technology, diplomacy, and the military, to call only part of the roll. And no one as aware as I am of the strength of the contrary forces, of the deeply ingrained mechanisms of the cold war mentality, could be very sanguine about our chances of escaping from this situation unscathed.

On the other hand, I have convinced myself, at least, that such a policy of graduated reciprocation in tension control is feasible for our time. True, it would require extraordinary sensitivity, flexibility, and restraint from leadership on all sides, as well as high-level strategic planning and execution, but this could be viewed as a challenge rather than a flaw. If it were successfully initiated, such a policy could, over the short term, increase the stability of the military environment and perhaps create an atmosphere in which more significant steps toward disarmament could be taken; over the long term, it might offer a model for international relations that is more appropriate to this age of nuclear technology. I can do no better than close with a quotation from Albert Einstein that might have been written today: "The unleashed power of the atom has changed everything except our ways of thinking. Thus we are drifting toward a catastrophe beyond comparison. We shall require a substantially new manner of thinking if mankind is to survive."

50 An Agenda for Action

Albert Carnesale, Joseph S. Nye, Jr., and Graham T. Allison _____

1. MAINTAIN A CREDIBLE NUCLEAR DETERRENT

- DO modernize the strategic triad.
- DON'T adopt a no-first-use policy.

To avoid war, it is necessary (though not sufficient) to maintain the capability of our military forces and the credibility of our political intentions and resolve. Our nuclear arsenal continues to play an important role in deterring aggression against the territory of the United States, our allies, and other areas of vital interest to us. There currently is rough parity in the U.S.–Soviet nuclear balance; but exactly what deters the Soviets is unknown to Americans, and is likely to remain so. Nevertheless, there seems little doubt that deterrence of deliberate nuclear or conventional attack on the American homeland is effective, robust, and stable. No U.S. or Soviet weapons program in progress or on the horizon will significantly alter the likelihood of such attacks, nor are any new capabilities within reach that would give either side a meaningful strategic advantage. Less hardy is deterrence of Soviet aggression against our allies or other areas of vital interest to us, because the threat to use nuclear weapons in response to attacks outside our homeland is inherently less credible. Our suggestions for actions to be taken and actions to be avoided are designed to ensure that Soviet leaders see no advantage in the balance of nuclear forces and to maximize the credibility of our nuclear deterrent.

Selection is reprinted from *Hawks, Doves, and Owls, An Agenda for Avoiding Nuclear War* (pp. 224, 225–246), edited by Graham T. Allison, Albert Carnesale, and Joseph S. Nye, Jr., by permission of W.W. Norton & Company, Inc. Copyright © 1985 by Graham T. Allison, Albert Carnesale, and Joseph S. Nye, Jr.

TABLE 50–1 Ten Principles for Avoiding Nuclear War

1. Maintain a credible nuclear deterrent
2. Obtain a credible conventional deterrent
3. Enhance crisis stability
4. Reduce the impact of accidents
5. Develop procedures for war termination
6. Prevent and manage crises
7. Invigorate nonproliferation efforts
8. Limit misperceptions
9. Pursue arms control negotiations
10. Reduce reliance on nuclear deterrence over the long term

Actions to Take

- **DO modernize the strategic triad.** The three legs of the strategic triad (land-based missiles, sea-based missiles, and long-range bombers and air-launched cruise missiles) comprise a diverse and redundant retaliatory force. Each component has unique properties, and their collective ability to survive attack and penetrate defenses is greater than that of each leg in isolation. The triad should be modernized as necessary to ensure that an adequate proportion would survive attack and be able to penetrate Soviet defenses. A modern ICBM force, smaller than the other legs of the triad, should be maintained to contribute to deterrence by the threat of reliable prompt use of small numbers of nuclear weapons against virtually any meaningful military targets and as a hedge against possible Soviet breakthroughs in antisubmarine warfare or air defenses. Such capabilities could be acquired by upgrading current Minuteman ICBMs or by deploying new ICBMs or by some combination of these modernizations. Over the longer term, consideration should be given to missile-carrying submarines smaller than the current versions.

• *DO put alliance politics first.* Deterrence depends not only on military capabilities, but also on perceived readiness to use force. The political cohesion of an alliance is essential to the credibility of its deterrent. In this connection, it is important for NATO to continue implementation of its intermediate-range nuclear force (INF) modernization program, unless an agreement is reached with the Soviets whereby NATO forgoes some of the planned INF deployments in return for similar reductions of Soviet forces. Political disputes that fractionate the alliance and weaken its resolve can be even more destructive than adverse changes in the military balance.

Actions to Avoid

• *DON'T adopt a no-first-use policy.* Rhetorical removal of the threat of intentional escalation to nuclear war in Europe, the Persian Gulf, or Korea would (if believed) psychologically enhance Soviet advantages in general purpose forces and increase the risk that the Soviets might attempt a conventional attack. If the current imbalance in conventional forces were corrected, so that the West could respond effectively to Soviet offensives without any perceived resort to nuclear weapons, then a strategy of no-first-use would be more attractive. There is no indication, however, that the West is likely soon to build up its conventional forces to that level. For the foreseeable future, a no-first-use declaration would be counterproductive militarily and would undermine essential alliance cohesion. Special effort should be made, however, to eliminate any requirements or operating procedures calling for early use of nuclear weapons in response to conventional aggression.

• *DON'T pursue a comprehensive freeze.* Alarm about the risk of nuclear war has increasingly been expressed in calls for a "comprehensive nuclear freeze." Unfortunately, however, a comprehensive freeze is not a good prescription for avoiding nuclear war. For example, because it is difficult to define and verify a freeze on defensive systems, most so-called "comprehensive" freeze proposals deal only with

offensive nuclear weapons. But an agreement that froze only offensive forces and not the corresponding defensive ones (including ballistic missile defenses, air defenses, and antisubmarine warfare) could lead to shifts in the offense-defense balance that would weaken the deterrent value of offensive retaliatory forces. In addition, by prohibiting all modernization of nuclear weapons systems, a comprehensive freeze would preclude changes that would reduce the risk of nuclear war, such as modification of long-range bombers to provide faster takeoff (and thus greater survivability) and replacement of large multiple-warhead ICBMs by small single-warhead models. Partial freezes that impose discriminating restraints on weapons technology can be both feasible and beneficial. The merits of such proposals must, of course, be judged on a case-by-case basis.

• *DON'T confuse MAD with a strategy.* Mutual assured destruction (MAD) describes a condition, not an objective. In this condition, each superpower can absorb a first strike and still retaliate massively against its adversary's population and industry. This condition exists today and is likely to persist for the foreseeable future. But MAD is not an objective of American policy. Its "mutuality" is unattractive to most American policymakers (and presumably to Soviets as well). Nor is MAD a military strategy, for it does not serve to guide U.S. targeting (which focuses primarily on Soviet military forces). Public understanding is not advanced by those who pretend that MAD is America's strategy or goal.

• *DON'T assume that cities can be defended.* In announcing his Strategic Defense Initiative (SDI) on March 23, 1983, President Reagan called for a defensive system that "could intercept and destroy strategic ballistic missiles before they reached our own soil or that of our allies" and thereby render nuclear weapons "impotent and obsolete." The long-term goal is understandable and readily shared, but in all likelihood mutual assured destruction will remain the condition of superpowers for decades to come. Because a substantial portion of each nation's population and industry is concentrated in a relatively small number of cities, and each city can be destroyed by a few nuclear weapons, their protection requires a perfect or near-perfect defense against all forms of nuclear delivery, including long- and short-range ballistic missiles and cruise missiles, manned bombers and, for that matter, fishing trawlers, civilian aircraft, and other means for covert delivery. There are sound military reasons favoring continued research on defensive systems, but it should not be assumed that such research will lead to an effective defense of cities.

2. OBTAIN A CREDIBLE CONVENTIONAL DETERRENT

- DO strengthen NATO and the RDF.
- DON'T provoke the Soviet Union.

The non-nuclear forces of the United States and its allies are currently inadequate to deter with high confidence or to defend against Soviet conventional attack in Europe, the Persian Gulf region, and other areas of vital interest. Thus the United States finds itself in effect threatening first use of nuclear weapons to counter conventional aggression. By choosing to rely on early nuclear use, the United States and its European and Japanese allies have opted for defense "on the cheap." Current political preferences make an early reversal of this policy unlikely, but it is not unaffordable. The Soviet Union enjoys no economic advantage over the United States. Quite the reverse: the U.S. gross national product (GNP) is roughly twice that of the Soviet Union. Moreover, the United States and its allies enjoy a combined GNP more than four times that of the Soviet Union and its allies. If the Western democracies and Japan rely on a cheaper, more dangerous, more nuclear-weapons-dependent defense, it is because they choose to accept that risk. Insufficient resources are not a plausible excuse.

Actions to Take

• *DO strengthen NATO and the RDF.* Because threats to use conventional force are more credible than threats to use nuclear weapons, improved general purpose forces would enhance deterrence even between the nuclear superpowers. The United States and its allies, each paying its fair share, should continue those conventional force improvements that reduce the chances that the Soviets could achieve rapid victory conventionally in vital areas like Europe and the Persian Gulf. Such improvements include the acquisition of a militarily meaningful Rapid Deployment Force (RDF) and additional airlift and sealift capacities, and upgrading of air defenses in Europe. Our objective should be to escape from

the position in which we have to threaten escalation to nuclear use; greater conventional capabilities will strengthen deterrence of Soviet aggression and reduce the dangers of conventional and nuclear war.

• *DO raise the nuclear threshold.* By developing and deploying conventional weapons systems capable of performing some of the functions now assigned to battlefield nuclear weapons, the United States and its allies can raise their threshold of nuclear use. This transition would be complemented by a reversal of the United States' practice of integrating battlefield nuclear weapons with general purpose forces. It must be recognized, however, that conventional forces alone cannot eliminate the risk of nuclear war. After all, the Soviets could choose to use nuclear weapons first.

Actions to Avoid

• *DON'T provoke the Soviet Union.* As the United States and its allies expand and improve their conventional forces, they should be wary of the dangers of threatening vital Soviet interests. Regardless of the peacefulness of the West's intentions, our offensive conventional capabilities should not be strong enough to pose plausible threats to Eastern Europe and the Soviet homeland. NATO should continue to adhere to a military strategy consistent with the fundamentally defensive character of its current forces. An offensive force posture and strategy, whether based on nuclear or advanced conventional technologies, even though intended to enhance deterrence could increase the risk of nuclear war by provoking the Soviets to preempt or by lowering their threshold for nuclear use.

• *DON'T pretend that nuclear weapons deter only nuclear war.* The proposition that the *only* military purpose of nuclear weapons is to deter the adversary's use of nuclear weapons is gaining acceptance as a new conventional wisdom. But we believe it is wrong. So long as nuclear forces are deployed in substantial numbers, they present an inescapable risk that any conventional war might escalate by design or by accident to a nuclear one. How much the United States should rely on the risk of nuclear escalation to deter conventional war is an appropriate topic for debate. That discussion is not advanced, however, by denying that the danger of nuclear escalation affects the calculations of a potential aggressor.

3. ENHANCE CRISIS STABILITY

- DO take decapitation seriously.
- DON'T adopt a launch-on-warning policy.

Though nuclear weapons remain essential for deterrence, our goal is to avoid their use. Nuclear weapons must be a last resort. Our preferred posture is one in which the Soviet Union can gain no advantage in striking first. One current problem is the apparent vulnerability of our fixed land-based ICBMs, which could be destroyed by only a fraction of the Soviets' large force of highly accurate multiple-warhead ICBMs. Our bombers are less vulnerable than our ICBMs, and our missile-bearing submarines at sea are virtually invulnerable. The weakest and most often overlooked element of our deterrent is the system for coordinating the use of the weapons themselves. It is critical to shape our nuclear forces to minimize incentives for preemption and allow time for diplomacy to work during a crisis.

Actions to Take

• *DO take decapitation seriously.* If there is a chink in our nuclear armor, it is the vulnerability of the command, control, and communications (C^3) structure associated with nuclear weapons. Particularly vulnerable are the people in the political chain of command, almost all of whom usually are located in Washington, D.C. A surprise or preemptive "decapitation" attack against the C^3 structure might be attempted in hopes that surviving weapons could not then be used in retaliation. The Reagan administration's Strategic Modernization Program gives highest priority to upgrading and improving the survivability of the C^3 system. That priority is well deserved.

• *DO send a top leader out of Washington during crises.* Given the danger of decapitation, it is essential that at least one of the seventeen constitutionally designated successors (and an appropriate staff) be outside of Washington in time of crisis. While it is contrary to the instincts of policy makers to be away from the action, at least one top official should be out of harm's way. In a serious crisis, it would be more important to the nation to have the vice president located in an alternative command post than in Washington trying to assist in managing the situation.

• *DO develop a survivable small ICBM.* The ICBM force is the most vulnerable leg of the strategic triad. To reduce the dangers of surprise or preemptive attack against these land-based missiles and to hedge against Soviet breakthroughs in antisubmarine warfare or air defenses, the United States should continue to develop a small ICBM (such as the "Midgetman") and to investigate the most effective modes in which it might be deployed (such as mobile launchers, deceptive basing, and defended silos). Even if ICBMs cannot be made reliably survivable, a modern ICBM force should be retained. The unique ability of ICBMs to perform prompt controlled attacks against a wide variety of targets is an important element of deterrence, and their deployment on land complicates any Soviet first strike against missiles and bombers.

Actions to Avoid

• *DON'T adopt a launch-on-warning policy.* Some have proposed a policy of launch-on-warning or launch-under-attack as a solution to the ICBM vulnerability problem. This cure is worse than the disease, for it would increase unacceptably the dangers of accidental or unauthorized launch. The United States should maintain the capability to launch on warning or under attack, and its declaratory policy should be sufficiently ambiguous that the Soviets could not be confident that it would not do so. But we should not adopt launch-on-warning or launch-under-attack as operational or unambiguous declaratory policy.

• *DON'T seek a first-strike capability.* Neither side could actually achieve a disarming first-strike capability, for the other side has the option of launching its strategic missiles on warning of, or during, an attack. Any attempt by the United States to acquire a disarming first-strike capability would encourage the Soviets to put their forces on a hair-trigger and would increase Soviet incentives to preempt in time of crisis, thereby significantly reducing our own security. Thus, we should not structure our forces to threaten the survival of the full spectrum of Soviet retaliatory forces.

• *DON'T plan for a nuclear demonstration shot in Europe.* Among NATO's contingency plans for responding to Soviet conventional aggression in Europe is a nuclear "shot across the bow" to demonstrate the alliance's resolve. But such a non-military use of nuclear weapons could have an effect quite different from the intended one. On the one hand, it could be seen as evidence of NATO's unwillingness to engage in a "real" nuclear war. On the other hand, if interpreted as a prelude to a substantial nuclear attack, it might induce an all-out preemptive strike by the Soviets. A nuclear demonstration shot in Europe is unlikely to serve NATO's interests.

4. REDUCE THE IMPACT OF ACCIDENTS

- DO reduce reliance on short-range theater nuclear weapons.
- DON'T use nuclear alerts for political signaling.

Accidents will happen. Broadly defined as unintended events, accidents are as certain as human fallibility and as Murphy's Law in large complex organizations. We protect against accident by maintaining reserve (not running systems at full capacity), redundancy (having more than one system to rely on), and time (introducing pauses that allow us to correct the effects of accidents). We protect against unauthorized use of nuclear weapons by special procedures and physical barriers such as permissive action links (special electronic combination locks). Given the irrationality of major nuclear war, accidents would be likely to play a significant role in the chain of events leading up to any such conflict. Thus it is important to find ways to introduce reserve, redundancy, and time into organizational procedures for dealing with nuclear crises.

Actions to Take

• *DO reduce reliance on short-range theater nuclear weapons.* Short-range theater nuclear weapons (such as nuclear artillery shells) would prove difficult to control centrally if conflict should arise. Most commanders in the field doubt that release authority would be received in time for their use against an attack. This reduces the deterrent value of these weapons. They do, however, pose a real danger of accidental or unauthorized use in peacetime and especially in the "fog of war." Conventional weapons based on emerging technologies will enable NATO to threaten more credibly to destroy targets, including massed Soviet armored divisions, currently assigned to short-range nuclear forces. Accordingly, we should reduce our reliance on these short-range weapons for deterrence and, to the extent feasible politically, withdraw them gradually from likely regions of conflict.

• *DO add safety devices and procedures.* Current safety devices and procedures such as permissive action links (PALs), weapons designs that prevent accidental nuclear detonation, and rules that require action by two or more people to arm each nuclear weapon should be maintained, improved, and extended. Of particular concern is the absence of PALs on the nuclear warheads on submarine-launched ballistic missiles, enabling launch of these armed weapons even in the absence of an express order from the president or his authorized successor. The United States should consider seriously the possibility of installing PALs on the nuclear weapons on SLBMs. Such PALs would reduce the danger of accidental and authorized use, but at the cost of increasing the potential effectiveness (and therefore the likelihood) of a Soviet decapitation strike. This cost could be reduced in several ways. For example, the PALs need not necessarily be active on all missile submarines or at all times. They might be relaxed on some of the submarines routinely and on most or all of them when ordered by higher authorities.

• *DO upgrade warning systems.* To protect against the danger of false alarms and to enhance confidence in "positive" signals of attack, the United States should maintain redundancy in its intelligence, surveillance, and communications systems. We should also explore with the Soviets the possibility of negotiating an agreement under which each side could place unmanned sensors in the missile fields of the other side.

Actions to Avoid

• *DON'T use nuclear alerts for political signaling.* Nuclear alerts are a dangerous form of communication, especially during crises. When some form of alert appears necessary to ensure the survival of our forces in case of an attack, preference should be given to low-level or partial alerts. Higher alert levels involve a deliberate release of the safety catches that ordinarily protect against accident or unauthorized use of nuclear weapons.

• *DON'T multiply crises.* It has been suggested that if the Soviets initiate a crisis in a region (or of a type) in which they have an advantage, the United States should respond by initiating another crisis in which it has the advantage. (For example, Soviet aggression against U.S. interests in the Persian Gulf region might be countered by U.S. action against Cuba.) Such action is likely to be counterproductive and possibly disastrous. The likelihood of accident goes up with the level of stress on people and systems in crisis, and the time available to correct accidents goes down. As the number of simultaneous crises rises, this danger increases geometrically rather than arithmetically.

5. DEVELOP PROCEDURES FOR WAR TERMINATION

- DO plan for ending a war if it begins.
- DON'T plan for early use of nuclear weapons.

Planning for terminating a nuclear war is a taboo subject. To the left it implies toleration of limited nuclear war; to the right it smacks of surrender. We wish to avoid all nuclear war, but if war should break out, there still may be a chance to avoid total holocaust. If a nuclear war ever occurs, a top priority will be to stop it. And since escalation of conventional war is the most likely path to nuclear war, war termination procedures should cover the full spectrum of conflict.

Actions to Take

• *DO plan for ending a war if it begins.* The greatest barriers to planning for war termination are emotional and political. Mere discussion of the subject attracts criticism from all quarters. Thinking about it only reinforces the importance of avoiding any war. If, however, despite our best efforts conventional or nuclear war should begin, we should have available plans and procedures to end it. Developing and practicing such plans and procedures is a distasteful but prudent task. It implies neither toleration of limited nuclear war nor belief that nuclear war can be won in any meaningful sense, only a recognition that some nuclear wars could be even more catastrophic than others.

• *DO develop survivable U.S.–Soviet communications.* Communication between the superpowers is clearly an essential component of any system for war termination. Yet the current Hot Line terminals would be destroyed by any attack on national capitals. The two sides jointly should provide the means and establish procedures for reliable, rapid, and effective communication between them not only in peacetime

and during political crisis, but also after armed conflict—even nuclear—has begun.

• *DO maintain civilian control over nuclear weapons.* Civilian control over military procedures, especially those associated with nuclear weapons, must be maintained in crises and, to the extent feasible, after war has begun. In particular, delegation of nuclear authority should be limited and conditioned so that it can be readily retrieved, even at the cost of increasing the consequences of decapitation. Negotiations over war termination can have meaning only if ceasefire orders can be issued, transmitted, received, and obeyed.

Actions to Avoid

• *DON'T plan for early use of nuclear weapons.* To provide opportunities for war termination on acceptable terms at the lowest possible levels of damage, preferably before escalation to nuclear war, effort should be made to avoid early use of nuclear weapons. In addition to appropriate plans and procedures, this effort will probably also have to include some strengthening and restructuring of conventional forces.

• *DON'T decapitate.* Deterrence undoubtedly is strengthened by the possibility that a United States retaliatory attack might include among its targets the Soviet political and military leaders and their C³ network. But if war should start, it is unlikely to be in the United States' interest to respond in a way that produces chaos on the other side. This could make it impossible to conduct the negotiations needed to end a war and could also eliminate Soviet leaders' ability to issue and transmit an order to halt hostilities. Thus, if the United States wishes to preserve the option of a negotiated settlement, it should not rely upon decapitation as part of a response to Soviet aggression.

6. PREVENT AND MANAGE CRISES

- DO prepare decision-makers to deal with nuclear crises.
- DON'T engage American and Soviet forces in direct combat.

Crises greatly increase the prospect of nuclear war. By definition a crisis means an increase in threat and stress and a compression of time. Both constrain rational options and reduce the ability to respond to the effects of accidents. Since World War II the United States and the Soviet Union have developed some de facto rules of prudence to prevent and contain crises. The superpowers have not engaged each other's forces in combat; they have not threatened each other's vital interests; and they have not used nuclear weapons against anyone. These rules represent a restraint of antagonism that should be recognized, enhanced, and extended. At the same time, it is clear that the U.S.–Soviet relationship is fundamentally competitive even during crises. Both nations wish to reduce the chances of intended or unintended war, but each also wishes to manipulate the fear of that outcome in order to deter or coerce the other side. The task of crisis prevention and management is thus more complex than it first appears. Nonetheless, initiatives in this realm can reduce risk.

Actions to Take

• **DO prepare decision-makers to deal with nuclear crises.** Nuclear decision-makers often are not experts on the subject. Many new political appointees with responsibilities related to nuclear weapons arrive at their jobs with little knowledge or background in U.S.–Soviet relations, nuclear weapons affairs, or crisis decision-making. They deserve help in preparing to deal with nuclear crises that might occur. We need to find more efficient ways of giving them information on nuclear deployments and practices, the kinds of crisis situations that might arise, and the mechanisms available for dealing with such crises. In addition it would be useful to offer some compilation of lessons learned from the experience of former officials in similar positions of responsibility. Active participation in crisis simulations can also be a valuable experience.

• **DO work with the Soviets to prevent and manage crises.** Discussions of crisis prevention and management with the Soviets could serve several useful functions. For example, such talks could help to sensitize the leaders to the issues involved and to the perspectives of the other side; to clarify perceptions of relative interests in specific geographical areas; and to reinforce and extend specific negotiated agreements like the U.S.–Soviet Incidents-at-Sea Agreement. In particular, the United States and the Soviet Union should seek to create a jointly staffed crisis-monitoring center along the lines proposed by Senators Sam Nunn and John Warner. Among its various virtues, the fact-finding role of such

a center could provide a useful mechanism for introducing a pause early in a crisis.

• **DO install bilateral hot lines between all nuclear powers.** Hot lines (or, more formally, direct communications links) offer means for timely exchange of information between heads of government in times of crisis. Such hot lines now exist between Washington-Moscow, London-Moscow, and Paris-Moscow. Similar bilateral direct communications links should be installed between all (or as many as possible) of the remaining pairs of capitals of acknowledged nuclear weapons states (namely Washington, Moscow, London, Paris, and Beijing).

Actions to Avoid

• **DON'T engage American and Soviet forces in direct combat.** The United States and the Soviet Union have not engaged in armed conflict with one another for more than six decades. Keep it that way. Escalation from conventional war to nuclear war, either intentionally or unintentionally, can best be prevented by avoiding conventional war. Special emphasis should be given to ensuring that surface ships and submarines armed with nuclear weapons neither threaten nor are threatened by the navy of the other side. A nuclear war at sea could quickly spread to land.

• **DON'T try to change rapidly the situation in Eastern Europe.** Eastern Europe is viewed by the Soviets as an essential geographical buffer to guard against (another) invasion from the West. At the same time, the United States and its Western allies have strong historical, cultural, and emotional attachments to the people and nations of Eastern Europe and are eager to free them from Soviet domination. Political instability and popular uprisings in the region inevitably will tempt us to take action. But the Soviets will perceive any attempt by the West to bring about rapid change in Eastern Europe as a most serious threat to their vital interests and will respond accordingly. Unfortunately, we must be patient and try to encourage desired changes over the long term.

• **DON'T use nuclear weapons against third parties.** The prohibition on use of nuclear weapons has lasted for forty years. Its value is obvious. Few events are more likely to cause a superpower crisis or to lead to a major nuclear war than the actual use of nuclear weapons.

7. INVIGORATE NONPROLIFERATION EFFORTS

- DO maintain security guarantees.
- DON'T be fatalistic about proliferation.

President John F. Kennedy's prediction that fifteen to twenty-five nations would have nuclear weapons by the 1970s has proven wrong. Today no more than seven states have nuclear weapons. The fact that thirty or forty other nations could have acquired nuclear weapons, but have chosen not to do so, is a considerable achievement of international relations and good sense, as well as good fortune. The risk of a catalytically induced nuclear war depends very much on how many independent fingers are on nuclear triggers. The spread of nuclear weapons would increase not only the danger that the superpowers would be drawn into local nuclear wars, but also the possibility of decapitation attacks by third parties against the United States or the Soviet Union. In addition, while nuclear terrorism would be unlikely to lead to a major nuclear war, its prospect could have catastrophic effects on an open society like ours, with its permeable borders.

Actions to Take

• *DO maintain security guarantees.* While several factors push countries in the direction of nuclear weapons, concern for national security clearly leads the list. Accordingly, the United States should maintain and reinforce its guarantees of security wherever credible, as in Europe, Japan, and Korea.

• *DO support the nonproliferation regime.* The Nuclear Nonproliferation Treaty and the International Atomic Energy Agency form the core of the international nonproliferation "regime"—an array of agreements, institutions, and practices that has contributed significantly to restraint. The Nuclear Suppliers' Group assists the regime by fostering cooperation among nuclear suppliers in maintaining controls over exports of materials and equipment that might be used to make nuclear weapons. While this regime is not perfect, it symbolizes the presumption against proliferation and provides an inspection system that helps to deter military use of civilian nuclear facilities. The regime should be supported and, whenever possible, strengthened.

• *DO explore sanctions against proliferators.* A nation considering the acquisition of nuclear weapons must take into account the potential adverse responses, including possible punitive measures. The stronger and more likely the international sanctions, the more powerful is the disincentive to proliferate. To this end, the United States should explore with others, including the Soviet Union, a plan for imposing specific agreed-upon political, economic, and security sanctions on countries that violate nonproliferation commitments or otherwise acquire nuclear explosives.

• *DO protect against nuclear terrorism.* The United States should improve its capabilities to gather intelligence on terrorist groups that might acquire nuclear weapons and should prepare to act against such nuclear threats if they emerge. These efforts should be pursued unilaterally as well as in cooperation with other interested countries.

Actions to Avoid

• *DON'T be fatalistic about proliferation.* Even though five, or six, or seven nuclear horses are out of the barn, more than 150 non-nuclear horses remain inside. It is well worth while to close the barn door, even if it cannot be nailed shut. Whether or not further proliferation is inevitable, we should strive to stop it or slow it. The slower the spread of nuclear weapons, the less destabilizing it will be and the better our chances for preventing their use.

8. LIMIT MISPERCEPTIONS

- DO meet regularly with Soviet leaders.
- DON'T treat nuclear weapons like other weapons.

Facts are not enough. They are filtered through the minds of policymakers. History offers many examples of misperceptions of adversaries' capabilities and threats. To recall an example from World War I, a major factor driving German action in 1914 was the German General Staff's conclusion that by 1916 the Russian military would acquire a capability for offensive action against Germany. In fact, the Russian General Staff had no such intention and could not imagine acquiring such a capability by 1916, or even 1926. Sound strategy must therefore target perceptions as well as reality.

Actions to Take

• *DO meet regularly with Soviet leaders.*
Regular discussions between American and Soviet officials at the summit, cabinet, high military, and working levels can contribute greatly to mutual understanding of how each side sees its own interests, the other's, and the risks. If such meetings were held at regular intervals they would become routine, thus reducing political pressure for tangible results from each session. Their purposes might best be served if the parties could agree in advance not to use these sessions for formal intergovernmental negotiations.

• *DO encourage non-governmental contacts with the Soviets.* Contact and exchange between Americans and Soviets other than government officials can play an important, if secondary, role in reducing misperceptions. Since our society is open and theirs closed, the United States is likely to learn more than the Soviets from such exchanges.

• *DO expect the unexpected.* A strategy for avoiding nuclear war must not be based on simple notions of what constitutes an adequate deterrent, on mirror-image models of the adversary, on psychology-free simulations of individual and group decision-making in crises, and on idealized computer calculations of the consequences of nuclear exchanges. Such devices can provide some insights into problems to be addressed and into possible solutions, but they are of little use for predicting the future. The events that might lead to nuclear war are unknown and unknowable: we must expect the unexpected.

Actions to Avoid

• *DON'T treat nuclear weapons like other weapons.* Political rhetoric and military training often suggest that nuclear weapons are no different from other instruments of war-fighting and should be used just as weapons have been used in the past. But nuclear weapons are not "normal," and we know it. They are weapons of terror. The danger that we might come to forget the truth is small, but there is some risk in confusing the Soviets about what we believe.

• *DON'T exaggerate military imbalances.*
Exaggerated statements about the existence, nature, extent, and importance of perceived or possible future Soviet military advantages often are made in seeking public and congressional support for defense programs intended to enhance deterrence. Ironically, such statements can themselves weaken deterrence by undermining the credibility of the current threat.

• *DON'T cut off communications as a sanction.* Soviet actions that anger us create domestic pressures for sanctions. Invariably in such situations, American leaders are tempted to reduce or even to cut off contacts with the Soviets. Such temptation should be resisted, for it is in times of worsened relations and heightened tensions that the communications links provided by official and non-governmental contacts are most needed.

9. PURSUE ARMS CONTROL NEGOTIATIONS

• DO preserve existing arms control agreements.
• DON'T oversell arms control.

Negotiated arms control has a variety of forms and functions. Some observers believe that comprehensive formal treaties to limit or reduce central force structures may be obsolete. But arms control can be informal as well as formal, and arms control negotiations are a form of communication and reassurance as well as constraint. Even if extensive formal agreements prove difficult to achieve, arms control talks can be used to limit or reduce specific threats, shape future forces, develop confidence-building measures, and increase transparency in the military competition. But arms control is unlikely to produce either miracles or calamities. Kept in that perspective, formal arms control has a modest but useful role to play in an overall strategy for avoiding nuclear war.

Actions to Take

• *DO preserve existing arms control agreements.* While arms control negotiations have been less productive than one might have wished, they have been far from fruitless. For example, the Nonproliferation Treaty, which provides for international inspections of nuclear facilities located in countries that do not have nuclear weapons, clearly serves U.S. interests. Indeed, the United States (as well as the Soviet Union and others) enjoy net benefits from existing arms control agreements, including the formally binding Limited Test Ban Treaty, Outer Space Treaty,

Accidents Measures Agreement, and Antiballistic Missile (ABM) Treaty, and the informally observed Threshold Test Ban Treaty, Peaceful Nuclear Explosions Treaty, SALT I Interim Agreement on Offensive Forces, and SALT II Treaty. The survival of these agreements and the preservation of the benefits associated with them require continuous vigilance. Particular care should be exercised to ensure that the activities associated with President Reagan's Strategic Defense Initiative remain in compliance with the ABM Treaty. If strategic defenses are ever to contribute significantly to protecting the territory of the United States and its allies, deep reductions and severe limitations on offensive forces almost certainly would be required. Such constraints are not likely to be accepted, except possibly in a highly cooperative arms control environment.

• *DO pursue crisis stability through arms control.* Explore the possibility of negotiating arms control agreements that enhance crisis stability with the Soviet Union. The following examples appear particularly attractive: a ban or limit on testing of antisatellite (ASAT) systems—especially high-altitude ASAT systems that threaten ballistic missile early warning satellites and communication satellites—could enhance each side's confidence that it would receive adequate warning of attack and be able to communicate with retaliatory forces; quantitative and qualitative constraints on long-range ballistic missiles with hard-target kill capabilities could make ICBMs less vulnerable; a comprehensive ban or gradually tightened limits on nuclear tests would constrain development of newer and potentially more destabilizing weapons; and a ban on forward deployment of short time-of-flight ballistic missiles (such as the Soviet SS-20 and the U.S. Pershing II) and a requirement that missile-carrying submarines "stand off" some specified minimum distance from the adversary's coast would increase the warning time available in case of attack on bomber bases and/or C³ installations.

• *DO reduce uncertainties through arms control negotiations.* Perhaps the most important potential contribution of arms control negotiations is to reduce uncertainties about the other side's current and likely future forces, practices, and intentions. Ongoing negotiations facilitate communication between responsible and informed representatives of governments and provide forums in which concerns can be expressed, data can be exchanged, ambiguities can be resolved, compliance can be addressed, confidence-building measures can be developed, and agreed-on limitations can be achieved. These factors, separately or in combination, can reduce uncertainties and constrain "worst case" planning on both sides.

Actions to Avoid

• *DON'T oversell arms control.* Public support is essential to progress in arms control. Such support is endangered when exaggerated claims are made about past arms control accomplishments and unrealistic expectations raised for future ones. Overselling arms control can result in dissatisfaction with useful agreements. It also runs the risk of lulling the public and elected officials into complacency, so that they are unwilling to invest adequately in defense.

• *DON'T abuse bargaining chips.* There is merit in the bargaining chip concept. The Soviets are more likely to give up something of value to them if we give up something of value in return. But the concept is distorted and abused when it is invoked to gain domestic support for funding weapons that would not be of value to us (that is, weapons whose costs exceed their benefits) or that we would not be willing to bargain away under any circumstances. Our weapons system development and acquisition programs should make sense in their own terms with or without arms control. Otherwise we may find ourselves without any bargain and stuck with the wrong chips.

• *DON'T restrict arms control to formal agreements.* The traditional objectives of arms control are to reduce the likelihood and consequences of war and the cost of preserving national security. Mutual restraints that serve these objectives can be enshrined in formal treaties, embodied in tacit understandings, or induced by unilateral actions. Each form has strengths and weaknesses relative to the others, and all can and should be used to play useful roles in achieving arms control objectives.

10. REDUCE RELIANCE ON NUCLEAR DETERRENCE OVER THE LONG TERM

- DON'T assume that nuclear deterrence will last forever.
- DO intensify the search for alternatives to deterrence.

Deterrence based on a threat of nuclear holocaust appeals to no one. Yet for forty years it seems to have worked, preventing not only nuclear war but also global conventional war. We see no reason to believe deterrence will soon fail. It may serve for many more decades, a century, or even longer. On the other hand, we do not believe that the current approach will succeed forever in avoiding major nuclear war. Unless human beings, our institutions, and the complex technological systems on which we now rely achieve perfection, eventual failure of some form appears assured.

Where might an alternative to deterrence be found? Three trails for exploration have been suggested: technology, politics, and social development. Technological advances might lead eventually to devices for countering nuclear weapons delivery systems or for neutralizing the nuclear weapons themselves. (The Strategic Defense Initiative may represent an early segment of this trail.) Politics offers the prospect of gradually transforming the nature of the relationship between the United States and the Soviet Union. (England and France have nuclear weapons, but we do not view them as threats to our survival.) The political trail might even take us beyond the current international system of sovereign states. Finally, the social development trail could lead to a world in which nuclear deterrence plays no role. It may seem utopian, but if we act creatively and deliberately to transform human society over the very long term into one in which nuclear threats no longer seem necessary to preserve peace, our descendants just might be able to eliminate the weapons rather than themselves.

Among these alternatives, we find the political trail the most promising. Despite deep differences in history, culture, values, and ambition, the United States and the Soviet Union share an inescapable common interest. That interest is to avoid a global nuclear war, for they would be the most ravaged victims. Over time, this fundamental interest might well serve as a foundation for cooperative actions that could transform the relationship between the superpowers.

In the near term, the two countries' shared concern provides a powerful incentive to work together in minimizing the prospects for unintended or catalytic nuclear war. Limiting misperceptions, reducing the danger of accidents, preventing and managing crises, and inhibiting the spread of nuclear weapons to additional states or to terrorists—these objectives all serve the common interest and are more likely to be achieved through cooperative action. Wise statesmanship that reduces mutual risks in the short run could eventually bring about changes in the U.S.–Soviet relationship as great as the change in U.S.–China relations over the past two decades. Such change would permit substantially reduced reliance on nuclear deterrence.

These observations offer only a little comfort. We see no certain way to escape some reliance on nuclear deterrence. Indeed, well-intended efforts to escape it before conditions are appropriate could make nuclear war more likely. Nonetheless, the search for less conventional, more imaginative alternatives for the long run must begin. Bold, creative approaches to the subject must be stimulated, nurtured, and rewarded. In particular, the community of defense and foreign policy specialists must resist cynicism toward nontraditional concepts, misplaced confidence that all of the important ideas have been examined, and condescension to newcomers from other fields. We intend to heed this advice as we join with others in exploring the realm of ideas beyond deterrence. In confronting the awesome challenge of avoiding nuclear war, the end as well as the beginning of wisdom is neither fear nor courage; it is humility.

51   What the U.S. Can Do

Robert McNamara _____

We live in a world of 40,000 nuclear warheads —with a destructive power 1 million times that of the Hiroshima bomb—divided roughly equally between the United States and Soviet Union. Even the most optimistic arms negotiators would not believe it likely that this total could be reduced by more than 50 percent in the next 10 or 15 years. Therefore, we and our children and our children's children will be living in a world with tens of thousands of nuclear weapons—a few hundred of which could destroy Western civilization for decades to come.

Neither side wants war with the other. But deterrence may fail—perhaps as a result of events on the periphery of NATO and the Warsaw Pact. If it does, under today's conditions there is a high risk of the use of nuclear weapons. We must act to reduce that risk. There is much that we can do.

We should begin by accepting two overriding principles. First, we must recognize that each side must maintain a stable deterrent—a nuclear arsenal powerful enough to discourage anyone else from using nuclear weapons. Neither the United States nor the Soviet Union should move in a way to destabilize the other's deterrent or to provide an incentive for a preemptive strike. That's absolutely imperative. Second, we must recognize that nuclear weapons have no military value whatsoever other than to deter one's opponent from their use. All arms negotiations, military strategies, war plans, weapons development and military-force structures should be based on that principle.

If we accept those two premises, we are well on the way toward reducing the risk of nuclear war. Still, there is much more we can do. Some of these steps would require agreement with the Soviet Union, but many could be taken unilaterally.

1. Negotiate a reduction in the ratio of nuclear warheads to missile launchers, ultimately moving to single-warhead missiles. This is very, very important, both to increasing the stability of deterrent forces and to reducing the temptation to launch a preemptive strike. The more warheads to launchers each side has, assuming a given level of accuracy, the greater the possibility that if one side launched an attack first, he could destroy the other's launchers and leave them with insufficient power to inflict unacceptable reciprocal damage. Under these circumstances, the Soviets, for example, might try to launch against us first because by doing so they could reduce the damage to themselves. If each of us put only one warhead on a launcher, that kind of calculus would be impossible.

2. Renounce the strategy of launch-on-warning. The great danger of launching on warning is that we may be responding to an attack that didn't occur—to an accident, a human or mechanical failure, or a simple misunderstanding. There is absolutely no reason to fear that if we don't launch on warning, we can't launch at all. That argument—if it ever was valid—is not valid today because our forces are invulnerable. The Scowcroft Commission proved there is no window of vulnerability. Even if the Soviets could destroy all of our land-based missiles, we would

still have our Polarises under the sea, and we would still have our bombers.

3. Announce that we would not retaliate against a nuclear strike until we had ascertained the source of the attack, the size of the attack and the intentions of the attacker. I term this a strategy of "no-second-use-until . . ." and it would apply to any strike against the West, including this country. This would further reduce the risk that we might be responding to something that we misjudged—an accident or an attack by a terrorist group, for example.

4. Strengthen command-and-control systems. We must ensure that under all circumstances our retaliatory capability is assured, and that we are capable of retaining control of our forces regardless of the size of an attack upon them. The administration is acting to strengthen these systems—but much more must be done.

5. Renounce the strategy of "decapitation" strikes. Publicly stating that we would spare the enemy's command-and-control apparatus during a nuclear exchange would be a very important step in reducing Soviet incentives to strike pre-emptively and would preserve the ability of the Soviets to terminate a nuclear conflict should one start.

6. Strengthen our conventional forces. Even in this period of fiscal austerity, nonnuclear forces could be strengthened substantially. Much could be done within the presently approved military budgets of NATO. This would permit the NATO members to substantially raise the nuclear threshold and greatly reduce the likelihood that nuclear weapons would be used in the early hours of a military confrontation in Europe.

7. Announce immediately a policy of no-early-first-use of nuclear weapons. Our present policy—with nuclear weapons deployed far forward on the eastern border of West Germany—carries the high risk that we would use them in the early hours of a military conflict. We should publicly state that a conventional attack by the Soviet Union would be met by NATO's conventional forces. If the Soviet attack could not be contained by such forces, only as a last resort would nuclear weapons be used by NATO. This no-early-first-use proposal has drawn a lot of opposition from political leaders in Europe who do not understand it and who fear that

it might tempt the Soviets into making incursions. But there is gathering support for it among many top military leaders. Gen. Bernard Rogers, the supreme allied commander in Europe, has indicated that he would be willing to consider a no-early-first-use policy.

Actually, no-early-first-use was part of the strategy of "flexible response" that we first proposed in the early 1960s. But when NATO finally approved "flexible response" in 1967, the ministers did not take the corollary action of strengthening their conventional forces in order to support a high nuclear threshold.

8. Propose that NATO heads of government announce that within five years, NATO's conventional forces will have been strengthened to the point where NATO will adopt a policy of "no-first-use" of nuclear weapons. This is a very controversial proposal. Some military and political leaders believe there is remaining deterrent value in the threat of first-use nuclear weapons. But that threat has become less and less credible in the last 20 years. As the Soviets have substantially expanded their retaliatory capabilities, it is becoming increasingly clear that if NATO initiated the use of nuclear weapons, it would almost surely lead to the destruction of Western civilization. There is less and less deterrent value to threatening to commit suicide.

More and more military and political leaders are saying this publicly. Field Marshal Lord Carver, the retired chief of the British Defense Staff, last year stated that first use of nuclear weapons by NATO would be "criminally irresponsible," because it would trigger a Soviet reaction that would destroy the West. Former Defense Secretary Melvin Laird and Adm. Noel Gayler, former commander in chief of U.S. forces in the Pacific, agree with Carver. And Gen. Johannes Steinhoff, the former commander of the German Luftwaffe, said under no circumstances would he recommend first use of weapons from German soil, because, of course, it would bring a devastating nuclear strike against Germany. Former Secretary of State Henry Kissinger, in Brussels in 1979, said it was wrong for the West Europeans to believe that we would ever initiate the use of strategic weapons against the Soviet homeland because it would be suicide for us to do so. He did not extend that statement to tactical weapons, but it is now generally recognized that a nuclear war, once started, will not remain limited.

9. After consultation with our allies, withdraw half of our 6,000 nuclear warheads now stockpiled in Western Europe. This could be done immediately. The atomic demolition munitions that are intended to block mountain passes and other "choke points" on potential Soviet invasion routes cause particular concern because, to be effective, they would have to be in place before the war actually began. That could aggravate the crisis and contribute to the likelihood of a war's actually starting. The nuclear-armed air-defense systems, which are old and unreliable, are also designed to be used at the onset of a conflict. Many of the other weapons are obsolete.

10. Redeploy to rear areas the remaining nuclear warheads deployed along West Germany's eastern border. This would reduce the vulnerability of those missiles to an enemy attack in the early hours of a conflict and reduce the temptation to use them rather than lose them to the enemy.

11. Negotiate with the Soviets to establish a nuclear-free zone—perhaps 60 miles wide—on both sides of West Germany's eastern border. This would build confidence on both sides that pressures for early use of nuclear weapons could be controlled.

12. Unilaterally halt development of destabilizing weapons systems and those that have no deterrent value. The neutron bomb, for example, has no deterrent value. The MX is a destabilizing system because it has a very high ratio of warheads to launchers—which means that it has a very high kill capability and, since it would be very easy to take out, it provides incentive for a pre-emptive strike. Similarly, the Pershing II missiles are destabilizing because the Soviets believe they could be used for a "decapitation" strike. There is a strong temptation for the Soviets to prevent such an attack by launching a preemptive strike.

13. Negotiate a ban on weapons in space. We are on the verge of a major new frontier in the arms race. We can gain no military advantage by crossing over it. And an attempt to do so will vastly increase our defense budget and run the risk of destabilizing the balance of Soviet and U.S. deterrent forces.

14. Introduce "permissive action links" into every NATO warhead. These devices—known as "PAL's"—would make it impossible for anyone to detonate the warhead without a specific electronic or mechanical input from the president. Having applied such controls to our own warheads, we should endeavor to obtain the agreement of the Soviets to apply similar devices to their warheads.

15. Negotiate a comprehensive test ban with the Soviets. With hindsight, the United States and its NATO allies would be more secure today if the limited-test-ban treaty of 1963 had been expanded then to a comprehensive test ban. We will be better off tomorrow if we negotiate such a ban today, along with the appropriate verification safeguards.

16. Strengthen nuclear nonproliferation programs. In particular, the United States, our allies and the Soviet Union should work to reduce the possibility that terrorists may obtain access to nuclear weapons. We need more discipline among the nations of the West that export nuclear technology to countries other than the existing nuclear powers. None of us has been as disciplined as the Soviet Union. . . .

17. Negotiate the establishment of a joint U.S.–Soviet information and crisis-control center. Sen. Sam Nunn of Georgia and the late Sen. Henry Jackson of Washington made similar suggestions. Nunn recommended the formation of a multinational crisis-management team of highly trained civilian and military personnel with access to top military and political leaders. It would be in operation 24 hours a day, 365 days a year, and its purpose would be to give leaders quick and reliable information about the size and source of any nuclear explosion. Such a watchdog group would encourage cooperation between the superpowers, even when political relations were strained, and it would significantly reduce the temptation of third countries or terrorist groups to use nuclear weapons.

18. Announce a strategy of lesser retaliation. McGeorge Bundy, the national-security adviser to Kennedy and Johnson, has suggested that any nuclear attack be met with a retaliatory strike at a lesser level, and I completely agree. If a nuclear war starts,

one must try to stop it; this lesser-response strategy would lead to a de-escalation rather than an escalation of any nuclear conflict. Strengthening our command-and-control system, and waiting to retaliate until we had verified the source and size of the attack, would ensure that we could make this sort of reasoned, rational response. Stating this as a policy would not reduce the deterrent value of the retaliatory threat. The damage that even a lighter nuclear response would inflict on the Soviets—or any potential enemy—would far outweigh any benefit they could hope to gain from launching an initial attack.

52 'No First Use' of Nuclear Weapons

Kurt Gottfried, Henry Kendall, and John M. Lee _____

The widespread misperception that the U.S.S.R. now has an overwhelming superiority in conventional forces has led some critics to dismiss the no-first-use option as utopian. As the conventional balance of forces is usually represented, it ignores the fact that NATO's task is to defend, not to attack. Although it is true that the Warsaw Pact is stronger in conventional arms than NATO, it must be remembered that in a conflict between armies of comparable competence an attacker must hold a substantial advantage to be confident of success. The disparity between the Warsaw Pact and NATO armies is not of such proportions. Furthermore, we believe NATO could mount an even more formidable conventional deterrent at or near current manpower levels with the adoption of an improvement program at a cost that is small compared with current expenditures. Such a program could be funded largely by reduced spending on nuclear weapons.

Under a no-first-use policy NATO's conventional forces would have to deter—and if necessary stop—a conventional Warsaw Pact attack without resorting to nuclear weapons. To that end the composition and structure of NATO's present forces would have to be modified and much larger stocks of supplies would have to be on hand.

The intelligence services of the Warsaw Pact would be fully aware of these developments. Although the Warsaw Pact leaders may never have absolute confidence in a NATO no-first-use declaration, they would probably be won over to a cautious belief that the new doctrine is actually in force. Similarly, from surveillance of Warsaw Pact military exercises and maneuvers, among other indicators, the NATO intelligence services would know whether the Warsaw Pact's recent no-first-use declaration was reflected in military training and planning.

Under the prevailing first-use policy many people in Western Europe are more frightened by their own defense than they are by the potential attack. This fear threatens the entire alliance with political paralysis and has created concern in military circles that NATO may already have a de facto no-first-use policy without any of the requisite preparation. A no-first-use policy that has been deliberately prepared and agreed on in peacetime would lead to more confident and coherent decisions in a crisis, a step that would in itself enhance deterrence.

Major changes in the tactical nuclear arsenal should also accompany the declaration of a no-first-use policy. Indeed, there is a consensus, encompassing many adherents of the current first-use policy, that the vast array of NATO tactical nuclear weapons based near the front presents a greater threat to NATO than it does to the Warsaw Pact. The problem is that in the face of a Warsaw Pact offensive there would be enormous pressure to use such weapons rather than to let them be overrun and captured. Under a no-first-use policy most of these systems would lose whatever reason for existence they now have.

It has been said that a no-first-use declaration would be tantamount to abandoning Europe and that the commitment to the present first-use policy is essential to linking the fate of the U.S. to that of its NATO allies. This assertion assumes that the immediate exposure to battle of some 300,000 American troops is a weaker link than the rather implausible promise to expose the U.S. to total devastation in the event of a Warsaw Pact incursion into Western Europe. A no-first-use policy would call for an enhanced U.S. commitment to a realistic and credible conventional defense of its European allies and should thereby engender increased confidence in the transatlantic "linkage." The U.S. would still continue to offer its allies a nuclear guarantee of the most profound nature: its ability to respond to a nuclear attack, which protects them from the threat of nuclear destruction.

A more concrete appraisal of the no-first-use option can be achieved by examining several possible scenarios. First, consider an all-out preemptive invasion of Western Europe by the Warsaw Pact during a crisis. The very existence of vast nuclear arsenals provides a measure of "extended deterrence" against the first use of nuclear weapons. Neither side, however, could be confident that large-scale nuclear war could be averted whatever the two sides' true intentions were before the outbreak of hostilities—even if nuclear escalation makes no military or political sense. Such an attack would therefore imply that the Warsaw Pact accepted some risk of the conflict's ultimately becoming nuclear.

Second, consider a limited thrust by the U.S.S.R. reaching for one or more lucrative prizes made more attractive by the withdrawal of the nuclear deterrent against conventional attack. Such a prize might be Hamburg; seizing it could give the Russians a strategically useful Atlantic port. Because it is within artillery range of the border, Hamburg might be vulnerable to sudden capture even with an improved NATO defense and with comparatively little risk of escalation, assuming NATO were to abide by its no-first-use declaration. An attack of this kind that left NATO essentially intact would be an extremely risky venture. Such a great gamble by the Warsaw Pact leaders would make sense only if the U.S.S.R. could count on the subsequent disintegration of a demoralized NATO. At least as likely an outcome would be an era of dangerous tension, the cessation of all East-West trade and resumption of the conflict after the West had rearmed itself to the teeth.

A third scenario is a 1914-style sequence of miscalculation and misperception that leads to war against the will and interests of the participants. This event could come about if NATO felt compelled to mobilize because of a massive influx of Russian troops to quell widespread unrest in the eastern European countries. Many senior officers and political leaders consider this sequence of events to be one of the most likely routes to conflict in Europe. A variant of the scenario involves the spillover of other hostilities between the U.S. and the U.S.S.R. (starting, for example, in the Middle East) into the European theater. In either case a no-first-use declaration would provide the time and relative calm to allow negotiations to begin before the conflict reached proportions comparable to an all-out invasion.

To summarize, a no-first-use strategy would be of some value in the event of a large-scale preemptive invasion by the Warsaw Pact; it might increase the likelihood of reckless adventures such as the surprise capture of a vulnerable NATO asset, and it would be distinctly beneficial in case of an inadvertent or spillover war. As long as the superpowers hold vast arsenals of long-range missiles a massive conventional attack—out of the blue, so to speak—appears to be quite improbable, and it will become progressively more improbable because space-based and airborne surveillance techniques will eventually provide all-weather, night-and-day, real-time intelligence over all areas relevant to the front. Although a limited attack against a target such as Hamburg cannot be ruled out, it would be militarily indecisive and a high-risk gamble from any point of view. Such an action does not conform to the pattern of great caution that has been characteristic of the foreign policy of the U.S.S.R. Blunders and misperceptions are by far the most probable causes of war. Given the ever-present danger of disastrous escalation, a no-first-use policy significantly increases military stability.

Although it is beyond the scope of this article, a similarly strong case can be made for adopting such measures elsewhere in the world. By reducing the risk of local nuclear wars, such measures could make escalation to global nuclear war less likely and thereby enhance the security of all nations.

At first it might appear that all the advantages of a declared no-first-use policy could be achieved by keeping the policy secret or, alternatively, by declaring a policy of "no early first use," according to which one would plan not to use nuclear weapons in the early stages of a conflict. The latter policy is indistinguishable from the present NATO policy, and, as we have argued, it shows little promise of producing the concrete military measures that would free NATO troops of their dependence on nuclear weapons. If the political and military benefits of a no-first-use policy are to be garnered, the policy must be publicly accepted by the leadership and citizenry of the NATO countries, otherwise the necessary improvements in military preparedness and the deterrent value of the new policy will never be realized. . . .

It is our thesis that the adoption of a no-first-use policy would be to NATO's military and political advantage, independent of actions by the U.S.S.R. and its allies, and that this decision is therefore not contingent on negotiations. Nevertheless, there are two other critical issues that are fundamental components of the European confrontation in their own right and can be addressed only by negotiations. If they could be resolved, they would significantly increase European security and diminish the political hurdles faced by a no-first-use policy. We refer here to the 10-year-old Mutual and Balanced Force Reduction (MBFR) negotiations, which seek to establish a stable conventional balance in Europe, and to proposals for a nuclear-weapon-free zone straddling the East-West border.

As currently conceived, the primary feature of an MBFR agreement would be the reduction of active-duty, ground-force manpower in central Europe to a ceiling of 700,000 men on each side, and a ceiling of 900,000 for ground-and air-force personnel combined. The agreement would also prohibit the introduction of additional military units into the regions affected, so that the force levels necessary for a successful attack would not be available. Proposals for verifying compliance and monitoring departures from normal patterns of military activity are under negotiation.

An MBFR treaty would reduce fears that the strengthening of NATO's conventional forces would simply trigger a conventional arms race. It would also provide a considerable measure of assurance that neither side was preparing for a conflict. If such a treaty were breached, that would give the NATO political leadership clear evidence of hostile intent and thereby justify intensified defensive efforts, including prompt mobilization.

The proposal for a nuclear-free zone in Europe that has received the broadest and most influential level of international support is the one made by the Independent Commission on Disarmament and Security Issues, which was chaired by Olof Palme, now prime minister of Sweden. The Palme commission issued a report in June, 1982, that called for a nuclear-weapon-free zone on each side of the central front, initially reaching almost to the midpoints of East Germany and West Germany. The zone would be extended gradually to include the entire European front between the two alliances [see "A Nuclear-Weapon-Free Zone in Europe," by Barry M. Blechman and Mark R. Moore; SCIENTIFIC AMERICAN, April, 1983]. In view of our earlier comments on the threat presented by forward-based nuclear systems, it is clear that the Palme commission's proposal would enhance the security of NATO and would form a natural complement to a no-first-use policy.

The essential requirement for completion of the MBFR negotiations is sustained support from top government officials on both sides. Strong political leadership on both the domestic and the international front would be necessary to turn a no-first-use declaration, an MBFR treaty and the Palme commission's recommendations into reality. Such a goal, if it could be achieved, would mark a major reduction in the risk of war in Europe.

The adoption of a no-first-use policy would have profound consequences. In contrast to arms-control measures, which rarely constrain the actual use of weapons, a no-first-use policy would transform the conceptual foundation on which military strategy and planning rest. A no-first-use regime, as defined in this article, would strengthen the cohesion of the NATO alliance and make relations with the U.S.S.R. less perilous in times of crisis, thereby markedly lowering the risk of nuclear war.

QUESTIONS FOR DISCUSSION

1. For each of McNamara's 18 policy proposals state whether you agree or disagree and explain why.

2. Propose several specific initiatives that could be taken today in the spirit of Charles Osgood's "graduated unilateral initiatives for peace."

3. Carnesale, Allison and Nye oppose the U.S. adopting a policy of "no first use" of nuclear weapons, while Gottfried, Kendall and Lee advocate no first use. Compare the reasons offered by the two sides in this debate and evaluate their arguments.

SUGGESTED READINGS

EVAN, WILLIAM M. "Unilateral Initiatives for Peace in the Middle East." *New Outlook: Middle East Monthly* 13 (July/August 1970): 7–15.

GALTUNG, JOHAN. *There are Alternatives! Four Roads to Peace and Security.* Nottingham, Eng.: Spokesman, 1984.

OSGOOD, CHARLES E. *Perspective in Foreign Policy.* 2nd ed., revised. Palo Alto, Calif.: Pacific, 1966.

SCOVILLE, Jr., HERBERT, "Reciprocal National Restraint: An Alternative Path," *Arms Control Today*, vol. 15, no. 5, June, 1985.

SHARP, GENE. *The Politics of Nonviolent Action.* San Diego, Calif.: P. Sargent, 1973.

Chapter XIV

Conversion of Military Industries to Civilian Uses

The conversion of military facilities and industries to civilian uses has been a subject of much discussion among analysts who study the economics of defense spending. These analysts mainly have concentrated on the economic opportunities for—and the barriers to—such conversion efforts. Though the economic and organizational barriers to conversion are substantial, most analysts have concluded that they are surmountable given a political mandate for disarmament. Of course, with international tensions high and the superpowers both avidly building new weapons systems, there is little basis for the hope that such a mandate will develop in the near future. Indeed, in comparison with the formidable obstacles that stand in the way of progress in arms control and disarmament, the problems of economic conversion seem trivial.

So why are we including a chapter on economic conversion? And why in the section on strategies for preventing nuclear war? For several reasons. First, some analysts propose that the conversion of military industries to civilian uses could be an important strategy for preventing nuclear war, since such conversion efforts could reduce domestic pressures for weapons production. Second, if a political mandate for arms control and disarmament ever develops, conversion will have to be addressed at that time. Thus, it is important at least to take note of the issue today.

We begin the chapter with a reading by Lloyd Dumas. Dumas contends that the domestic pressures behind the nuclear arms race can only be reduced if the peace movement addresses the issue of converting military industries to civilian uses. Dumas argues that no weapon should ever be built for economic reasons. But he fears that economic motives will continue to stimulate the arms race as long as people, firms, and communities are financially dependent on military contracts. Thus, he argues that economic conversion is an important strategy for checking the arms race, one which the nation can no longer afford to neglect.

Next, we turn to an article by Seymour Melman that examines the practical barriers to conversion that face military contractors. Melman argues that firms can become so dependent on defense contracts that they "reach a point of no return." Melman presents a case history of Boeing-Vertol's attempt to enter the market for subway cars, a project that failed because of the firm's inability to adapt to the civilian market.

Finally, economist Judith Reppy briefly discusses the prospects for conversion. Reppy argues that while "economic considerations play a part in the opposition in the United States towards any policy of disarmament, the most serious obstacles lie elsewhere."

53   Economic Conversion as a Strategy for Peace

Lloyd J. Dumas _____

ECONOMIC CONVERSION AS A STRATEGY FOR SOCIAL CHANGE

The term "economic conversion" has been used here to refer to the transfer of labor, capital and other productive resources from unproductive military use to alternative civilian-oriented activity. The problem, of course, is to assure that this transfer of resources takes place as smoothly as possible, with minimal economic and social disruption. And we have seen that it *is* a problem, despite the enormous economic and social benefits that would potentially flow from such a transfer. For once resources have been occupied in one particular use for a significant period of time, there is a tendency for them to become less flexible, more specialized. This economic stiffening of the joints can generally be overcome without great difficulty if approached properly, particularly in the case of labor. But it will not happen automatically. Careful attention is required for the conversion process to be smooth and effective.

It is true that economic conversion, so defined, is but a special case of the broader problem of "economic transition," the transfer of productive resources among any specified set of alternative uses (a vastly understudied problem made vital by the inherently dynamic nature of economies). Yet, it is a particularly important special case because of the economically parasitic effects of the production of military goods and services,

not to mention the devastating effects of their use, made ever more likely by their continued development and accumulation. There is no other transfer of resources that stands as such a crucial prerequisite to both economic viability and physical survival.[1]

But why discuss conversion now? Isn't it a little like locking the barn door before the horse is purchased? There are no plans for reducing the military budget, much less for even partial disarmament. Quite the contrary, the Carter Administration, which carried out year-by-year expansions in the military budget above the rate of inflation, has been replaced by the Reagan Administration which is even more militaristic and appears deeply committed to a far larger and more dangerous escalation of the arms race. The Cold War, restarted by the Carter Administration, is being pursued with such vigor and enthusiasm by President Reagan that confrontation and "hot war" seem even more likely. Another Vietnam War lies waiting in the wings in Latin America and/or Africa, with apparently significant public support. The vested interests that support the continuation of the present extraordinarily high levels of military spending are no less powerful, and in fact seem to have not only seized the initiative, but also many of the critical seats of power. What is the point of talking about conversion now?

Changes in the status quo that go against the "conventional wisdom" are virtually always viewed as threats by the mainstream of society, regardless of how beneficial they may be. And any world view that faces off against the conventional wisdom no matter how logical, no matter how rooted in reality, must always contend not only with societal inertia but also with the outright hostility which inevitably arises from

Excerpted with permission from Lloyd J. Dumas, "The Political Economy of Reversing the Arms Race," Lloyd J. Dumas, ed., *The Political Economy of Arms Reduction* (pp. 145–147, 160). (Washington, D.C.: American Association for the Advancement of Science, 1982.) Copyright © 1982 by Westview Press.

being perceived as a threat. It is therefore necessary, if one is to be effective in advocating social directional changes of this type, to find a strategy for removing enough of this threat perception to permit people to allow themselves to listen to what is being said. Belief in the moral and intellectual persuasiveness of the argument being advocated should never be allowed to blind one to the necessity of reducing threat perception. It is simply not possible, no matter how obvious the case being argued, to persuade anyone who is not listening.

Economic conversion is a strategy for making peace possible by concretely reassuring those who directly fear loss of their own jobs as a result of cutbacks in military spending, as well as the much larger segment of the population who fear that such cutbacks will generate unemployment (or broader economic recession or depression.) . . .

[P]ersistently high levels of military spending have been and continue to be enormously damaging to the economies of both the U.S. and the U.S.S.R. The idea that high military expenditures are detrimental to any economy may not yet have penetrated the consciousness of the wider public. But it is nevertheless true. Hence, economic conversion can be understood as a crucial positive policy for economic redevelopment and reconstruction. Seen in that light, it is not only not threatening, nor merely reassuring, but a positively attractive and encouraging approach.

Furthermore, . . . the economic conversion problem, though it is certainly complex . . . , is without question solvable, whether in the context of a fundamentally socialist or market capitalist oriented economic system. It is possible, given careful advanced planning, to convert resources currently involved in military activity to productive civilian use—not merely to create the same total number of new civilian jobs as the number of military jobs lost, but to create the kind of civilian jobs which will productively absorb those specific people released from military activity, and to assure a smooth transition between the two. One possible model for institutionalizing the process of advance contingency planning for conversion, embodied in the proposed Defense Economic Adjustment Act, has been described and discussed. And the origins, nature and history of one set of alternative product plans, the Lucas stewards "Corporate Plan," has also been set forth. It should be clear then that economic conversion is not merely a nice

idea, but a hardnosed, down-to-earth policy.

Of course, the current consensus in support of large military budgets in the U.S. is not based solely on the belief that military spending is economically beneficial and/or that the transition to lower levels of military spending would in itself be unacceptably disruptive. There are also serious questions of military national security involved.[2] Yet the political power of the perceived economic threat of reduced military spending is not to be underestimated. It is, in fact, clearly understood by the military and military industry. Even a cursory glance at press accounts of the pro- and anti-B1 bomber campaigns, for example, will reveal that the debate centered, not on the strategic value of the B1, but on the economic effects (particularly the job issue). The political importance of the job argument can also be verified by noting that virtually every newspaper account of any curtailment of military activity, whether a base closure or contract cancellation, always contains a statement about job loss, if not in the headline, then in the first sentence.

Just how much of the support for large military budgets would evaporate if planning for conversion rendered the jobs argument irrelevant is difficult to say. But one thing is absolutely clear. The debate on weapons systems, military posture, etc. would be moved from the arena of myopic economics into the areas of appropriate political behavior and legitimate military requirements where it belongs. The military is no social economic welfare agency, nor should it be. National security issues should not be unnecessarily entangled in local economic dependencies. No military project need ever, or should ever, be funded for economic reasons. There are always more effective and more generally productive ways of creating or maintaining jobs and income in a local community than by building unnecessary military hardware or keeping an unneeded base open. . . .

Economic conversion is a viable strategy for making peace possible. It is very much a hardnosed, pragmatic approach. The plain fact is that the nation's economy will never more than temporarily emerge from the deepening morass of stagflation until it is relieved of the crippling burden of heavy military spending. Furthermore, national security will continue to deteriorate as long as we persist in the fantasy that our safety can be assured by adding ever more sophisticated weaponry to the nearly incomprehensible pile of mutually destructive capability we have already amassed. Yet until the fear of unemployment and other severe economic disruption can be permanently laid to rest, it will be exceedingly difficult to develop the political wherewithal required to transfer resources from the military to the civilian sector. And this is the crucial role of economic conversion.

NOTES

1. See Dumas, L.J. "Holocaust by Accident" in *To Avoid Catastrophe*, M.P. Hamilton, ed. (Eerdmans, Grand Rapids, 1977.)
2. See L.J. Dumas, "National Insecurity in the Nuclear Age," and "Human Fallibility and Weapons," in *The Bulletin of the Atomic Scientists* (May 1976 and November 1980, respectively.)

54   The Boeing-Vertol Experience

Seymour Melman ———————————————————————

During the 1970s, two military industry contractors attempted to change over part of their production facilities and labor forces to civilian work: the Rohr Corporation of Chula Vista, California, and Boeing-Vertol, a division of the Boeing Company located near Philadelphia, Pennsylvania. Rohr built the BART (Bay Area Rapid Transit) system for San Francisco, as well as the Washington, D.C., subway system, acting as general contractor for the rolling stock and the control equipment. Boeing-Vertol, starting in 1971, undertook to design and then produce electric trolley cars and subway cars. Both firms displayed a severely limited competence in the manufacture of civilian vehicles. I shall discuss the Boeing-Vertol experience, since many of the key problems are similar, and the Rohr Corporation case has been extensively reported.[1]

Stimulated by potential subsidies from the federal government's Urban Mass Transportation Administration, Boeing-Vertol bid, in 1971 and thereafter, won orders for electric trolleys and subway cars in the United States. The company was, in fact, the frontrunner in a national competition to design such vehicles, and its management hoped that its product would set the national standard. Boeing-Vertol had reached a peak of production during the Vietnam war, when its 13,500 employees were producing helicopters for the military. But this business had dropped off and by 1978 4,300 workers, engineers and administrators were operating the design, production and assembly shops that spread across a 180-acre tract along the Delaware River.

Two-thirds of Boeing-Vertol's employees were then still on helicopter production, but the remainder were working on light-rail vehicles and stainless steel rapid-transit cars. The firm had received orders for 275 trolleys from the transportation agencies of Boston and San Francisco. Also, 200 stainless steel rapid-transit cars were on order for Chicago. The seventy-one-foot trolleys are of particular interest in this discussion, since their design and production involved many innovations.

No trolley cars were built in the United States after 1952. Thus, by 1978, all such vehicles in use in the United States, about 1,200, were of vintage design, the majority being more than thirty years old. The hope was that these represented a definite replacement market, with prospects for a lot more orders when the worth of a modern electric-powered light-rail vehicle had been demonstrated.

The electric public carrier designed by Boeing-Vertol was downright handsome: sleek, articulated at the center to permit easy negotiation of sharp curves. Its windows were large; it was well lit, had comfortable seats, air-conditioned interior; it was quiet and speedy. The motorman's console was comfortably designed, with radiotelephone linkage for easy system control. Riders and motormen were pleased with the new vehicles. The Boston press carried comments from riders and operators who welcomed the elegant successor to the noisy, jerky, drafty and slow trolley cars of an earlier era.

To design and construct the vehicles, Boeing-Vertol assembled a team of eighty engineers who, with one exception, came from the aerospace departments of the firm. These professionals and their managers saw themselves as transferees from the high technology of aerospace to a field of comparatively low technology. Deciding that the technical transition should be easy enough, these sophisticates of high technology proceeded to conduct the project on a "systems engineering" pattern. Design tasks were subdivided among the engineering group and a small team was dispatched on brief visits to European plants that were manufacturing rail vehicles. The Boeing engineers sought to make a major technological leap by assigning key components to a network of seventeen subcontractors in the United States and other countries. They thus established themselves as system designers and assemblers, leaving the principal functional work to specialized subcontractors. German firms supplied electrical equipment and a company in Yokohama supplied not only the "truck" frames carrying the driving motors, brakes, etc., but also the welded steel car body. In that way the Boeing-Vertol engineers arranged a "transfer of technology" in the form of the detailed know-how embodied in the equipment supplied by the various contractors. In other words, the engineering staff attempted to skip an otherwise long learning period and to dodge the manufacturing problems they might have encountered if they had tried to design and produce many of these components themselves.

However, as the Boeing-Vertol engineers became involved in other aspects of the design and subsequent tasks, they ran into some of the specific and unique requirements of this class of equipment. For example, trolley-car doors, which, unlike those on airplanes, are opened and closed thousands of times a week, impose special design criteria of simplicity and durability. However, there was no way to learn the art of trolley-car design from other American firms, or from engineers who might be hired away from them. Also—such was the boundless self-confidence of the aerospace team that took charge of this project—it seemed unnecessary to call on anyone else to advise them on how to "bring automation" to an area long neglected in the United States. Finally, no American university had been training engineers for this long-dead industry.

Starting in 1976, thirty-three of the new light-rail vehicles were put in operation on the "Green Line" of the Massachusetts Bay Transportation Authority. A succession of difficulties began to show up rather quickly, and by December 1977 about seventy-two essential modifications had been recognized and were agreed by both MBTA and Boeing-Vertol to be the responsibility of the vendor. Most of the changes were minor, but there were some major, intractable problems. The cars derailed repeatedly on tight curves, and successive modifications of the truck and wheel adjustment in the center section of the vehicle failed to achieve a durable "fix." The doors on the original cars, designed and built abroad, had 1,300 parts and failed repeatedly. Boeing-Vertol did its own redesign, scaling down the complexity of the door mechanism to about 600 parts. The vehicle was subject to repeated delays under certain emergency conditions. For example, when air pressure was lost, the brakes went on in emergency pattern. But to release the brakes, maintenance men had to unwind six sets of brakes mechanically with a special tool, a job that took twenty minutes or more, often in a cramped subway area. Certain maintenance requirements had been overlooked. The car batteries were not arranged for easy roll-out and required time-consuming physical disconnection for servicing. Similarly, no provision had been made for "quick disconnects" to allow servicing of the air-conditioning system without cutting and then resoldering piping, a long and costly process.

In their first year and a half of operation, the new vehicles were involved in more than 100 reported derailments. The MBTA reported that it had been forced to assign more maintenance personnel to keep "fifty-odd LRVs going on the Green Line than . . . to maintain 220 rapid transit cars on the Red, Blue and Orange Lines." MBTA's director of operations said, "Everybody was taken by surprise by the LRV's rate of failure. They were supposed to be reliable, but it just wasn't true."[2] . . .

What went wrong? What were the crucial elements of the Boeing-Vertol failure to produce a competent vehicle? The answer is important, because Boeing-Vertol's practices reflected normal operation procedure in much of military industry.

Boeing-Vertol applied "state-of-the-art" technology to the separate components, which they then matched together in their design. Design practice was somewhat tempered by the brief visits abroad, but on the premises of Boeing-Vertol there was no senior engineering staff with long experience in this class of vehicle design or production. The idea of sending a team to be trained abroad, or engaging foreign experts to train the staff outside Philadelphia, was evidently unthinkable. So the Boeing-Vertol staff got the benefit of "on-the-job" training without the benefit of direction by experienced hands. It accepted the new vehicle assignment as a case of low technology, by comparison with the aerospace high technology with which it was familiar. This technological chauvinism blinded the Boeing-Vertol staff to the need for a definition of the difference between criteria appropriate in aerospace and in civilian vehicle design. Subcontractors were relied upon for primary functional components on the assumption that the quality of individual parts would assure their competent function in combination—an idea that makes no sense on theoretical grounds, nor in varied engineering experience.

The Boeing-Vertol management/engineering team was prepared to accept "sophisticated" designs in many components, when what was needed was rugged simplicity. In many aspects of the vehicle design Boeing-Vertol overlooked ease and economy of maintenance, major issues in mass transit vehicles intended for long lives of reliable service. The firm assumed spare parts would be as readily available in the future as they had been in conjunction with original orders. There was no clear justification for that optimism, especially with respect to vendors scattered all over the world.

Boeing-Vertol, believing that full service testing of prototype equipment was dispensable, practiced the familiar military strategy of "concurrency." Indeed, the light-rail vehicles were put into production straight from the drawing board.

Working for the Department of Defense, military contractors have had repeated experience of major maintenance and reliability problems with complex military products. These difficulties have been smoothed over by redesign, retrofitting of new components, assigning extensive maintenance time and equipment, retiring the equipment earlier than planned, or by some combination of these expedients. In the military market, equipment failures customarily occur under conditions of restricted access—behind barbed wire, on ships at sea, at remote air bases. Boeing-Vertol's light-rail vehicles sailed in full public view and to the inconvenience of a great many passengers. The press soon discovered that there was a real story in "the cars that couldn't."

From the civilian technology and civilian service viewpoint, the Boeing-Vertol experience is a saga of managerial and engineering arrogance and incompetence. It also closely resembles the performance of aerospace firms on military contracts. The C-5A and missile programs come immediately to mind. That is why it is so important to estimate accurately the capability for weaning military industry engineers, managers and blue-collar workers from their accustomed professional ways. And that also is why it is cause for very serious concern that, until now, no major military-serving enterprise has demonstrated an autonomous ability to carry out the sort of occupational switch that is needed to go civilian. Economic conversion is therefore an important policy idea that has yet to be proved in operation by American industry. If such capability can be shown, there may be at least a fighting chance to turn the vast resources of the military economy to productive use. If it cannot be shown, there is no prospect for success without a complete dismantling of military-serving firms and a regrouping of people in order to break the military industry pattern. . . .

The story of Boeing-Vertol's light-rail vehicle program in Boston is also the story of the Morgantown, West Virginia, people mover; the BART system of San Francisco; the Washington, D.C., subway; and the Grumman venture in city buses.[3] . . .

NOTES

1. See e.g. *Investigation of the Operations of the Bay Area Rapid Transit with Particular Reference to Safety and Contract Administration,* Legislative Analyst, State of California, State Capitol, Sacramento, November 9, 1972; The State of California Senate, Public Utilities and Corporations Committee, *Report on Safety of the Bay Area Rapid Transit Automatic Train Control System,* January 31, 1973, State Capitol, Sacramento, California.

2. Boston *Globe,* December 6, 1978.

3. On the Morgantown, West Virginia, story, see *Railway Age,* September 8, 1975, and *Business Week,* March 16, 1974. The Morgantown, West Virginia, people mover saga reads as either more industrial tragedy or high comedy, depending on the reader's mood.

55   Prospects for Conversion

Judith Reppy

The US defence industry . . . is a large industry, but not dominant in the context of the whole economy. Spending is high, but it is less than 6 per cent of GNP. The major defence contractors are large firms, but not the largest ones in the United States. The very large US companies such as General Motors, American Telephone and Telegraph and the major oil firms do appear on the list of 100 top Department of Defense (DOD) prime contractors, but their defence business is only a small fraction of their total sales. Furthermore, the United States enjoys the advantage of a fully articulated economy, in the sense of a complete set of industries connected by relatively free markets, and thus it possesses an inherent degree of flexibility that may be lacking in centrally controlled economies or less-developed countries. A priori it seems that changes in government spending for new weapons, either increases or decreases, could be accommodated by the economy with little difficulty.

What is true for the whole, however, is not necessarily true in detail. The defence industry is really a collection of segments of distinct industries and the effects of defence spending differ by sector. . . . Thus, increased spending for communications equipment would increase demand for the output of firms in the electronics industry and the electronics divisions of the aerospace firms. The electronics industry is not heavily dependent on the DOD market and a change in DOD demand would be a small perturbation of its total sales. But if skilled engineers are in short supply to the industry (and

Excerpted with permission from Judith Reppy, "The United States," in Nicole Ball and Milton Leitenberg, *The Structure of the Defense Industry* (pp. 45–47). Copyright © 1983 by Croom Helm Ltd.

they are), and the DOD demand is for products requiring custom-designed chips (and it is), then it may be more difficult for the electronics industry to expand output of defence-related items than for an industry already heavily committed to the DOD market but with excess capacity.

Turning to the problems of economic conversion, the economic difficulties of adjusting to reduced military spending are often thought to constitute a powerful political argument against any move towards disarmament. Decreases in levels of defence spending will have considerable impact for particular industries, regions and occupations precisely because changes are rarely made evenly across the board, but rather are concentrated in specific programmes. Just as closing a military base may have a serious impact on its local economy, reductions in procurement programmes can affect strongly those companies that are involved in the specific programmes. The regional grouping of defence contractors, in turn, insures the uneven regional impact from changes in defence spending.

Similarly, the effects on employment will vary by occupation. The largest effects are likely to be found among the scientists and engineers, for whom defence jobs represent one quarter of total employment. Lloyd Dumas has argued that the long-run diversion of scientific resources into military-related research in the US has caused a deterioration in civilian technology, and that conversion of these resources (mostly scientists and engineers) from military to civilian-oriented work is inhibited by the degree of specialization that marks military R&D.[1] The straightforward identification of military-related employment with a burden on the civilian economy must be modified, however, by recognition of the role played by the defence-related demand for scientists and engineers in expanding the supply of scientifically-trained people. The availability of well-paying jobs in the defence industry has attracted people to engineering as a career, and federal programmes have helped to pay for their education. Thus, not all of the scientists and engineers employed in defence-related work can be regarded as having been taken away from the civilian economy.

The analysis is further complicated on the demand side. The level of alternative employment in civilian industry is conditioned by national practices in the use of engineering skills; for example, Japanese firms employ more engineers on the floor, that is, directly involved in the production process, than do US firms. Nevertheless, the US has 58.7 scientists and engineers per 10,000 labour force population and, even if this number is reduced by one-quarter to adjust for defence-related work, the figure for the US is exceeded only by that for Japan among the OECD nations.[2] It appears that a shift in resources from military to civilian-oriented R&D will require stimulating civilian demand as well as retraining specialized defence engineers to function in the civilian marketplace.

These considerations serve to strengthen Dumas's argument that conversion of defence resources to civilian use will require careful planning in order to minimize the cost to those industries and workers that are heavily involved in defence work. These potential costs are a barrier to disarmament policies to the extent that the narrow interests of the defence industry can be translated into effective political pressures for maintaining a large defence programme. Fears of lost jobs and income from cancelled projects are a potent political force in the localities affected. The pluralist character of the US society bestows power on coherent, well-organized groups, power that in the case of defence spending is not balanced by the diffused interests that are harmed by high levels of defence spending. The close ties between defence contractors and the Pentagon and Congress make the translation of economic interest into political decisions particularly easy. An additional factor is the general bias in the US economy towards growth, so that policies that would reduce rather than increase markets are suspect. Defence company executives are not likely to regard growth in other parts of the economy as compensation for negative growth rates in their own companies.

Nevertheless, this list of obstacles to conversion would not form a serious barrier to disarmament if political conditions were suitable. As argued above, the level of defence-related activity is small relative to the whole economy, and cutbacks in the scale likely to be caused by any arms control agreement could be easily absorbed through compensatory policies directed at the industries most affected. Unfortunately, political conditions have rarely been suitable in the post-World War II period. While economic considerations play a part in the opposition in the United States towards any policy of disarmament, the most serious obstacles lie elsewhere.

NOTES

1. Lloyd J. Dumas, Disarmament and Economy in Advanced Industrialized Countries—The US and the USSR *Bulletin of Peace Proposals*, 12:1 (1981): 5–6.

2. National Science Foundation, *National Patterns of Science and Technology Resources, 1980,* NSF 80–308, Table 18. Some countries outside the OECD report higher figures, for example, the Soviet Union and Israel.

QUESTIONS FOR DISCUSSION

1. Dumas suggests that the peace movement should address the problem of economic conversion. Summarize and evaluate his argument.

2. What are the pros and cons of initiating an economic conversion program?

3. What lessons can be drawn from Melman's analysis of Boeing-Vertol's attempt to enter the trolley car market?

4. Compare and contrast the views concerning economic conversion of Dumas, Melman, and Reppy.

SUGGESTED READINGS

ADAMS, GORDON. "Economic Conversion Misses the Point." *Bulletin of the Atomic Scientists*. (February 1986): 24–28.

BALL, NICOLE and MILTON LEITENBERG. *The Structure of the Defense Industry*. London: Croom Helm, 1983.

GORDON, SUZANNE and DAVE McFADDEN, eds. *Economic Conversion*. Cambridge: Ballinger, 1984.

GORGOL, JOHN FRANCIS. "A Theory of the Military-Industrial Firm." In Seymour Melman, ed. *The War Economy of the United States: Readings on Military Industry and Economy*, New York: St. Martin's Press, 1971, 60–71.

MELMAN, SEYMOUR. *The Permanent War Economy: American Capitalism in Decline*. New York: Simon and Schuster, 1974.

Chapter XV

International Law

Since the beginning of the nuclear age, many have believed that international law and international cooperation offer the best long-term hope for averting nuclear catastrophe. Even prior to the first test of the atomic bomb in New Mexico, a group of scientists accurately assessed the risk that a nuclear arms race would ensue after the end of World War II. In a report to the Secretary of War, dated June 11, 1945, J. Franck and six other physicists argued as follows:

> [S]cience . . . cannot promise . . . efficient protection against the destructive use of nuclear power. This protection can come only from the political organization of the world. Among all the arguments calling for an efficient international organization for peace, the existence of nuclear weapons is the most compelling one. In the absence of an international authority which could make all resort to force in international conflicts impossible, nations could still be diverted from a path which must lead to total mutual destruction, by a specific international agreement barring a nuclear armaments race . . . We cannot hope to avoid a nuclear armament race either by keeping secret from competing nations the basic scientific facts of nuclear power or by cornering the raw materials required for such a race. . . . Unless an effective international control of nuclear explosives is instituted, a race for nuclear armaments is certain to ensue following the first revelation of our possession of nuclear weapons to the world.

In the aftermath of Hiroshima and Nagasaki, the nuclear arms race predicted by Franck and his colleagues occurred; international cooperation to control nuclear weapons remained a hopeful vision. In today's world of heavily-armed sovereign states, the prospects for international law showing a way out of the arms race look bleak. The United Nations has not succeeded as a peace-keeping organization, and international organizations, such as the World Court, lack the power to enforce their rulings. Nevertheless, many believe that a fuller appreciation of international obligations could help national leaders make decisions that would promote more lawful relations between states, thus contributing to international security. And the hope that international law might someday be able to offer security and peace has not vanished.

This chapter briefly considers nuclear weapons and international law. In the first reading, Francis A. Boyle argues that nuclear weapons are illegal under international law, charging that the use of nuclear weapons on civilian populations would constitute genocide under the Nuremberg Principles. Finally, William M. Evan discusses "UN Governance and the Maintenance of Peace." Evan analyzes the constraints that limit the UN's ability to keep the peace. He proposes that new forums—representing such entities as international professional and scientific associations, multinational enterprises, universities, and supranational regional organizations —should be added to the structure of the UN. Such "transnational forums," he argues, can contribute to the peaceful resolution of international conflict.

56 International Law and Nuclear Deterrence

Francis A. Boyle

The author submits that at any . . . future war crimes tribunal held after a nuclear holocaust the judges would rule unanimously that as of 1985 the use of nuclear weapons was absolutely prohibited under all circumstances by both conventional and customary international law. Therefore, all Soviet and American government officials and military officers who either launched or waged a nuclear war would be guilty of war crimes, crimes against humanity, crimes against peace, grave breaches of the Geneva Conventions, and genocide, at a minimum, and would not be entitled to the defenses of superior orders, act of state, duress, necessity, etc. They could thus be quite legitimately and most severely punished as war criminals, up to and including the imposition of the death penalty. . . .

THE U.S. GOVERNMENT'S ARGUMENT FOR THE LEGALITY OF USING NUCLEAR WEAPONS

The official position of the United States government asserting the permissibility of using nuclear weapons for the purposes of legitimate self-defense has historically been based on the rationale enunciated in paragraph 35 of the 1956 Department of the Army Field Manual 27–10 on *The Law of Land Warfare*:[1]

> The use of explosive "atomic weapons," whether by air, sea, or land forces, cannot *as such* be regarded as violative of international law in the absence of any customary rule of

Excerpted with permission from Francis A. Boyle, "The Relevance of International Law to the 'Paradox' of Nuclear Deterrence," unpublished manuscript copyright 1985 by Francis A. Boyle.

international law or international convention restricting their employment. [Emphasis added.]

To the same effect is paragraph 613 of the 1955 Department of the Navy Field Manual NWIP 10–2 on *The Law of Naval Warfare*:[2]

> There is at present no rule of international law expressly prohibiting States from the use of nuclear weapons in warfare. In the absence of express prohibition, the use of such weapons against enemy combatants and other military objectives is permitted.

According to the United States government, if the actual use of nuclear weapons is permissible in legitimate self-defense under article 51 of the United Nations Charter, then *a fortiori* it is certainly lawful merely to threaten their use in order to deter an offensive nuclear or conventional attack by the Soviet Union upon America or the European members of the NATO alliance.

Although there exist substantial differences between these two formulations of the American rationale purporting to justify both the use of nuclear weapons and, by implication, the threat of their use (which will be analyzed below), these phraseologies are motivated by the same underlying conception of international law and its relationship to state sovereignty: Namely, that state conduct which is not expressly prohibited by a positive norm of international law is therefore permitted. This doctrine is known in the international legal studies profession as the "prohibitive" theory of international law. It stands in contrast to the diametrically opposed "permissive" theory, which holds that a state is free to do only that which it is expressly permitted to do by a positive norm of international law.

By definition, adherence to the "prohibitive" theory creates an almost irrefutable presumption in favor of state sovereignty at the expense of international law whenever the latter is silent, and thus concedes an enormous degree of freedom and discretion to governments in their conduct of international relations. Whereas the "permissive" theory is purposefully intended to severely restrict the scope of state sovereignty within the presumably well-defined boundaries of international law. Quite predictably, therefore, for reasons of national self-interest the member states of the international community have generally subscribed to the "prohibitive" theory of international law as the correct approach, and have repudiated the "permissive" theory as utopian speculation by academic theorists that is at gross variance with the facts of international life. In recognition of, or perhaps in deference to, this well-nigh universal sentiment espoused by the governments of the world community, the Permanent Court of International Justice long-ago adopted the "prohibitive" theory and expressly rejected the "permissive" theory as the proper formulation of the relationship between international law and state sovereignty in the famous case of the *S.S. Lotus* (1927).[3]

These two quite peremptory statements by the U.S. Army and the U.S. Navy have been routinely trotted out and cited by government lawyers, governmental apologists among international lawyers in academia or private practice, and other supporters of U.S. nuclear weapons policy to justify whatever was (and currently is) the then fashionable U.S. nuclear deterrence doctrine as being essentially consistent with, or at least not in violation of, the requirements of international law. By successfully propagating the general belief that American nuclear deterrence policy creates no serious problems under international law, these two statements have either directly or indirectly exercised a profound influence upon international lawyers, government officials, professional academics, the military establishment, and through the medium of these elite groups, upon U.S. public opinion. Even more insidiously, these two statements have contributed to the development of the facile yet erroneous opinion among such elite groups that U.S. nuclear deterrence policy is a matter concerning the highest national security interest of America and thus the entire "Free World," and which therefore must exist as some metaphysical entity above and beyond the domain of international law. In other words, international legal considerations are incorrectly deemed to be essentially "irrelevant" when it comes to any evaluation of the propriety of the threat to use nuclear weapons by the United States government.[4]

Moreover, despite all the various evolutionary stages U.S. nuclear deterrence doctrine has proceeded through since 1955, the purported legal justification has remained the same. America's rationale for the legitimacy of its threat to use nuclear weapons has remained untouched by time and uninfluenced by technological advances in nuclear weaponry, strategy, and destructiveness for over three decades. These unilateral and self-serving policy pronouncements by two branches of the U.S. armed services have essentially been spared from systematic examination and authoritative critique from the time of their original promulgation during the Eisenhower Administration operating under its doctrine of "massive retaliation"[5] to the Kennedy Administration and its doctrine of "mutual assured destruction" (MAD)[6] through the Johnson Administration and its doctrine of "flexible response" for NATO[7] and the Nixon Administration with its "Schlesinger Doctrine"[8] until the Carter Administration's Presidential Directive 59[9] (that naively contemplated the possibility of America "fighting" a "limited" nuclear war), which was, in turn, essentially endorsed and embellished upon by Secretary of Defense Caspar Weinberger's 1982 Five-Year Defense Guidance Statement, that boldly proclaimed the objective of America "prevailing" in a "protracted" nuclear war.[10] Common sense dictates that over a quarter century of history demands a re-examination of the rationale behind the alleged legality of U.S. nuclear weapons deterrence policy. . . .

THE RELEVANCE OF THE NUREMBERG PRINCIPLES TO NUCLEAR DETERRENCE

Article 6(a) of the 1945 Charter of the International Military Tribunal subsequently established at Nuremberg to prosecute and punish Nazi war criminals defined the term "crime against peace" to mean "planning, preparation, initiation or waging of a war of aggression, or a war in violation of international treaties, agreements or assurances, or participation in a common plan or conspiracy for the accomplishment of any of the foregoing." Nuremberg Charter article 6(b) defined the term "war crime" to include "murder, ill-treatment or deportation to slave labour or for any other purpose of civilian population of or in occupied territory, murder or ill-treatment of prisoners of war or persons on the seas, killing of hostages, plunder of public or private property, wanton destruction of cities, towns or villages, or devastation not justified by military necessity." Article 6(c) of the Nuremberg Charter defined the term "crime against humanity" to include "murder, extermination, enslavement, deportation, and other inhumane acts committed against any civilian population."

Article 6 also provided that leaders, organizers, instigators, and accomplices participating in the formulation or execution of a common plan or conspiracy to commit crimes against peace, crimes against humanity, and war crimes are responsible for all acts performed by any persons in execution of such plan. Article 7 of the Nuremberg Charter denied the applicability of the "act of state" defense to them by making it clear that the official position of those who have committed such heinous crimes "shall not be considered as freeing them from responsibility or mitigating punishment." Finally, article 8 provided that the fact an individual acted pursuant to an order of his government or of a superior shall not free him from responsibility, but may be considered in mitigation of punishment if justice so requires.

The principles of international law recognized by the Charter of the Nuremberg Tribunal and the Judgment of the Tribunal[11] itself were affirmed by a unanimous vote of the United Nations General Assembly in Resolution 95(1) on December 11, 1946.[12] Since that time, the Nuremberg Principles have universally been considered to constitute an authoritative statement of the rules of customary international law dictating individual criminal responsibility for crimes against peace, crimes against humanity, and war crimes.[13] Under the general principle of customary international law creating "universality" of jurisdiction for the prosecution and punishment of those alleged to have committed such heinous offenses,[14] all U.S. and Soviet government officials and members of the U.S. and U.S.S.R. military forces who might order or participate in a strategic nuclear attack upon the Soviet Union could lawfully be tried by any government of the world community that subsequently obtains control over them for crimes against peace, crimes against humanity and war crimes, *inter alia.*

The very existence of such heinous offenses and of personal criminal responsibility for the commission thereof is expressly recognized and affirmed by paragraph 498 of that same 1956 U.S. Army Field Manual on *The Law of Land Warfare.*[15] Yet simultaneously and quite inexplicably the Manual apparently asserts the non-illegality of using nuclear weapons during wartime in paragraph 35! Furthermore, paragraph 500 thereof expressly provides that: "Conspiracy, direct incitement, and attempts to commit, as well as complicity in the commission of, crimes against peace, crimes against humanity, and war crimes are punishable."[16]

Does not contemporary U.S. nuclear deterrence policy constitute planning, preparation and conspiracy to commit crimes against peace, crimes against humanity, and war crimes? Are not the nuclear decision-makers of the Reagan and Gorbachev administrations thus subject to personal criminal responsibility and punishment under the Nuremberg Principles for currently pursuing the development of a U.S. "protracted nuclear war-prevailing" capability? In any event, does there not exist an incredible inconsistency if not a serious incompatibility between paragraph 35 of the 1956 U.S. Army Field Manual, on the one hand, and paragraphs 498, 499,[17] 500, and 501,[18] *inter alia*, on the other? If so, what are the ramifications of this gross discrepancy for both the validity and the effectiveness of the contemporary U.S. nuclear deterrent in theory and practice?

At the very minimum, under the Nuremberg Principles, the U.S. nuclear destruction of Soviet civilian population centers would be absolutely prohibited under all circumstances.[19] This proposition would be true even if such a countercity attack was undertaken as a measure of retaliation in response to a prior nuclear attack against U.S. population centers by the Soviet Union.[20] But if the actual destruction of civilian population centers is prohibited under all circumstances, how can a theory of strategic nuclear deterrence that threatens to destroy cities be justified under international law?

The simplistic answer to this objection would be that the Nuremberg Principles apply only to the actual use of nuclear weapons during wartime. Hence, arguably, it is perfectly lawful for a state in peacetime to threaten to do something that would be completely unlawful to do in wartime, especially if the purpose of the peacetime threat is to prevent a nuclear or conventional war in the first place. This proposition is the cornerstone of the alleged "paradox" concerning the legality *vel non* of strategic nuclear deterrence.

Of course this rationale fails to account for the existence of the inchoate crimes incidental to war crimes, crimes against peace and crimes against humanity (viz., planning, preparation, conspiracy, incitement, attempt, complicity) that can be committed by government officials during peacetime and can thus create individual criminal responsibility for the commission thereof even before the outbreak of war. The primary purpose for recognizing the existence of such inchoate crimes with respect to war crimes, crimes against peace and crimes against humanity was to deter, prevent, or forestall the commission of the substantive offenses in the first place.[21]

Once again, the simplistic response to this objection would be that the recognition of such inchoate crimes with respect to nuclear deterrence is counterproductive to maintaining a credible nuclear balance between the two superpowers that is supposedly necessary to preserve world peace from nuclear Armageddon. According to this rationale, the application of the concept of inchoate crimes from the Nuremberg Principles to the issue of nuclear deterrence would weaken the credibility of the deterrent itself and therefore increase the risks of war. In other words, this argument reduces itself to the bald-faced and reprehensible Machiavellian proposition that the ends justify the means. Yet the rules of international law have been formulated precisely for the purpose of evaluating the propriety of both the ends and the means of international behaviour pursued by governments and foreign policy decision-makers alike. That point was made quite clear by the Nuremberg Tribunal to the Nazi war criminals. It would also be made quite clear by a Nuclear Holocaust Tribunal to any surviving American and Soviet civilian and military leaders. . . .

IS IT LAWFUL TO POSSESS NUCLEAR WEAPONS?

The final question that needs to be addressed concerning the relevance of international law to the so-called paradox of nuclear deterrence is whether or not it is lawful for a state even to possess nuclear weapons. A great deal has been said about this subject on both sides of the dispute. The author submits, however, that the question itself is completely speculative and

misdirected, if not outrightly misleading. It obfuscates the fact that today's acknowledged nuclear weapons states (viz., United States, Great Britain, France, Soviet Union, People's Republic of China) do not simply possess nuclear weapons. Rather, they have actively deployed nuclear weapons in enormous numbers and varieties by attaching them to delivery vehicles that are interconnected with sophisticated command, control, communication and intelligence (C³I) networks.[22] Such nuclear weapons systems are ready for almost instantaneous launch upon immediate notice. Hence the only meaningful question concerns the legality of modern nuclear weapons *systems* as they are currently deployed and programmed for use.

If the nuclear weapons states had actually kept all their nuclear devices stored in warehouses where they were separated from their respective delivery vehicles, it might be pertinent to answer the question whether or not such mere possession of nuclear weapons was legal under international law. Yet that historically has not been the case. The nuclear weapons systems maintained by all the world's nuclear weapons states, and especially by the two superpowers, are far beyond this stage of mere possession, and have been at the point of deployment and preparation for immediate use in a thermonuclear war for quite some time. As pointed out earlier in this article, under the Nuremberg Principles, such planning, preparation and conspiracy to commit crimes against peace, crimes against humanity and war crimes, *inter alia*, constitute international crimes in their own right.

The appropriate analogy from domestic law to be applied here is not the hand gun kept in the bedroom bureau drawer for the purposes of legitimate self-defense against a home intruder. But rather, a shotgun that is fully loaded and pointed at the head of another human being, with the safety catch off, the hammer cocked, the firing mechanism set on a hair-trigger, and the assailant's finger ready, willing and able to twitch at an instant's notice or even because of a mistake or an instinctual reflex. This is clearly illegal behavior under the domestic criminal legal system of any state in the world community today, and therefore under international law as well, since it violates a general principle of law recognized by all civilized nations.[23]

In any jurisdiction within the United States of America, such criminal activity purposely and knowingly engaged in by two individuals with respect to each other would render both guilty of aggravated assault, assault with a deadly weapon, and reckless endangerment of a human being, *inter alia*. Moreover, as would be true for dueling, Russian Roulette, or playing "chicken" with automobiles, the fact that two or more individuals voluntarily participated in such a joint criminal enterprise would not excuse anyone from personal responsibility. In the case of modern nuclear weapons systems, the two nuclear superpowers have both committed and are continuing to commit on an everyday basis the international crime of recklessly endangering the entire human race. They cannot exonerate themselves from joint and several criminal responsibility for such illegal behavior by invoking the unlawful conduct of their co-felons.

So much then for the argument made by some international law professors that just because five states in today's world community already possess and deploy nuclear weapons systems and several more are diligently pursuing policies designed to acquire a nuclear weapons capability, their behavior somehow negates the existence of international legal rules prohibiting the possession and deployment of nuclear weapons and related delivery and C³I systems.[24] Since when have a small band of criminals been permitted to argue that their own lawless conduct destroys the validity of the very laws they have violated? The maxim *ex injuria non oritur jus* is a general principle of law recognized by all civilized nations, and therefore a rule of international law as well.[25]

The repeated commission of criminal acts by a few miscreant states cannot create a right for them to continue to do so unless, perhaps, the rest of the international community might agree to abrogate the applicable rules of law. To the contrary, as of January 1, 1984 there were 124 state parties to the 1968 Treaty on the Non-Proliferation of Nuclear Weapons (NPT), article 2 of which prohibits non-nuclear weapons state parties from acquiring a nuclear weapons capability.[26] The fact that of the five acknowledged nuclear weapons states, only three (United States, Great Britain, Soviet Union) are parties to the NPT does not mean that the non-nuclear weapons state parties have thereby implicitly consented to the legality of their possession and deployment of nuclear weapons and related delivery and C³I systems. Even if the NPT were to be abrogated by the non-nuclear weapons state parties because the nuclear weapons state parties have already committed a material breach

of the treaty by failing to perform their obligations under article 6,[27] the possession and deployment of nuclear weapons and their related systems would still remain illegal because it violates the various rules of international law enumerated above.

Indeed, any international agreement purporting to legalize the possession and deployment of nuclear weapons and their related systems would violate a peremptory norm of international law and thus be void in accordance with article 53 of the 1969 Vienna Convention on the Law of Treaties.[28] If piracy, slavery, armed aggression, crimes against peace, crimes against humanity, war crimes, and genocide are universally considered to violate *jus cogens*, then *a fortiori* the threat by the two nuclear superpowers to exterminate the entire human race, coupled with their imminent capability to do so, must likewise do the same. International law professors must face up to the fact that for them to argue that the present system of nuclear deterrence as practiced by the two superpowers and their nuclear cohorts is lawful, they must in essence deny the very existence of such a phenomenon known in the international legal studies profession as a peremptory norm of international law. This author seriously doubts that such would be the intention of even those who are most fervently committed to promoting the abstract proposition that nuclear deterrence is legal. . . .

NOTES

1. Department of the Army, Field Manual 27–10: The Law of Land Warfare 18 (1956).

2. Office of the Chief of Naval Operations, Department of the Navy Field Manual NWIP 10–2: The Law of Naval Warfare (1955).

3. S.S. "Lotus" (Fr. v. Turk.), 1927, P.C.I.J., Ser. A, No. 9.

4. *Cf.* Boyle, *The Irrelevance of International Law*, 10 Cal. W. Int'l L. J. 193 (1980).

5. *See, e.g.*, L. Freedman, The Evolution of Nuclear Strategy 76–91 (1981); P. Peeters, Massive Retaliation: The Policy and its Critics (1959).

6. *See* Freedman, *supra* note 5, at 227–44. *See generally* Martin, *The Role of Military Force in the Nuclear Age*, in Strategic Thought in the Nuclear Age 4–7 (L. Martin ed. 1979); D. Snow, Nuclear Strategy in a Dynamic World 57–58 (1981).

7. *See* Freedman, *supra* note 5, at 285–86. *See also* Harvard Nuclear Study Group, Living with Nuclear Weapons 85, 92 (1983); Stanford Arms Con-

trol Group, International Arms Control 205–07 (C. Blacker & G. Duffy eds. 1984).

8. *See* L. Freedman, *supra* note 5, at 377.

9. See R. Scheer, With Enough Shovels: Reagan, Bush & Nuclear War 11–12 (1982). *See also* President Carter's Remarks at the Annual Convention of the American Legion, 16 Weekly Comp. Pres. Doc. 1549, 1553 (Aug. 21, 1980).

10. See R. Scheer, *supra* note 9, at 8, 32. *See also* Bethe, Gottfried & Currey, The Five Year War Plan, N.Y. Times, June 10, 1982, at A31, col. 1; N.Y. Times, May 30, 1982, at Al, col. 1.

11. XXII Trial of the Major War Criminals Before the International Military Tribunal 411–589 (1948).

12. G.A. Res. 95(I), U.N. Doc. A/236, at 1144 (1946).

13. *See* I. Brownlie, International Law and the Use of Force by States 154–213 (1963). *See also* R. Woetzel, The Nuremberg Trials in International Law 232–35 (1962).

14. *See, e.g.*, Attorney General of Israel v. Eichmann, Criminal Case No. 40/61, District Court of Jerusalem, Judgement of Dec. 11, 1961, *reprinted in* 56 Am. J. Int'l L. 805 (1962), 36 I.L.R. 5 (1962).

15. The Law of Land Warfare, *supra* note 1, ¶ 498, at 178.

16. *Id.*, ¶ 500, at 178.

17. *Id.*, ¶ 499, at 178.

18. *Id.*, ¶ 501, at 178–79. *See also Application of Yamashita*, 327 U.S. 1 (1946).

19. Nuremberg Charter, art. 5(c).

20. See, e.g., Falk, Meyrowitz, and Sanderson, Nu-

clear Weapons and International Law 30–32, 45, 50–51, 63–71 (Oct. 1981); Rubin, *Nuclear Weapons and International Law*, 1984 Fletcher Forum 53–57; Weston, Nuclear Weapons Versus International Law: A Contextual Reassessment, 28 McGill L.J. 585 (1983).

21. II Trial of the Major War Criminals Before the International Military Tribunal 104–05 (1948).

22. P. Bracken, The Command the Control of Nuclear Forces 212 (1983).

23. I.C.J. Stat. art. 38, para. 1(c): "1. The Court, whose function is to decide in accordance with international law such disputes as are submitted to it, shall apply:. . .c. the general principles of law recognized by civilized nations;" *reprinted in* S. Rosenne, Documents on the International Court of Justice 77 (1974).

24. Reisman, *Nuclear Weapons in International Law*, 4 N.Y.L. Sch. J. Int'l & Comp. L. 339, 342 (1983).

25. Brownlie, *Some Legal Aspects of the Use of Nuclear Weapons*, 14 Int'l & Comp. L. Q. 437, 451 (1965).

26. Treaty on the Non-Proliferation of Nuclear Weapons, July 1, 1968, 21 U.S.T. 483, T.I.A.S. No. 6839, 729 U.N.T.S. 161.

27. *Id.* at art. 6:

28. Vienna Convention on the Law of Treaties, May 23, 1969, U.N. Doc. A/Conf. 39/27, at 289 (1969), [1980] Gr. Brit. T.S. No. 58 (Cmd. 7964) (entered into force Jan. 27, 1980), *reprinted in* 8 Int'l Legal Mat. 679 (1969); 63 Am. J. Int'l L. 875 (1969).

57   U.N. Governance and the Maintenance of Peace

William M. Evan _____

The founding fathers of the United Nations, in designing its structure and function, brought to bear pre-World War II and pre-Nuclear Age preconceptions about international relations. The product of a series of wartime conferences, especially at Dumbarton Oaks in August 1944 and at the Yalta Conference in February 1945, the Charter of the United Nations was the subject of deliberations at the conference in San Francisco in April 1945. It would have been difficult, though not impossible, for the framers of the Charter to envision the massive movement for decolonization that was about to emerge at the end of World War II. As for the Nuclear Age, since the Charter was signed on June 26, 1945, it preceded the first test of the atomic bomb at Alamagordo on July 16, 1945 and the dropping of the atomic bombs on Hiroshima and Nagasaki on August 6 and 9, 1945.

These two watershed events, the movement for decolonization and the dawn of the Nuclear Age, soon created a governance crisis for the United Nations, on the one hand, and, on the other hand, erected obstacles to achieving its objectives, as set forth in Article 1 of the Charter, "to maintain international peace and security." Thus, forty years after the founding of the United Nations, the Charter, which is unchanged, is out-of-phase with the realities of the international system and the Nuclear Age.

THE GOVERNANCE CRISIS

The principal organs of the United Nations, such as the Security Council, the General Assembly and the International Court of Justice, were adopted from its predecessor, the League of Nations. And like the League, the U.N. is a voluntary association of sovereign nation-states. Article 2 of the Charter declared "the organization is based on the principle of sovereign equality of all its members." In addition, as Röling has pointed out, the Charter sought to preserve the colonial system by stipulating provisions—in Chapters XI, XII and XIII which deal with "non-self-governing territories" and "trusteeship systems"—for "good colonial administration" (Röling, 1979: 26).

The doctrine of sovereignty had profound consequences for the design and functioning of the United Nations. Beginning with the concept of nation-state membership, each state was accorded one vote in the General Assembly. In 1946, when the General Assembly met for its first session, the large and powerful states constituted a majority among the 51 member states. As a result of decolonization, however, the membership in the U.N. changed radically within 15 years of its founding. By 1961, African, Asian, Central and South American states comprised more than a two-thirds majority. By 1976, with the admission of more newly-established independent states, some of which were "ministates," the African, Asian, Central and South American states numbered almost three-fourths of the 147 member states (Jacobson, 1977: 61). And with the further growth of U.N. membership to 159 states by 1984, this pattern has been further reinforced.

As policy conflicts multiplied between the de-

Reprinted from William M. Evan, "U.N. Governance and the Maintenance of Peace," in *World Encyclopedia of Peace* (London: Pergamon Press, 1986). Copyright 1986 by William M. Evan.

veloped and less developed countries (LDCs), a number of overlapping coalitions or blocs emerged which tended to weaken the role of Western states.

> The organization's 1984 membership of 159 states is grouped into blocs, which roughly approximate political parties. The Group of 77 (or Developing Nations bloc) consists of some 120 states. Next largest, and more influential because better organized, is the Non-Aligned Movement which claims 99 members. Also large and often cohesive is the 50-member African Group. The Islamic Conference has 41 member-countries, but is usually divided except on the Palestine question. Lacking in cohesion, too, are the Asian Group (39 members) and the Latin American Group (33 members), both of which have pro-Soviet adherents who actively prevent the groups from taking consensual positions of which Moscow disapproves. The Western European "and Others" Group is smaller (22 members) but acts mostly in concert. The Eastern European Group (11 members) is strained because three members (Albania, Romania, Yugoslavia) often refuse to take their cues from the Kremlin. The Arab Group (21 countries) is usually divided between shifting alliances of radical and moderate regimes. The smallest groups—the five Nordics, the six-member Association of Southeast Asian Countries, and the 10-member European Community—are perhaps the most cohesive. (Franck, 1985: 246–247)

With the tendency for some of these coalitions to enter into an alliance with Soviet bloc countries in the General Assembly and in other U.N. organs, the Western industrialized member states have frequently been outvoted on an array of issues. A dramatic illustration of this tendency is the General Assembly resolution on the New International Economic Order in 1974. Understandably, the LDCs had much to gain from the passage of this resolution, while the developed countries were in a position of relinquishing some of their economic advantages and resources.

The recurrent conflicts in the U.N. involve a demand on the part of LDCs for reapportionment of political power (Gregg, 1977). The General Assembly, where the LDCs often defeat the policies of Western developed countries because of their numerical preponderance, has become a paradigm for restructuring the governance of the other U.N. forums. The egalitarian principle

of one state, one vote is advocated by LDCs for other U.N. organs, especially the World Bank, the International Monetary Fund, and the United Nations Conference on Trade and Development. In effect, the LDCs want to restructure the governance system of the U.N. in the direction of a centralized forum with a broad mandate in which all member states can participate and thus assure themselves a majority vote. In contrast, the developed Western states prefer decentralized and functionally-specific forums involving only those member states with a direct interest in the issues (Gregg, 1977).

Thus, the developed Western states, because of their minority status, find themselves in a paradoxical position of opposing the Western egalitarian voting principle and arguing in favor of "weighted voting" in accordance, for example, with the economic importance of the member state and its financial contribution to the U.N. budget. Cast in these terms, the conflicts between the developing and developed countries pose a serious challenge to the future of the U.N. with little likelihood that they will be resolved to the satisfaction of all member states.

MAINTENANCE OF PEACE

Another challenge, which the U.N. has thus far failed to meet, pertains to its raison d'être—as articulated in Article 1 of its Charter—of "maintaining international peace and security." Almost from its very inception, the U.N. has wrestled with the problem of forestalling the nuclear arms race between the superpowers and initiating a process of disarmament by passing resolutions and establishing committees and commissions (U.N. Department of Public Information, 1979). As early as 1952, the General Assembly created the Disarmament Commission which, in 1961, paved the way for the Eighteen-Nation Committee on Disarmament, the membership of which was subsequently enlarged in 1969 to 26 and in 1975 to 31. And beginning in 1959, the General Assembly has included on its agenda the item of "General and Complete Disarmament," culminating in the convening of Special Sessions on Disarmament in 1978 and 1982. With the aid of the Committee on Disarmament, the treaty on the Non-Proliferation of Nuclear Weapons was drafted and overwhelmingly approved by the General Assembly in 1968. Article VI of this treaty obligates the nuclear weapons states to negotiate an end to the arms race and a treaty on "general and complete disarmament" under effective international controls. Notwithstanding this record of persistent and admirable efforts to promote peace, the nuclear arms race not only continues into the mid-1980s, but has accelerated, thereby steadily increasing the risk of nuclear war.

To make matters worse, the U.N. has not succeeded in its peacemaking mandate (Forsythe, 1977), that is, in implementing its Charter provisions in Chapters VI and VII for the "pacific settlement of disputes" and for actions in response to "breaches of the peace" and "acts of aggression." Thus, since 1945 about 148 local wars have been waged, all of them in the Third World and involving many millions of victims (Kende, 1985; Soedjatmoko, 1985). Perhaps one of the most destructive wars is the five-year old Iran-Iraq war which has thus far eluded all efforts at negotiation, conciliation and mediation, such as are provided in Article 33 of the Charter. Another serious breach of the peace is terrorism by states and non-state actors. Without the establishment of an International Criminal Court of Justice, all efforts by states to deal with this problem bilaterally and according to their domestic laws are unlikely to succeed.

In contrast to the U.N.'s failure in peacemaking, its efforts at peacekeeping has met with some measure of success. U.N. peacekeeping in Zaire, Israel, Egypt, Cyprus and the Golan Heights illustrates the utility of interposing U.N. forces to end hostilities and enforce cease-fire and truce agreements (Finger, 1977). Ironically, U.N. peacekeeping is hampered by inadequate funding, the lack of a clear Charter mandate and by political disputes between East and West as to the objectives of peacekeeping operations (Finger, 1977).

That the U.N. has largely failed in its noble mandate of "maintaining international peace and security" is due to a number of severe constraints under which it operates. Of fundamental importance is the doctrine of national sovereignty. This is reflected in many provisions of the Charter, for example, the "domestic jurisdiction" provision in Article 2 (Rajan: 1982) and the inadequate provisions in Chapter XIV regarding the jurisdiction of the International Court of Justice and the enforcement of its judgments. It is also reflected in the tendency of the superpowers, in their struggle to protect and enlarge their respective spheres of influence, to subordinate international law to geopolitical objectives. An additional and related factor of critical consequence for the functioning of the U.N. is a structural failure, viz., that it confines membership to nation-states.

NEW U.N. FORUMS FOR PEACE

The sovereignty assumption that each nation-state should have supreme authority over its internal and external relations prompted the framers of the U.N. Charter to confine membership to the nation-state (Jacobson, 1977: 60). They evidently did not conceive of an international system, following World War II, that might include actors other than nation-states. Elsewhere I have considered the rationale for the concept of "transnationalism" and "transnational forums for peace" (Evan, 1962).

> Actions undertaken by entities larger than nations or smaller than nations and outside the framework of nation-states, I shall call "transnational." This concept, partially based on Jessup's idea of "transnational law," subsumes modes of action of "supranational" and "infranational" bodies. (Evan, 1962: 395)

In recent years political scientists and students of international relations have acknowledged that a "state-centric" model no longer suffices to describe and analyze the international system because of the emergence of diverse transnational actors (Keohane and Nye, 1972). In light of this realization, I would like to consider, once again (Evan, 1962), the rationale for incorporating within the present structure of the United Nations new transnational forums for peace.

> The addition of new organs of a transnational character would add other voices to those now heard in U.N. deliberations. A multiplicity of voices, especially in a crisis, may generate ideas for new alternatives and bring pressure to bear on governments to entertain new alternatives, thus facilitating the resolution of conflicts. (Evan, 1962: 396)

In the interest of avoiding or at least minimizing ideological controversies, I would like to entertain a proposal for adding to the U.N. governance structure four transnational forums for peace: 1) a forum for regional supranational communities, 2) a forum for international scientific and professional associations, 3) a forum for multinational enterprises and 4) a forum for universities.

A Forum for Regional Supranational Communities. Among supranational entities that can conceivably contribute ideas and mobilize resources for a peaceful resolution of international conflicts are regional supranational communities which seek to promote the common economic objectives of a group of nations. Since 1949, with the establishment of the Council for Mutual Economic Assistance consisting of the USSR and Eastern European communist countries, a number of supranational experiments in the integration of the economies of several sets of countries have been undertaken. In 1952 the European Coal and Steel Community was formed and paved the way, in 1958, for the establishment of the European Economic Community. Since then other regional communities have come into being, e.g., the Central American Common Market (1960), the Caribbean Community and Common Market (1973) and the Economic Community of West African States (1975).

A Forum of International Scientific and Professional Associations. Another category of supranational actors is the international scientific and professional association (Evan, 1981). Since the nineteenth century there has been a marked growth of such organizations, and increasingly such organizations are beginning to address global problems such as hunger, environmental deterioration, the exhaustion of non-renewable sources of energy and the threat of nuclear war from a scientific and professional vantage point. Examples of such organizations are the International Council of Scientific Unions, which is a federation of international physical and biological associations, and the International Social Science Council, which is a federation of international social science associations. In the various professions which apply science and technology such as medicine, law, engineering, and architecture, there are numerous international associations (Evan, 1974) as well as federations of such organizations, e.g., World Medical Association, International Dental Federation, International Union of Architects and the Union of International Engineering Organizations.

Of particular relevance for the problem of maintaining peace are two international organizations, one of scientists and the other of professionals. The first is the "Pugwash Conference on Science and World Affairs," founded by Einstein and Russell in 1955. Meeting periodically since 1957, members of Pugwash—scientists from East and West—have inquired into technical aspects of arms control and disarmament and have developed proposals that have contributed to the drafting of several significant treaties, notably the Limited Test Ban Treaty of 1962, the Nuclear Non-Proliferation Treaty of 1968, and the Convention Barring the Development, Manufacture and Stockpiling of Biological Weapons of 1972 (Evan, 1981). The other noteworthy organization is the International Physicians for the Prevention of Nuclear War. Established in 1980 by American and Soviet physicians, this organization now has a membership of 135,000 in 41 countries. The purpose of this organization is to disseminate scientific information on the potential effects of nuclear warfare and thus increase public awareness of its catastrophic consequences.

A Forum of Multinational Enterprises. In contrast to the two previous forums which are *supranational* in character, a forum of multinational enterprises is *subnational*. The parent headquarters of such enterprises—which have greatly multiplied since World War II (Stopford and Dunning, 1983)—are based in a given country in which they are legally incorporated; however, they have the distinctive feature of having established manufacturing and/or marketing subsidiaries in a variety of countries around the world. Although this is more typical of large-scale Western capitalist enterprises than of socialist enterprises, it is also the case that the latter have in recent years entered into co-production contracts and joint ventures with firms in the West (Perlmutter, 1969, 1980) and have also established marketing organizations in capitalist countries. In so doing, both capitalist and socialist multinational enterprises have developed a common interest in promoting international trade. And in as much as the promotion of international trade tends to create economic interdependence between nations, it can become a source of international integration (Evan, 1974), which, in turn, would encourage the management, if not the resolution, of international conflicts.

A Forum of Universities. Virtually each of the 159 member-states of the United Nations has one or more universities. If we include only those multi-college entities with research and graduate programs, there are probably several hundred such organizations throughout the world (World Guide to Universities, 1976). Notwithstanding cultural and ideological differences among universities, what they share in common is a commitment to the development and transmission of knowledge in the sciences, humanities and the arts. Since the Middle Ages, when the earliest universities were founded in Italy, France, and England, there has evolved the rudiments of a shared universe of discourse which transcends national and ideological boundaries. It is the transnational heritage of higher learning, with a commitment to rationality, that can be drawn upon for a rational approach to the management of international disputes and the strengthening of international order.

The foregoing brief discussion of the four proposed transnational forums for peace leaves unanswered many questions pertaining to membership criteria for each forum and the governance structure of each forum. These questions entail complex issues that must be carefully addressed if these forums—assuming that they are ever implemented—are to promote conflict management instead of further politicizing debates on international disputes.

CONCLUSION

Admittedly, a proposal for new transnational forums for peace, given the present structure of the international system in the 1980s, is visionary. But that is surely not a justification for dismissing it as infeasible. There are at least two relevant considerations. First, Article 22 of the Charter has a direct bearing on the proposed transnational forums:

> "The General Assembly may establish such subsidiary organs as it deems necessary for the performance of its functions."

Persuading the General Assembly to establish transnational forums for peace is substantially easier than invoking the more complicated provisions for amending the Charter set forth in Article 108. Hence, if such a proposal were advanced by one or another member-state, preferably by several member-states cutting across the various political coalitions, it could be included as an item on the agenda of a future session of the General Assembly. Second, by establishing such transnational forums, the governance crisis in the General Assembly arising from the one state, one vote principle might be somewhat mitigated. While maintaining the egalitarian and majoritarian voting principle and

avoiding the introduction of "weighted voting," each of the four proposed transnational forums would probably have a different mix of organizations from East, West, North and South. The resulting composition of the transnational forums would very likely promote "cross-cutting" cleavages across the political coalitions (Coser, 1976), which could encourage the consideration of policy alternatives not entertained by the General Assembly. Especially in the event of an international crisis, the addition of transnational voices could facilitate the resolution of conflicts threatening world peace.

By inquiring into the issues raised in this essay, scholars in international law concerned with strengthening the rule of law may eventually and indirectly be instrumental in persuading the General Assembly to debate the merits of establishing transnational forums for peace. As Roling, the late distinguished Dutch international legal scholar, stated:

> The United Nations will need the support of scholars in the near future more than ever, because it will grow more and more unpopular. . . . Insight will be necessary, in the defense of United Nations actions, and even perhaps courage. Students and scholars should be prepared for this coming controversy, where the demands of narrow nationalism should be opposed and answered by the demands of humanity as a whole. (Röling, 1979: 36).

REFERENCES

COSER, LEWIS A., *Functions of Social Conflict*. Glencoe, Ill.: Free Press, 1956.

EVAN, WILLIAM M., "Transnational Forums for Peace," in Quincy Wright, William M. Evan and Morton Deutsch, eds., *Preventing World War III*, New York: Simon and Schuster, 1962, pp. 393–409.

EVAN, WILLIAM M., "Multinational Corporations and International Professional Associations," *Human Relations*, 27 (November 6, 1974), pp. 587–625.

EVAN, WILLIAM M., "Some Dilemmas of Knowledge and Power: An Introduction," in William M. Evan, ed., *Knowledge and Power in a Global Society*, Beverly Hills, California: Sage Publications, Inc., 1981, pp. 11–25.

FINGER, SEYMOUR MAXWELL, "The Maintenance of Peace," in David A. Kay, ed., *The Changing United Nations: Options for the United States*, Vol. 32, No. 4, New York: The Academy of Political Science, 1977, pp. 195–205.

FORSYTHE, DAVID P., "United Nations Peacemaking", in David A. Kay, ed., *The Changing United Na-*

tions: Options for the United States, Vol. 32, No. 4, New York: The Academy of Political Science, 1977.

FRANCK, THOMAS M., *Nation Against Nation*. New York: Oxford University Press, 1985.

GREGG, ROBERT W., "The Apportioning of Political Power," in David A. Kay, ed., *The Changing United Nations: Options for the United States*, Vol. 32, No. 4, New York: The Academy of Political Science, 1977, pp. 69–80.

JACOBSON, HAROLD K., "The United Nations and Political Conflict: A Mirror, Amplifier, or Regulator?" in David A. Kay, ed., *The Changing United Nations: Options for the United States*, Vol. 32, No. 4, New York: The Academy of Political Science, 1977, pp. 56–68.

KENDE, ISTVAN, "Local Wars Since 1945," in *World Encyclopedia of Peace*.

KEOHANE, ROBERT O. and JOSEPH S. NYE, JR., *Transnational Relations and World Politics*, Cambridge, Mass: Harvard University Press, 1972.

PERLMUTTER, HOWARD V., "Emerging East-West Ventures: The Transideological Enterprise," *Columbia Journal of World Business*, Vol. IV (September-October 1969), pp. 39—50.

PERLMUTTER, HOWARD V., "The Future of East-West Industrial Cooperation," in Paul Marer and Eugeniusz Tabaczynski, eds., *Polish-US Industrial Cooperation in the 1980s: Findings of a Joint Research Project*. Bloomington, IN: Indiana University Press, 1980, pp. 187–204.

RAJAN, M.S., *The Expanding Jurisdiction of the United Nations*. New York: Dobbs Ferry: Oceana Publications, Inc, 1982.

RÖLING, BERT V. "The United Nations—A General Evaluation," in Antonio Cassese, ed., *U.N. Law/ Fundamental Rights*. Alphen aanden Rijn—the Netherlands: Sijthoff and Noordhoff, 1979, pp. 23–38.

SOEDJATMOKO, "Patterns of Armed Conflict in the Third World," 64th Nobel Symposium on "The Study of War and Peace," Noresund, Norway, June 24–28, 1985.

STOPFORD, JOHN M. and JOHN H. DUNNING, *The World Directory of Multinational Enterprises, 1982–83*. Detroit, Michigan: Gale Research Co., 1983.

U.N. DEPARTMENT OF PUBLIC INFORMATION, *Everyone's United Nations*, 9th edition. New York: United Nations.

World Guide to Universities. 2nd edition. Munich: Verlag Dokumentation Saur 1976.

QUESTIONS FOR DISCUSSION

1. Imagine you are the prosecutor at an international tribunal following a nuclear war that killed 113 million people. The defendants, a group of U.S. and Soviet officials, are charged with war crimes, as a result of having ordered nuclear attacks on civilian populations. How would you press your case? What precedents from international law would you invoke?

2. Now imagine that you are the defense attorney. How would you defend the actions of the officials? What legal arguments would you make?

3. How can the transnational forums proposed by Evan contribute to international understanding and peace?

SUGGESTED READINGS

BOYLE, FRANCIS A. *World Politics and International Law*. Durham, N.C.: Duke University Press, 1985.

CLARK, GRENVILLE and LOUIS B. SOHN. *Introduction to World Peace through World Law*, 4th ed. Cambridge: Harvard University Press, 1984.

EVENSEN, J. "The Establishment of Nuclear Weapon-Free Zones in Europe: Proposal on a Treaty Text," in Sverre Lodgaard and Marek Thee, *Nuclear Disengagement in Europe*. Philadelphia: Taylor and Francis, 1983.

FERENCZ, BENJAMIN. *Enforcing International Law: A Way to World Peace: A Documentary History and Analysis*. Dobbs Ferry, N.Y.: Oceana, 1983.

MILLER, ARTHUR SELWIN and MARTIN FEINRIDER, eds. *Nuclear Weapons and Law*. Westport, Conn.: Greenwood Press, 1984.

WESTON, BURNS H. RICHARD A. FALK, and ANTHONY A. D'AMATO. *International Law and World Order*. St. Paul, Minn.: West Publishing Co., 1980.

Selected Glossary

A-Bomb. See *Atomic bomb.*

ABM. See *Antiballistic missile.*

ABM Treaty. See *Antiballistic missile treaty.*

Accidental nuclear war. A military conflict involving the detonation of nuclear weapons that results from technical malfunction, human error, unauthorized actions of military personnel or some combination of these factors. (See also *Unintentional nuclear war.*)

Air-launched cruise missile (ALCM). A cruise missile that can be launched by an airplane. (See also *Cruise missile.*)

Antiballistic missile (ABM). A missile designed to counter an enemy's intercontinental ballistic missile by intercepting and destroying it before it reaches its target.

Antiballistic missile treaty of 1972 (ABM Treaty). One of the treaties between the U.S. and the USSR passed in 1972 as part of the SALT I agreements. The ABM Treaty permits each side to establish ABM defenses at two sites. A 1974 protocol to the treaty further restricts each side to deploying ABMs at only one site.

Antisatellite weapon. A weapon designed to destroy satellites or render them inoperative. Potential targets include enemy communication, surveillance and hunter-killer satellites.

Antisubmarine warfare (ASW). Military techniques and technologies for detecting, destroying or reducing the effectiveness of enemy submarines.

Arms control. Efforts to control the arms race through treaties, agreements, or other measures designed to regulate the numbers, types or deployment patterns of weapons and troops.

Arms race stability. A situation in which neither side perceives an incentive to develop new weapons systems. (Compare *Crisis stability.*)

ASAT. See *Antisatellite weapon.*

ASW. See *Antisubmarine warfare.*

Atomic bomb (A-bomb). A weapon that derives its explosive power from the energy of nuclear fission.

Ballistic missile. A missile that is propelled into space by rocket boosters.

Ballistic missile defense (BMD). Weapon systems whose mission is to destroy ballistic missiles before they reach their targets. Ground-based ABMs are one type of BMD system (see *Antiballistic missile*). In addition, there are proposals for a space-based BMD system (see *Strategic Defense Initiative* and *Star Wars.*)

Battlefield nuclear weapons. See *Tactical nuclear weapons.*

BMD. See *Ballistic missile defense.*

C³I. See *Command, control, communications and intelligence systems.*

CEP. See *Circular Error Probable.*

Circular Error Probable (CEP). A measure of missile accuracy. If a missile is aimed at a target, the CEP is equal to the radius of a circle around the target within which the missile has a 50 percent chance of landing.

Collateral damage. Damage caused by military action to populations and property that are not the intentional targets of the attack. For example, a nuclear attack designed to destroy missile silos may cause significant collateral damage to civilians.

Command, control, communications, and intelligence (C³I) systems. The organizational and technological systems, the personnel, and the procedures for acquiring and disseminating information, making decisions, issuing orders, and planning, directing, evaluating and coordinating military operations.

Comprehensive Test Ban Treaty (CTBT). A proposed treaty that would ban the testing of nuclear weapons underground or anywhere else. (Compare *Limited Test Ban Treaty of 1963*.)

Conventional forces. Military forces that do not utilize nuclear, chemical or biological weapons.

Counterforce attack. A military attack directed at the enemy's military systems, troops or facilities. (Compare *Countervalue attack*.)

Counterforce capability. The ability to successfully mount a counterforce attack. Frequently used to refer to the ability to undertake a successful strike at the enemy's strategic nuclear weapons systems.

Countervalue attack. A military attack directed at the enemy's civilian population and industrial capacity, e.g., a nuclear attack on cities. (Compare *Counterforce attack*.)

Crisis stability. A strategic situation in which neither side would feel an urgent need to decide quickly whether to use nuclear weapons if an international crisis occurred. A situation of crisis instability, in which the nations felt a need to decide quickly, could result if the nations believed that their strategic forces were vulnerable to preemptive attack. (Compare *Arms race stability*.)

Cruise missile. A small guided missile that flies through the earth's atmosphere, supported by aerodynamic lift. In an effort to evade air defenses, a cruise missile can follow a flight path quite close to the ground, while maneuvering around obstacles. Cruise missiles have a range of from 1000 to 3500 kilometers, depending on the type. (See also *Air-launched cruise missile* and *Ground-launched cruise missile*.)

Détente. A warming of relations between the superpowers, designed to place limits on conflict while seeking points of mutual cooperation and accommodation.

Deterrence. A strategic doctrine that seeks to prevent enemy attacks through the threat of retaliation.

Disarmament. Bilateral or multilateral agreements or unilateral policies to reduce or eliminate weapons or certain types of weapons. (Compare *Arms control*.)

Economic conversion. The conversion of military firms and facilities to non-military uses.

Electromagnetic pulse (EMP). A powerful burst of electromagnetic radiation caused by a nuclear explosion. EMP can destroy electronic equipment.

EMP. See *Electromagnetic pulse*.

Enhanced radiation warhead. See *Neutron bomb*.

Escalate. To expand a conflict, e.g., by intensifying an attack, expanding the geographic area of conflict, etc. **Escalation** is the process through which military conflict expands.

First strike capability. The ability to attack first, destroy a large fraction of the enemy's strategic forces, and thus severely undermine the adversary's ability to respond with a retaliatory strike. See *Preemptive strike, Retaliatory strike* and *Second strike capability*.

First-use. A nation's military policy that states that under certain circumstances, the country would be the first one to employ nuclear weapons during a conflict.

Fissile material. Material (e.g., Uranium-235 and Plutonium-239) that can sustain an explosive nuclear chain reaction and is required for the manufacture of nuclear weapons.

Ground-launched cruise missile (GLCM). A cruise missile that can be fired from ground-based launchers. (See *Cruise missile*.)

H-Bomb. See *Hydrogen bomb*.

Hotline. A telecommunications link between the White House and the Kremlin for use during nuclear crises or other emergencies. It is hoped that communications over the hotline could help control a nuclear crisis and thus reduce the likelihood of accidental or unintentional nuclear war.

Hydrogen bomb (H-bomb). A weapon that derives its explosive power from the energy of nuclear fusion.

ICBM. See *Intercontinental ballistic missile*.

Intercontinental ballistic missile (ICBM). A land-based ballistic missile capable of striking targets at intercontinental ranges.

Intermediate-range ballistic missile (IRBM). A ballistic missile with a range of 2,800 to 5,500 kilometers.

Iron triangle. A pattern of interorganizational exchange and linkages between officials in the Department of Defense, members of Congress involved in military appropriations, and firms that are major military contractors. Many analysts believe that the iron triangle has far-reaching effects on military procurement and policy. See *Military-industrial complex.*

Kiloton. An explosive force equivalent to one thousand tons of TNT.

Launch-on-warning. A policy that states that a nation will launch nuclear weapons upon learning (e.g., from surveillance satellites) that a nuclear attack has been launched by the other side, rather than waiting for the enemy missiles to hit before responding. Such a policy might be motivated by a desire to prevent an enemy believed to have first strike capability from completing a preemptive strike.

Limited Test Ban Treaty of 1963. A treaty passed in 1963 that bans the testing of nuclear weapons in the atmosphere, in outer space and underwater.

MAD. See *Mutual assured destruction.*

Manhattan Project. The secret U.S. project during World War II that designed and manufactured the first atomic bomb.

Megaton. An explosive force equivalent to one million tons of TNT.

Military-industrial complex. The network of officials from the Pentagon and from private military contractors. See *Iron triangle.*

MIRV. See *Multiple independently targetable reentry vehicle.*

Mobile missile. A ballistic or cruise missile that can be transported by aircraft, ships or land-based launchers. Mobility is supposed to enhance the survivability of a missile by making it harder to detect, target and destroy.

Multilateral initiative. A cooperative action, such as an arms control treaty, involving two or more nations in a collective effort to reduce the likelihood of war. (Compare *Unilateral initiative.*)

Multiple independently targetable reentry vehicle (MIRV). A missile payload consisting of multiple warheads that can be delivered to separate targets.

Mutual assured destruction (MAD). A situation existing when both sides possess the capability to inflict massive damage in a retaliatory countervalue attack even after absorbing a full-scale counterforce strike.

Neutron bomb. A nuclear weapon designed to use radiation to attack enemy ground troops, while producing reduced explosive blast, thus limiting collateral damage to the surrounding area.

NPT. See *Nonproliferation Treaty.*

Nuclear winter. A period of low temperatures and extended darkness that some scientists believe would result from smoke and dust particles blocking sunlight in the aftermath of a nuclear war.

Permissive action links (PAL). Electronic systems that would ensure that nuclear warheads could only be armed if a positive action is taken by the proper governmental authority, e.g., the president.

Plutonium. See *Fissile material.*

Preemptive strike. A nuclear attack initiated on the assumption that an enemy nuclear attack is about to take place and designed to prevent the enemy attack or reduce its impact. See *First strike capability.*

Proliferation. The spread of nuclear weapons. **Horizontal proliferation** refers to the spread of nuclear weapons to new nations, thus increasing the number of nuclear powers. **Vertical proliferation** refers to increases in the sizes of the nuclear stockpiles of current nuclear powers.

Retaliatory strike. A nuclear attack launched in response to a nuclear attack by an adversary. See *Second strike capability.*

SALT I and **SALT II.** See *Strategic arms limitation talks.*

SDI. See *Strategic defense initiative.*

Second strike capability. The ability to absorb an enemy first strike and still have enough usable weapons to mount a devastating retaliatory strike. See *First strike capability.*

Silo. An underground facility for the launch of ballistic missiles.

Submarine-launched cruise missile (SLCM). A cruise missile capable of being launched from a submarine. See *Cruise missile.*

Submarine-launched ballistic missile (SLBM). A ballistic missile that is deployed in—and can be launched from—a submarine.

START. See *Strategic arms reduction talks.*

Strategic arms limitation talks (SALT). Nuclear arms control negotiations between the U.S. and the Soviet Union that began in 1970. The **SALT I** talks resulted, among other things, in the signing of the ABM Treaty in 1972. In **SALT II**, U.S. and Soviet negotiators reached an agreement proposing limitations in nuclear weapons systems, but ratification of the treaty was blocked by the U.S. Senate.

Strategic arms reduction talks (START).

(START). Negotiations on strategic arms currently being conducted by the U.S. and Soviet Union.

Strategic bomber. A multi-engine aircraft with intercontinental range capable of delivering nuclear bombs.

Strategic nuclear forces. Nuclear weapons and delivery systems designed for the destruction of an enemy's military, political, and economic capacity or for the destruction of cities, and the defensive systems designed to counteract those systems. See *Strategic Triad.*

Strategic Defense Initiative (SDI). A U.S. military program, begun by President Reagan, that seeks to develop "strategic defenses," especially space-based missile defense technology. See *Space-based missile defense.*

Strategic Triad. The three major types of weapons systems in U.S. strategic nuclear forces: land-based missiles, submarine-based missiles, and strategic bombers.

Submarine launched ballistic missile (SLBM). A ballistic missile deployed on, and launchable from, a submarine.

Submarine launched cruise missile (SLCM). A cruise missile transported and launched from a submarine. See *Cruise missile.*

Superbomb. See *Hydrogen bomb.*

Survivability. The ability of a weapon system to weather a first strike and successfully retaliate.

Tactical nuclear weapons. Nuclear weapons designed for attacking conventional or nuclear forces in close quarters. Tactical nuclear weapons can be packaged in a number of ways, including in short-range missiles, in artillery shells, and in bombs, land mines, and demolition munitions.

Theater nuclear weapons. Nuclear forces deployed in particular regions, or "theaters of operation," such as Europe, for use in combat within that region. Theater nuclear weapons do not have intercontinental range, and they vary from long-range theater forces to battlefield nuclear weapons.

Thermonuclear weapon. See *Hydrogen bomb.*

Unilateral initiatives. Measures to promote peace or reduce the risk of nuclear war that can be taken by one nation unilaterally, i.e., without the cooperation of other nations. (Compare *Multilateral initiatives.*)

Unintentional nuclear war. Nuclear war resulting from misjudgment, miscalculation, or panic of high government officials during a crisis situation. (Compare *Accidental nuclear war.*)

Uranium. See *Fissile Material.*

Verification. Efforts to ensure compliance with arms control agreements, including inspection, surveillance, and monitoring of the adversary's activities.

War-fighting. Doctrine emphasizing procedures for conducting a nuclear war with an emphasis on combat strategy rather than war prevention. Compare *Deterrence.*